T0207106

Apple Device Management

A Unified Theory of Managing Macs, iPads, iPhones, and Apple TVs

Second Edition

Charles Edge
Rich Trouton

Apress®

Apple Device Management: A Unified Theory of Managing Macs, iPads, iPhones, and Apple TVs

Charles Edge
Minneapolis, MN, USA

Rich Trouton
Middletown, MD, USA

ISBN-13 (pbk): 978-1-4842-9155-9
ISBN-13 (electronic): 978-1-4842-9156-6
https://doi.org/10.1007/978-1-4842-9156-6

Managing Director, Apress Media LLC: Welmoed Spahr
Acquisitions Editor: Susan McDermott
Development Editor: James Markham
Coordinating Editor: Jessica Vakili

Distributed to the book trade worldwide by Springer Science+Business Media New York, 1 NY Plaza, New York, NY 10004. Phone 1-800-SPRINGER, fax (201) 348-4505, e-mail orders-ny@springer-sbm.com, or visit www.springeronline.com. Apress Media, LLC is a California LLC and the sole member (owner) is Springer Science + Business Media Finance Inc (SSBM Finance Inc). SSBM Finance Inc is a **Delaware** corporation.

For information on translations, please e-mail booktranslations@springernature.com; for reprint, paperback, or audio rights, please e-mail bookpermissions@springernature.com.

Apress titles may be purchased in bulk for academic, corporate, or promotional use. eBook versions and licenses are also available for most titles. For more information, reference our Print and eBook Bulk Sales web page at http://www.apress.com/bulk-sales.

Any source code or other supplementary material referenced by the author in this book is available to readers on the Github repository: https://github.com/Apress/Apple-Device-Management. For more detailed information, please visit http://www.apress.com/source-code.

Printed on acid-free paper

Table of Contents

About the Authors

Charles Edge is the Chief Technology Officer of venture capital firm Bootstrappers.mn. He holds 30 years of experience as a developer, administrator, network architect, product manager, and CTO. He built the team that developed an Apple-focused MDM and has code-level experience with security and cryptography on the Apple platforms. He is the author of 20+ books and more than 6000 blog posts on technology and has served as an editor and author for many publications. Charles also serves on the board of multiple companies and conferences and frequently speaks at industry conferences around the world, including DefCon, BlackHat, LinuxWorld, the Apple Worldwide Developers Conference, and a number of Apple-focused conferences. Charles is also the author of krypted.com and a cohost of the Mac Admins Podcast and the History of Computing Podcast.

Rich Trouton has been doing Macintosh system and server administration for 20 years and has supported Macs in a number of different environments, including university, government, medical research, advertising, and enterprise software development. His current position is at SAP, where he works with the rest of the Apple CoE team to support SAP's Apple community.

About the Technical Reviewer

Ahmed Bakir is a career iOS developer, entrepreneur, and educator. He is the author of three books on iOS development, including *Program the Internet of Things with Swift for iOS*, which ranked #3 on Amazon. In 2009, he started his consulting business, devAtelier, where he worked on mobile apps for a wide range of clients ranging from startups to Fortune 500 companies. He has been a senior or lead developer on over 20 apps, including ones for major brands like UNIQLO and KFC. In 2015, he developed and taught a mobile programming certificate program for the University of California San Diego's extension program. Ahmed is currently building cool stuff in Tokyo! You can find him online at `www.devatelier.com`.

Preface

Apple distributed 25 releases of the Mac operating system across 35 years. Then came iPhone, iPad, Apple TV, a watch, and a HomePod. The success of the iPhone and the unique challenges to manage mobile devices mean that new paradigms in device management had to be established. This meant the world of managing Apple devices had to change. That evolution was inevitable, from the second the iPhone sales doubled those of the Mac, and has only gotten more and more clear.

That evolution in device management is now undeniable and irreversible. The end result of that evolution is a fate not yet determined. But change is afoot. This book is meant to codify those changes and identify best practices.

Who This Book Is For

Simply put, this book is for administrators of organizations that want to integrate with the new Apple. Many organizations have started building what's next. And many complain about aspects of how they have to build out infrastructure and services. But the world's most valuable company has shown no desire to allow exceptions.

This book outlines what organizations need to achieve work effectively with the Apple platform and includes not only infrastructure but a mode of thinking that you have to adopt to find success, a mode of thinking that forces you to leave 30 years of IT dogma at the door. And you can feel free to complain, but the faster you embrace, the faster you find success with the platform.

This book is here to help you embrace the new style of management. Because it's not going anywhere.

Chapters at a Glance

This book provides guidance. This guidance is split up into a number of chapters that provide insights for each larger theme of Apple device management. Most will go through the philosophy and design of the Apple device management story. Unless specified in the title, we work to unify that management story across the operating systems, covering iOS, macOS, and tvOS, noting the differences within each chapter.

Chapter 1: The Evolution of Apple Device Management

How did we get here? It helps to understand the history of how Apple management has evolved in the past 20+ years. Understanding where we have come from should make you more accepting of Apple's choices and help you better understand where Apple, third-party software vendors, and the IT community are taking us. Chapter 1 provides the background to get us started.

Chapter 2: Agent-Based Management

There is no such thing as an agentless management solution. In this chapter, we'll look at management agents that do not include MDM, as well as when you will need to use an agent as opposed to when to use other options.

Chapter 3: Profiles

A profile is a file that can be used to configure settings on a Mac or iOS device. Once you install a management solution, you can deploy those profiles on a device, or you can deploy profiles on Macs using scripts. We'll cover how to craft profiles and install them so you can get most necessary settings on devices.

Chapter 4: MDM Internals

What is Mobile Device Management and how does it work under the hood? By understanding how MDM works, you will understand what needs to happen on your networks in order to allow for MDM, as well as the best way to give the least amount of access to the servers or services that are necessary.

Chapter 5: iOS Provisioning

This chapter covers how to prepare iOS, tvOS, and iPadOS devices for deployment, including working with profiles, MDM, Apple Configurator, the App Store, and other tools to set up these devices.

Chapter 6: Mac Provisioning

Setting up Macs has been a bit of a moving target, starting with the end of traditional imaging and the rise of zero-touch deployments using DEP. This chapter covers how to provision Macs for deployment using a variety of methods, including tools from both Apple and third parties.

Chapter 7: Endpoint Encryption

Now that the Mac or iOS device has been set up, folks will start adding data to them which needs to be protected. Encryption provides that protection, and this chapter covers how it works, how to enable it, and how to manage it for all of your Apple devices.

Chapter 8: Securing Your Fleet

An administrator can lock down devices so they're completely secure by turning them off and smashing them with a hammer. Security is table stakes in order to grow your device population. Every organization has their own security posture, and so once you get settings and apps on devices, we will take you through applying your security posture to customize the settings on Apple devices.

Chapter 9: A Culture of Automation and Continuous Testing

Deploying settings on devices without first testing those settings can cause your coworkers to have no idea where things are on their devices, get kicked off of networks, or many other things that will cause you to get coal during your office Secret Santa. As you deploy more and more iterations of systems, settings configurations, and software loads, you won't be able to manually test everything. In this chapter, we'll work on getting standard QA environments built out, so you can test without having to manually test everything.

Chapter 10: Directory Services

Active Directory was once the bane of many Mac Admins' existence. But in recent years, the problem of binding and existing in an Active Directory environment has been mostly a nonissue. In fact, these days, the biggest concern isn't how but why, given that there is now a bevy of options for dealing with directory services. In this chapter, we go through how to get Macs to work with Active Directory and function as a first-class citizen on predominantly Windows networks.

Chapter 11: Customize the User Experience

You can't cover device management without discussing one of the main reasons why people actually want to manage devices: to make the lives of their coworkers better. The book has thus far been about deployment and the finer technical details. We'll look at techniques and tools to leverage some of the things you've learned how to do in order to deliver world class support and enablement workflows.

Chapter 12: Identity and Device Trust

Federated identities are important as they keep us from putting our passwords over networks. This allows us to more easily access resources on networks and be more secure at the same time. What can be better? In this chapter, we cover common federated identity solutions and how to leverage them in new ways.

Chapter 13: The Future of Apple Device Management

By this point, you've likely stopped caring and just want the authors to wrap it up already. We get that. But in case you're still reading, you'll find a little prognostication for things to consider future-proofing your deployments.

Think Different

How cliché can we be? Obviously very much so. But there's an important concept that needs to be addressed, and that's attitude. Apple is forging their own path in IT. They trade spots with Amazon, Google, and Microsoft as the wealthiest company to ever exist. And they will not be constrained by 30 or more years of dogma in the IT industry. Or at least that's the way they often portray their perspective on the industry (which is real, but also a little spin).

As you'll see in Chapter 1, Apple is actually going about mass device management in much the same way it has since the 1980s. The screens look similar, the options look similar, sometimes with the same words. But due to the private data on systems and the ease of identity theft, there's much more of a focus on end-user privacy. Still, Apple devices aren't Windows devices. But they are increasingly sharing a code base made simpler by shared Swift and SwiftUI frameworks, and this has led to more similar management techniques than ever before.

The most important thing to consider is whether you want to try to shoehorn Apple devices into outdated modes of device management or whether you are ready to embrace Apple's stance on management. If you aren't ready to embrace the Apple way, then you might not be ready to manage Apple devices.

CHAPTER 1

The Evolution of Apple Device Management

Once upon a time, in a land far, far away, the Mac existed in a vacuum. Unmanaged and left behind in the grand scheme of the corporate enterprise, it was at best overlooked by Windows-centric IT departments and, at worst, marked for retirement and removal. In those times, it was common to see a network of Macs run as a silo, often with a dedicated cable modem for Internet access and sometimes even with a dedicated mail server to support the creatives. And yes, the Mac was almost exclusively used by teams of creatives like graphic designers and video editors.

The Mac platform seemed close to death in the late 1990s, as Apple's sales slumped and Microsoft's offerings dominated the consumer and enterprise markets. Microsoft embraced corporate and large-scale use and they released a number of tools like Active Directory and policies that a generation of administrators began to consider synonymous with enterprise management. Meanwhile, Apple released a few tools to help manage devices, but nothing with as granular options to control devices en masse as Microsoft had. Gradually, deployments of Apple equipment shrank to small workgroups with one exception: education.

C. Edge and R. Trouton, *Apple Device Management*,
https://doi.org/10.1007/978-1-4842-9156-6_1

Schools around the world continued to embrace the Apple platform throughout the tough times at Apple. During those times, anyone with large-scale Apple management experience almost certainly worked at a school or for a school district. But everything started to change with the advent of the iPhone. Suddenly, enterprises looked to education for guidance on how to deploy large numbers of Apple devices, CIOs asked their IT departments why IT wouldn't support the CEO's new MacBook Air, staff at some schools started to get jobs at large companies, and some of the requirements we faced started to change as corporate compliance became a new challenge.

> *The more things change, the more they stay the same, but not exactly. When Apple asked me to take over updating the Directory Services course and book, we used Mac OS X Server to keep management, identity, and authorization settings in the same place: Open Directory. But most wanted to leverage identity and authorization stored in another directory (LDAP or Active Directory). Then it seemed like no one cared about Directory Services any more and the focus was on moving from directory-based management (Workgroup Manager) to MDM. Now we're learning more about integrating MDM solutions with various 3rd party Identity Providers (IdPs). The fun part of this job is trying to figure out... What's next?*
>
> —Arek Dreyer, Dreyer Network Consultants and the author of several books on macOS and macOS Server

There are about as many reasons for this change as there are Apple fans. But the change is undeniable. The rise of Apple in the enterprise and the growth led to a number of innovations from Apple. The management story completely changed when Mac OS X was released and slowly evolved into what we now call macOS. But it started long before that.

In this chapter, we'll look at this management story - beginning in the dark ages, through the Renaissance that was the emergence of Mac OS X rising like a phoenix from the ashes of NeXT and into the modern era of macOS and iOS management. That story begins with the Apple II.

The Classic Mac Operating Systems

The Apple II was released in June of 1977 and changed the world, long before the Mac. It was one of the first mass-produced and therefore actually accessible computers. Back then, if environments had more than one computer, device management meant someone walked around with floppy disks that were used to boot the computer. Large-scale device management didn't become a thing until much, much later.

The Macintosh was released in 1984 and marked the first rung of the upward climb to where we are today. Between Apple's System 6 and Mac OS 9 operating systems, Mac management over the network often used the AppleTalk network protocol (which was released in 1985 but only went away in 2009 with Mac OS X Snow Leopard) instead of TCP/IP. In addition to being unsupported by any other platform (although Windows NT Server shipped with a connector and there were third-party tools that could bootstrap a service to host AppleTalk), AppleTalk's methods of network communication were viewed by many as being unnecessarily "chatty," which caused networks to slow down. This reputation, other Apple-specific characteristics, and the difficulty of managing Apple devices using Microsoft management tools led to the opinion that many old-timer IT execs still have today: "Apple devices don't play nice on corporate networks." They always did, just in a different way than Windows.

Network Protocols

Many of those older IT execs still have questions about whether or not Apple devices will cause problems on modern networks. If an Apple device can hurt a network, then the network has problems. It is true that once upon a time, Apple devices could spew AppleTalk traffic on the network that caused packet storms or other problems. But then, so could IPX or NetBIOS, which were initially released in 1983. The developers of these protocols learned a lot about how to network computers in the past 40 years.

Networking capabilities were initially built into the Apple Lisa in 1983 and initially called AppleNet. AppleNet was replaced by AppleTalk in 1985, and Apple finally dropped support for AppleTalk in 2009, although its use had slowed since the introduction of Mac OS X. Apple was able to join TCP/IP networks in 1988 with the release of MacTCP, which provided access to most types of devices that a Mac would connect with provided there was an agent that could decipher typically socket-based communications for each protocol.

Before Mac OS X, the Chooser was a tool used to connect to network file servers and printers. Shown in Figure 1-1, the Chooser would scan the network for AppleTalk devices and display them, which allowed users to "choose" a device to mount. Those mounts were synonymous with drive letter maps to network shares in Windows and mounted NFS shares for Unix and Linux. Because networks grew and discovery protocols didn't always find devices on the network, users could also enter a custom IP address to connect to if the host didn't show up in the list. The custom IP could also be used to connect to other LANs or over a WAN, provided port 548 was open on a host.

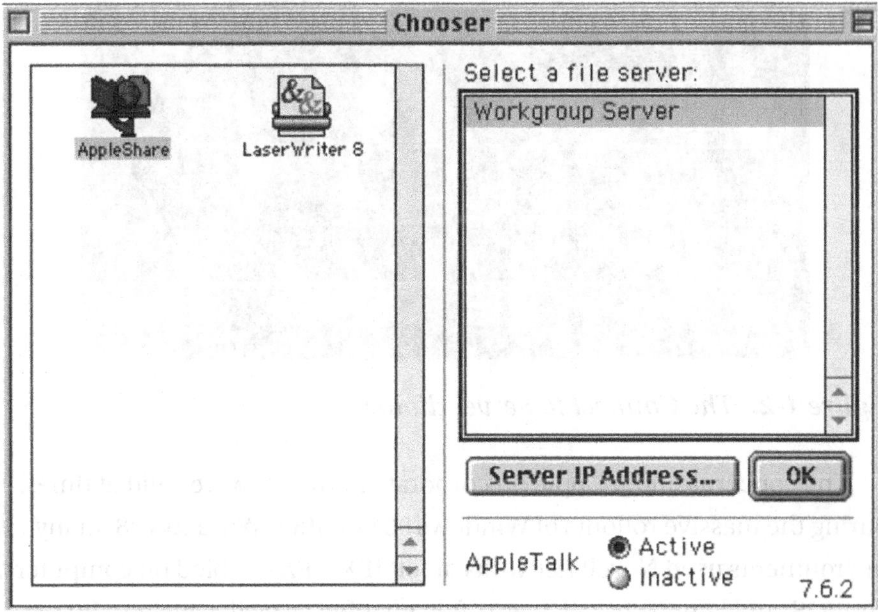

Figure 1-1. *The 1990s era Chooser*

With the advent of Mac OS X in 2001, the Chooser was replaced with the Connect to Server option (Figure 1-2), which had everything required to connect to file servers, WebDAV, and FTP servers available in most standard TCP/IP environments. Apple added Rendezvous to Mac OS X beginning in 2002, which allowed Macs to find devices and services over TCP/IP. Renamed to Bonjour in 2005, this zero-configuration technology uses mDNS (multicast Domain Name System) to allow users to locate (or browse) and connect to devices or services on networks with the same level of convenience that AppleTalk offered but with built-in support for the traditional Windows SMB (Server Message Block)services.

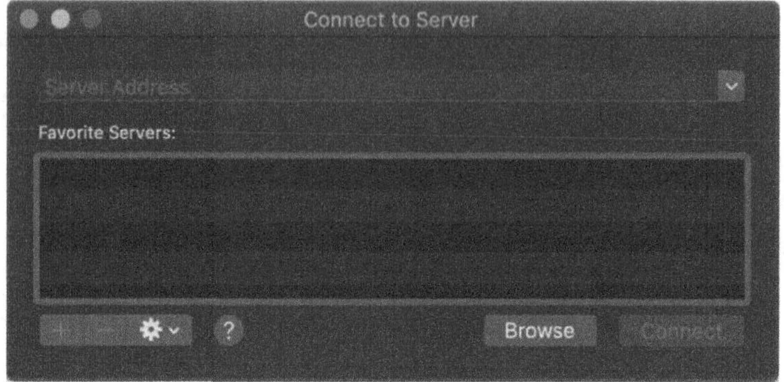

***Figure 1-2.** The Connect to Server dialog*

The concerns about Apple on corporate networks were valid at times. During the massive rollouts of Windows 95 and then Windows 98, many environments used Novell networks or left IPX/SPX enabled on computers. NetBIOS, and later NetBEUI, were often enabled as well, causing a lot of traffic going over older hubs. When you added AppleTalk into that mix, there could legitimately be just too much traffic for the network equipment of that era. Luckily, AppleTalk is long behind us. Additionally, many switching environments started to ship with Spanning Tree Protocol (STP) enabled during the 2000s. Macs could have issues with Spanning Tree Protocol, especially if AppleTalk had not been disabled. However, Mac OS X slowly phased AppleTalk out in favor of newer protocols like Apple Filing Protocol (AFP) and later SMB. Even AFP became a "legacy" protocol as Apple transitioned the default protocols to SMB over time, and by the mid-2000s, AppleTalk was only there for backward compatibility with old hardware and software.

Once file services (and print services as AppleTalk gave way to standard LPR and other types of printers) were more compatible with other vendors, Apple could turn their attention to more important services. Larger environments naturally looked toward how they could manage devices over that same network connection used for files and printers.

Early Device Management

Devices weren't managed as intricately initially as they are today. Not only were the network protocols different, but the technology stack was wildly different; there weren't nearly as many devices being managed from a central location, and we didn't have 30–40 years of IT wisdom on how to make the lives better for our coworkers, students, or even ourselves. There also wasn't the expectation of privacy that there is today, which is a key element for managing Apple devices, as we'll cover over the next few hundred pages. Maybe administrators managed extensions (as Desk Accessories) with Font/DA Mover or launchers. This allowed a school or other environments to install fonts and things like screensavers - but Apple-provided tools for centralized management of Macintosh settings by and large weren't available reliably until the 1990s.

Apple's At Ease was an alternative desktop environment released for System 7 in 1991, which provided a simplified desktop environment for multiple users to use and share files, functionality not otherwise supported in the Mac at that time. As At Ease evolved, Apple also released At Ease for Workgroups, which provided client configuration options and a restricted Finder mode. It also allowed for home folders that could be stored on an AppleShare IP Server and with eMate the ability to hand in homework for classes (Figure 1-3). That restricted Finder mode later evolved into a (mostly) multiuser operating system environment in Mac OS 9 and the Simple Finder, which is still around today in modern macOS.

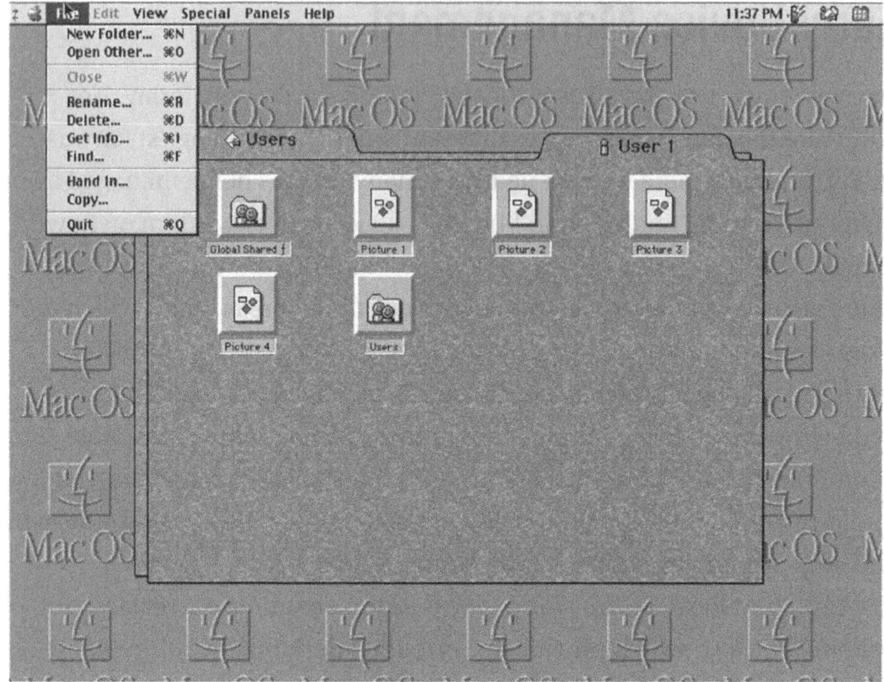

***Figure 1-3.** Handing in homework in a managed environment*

The following are few important things to keep in mind as this story evolves through the years:

- At one point, At Ease was a unified tool to manage file shares, printers, settings on devices, and mobile devices (the Newton).
- At Ease provided some semblance of multiple users, but the actual operating system of the Mac didn't interpret those the way it does today.
- Many of the philosophies available in At Ease are still the same, even though the way those are implemented on devices is now quite different, due to a shift from AppleTalk, Ethernet, Wi-Fi, and then devices that could exist outside a Local Area Network.

- eMate (Figure 1-4) was used to exchange data with devices, including the Newton (when using Apple Newton Works), which made it the ancestor of Apple Classroom (albeit a less feature-rich ancestor).

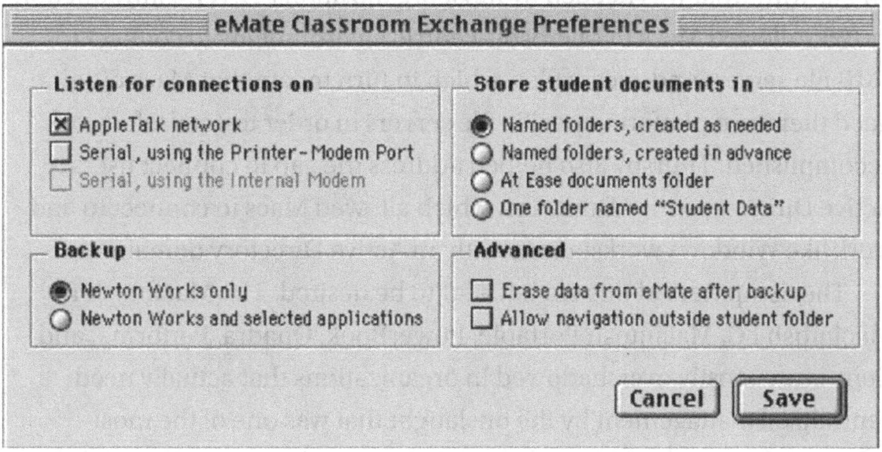

***Figure 1-4.** Settings for eMate management are similar to Classroom settings*

At Ease didn't solve every problem for every use case. Another important shift from this era was the first wave of third-party device management solutions. In August of 1991 (the same year the Internet was born), netOctopus was launched at Macworld in Boston. This kicked off an era of third-party tools that allowed organizations to manage Apple devices. By 1993, when FileWave was released, Apple allowed and even gave active thought to how to put things (like files) in places on Macs. That was the infancy of a centralized command and control environment. The same happened in Windows, where in Windows 3, an administrator could edit .ini files from a central location. That evolved into .zap files and similar formats (now .mst files) that could be distributed from a central location in the upcoming Windows 95 era and beyond. Companies that built similar tools for Windows management exploded over the next decades, while many who focused on the Mac wouldn't see such meteoric growth until the iPhone.

The next major third party to enter the picture was Thursby Software. They released DAVE, a file and printer sharing tool for the Mac, which bridged the gap to SMB/CIFS shares from Windows servers. Microsoft had an AFP server called File Sharing Services for Mac, but it was never on par with what was needed by most organizations. DAVE's introduction in 1996 allowed Macs in Microsoft-centric environments to connect to SMB file servers and access files, which in turn meant that Macs didn't need their own platform-specific file servers in order to get useful work accomplished. Thursby also helped address the gap to connect users to Active Directory with ADmitMac, which allowed Macs to connect to and work like Windows workstations with an Active Directory domain.

The computers of this era left a lot to be desired. The Macintosh II, Macintosh LC, Macintosh Portable, PowerBook, Quadra, Performa, and Centris are mostly overshadowed in organizations that actually need centralized management by the onslaught that was one of the most substantial technological revolutions in history, the PC era. But all that was ready to change.

NeXT

Steve Jobs left Apple in 1985 and started his next company, aptly named NeXT. The first NeXT computers shipped in 1988, with the NeXTSTEP operating system at the core of what would later become Mac OS X when Apple acquired NeXT and brought Steve Jobs back. Therefore, the management ecosystem in NeXT set the tone for how Macs were managed into the modern era.

The most important thing that happened on a NeXT computer was that the first web page was served on a NeXT computer by Tim Berners-Lee in August 6, 1991, at the European Organization for Nuclear Research, CERN. Doom was developed on NeXT - which ushered in a whole new era of gaming. When Steve Jobs returned to Apple in 1997, NeXT's workstation technologies had matured enough that Apple could begin to replace Mac OS 9 with Mac OS X (which would later evolve into macOS). The NeXT had many obvious user interface similarities to the Mac, as seen in Figure 1-5.

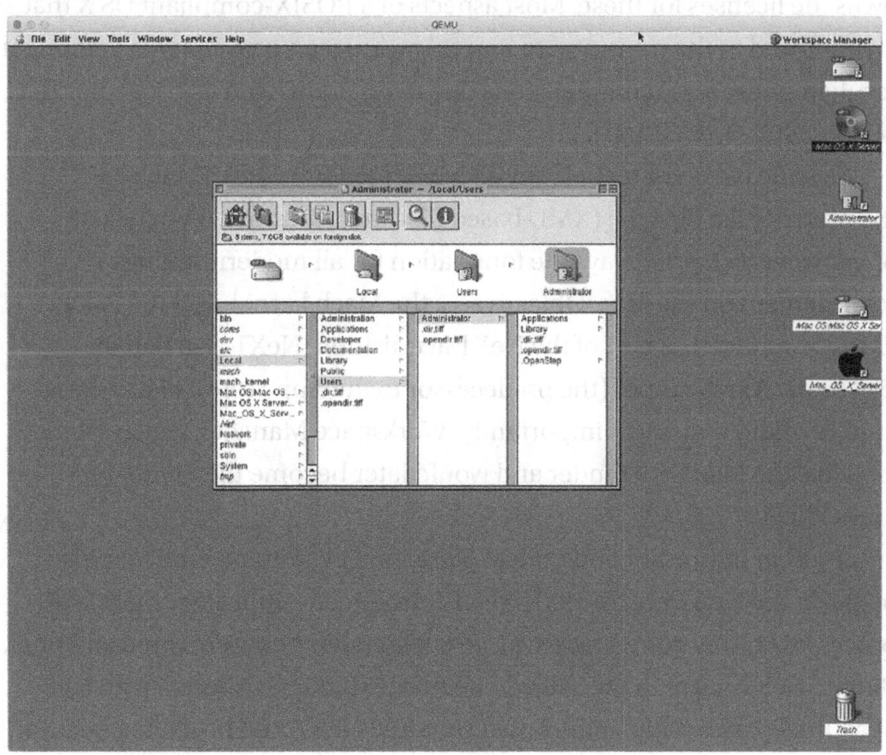

Figure 1-5. NeXT (a.k.a. The Inbetween)

As it pertains to the concept of device management, several important things came from NeXT that would later influence the Mac and then iOS. The most important is the object-oriented nature of NeXTSTEP, and the second is the development environment. Ironically, the Unix-derived nature of OPENSTEP is what brought the modern Mac so far, so fast. And the "open" components of the operating system have actively been removed piece by piece as large portions of open source code within the

Mac are being removed as well. Still, Darwin, Xcode, and parts of iOS are still hosted and regularly updated on opensource.apple.com, and WebKit and Swift are successful open source projects from Apple. However, Apple owns the licenses for these. Most aspects of a POSIX-compliant OS X that are removed in the transition to macOS are instead components that might result in future legal complications due to different licensing schemes (e.g., MIT vs. GPLv2 vs. GPLv3).

Specific pieces of technology also emerged from NeXT, such as the property list file type (XML-based files that can store key-pair sets of information), which lays the foundation for all modern settings management on the Mac. Objective-C, the Mach kernel, and the Dock likewise surfaced as part of the NeXT acquisition. NeXT also had the Electronic AppWrapper (the predecessor to the App Store), Mail, Chess.app, TextEdit, and, most importantly, Workspace Manager, which seemed a bit like the Mac OS 9 Finder and would later become the Finder for Mac OS X.

Another important and critical part of the evolution of the Mac also began in the NeXT era. In 1991, NeXT introduced support for the 80486 processor. At this point, there was no partnership between Apple and Intel. But the NeXT move to the x86 architecture (Marklar) ushered in an era of an Intel partnership, once Apple acquired NeXT and began to plan the introduction of the new operating system that lasts to this day (although there was a PowerPC chipset port in there through the Rhapsody era). The x86-based architecture did more than make it easier for Apple to buy ready-built chips from Intel; it introduced better virtualization of Windows for the Mac and made those Directors of IT stop and think that suddenly Apple played nice and maybe could be trusted to show up on their networks.

Mac + Unix = Mac OS X

Apple started to integrate NeXT technologies with a new operating system with the code name Rhapsody. Rhapsody included many of the tools administrators still use today. The transition to Mac OS X introduced a more Unix-oriented management framework, which replaced the single-user model in Mac OS 9 and earlier. Mac OS X was a true multiuser experience and marked the start of what would evolve into management policies.

New policy-based management was introduced in the form of Managed Preferences, or MCX (Managed Computing for X). These are still available in /System/Library/CoreServices/ManagedClient.app and allow administrators to prepopulate global system preference domains or control the settings applied in those keys. Those preferences were similar to how the registry in Windows worked and similar to how traditional Mac administrators blocked access to resources like Control Panels in At Ease. For many years, Managed Preferences was the main way that administrators controlled settings on a Mac, and MCX provided a framework that later tools leveraged to provide centralized management of a Mac's settings.

With policy controls available on a multiuser computer, the Mac continued to iterate toward a first-class corporate citizen. Developers at Apple added flags to the `dsconfigad` command that is used to bind Macs to Active Directory. Developers added DFS integration along the way. Additionally, standard LDAP implementations, and the ability to natively connect to file shares was bolstered with the ability to manage these from a centralized location.

> *The course of my professional life changed when we realized that while Apple had provided a great tool in At Ease, but that we could go further. Apple has always given customers a product that can get the job done in isolated circumstances, but often wants third party developers to step in and handle use cases that aren't exactly what they have in mind. We saved customers time and provided a better experience with netOctopus. Much the same way that modern deployments tend to leverage one of the many third party products instead of Apple's Profile Manager today.*
>
> —Martin Bestman, founder of netOctopus

The Bondi Blue iMac was released in 1998, shortly after Steve Jobs returned to Apple. This led to a quick increase in the number of devices managed in larger environments. Mac Admins soon began to employ the second major wave of third-party Apple device management solutions. These built on the frameworks that came to the Mac from NeXT, which still managed the way things appeared on a Mac but went further and allowed for software packages (.pkgs) and centrally managed preference files.

The first major open source project used to manage Macs was released in 2002. Radmind was initially developed at the University of Michigan. The Casper Suite 1.0 was also released in 2002, which evolved into what's now known as Jamf Pro. At this point, device management was mostly about how administrators could initially deploy a Mac in a known state, known as imaging, and how to use packages or similar data constructs to deploy additional information and settings onto devices, as you can see in Figure 1-6, which shows Casper 1.0's package selection screen.

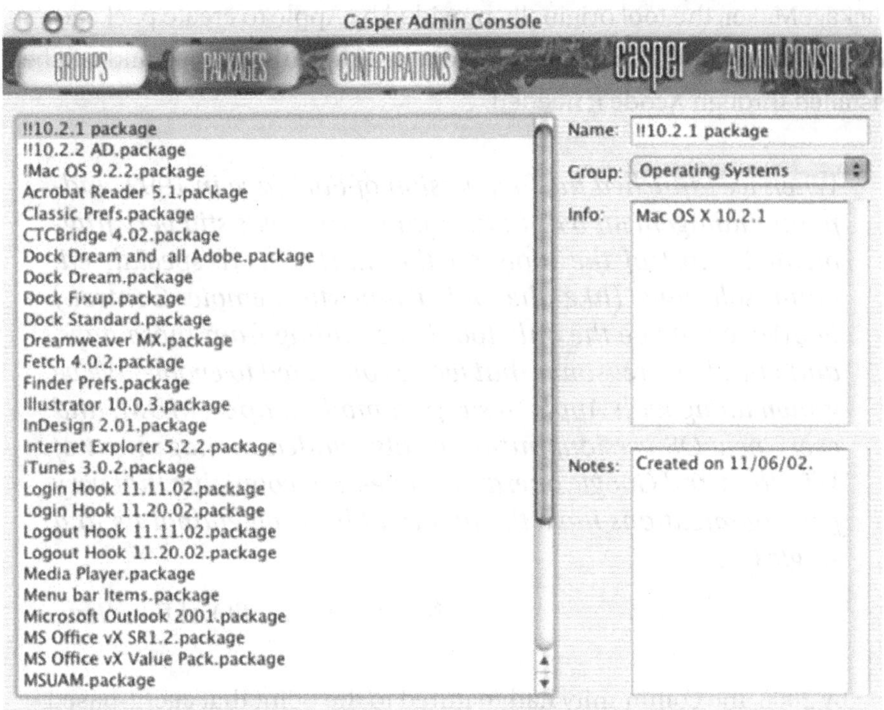

Figure 1-6. *The Casper Admin Console from the Casper 1.0 User's Guide*

These tools used an agent (or daemon usually) on devices to communicate back to a server and pull down objects to be deployed. That agent pulled commands or configurations down to devices. FileWave and Radmind took a more file-based approach, where they dropped a "set" of files in a location on a filesystem in order to deploy a change on a system. NetOctopus and Jamf used native Apple technologies, like software packages (pkgs), to make changes on devices instead.

Later, Apple started to implement an agentless technology called Mobile Device Management (MDM), which is covered later in this chapter (and there's an entire chapter on MDM later in the book). Packages are still used to configure settings, install software, and perform other tasks.

PackageMaker, the tool originally provided by Apple to create packages, was removed from the operating system in 2015, although it could still be installed through Xcode if needed.

> *When we launched the first version of FileWave in 1992, endpoint management was in its infancy, and was still very fragmented. Most of the tools on the market were specialized, point solutions (like the old Timbuktu Remote Control.) FileWave may be the only tool left standing from those days, and I think the reason is that we've continued to evolve. We've grown along with Apple to support modern apps, MDM, and every new OS version, but we've also added management of Windows and Google operating systems, recognizing that very few organizations have the luxury of limiting endpoints to a single OS.*
>
> —Nurdan Eris, CEO of FileWave

By 2008, the community had matured to the point that agent-based management had matured to be on par with what was available for Windows systems through tools like Altiris. In fact, Altiris and other Windows management solutions had agents available for the Mac. Tools with a stronger focus on Apple, such as FileWave, Jamf, and LANrev, could manage Macs as first-class citizens on corporate networks.

In 2008, Greg Neagle began to work on an open source agent for Mac management called Munki. The first public code commits came in early 2009, which opened the way for an open source alternative to Mac management. The use of Munki has grown over the years, and so centralized management has been accessible to environments that previously couldn't afford it or who needed more customizable workflows than those available with the third-party solutions. With the advent of MDM, Munki also plays a pivotal role in adding agent-based options for environments that also use MDM. Most importantly, Munki brought an almost DevOps-style focus to Apple administration that allowed many administrators to manage Macs in much the same way they manage code.

Management is now a set of policy-driven actions used to achieve a certain amount of idempotency on Apple devices, or the known state a device is in. The first management tasks were to control the way a system looked and the experience a user had to access the applications and data they needed. Some lost their way for a while, if only to make the job easier. Yet since the advent of iOS, they have started to rediscover that goal to improve the user experience, not control it. The less that changed on the operating system, the more control is passed to the user. Therefore, while there's still a gap in understanding the exact state of a device, administrators now have a good ecosystem that allows for policies that don't destroy the experience Apple crafts for devices.

Server

Apple has had a server product from 1987 to 2022. At Ease had some file and print sharing options. The old AppleShare (later called AppleShare IP, shown in Figure 1-7) server was primarily used to provide network resources for the Mac from 1986 to 2000; file sharing was the main service offered. Apple also took a stab at early server hardware in the form of the Apple Network Server, which was a PowerPC server sold from 1996 to 1997 that ran the AIX operating system. AppleShare IP worked up until Mac OS 9.2.2. In an era before, as an example, mail servers required SMTP authentication, AppleShare IP was easily used for everything from printer sharing services to mail services. An older Quadra made for a great mail server so a company could move from some weird email address supplied by an ISP to their own domain in 1999.

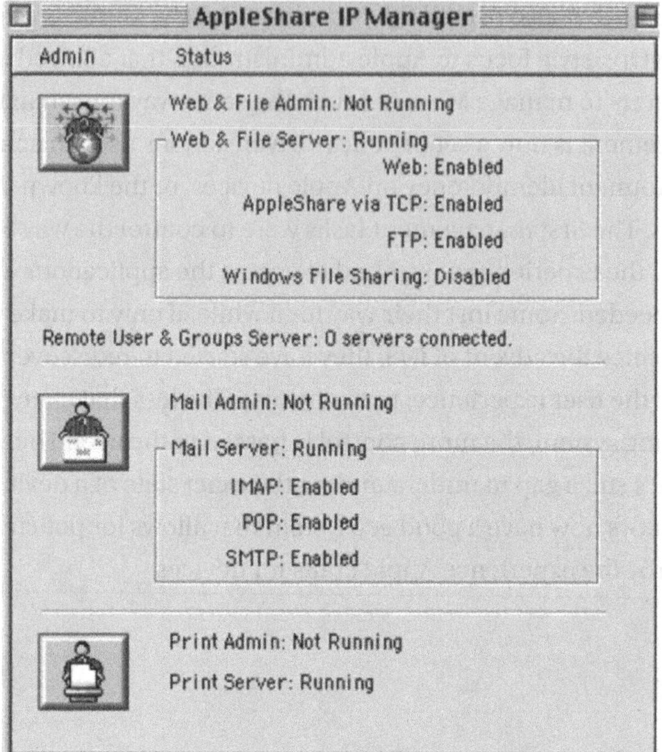

***Figure 1-7.** Early Apple servers were pretty easy to manage*

Meanwhile, services that provided sockets so other systems could access that data were a central need for NeXTSTEP and OPENSTEP systems. The UNIX underpinnings made it possible to compile a number of open source software packages, and as mentioned earlier in this chapter, the first web server was hosted on a NeXTcube. After NeXT was acquired by Apple, AppleShare IP and services from NeXT were made to look and feel similar and morphed into Mac OS X Server.

The first few releases of Mac OS X Server represented a learning curve for many classic Apple admins and in fact caused a generational shift in who administered the systems. John Welch wrote books in 2000 and 2002 that helped administrators get up to speed. The Xserve was released in 2002, and the Xserve RAID was released in 2003. It took time, but a community began to form around these products. The late Michael Bartosh compiled a seminal work in *Essential Mac OS X Panther Server Administration* for O'Reilly Media in 2005. Charles Edge (coauthor of this book) released *The Mac Tiger Server Little Black Book* in 2006.

Up until this point, Apple never publicly acknowledged that businesses or enterprises used their devices, especially for servers. They purchased advertising for the first time to promote the Xserve. Apple continued to improve the product with new services up until 2009 with Mac OS X Server 10.6. At this point, Apple included most services necessary to run a standard IT department in the product. These included the Web (in the form of Apache), mail, groupware, DHCP, DNS, directory services, file sharing, and even web and wiki services. There were also edge case services such as Podcast Producer used to automate video and content workflows. Xsan provided administrators with a storage area network (SAN) in the form of the StorNext clustered filesystem. Apple also acquired a company called Artbox in 2009, whose product was rebranded as Final Cut Server.

That was a turning point. As seen in Table 1-1, around that same time, Apple was ready to release the iPad in 2010 (although arguably the Knowledge Navigator was the first iteration, conceptualized in 1987). The skyrocketing sales of the iPhone led to some tough decisions. Apple no longer needed to control the whole ecosystem with their server product and instead began to transition as many teams as possible to work on higher profit margin areas. They reduced the focus on areas that took attention away from valuable software developers. Rather than solve problems many other vendors had already solved better, those engineers could develop great Application Programming Interfaces (APIs) that third parties could build products around.

Table 1-1. *macOS Server Is Now Used to Host Far Fewer Services Than It Once Did*

10.3	10.4	10.5	10.6	10.7	10.8	10.9	10.1	10.11	10.12	10.13
2003	**2005**	**2007**	**2009**	**2011**	**2012**	**2013**	**2014**	**2015**	**2016**	**2017**
15	19	24	24	22	18	21	21	21	21	14
AFP	AFP	AFP	AFP	AFP	AFP	AFP	AFP	AFP	AFP	
NFS	NFS	NFS	NFS	NFS	NFS	NFS	NFS	NFS	NFS	
Web	Web	Web	Web	Web	Websites	Websites	Websites	Websites	Websites	Websites
Open Directory	Open Directory	Open Directory	Open Directory	Open Directory	Open Directory	Open Directory	Open Directory	Open Directory	Open Directory	Open Directory
NetBoot	NetBoot	NetBoot	NetBoot	NetBoot	NetInstall	NetInstall	NetInstall	NetInstall	NetInstall	NetInstall
FTP	FTP	FTP	FTP	FTP	FTP	FTP	FTP	FTP	FTP	
Windows	Windows	SMB	SMB	SMB	SMB	SMB	SMB	SMB	SMB	
Mail	Mail	Mail	Mail	Mail	Mail	Mail	Mail	Mail	Mail	Mail
DNS	DNS	DNS	DNS	DNS	DNS	DNS	DNS	DNS	DNS	DNS
DHCP	DHCP	DHCP	DHCP	DHCP		DHCP	DHCP	DHCP	DHCP	DHCP
VPN	VPN	VPN	VPN	VPN	VPN	VPN	VPN	VPN	VPN	VPN

	Software Updates	Software Updates	Software Updates	Software Updates	Software Updates	Software Updates	Software Updates	Software Updates	Software Updates	Software Update
	iChat	iChat	iChat	iChat	Messages	Messages	Messages	Messages	Messages	Messages
		iCal	iCal	iCal	Calendar	Calendar	Calendar	Calendar	Calendar	Calendar
		Wiki	Wiki	Wiki	Wiki	Wiki	Wiki	Wiki	Wiki	Wiki
			Address Book	Address Book	Contacts	Contacts	Contacts	Contacts	Contacts	Contacts
				Time Machine	Time Machine	Time Machine	Time Machine	Time Machine	Time Machine	
				Profile Manager	Profile Manager	Profile Manager	Profile Manager	Profile Manager	Profile Manager	Profile Manager
					Xsan	Xsan	Xsan	Xsan	Xsan	Xsan
						Caching	Caching	Caching	Caching	
						Xcode	Xcode	Xcode	Xcode	
	Web Objects	Web Objects								

(*continued*)

Table 1-1. *(continued)*

10.3	10.4	10.5	10.6	10.7	10.8	10.9	10.1	10.11	10.12	10.13
Application Server	Application Server	Tomcat	Tomcat							
Print	Print	Print	Print							
QTSS	QTSS	QTSS	QTSS							
NAT	NAT	NAT	NAT	NAT						
	Xgrid	Xgrid	Xgrid	Xgrid						
		RADIUS	RADIUS	RADIUS						
		Podcast	Podcast	Podcast						
			Mobile Access							
		MySQL								

In 2009, the Xserve RAID was discontinued, and the Xserve was canceled the following year. The next few years saw services slowly removed from the server product, which coincides with an increased frequency in legal disputes over usability of open source code licensed with specific types of licenses. The Mac OS X Server product was migrated to just an app on the App Store, as seen in Figure 1-8. At that point, macOS Server was meant primarily to run Profile Manager and be run as a metadata controller for Xsan. Products that used to compete with the platform were then embraced by most in the community. Apple let Microsoft or Linux-based systems own the market to provide features that are often unique to each enterprise and not about delighting end users.

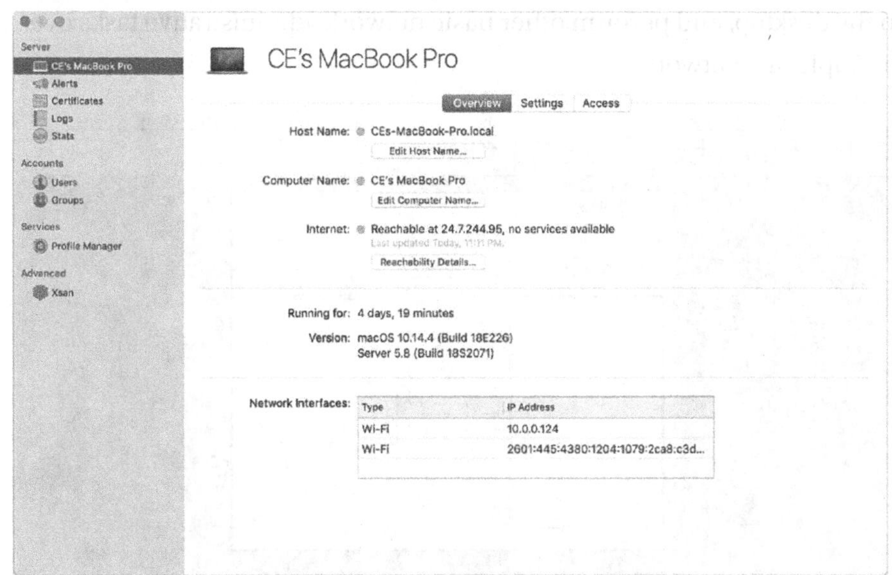

***Figure 1-8.** The simplified macOS Server app*

macOS Server was canceled in April of 2022. Today, server products that try to do everything for everyone seem like a distant memory for many at Apple. There is instead a keen eye toward how to make the lives of Apple devices better and provide a clean experience for users. This can be seen by the Caching service built into macOS (moved there from macOS Server) and how some products, such as Apple Remote Desktop, are still maintained.

Apple Remote Desktop

By 1997, the Apple Network Administrator Toolkit, which was used to install At Ease, also came with the Apple Network Assistant. Shown in Figure 1-9, the Apple Network Assistant will look very similar to modern users. Mac Admins could remotely control the screen of a Mac, lock screens, share your screen, copy files, remotely open apps, send messages to the desktop, and perform other basic network administrative tasks over an AppleTalk network.

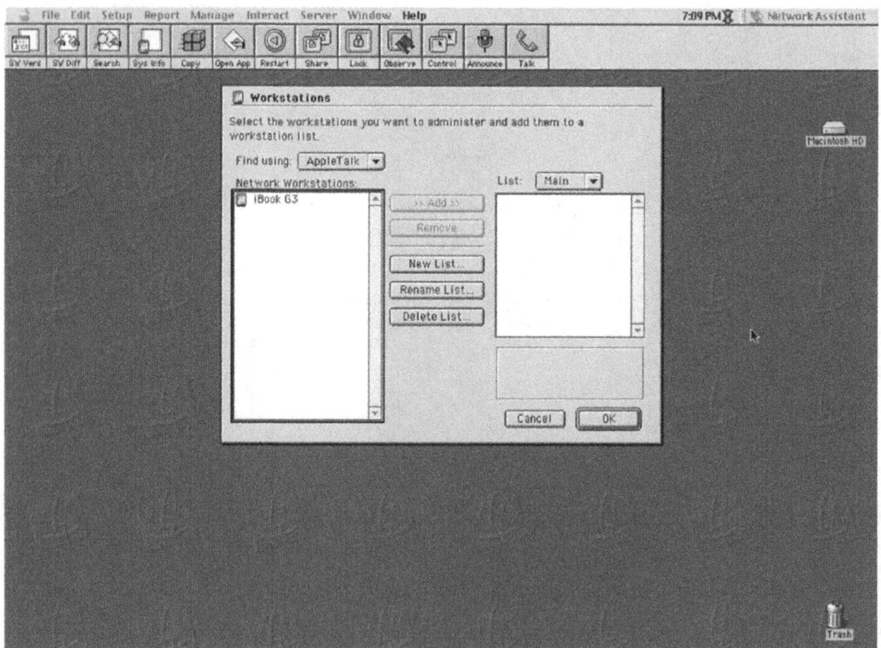

Figure 1-9. *Network Assistant, the ancestor of Apple Remote Desktop*

After the introduction of Mac OS X, Apple released a new tool called Remote Desktop in 2002. Remote Desktop, which is still available on the Mac App Store today, allows administrators to take over the desktop of client systems, send shell scripts to Mac clients, and perform a number of other tasks that are useful for point-in-time management. Remote Desktop also works well when used in conjunction with these other tools as those are mostly used for imaging, software configuration management, and deployment. Most of the functionality from Apple Network Assistant was brought into Apple Remote Desktop (ARD), as well as the Virtual Network Computing (VNC) protocol, and a new ARD protocol was built to find and control clients over the User Datagram Protocol (UDP).

> *Apple's Remote Desktop allows administrators to control Macs and send scripts to devices. This was great for a lot of environments and well priced! As organizations grew and their needs matured, ARD made it easy to transition into more traditional management solutions because the packages and scripts were great foundational technologies we could build on.*
>
> —Chip Pearson, cofounder, Jamf Software

By 2004, it was clear that there were some better options than a UDP-based protocol to perform screen control. Apple Remote Desktop 2 was built on top of Virtual Network Computing (VNC) but does much more. It also comes with a task server, so it can queue up commands to be sent out. While Remote Desktop can make a specific immediate change or action on a computer, it also provides a great entry point into management tools and makes it easy to test unattended installations.

Now on version 3.9.5 (Figure 1-10), Apple Remote Desktop has gone through a number of different places in the Apple ecosystem. Management commands have transitioned to APNs-based workflows for other products, and Apple Remote Desktop only allows connectivity over a LAN unless you open ports to control devices from incoming WAN connections. Other tools such as Bomgar, TeamViewer, GoToMyPC, Splashtop, ISL, and a host of other solutions can do this; it's no surprise that Apple hasn't made such a large investment into a refactor for a product that now costs $79.99 on the Mac App Store and has only 1.7 star out of 5 star ratings. Furthermore, Apple Remote Desktop gets away from a slightly more modern way of thinking at Apple: users should explicitly approve any invasion into their privacy.

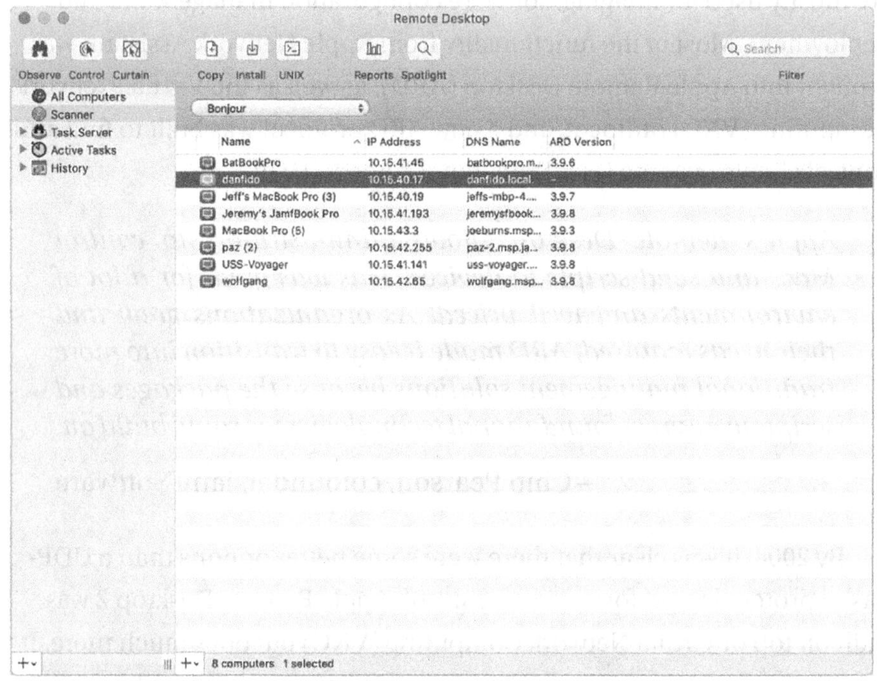

***Figure 1-10.** Apple Remote Desktop still has much of the functionality from Network Assistant*

Ecosystem Coexistence

With the release of a more modern and flexible operating system, Apple introduced multiple users. This feature led to the ability to have one of those users be sourced from a directory services account. These accounts then gave users the ability to log in to their local computer with the same password used on servers to access their mail and other services provided by an organization.

MCX was developed to use with Apple's Open Directory directory service built into Mac OS X Server. Administrators could also get policy data via directory services in the form of an extended Active Directory schema that contained MCX data, which is much easier to manage en masse than the local MCX referenced earlier. The reason is that both used similar Lightweight Directory Access Protocol (LDAP) implementations. Not all organizations could extend their schemas (no Active Directory administrator wants to extend their schema), and so techniques were also developed to bind client computers to both Active Directory and Open Directory and allow users and groups hosted in Active Directory to be nested inside Open Directory in order to deploy Managed Preferences to clients without extending the Active Directory schema. This was known as the Magic Triangle.

ADmitMac wasn't the only option to get policy information via a third party. Centrify was released in 2005. They allowed administrators to use a more centrally managed solution to deliver policies to the Mac. Centrify has since focused much of their efforts to be an Identity Provider (IdP). Quest Authentication Services was also introduced to help deploy policies. The easier Apple made it to work with directory services, the less each of those solutions was needed, and by 2011 some fizzled out. The policies were always a tough sell to IT departments (even though many had extended their schema dozens of times for other products like Cisco integration with Active Directory). Environments that wouldn't extend schemas typically also wouldn't add Apple servers for a supplemental directory service. In the past few releases of macOS, MCX has slowly been deprecated in favor of profile-based management, which evolved from a time when Apple started to rethink policy-based management for iOS.

> *Apple's MCX was a powerful and flexible way for admins to manage the settings of Apple and third party software. Apple's preferred replacement, configuration profiles, lacks some of the flexibility present in MCX. Many of us hoped that over time, Apple would add the missing features back into configuration profiles, but that seems unlikely now. Back to badly written shell scripts!*
>
> —Greg Neagle, creator of Munki and coauthor of *Enterprise Mac Managed Preferences*, from Apress

Many Apple admins' jobs were once to manage servers. Those jobs now shifted, and now administrators moved to manage cloud services and the states of devices, first with directory services and MCX and then toward more modern management techniques, such as the ones initially introduced to manage iPhones and iPads. This is where profiles enter into the picture, which cover a lot of needs of an administrator, but not all.

iOS Device Management

The presence of the Mac in the enterprise continued to grow, but another big change was on the way. A corporate dogma that evolved out of the Windows ecosystem became a model of how the business of IT was done. Apple developers worked to support the traditional methodologies but rethought the paradigm and started to go their own way. This was made possible by the newfound dominance of the iPhone that accessed Exchange servers and the fact that suddenly employees showed up with these devices and used them at work. Suddenly, companies needed to manage the OS that ships on iPhone, iOS.

The original iPhone was released in 2007, and iOS management initially occurred manually through iTunes. Most needed to deploy apps for schools, so the deployment options started with the ability to drag an app onto a device to install it onto phones over USB cables. Some settings were exposed to iTunes. Back then, iOS devices were registered with Apple when they were plugged into iTunes to use it. Administrators could also back up and restore a device with iTunes, which came with some specific challenges, such as the account used to buy an app would follow the "image" to the new device. Additionally, if the backup was encrypted or not determined, what was stored in the backup and some information might have to be reentered. This led to profiles.

Profiles were created with a new tool called the iPhone Configuration Utility, released in 2008. A profile is a small .xml file that applies a given configuration onto an iOS device. This was necessary because a new generation of Apple developers wanted to control what could be done on iOS devices. One of those configurations was the ability to install an app over the air that was hosted on an organization's own web server, provided the .ipa mime type on the web server was defined. This basically mirrored what the App Store did and paved the way for internal app stores and profiles that were hosted on servers, both of which could be installed through in-house app stores, which hosted .ipa files.

> *Profiles were a huge paradigm shift. Instead of growing a library of scripts that customers needed to learn, modify, and deploy, profiles allowed us to start moving in a unified direction for configuring settings across the OS and applications, on both iOS and macOS. I think it's representative of why adoption of Apple has been so strong: they are able to re-architect major aspects of the platform relatively quickly, which allows them to remove barriers to adoption rapidly.*
>
> —Zach Halmstad, cofounder, Jamf

iPhone OS 3.1, released in 2009, came with the mail client in iOS that read and respected any Exchange ActiveSync (EAS) policies. These were policies configured on an Exchange server that gave the institution the ability to limit various features of the device, such as the ability to restrict the use of the camera or to force a password to wake a device up. EAS policies had been introduced by Microsoft in 2005, as part of the Exchange 2003 SP2 release, but had mostly been used to manage Windows Mobile devices.

At this point, Apple got larger and larger deployments, and it quickly became clear that it was no longer tenable to plug devices into iTunes and wait for long restores through legacy monolithic imaging solutions. The first iteration of iOS device management techniques that survives to this day was through profiles which gave control over most of what was available through EAS policies and added additional features. The success of the iPhone 4 in 2010 and the iPhone 4s in 2011 meant administrators needed better tools than iTunes restores and iPhone Configuration Utility to apply profiles. In 2012, the ability to create profiles and apply them to devices was moved into a new tool called Apple Configurator, which is still used to build custom profiles.

Apple Configurator could do a lot more than install profiles. Apple Configurator also allowed administrators to back up, restore, and install apps with Volume Purchase codes from the App Store. These were like coupon codes. Administrators could also build complex workflows that Configurator called Blueprints to do all of these automatically when a device was plugged in. Those options were expanded over time to include automatic enrollment into a Mobile Device Management Solution and the ability to supervise unsupervised devices (which we'll cover throughout the book).

Mobile Device Management

Apple Push Notifications were introduced in 2009. Those allowed devices to be alerted when there was data available for a given app. The MDM agent was built on top of that technology the following year. MDM, short for Mobile Device Management, was introduced in 2010, along with iOS 4. Initially, MDM was used to manage profiles on iOS, thus why Apple called their MDM service in macOS Server Profile Manager. In addition to managing profiles, three actions were supported in that original release: locate, lock, and wipe.

Since the initial release, MDM capabilities have grown over the years, as shown in Table 1-2. Each update brings more into MDM and means device administrators have to script and perform custom workflows to manage various features.

Table 1-2. *MDM Capabilities by OS, per Year*

iOS Version	macOS Version	Year	New Capabilities
4	N/A	2010	Volume Purchase Program (VPP), Mobile Device Management (MDM), MDM for the Mac
5	10.7	2011	Over-the-air OS updates, Siri management, disable iCloud backup
6	10.8	2012	APIs for third-party developers, Managed Open In, device supervision
7	10.9	2013	Touch ID management, Activation Lock bypass, Managed App Config
8	10.10	2014	Device Enrollment Program, Apple Configuration enrollments
9	10.11	2015	Device-based VPP, B2B app store, supervision reminders, enable and disable apps, home screen control, kiosk mode/app lock
10	10.12	2016	Restart device, shut down device, Lost Mode, APFS
11	10.13	2017	Classroom 2.0 management, Managed Face ID management, AirPrint. Add devices to DEP, QR code-based enrollment with some MDMs, User-Approved Kernel Extension Loading for Mac, user approval of MDM enrollment for Mac

(*continued*)

Table 1-2. *(continued)*

iOS Version	macOS Version	Year	New Capabilities
12	10.14	2018	Apple Business Manager, OAuth for managed Exchange accounts, managed tvOS app installation, password autofill restrictions
13		2019	Content Caching configuration, Bluetooth management, autonomous single app mode, OS update deferral, automatic renewal of Active Directory certificates
14		2020	Mark each managed app as removable, profile integration with the fonts API, the ability to manage home screen layouts in Apple Configurator, managed domains in Safari (for uploads), the ability for users to remove Exchange accounts (if they remove the profile), restriction for Unlock iPhone with an Apple Watch
15		2021	Managed Pasteboard restriction, the ability for personal iCloud and Managed Apple ID accounts to use the files app. The single sign-on payload can use specific Kerberos KDCs, Face ID and Touch ID for the single sign-on extension, restriction for iCloud Private Relay, Managed Apple ID enrollment flow, MDM-managed apps from user enrollment
16		2022	Sign in with Apple for education and offices, managed per-app networking, default domains, improved managed software updates, Platform single sign-on (SSO) with user enrollment SSO, Improved OAuth 2 support, Managed Device Attestation via the certificates generated on the Secure Enclave that secure communications with MDM, VPN, and 802.1X

Apple continues to evolve the device management toolset made available through MDM. The transition also makes the Mac more and more similar to iOS, sometimes disrupting traditional agent-based management when features that tap into then-unsupported areas of the filesystem are introduced. At the same time, the original programs had too many acronyms and were too disconnected - therefore much more difficult to access for new administrators of the ecosystem, who continue to flood in more rapidly than ever to support the platform.

Apple Device Management Programs

The App Store is arguably the reason that iOS is so popular. "There's an app for that" became the popular catchphrase for television commercials. The App Store debuted in 2008, the day before the iPhone 3G was released. It launched with 500 apps and grew to well over 2 million.

The App Store created a cultural shift in how people use computers. Need an app to manage HR operations? There's an app for that. Need an app to look up CIDR tables? There's an app for that. Need an app to make fart sounds? Obviously, that was one of the first apps. Businesses and schools started to use these devices at scale. But there was a gap: in order to get apps to users, administrators had to install them as an App Store user. That meant users used their own accounts to install VPP codes or got gift cards which came with tons of legal and accounting problems, as these apps were basically gifted to personal accounts and could be counted as income.

As with all things, large customers wanted a way to buy apps en masse. The Volume Purchase Program (VPP) was introduced to the App Store in 2010, which allowed customers to purchase apps in bulk. The VPP was akin to large tables of gift codes that were doled out to users, which could be done through Apple Configurator with a fancy spreadsheet. That evolved into revocable codes and then the ability to assign apps over the air, which still required a user to associate their personal Apple ID to an organization (although apps were revocable so it could be reclaimed when employees left an organization). The VPP allotments could then be managed over the air with a Mobile Device Management solution. Recent enhancements included a B2B app store, which has apps that aren't publicly available, and device-based VPP, which ties apps to devices enrolled into an MDM automatically at setup. That's done through what was once called DEP.

The Device Enrollment Program (DEP) was launched in 2014 and is now referred to as "automated enrollment." Organizations need to either be a school or have a DUNS number from Dun & Bradstreet (in order to prove they are a legitimate company) to participate. Enrollment via automated enrollment proves that an organization owns a device, and so Apple provides special management features that allow greater control by a centralized device management solution, such as the ability to force a device background or the ability to skip the confirmation screen before an app is being deployed on a device. Automated enrollment links a purchase order to an organization's Apple management accounts, so initially only supported the ability to work with a few official Apple resellers. Apple recognized that some devices weren't a part of DEP for various reasons, so added the ability to enroll iOS devices into DEP through Apple Configurator in 2018.

All of these acronyms can provide unnecessary friction to learn how to work with Apple. Therefore, Apple School Manager (ASM) was released in 2016, which also added the Classroom app into the mix - teachers could manage various features on Apple devices via the app. ASM provides a single portal to manage these Apple services as well as a means to manage classroom rosters. This makes it easier to find everything necessary to set up MDM services. Apple Business Manager was released in 2018, which centralized all of the ASM options applicable to businesses into a new program. As with ASM, organizations now have a single location to obtain VPP tokens and assign servers for automated enrollment-based devices associated with a given account.

Enterprise Mobility

All of the solutions referenced need a third-party device management tool. The first real mobile management solution to gain traction was SOTI, which launched in 2001 to leverage automation on mobile devices. They got into device management when those options became available for each platform. More and more IT departments wanted "over-the-air" management, or OTA management. AirWatch, founded by John Marshall in 2003 as Wandering Wi-Fi, was the first truly multiplatform device management solution that included iOS device management. Jamf, Afaria (by SAP), and MobileIron, founded by Ajay Mishra and Suresh Batchu, in 2007, also built similar OTA profile delivery techniques based on the original MDM spec that Apple introduced for OTA management.

At this point, most OTA management tasks (such as issuing a remote wipe or disabling basic features of devices) were done with Exchange ActiveSync (EAS). As seen in Figure 1-11, administrators could control basic password policies as well as some rudimentary device settings such as the ability to disable the camera. With this in mind, Apple began to write the initial MDM specifications, which paved the way for an entire IT industry segment to be born.

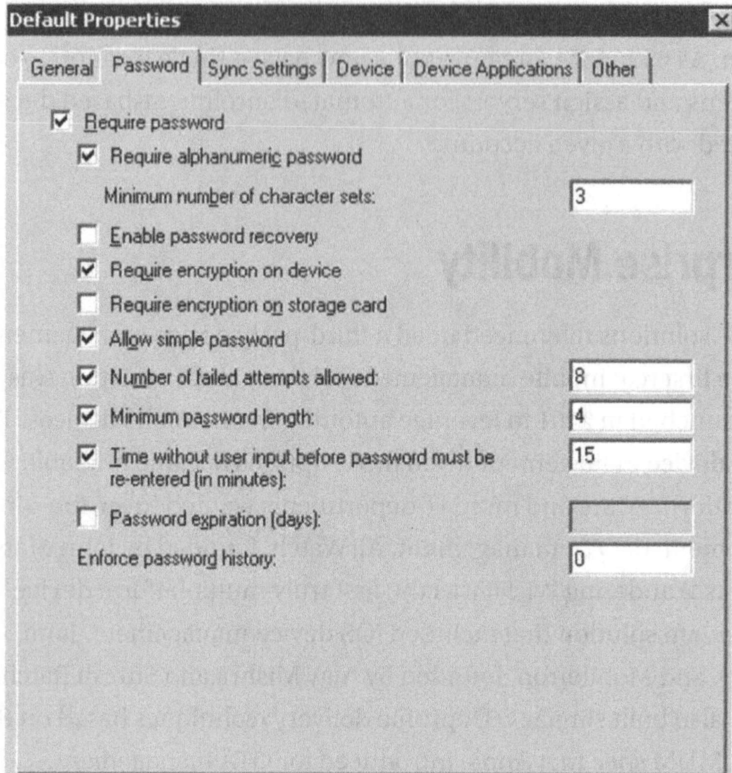

***Figure 1-11.** Exchange ActiveSync policies*

This was the landscape when the first edition of the *Enterprise iPhone and iPad Administrator's Guide* was released by Apress in 2010. Additional MDM solutions soon followed. TARMAC was released in 2011, which could manage iOS devices from a Mac. AppBlade and Excitor were also released in 2011. Over the course of the next 10+ years, MDM became one part of a number of other lovely acronyms:

- Mobile Content Management, or MCM, is a system of distributing content to mobile devices.
- Mobile Identity Management, or MIM, refers to a centralized identity provider hosting SAML or OAuth services.

- Enterprise Mobility Management, or EMM, gets more into managing apps and content that gets put on devices.
- Unified Endpoint Management, or UEM, brings traditional laptops and then desktops into the management feature, merging EMM with traditional device management.

A pivotal moment for Apple device management came in 2011, when BlackBerry announced support to manage Apple devices with their BlackBerry Enterprise Server (BES), which had been created in 1999 to manage BlackBerry devices. This represented a legitimization of sorts for Apple mobile devices in enterprise environments and also an opportunistic play for licensing due to the fact that the devices became such a mainstay in the enterprise. A shift toward UEM began at BlackBerry, which continued until 2018, when BlackBerry Enterprise Server was renamed to BlackBerry Unified Endpoint Manager. By then, BlackBerry was no longer a leading phone manufacturer.

An explosion of MDM providers has occurred since BlackBerry added Apple to their platform, to keep up with the demands of the market. FileWave and LANrev added MDM to their products in 2011 with new iOS vendors NotifyMDM and SOTI entering into the Apple device management family. Then Amtel MDM, AppTrack, Codeproof, Kony, ManageEngine (a part of Zoho Corporation), OurPact, Parallels, PUSHMANAGER, ProMDM, SimpleMDM, Sophos Mobile Control, and Tangoe MDM were released in 2012. MaaS360 was acquired by IBM in 2013, the same year auralis, CREA MDM, FancyFon Mobility Center (FAMOC), Hexnode, Lightspeed, and Relution were released and when Endpoint Protector added MDM to their security products. Citrix also acquired Zenprise in 2013 to introduce XenMobile. Jamf Now (originally called Bushel), Miradore, Mosyle, and ZuluDesk (acquired by Jamf in 2018 and being rebranded to Jamf School) were released in 2014, which also saw

VMware acquire AirWatch for $1.54 billion dollars and Good Technology acquire BoxTone, beefing up their Apple device management capabilities. The year 2014 also saw Microsoft extend Intune to manage iOS devices.

> *Working every day to boost our users' experiences with the most powerful, intuitive and elegant devices is amazing. As an Apple-only MDM provider, we have the joy of working every day with the most innovative company in the world and with the most advanced customers in the market. It's all about working 24x7 with the best people in the computer world and we love it!*
>
> —Alcyr Araujo, founder and CEO of Mosyle

Things quieted down a bit, as vendors struggled to keep up with near-constant updates from Apple. In 2016 after Apple started to publish the MDM specifications guide freely, an open source MDM called MicroMDM was initially committed to GitHub, which made it easier for organizations to build their own fork or implement services atop MicroMDM should they choose. Others crept on the scene as well in those years, such as Absolute Manage MDM, AppTech360, Avalanche Mobility Center, Baramundi, Circle by Disney, Cisco Meraki (by way of the Cisco acquisition of Meraki), Kaseya EMM, SureMDM, Trend Micro Mobile Security, and many others. Some focus on specific horizontal or vertical markets, while others focus on the ability to integrate with other products (like those in a company's portfolio). With such a wide field of MDM solutions, Apple focused on a great API and did not spend a ton of time on specific features needed for every possible market in their own product called Profile Manager (a part of macOS Server).

A number of family or residential MDM providers have also sprung up, which include Circle by Disney. The one market Apple has not made MDM available to has been the home. Apple has a number of tools they believe help families manage devices, such as Screen Time (built into every Apple device). It's been touted as a violation of user privacy to deploy MDM for home environments and in fact is a violation of the Apple Push Notification (APNs) terms of service. Apple has also limited what vendors can do in the home space. For example, OurPact, initially launched in 2012, was shut down in 2019 along with a number of other Screen Time apps as they used MDM to control various functions of iOS devices. Some of those have been restored to the app stores, but Apple has gotten more specific about requirements for future acceptance.

MDM isn't the only feature that began on iOS and ended up on the Mac. In fact, so many options shifted over that the name of the operating system used on Macs was even changed.

iOS + Mac OS X = macOS

Apple once dedicated an entire keynote to "Back to the Mac." macOS shows a slow unification of features from iOS. This isn't to say that the operating systems will eventually merge (in fact, Apple has stated they will not and instead split iPadOS from iOS), but concepts inarguably do continue to come to the Mac from iOS.

This began with the App Store, released for iOS and then for Mac in 2011 with Mac OS X 10.6.6. Software updates were later moved to the App Store, which unified how updates are centralized. Software updates for iOS have always been free. Up until 2013, major operating system releases were not free for the Mac. Mavericks was free as was every operating system thereafter. Updates for iOS have always been free (except a couple of releases for the iPod Touch, which were legal and accounting issues more than technical or marketing issues). This is one of the larger shifts in architecture from iOS that has changed not only the Mac but the entire IT industry (although while Microsoft hasn't made Windows free as of the time of this writing, it is very easy to legitimately get it for free now).

One More Thing: tvOS

The Apple TV initially ran a modified version of Mac OS X 10.4 in 2007. It was a great idea but a little too early to market. For example, it had a spinning disk and almost invited people to "hack" the device. So in 2010, the TV project started over with tvOS, initially introduced as a modified iOS 4 for the second-generation Apple TV. The operating system has evolved since then to be very similar in terms of management to iOS, albeit a bit more restrictive in terms of low-level functionality exposed to users (there naturally aren't as many features on the OS).

Initial management for tvOS came in Apple Configurator, which you would need to plug a device into in order to load an 802.1x certificate. You can plug devices into Apple Configurator and deploy profiles (including 802.1x configuration and MDM enrollment profiles). Later, we were able to load devices into DEP so we could manage them over standard MDM. Management commands can be a bit different, so not all MDM providers support tvOS, but as management of the platform matures, more and more do.

Imaging Is Dead?

NetBoot shipped in 1999 at Macworld. NetBoot allowed an administrator to boot a computer to an image stored on a centralized server. NetBoot was cool but was only adopted in niche environments; given the rapid acceleration of the desktop and the less rapid acceleration of the servers, networks and disk drives used to host and facilitate access to NetBoot servers.

Apple Software Restore then shipped in 2002. It had existed since the Mac Classic days as an internal restore tool, but after the public release, the combination of these formed the foundation of the imaging story for the

Mac for the next 15 years. Administrators with a fleet of devices to image could boot a Mac to a NetBoot volume and then, since the hard drive wasn't being used, could reformat the drive and restore an image to it.

An "image" refers to a digital replica. "Imaging" is when an admin takes a snapshot of the boot volume (and other volumes as well) of a device and then replicates that snapshot onto other devices. The Mac community has often referred to this practice as "monolithic imaging" and usually involved a Mac configured just how someone wants it. That image is captured with a tool like the `asr` command, which is built into the Mac.

Monolithic imaging first became a common practice around 2004 and evolved so you could stream that image over a network and lay those bits down on a hard drive. Other evolutions involved scripts that ran to normalize the volume or customize the image that could be applied to computers at imaging time like a computer name and other per-device settings. Additional post-flight scripts performed additional tasks on the image which hadn't been booted, as well as install standard Apple packages during the imaging process.

Imaging then became modular, and tools such as AutoDMG (`https://github.com/MagerValp/AutoDMG`) were released to build images, and DeployStudio (shown in Figure 1-12) was released to deploy images – both to address issues administrators found with the built-in NetBoot, NetInstall, and NetRestore tools from Apple. These allowed admins to build a master out of packages and dmg files that were then synthesized into an image. As seen in Figure 1-13, these workflows started out a little tough to use but quickly became GUI-driven and much more accessible to new administrators.

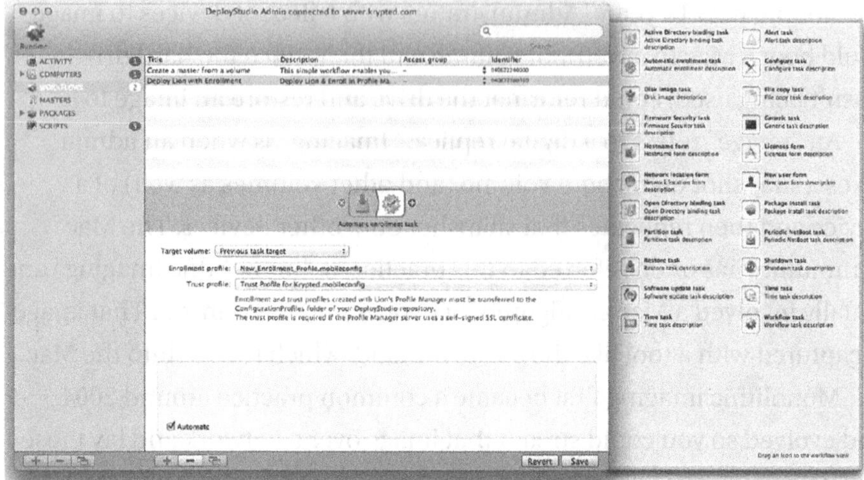

Figure 1-12. *DeployStudio*

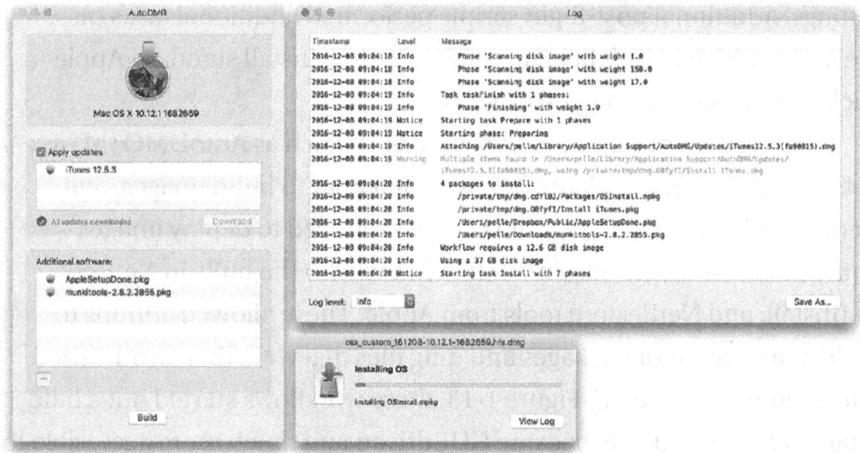

Figure 1-13. *AutoDMG*

The methodologies continue to evolve. The device security landscape has changed in such a way that Apple doesn't seem so friendly to tools that put bits on devices in an arbitrary fashion. Filesystems don't change often. Apple introduced HFS in 1985 to replace the Mac File System. It went through a few revisions over the decades and most notably became

HFS+ in 1998. It then makes sense that Apple would move toward a common filesystem across all operating systems. This led to APFS (Apple File System) filesystem being introduced on March 27, 2017, for iOS and then rolled out to tvOS and watchOS. By September of that year, it came to the Mac in macOS 10.13.

> *With the move away from imaging I thought for sure that apfs would be the death knell for AutoDMG. Apple has a long tradition of not discussing upcoming changes in public, so listening closely to what they announce at WWDC is critical - and always, _always_, test the betas. In the end apfs turned out to be quite uneventful for AutoDMG itself and the surrounding ecosystem had to bear the brunt of the changes.*
>
> —Per Olofsson, creator of AutoDMG

The introduction of APFS to iOS and then macOS gives Apple software engineers a lot of options around how to slice disks, how to leverage volumes to provide device management options, and potentially how to freeze portions of the Mac filesystem from being edited. Most importantly, it means Apple administrators need to embrace a whole new way of device management.

Once volumes are prepared, admins can use tools like Apple Configurator to explode an ipsw file onto an iOS device. An ipsw is signed by Apple, cannot be altered, and is similar to the old monolithic restore process with the exception that administrators can't install anything into the image before applying the image to devices. The Mac process of imaging evolved to how it's done in iOS (shocking). Boot a Mac to a network volume (now hosted on the App Store); the operating system is downloaded and installed onto the Mac (now hosted on the App Store). An alternative method is to use the createinstallmedia command to build an operating system installer that can then be used to install Macs without the recovery partition/App Store.

macOS – Unix = appleOS

As it is said with the viking legend of Ragnarok, someday we will return to our roots. Mac management lost part of what makes it work so well in a corporate environment. From 10.2 and on, the Mac community gained momentum, with multiuser operating systems; fast user switching; Active Directory integration; good information security policies; mass deployment techniques on par with Windows, if not better; and a number of other features that made the Mac a first-class citizen.

Apple always played catch-up though. At some point, companies have to realize that the goalpost continues to move to be a first-class citizen on corporate networks. The success of iOS taught Apple that they can redefine corporate dogma rather than just play catch-up - suddenly rather than have their developers told what they did was wrong, they could define where the goalposts went. That mentality started to leak into the Mac. Part of that redefinition is SIP.

System Integrity Protection, or SIP, is a mode for macOS where full sandbox controls are implemented in such a way that parts of the operating system can't be written to, even if privileges are elevated to a superuser account. There are other aspects of SIP such as how memory is handled more securely and how dynamic libraries can't be loaded into apps - but the most noticeable aspects for many administrators involved the inability to write into /System folders and/or remotely set NetBoot targets. This philosophy comes from the fact that iOS is arguably one of the most secure operating systems ever conceived (built on generations of learning from previous secure operating systems via its origins as the Darwin UNIX core of macOS).

There are a number of features in iOS that provide such a high level of security on the platform, although arguably the most important is how apps are sandboxed. Every iOS app comes with its own sandbox, which means that apps can communicate with one another, but only if they have what are called entitlements, to do so, which typically involve a prompt so a user can allow a temporary connection between apps through a share sheet or an entitlement to use the app. Consider how many apps ask to use the Camera or access the Desktop. Over the past few years, this design philosophy was added to the Mac with special use cases allowing for various technologies that require their own type of kernel access (like a virtualization framework).

To distribute apps through the Mac App Store for 10.14.4 and below, developers need to turn on an App Sandbox and have entitlements defined for apps in more and more cases. Higher versions of the operating system actually require certain entitlements be explicit in order for the app to get notarized by Apple. Apps that aren't notarized then can't be opened. For macOS Catalina, an app does not yet have to be sandboxed to be notarized. The only requirement is to be set as a "hardened runtime."

Apple has sandboxed part of the operating system. Sandboxing and other security measures are discussed in more depth throughout the book, but there are other ramifications to how the technology is implemented. In a POSIX-compliant Unix environment, administrators with an appropriate level of privileges (e.g., root access) have historically done whatever they want on a device. They're often called superusers for just this reason. With sandbox, Apple can restrict any type of user from writing to certain directories on the filesystem. While macOS has been certified as compatible with the Single UNIX Specification version 3, or SUSv3 for short, this is more tied to the core of macOS, Darwin, than the layer that an end user interacts with.

Each variant of an operating system seems to have their own way to deal with device drivers, probably more true for UNIX-compatible operating systems than any others. The concept of an extension dates back to the Mac OS Classic era. An extension was a file that basically provided kernel access, which allowed devices to be plugged into computers. Mac OS 9 had a tool called the Extension Manager, which allowed a user to turn these drivers on and off easily. If an extension caused a computer to become unbootable, you could easily boot the computer into safe mode, drag all the extensions out of their folder and into a folder called Disabled Extensions on the desktop, and reboot and viola – the system was good.

In Mac OS X and later macOS, a kernel extension (often referred to as a kext) is code loaded directly into the kernel of the Mac. This allows much lower-level access that's typically necessary for software that needs to interrupt processes (such as security software) or software that interfaces with physical devices where Apple doesn't provide an API for doing so. Most operating systems have something of this sort, for example, on Windows there are Kernel-Mode Extensions.

Given how low-level kexts can run, there's always been a concern about the security of a kext. Kexts required a signature as of 2013 (Maverick). Apple went further to restrict kexts in High Sierra, when Secure Kernel Extension Loading forced a user to accept a kext. Apple disabled synthetic clicking on this screen, so administrators couldn't programmatically accept their own kext. The exceptions are that an MDM can preemptively enable a kernel extension, and the `spctl kext-consent add` command can do so if you have administrative access on a client computer.

Kernel extensions and MDM enrollments cannot complete without the acknowledgment from a user of what is happening. In general, to force acceptance of kernel extensions and MDM enrollments is another step toward a more iOS-centric Mac. This isn't to say that admins will lose the ability to access a command line or write code, but as the distribution of Macs increases, those are made more difficult. Management options need to be simpler so they're more accessible, while also more secure, to keep users safe. While the kernel extension is a uniquely Apple solution, sandbox is actually derived from the sandbox facility in BSD, a core part of trusted BSD. Based on how future options are implemented, admins could still have fully manageable and nerdy tools without the need to sacrifice attributes of the Apple experience they hold so dear, like privacy.

Moving Away from Active Directory

One of the main reasons the Mac was accepted as a standard in many companies was the ability to work within standard Active Directory environments. From Mac OS X 10.2.x until today's macOS versions, many Mac Admins spent countless hours to refine and perfect their Active Directory bind scripts. Out of that wealth of knowledge about how every part of Active Directory worked, some also realized that it might be wrong to use Active Directory with the Mac. There were some advantages to Macs directly connected to an Active Directory domain, like users could get Kerberos tickets and have password management; it also introduced issues like how to keep login keychain passwords and FileVault account passwords in sync with the password used for the user's Active Directory account. These password problems were solved by local accounts on the Mac, but local accounts were unable to communicate at all with the AD domain.

The open source NoMAD project was introduced in 2017 by Joel Rennich and represented a seismic shift in how people charged with managing Apple devices thought about Active Directory and how their Macs should connect to it. NoMAD, short for No More AD, was a project that allowed admins to obtain Kerberos tickets from Active Directory and do many of the common tasks required in an Active Directory environment, without the need to "bind" the machine to the domain. This new approach of middleware that handled the connections to Active Directory allowed the use of local accounts on the Mac, addressing the password problems, while still enabling NoMAD-equipped Macs to obtain Kerberos tickets and password management from the AD domain.

> *As the father of the Magic Triangle(tm) I get that it's a bit weird to be telling you not to bind anymore... but those days are done. The modern Mac is primarily a single user system that barely, if ever, touches the corporate network anymore, so we should stop acting like a persistent LDAP bind is doing anybody any favors.*
>
> —Joel Rennich, founder of NoMAD and director of Jamf Connect, Jamf

NoMAD was sold to Jamf in 2018, and portions are now part of a proprietary product called Jamf Connect. Since the early days of NoMAD, the paid version of NoMAD Login Window (now called Jamf Connect) has since expanded to allow for Smart Card authentication and now works with federated identity providers such as Azure AD, Okta, Ping, and Google.

Rennich introduced NoMAD. In terms of his place in the Apple device management history books, though, almost as importantly, he founded a website called afp548.com. In doing so, he and his cohort Josh Wisenbaker established the foundation blocks for what has evolved into the latter-day Apple admin community. Both went to work for Apple, and others took up the mantle to help forge that community for years to come (both have since left Apple).

The Apple Admin Community

There is a strong community of Apple administrators, which often self-identify as Mac Admins. The community idea is fairly Apple-centric - back to when Guy Kawasaki started the concept of evangelizing the platform as Apple's Chief Evangelist from 1983 to 1987. There are a variety of ways to interact with the community, which include going to conferences, attending user groups, and interacting with the community online (e.g., via Slack).

Conferences

The MacAdmin community initially grew out of Macworld and the Apple Worldwide Developers Conference (WWDC), which both started in 1987. The community slowly matured; people often met in sessions, expo booths, and then bars (e.g., one called Dave's). Those were around the conferences up until 2009 when Apple announced their final year as a sponsor of the conference. Many Apple products had been announced at Macworld, but that would shift to WWDC in the future. Many of the people who met in person moved those relationships online, like IRC channels dedicated to Mac management. Some who joined those lists created online relationships that led to people getting a chance to meet in person at the next event they went to.

The explosion of iPhones shifted WWDC to be less focused on administration topics and much more focused on software development (after all, it is a "developers" conference). WWDC also became so popular that Apple began to sell tickets in a lottery, and less and less admins could actually go. After the administrative sessions ended at WWDC (for a bit), a new era of conferences began to be created in the vacuum. MacSysAdmin in Gothenburg, Sweden, was introduced in 2009. Once again, the MacAdmin team at Penn State University (PSU) stepped up and created the PennState MacAdmins Conference in 2010.

> *From the earliest days of Macintosh, there's always been something special about those that were creating or supporting Apple technologies. That community, the Apple technical community, has always been at the core of MacTech. It's the reason that we created the live, in-person MacTech events more than a decade ago. Some 150+ days of events later, the community continues to come together for an amazing experience, seeing incredible speakers and content, and engaging*

in the ever popular "hallway track". Those awesome face-to-face interactions both bond and power an exceptional community. As we move into the second decade of MacTech's live events, we'll continue to enable the community to come together in this unique way.

—Neil Ticktin, CEO, MacTech

A number of other vendors have also built up conferences, and parts of the community have fragmented off into the conferences that most fit their needs. This is to be expected when there are multiple generations of engineers who use a variety of different ecosystems to manage products. People need to find more focused content for their specific jobs, especially since many tasks have become vendor or open source product-centric. A quick overview of the conferences available is as follows:

- **ACES Conference**: ACES is a conference for Apple consultants so people who are members of the Apple Consultants Network (or ACN). ACES is a solid introduction for many with a mix of the business side of a consulting or managed service firm and the technical aspects of what consultants might need to know. This combination of soft and technical skills is common at conferences, but the focus on how to run a small business is unique.
- **Addigy Innovate**: A conference for those who use Addigy products to manage their fleets of Apple devices. This includes topics like identity, security, initial setup, and long-term management of devices.
- **Command-IT**: 2018 was the first year of the Command-IT conference in France! Sessions are fairly broad and highly informative. More at `www.command-it.fr`.

- **FileWave Conference**: The FileWave Alliance Conference focuses on the latest and greatest with FileWave and provides systems administrators of FileWave environments with access to developers, deployment information, etc.
- **Jamf Software's JNUC (Jamf Nation User Conference)**: A conference primarily geared at the Apple Administrator who uses Jamf products for their administrative efforts. There are some sessions on general administrative topics, such as what a plist is and general shell scripting. It's a must for admins who spend a lot of their days in Jamf Pro (or other Jamf products). Traditionally held in Minneapolis, the conference moved to San Diego for 2022.
- **MacAdminsUA**: A conference held in the Ukrainian city of Kyiv. On hold for obvious reasons. Past sessions included topics on consulting, security, and of course the latest requirements with tech like Apple Business Manager (keep in mind that not all features are available in all countries). Find more on it at `https://macadmins.org.ua`.
- **Mac Admin and Developer Conference UK**: MacADUK is a conference for Apple administrators and developers, with a lot of sessions and good content, held in London.
- **MacDevOps YVR**: MacDevOps is a conference based in Vancouver, with sessions that range across the DevOps build train. YVR is definitely for those who are deeper into automation (e.g., want to script every aspect of the management experience).

- **MacSysAdmin**: All things Apple, in Sweden. This conference is held in the fall in Göteborg, Sweden, with great content that spans the tasks a Mac Admin has to cover. There are lots of really good content, with a very global perspective. Network with other career-oriented Mac Admins in a relaxed atmosphere.
- **MacTech**: This conference is a good look at how environments grow and how administrators can grow into new roles. There are some consultants, but in general the focus has been on tips and tricks ranging from small to large deployment sizes. MacTech Conference is held in LA, so don't forget the wetsuits.
- **Mobile World Congress**: Most presenters at a show like this will be less technical, more business analysts, and more interested in the why and results than the how. It's a good group but different from those who spend all of their time integrating systems. Held in early May, with smaller shows globally, later in the year. For a sampling of sessions, check out their YouTube channel at `www.youtube.com/user/GSMAOnline/playlists`.
- **MobileIron Live**: MobileIron has a new(ish) conference. Since they were acquired by Ivanti, the conference has added three smaller conferences. environments who use MobileIron (and other Ivanti products integrated with MobileIron) to manage Apple devices, definitely worth a look.
- **Objective by the Sea**: Security is a topic that has come up from time to time at MacAdmin conferences. Patrick Wardle put together a lineup of speakers for the first

few and the sessions for past conference sessions are online. Probably one of the deepest technical conferences for those in information security.

- **Penn State MacAdmins Conference**: Held at the Penn Stater Hotel and Conference Center in State College, PA. Penn State MacAdmins emerged during a time of uncertainty with WWDC and systems administration topics. The same team had created the infamous MacEnterprise list that Penn State runs. The use of the list has trickled off while the conference itself has grown. It's priced well, vendor agnostic, and run by one of the most talented MacAdmin teams around.
- **VMworld (formerly AirWatch Connect)**: A conference for people who manage heterogeneous mobile deployments that rely on Workspace ONE and AirWatch.
- **WWDC**: Everyone knows about Apple's Worldwide Developer Conference. It continues to get more and more difficult to get tickets to the conference, although with a pivot to more of an online conference, attendees can watch the videos they want to see wherever they want, rather than have to make choices about which sessions would be better than others. This is a must for engineers who build third-party tools, and what a Mac Admin sees in a WWDC session is likely not to ship for a few months in management tools. Still, watch the sessions online at a minimum and save any continuing development/training funds to check out one of the other conferences.

- **X World**: Originally part of the AUC in Australia, X World has topics ranging from Munki to Casper. Initially a very education-centric conference, there were Apple administrators from around Australia gathered to share their knowledge and green information from others on managing large numbers of Apple systems. And the organizers and delegates are pretty awesome people to hang out with. Great networking.

Online Communities

The Apple administrative community began to emerge in 2001 and congealed around a few specific places. One was the Mac Enterprise listserve, from Penn State University. Another was the Mac OS X Server list from Apple. These were active communities that were really sometimes very long email threads, but we all got to know each other. Another was afp548. The port for the Apple File Protocol hosted by Mac OS X Server is 548. The afp548.com website was launched in 2002 by Joel Rennich. It had a little more focus around the server product and later around directory services and imaging or large-scale deployment practices. Both Mac Enterprise and afp548.com are important as they represented the creation of a community built around Apple Administration that wasn't controlled by Apple (like the forums on Apple's own support sites).

Over time, email lists can grow unwieldy. Many conversations moved to specialized lists, chat rooms, Twitter, or bulletin boards. For example, in 2011, Jamf created a message list but eventually moved that over to a web portal that now boasts over 40,000 active users and over 30,000 discussions. Other vendors created message boards and communities as well, and the community appeared to fragment for a time. Then came the MacAdmins Slack channel.

The Mac Admins Slack is a unique online community for a few reasons. There is a general sense of thoughtfulness among members. Time and time again I see someone go to lengths to help another member that they have no prior connection with, just for the good of the community. Likewise, there's a strong sense of authenticity. Vendors, like us, can become involved, but we're really there to support the community and not to treat it like a promotional channel. It's also not just a slack. It's a podcast, it's local meetups, and more. Connections may initially be made online, but they can grow outside of it. The community extends far beyond a particular slack channel. The Slack is just a touch point.

—Taylor Boyko, founder and CEO at SimpleMDM

The MacAdmins Slack instance was introduced in 2015. Since then, "Slack" as it seems to lovingly be called has grown to over 50,000 users who have sent over 18 million messages. As can be seen in Figure 1-14, these Apple admins discuss everything from upcoming betas to DEP deployments, imaging, and even local groups for each major city and/or country in the world. More focused than checking for #macadmins on Twitter, more history than IRC, and a great place to ask a polite question and potentially save weeks of hunting for the answer to a problem.

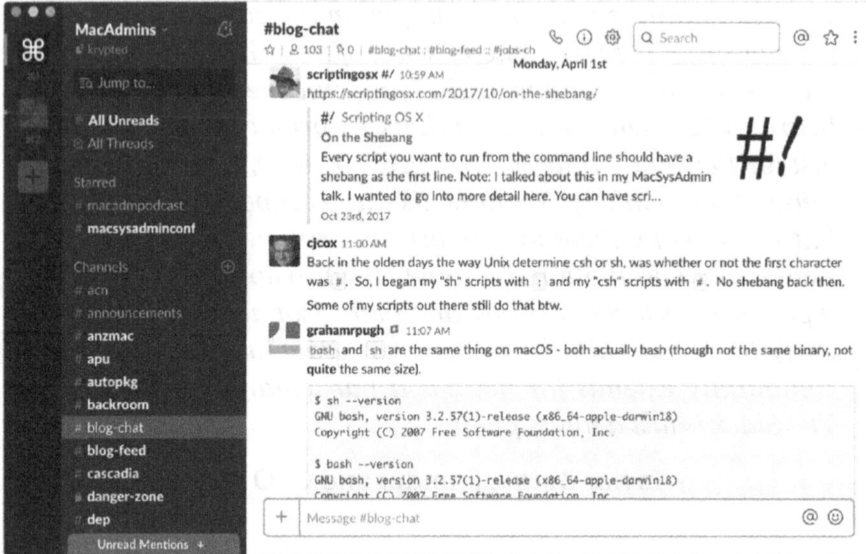

Figure 1-14. *The MacAdmins Slack*

The MacAdmins Slack channel is one of the most important things to happen to the MacAdmins community. With over 1100 channels to follow, Slack could further fragment admins, but the fact that so many people are in a lot of different channels actually brings more people together in better contexts. Slack is real time; digest emails always felt a bit less inclusive, and it can be easier not to take something out of context when catching up through a week's worth of digests.

User Groups

Apple has a long and rich tradition of sponsoring, facilitating, helping out with, and sometimes just tolerating user groups. There have been Macintosh user groups since there has been a Mac. Over time, those charged with larger-scale care and feeding of devices have split off into their own, professional user groups. Simply search for a city name followed by MacAdmins, and user groups or meetups with an established local chapter to get involved in can often be found.

Some available at the time of this writing include the following:

- **Apple Admins of LA and OC**: `www.meetup.com/Los-Angeles-Mac-Meetup/`
- **Austin Apple Admins**: `www.austinappleadmins.org`
- **Boston Mac Admins**: `www.meetup.com/bostonmacadmins/`
- **Calgary MacDeployment Meetup**: `http://macdeployment.ca`
- **Chicago Mac Admins**: `www.chicagoappleadmins.org`
- **Colorado iOS Admins**: `http://coiosadmin.tumblr.com`
- **Denver Mac Admins**: `www.meetup.com/Denver-Mac-Admins/`
- **London Apple Admins**: `www.londonappleadmins.org.uk`
- **MacAdmin Monthly**: `www.macadminmonthly.org`
- **[MacSysAdmin] Bier**: `http://macsysadmin.ch`
- **MacBrained**: `http://macbrained.org`
- **MacDMV (The DC Metro area Mac Admins group)**: `www.macdmv.com`
- **NW Apple Administrators (Portland)**: `www.meetup.com/NW-Apple-Administrators-Eng-Architects-Support-JAMF-Casper/`

- **Perth Apple Admins**: www.meetup.com/Perth-Apple-Admins/
- **Philly Mac Admins**: www.meetup.com/Greater-Philadelphia-Area-Mac-Admins/
- **Providence Apple Admins**: www.meetup.com/providenceappleadmins/
- **Apple Admins of Seattle and the Great Northwest**: www.meetup.com/Seattle-Apple-Admins/
- **Sydney Mac Admins Meetup**: www.meetup.com/Sydney-Mac-Admins/
- **Twin Cities Mac Admins Group**: https://twitter.com/mspmacadmns

More come online all the time (some exist solely online). Many now start out of MacAdmins Slack channels or organize around those. The topics always change, but many of those discussed build up to form a set of best practices that can be summarized in a line in a balanced scorecard, one way to easily visualize how an organization tracks performance of any initiative over time. To see one of those, skip ahead to Chapter 12.

Summary

Apple's pace of innovation in the early days was astounding. Those first few years can be read about in plenty of business books. That seemed to trail off for a while. After Mac OS X came along, the first ten years seemed to be trying to find an identity for administration. "Words matter" quite a bit at Apple. In 2008, Steve Jobs said, "Why would I do anything for that orifice called the CIO?" This sums up that period of time. Yet that is classic sales – Apple didn't have a great story to tell for larger-scale management yet.

The Apple administrative community pushed, and Apple learned what larger organizations actually needed the devices to do and figured out how to do those tasks (such as integrate with Active Directory) in a way that preserved Apple values while still providing the tools needed to manage devices en masse.

The pace for administrators over the past ten years has been substantial. Always-on Internet, the explosion in the number of devices each user has, and the way devices are used (like to stream music over a HomePod) were barely even conceivable when the Mac was released. Always-on Internet for every device has caused that type of change in almost every industry - not just at Apple. The evolution to allow for more device management has been a learning experience, both for Apple and for the community of users and administrators they serve.

> *Perhaps what I respect about Apple most is that they know who they are. Their focus on the individual has been relentless. In the face of many telling them to do something different, Apple stays true to their DNA.*
>
> —Dean Hager, CEO Jamf

The tipping point in that evolution was when Apple forged a partnership with IBM in 2014, with Ginni Rometty and Apple CEO Tim Cook (who spent 12 years at IBM) who did interviews (e.g., for CNBC) and were filmed on a walk around campus, looking all kinds of pensive. Since then, a newfound focus on business has tightened and so enterprise adoption has exploded. After all, the largest fleet of devices in the world is the culmination of all the iPads, iPhones, and MacBooks in homes around the world.

As seen throughout this chapter, the more things change, the more they stay the same. The names of the tools have changed: At Ease led to Macintosh Manager, which led to Workgroup Manager, and eventually became what was Profile Manager. In a more SaaS-oriented world, Profile

Manager then became Apple Business Essentials (not the code but the very idea of an Apple-branded MDM). The back-end technology for management has changed with each of those names, where we now have MDM as the predominant way to manage devices - and some tools still have agents. While the look and feel of the tools has changed, the mission of each hasn't changed all that much, much as the buttons still say many of the same words from Apple Network Assistant all the way through to Apple Remote Desktop 3.9.

In this chapter, we laid out the timeline of when various features and components were released. We can't cover all of the items in this book at the level they deserve, especially given the number of vendors and talented engineers that now work in the Apple space. When that first book on managing Macs in the Enterprise was released, there were about half a dozen management MDM vendors; today, there are well over ten times that, some by companies with valuations in the billions. That doesn't include the rest of the ecosystem like security tools, backup software, groupware, and other entire software categories this chapter skipped right over. It is possible to look at general themes and provide guidance around each. This guidance begins in Chapter 2, when we look at what the agent-based management solutions do to help manage Macs.

CHAPTER 2

Agent-Based Management

This chapter is about agents that can run on a Mac. Agents are services, or programs, that run on devices. These agents are specifically designed to give a systems administrator command and control over a Mac and are usually agents that start a listener on the Mac or tell the Mac to log in to a server and pull down management tasks from that server on a routine basis. These give administrators the ability to control various aspects of computers from a centralized server. Commands are sent to the device from the server or pulled from the server and run on devices.

Over the past few years, Apple developers have started to reduce the importance of agents on the Mac. They do this when they remove capabilities from agents and/or make it easier to disable them. Agents are still an important aspect of macOS management, and so it's important to understand what an agent is, what it does, and when to use one. Device management tools use agents, security software uses agents, and a number of tools use agents to track the licensing of their software on devices. Agents can do less and less with every passing year, but they are still necessary.

One place where "less and less" has been problematic is device management. Just keep in mind that any time a task can be done with an agent or MDM, make sure to use the MDM unless there's a really good reason to use an agent. The Mac isn't quite back in the era of Desk

C. Edge and R. Trouton, *Apple Device Management*,
https://doi.org/10.1007/978-1-4842-9156-6_2

Accessories from System 7, but the platform is in an era where user consent is more and more important for tasks that could violate user privacy - even for various tasks that would be performed on devices we can prove the organization owns.

Neither iOS nor tvOS allows for custom agents, but agent-based management is (at least for now) a critical aspect of how to manage macOS devices. In this chapter, we'll review common agents designed for the Mac and what they do. We'll cover MDM, which is an agent-based management environment provided by Apple in the next chapter, and provide much more information around how MDM works. MDM has been referred to as "agentless" at times, but that really means it's just an agent provided by Apple.

Daemons and Agents

As mentioned, an agent is a process that runs on a device. These run persistently and so they're always running. When a daemon or agent is configured, they can be flagged to restart in case they stop. To see a few built-in agents, open System Settings and go to the Sharing System Setting pane. As seen in Figure 2-1, those are often for sharing resources over a network. Let's turn File Sharing on for just a moment

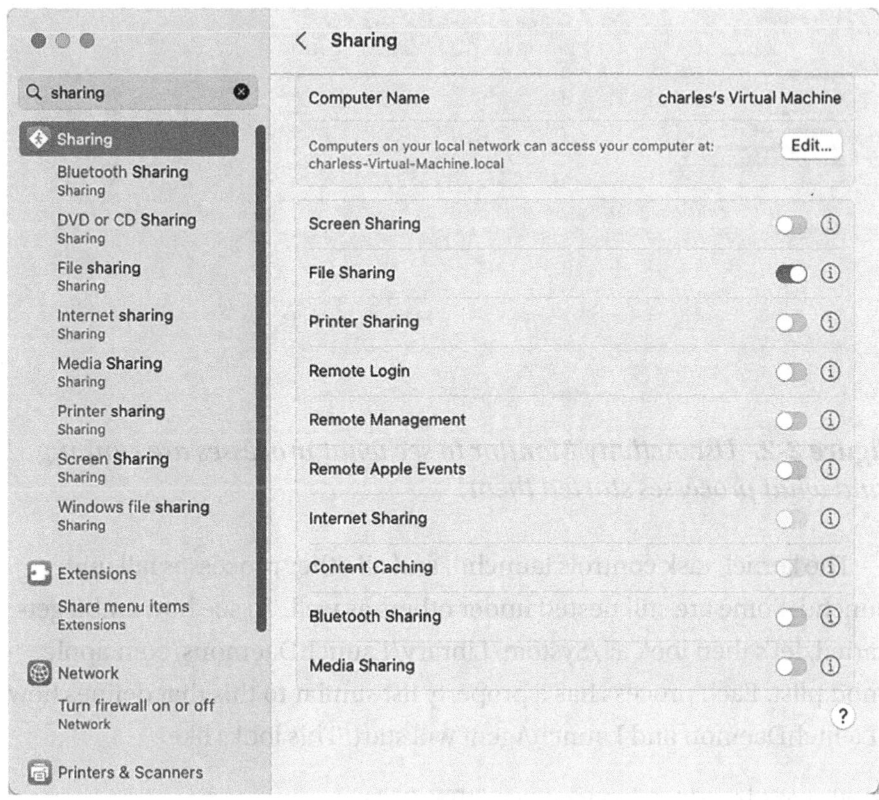

***Figure 2-1.** The Sharing System Setting pane*

Each of these agents is a LaunchDaemon or LaunchAgent that loads on the computer - for this example, we'll start File Sharing with Windows File Sharing enabled. The first process that starts on a Mac is launchd, which is then responsible for starting, stopping, and controlling all subsequent processes based on the .plist file that defines them. This includes all services required to make the operating system function. The easiest way to see this is to open Activity Monitor from `/Applications/Utilities` and select "All Processes, Hierarchically" from the View menu. Here, search for the file (Figure 2-2) and note that it's been started, has a PID of 194, and runs as root. The PID is the process ID.

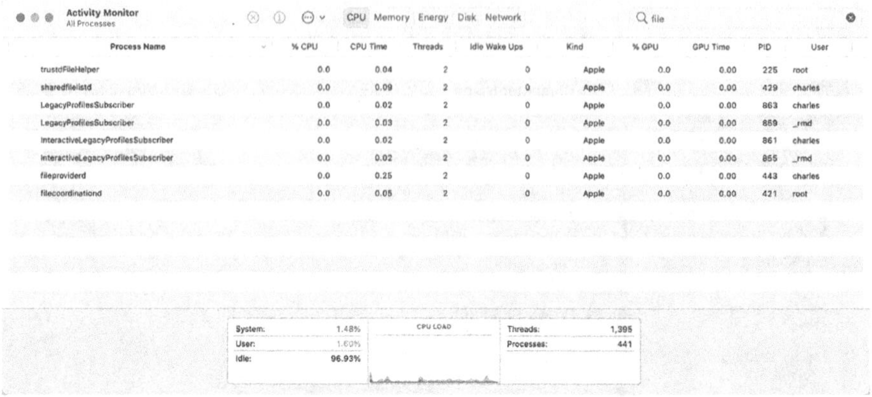

***Figure 2-2.** Use Activity Monitor to see what processes are running (and what processes started them)*

The kernel_task controls launchd, and all other processes fall under launchd. Some are still nested under others as well. To see how smbd gets started, let's then look at /System/Library/LaunchDaemons/com.apple.smbd.plist. Each process has a property list similar to this that defines how a LaunchDaemon and LaunchAgent will start. This looks like

```
<?xml version="1.0" encoding="UTF-8"?>
<!DOCTYPE plist PUBLIC "-//Apple//DTD PLIST 1.0//EN" "http://
www.apple.com/DTDs/PropertyList-1.0.dtd">
<plist version="1.0">
<dict>
        <key>EnableTransactions</key>
        <true/>
        <key>Disabled</key>
        <true/>
        <key>Label</key>
        <string>com.apple.smbd</string>
        <key>MachServices</key>
        <dict>
```

```
                <key>com.apple.smbd</key>
                <dict>
                        <key>HideUntilCheckIn</key>
                        <true/>
                </dict>
        </dict>
        <key>ProgramArguments</key>
        <array>
                <string>/usr/sbin/smbd</string>
        </array>
        <key>Sockets</key>
        <dict>
                <key>direct</key>
                <dict>
                        <key>SockServiceName</key>
                        <string>microsoft-ds</string>
                        <key>Bonjour</key>
                        <array>
                                <string>smb</string>
                        </array>
                </dict>
        </dict>
</dict>
</plist>
```

In the preceding example, note that the /usr/sbin/smbd binary is loaded and the LaunchDaemon controls the binary. LaunchDaemons can run even without a user logged in. LaunchDaemons cannot display information with the graphical interface of a Mac; but they can provide data to apps that have graphical interfaces. The plist files are stored in the /System/Library/LaunchDaemons folder (for those provided by Apple) and /Library/LaunchDaemons (for the rest). There are also LaunchAgents, which run on behalf of a user and therefore need the user to be logged in to run. LaunchAgents can display information through the window server if they are entitled to do so. As with LaunchDaemons, LaunchAgents are controlled by property lists. The configuration plist files are stored in the /System/Library/LaunchAgents and /Library/LaunchAgents, and user launch agents are installed in the ~/Library/LaunchAgents folder.

Next, let's look at a common graphical interface for managing LaunchDaemons and LaunchAgents, Lingon.

Use Lingon to See and Change Daemons and Agents Easily

Lingon is a tool available on the Mac App Store at `https://itunes.apple.com/us/app/lingon-3/id450201424`. Install Lingon to be able to quickly and easily manage LaunchDaemons and LaunchAgents. It can also be downloaded through Peter Borg's site at `www.peterborgapps.com/lingon`. The version there has more features and control over system-level daemons and agents.

On first open, Lingon shows a list of non-Apple services installed on the system. In Figure 2-3, notice that you see two for Druva, one for Tunnelblick, and one for an older version of macOS Server.

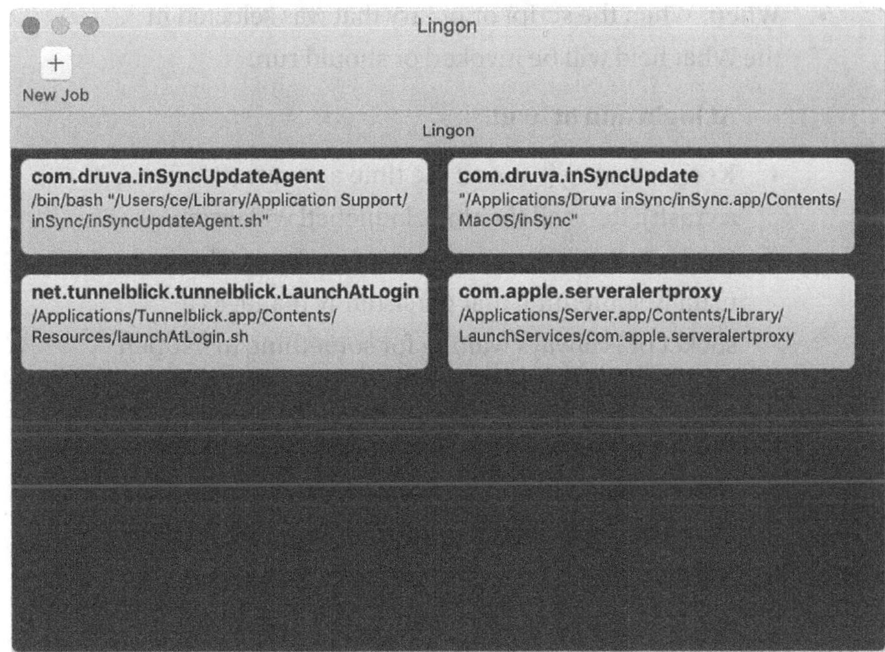

***Figure 2-3.** The Lingon agent browser screen*

Create a new one by clicking New Job. At the New Job screen shown in Figure 2-4, there are the following fields:

- **Name**: The name of the script. This can be something simple like Pretendco Agent but is usually saved as com.Pretendco.agent.
- **What**: App or even just an arbitrary command like "say hello" if the command is short and simple.

- **When**: When the script or binary that was selected in the What field will be invoked or should run.
    - **At login and at load**.
    - **Keep running** (runs all the time and restarts after a crash): Runs all the time. launchctl will watch for the process to terminate and restart it. This is usually something that persistently manages a socket or is always waiting for something to happen on a system.
    - **Whenever a volume is mounted**: This is similar to watching for a file to change given that it's watching /Volumes, but when a volume mounts, the process will run.
    - **Every**: Runs the script or process at a regularly scheduled interval, like every 90 seconds or once an hour.
    - **At a specific time**: Runs the specified process at a given time on a schedule (this is similar in nature to how cron jobs worked).
    - **This file is changed**: Defines a path to a file so that if the LaunchDaemon notices a file has changed, the desired script will run. This is pretty common for scripting automations, such as "if a file gets placed in this directory, run it through an image converter.
- **Save & Load**: Saves the LaunchAgent or LaunchDaemon, provides the correct permissions, and attempts to load.

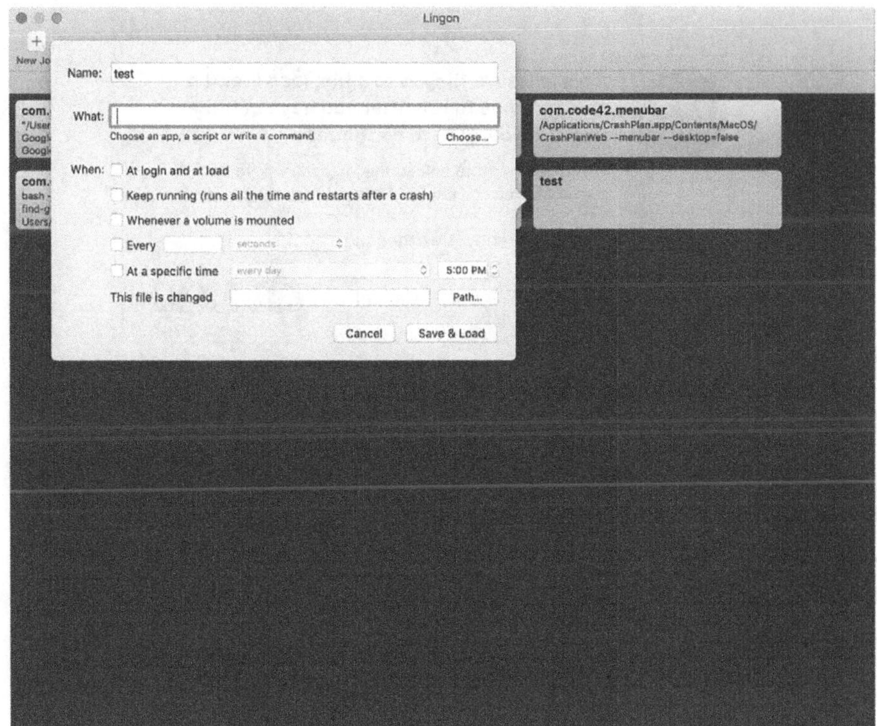

***Figure 2-4.** Provide a name and location for a script or app to daemonize it*

Next, click **Save & Load** and you'll be prompted that the service will run even after you close Lingon (Figure 2-5). The reason for this is that when you save your entry, the Lingon app creates a LaunchDaemon and starts it.

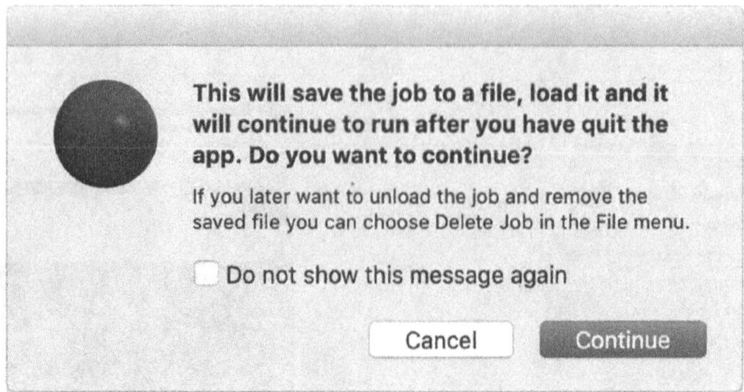

Figure 2-5. *Save your new agent or daemon*

If you select a job and then select "Copy Job to Clipboard" from the Job menu, then you can open a new document and paste the contents of what would be in a property list in. By default, the new LaunchAgent is saved in ~/Library/LaunchAgents/ so you can also easily just view it with cat once saved.

Now that we can create and delete LaunchAgents and LaunchDaemons, you know how to create an agent if you need to or stop one from processing if it's running on a host. Now that we've described what goes into building a daemon or agent, let's look at controlling them so we can then show how you interface with those used to send management commands to macOS devices.

Controlling LaunchDaemons with launchctl

Earlier, when we showed Activity Monitor, we could have stopped the process we were looking at. Doing so means that if the process is set to do so, it can start up again. It's possible to add, edit, delete, and load these with the launchctl command. Using launchctl is pretty straightforward. In the following example, we'll look at disabling the disk arbitration daemon to show how to control a LaunchDaemon with launchctl. To disable disk arbitration, first run the following command to obtain a list of currently running launchd-initiated processes:

```
launchctl list
```

That's going to output a few too many so let's constrain our search to those that include the string "shazam":

```
launchctl list | grep shazam
```

You'll now see a PID and the name of the process, similar to when looking at these in Activity Monitor. Next, go ahead and stop it, again using launchctl, but this time with the stop option and the exact name:

```
launchctl stop com.apple.shazamd
```

Once stopped, let's verify that shazamd is no longer running:

```
ps aux
```

Once you have completed your tasks and want to reenable shazam, it's possible to reboot or restart it with the start option in launchctl:

```
launchctl start com.apple.shazamd
```

Finally, this process is not persistent across reboots. If you will be rebooting the system, unload shazam and then move the plist from /System/Library/LaunchDaemons/com.apple.shazamd.plist. For example, to move it to the desktop, use the following command:

```
mv /System/Library/LaunchDaemons/com.apple.shazamd.plist ~/
Desktop/com.apple.shazamd.plist
```

If the launchd job you're trying to manage doesn't start, check out the system.log for a more specific error why:

```
tail -F /var/log/system.log
```

For more on LaunchDaemons, see the Apple developer documentation at `https://developer.apple.com/library/archive/documentation/MacOSX/Conceptual/BPSystemStartup/Chapters/CreatingLaunchdJobs.html` or check launchd.info, a site where you can see additional information.

Now that we've looked at LaunchDaemons and LaunchAgents, let's review what each has access to before we move on to looking at some of the commercial and open source distributions of management agents.

Deeper Inspection: What Does the App Have Access To?

Apps must be signed. Not all persistent binaries need to be signed but all should be, and all should also have a corresponding sandbox profile (although even Apple hasn't gotten around to signing everything that comes bundled with the operating system). To see a detailed description of how an app was signed:

```
codesign -dvvvv /Applications/Firefox.app
```

This also gives you the bundleID for further inspection of an app. There are then a number of tools to use to check out signing and go further into entitlements and sandboxing. For one, check the /usr/share/sandbox directory and the more modern /System/Library/Sandbox/Profiles/ and Versions/A/Resources inside each framework for a .sb file – those are the Apple sandbox profiles. Additionally, to see what each app has access to with the codesign command:

```
sudo codesign --display --entitlements=- /Applications/
Safari.app
```

When building and testing sandbox profiles for apps to compile, you may want to test them thoroughly.

As of 10.14, any app looking to access Location Services, Contacts, Calendars, Reminders, Photos, Camera, Microphone, Accessibility, the hard drive, Automation services, Analytics, or Advertising kit will prompt the user to accept that connection. This is TCC, or Privacy Preferences. You can programmatically remove items but not otherwise augment or view the data, via the tccutil command along with the only verb currently supported, reset:

```
tccutil reset SERVICE com.smileonmymac.textexpander
```

Third-Party Management Agents

There are a number of tools that other people or organizations have built that enable you to tap into the power of the macOS command line. Organizations like Addigy, FileWave, Jamf, MobileIron, and VMware all have agents. And Munki has become a popular open source management agent for a number of reasons. We'll start our look at agents with one of the more recently added, given how it's built: Addigy.

Addigy

Addigy is a management solution for iOS and macOS. As Addigy was developed somewhat recently, the developers make use of a number of open source components to form a management solution that can track what's on a device (or monitor inventory), deploy new software to a device, remove software from a device, run scripts remotely, and other tasks. The ability to do this en masse is derived by having an agent running on client systems and having that agent be able to talk back to a centralized management server. The Addigy agent is available by navigating to the Add Devices button in the sidebar (Figure 2-6).

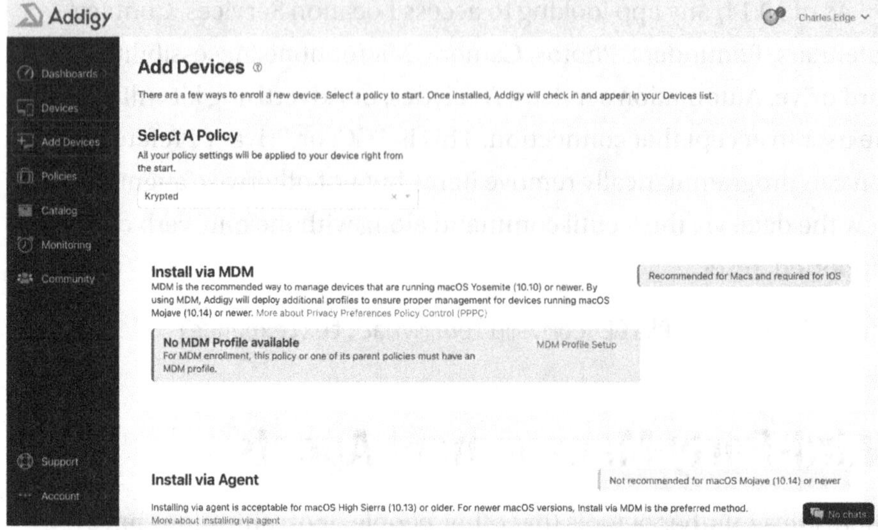

***Figure 2-6.** Download the Addigy Agent*

As seen in Figure 2-7, there are different options to install the agent (other than with MDM, which we cover in more depth throughout the rest of the book). Install with Terminal downloads a shell script that runs an installer, whereas the package option downloads a package.

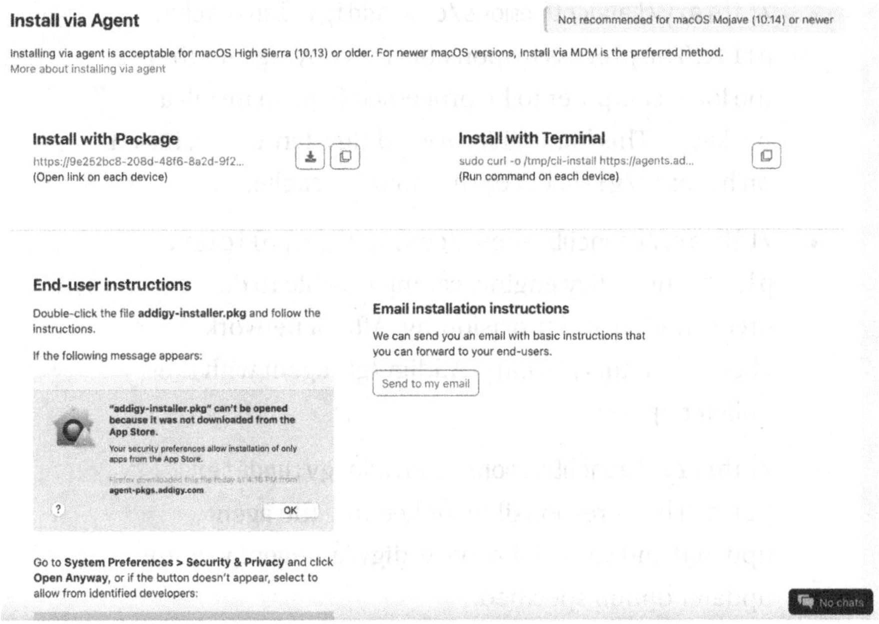

***Figure 2-7.** Scripted or package deployment*

As with many software packages today, the Addigy agent consists of a few different components. The package will install a number of LaunchDaemons and LaunchAgents according to the services you use in your environment. These services are as follows:

- `/Library/LaunchDaemons/com.addigy.agent.plist`: The Addigy agent, responsible for controlling other services running on the system. This calls /Library/Addigy/go-agent with the agent option.
- `/Library/LaunchDaemons/com.addigy.collector.plist`: The Collector, which maintains inventory and reports information back to the server. This calls /Library/Addigy/collector.

- `/Library/LaunchDaemons/com.addigy.lan-cache.plist`: The process responsible for copying files to the local computer to be processed (e.g., to install a package). This loads /Library/Addigy/lan-cache, based on `https://github.com/bntjah/lancache`.
- `/Library/LaunchDaemons/com.addigy.policier.plist`: The policy engine, calling Ansible to do orchestration and provisioning. After a network check, this runs /Library/Addigy/go-agent with the policier option.
- `/Library/LaunchDaemons/com.addigy.updater.plist`: This is responsible for keeping the agent updated and calls /Library/Addigy/go-agent with the updater option specified.
- `/Library/LaunchDaemons/com.addigy.auditor.plist`: Addigy's audit tool, which can be used to get custom facts about the state of a host.
- `/Library/LaunchDaemons/com.addigy.watchdog.plist`: Throttles processes if their CPU usage gets too high.
- `/Library/LaunchDaemons/screenconnect-92fde59311b74250.plist`: Addigy's screen connection agents.
- `/Library/LaunchAgents/screenconnect-92fde59311b74250-launch-prelogin.plist`: Addigy's screen connection agents.
- `/Library/LaunchAgents/screenconnect-92fde59311b74250-launch-onlogin.plist`: Addigy's screen connection agents.

To load or unload any of these, we'll use the launchctl command as we did earlier in the chapter. For example, to unload the Go agent:

```
sudo launchctl unload /Library/LaunchDaemons/com.addigy.lan-
cache.plist
sudo launchctl load /Library/LaunchDaemons/com.addigy.lan-
cache.plist
```

In addition, there are a number of supporting files located in /Library/Addigy, including auditor-facts, which has information obtained by the auditor, /Library/Addigy/ansible/status.json which is the main ansible inventory file, and /Library/Addigy/user-job which runs shell scripts on behalf of the user.

Larger files, such as packages, are then cached to the client systems with LANCache. To see what resources the LANCache daemon is using, use ps to view processes and then grep the output for lan-cache as follows:

```
sudo ps aux | grep -v grep | grep lan-cache
```

A similar incantation of the command can be used to view the resources being used by any of the agents we'll cover in this chapter. In general, if you notice a trend here, we use launchctl to check what binaries are called by the agents and then use the command structures for each agent to get more details, troubleshoot, and learn how to most efficiently deploy management to devices. For example, know where that LANCache binary is; we can see what peers are visible to a device using lan-cache along with the peers verb, as you can see here:

```
/Library/Addigy/lan-cache peers
```

One great aspect of LANCache is that it's used to speed up downloads for many clients. By caching updates on peers, the download is faster, and organizations reduce the bandwidth required to download assets, making the Internet seem faster during a large deployment push. To set a device as a proxy for peers, use the -peer-proxy options with that binary along with the -set-proxy-setting as follows:

```
/Library/Addigy/lan-cache -peer-proxy -set-peer-proxy-setting
```

One of the reasons we placed the Addigy agent first is that it's a simple, efficient, and transparent architecture. The other is of course that it alphabetically comes first, and when we list vendors, we try to do so alphabetically. But the main components of the agent and with others will be that there's a process for connecting to the server and orchestrating events, another process for downloading updates, and a final process for executing and reporting. More daemons just means more logic behind the scenes and more options. But more daemons or agents also means more CPU usually.

The use of LANCache is a really great feature, provided there's a checksum validation at installation of packages as it improves the experience but also keeps the bandwidth required to host assets for customers low. Caching updates on client devices is not a new concept. FileWave has supported "Boosters" for well over a decade. Notice that the "agent" for every tool we cover isn't just a single binary or script that runs in the background, but is a collection of a few that do various tasks. In the next section, we'll look at the FileWave agent in more depth.

FileWave

FileWave is a management solution for iOS, macOS, and Windows. FileWave deploys software to client Macs using what's known as a fileset, or a set of files. These filesets are referenced using a manifest on a FileWave server, and the FileWave client, or agent, looks to the server manifest for a list of any actions it needs to perform. If a fileset needs to be installed, the FileWave client is provided with a path to access the fileset using the manifest file and retrieves the files necessary for installation using a FileWave booster or distributed repository that hosts those files.

The FileWave client agent is primarily made up of an app, located at /usr/local/sbin/FileWave.app; a preference file, located at /usr/local/etc/fwcld.plist; and a control script, found at `/sbin/fwcontrol`. These tools log to /var/log/ using log files that begin with the name fwcld. The scripts are started up using /Library/LaunchAgents/com.filewave.fwGUI.plist and /Library/LaunchDaemons/com.filewave.fwcld.plist.

Let's start with a pretty basic task; let's get the status of the agent:

```
sudo /usr/local/sbin/FileWave.app/Contents/MacOS/fwcld -s
```

The output will be similar to the following:

```
***************************
**FileWave Client Status**
***************************

User ID: 2243
Current Model Number: 134
Filesets in Inventory:
1. Enroll Macs into MDM, ID 25396 (version 2) - Active
2. OSX App - Lingon, ID 846 (version 3) - Installing via Mac
   App Store (can take some time)
3. Firefox.app, ID 1133 (version 7) - Active
4. FileWave_macOS_Client_14.7.0_317xyz, ID 24000 (version
   1) - Active
5. FileWave_macOS_Client_14.8.0_076xyz, ID 21000 (version
   1) - Active
```

The preceding data shows the user and the filesets the device has, the versions of those filesets, and the status of each. Another task you can do with the fwcld would be to set some custom information into a field and then save that up to a server. Supported fields to do so are custom_string_01, custom_integer_01, custom_bool_01, and custom_datetime_01, where there are 20 slots for each and they contain a string (or a standard varchar), number, a Boolean (so 0 or 1), and a date. In the following example, we'll take some information telling us if a login hook is installed and send that into the ninth available string value:

```
/usr/local/sbin/FileWave.app/Contents/MacOS/fwcld -custom_
write -key custom_string_09 -value `defaults read com.apple.
LoginWindow`
```

As seen in the earlier example, we've sent information about a device back to a server. We can then build automations at the server that send further instructions to the client. For example, if there's no login hook, install one. The FileWave manual will be a better guide to getting started using the command line and scripts to help manage FileWave. That can be found at `www.filewave.com`.

The Once Mighty Fleetsmith

Fleetsmith was acquired by Apple, and the team helped build out better APIs for built-in management options. However, it's still worth mentioning in a book like this as it had features still not replicated by other solutions (but that an enterprising admin could build themselves) and an agent built on open source software in ways enterprising engineers could build another agent (and some third-party tools have been built similarly).

As with many of the agent-based management solutions, Fleetsmith was a solution that could run as an MDM for the Mac alongside an agent, which Fleetsmith referred to as Fully Managed. Fully Managed devices could be remotely locked, have kernel extensions whitelisted, and be remotely erased via MDM. Fleetsmith could also run with just an agent and no MDM initially. The agent was downloaded in a similar way as the Addigy agent is downloaded, as seen in Figure 2-8.

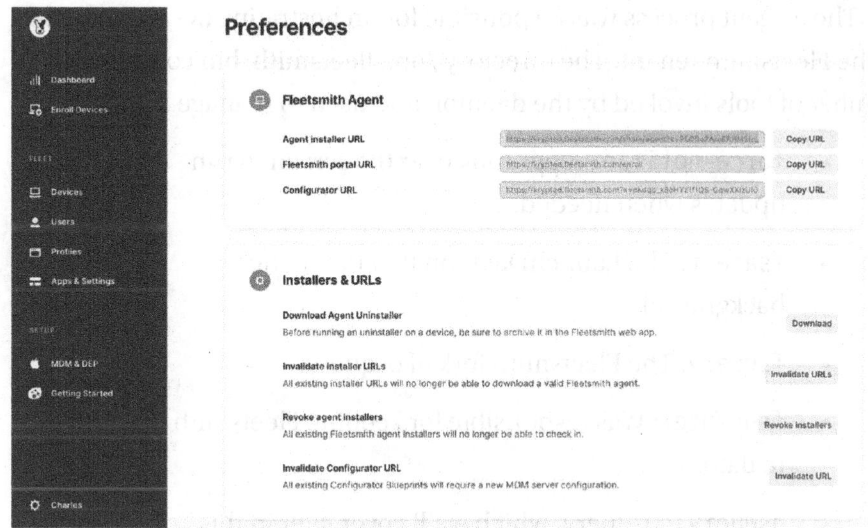

***Figure 2-8.** Download the Fleetsmith installer*

Once the package was downloaded, it could be run, and a number of assets were loaded on client computers. As with many of the “agents,” Fleetsmith had three LaunchDaemons:

- `com.fleetsmith.agent.plist`: Invoked the /opt/fleetsmith/bin/run-fsagent shell script, which logged to /var/log/fleetsmith and invokes the agent daemon
- `com.fleetsmith.query.plist`: Started /opt/fleetsmith/bin/fsquery, a customized osquery daemon
- `com.fleetsmith.updater.plist`: Started /opt/fleetsmith/bin/fsupdater, a Go daemon that kept software up to date

The fsagent process was responsible for orchestrating events on behalf of the Fleetsmith tenant. The directory /opt/fleetsmith/bin contained a number of tools invoked by the daemon and used to manage devices:

- `force-notifier.app`: Took over the screen to run updates when needed.
- `fsagent`: The LaunchDaemon that ran in the background.
- `fsquery`: The Fleetsmith fork of osquery.
- `fsupdater`: Was responsible for keeping Fleetsmith up to date.
- `osqueryi`: osquery, which we'll cover later in this chapter, is distributed in order to provide inventory information for Fleetsmith.
- `run-fsagent`: Started the agent.

The /opt/fleetsmith/data directory stored the agent.log, downloads directory, and a store.db sqlite3 database. All of this was used as small components to accomplish the tasks servers instructed clients to perform. As an example, to manage Google Chrome in Apps (Figure 2-9), users could enable the app to be managed and then configure the settings to be pushed to the app.

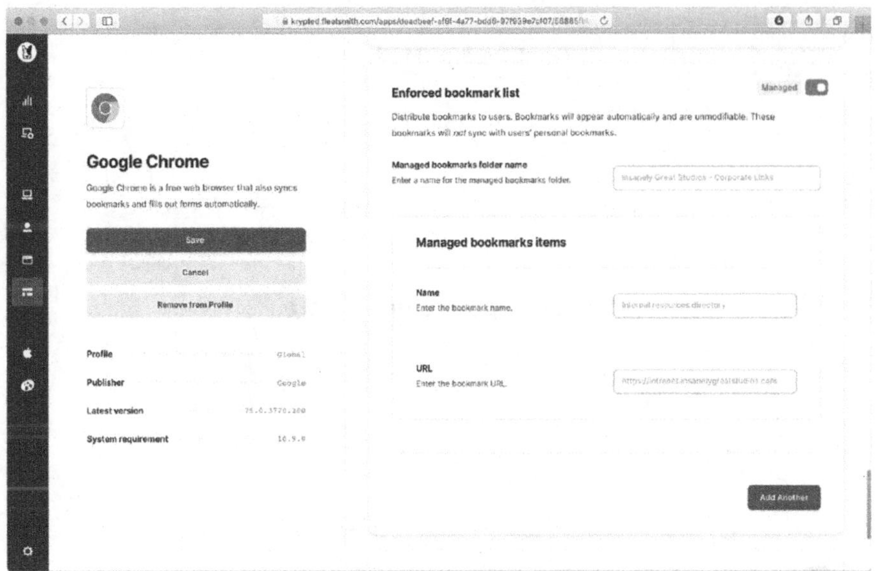

***Figure 2-9.** Manage Google Chrome with Fleetsmith*

The Fleetsmith agent then installed the Chrome app. The Fleetsmith app from /Applications showed apps as "All your apps are up to date" (Figure 2-10) provided they were running the latest version.

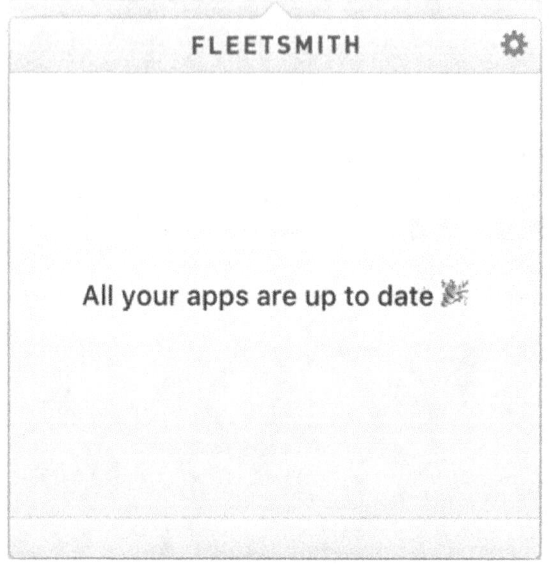

Figure 2-10. *The Fleetsmith app in the menu bar*

Addigy is (and Fleetsmith was) built on Go-based agents that included components from the open source community. Fleetsmith bolted on a lot of keys and certificates to further secure the communication channel and added a lot of logic on top of osquery. All of this could be done by any company and is likely to be replicated, especially given the open source solutions that can handle the MDM management stack. Perhaps one of the top names in device management is Jamf. Next, we'll look at the jamf "binary" – which is one of the older agents but also one of the most widely distributed.

Jamf

Since the early days when it was called The Casper Suite, Jamf Pro has always had a binary that ran on a computer. That binary currently lives at /usr/local/jamf/bin/jamf, and it executes most of the non-MDM-based tasks that Jamf Pro sends to the agent. The "agent" is an oversimplification. There are others, which include

- `/usr/local/jamf/bin/jamfagent`: The agent for processing user work and report on user data.
- `/Library/Application Support/JAMF/JAMF.app/Contents/MacOS/JamfDaemon.app`: A bundle that contains the Jamf Pro daemon, for more global instructions (the Jamf.app is an app bundle that keeps all this together).
- `/Library/Application Support/JAMF/JAMF.app/Contents/MacOS/JamfAAD.app`: For the Azure Active Directory integration.
- `/Library/LaunchDaemons/com.jamfsoftware.task.1.plist`: Manages checking into Jamf Pro. Additionally, there are some symbolic links for either backward compatibility or to provide paths to files in various locations, according to the file.

Additionally, there are a number of daemons and agents that are not compiled binaries. The daemons are the global processes. /Library/LaunchDaemons/com.jamfsoftware.startupItem.plist launches a check-in script, and the daemon /Library/LaunchDaemons/com.jamfsoftware.jamf.daemon.plist collects application usage, FileVault data, network state changes, and restricted software as well as performs actions from Self Service. To manage check-ins to the servers, /Library/LaunchDaemons/com.jamfsoftware.task.1.plist is run routinely. /Library/LaunchAgents/com.jamf.management.jamfAAD.clean.agent.plist cleans up artifacts from Azure AD IDs, and /Library/Preferences/com.jamf.management.jamfAAD.plist is used to retain preferences of Azure AD information.

All of this is logged to /var/log/jamf.log. So the binary is handling non-MDM communications back to the server but also enables you to script various tasks quickly.

Manage User Accounts with Jamf

You can then add a new user, using the createAccount verb. To do so, run the jamf binary using the createAccount verb. This verb provides for a number of options, including a short name (-username), a full name (-realname), a password (-password), a home directory (-home), and a default shell (-shell). If you want the user to be an admin of the system, you can also add an -admin option. In the following, we'll string it all together:

```
/usr/sbin/jamf createAccount -username charlesedge -realname
"Charles Edge" -password mysupersecretpassword -home /Users/
charlesedge -shell bash -admin
```

Or if you need to, you can easily delete an account using the `deleteAccount` verb. Here, use the -username operator to define a given user that you'd like to remove. That username is defined as the short name (or what dscl shows) of a given user. For example, to remove the user we just created (charlesedge), run the following command:

```
/usr/sbin/jamf deleteAccount -username charlesedge
```

You can then provide a pop-up on the screen that you completed that action using the `displayMessage` verb along with the -message option to indicate what was done:

```
/usr/sbin/jamf displayMessage -message "charlesedge has been
deleted"
```

Once an action is complete, it's always a good idea to perform a quick recon again to make sure everything is registered back to the server:

```
/usr/sbin/jamf recon
```

More Automation Through the Jamf Framework

The Jamf Framework is also capable of performing a number of tasks that the developers have provided, to make it easier to configure devices on your network. To get started, let's see all of the options. As with many binaries, if you have any questions, you can use the help verb to see what all it can do:

```
/usr/sbin/jamf help
```

If you need more information on a given verb, run the help verb followed by the one you need more information on:

```
/usr/sbin/jamf help policy
```

You can also automate standard tasks. The following command will unmount a mounted server called mainserver:

```
jamf unmountServer -mountPoint /Volumes/mainserver
```

Or change a user's home page in all of their web browsers:

```
sudo jamf setHomePage -homepage www.krypted.com
```

The following command can be used to fire up the SSH daemon:

```
sudo jamf startSSH
```

The following command can be used to fix the By Host files on the local machine:

```
sudo jamf fixByHostFiles -target 127.0.0.1
```

The following command can be used to run a Fix Permissions on the local machine:

```
sudo jamf fixPermissions /
```

The following can be used to flush all of the caches on your local system:

```
sudo jamf flushCaches -flushSystem
```

The following can be used to run a software update on the local system:

```
sudo jamf runSoftwareUpdate
```

The following can be used to bind to an AD environment (rather than dsconfigad) but would need all the parameters for your environment put in as flags in order to complete the binding:

```
sudo jamf bindAD
```

The jamf binary can also poll for a list of printers using the listprinters verb:

```
sudo jamf listprinters
```

The output looks like this:

```
MSP Lobby HP MSP_LobbyLobby lpd://192.168.12.201/ HP 6490
C5250 PS
```

As noted by the number of agents and daemons, there can be a bit of cruft spread throughout the system, especially for devices that have been enrolled in Jamf for some time. Therefore, the removeFramework option can be used to fully clean out the Jamf artifacts from a device (of course the device cannot check in once run):

```
/usr/local/bin/jamf removeFramework
```

In general, most of the agents will provide a few options. The Jamf binary goes a bit deeper than most, which makes Jamf the more advanced third-party Mac management tool available. It does still wrap a lot of shell commands that administrators can send through any management tool, which some admins have chosen to build on their own – either with the assistance of open source tools or as open source tools altogether. The top open source tool for Mac management is another common tool called Munki, which we'll cover in the next section.

Munki

Munki is an open source device management framework originally developed by Greg Neagle and available via GitHub at `https://github.com/munki/munki`. Munki was initially designed to be similar to the Apple Software Update Server but for third-party products. The design is elegant in that simplicity. The client downloads one or more manifests and one or more catalogs, and a client computer takes its updates from the manifest(s) and catalog(s). As the project has gained traction and a greater level of maturity, a number of enhancements have been made; but you have to love that core concept that a client picks up a dictionary of information about the state the client should be in and then takes action based on that, including installing profiles, updating default domains, and of course installing software updates.

Munki runs an agent on client computers. As with many "agents" these days, it's split up between a number of LaunchDaemons and LaunchAgents, each built for a specific task. There are four LaunchDaemons and three LaunchAgents, as well as a number of scripts that do specific tasks. As with a few of the tools we cover, Munki comes with an app that can be used to allow users to perform a number of tasks themselves.

Munki LaunchDaemons

As is a good practice, each task that the Munki client requires is a separate program, with the four tasks that require root privileges being run as LaunchDaemons and three LaunchAgents for the things visible in the Managed Software Center GUI. In this section, we'll look at what each of the LaunchDaemons does:

- `/Library/LaunchDaemons/com.googlecode.munki.managedsoftwareupdate-check.plist` causes managedsoftwareupdate to run approximately once an hour in the background to check for and possibly install new updates. This controls background task scheduling with the supervisor (/usr/local/munki/supervisor) to make sure it wasn't removed and adds a delay to triggered managed softwareupdate events (/usr/local/munki/managedsoftwareupdate). This allows the local agent to process catalog changes and run unattended installations of software.
- `/Library/LaunchDaemons/com.googlecode.munki.managedsoftwareupdate-install.plist`: Runs cached updates when user notification is required. The managedsoftwareupdate-install launchdaemon runs cached updates for Managed Software Center. This involves a sanity check that /private/tmp/.com.googlecode.munki.managedinstall.launchd is present. If so, managedsoftwareupdate runs using the -installwithnologout option when invoked.

- `/Library/LaunchDaemons/com.googlecode.munki.managedsoftwareupdate-manualcheck.plist`: Gives Managed Software Center the ability to scan servers for updates to the Munki manifest file. Requires the /private/tmp/.com.googlecode.munki.updatecheck.launchd trigger file is present.
- `/Library/LaunchDaemons/com.googlecode.munki.logouthelper.plist`: Notify users when the force_install_after_date approaches. This is done by invoking Managed Software Center which can terminate a user session, which uses the /usr/local/munki/logouthelperutility script.

Munki also comes with a number of LaunchAgents, which include the following:

- `/Library/LaunchAgents/com.googlecode.munki.ManagedSoftwareCenter.plist`: Used to open Managed Software Center in the user context when user notification is required.
- `/Library/LaunchAgents/com.googlecode.munki.MunkiStatus.plist`: Calls MunkiStatus in the Contents/Resources directory of the Managed Software Center app bundle and is used for notifications on top of the login window.
- `/Library/LaunchAgents/com.googlecode.munki.managedsoftwareupdate-loginwindow.plist`: Processes user tasks at the login window. Can be triggered by /Users/Shared/.com.googlecode.munki.checkandinstallatstartup, /private/tmp/com.googlecode.munki.installatlogout, or /Users/Shared/.com.googlecode.munki.installatstartup.

The architecture of what processes are used to run what services are pretty telling, not only about how the product works but also how to troubleshoot that product. The fact that each task that will be performed has been pulled off into a separate daemon or agent speaks to preserving the security of managing endpoints using the least amount of privileges available and avoids requiring a kext always be loaded in order to orchestrate all of these tasks. Most, though, are in support of processing the manifest, catalog, and pkginfo plist files, which we'll cover in the next section.

Customizing a Munki Manifest

The manifest is where the Munki agents take their instruction sets from. Now that we've looked at the components of Munki, let's look at that format, the manifest, catalog, and pkginfo plist files, and the keys in those files that go to each client. Keep in mind that Munki was initially built to replicate what Apple did for Software Update Services where there is a manifest file distributing packages to install on clients. Therefore, Munki has catalogs of all software to be installed.

Over time, the scope of the project grew to include groupings of different client computers that received different manifest files and an app that allowed end users to install their own software, which we'll cover in more detail in Chapter 11.

Manifests are standard property lists. We'll cover manipulating property lists further in Chapter 3, but for now, think of them as simple XML files that have a collection of keypairs. Those are a simple list of the items to install or verify their installation or to remove or verify their removal. The manifest contains a list of one or more catalogs, defined using a catalogs array, along with an array of packages to install or just update if they are found on disk, which are a number of arrays for how you want the Munki agent to handle items listed. These include the following arrays:

- **managed_installs**: Munki will install these items and keep them up to date.
- **managed_uninstalls**: Munki will remove these items.
- **managed_updates**: Munki will update these items, if present, whether or not they were installed by Munki.
- **optional_installs**: Munki will allow users to install these items optionally and keep them up to date once installed (e.g., using Managed Software Center).
- **featured_items**: Items listed at the top of Managed Software Center.

Munki Managed Installs

The managed_installs key is the first and so arguably one of the most important things Munki does. As mentioned, managed installs are software that is required to be deployed to a device. Once deployed, the software must be kept up to date in alignment with the catalog. You can see this in practice using the following manifest, which instructs the client computer to install Quickbooks, Slack, and Office from the Accounting catalog:

```
<?xml version="1.0" encoding="UTF-8"?>
<!DOCTYPE plist PUBLIC "-//Apple Computer//DTD PLIST 1.0//EN"
"http://www.apple.com/DTDs/PropertyList-1.0.dtd">
<plist version="1.0">
<dict>
   <key>catalogs</key>
   <array>
      <string>production</string>
   </array>
```

```
    <key>managed_installs</key>
    <array>
       <string>Quickbooks-2019</string>
       <string>Slack-3.3.8</string>
       <string>Office-16.23</string>
    </array>
</dict>
</plist>
```

Many environments use a production catalog and a testing catalog, where the testing catalog is populated by an automated packaging tool such as AutoPKG. Once software has been tested and validated as safe for distribution, it's then added to the production catalog. Testing machines can then use the testing catalog to install software, instead of the safer production catalog. You can have multiple catalogs listed by adding items to the catalogs array. The following example shows adding a testing catalog above the production catalog. Doing so causes the Munki agent to search the testing catalog for the packages defined in the managed_installs array before trying to install those software titles or scripts from the production catalog, making for a seamless transition when the software you are testing is promoted to production.

```
<?xml version="1.0" encoding="UTF-8"?>
<!DOCTYPE plist PUBLIC "-//Apple Computer//DTD PLIST 1.0//EN"
"http://www.apple.com/DTDs/PropertyList-1.0.dtd">
<plist version="1.0">
   <dict>
        <key>catalogs</key>
        <array>
            <string>testing</string>
            <string>production</string>
        </array>
```

```
        <key>managed_installs</key>
        <array>
            <string>Firefox-104.0.2</string>
            <string>Chrome-105.0.5195.102</string>
        </array>
    </dict>
</plist>
```

It's usually a good practice to deploy software without version numbers or, if there are version numbers, to only use major release numbers. In the preceding example, we've actually piped the point release version number for testing. This allows you to keep track of software during testing that's destined for your production catalog. This catalog isn't always exclusive for software you installed.

Updating Software That Munki Didn't Install

There are a number of reasons to patch software that Munki didn't install. Chief among them are security patches. But also, the general performance of a system can be greatly improved by treating a piece of software Munki didn't install as you would treat other managed software. This is referred to as a managed update in Munki and defined using a managed_updates option.

The `managed_updates` array is handled similarly to managed_installs but looks for a software title on the host and runs an updater only if that title is found. For example, if you don't deploy Firefox, Chrome, or the Microsoft Edge browser, you might still want to keep those patched if you find your users install them. Running an inventory through a tool like osquery (described later in this chapter) will supply you with a list of software on the computers in your deployment and can then be used to find any software you would like to either move into your managed catalog or at least keep updated.

The following example is similar to the previous example but using managed_updates for these pieces of software installed by users outside of the Munki deployment:

```
<?xml version="1.0" encoding="UTF-8"?>
<!DOCTYPE plist PUBLIC "-//Apple Computer//DTD PLIST 1.0//EN"
"http://www.apple.com/DTDs/PropertyList-1.0.dtd">
<plist version="1.0">
   <dict>
        <key>catalogs</key>
        <array>
            <string>production</string>
        </array>
        <key>included_manifests</key>
        <array>
            <string>accounting </string>
            <string>allusers</string>
        </array>
        <key>managed_updates</key>
        <array>
            <string>Chrome</string>
            <string>Firefox</string>
        </array>
    </dict>
</plist>
```

The exception to updating a package would be if it's been slated to be removed on a computer. If a piece of software is scheduled for removal, it will not be updated. As deployments grow, you need more complicated logic on client systems in order to handle the added burden that additional groups and iterations put on an environment. This has led to nesting manifests.

Nested Manifests

You can nest manifests. Much as you can do an include in an Apache configuration, you can logically group manifests of files. If you have a user in the accounting group, then you can create a manifest just for accounting, along with a manifest that all of the users receive. In the following example, we'll remove the testing catalog and add an array of manifests to include, adding the accounting and allusers manifests and install Chrome as well, which wouldn't be included for other devices:

```
<?xml version="1.0" encoding="UTF-8"?>
<!DOCTYPE plist PUBLIC "-//Apple Computer//DTD PLIST 1.0//EN"
"http://www.apple.com/DTDs/PropertyList-1.0.dtd">
<plist version="1.0">
   <dict>
        <key>catalogs</key>
        <array>
            <string>production</string>
        </array>
        <key>included_manifests</key>
        <array>
            <string>accounting </string>
            <string>allusers</string>
        </array>
        <key>managed_installs</key>
        <array>
            <string>Chrome</string>
        </array>
    </dict>
</plist>
```

The preceding manifest includes two other manifests. Consider this akin to having nested groups. Those manifests specifically meant to be included in other manifests should not typically include a catalog, given that the catalog is defined in the parent manifest. In the following example, see an example of a manifest built to be included:

```
<?xml version="1.0" encoding="UTF-8"?>
<!DOCTYPE plist PUBLIC "-//Apple Computer//DTD PLIST 1.0//EN"
"http://www.apple.com/DTDs/PropertyList-1.0.dtd">
<plist version="1.0">
<dict>
   <key>managed_installs</key>
   <array>
      <string>Quickbooks-2022</string>
      <string>Slack</string>
      <string>Office-16.64</string>
   </array>
</dict>
</plist>
```

The preceding manifest is similar to the earlier example, defining Quickbooks, Slack, and Office but without listing the catalogs. This simple approach allows administrators to push out small changes, managing universal software and then either aligning a computer with a job function or, as the deployment grows, allowing for more complicated hierarchies. This is similar to Apple allowing for nested Software Update Servers, where you can limit software to be deployed on child servers. While the Apple technique is no longer supported, Munki has filled much of the gap for third parties and continues this tradition.

Removing Software with Munki

Managed installs get software and packages on devices and keep software updated. Managed uninstalls remove software. This is defined in the same property lists but with a managed_uninstalls array followed by a list of titles in the form of strings. Obviously, software must be installed in order to be uninstalled. Provided that a software title is installed that should be removed, the following example builds on the previous, keeping any software defined in the accounting and allusers manifest installed, keeping Chrome installed but also defining that the Symantec software will be removed any time it's encountered:

```
<?xml version="1.0" encoding="UTF-8"?>
<!DOCTYPE plist PUBLIC "-//Apple Computer//DTD PLIST 1.0//EN"
"http://www.apple.com/DTDs/PropertyList-1.0.dtd">
<plist version="1.0">
   <dict>
        <key>catalogs</key>
        <array>
            <string>production</string>
        </array>
        <key>included_manifests</key>
        <array>
            <string>accounting </string>
            <string>allusers</string>
        </array>
        <key>managed_installs</key>
        <array>
            <string>Chrome</string>
        </array>
<key>managed_uninstalls</key>
    <array>
        <string>Symantec</string>
```

```
    </array>
    </dict>
</plist>
```

The preceding example is mostly used to retire software, plan for major updates, and pull back any software accidentally released.

Optional Software Installation

Optional software are software titles that users can optionally install through Managed Software Center. If a user installs an optional software title, a package is installed as an administrator. Optional software is defined in manifests using an optional_installs array and then a number of packages, by name.

The following example builds off of our accounting include from earlier, listing VPN, Okta, Druva, and Zoom as optional installations:

```
<?xml version="1.0" encoding="UTF-8"?>
<!DOCTYPE plist PUBLIC "-//Apple Computer//DTD PLIST 1.0//EN"
"http://www.apple.com/DTDs/PropertyList-1.0.dtd">
<plist version="1.0">
<dict>
   <key>managed_installs</key>
   <array>
      <string>Quickbooks-2019</string>
      <string>Slack</string>
      <string>Office-16</string>
   </array>
    <key>optional_installs</key>
    <array>
        <string>VPN</string>
        <string>Okta</string>
        <string>Druva</string>
```

```
        <string>Zoom</string>
    </array>
</dict>
</plist>
```

Any software installed using an optional install is stored in a locally stored manifest file that is also reviewed by Munki, located at /Library/Managed Installs/manifests/SelfServeManifest. As you might guess, if a title is listed in optional installs and managed installs, the package will be a required install. Managed Software Center then has the logic not to list that package as an optional install. The beauty of these types of installs is that users don't need administrative privileges. We'll get into packaging further in Chapter 6, but because anything can be put in a package, you can also deploy automations using Managed Software Center this way. Therefore, basic support tasks that might otherwise require administrative privileges such as clearing print queues, installing certain printers, and clearing caches can then be deployed without a user being made an administrator or without a remote control session to the computer.

If an item is installed through an optional install, then it is treated as a managed install. Because the software is optional, it can be removed through Managed Software Center. If the optional install is then removed, it is treated as a managed uninstall. A type of optional item is a featured item.

Featured Items

The featured_items array indicates software that is listed at the top of Managed Software Center in the Featured section. Featured items are a subset of optional installs so should be listed in both places. Manifests may also have a featured_items key:

```
<?xml version="1.0" encoding="UTF-8"?>
<!DOCTYPE plist PUBLIC "-//Apple Computer//DTD PLIST 1.0//EN"
"http://www.apple.com/DTDs/PropertyList-1.0.dtd">
```

```
<plist version="1.0">
<dict>
   <key>managed_installs</key>
   <array>
      <string>Quickbooks-2022</string>
      <string>Slack</string>
      <string>Office</string>
   </array>
    <key>optional_installs</key>
    <array>
        <string>VPN</string>
        <string>Okta</string>
        <string>Druva</string>
        <string>Zoom</string>
    </array>
<key>featured_items</key>
    <array>
        <string>Okta</string>
        <string>Druva</string>
        <string>Zoom</string>
    </array>
</dict>
</plist>
```

One of our favorite aspects of Munki admins is that most know more than anyone else has ever known about anything; therefore, there will be a lot of disagreement on this explanation of manifest files. That is fine. Now that we've created manifests, let's move on to getting the first catalog created and getting some software imported into it for distribution.

Building a Repository and a Catalog of Software

Munki is a tool designed for installing software. The catalog is a list of software titles available for installation. The catalog is stored locally at /Library/Managed Installs/catalogs but can be downloaded from the server when it's changed and used to provide catalogs using a web service and items are imported into the catalog using munkiimport, by default installed at /usr/local/munki/munkiimport. The munkiimport script is a python script that acts as an assistant for importing disk images (.dmg files), packages (.pkg files), manual configuration profiles (which have been partially deprecated since macOS 10.15), and application bundles (.app files) into your repo.

A repository's location is configured, along with other global configuration options for `munkiimport`, using a -configure option for munkiimport. Simply run that option and follow the interactive shell:

```
/usr/local/munki/munkiimport --configure
```

When prompted, provide a URL for your repo, which we're using as /usr/local/var/www/munki_repo in this demonstration. The repo is set such that when the user runs munkiimport, imports will go to that location by default. The preferences set by the --configure option are stored in ~/Library/Preferences/com.googlecode.munki.munkiimport.plist. The repo should be provided as file://usr/local/var/www/munki_repo for our example location, although you could use an afp:// or smb:// mount instead or use one of the file-handler options to store your repo in an AWS or GCS file store.

Next, we're going to create a PkgInfo property list based on a standard installer package that lists the catalogs an installer is a member of and other metadata about the installer. In this example, we'll create the Zoom installer we used in the manifest earlier in this chapter: the PkgInfo plist. PkgInfo files are stored in the pkgsinfo directory inside the munki_repo.

The PkgInfo file is generated when using munkiimport to import an installer. To import software, we'll use munkiimport along with options that allow the script to run without providing the information in these options interactively. This involves answering some basic questions about the software, including the name, name that should be displayed when installing, the category of software, the version of the package being imported, the organization that made the software, whether the software can be installed/uninstalled in an unattended fashion, and a -c option which defines what catalogs the software should be placed into:

```
munkiimport ~/Desktop/zoom.pkg --name=Zoom --displayname=Zoom
--description="Our conferencing software"  --category=Productivity
--developer=Zoom --pkgvers=4.6.4 -c allusers --unattended_install
--unattended_uninstall
```

Because we didn't specify an -n option, we will still have some interactive steps to provide information about our installer. We'll show these steps so you can better understand what's happening behind the scenes:

```
Import this item? [y/n] y
Upload item to subdirectory path []: apps/zoom
Path pkgsinfo/apps/Zoom doesnt exist. Create it? [y/n] y
No existing product icon found.
Attempt to create a product icon? [y/n] y
Attempting to extract and upload icon...
Imported icons/Zoom.png.
Copying zoom.pkg to repo...
Copied zoom.pkg to pkgs/apps/zoom/zoom.
Edit pkginfo before upload? [y/n]: n
Saved pkginfo to pkgsinfo/apps/Zoom/Zoom-4.4.53590..plist.
Rebuild catalogs? [y/n] y
Rebuilding catalogs at file://usr/local/var/www/munki_repo
Created icons/_icon_hashes.plist...
```

All of the preceding options can be added as additional parameters to your installer. This shows the amount of work being done each time you run a munkiimport, even creating an icon. The one important option is to rebuild catalogs. Answering yes to that option will result in a new catalog files being built based on pkginfo files.

The software itself is also then imported into the repo, and if successful, the pkginfo file will open in the editor you defined in the --configure step for your user. Now that we have a repo, a catalog, and manifests, let's distribute the manifest to client devices that need to install software.

Distributing the Manifest File

We've described manifests and catalogs, but how is a device provided with a manifest? Upon installation, the Munki agent will look to a SoftwareRepoURL key for the main repository of manifests. If Munki's SoftwareRepoURL preference is not defined, the Munki client will attempt to detect a Munki repo based on some common defaults. That web host should have a valid TLS certificate and host the URL via https in order to protect against any man-in-the-middle attacks. Munki is architected such that the administrator points the Munki client to the server and that the host running Munki implicitly trusts that server. Therefore, it's not recommended to deploy Munki without https in order to ensure the authenticity of catalogs being deployed. Failure to do so could cause résumé-generating events.

If no SoftwareRepoURL is defined, Munki will go through a search order looking for a repository of manifests. This follows the following search order, where $domain is a search domain for a client:

- `https://munki.$domain/repo`
- `https://munki.$domain/munki_repo`
- `http://munki.$domain/repo`

- `http://munki.$domain/munki_repo`
- `http://munki/repo`

Once Munki finds a repo, there is usually a manifest for all devices at that URL. This is the site_default manifest, and if a manifest is not found, that uses a better option. The URL for that site_default for a domain name of pretendco.com might then be `https://munki.pretendco.com/repo/manifests/site_default`. Those better options in order of priority would be a unique identifier for Munki known as the ClientIdentifier, a fully qualified hostname (e.g., the output of scutil --get HostName), a local hostname (e.g., the output of scutil --get LocalHostName), or the serial number. The file for a computer's hostname using that pretendco.com domain name from earlier but with a hostname of client1234 might then be `https://munki.pretendco.com/repo/manifests/client1234.pretendco.com`.

The manifest can be created manually or using a device management tool. For example, some organizations use puppet, chef, VMware AirWatch, or Jamf Pro to distribute the Munki manifest files and settings that point to manifest files. While it might seem like these other tools can manage the software on devices natively, it's worth noting that these other tools are more about state and policy management, where Munki is about managed software. The power of Munki is the fact that it has such a narrow set of duties. For smaller environments, managing software and leveraging some payload-free packages is often all they need. For larger environments with a state management tool, Munki perfectly complements their other tools, and engineers tasked with the management of large fleets of devices are accustomed to scripting middleware for their organization's specific needs.

Many software packages are updated every couple of weeks. According to how many software titles a given organization is managing, it can be a challenge to maintain an extensive software catalog. Therefore, AutoPkg is often used alongside Munki to automatically build packages and put them in your testing catalog. We cover AutoPkg more in Chapter 7, when we review preparing apps for distribution. Now that we've covered Munki, and how Munki keeps devices up to date, let's move to a tool often used to complement Munki but built more for tracking the state of a device than systems orchestration: osquery.

osquery

Facebook open sourced osquery, a tool they initially used to monitor servers, at `https://osquery.readthedocs.io/en/stable/`. Since then, a number of developers (including those responsible for each platform internally at Facebook) have built additional capabilities for managing a specific platform. This makes osquery capable of being used as part of the management stack of a variety of platforms, without having to learn the internals for each of those platforms. The point of osquery is to obtain information about a system.

The osquery framework is multiplatform and tracks all the information about a system in a simple SQL database, so that devices can run lookups efficiently on behalf of a process that calls a lookup. This makes otherwise costly (in terms of processing power) processes run quickly, meaning an organization can obtain more data about devices in a central location at a higher frequency, without impacting the performance of the device being monitored. This would include common settings used on a Mac, the daemons running, how a device is configured, and the version of software. But you can get lower level and analyze processes running, view network sockets, compare file hashes, and find any other fact required about a device at a given time.

When osquery is installed, the following files are deployed to the device:

- `/private/var/osquery/io.osquery.agent.plist`: The configuration preferences for the osquery daemon.
- `/private/var/osquery/osquery.example.conf`: The customized settings for each organization running osquery.
- `/private/var/log/osquery/`: Log files are stored in this directory and written as to the specified parameters in the configuration file.
- `/private/var/osquery/lenses`: A record of a rest call stored in Augeas' tree (thus the .aug files).
- `/private/var/osquery/packs`: A set of queries configured with standard .conf files.
- `/opt/osquery/lib/osquery.app` (moved from /usr/local/lib/osquery/ in version 3): The directory for the command tools for osquery.
- `/usr/local/bin/osqueryctl`: Symlink to a control utility to wrap basic tasks, like starting the LaunchDaemon.
- `/usr/local/bin/osqueryd`: The main osquery daemon, which starts the process.
- `/usr/local/bin/osqueryi`: Provides a SQL interface to test queries. By default, comes with a number of built-in tables populated with more information than most can consume (more data is always a good thing).

Now that we've looked at the osquery components, let's get it installed and check SQL to see what data we now have at our fingertips.

Install osquery

The osquery software package for Mac is available at osquery.io/downloads. The default package creates the files mentioned in the previous section. Then you'll want to create a configuration file from the example:

```
sudo cp /var/osquery/osquery.example.conf /var/osquery/
osquery.conf
```

When you edit this file, it's a standard json file. Look for lines that begin with a // as those that are commented out. For this example, we're going to uncomment the following lines by simply deleting the // that the lines begin with and then change the /usr/share/ to /var given that packs have moved (note the exact path to each file may be different based on the version of osquery run and how it was compiled):

```
//
"osquery-monitoring": "/usr/share/osquery/packs/osquery-
monitoring.conf",
//
"incident-response": "/usr/share/osquery/packs/incident-
response.conf",
// "it-compliance": "/usr/share/osquery/packs/it-
compliance.conf",
// "osx-attacks": "/usr/share/osquery/packs/osx-attacks.conf",
```

So those four lines should then read

```
"osquery-monitoring": "/var/osquery/packs/osquery-
monitoring.conf",
"incident-response": "/var/osquery/packs/incident-
response.conf",
"it-compliance": "/var/osquery/packs/it-compliance.conf",
"osx-attacks": "/var/osquery/packs/osx-attacks.conf",
```

We'll also uncomment this line in the same way, by removing the //:

```
//"database_path": "/var/osquery/osquery.db",
```

The osqueryd daemon provides you with queries run on a schedule. The daemon then aggregates the results of those queries and outputs logs. The following is an example query from the configuration file. Here, we're looking for hostname, cpu, and memory from the system_info table. We also include the schedule for how frequently osqueryd updates the database per query using an interval option in seconds.

```
"system_info": {
// The exact query to run.
"query": "SELECT hostname, cpu_brand, physical_memory FROM
system_info;",
//
The interval in seconds to run this query, not an exact
interval.
      "interval": 3600
    }
```

We're not going to make any changes to any of the example queries just yet. Now that we've customized the configuration file, we'll copy the LaunchDaemon to /Library/LaunchDaemons and start it:

```
sudo cp /var/osquery/com.facebook.osqueryd.plist /Library/
LaunchDaemons/
```

Once you've copied the file, we'll start the LaunchDaemon:

```
sudo launchctl load /Library/LaunchDaemons/com.facebook.
osqueryd.plist
```

The footprint for osquery is slight. As an example of this, to remove osquery simply stop the processes and remove /Library/LaunchDaemons/com.facebook.osqueryd.plist. Then remove all files from /private/var/log/

osquery, /private/var/osquery, and /usr/local/bin/osquery and then use pkgutil to forget the osquery package was used using pkgutil:

```
pkgutil --forget com.facebook.osquery
```

To deploy osquery en masse, edit your own templates, script any additional installation steps as a postflight script, and repackage them for distribution. This can be more work for some environments than a third-party package that is purchased or could be less for some environments based on the scale and complexity requirements. Now that we have osquery running on a system, let's look at running queries with osquery.

Running osquery

The best way to understand the real value of osquery is to use osqueryi as a stand-alone tool to query facts about a device. Architecturally, anything you report on locally is then available on the server as well or easily piped to a Security Information and Event Management (SIEM). In fact, if you're threat hunting, doing research to write this book, or just obsessive compulsive about tracking your own personal device performance, you can run osquery locally.

First, we'll start the osquery daemon, which now that everything is installed should be started, but just in case, we'll use the following:

```
/usr/local/bin/osqueryctl start
```

Events and facts about devices are stored in a SQL database at /var/osquery/osquery.db (by default), and the schema for the tables in that database is documented at `https://osquery.io/schema/3.3.2`. The osqueryi binary can then be used to perform SQL queries. This is an interactive SQL shell and can be invoked by simply calling the file:

```
/usr/local/bin/osqueryi
```

Once in the interactive shell, just run a .SCHEMA command to see the lay of the land:

```
osquery>.SCHEMA
```

There are way too many attributes that are tracked than we have pages to go through them in this book. See `https://link.springer.com/book/10.1007/978-1-4842-1955-3` for a great book on SQL queries.

For osquery specifically, use the link to the official schema to easily find information about what's being tracked. It's a much prettier map. Next, we'll provide a few samples just to show the power of osquery. The first is from sample documentation, but it's one of the most common. This query shows the USB devices that are plugged into a computer:

```
osquery>SELECT vendor, model FROM usb_devices;
```

The output would be as follows:

```
+------------+----------------------------------+
| vendor     | model                            |
+------------+----------------------------------+
| Apple Inc. | AppleUSBXHCI Root Hub Simulation |
| Apple Inc. | AppleUSBXHCI Root Hub Simulation |
| Apple Inc. | AppleUSBXHCI Root Hub Simulation |
| Apple Inc. | iBridge                          |
+------------+----------------------------------+
```

The preceding example is a standard SQL result set. It shows all USB devices on the bus. You can also use the WHERE clause to extract only those records that fulfill a specified criterion. The WHERE syntax uses a SELECT followed by the column and then a FROM for the table but now adds a WHERE at the end so you can specify table_name WHERE a column name is - and this is where it becomes powerful because it's where it is either something in the data set or a comparative between columns. To show what this expands to fully:

```
osquery> SELECT vendor, model FROM usb_devices WHERE vendor
!='Apple Inc.';
```

As you can see, we used single quotes around text. We could have also used double quotes. You do not need to quote numbers, but do need to quote strings. The following operators are available when using a WHERE clause:

- = Equal
- <> or != Not equal to
- > Greater than
- **IN** Indicates multiple potential values for a column
- < Less than
- >= Greater than or equal
- <= Less than or equal
- **BETWEEN** Between an inclusive range
- **LIKE** Looks for a provided pattern

What would this look like in your configuration file?

```
{
  "usb_devices": {
    "query": "SELECT vendor, model FROM usb_devices;",
    "interval": 60
  }
}
```

In the preceding query, notice that we are running a standard SELECT statement. Most tasks executed against a SQL database are done with SQL statements. Think of statements as a query, an insert, a change, or a delete operation. For example, to see all data in the tables, select all of the records from a database using the SELECT statement.

Notice that this is just the name of a query (any old name will work) followed by a query, which is a standard SQL query, followed by an interval. This would run once a minute. Another option would be to list the amount of free space on Time Machine destinations once an hour:

```
{
  "time_machine": {
    "query":
    "SELECT bytes_available from time_machine_destinations;;",
    "interval": 60
  }
}
```

The ORDER BY keyword in a SQL SELECT statement is used to sort a given result set based on the contents of one or more columns of data. By default, results are in ascending order, but you can use either ASC or DESC to indicate that you'd like results sorted in ascending or descending order, respectively.

```
SELECT * FROM shared_folders ORDER BY name DESC
```

Now that we've looked at queries, let's move to how the logging and reporting functions work so we understand how drift is tracked.

Logging and Reporting

The SQL result set we looked at earlier ends up getting tracked in the osquery database as a field in json. Each time the query runs, a new row is created in the table. The rows are empty until a change occurs the next time the query is told to run. The contents of the first run would appear as follows:

```
[
{"model":
"XHCI Root Hub SS Simulation","vendor":"Apple Inc."},
```

```
{"model":
"XHCI Root Hub USB 2.0 Simulation","vendor":"Apple Inc."},

{"model":
"XHCI Root Hub SS Simulation","vendor":"Apple Inc."},

{"model":
"Bluetooth USB Host Controller","vendor":"Apple Inc."}
]
```

Until a new device is added, no results are logged. But once I insert a USB drive, I would then see an entry that looks like the following:

```
[
  {"model":"WD Easystore USB 3.0","vendor":"Western Digital"}
]
```

There's plenty of extensibility. Each deployment then has the option to add decorations, lenses, or additional packs. Now that we understand some basics about running these queries and automating them, let's just do a quick check on shared folders:

```
osqueryi --json "SELECT * FROM shared_folders"
```

The output is then as follows:

```
[
  {"name":"CE's Public Folder","path":"/Users/ce/Public"},
  {"name":"molly's Public Folder","path":"/Users/molly/Public"}
]
```

This information can quickly and easily be picked up as inventory from other tools with agents, such as munki, Jamf Pro, Addigy, or Fleetsmith. As noted previously, Fleetsmith came with the ability to direct osquery information from managed clients into a server. Now that we've covered osquery, let's look at another open source agent called Chef.

Chef

The purpose of osquery is to obtain information about devices. But an orchestration tool is required as well for large-scale systems administration. Chef is a tool originally built by Jesse Robbins to do server builds and is now maintained at `https://chef.io`. Chef uses a recipe to perform a configuration task. These recipes are organized into cookbooks.

> *Managing clients is harder than managing servers. Your server isn't likely to get up and walk away, doesn't have a rouge root user, and will never connect to Starbucks wi-fi.*
>
> —Mike Dodge, Client Platform Engineer, Facebook

The most complete list of cookbooks available for the Mac can be obtained through the Facebook Client Platform Engineering team's GitHub account at `https://github.com/facebook/IT-CPE`. Reading through these should provide a good understanding of the types of things that Facebook and other IT teams do to automate systems and get up to speed on how to orchestrate various events on the Mac.

Install Chef

We don't go into detail in this book on how to set up a Chef instance and get client systems to connect to it. That's an entire book of its own. But we do review the Chef client in this section. To install the client, download the installer from `https://downloads.chef.io/chef-client/`. When you install the package, chef-apply, chef-client, chef-shell, and chef-solo will be installed in /usr/local/bin.

To clone the repo mentioned earlier from Meta/Facebook (as of the time of this writing, that repo was last updated less than three weeks ago, so it's an active community-run asset), use the following command (which would copy it to /Users/Shared/ChefAssets):

```
git clone https://github.com/facebook/IT-CPE /Users/Shared/
ChefAssets
```

Once installed, there will be a company_init.rb script at /Users/Shared/ChefAssets/chef/cookbooks/cpe_init/recipes. There's also a /Users/Shared/ChefAssets/chef/tools/chef_bootstrap.py bootstrap script. Next, customize the chef server URL and the organization name (which should match that of the chef server), and provide any certificates necessary. The main settings are in the header of the script:

```
CLIENT_RB = """
log_level              :info
log_location           STDOUT
validation_client_name 'YOUR_ORG_NAME-validator'
validation_key
File.expand_path('/etc/chef/validation.pem')
chef_server_url        "YOUR_CHEF_SERVER_URL_GOES_HERE"
json_attribs           '/etc/chef/run-list.json'
ssl_ca_file            '/etc/chef/YOUR_CERT.crt'
ssl_verify_mode        :verify_peer
local_key_generation   true
rest_timeout           30
http_retry_count       3
no_lazy_load           false
```

Additionally, look for any place that indicates MYCOMPANY and replace that with the name of the organization to personalize the installation. Also, make sure that if using chef to bootstrap a Munki installation, the correct URL is defined in SoftwareRepoURL:

```
# Be sure to replace all instances of MYCOMPANY with your
actual company name
node.default['organization'] = 'MYCOMPANY'
```

```
prefix = "com.#{node['organization']}.chef"
node.default['cpe_launchd']['prefix'] = prefix
node.default['cpe_profiles']['prefix'] = prefix
# Install munki
node.default['cpe_munki']['install'] = false
# Configure munki
node.default['cpe_munki']['configure'] = false
# Override default munki settings
node.default['cpe_munki']['preferences']['SoftwareRepoURL'] =
  'https://munki.MYCOMPANY.com/repo'
```

The logs are written to /Library/Chef/Logs/first_chef_run.log when the script runs. The supporting files for chef will also be at /etc/chef, including certificates that secure communications, a client.rb file that contains the information you supplied the bootstrap.py. Provided it completes, you'll then have a working quickstart.json file at /Users/Shared/ChefAssets/chef and a working run-list.json file that includes any recipes you want to run. You'll also have a /var/chef/cache for caches.

The quickstart script can then be as simple as the following:

```
{
  "minimal_ohai" : true,
  "run_list": [
    "recipe[cpe_init]"
  ]
}
```

Cookbooks should be ordered in the run-list from least specific to most specific. That company_init.rb recipe defined the defaults for an organization with all of the CPE cookbooks provided. The cpe_init entry in the quickstart.json loads those recipes called in that init, which by default includes a platform run-list, a user run-list, and a node customization run-list. To know what anything is doing when it's being called, simply look at the depends lines and then read the resource ruby script for each, such as /Users/Shared/ChefAssets/chef/cookbooks/cpe_hosts/resources/cpe_hosts.rb. Once everything is in place, it's time to grill out with chef. Let's simply run the chef-client along with the -j to specify your json file:

```
sudo chef-client -z -j /Users/Shared/ChefAssets/chef/
quickstart.json
```

Edit a Recipe

Chef then verifies each resource in each included cookbook has been configured as defined and resolves any drift found in the current system. One of the most important things about a tool like chef is how configurable it is. Simply cat the /Users/Shared/ChefAssets/chef/cookbooks/cpe_munki/resources/cpe_munki_local.rb file to see how munki is installed and note that. Now that chef is running, let's edit a recipe. To do so, edit that /Users/Shared/IT-CPE/chef/cookbooks/cpe_init/recipes/company_init.rb recipe in your favorite text editor to add the following lines to the bottom of the file:

```
node.default['cpe_autopkg']['repos'] = [
  'recipes',
  'https://github.com/facebook/Recipes-for-AutoPkg.git'
]
```

This adds the recipes from the Meta team to an autopkg instance running on the host. Other parts of the recipe will allow you to install autopkg and customize it, so you don't have to do all the steps we'll follow in a manual installation later in this book. Programmatic deployment of tools and configuration provides for a consistent experience. Once you've configured the change to the client init, rerun the chef-client:

```
sudo chef-client -z -j /Users/Shared/ChefAssets/chef/
quickstart.json
```

These also write profiles, which you can then see in System Preferences. Meta was one of the first to publish cookbooks for Chef and an early proponent of Chef for large-scale Mac orchestration. A few others have also open sourced their cookbooks, which gives a number of options to choose from. And cookbooks can be obtained from multiple vendors. A few include the following:

- `http://chef-osx.github.io/`
- `https://github.com/microsoft/macos-cookbook`
- `https://github.com/pinterest/it-cpe-cookbooks`
- `https://supermarket.chef.io/cookbooks/macos`
- `https://github.com/uber/cpe-chef-cookbooks`

The social community of Chef administrators and how they share cookbooks makes for a good reason to look into these types of workflows. Chef is open source and there are a lot of different methodologies around its use and deployment. The examples in this chapter have mostly been developed around a model that Apple began back in Software Update Server when they provided us with a manifest URL. Mac admins have been using a similar manifest, init script, etc., to deploy settings, apps, and operating systems ever since. Some organizations have developed integrations with Chef that go beyond this and leverage a chef server.

In the preceding example, we're providing those certificates and the chef-client to endpoints from a central location, configuring what is required for a client to be able to communicate back to a server. The steps we followed in the previous examples can be strung together into an installer package. But being able to automatically deploy one and keep clients up to date automatically makes for a much simpler experience. This is where an orchestration tool like Puppet can come in handy.

Puppet

The tools covered in the previous sections are just a few in a red ocean that includes a large number of client management tools available for the Mac. We've seen Puppet, Vagrant, and other open source projects used to orchestrate events on the Mac in much the same way they would orchestrate events on a large farm of Linux servers.

The Puppet installer for Mac is available at `https://downloads.puppetlabs.com/mac/`, and when installed using a standard software package, the puppet-agent is used to orchestrate events on Macs. A number of other binaries for puppet can be found in /opt/puppetlabs/bin/. The service can be managed using launchctl or the puppet binary. For example, if puppet is stopped, it can be started using

```
sudo /opt/puppetlabs/bin/puppet resource service puppet
ensure=running enable=true
```

Configure changes to some of the ways the agent runs with settings found at `https://puppet.com/docs/puppet/5.5/config_important_settings.html`. The most important is to sign a certificate that's then used to establish communications with the server. This is done using the puppet command-line utility followed by the cert option and then the sign verb for that option, followed by the name of a certificate that's generated, as follows:

```
sudo /opt/puppetlabs/bin/puppet cert sign com.puppet.
pretendco8734
```

These need to match with the server entry in the puppet.conf directory. We don't want to oversimplify a full-blown puppet deployment. Getting a client to connect to a server is pretty straightforward. The real value in any of these tools comes in the form of how much time they save you once deployed. Puppet has nine configuration files, such as auth.conf and puppetdb.conf, for a reason. We won't go into each of them (especially since our publisher has an entire book on the subject available at `www.apress.com/gp/book/9781430230571`).

Logs are then saved to /var/log/puppetlabs/puppetserver/puppetserver.log. This walk-through follows the same general standard as Chef and Munki. But each is really built for something specific. Puppet is for immediate orchestration. Munki is for software distribution. Chef is for keeping a device in a known state. Osquery is for keeping inventory of settings and events. There's overlap between some of the options, but if you squint enough, the basic methodology and management principles across them are, in a very oversimplified way, similar. One such similarity is that most administrators of these tools prefer to check changes in and out using a tool called git.

Use Git to Manage All the Things

Git is a version control system (or tool) that can be used to manage files including code that is then version controlled so you can see changes over time. The main page indicates it's actually the stupid content tracker. Git is good at tracking changes between files and allowing administrators to check code or files out and then check them back in when finished working. This is well suited to a workflow where you want someone else to review your changes before they get applied to a large fleet of devices. This makes git a common complement to chef, osquery, and munki deployments.

Ultimately though, git is a command with some verbs. Let's start with the init verb, which creates an empty git repository in the working directory (or supply a path after the verb):

```
git init
```

Now let's touch a file in that directory:

```
touch newfilename
```

Once a new file is there, with that new repo as the working directory, run git with the status verb:

```
git status
```

You now see that you're "On branch master" – we'll talk branching later. You see "No commits yet" and hey, what's that, an untracked file! Run git with the add verb, and this time you need to specify a file or path (I'll use . assuming your working directory is still the directory of your path):

```
git add .
```

Now let's run the status command; again, the output should indicate that you now have a staged file (or files). Now let's run our first commit. This takes the tracked and staged file that we just created and commits it. Until we do this, we can always revert back to the previous state of that file (which in this simple little walk-through would be for the file to no longer exist).

```
git commit -m "test"
```

Now let's edit our file:

```
echo "This is an example." > newFile'
```

This time, let's run git with the diff verb:

```
git diff
```

You can now see what changed between your file(s). Easy, right? Check out the logs to see what you've been doing to poor git:

```
git log
```

There's a commit listed there, along with an author, a date and timestamp, as well as a name of the file(s) in the commit. Now, let's run a reset to revert to our last commit. This will overwrite the changes we just made prior to doing the diff (you can use a specific commit by using it as the next position after —hard, or you can just leave it for the latest actual commit):

```
git reset –hard
```

This resets all files back to the way it was before you started mucking around with those poor files. OK, so we've been working off in our own little world. Next, we'll look at branches. You know how we reset all of our files in the previous command? What if we had 30 files and we just wanted to reset one? You shouldn't work in your master branch for a number of reasons. So let's look at existing branches by running git with the branch verb:

```
git branch
```

You see that you have one branch, the "* master" branch. To create a new branch, simply type git followed by the name of the branch you wish to create (in this case, it will be called myspiffychanges1):

```
git branch myspiffychanges1
```

Run git with the branch verb again, and you'll see that below master, your new branch appears. The asterisk is always used so you know which branch you're working in. To switch between branches, use the checkout verb along with the name of the branch:

```
git checkout myspiffychanges1
```

I could have done both of the previous steps in one command, by using the -b flag with the checkout verb:

```
git checkout -b myspiffychanges1
```

OK now, the asterisk should be on your new branch, and you should be able to make changes. Let's edit that file from earlier. Then let's run another git status and note that your modifications can be seen. Let's add them to the list of tracked changes using the git add for the working directory again:

```
git add .
```

Now let's commit those changes:

```
git commit -m "some changes"
```

And now we have two branches, a little different from one another. Let's merge the changes into the master branch next. First, let's switch back to the master branch:

```
git checkout master
```

And then let's merge those changes:

```
git merge myspiffychanges1
```

OK – so now you know how to init a project, branch, and merge. Before we go on the interwebs, let's first set up your name. Notice in the logs that the Author field displays a name and an email address. Let's see where that comes from:

```
git config -list
```

This is initially populated by ~/.gitconfig so you can edit that. Or let's remove what is in that list:

```
git config --unset-all user.name
```

And then we can add a new set of information to the key we'd like to edit:

```
git config user.name "Charles Edge" --global
```

You might as well set an email address too, so people can yell at you for your crappy code some day:

```
git config user.email "chuckufarley@me.com" --global
```

Next, let's clone an existing repository onto our computer. The clone verb allows you to clone a repository into your home directory:

```
git clone https://github.com/autopkg/autopkg
```

The remote verb allows you to make a local copy of a branch. But it takes a couple of steps. First, init a project with the appropriate name and then cd into it. Then grab the URL from GitHub and add it using the remote verb:

```
git remote add AutoPkg https://github.com/autopkg/autopkg.git
```

Now let's fetch a branch of that project, in this case, called test:

```
git fetch test myspiffychanges1
```

Now we'll want to download the contents of that branch:

```
git pull myspiffychanges1
```

And once we've made some changes, let's push our changes:

```
git push test myspiffychanges1
```

Now that you've deployed agents, MDM is a great complement to what agents can do, so we'll cover the concept of User-Approved MDM in order to have less button mashing happening by our end users.

The Impact of UAMDM and Other Rootless Changes to macOS

Many of the third-party and open source tools use binaries that have been forced to evolve over the years due to the Mac becoming less like a Unix or Linux and more like an iOS (which is arguably one of the safest operating systems available). Until macOS High Sierra, some MDM functions would not run as well on personally owned Macs as on iOS devices owned by a company. This is because the iOS counterparts had supervision and Macs did not. As of High Sierra and beyond, Macs owned by a company, school, or institution can now be managed in a similar fashion as supervised iOS devices are managed because of the introduction of UAMDM. User-Approved MDM (UAMDM) in macOS 10.13.4 changed that by putting certain management privileges in a special category. The use of these special management privileges required both the use of an MDM solution and for that MDM solution to support User-Approved MDM. As of macOS Mojave 10.14.x, these special management privileges are the following:

- Approval of third-party kernel extension loading (less of an issue now that kernel extensions aren't used, but the same logic now applies to system extensions and other apps that require entitlements)
- Approval of application requests to access privacy-protected data and functionality
- Autonomous Single App Mode

For Mac environments which had traditionally not used MDM management solutions, this meant for the first time that an MDM solution was absolutely necessary for certain management functions to happen (unless SIP is disabled). Moreover, there are two ways to mark a Mac as being user approved:

- Enrolling the Mac in Apple's Automated Device Enrollment, or ADE, formerly called the Device Enrollment Program (DEP). Enrollment of a Mac into ADE means that Apple or an authorized reseller has designated that Mac one that is owned by a company, school, or other institutions. Since this Mac is now explicitly not a personally owned device, it gets UAMDM and other benefits that allow certain binaries to run in privileged ways automatically.
- Having a human being click an approval button on the MDM profile issued by an MDM server which supports UAMDM. Notice that this cannot be scripted with graphical scripting tools as Apple blocks "synthetic clicking" on these screens to protect the privacy of end users.

The automatic granting of UAMDM to ADE-enrolled Macs means that ADE (and so MDM) is now almost a requirement for most organizations. The combination of UAMDM's reserving of management privileges and the necessity of using MDM to employ those privileges means that using an MDM solution to manage Macs has moved from the "useful, but not essential" category to the "essential" category.

The rise of MDM management may signal the diminishment of using agents to manage Macs, but that has been a slow progression, and as seen in this chapter, agents are still quite beneficial. As more MDM management options become available every year, the more an MDM solution can use Apple's built-in MDM management functionality to manage Macs in place of using a third-party agent to manage the Mac, the more future-proofed a deployment is likely to be. While agents likely won't disappear overnight, the areas where they provide management value will shrink over time.

Rootless

The challenge with what some of these agents are doing is that they are operating in a way that is becoming challenging to keep up with the rapid pace of change at Apple engineering. Given the prevalence of some of these tools, Apple provides a group of apps that are whitelisted from many of the sandboxing requirements, which they call rootless. Some files need to be modifiable, even if they're in a protected space. To see a listing of Apple tools that receive this exception, see /System/Library/Sandbox/rootless.conf:

```
cat /System/Library/Sandbox/rootless.conf
```

The degree with which each entry in the rootless.conf file is exempt varies. In addition to the list of SIP exceptions listed others can be found in the rootless.conf file.

Frameworks

Another aspect to be aware of when considering agents is the frameworks used in the agent. Frameworks are also sometimes important to consider as they're added into apps and have to be approved for use by a user via an extension that loads the framework. A framework is a type of bundle that packages dynamic shared libraries with the resources that the library requires, including files (nibs and images), localized strings, header files, and maybe documentation. The .framework is an Apple structure that contains all of the files that make up a framework.

Frameworks are stored in the following location (where the ∗ is the name of an app or framework):

- /Applications/∗contents/Frameworks
- /Library/∗/
- /Library/Application Support/∗/∗.app/Contents/

- /Library/Developer/CommandLineTools/
- /Library/Developer/
- /Library/Frameworks
- /Library/Printers/
- /System/iOSSupport/System/Library/PrivateFrameworks
- /System/iOSSupport/System/Library/Frameworks
- /System/Library/CoreServices
- /System/Library/Frameworks
- /System/Library/PrivateFrameworks
- /usr/local/Frameworks

If you just browse through these directories, you'll see so many things you can use in apps. You can easily add an import followed by the name in your view controllers in Swift. For example, in /System/Library/Frameworks, you'll find the Foundation.framework. Foundation is pretty common as it contains a number of APIs such as NSObject (NSDate, NSString, and NSDateFormatter).

You can import this into a script using the following line:

```
import Foundation
```

As with importing frameworks/modules/whatever (according to the language), you can then consume the methods/variables/etc. in your code (e.g., let url = NSURL(fileURLWithPath: "names.plist").

The importance of frameworks here is that you should be able to run a command called otool to see what frameworks a given binary is dependent on in order to better understand what's happening:

```
otool -L /usr/bin/lldb
```

Additionally, you can use an open source project called looto to see what is dependent on binaries in order to better understand how tools interact with other tools or with their own various frameworks. This is one of a number of open source tools that many administrators will need to understand at some point in order to have a well-rounded perspective on device management.

For noncompiled apps, dynamic libraries (.dylib) can be dangerous and therefore should no longer be used where possible. Most Swift apps now disable the ability to add a dylib by default due to the number of security flaws they have been used to implement.

Miscellaneous Automation Tools

There are also a number of automation tools that are easily called by agents that make planning and implementing a deployment easier by providing more flexible options to administrators for specific tasks. There are plenty of other tools described throughout the book, but these are specifically designed to help extend what agents can do.

The first tool we'll cover is outset from Joseph Chilcote and available at `https://github.com/chilcote/outset/`. Outset processes packages and scripts at first boot and user logins. Outset is comprised of two launchd items that call loose packages or scripts in individual folders either at startup or user login. To add more tasks to the startup and login processes, add new items to the appropriate folders. Outset handles the execution.

If your Macs need to routinely run a series of startup scripts to reset user environments or computer variables, then making launchd plists may be burdensome and difficult to manage. And plists execute asynchronously, which means startup and login processes may not run in the same order every time.

The next tool is dockutil, available at `https://github.com/kcrawford/dockutil`. Dockutil makes it easier to manage the Dock on a Mac. Users need the right tools to do their jobs, and a thoughtfully crafted dock helps them find those tools. They need access to applications, their home folders, servers, and working directories. Dockutil adds, removes, and reorders dock items for users. The script allows an administrator to adjust dock settings to adjust the view of folders (grid, fan, list, or automatic), adjust the display of folders to show their contents or folder icons, and set folder sort order (name, date, or kind).

The last tool we'll cover is duti, available at `http://duti.org/index.html`. Duti makes it easier to set default applications for document types and URL handlers/schemes. Enterprises often incorporate Macs into complex workflows that require consistent behaviors. If a workflow requires using the Firefox browser instead of Safari or using Microsoft Outlook instead of Apple's Mail application, Andrew Mortensen's duti can ensure the correct applications respond when opening a URL or new email message.

Note A much more comprehensive list of these tools can be found in Appendix A.

Duti's name means "default for UTI" or what Apple calls Uniform Type Identifiers. Every file type such as an HTML page or Microsoft Word document has a UTI, and developers constantly create their own new UTIs. Duti reads and applies UTI settings to pair applications with UTIs.

Summary

There are a number of agent-based solutions on the market that make managing Macs en masse possible. Some of these are proprietary, and others are open source. Most management agents should be paired with a Mobile Device Management (MDM) solution, which we cover further in Chapter 4. The focus here is on the Mac, simply because we cannot install "agents" on iOS, iPadOS, and tvOS devices (without some serious breaking of the devices).

These agents are typically used for device inventory, deploying software, keeping software up to date, managing settings, user notification, and a number of other tasks. The term "agent" is often an oversimplification. Each "agent" usually comes with anywhere between one and five LaunchAgents and LaunchDaemons. This is because each task should be run independently. These tasks usually invoke other tasks, preferably with native Swift frameworks but often by simply "shelling out" a command-line tool built into macOS. As an example, you can install profiles manually using the profiles command, which any agent-only management tool will use for profile management, given that some tasks require a profile. We'll cover profiles in detail in Chapter 3.

More and more of these settings are now prompting users. Thus, we need to use an MDM solution to limit the number of prompts on behalf of the user and to get our management agents on devices without too much work from line tech support.

Now that we've covered agents, we'll dig into MDM further in Chapter 4. But first, we'll explore profiles even further in Chapter 3, so you can get more done with both agents and MDM.

CHAPTER 3

Profiles

A profile is an xml file. This file, when installed on a device, configures the device to act in a certain way. Profiles began back in the iPhone Configuration Utility (the precursor to Apple Configurator) and have since moved to being the way you manage various settings on Apple operating systems like iOS, iPadOS, macOS, and tvOS.

When configuring iOS devices to use the settings you want, there's generally three ways to go, restoring devices and manually configuring settings and profiles. For the Mac, you have another option, scripting changes with defaults.

Manual configuration can be done by anyone and doesn't require any management infrastructure at all, but it's generally time-consuming and requires having the device in front of the person doing the configuration, and, frankly, people make errors.

In contrast, profile configuration usually requires some sort of Mobile Device Management solution infrastructure but can also be done with nothing more than Apple's Configurator app. Settings configuration via a profile is quick, the settings can be applied to multiple devices simultaneously, and (assuming the profile was configured correctly) a profile will apply the desired settings consistently and without errors.

Scripted configuration changes can be done in a number of ways. You can install a profile from the command line. But you can also edit a defaults domain, which is based on a property list file that can also be edited manually. We'll cover manipulating settings using the defaults

C. Edge and R. Trouton, *Apple Device Management*,
https://doi.org/10.1007/978-1-4842-9156-6_3

command further in Chapter 10. In this chapter, we will perform some manual configurations and then look at how to perform some of those same tasks using profiles, to better understand how profiles work and look at doing scripted management of profiles. Along the way, we'll look at the contents of a profile.

Manually Configure Settings on Devices

The manual configuration of settings on devices is done using System Settings on the Mac or using the Settings app on iOS. We'll start by looking at using the Settings app to configure a newer feature called Downtime. Downtime restricts anything but phone calls from working on an iOS device, and settings to Downtime are synchronized to iCloud applying them to all devices that have been configured using a given iCloud account.

To get started, first open the Settings app on an iOS or iPadOS device. This is where all settings are configured, such as Wi-Fi and privacy settings. From there, tap on the Screen Time setting. In Screen Time, you'll find Downtime (Figure 3-1); tap on that.

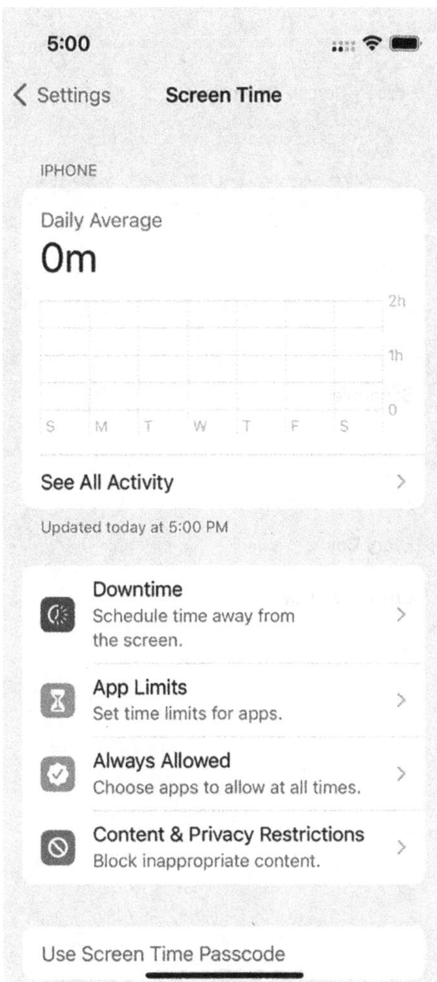

***Figure 3-1.** Tap **Downtime** to configure Downtime settings*

Now that you're in the Downtime settings, tap the Scheduled button to turn on the ability to set time away from your device. Once done, click the Start field and set a time. Then tap the End time to configure when you'll get alerts again (Figure 3-2).

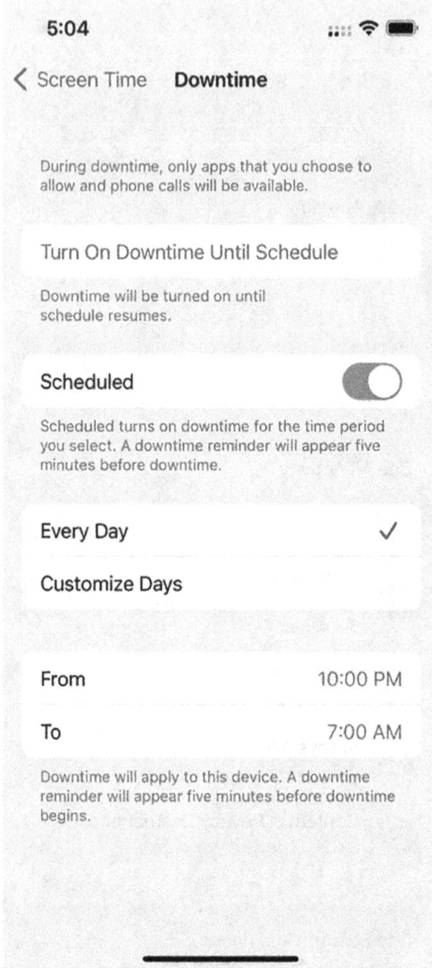

Figure 3-2. *Configuring Downtime settings to schedule time away*

Tap back on Screen Time in the upper left-hand corner of the screen. Now, let's set up an app limit for social apps (because really, most of us are on those way too much) (Figure 3-3):

- Open Settings.
- Tap Screen Time.

- Tap Add Limits.
- Tap an app category (e.g., Social).
- Set the number of hours you can use that type of app (note, if you set 23 hours and 59 minutes, you are totally cheating).
- Tap Add.

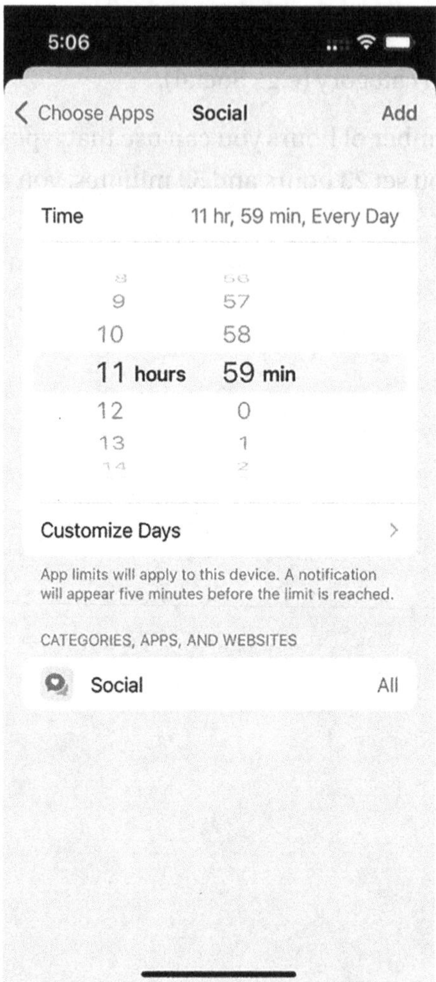

Figure 3-3. *Configuring App Limit settings to restrict time spent on social media*

Should you want to remove those limits you created, just tap Delete Limit. Or better, just configure apps that are allowed to bypass the limits you've made by tapping Always Allowed and adding apps that are always allowed to work. This allows you to limit all your apps except, as an example, Maps and Camera.

Another option in Screen Time is Content and Privacy Restrictions (Figure 3-4). To configure these

- Open Settings.
- Tap Screen Time.
- Tap Content & Privacy Restrictions.
- Turn Content & Privacy Restrictions on by tapping the slider.
- Tap iTunes & App Store Purchases.

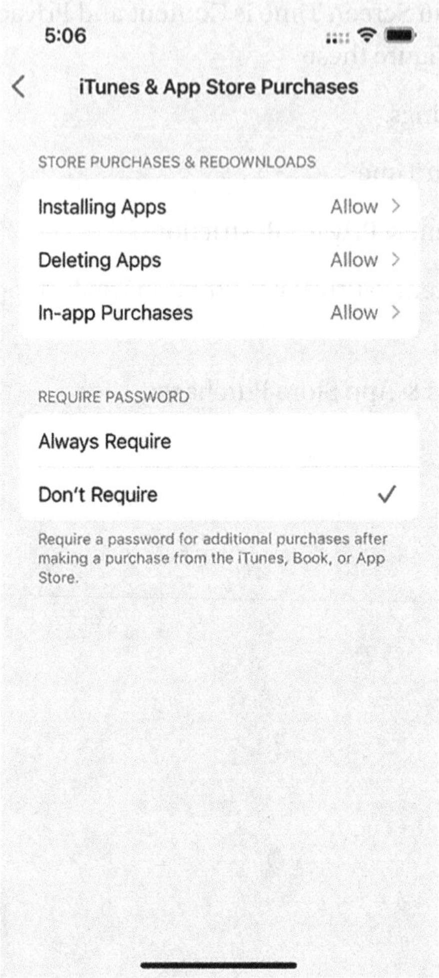

Figure 3-4. *Restricting iTunes and App Store purchases to desired categories*

Here, you can limit installing apps, deleting apps, or making in-app purchases on the device (Figure 3-5). You can also just force a password in order to make any purchase from iTunes, Book Store purchases, or App Store purchases:

- Tap the back button.

- Tap Allowed Apps.
- Use the indicator light to disable any app you don't want to be able to access on this profile.
- Once all apps are configured, tap the back button.
- Tap Content Restrictions.

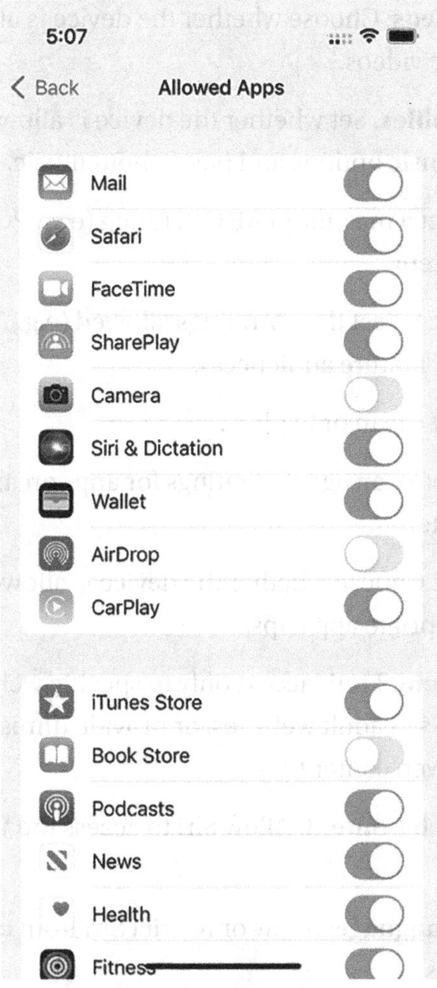

***Figure 3-5.** Restricting apps which can be used on this iOS device*

There are a lot of content restrictions available (Figures 3-6 and 3-7). Most are mirrored with a profile and so can be controlled by an MDM as well:

- **Music, Podcasts, News, Fitness**: Select whether or not explicit content is allowed (and by content we really mean music, podcasts, and news).
- **Music Videos**: Choose whether the device is allowed to play music videos.
- **Music Profiles**: Set whether the device is allowed to publish music options and posts about music.
- **Movies**: Set a maximum AFTRA rating (e.g., PG-13 or R) for content.
- **TV Shows**: Select the TV ratings allowed (e.g., TV-G or TV-MA for mature audiences).
- **Books**: Set Clean or Explicit.
- **Apps**: Choose an age that ratings for apps are most appropriate.
- **App Clips**: Choose whether the device is allowed to use age-appropriate app clips.
- **Web Content**: Limit access only to specific websites, limit access to adult websites, or provide unrestricted access to web content.
- **Web Search Content**: Allow Siri to access the Web to search.
- **Explicit Language**: Allow or restrict Siri from using dirty words.

- **Multiplayer Games**: Allow or deny access to multiplayer games.
- **Connect with Friends**: Allow or deny access to add friends within the Game Center app.
- **Screen Recording**: Allow or deny access to screen recordings.
- **Nearby Multiplayer**: Choose whether the "nearby" setting can be enabled.
- **Private Messaging**: Allow or deny voice chat or the ability to receive custom messages with game and friend invitations.
- **Avatar & Nickname Changes**: Choose whether Game Center avatars or nicknames can be changed.

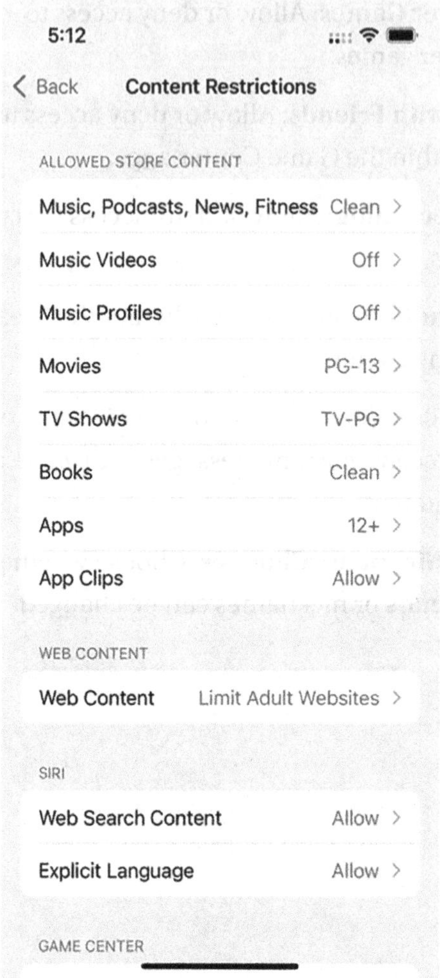

***Figure 3-6.** Restricting iTunes, App Store, and web content settings to desired categories*

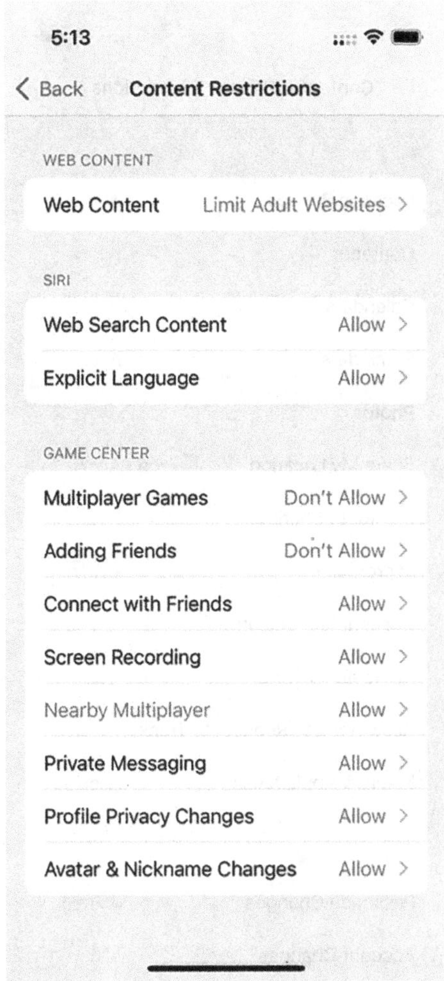

***Figure 3-7.** Restricting Siri and Game Center content settings to desired categories*

Next, go back and in the privacy section, configure what apps are able to access Location Services, Contacts, Calendars, Reminders, Photos, Share My Location, Bluetooth Sharing, Microphone, Speech Recognition, Apple Advertising, Allow Apps to Request to Track, and Media & Apple Music (Figure 3-8).

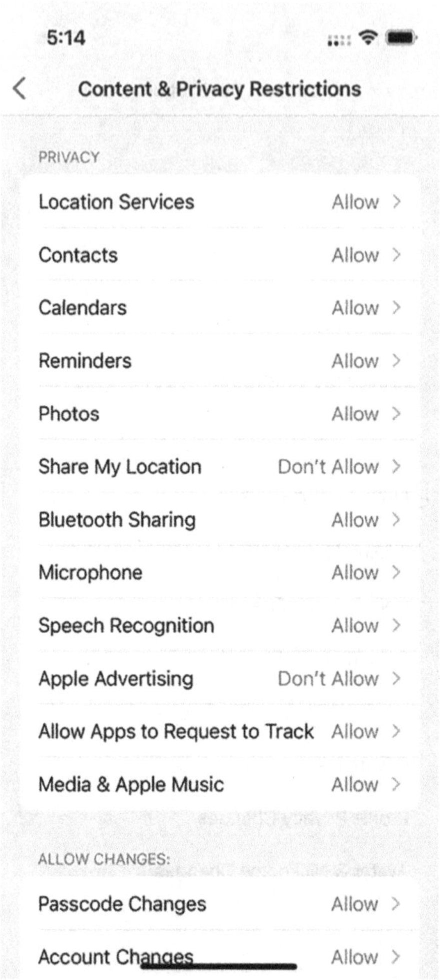

Figure 3-8. *Restricting app access to desired settings*

Under allow changes, configure whether you'll be able to make changes to Passcode Changes, Account Changes, Cellular Data Changes, Reduce Loud Sounds, Driving Focus, TV Provider, and Background App Activities (Figure 3-9).

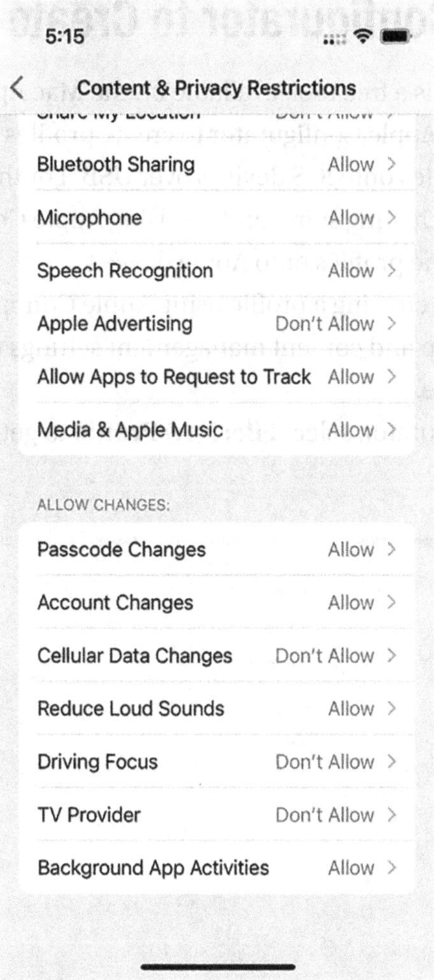

Figure 3-9. *Restricting changes which can be made to specified settings*

That's a ton of work, and if you have more than one device to apply these changes to, it gets tedious and tiresome around device number 2. There's a better way though, which is to use a management profile to configure a device. Let's look at that next.

Use Apple Configurator to Create a Profile

Apple Configurator is a free tool, available on the Mac App Store from Apple. You can use Apple Configurator to create profiles and manage the deployment of profiles onto iOS devices over USB. For the purposes of this chapter, we will be creating some profiles using Apple Configurator and then install one of the profiles onto Apple devices.

First off, let's try creating a profile using Apple Configurator which sets the same kind of app and content management settings that we had earlier set with Screen Time.

In Apple Configurator, select **File: New Profile** to get started (Figure 3-10).

Figure 3-10. *Creating a new management profile in Apple Configurator*

A new profile creation window should open, with Configurator defaulting to showing the **General** section (Figure 3-11).

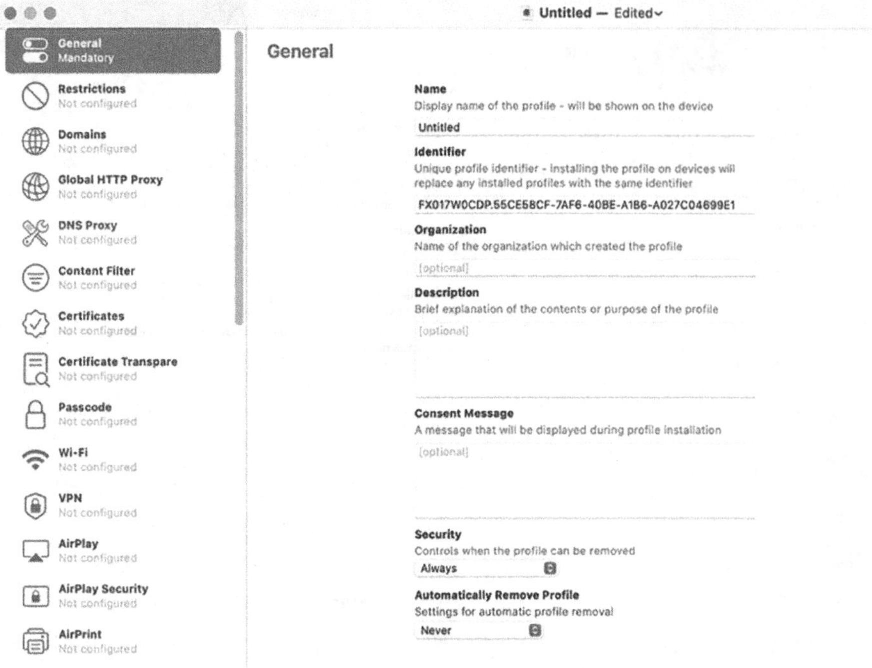

Figure 3-11. *Viewing the new management profile template in Apple Configurator*

The **General** section is where the identifying information for the new profile should be entered (Figure 3-12). In this example, the following information is being used:

- Name: **Screentime Controls**
- Organization: **Company Name**
- Description: **This profile sets app and content restrictions on managed iOS and iPadOS devices**

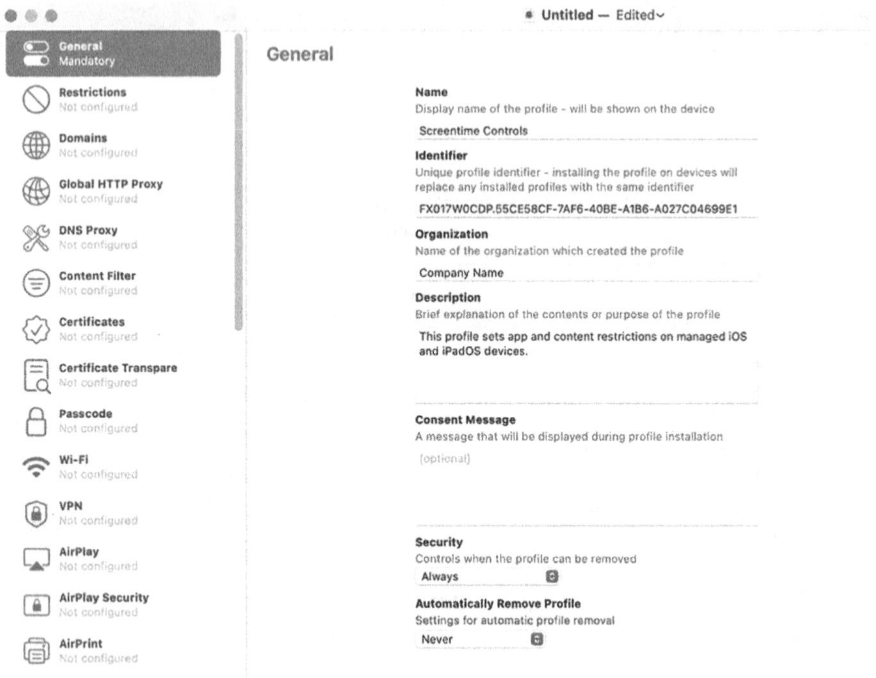

Figure 3-12. *Adding identification information to the new profile*

If needed, additional information and settings can be entered. For example, by default the **Security** settings allow the profile to be removed at any time. These settings can be altered to the following:

- **With Authorization**: This setting requires that a password be entered before the profile can be removed.
- **Never**: This setting means that the profile can never be removed. Only wiping and resetting up the device will erase it from the device.

The settings which match those found in Screen Time are found under the **Restrictions** payload section of the profile. To access these settings, click **Restrictions** and then select the **Configure** button (Figure 3-13).

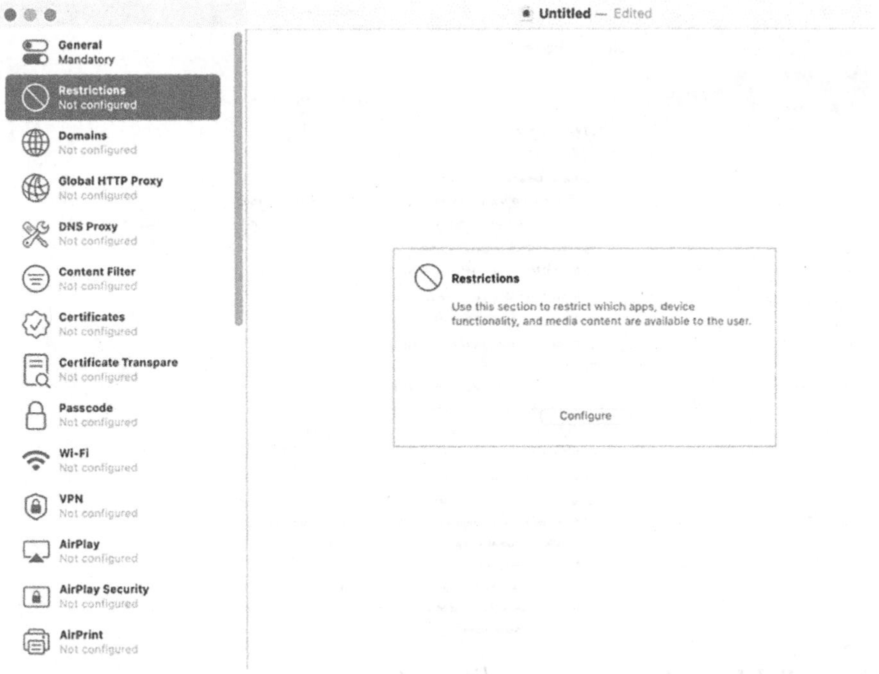

***Figure 3-13.** Enabling the **Restrictions** payload of the new profile*

Once the Restrictions payload is enabled, you can set the desired app and content restrictions for your devices (Figures 3-14 to 3-16).

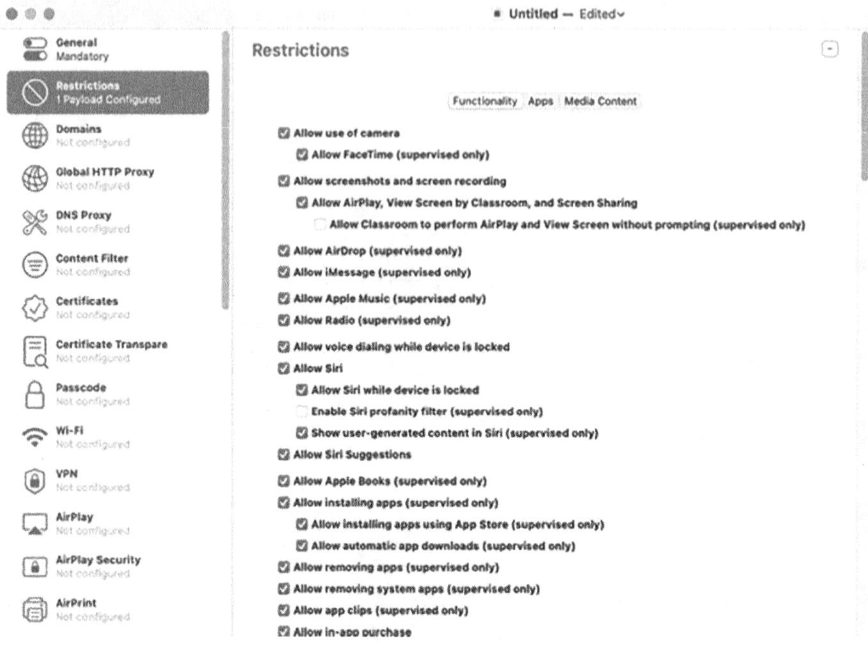

***Figure 3-14.** Setting functionality restrictions*

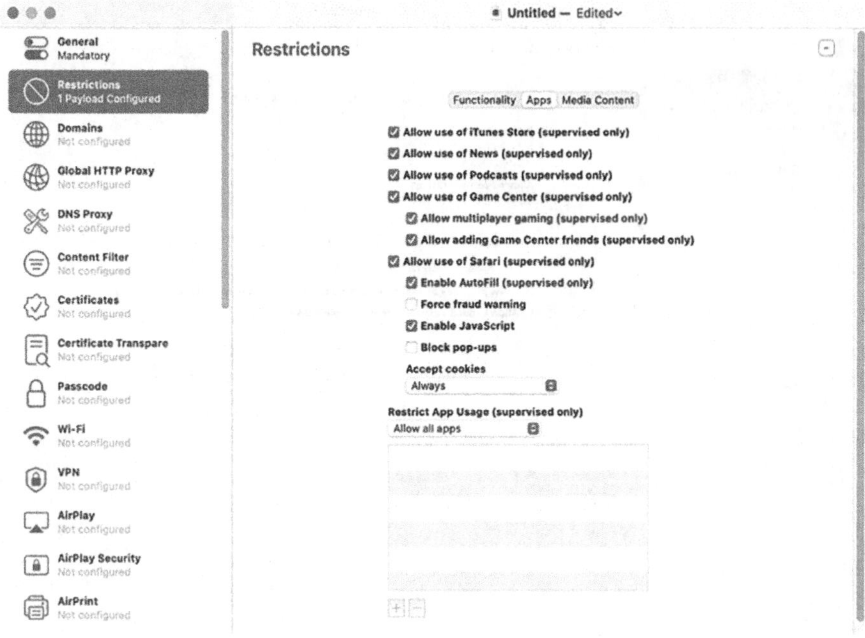

Figure 3-15. *Setting app restrictions*

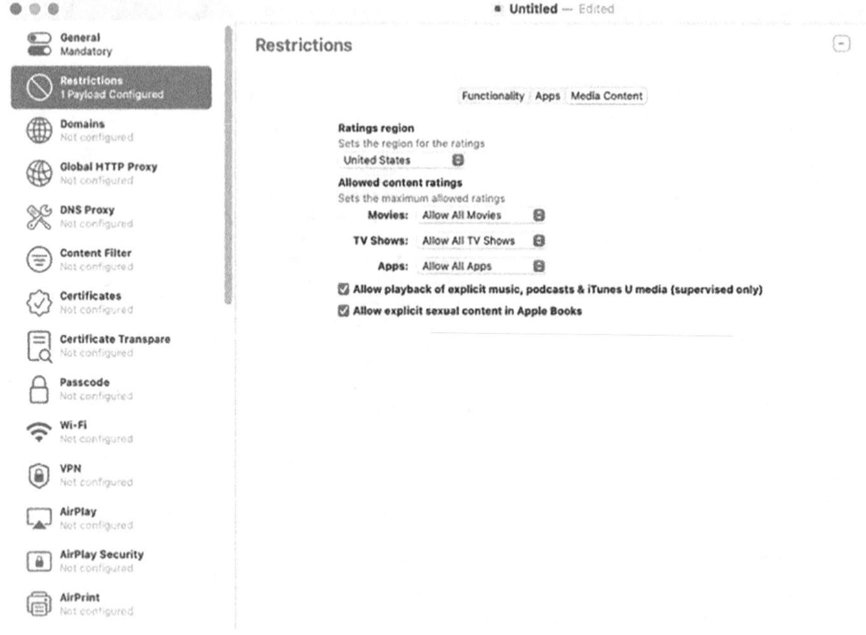

Figure 3-16. *Setting media content restrictions*

Once all the desired settings have been configured in the **Restrictions** payload, save the profile by selecting **Save** under the **File** menu (Figure 3-17).

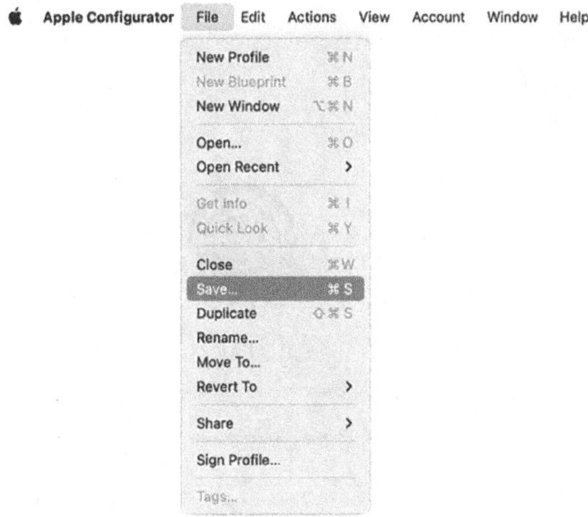

Figure 3-17. Saving a management profile in Apple Configurator

You'll then be prompted to save the profile with a desired name to a desired location, such as the Desktop, so it's easy to find (Figures 3-18 and 3-19).

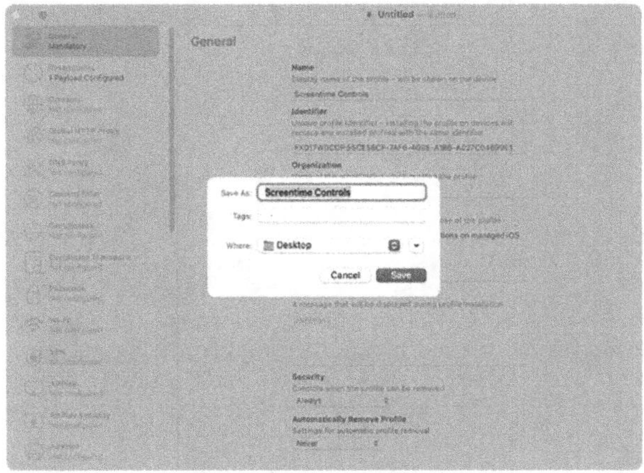

Figure 3-18. Saving a management profile to chosen location with desired name

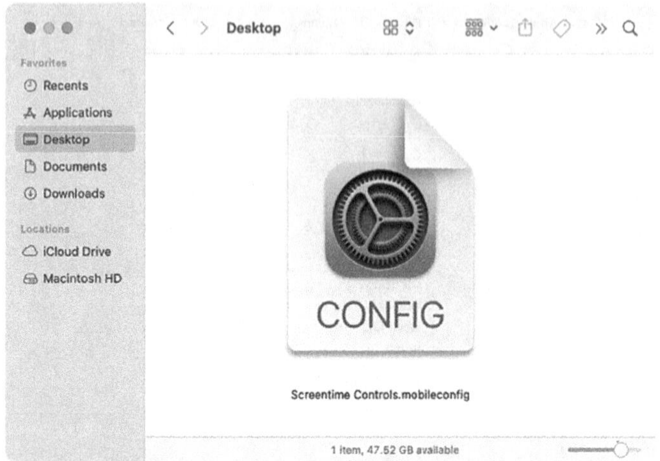

Figure 3-19. *Saved management profile in chosen location*

Once the name and location have been chosen, the profile will be saved as an XML-formatted document with a ***.mobileconfig*** file extension (Figure 3-20).

```
<?xml version="1.0" encoding="UTF-8"?>
<!DOCTYPE plist PUBLIC "-//Apple//DTD PLIST 1.0//EN" "http://www.apple.com/DTDs/PropertyList-1.0.dtd">
<plist version="1.0">
<dict>
	<key>PayloadContent</key>
	<array>
		<dict>
			<key>PayloadDescription</key>
			<string>Configures restrictions</string>
			<key>PayloadDisplayName</key>
			<string>Restrictions</string>
			<key>PayloadIdentifier</key>
			<string>com.apple.applicationaccess.1C4DD952-8B74-4810-B005-E12D00B37A83</string>
			<key>PayloadType</key>
			<string>com.apple.applicationaccess</string>
			<key>PayloadUUID</key>
			<string>1C4DD952-8B74-4810-B005-E12D00B37A83</string>
			<key>PayloadVersion</key>
			<integer>1</integer>
			<key>forceEncryptedBackup</key>
			<false/>
			<key>forceITunesStorePasswordEntry</key>
			<false/>
			<key>forceLimitAdTracking</key>
			<false/>
			<key>forceWatchWristDetection</key>
			<false/>
			<key>forceWiFiPowerOn</key>
			<false/>
			<key>forceWiFiWhitelisting</key>
			<false/>
			<key>ratingApps</key>
			<integer>1000</integer>
			<key>ratingMovies</key>
			<integer>1000</integer>
			<key>ratingRegion</key>
			<string>us</string>
			<key>ratingTVShows</key>
			<integer>1000</integer>
			<key>safariAcceptCookies</key>
			<integer>2</integer>
			<key>safariAllowAutoFill</key>
			<true/>
			<key>safariAllowJavaScript</key>
			<true/>
		</dict>
	</array>
	<key>PayloadDescription</key>
	<string>This profile sets app and content restrictions on managed iOS and iPadOS devices.</string>
	<key>PayloadDisplayName</key>
	<string>Screentime Controls</string>
	<key>PayloadIdentifier</key>
	<string>FX017W0CDP.55CE58CF-7AF6-40BE-A1B6-A027C04699E1</string>
	<key>PayloadOrganization</key>
	<string>Company Name</string>
	<key>PayloadRemovalDisallowed</key>
	<false/>
	<key>PayloadType</key>
	<string>Configuration</string>
	<key>PayloadUUID</key>
	<string>3C09FDA9-A0C8-41B7-B446-18B663669AD7</string>
	<key>PayloadVersion</key>
	<integer>1</integer>
</dict>
</plist>
```

Figure 3-20. *Saved management profile opened in text editor*

Now that the desired settings have been applied to the saved management profile, this profile can now be applied to multiple iOS devices via Apple Configurator or via a Mobile Device Management (MDM) server.

On each device, the profile will set the configured settings in a consistent and repeatable fashion, eliminating the tedium and errors involved in setting these settings manually via Screen Time.

Let's take another look at the process of creating a profile which will be usable on both macOS and iOS. Apple Configurator can again be used to build the profile (Figures 3-21 and 3-22).

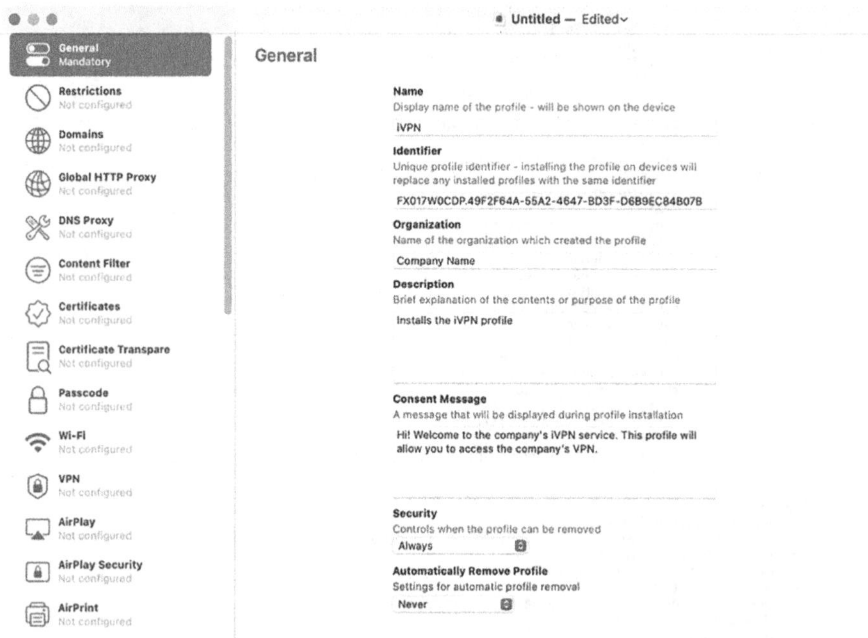

Figure 3-21. *Adding identification information to the new profile*

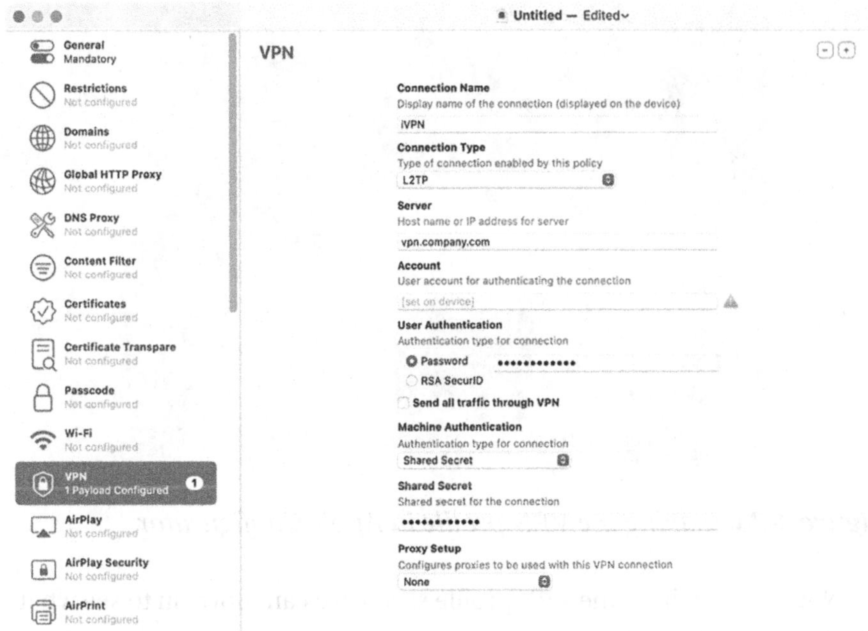

***Figure 3-22.** Setting the VPN payload settings*

Once you've filled in the appropriate information for the VPN profile, click File and then Save from within Apple Configurator. Next, provide a name and location for the profile and then click Save (Figure 3-23).

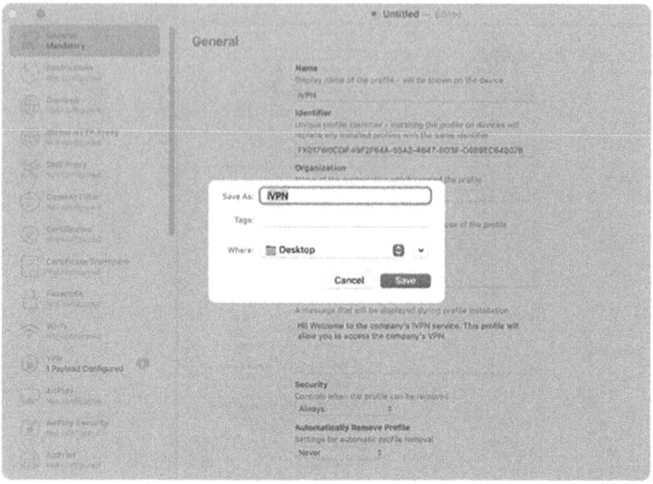

Figure 3-23. Saving the VPN profile in Apple Configurator

Now that you have the VPN profile saved, we can move on to see what all is in the profile in the next section.

View the Raw Contents of a Profile

A raw profile will contain a header, which contains a signature, and a bunch of XML. The easiest way to view the contents is to use the cat command. Here, we'll do a simple cat command of the file:

```
cat ~/Desktop/iVPN.mobileconfig
```

The contents will look as follows:

```
<?xml version="1.0" encoding="UTF-8"?>
<!DOCTYPE plist PUBLIC "-//Apple//DTD PLIST 1.0//EN" "http://
www.apple.com/DTDs/PropertyList-1.0.dtd">
<plist version="1.0">
<dict>
        <key>ConsentText</key>
```

```
<dict>
        <key>default</key>
        <string>Hi! Welcome to the company's iVPN
        service. This profile will allow you to access
        the company's VPN.</string>
</dict>
<key>PayloadContent</key>
<array>
        <dict>
                <key>IPSec</key>
                <dict>
                        <key>AuthenticationMethod</key>
                        <string>SharedSecret</string>
                        <key>LocalIdentifierType</key>
                        <string>KeyID</string>
                        <key>SharedSecret</key>
                        <data>
                        UGFzc3dvcmQxMjM0
                        </data>
                </dict>
                <key>IPv4</key>
                <dict>
                        <key>OverridePrimary</key>
                        <integer>0</integer>
                </dict>
                <key>PPP</key>
                <dict>
                        <key>AuthPassword</key>
                        <string>SooperSekritPasswordGoe
                        sHere</string>
                        <key>CommRemoteAddress</key>
```

```
                        <string>vpn.company.
                        com</string>
                </dict>
                <key>PayloadDescription</key>
                <string>Configures VPN
                settings</string>
                <key>PayloadDisplayName</key>
                <string>VPN</string>
                <key>PayloadIdentifier</key>
                <string>com.apple.vpn.managed.0382A626-
                CCC7-4D39-84E9-3FAE2EC7D6DA</string>
                <key>PayloadType</key>
                <string>com.apple.vpn.managed</string>
                <key>PayloadUUID</key>
                <string>0382A626-CCC7-4D39-84E9-
                3FAE2EC7D6DA</string>
                <key>PayloadVersion</key>
                <integer>1</integer>
                <key>Proxies</key>
                <dict>
                        <key>HTTPEnable</key>
                        <integer>0</integer>
                        <key>HTTPSEnable</key>
                        <integer>0</integer>
                </dict>
                <key>UserDefinedName</key>
                <string>iVPN</string>
                <key>VPNType</key>
                <string>L2TP</string>
        </dict>
</array>
```

```
        <key>PayloadDescription</key>
        <string>Installs the iVPN profile</string>
        <key>PayloadDisplayName</key>
        <string>iVPN</string>
        <key>PayloadIdentifier</key>
        <string>FX017WOCDP.49F2F64A-55A2-4647-BD3F-D6B9EC84B07B
        </string>
        <key>PayloadOrganization</key>
        <string>Company Name</string>
        <key>PayloadRemovalDisallowed</key>
        <false/>
        <key>PayloadType</key>
        <string>Configuration</string>
        <key>PayloadUUID</key>
        <string>29AD26BC-7B99-4116-94E6-618507C2FBF7</string>
        <key>PayloadVersion</key>
        <integer>1</integer>
</dict>
</plist>
```

Profile keys must follow a standard, where Apple defines the keys and administrators and software developers place the keys with payloads in the keys in profiles. The official profile reference guide is available at `https://developer.apple.com/documentation/devicemanagement/profile-specific_payload_keys`. No guide to these keys can be complete without mentioning the companion reference, built by @Mosen and available at `https://mosen.github.io/profiledocs/`. This reference describes some of the available settings that Apple doesn't include in the official reference. Always assume that anything Apple doesn't document is intended that way (as with private APIs) and can be changed at the drop of a hat.

Once you have created a profile, it's time to install the profile, which we'll cover in the next section.

Install a Profile on macOS

There are a number of ways to install a profile on macOS. The first and easiest is to just open the profile. When opened, you will be prompted to install a profile. To install a profile, just walk through the steps to install. To do so on macOS, start by clicking **Install...**, as seen in Figure 3-24.

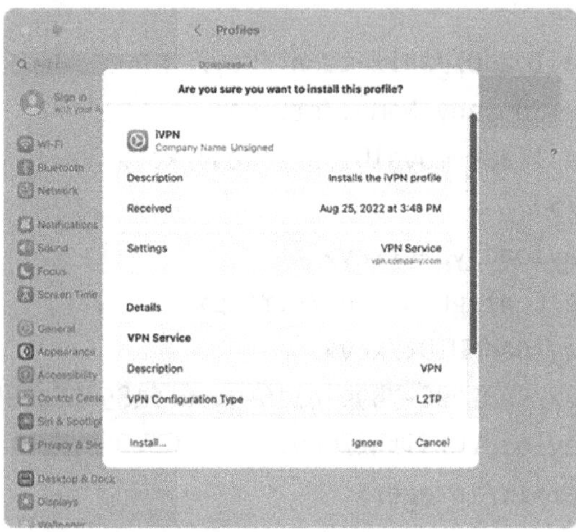

Figure 3-24. *Installing a profile on macOS*

Because we didn't sign the profile with a trusted certificate, we're prompted to install an unsigned profile, as seen in Figure 3-25. It's best not to install unsigned profiles unless you have to. Click Show Details to see a description of what the signing status means.

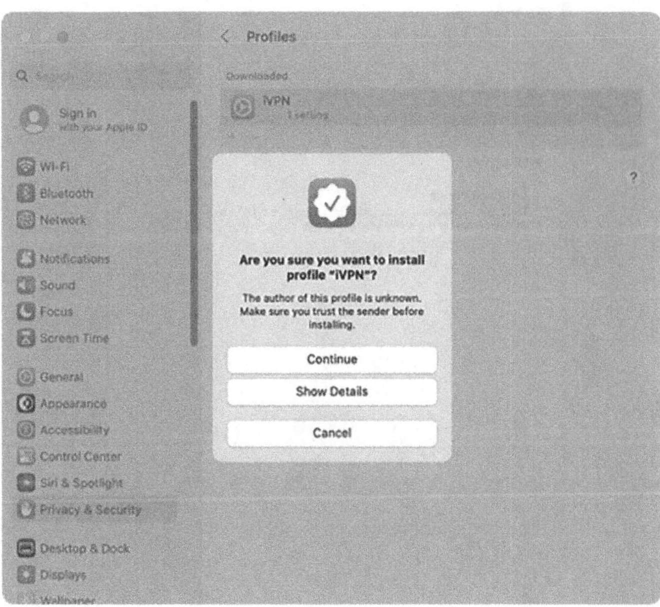

Figure 3-25. *Warning about installing an unsigned profile on macOS*

The additional details (Figure 3-26) are really just there to allow a user to understand why a yellow icon is in front of them. We haven't noticed that many users actually avoid clicking things with yellow icons though. It's still best to distribute signatures or use legitimately obtained public certificates though, if only to future-proof your deployment. Click Continue to proceed.

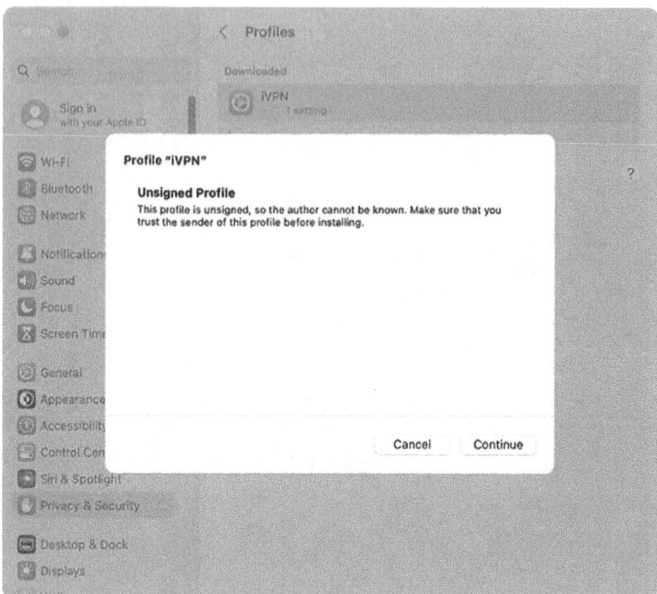

Figure 3-26. *Additional details about installing an unsigned profile on macOS*

Then you'll see the installation message that we provided while creating the profile as seen in Figure 3-27. Here, click Install to complete the process.

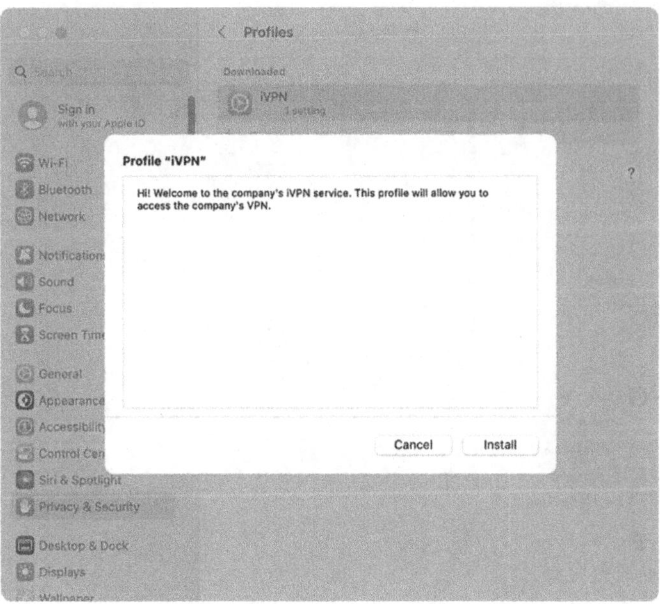

***Figure 3-27.** Consent message to install VPN profile*

Voilà, as you can see in Figure 3-28, you've now installed the profile. Later in this chapter, we'll cover how to install the profile automatically via the profiles command. Now that we've installed the profiles on the Mac, we'll get the profile setup on an iOS device.

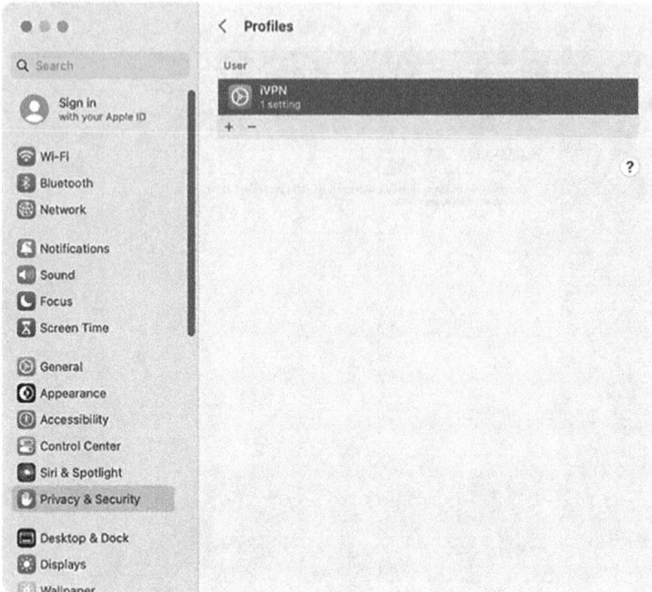

Figure 3-28. *The installed VPN profile*

Tip The power of profiles makes them a potentially dangerous way to receive compromised settings. When you install an MDM profile, you can disable the ability to deploy settings using a manual profile (and probably should do so). Or if you are using an agent-only management environment, make sure to know what profiles are on your Apple devices by checking them routinely.

Install a Profile on iOS

As with macOS, you can install a profile on iOS simply by opening the profile. In fact, the first management tools (before MDM) for iOS were apps that just had links to profiles, and getting mail settings on a device meant tapping on a profile to install a .mobileconfig file that then gave you your mail settings. Today, profiles can be stored on a web server and opened, emailed to users, or deployed automatically using an MDM solution, with installation via MDM being the only "silent" way to deploy a profile. In this case, the profile being installed is the unsigned VPN profile used in the previous macOS example, deployed via email or through a web page (or silently via MDM).

Once the profile is downloaded onto the iOS device and selected for installation, click the **Install** button in the upper-right corner of the screen, as seen in Figure 3-29.

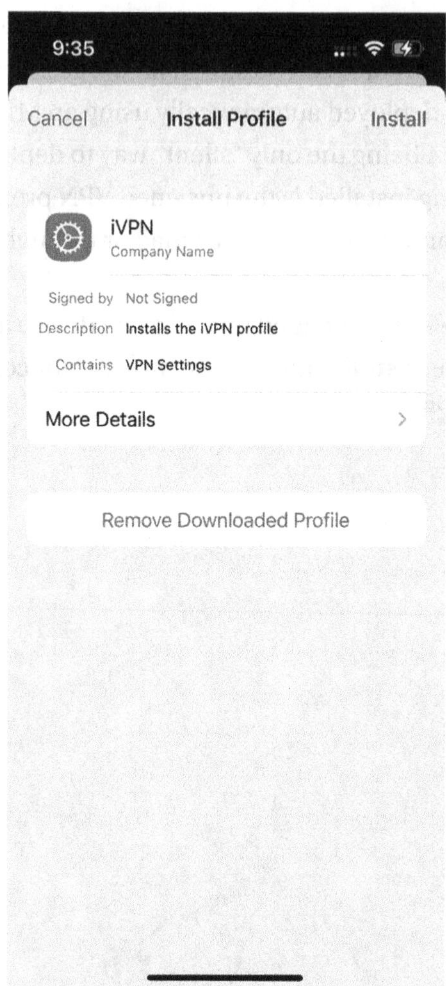

***Figure 3-29.** Installing a profile on iOS*

Installing a profile requires a passcode be entered, when using one on a device (at this point everyone should be). Next, enter the passcode as shown in Figure 3-30.

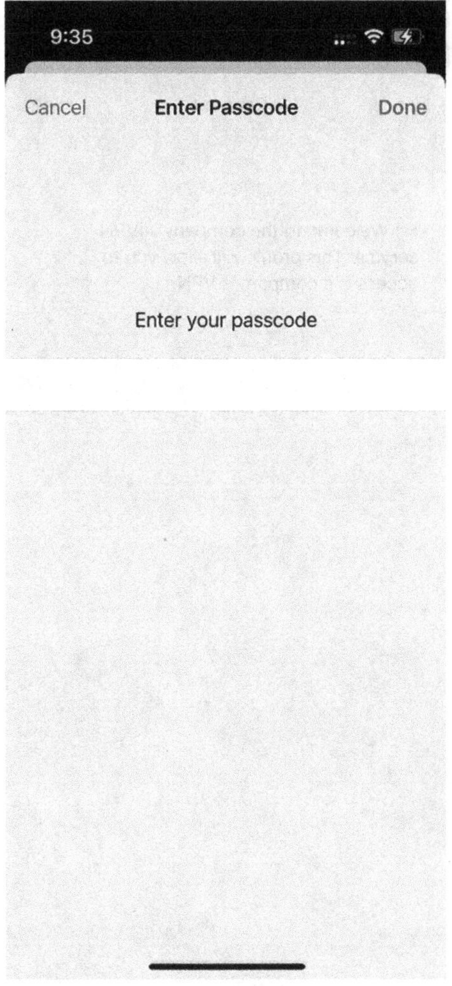

Figure 3-30. *Entering the passcode for the iOS device to authenticate installing a profile*

Since we added the additional consent step as part of the profile we created earlier, consent must be granted as part of installing the profile, which can be seen in Figure 3-31. This is in addition to the other usual steps and optional when creating profiles.

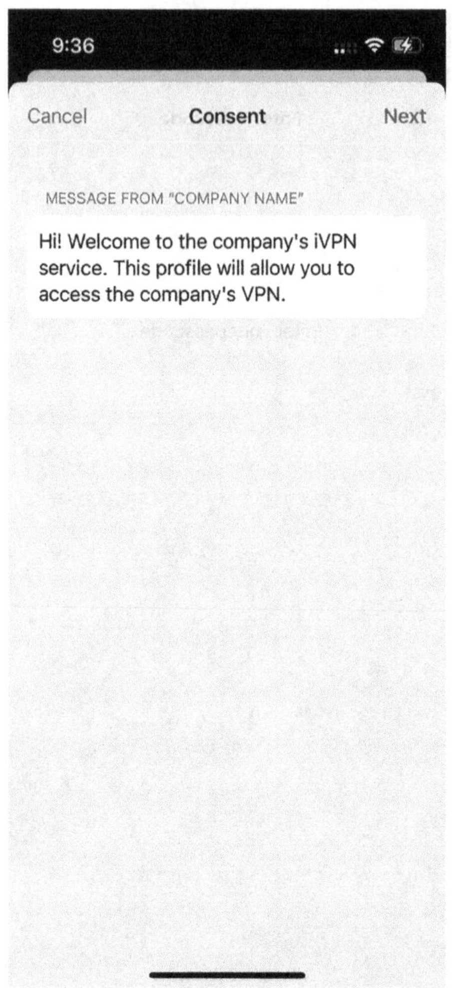

Figure 3-31. *Granting consent to installing the profile*

As with macOS, there will be a warning about installing an unsigned profile (Figure 3-32). If you use a valid signature that the device recognizes, then this won't appear. But it's important to drive home the fact that you need to sign profiles and show why. It's possible that some day in the future Apple developers will remove the ability to install unsigned profiles. Tap Install in order to proceed to the next step.

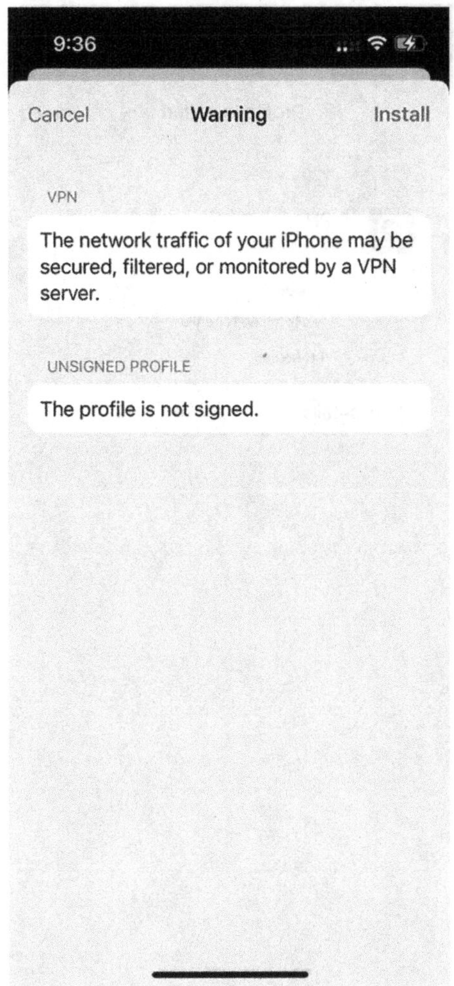

Figure 3-32. *Warnings about installing the profile on iOS*

Additional warning will be given about the capabilities that the profile is enabling on the iOS device. After the warning, iOS will prompt you to install the profile. The profile is now installed, and its new settings take effect, as you can see in Figure 3-33.

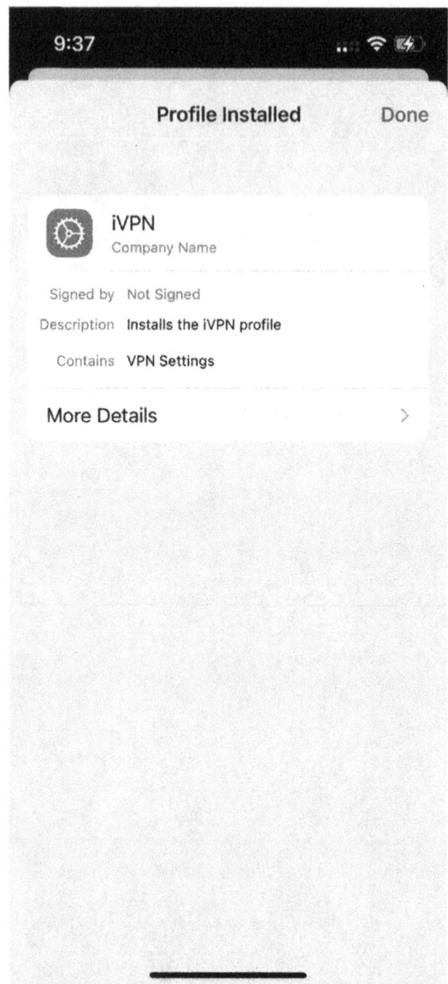

Figure 3-33. *iOS profile installation completed*

Install a Profile on tvOS

To install a profile on tvOS, profiles can be installed from a web server or Apple Configurator or by using an MDM. If using Apple Configurator, it may need to first pair Apple Configurator with the Apple TV. Apple has a knowledge base article explaining the process, available at `https://support.apple.com/HT208124`. Once paired, the Apple TV should show up as an available device in Apple Configurator, as shown in Figure 3-34.

***Figure 3-34.** Apple Configurator showing a paired Apple TV*

Double-click the Apple TV in Apple Configurator, and it will display information about the Apple TV. As you can see in Figure 3-35, Apple Configurator can be used to install Profiles, and you can see the logs of what is being deployed using the Console, useful for troubleshooting problems if they arise.

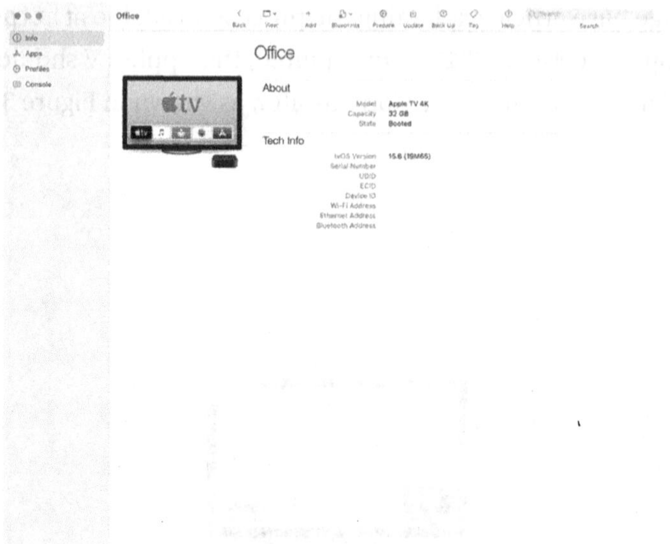

***Figure 3-35.** Apple Configurator showing Apple TV information*

Select the **Profiles** option to install profiles onto the Apple TV, and then click Add Profiles (Figure 3-36).

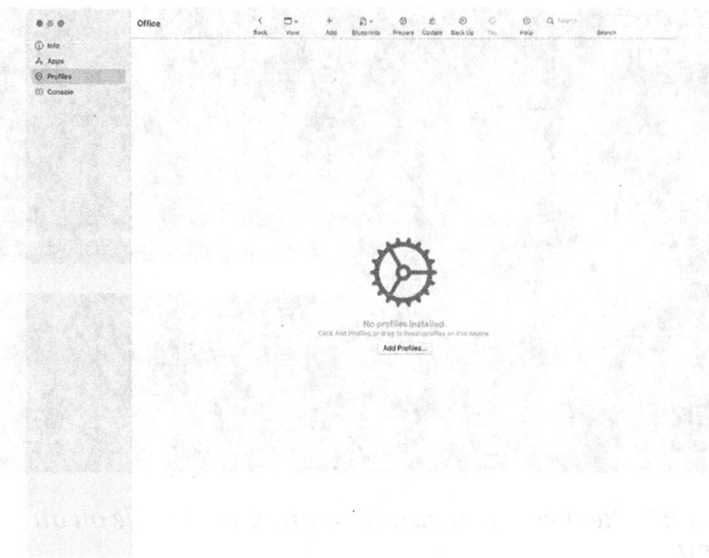

Figure 3-36. *Apple Configurator showing Apple TV profile installation window*

For some profiles, it may be necessary to install them using the Apple TV user interface. In Figure 3-37, we show an unsigned profile to control AirPlay settings is being installed onto the Apple TV - another good reason to make sure profiles are signed with valid third-party certificate providers.

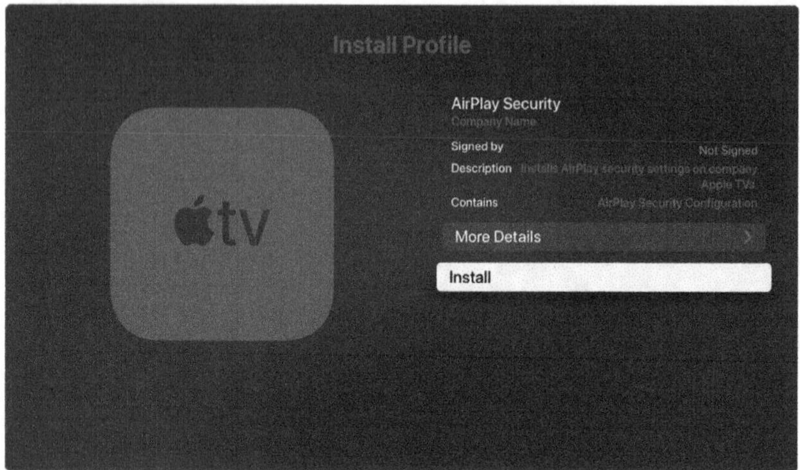

Figure 3-37. *Requesting to install an unsigned profile on an Apple TV*

Since the profile is unsigned, there will be warnings and additional install confirmations in order to install it (Figure 3-38).

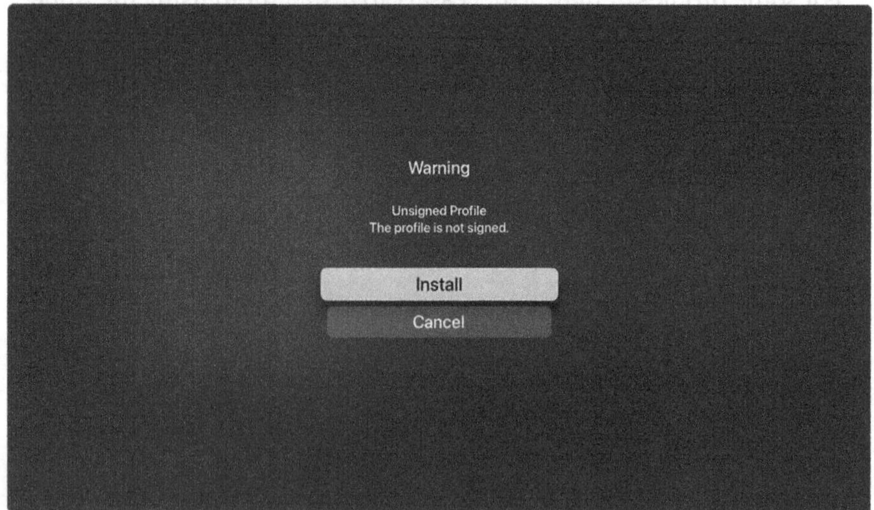

Figure 3-38. *Notification that the Apple TV profile is not signed*

To install a profile manually, one dialog that can't be skipped is the standard Install Profile screen (Figure 3-39). Click Install to proceed.

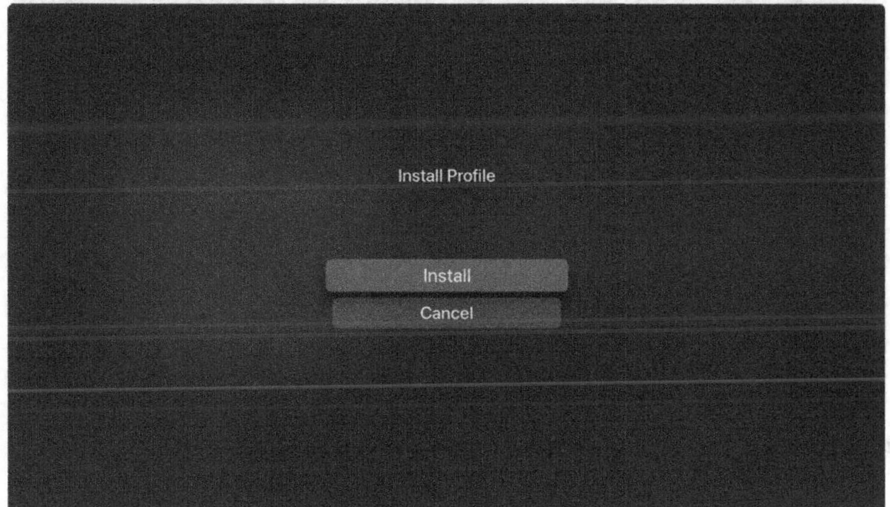

***Figure 3-39.** Confirming installation of unsigned profile*

As with installing profiles on the other operating systems, you then see a screen showing the profile and a brief summary of what is contained in the profile (Figure 3-40). Using the Apple TV remote, select More Details for a more granular look at what's in the profile, or tap Done to be finished with the profile installation.

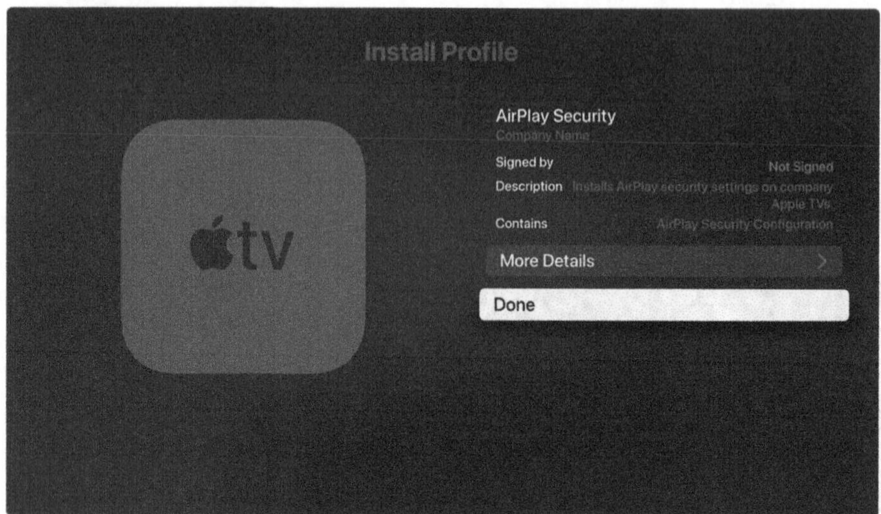

Figure 3-40. *Completion of the installation process*

Once the profile installation process is installed, the profile's settings should now take effect on the Apple TV; if you've configured certificates, those will be available to join a network, or if you've configured security settings, you'll then be prompted to enter passcodes or notice that certain restrictions have been enforced.

View a Profile from macOS

Transparency is important to the profile development team. Any setting implemented on systems should be available to view on devices where profiles are installed. This shows up again and again, whether around user acceptance of certain screens or just seeing why a user doesn't have the ability to see a given system preference. It's also an important troubleshooting step for those in the field trying to figure out why a given feature doesn't work on a device.

To view the profiles installed on a Mac, open System Settings and then select Privacy & Security. From there, you will see an entry for Profiles, as seen in Figure 3-41.

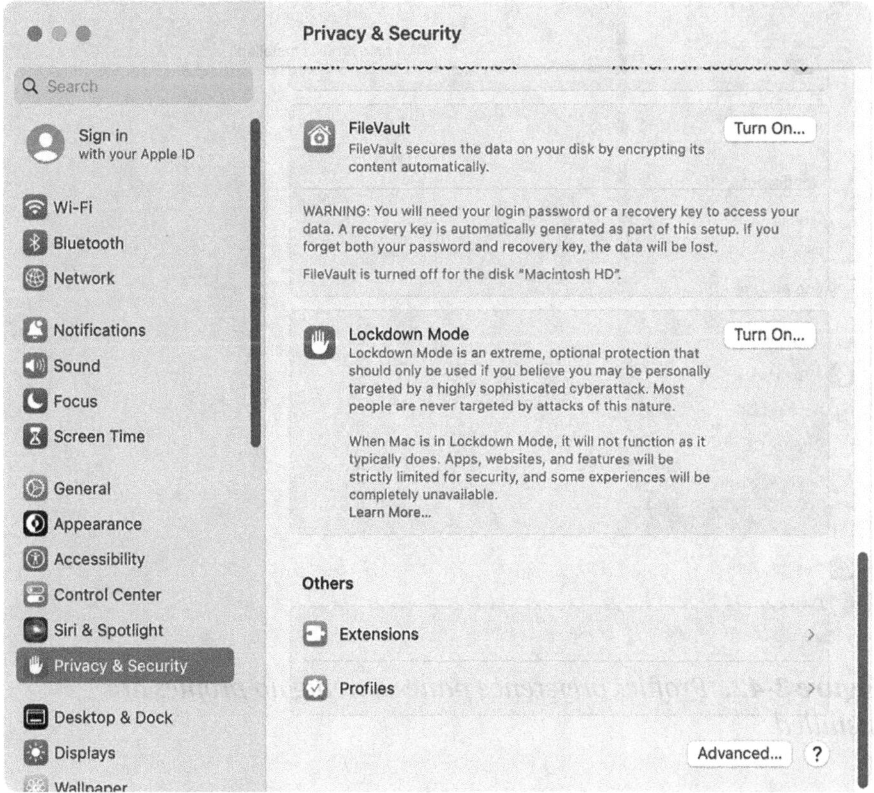

Figure 3-41. *Profiles preference pane appearing in System Settings*

If no profiles have been installed, the Profiles preference pane will display that no profiles are installed, as seen in Figure 3-42.

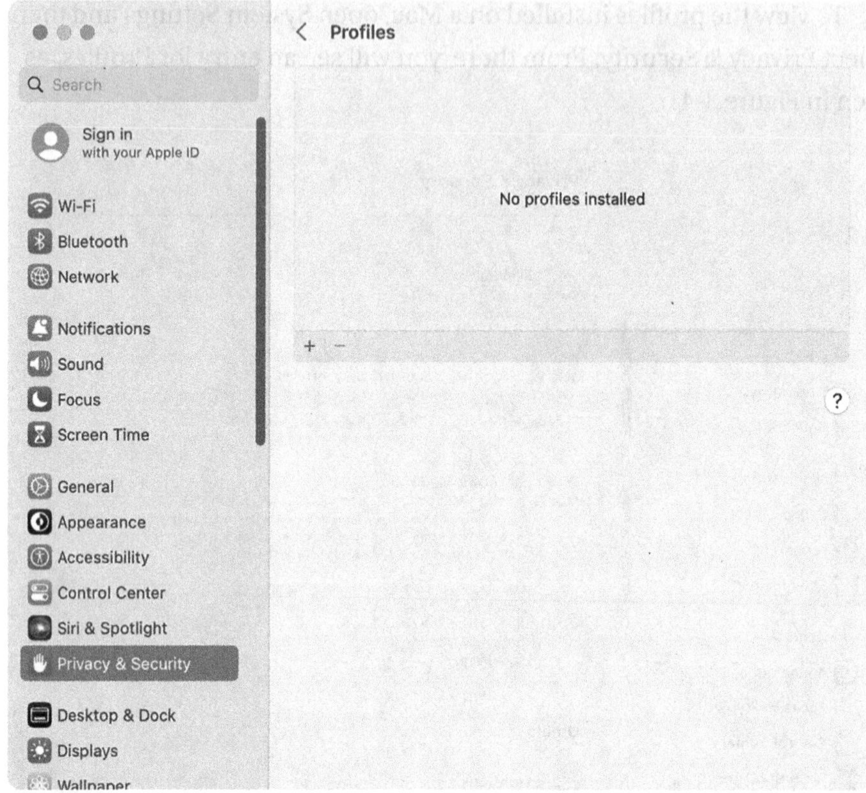

***Figure 3-42.** Profiles preference pane showing no profiles are installed*

Once the Profiles preference pane is open, if one or more profiles are installed, you can click a profile to see the contents. In the example shown in Figure 3-43, we can see that the description made for the profile can be seen, as well as when the profile was installed, and the settings that were put into the profile.

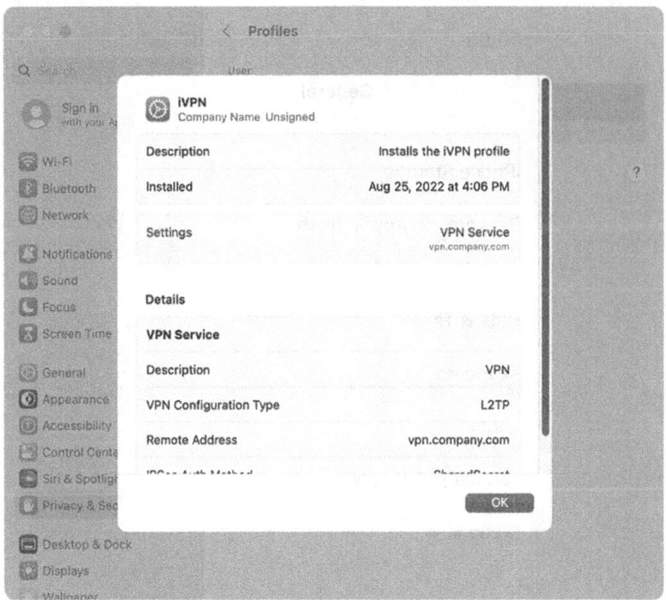

***Figure 3-43.** Viewing profile details via System Settings*

View a Profile from iOS

As with the Mac, the restrictions or settings pushed to a device should be able to be viewed at any time. Therefore, once a profile on an iOS device is installed, you can view the contents of the profile using the Settings app. To do so, open Settings and then tap General and scroll to the bottom of the screen to see the "VPN & Device Management" option, as shown in Figure 3-44. On older versions of iOS, this option may be named "Profiles & Device Management."

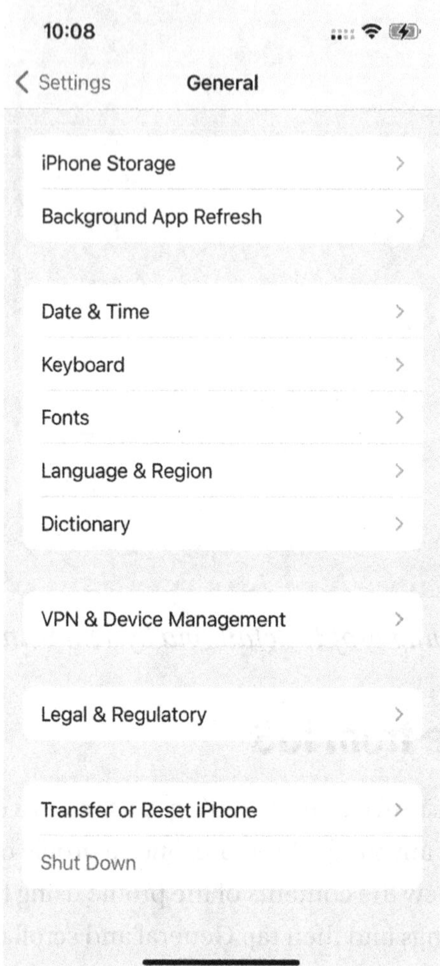

Figure 3-44. *Viewing profile location via Settings.app's General settings*

When you tap **VPN & Device Management**, the profiles that are installed on the iOS device are displayed, as seen in Figure 3-45.

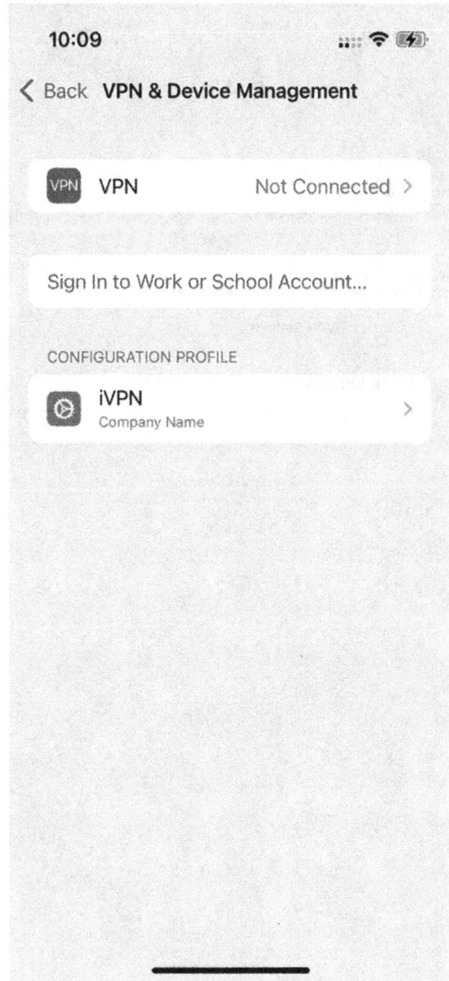

***Figure 3-45.** Viewing installed profiles on an iOS device*

Tap a profile to see the signing authority for the profile, the organization that deployed the profile, the description we created when creating the profile, and the type of payload (in the Contains) field, as seen in Figure 3-46. You can also tap the More Details to see information about the specific settings deployed or the Remove Profile if the profile has been set to removable.

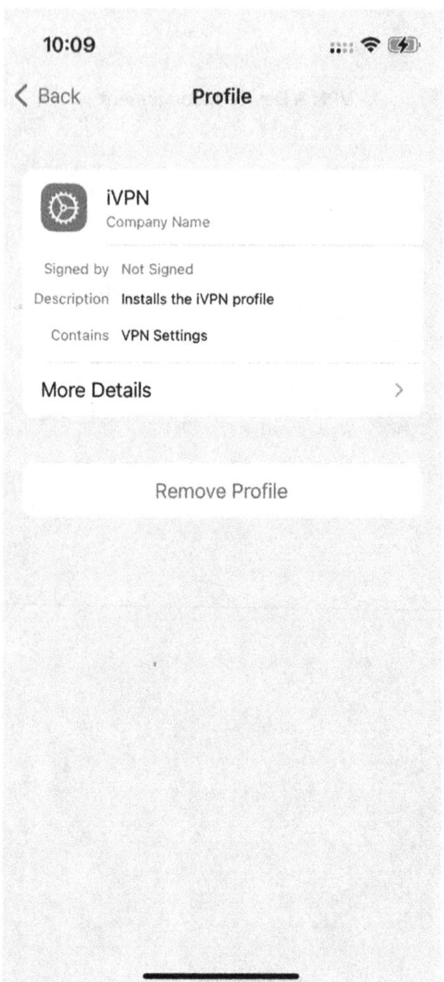

***Figure 3-46.** Viewing profile details on an iOS device*

Again, being transparent about what policies are enforced on a device is key. And this philosophy transcends all platforms that are manageable through profiles, including the newcomer to the profile world: tvOS.

View a Profile from tvOS

As with macOS and iOS, once you've loaded a profile on a tvOS device, you can view the contents of the profile. Doing so is done using the Settings app. This process is similar to the process for iOS devices. To get started, open the Settings app. Once Settings is open, use the Apple TV remote to select General and then scroll to the bottom of the screen, where you'll see the Profiles listed (shown in Figure 3-47).

Figure 3-47. *Viewing profile location via Settings.app's General*

To view the profiles, select the profile as shown in Figure 3-48.

***Figure 3-48.** Viewing installed profiles on a tvOS device*

Use the remote for the Apple TV to select that profile, and you'll be able to see the signer, description, and contents, and select More Details to see each setting broken down separately or Remove Profile to remove the profile (Figure 3-49). These are the same options you see in macOS and iOS, indicating the developers want a similar experience and full transparency across platforms.

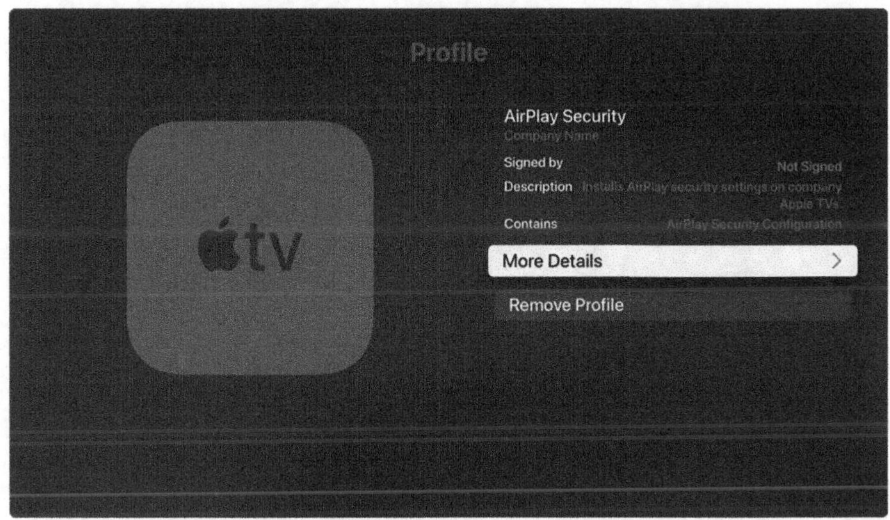

Figure 3-49. *Viewing profile details on a tvOS device*

Now that we've gone through looking at what settings and policies have been enforced on devices, let's move to removing those, provided the option to do so is available.

Remove a Profile on macOS

While we've focused on managing profiles manually in this chapter, in the next chapter, we will turn our attention toward leveraging those profiles over the air using a Mobile Device Management (MDM) solution. One reason to look at an MDM is that profiles can more dynamically be managed. Once we've enrolled devices into an MDM, it's a good idea to only push settings out using the MDM. Therefore, in the following example, we're going to remove the VPN profile installed previously.

To do so, open the Profiles preference pane and click the profile again. Then click the minus sign underneath the list of profiles. You'll then be prompted to confirm that you wish to remove the profile, as seen in Figure 3-50.

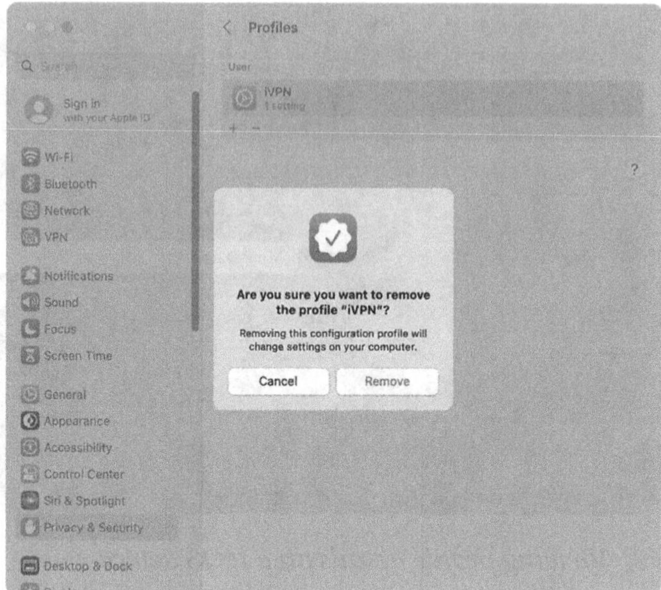

Figure 3-50. *Removing a macOS configuration profile*

To remove the profile, click Remove and you'll be prompted to confirm using Touch ID (see Figure 3-51) or via standard authentication.

Figure 3-51. *Using Touch ID to authenticate profile removal*

For most restrictions and settings, you'll then immediately see the device change. Another benefit of profiles is that most change immediately when enforced or removed, rather than needing to wait for a restart or a new login event.

Remove a Profile on iOS

The process is similar in iOS. To remove a profile on iOS, use the Settings app. Once Settings is open, tap General and scroll to the bottom of the screen and tap "VPN & Device Management" as shown in Figure 3-52.

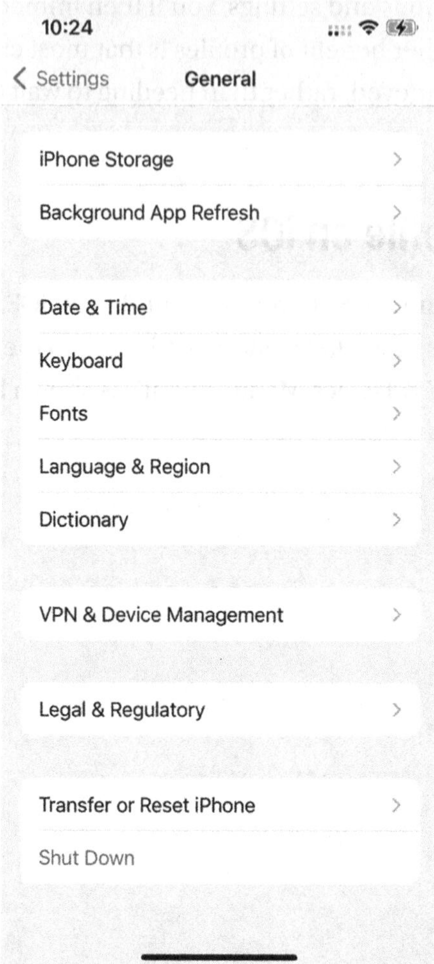

***Figure 3-52.** Viewing profile location via Settings.app's General settings*

Once you find the profile to remove, tap the red **Remove Profile** button shown in Figure 3-53 to start the remove process.

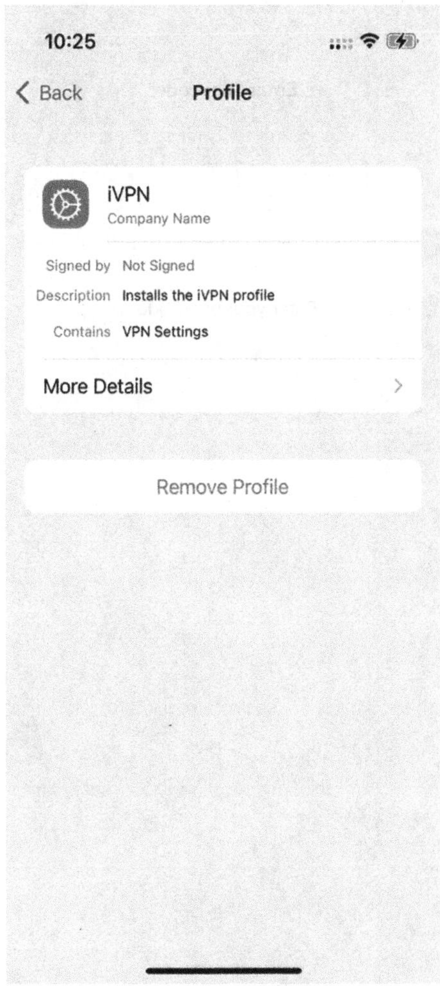

Figure 3-53. *Removing profile from the iOS device*

To authenticate removal of the profile, the device passcode and/or the profile passcode (if that option enabled on the profile) will need to be entered (Figure 3-54).

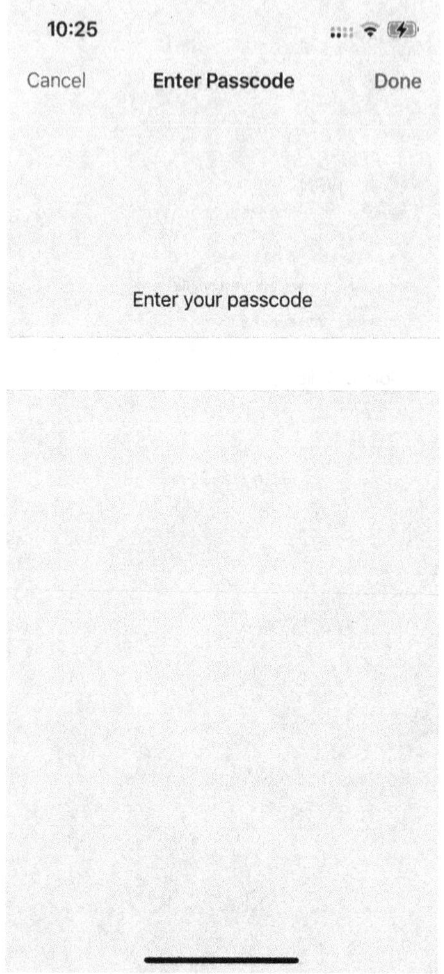

Figure 3-54. *Entering the passcode for the iOS device to authenticate installing a profile*

As the last step, the profile removal needs to be confirmed. Here, tap the red Remove button (Figure 3-55).

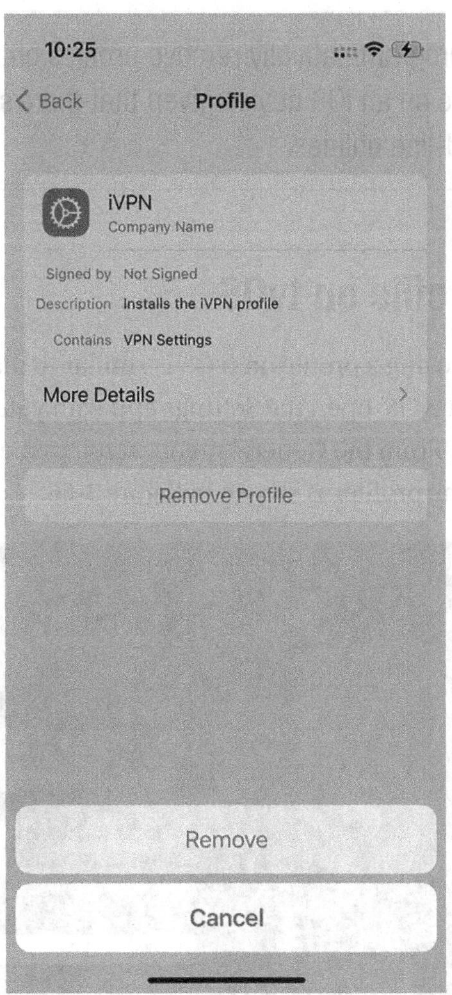

Figure 3-55. *Confirmation of profile removal*

As with Mac, the profile is removed, and any restrictions should immediately change. The profile is no longer listed in the list. All of this is, of course, dependent on the profile having been marked as removable when created. If the profile wasn't, then you would have to erase the iOS device in order to remove it.

Note You can programmatically remove profiles on the Mac, but that's not possible on an iOS device given that there's no root account and no command-line utilities.

Remove a Profile on tvOS

The process of removing a profile on tvOS is similar to that of iOS. To remove a profile on tvOS, open the Settings app with your Apple TV remote and select General. From the General menu, scroll to the bottom of the screen and select the profile, as shown in Figure 3-56.

***Figure 3-56.** Viewing profile location via Settings.app's General settings*

Once the profile is located, click the **Remove Profile** button (shown in Figure 3-57) to start the removal process.

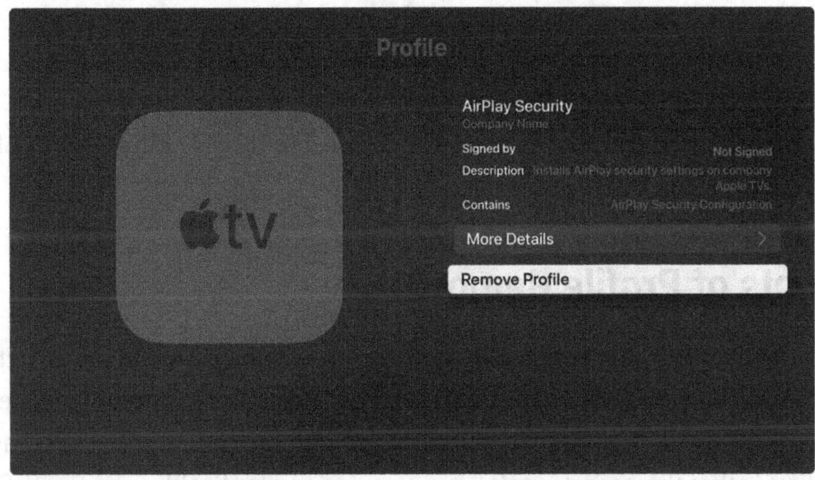

***Figure 3-57.** Removing profile from the iOS device*

Figure 3-58 shows the confirmation dialog. Here, simply highlight Remove with the Apple TV remote and hit the button.

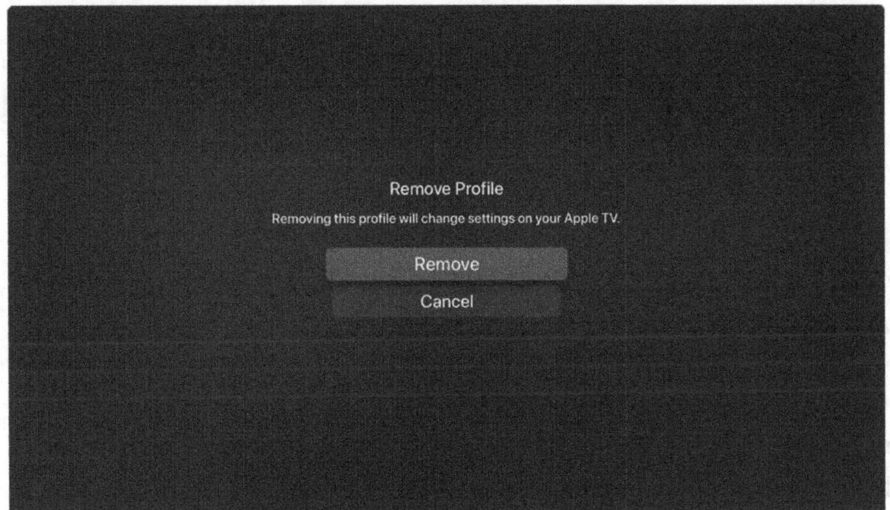

***Figure 3-58.** Confirmation of profile removal*

As with iOS, the effects of the profile are immediately removed, so any apps that might have been disabled will appear, and any settings or assets provided by the profile, such as a certificate to join the network, will immediately be removed from the device. We'll cover other effects of profile removal in the next section.

Effects of Profile Removal

Once the profile is deleted, it will no longer be displayed on the device. If you cannot authorize the computer to authenticate the action being taken, then the removal of the profile will fail. This can happen for a few reasons. The first is that the user doesn't have permissions to disable a given profile.

The second is that the profile has been identified as a profile that can't be removed because it was marked as such (e.g., except by the system that deployed the profile). This would have been done back in Apple Configurator, in the General screen of the profile, as seen in Figure 3-59.

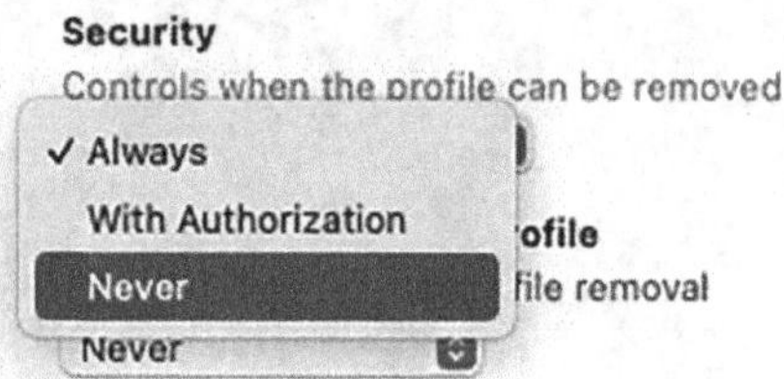

***Figure 3-59.** Using Apple Configurator to mark a profile as nonremovable*

You can restrict profile removal, but you can also restrict profile installation. This is a common means of trying to get in front of malware that deploys a profile to direct traffic through a proxy or locks down a device as a means of trying to extort money from a user (otherwise referred to as ransomware). Profiles are the best tool we have to automate the setup of iOS devices. But as with most valuable tools, profiles can be quite dangerous. We've seen bad actors post profiles to their sites, masquerading as apps, that when applied routed all traffic from the device through the attacker's proxy. This restriction is done via an MDM solution.

Now that we've looked at dealing with profiles using the common graphical tools available, let's get a better understanding of what those buttons are doing when you click, tap, and select them by diving into the command that is used to manage them in macOS environments in the next section of this chapter.

Use the Profiles Command on macOS

Once created, manage profiles on macOS using the aptly named command-line tool, profiles. This tool is unique to macOS in that it provides a mechanism to automate many tasks, such as managing features through profiles without an MDM, where possible, in order to automate the process of joining MDMs. iOS and tvOS do not have equivalent native tools and must use an MDM or external tools like Apple Configurator to manage profiles without manually tapping or selecting so many dialog boxes in the user interface.

The profiles command comes with a number of verbs or actions that can be performed and then options. The options define how those verbs are interpreted. The verbs include the following:

- **status**: Indicate if profiles are installed
- **list**: List profile information
- **show**: Show expanded profile information
- **remove**: Remove profile
- **sync**: Synchronize installed configuration profiles with known users
- **renew**: Renew configuration profile installed certificate

- **version**: Display tool version number

Some of the options are available for all verbs, others not so much. The options include the following:

- **-type=**: Type of profile; either "configuration," "provisioning," "enrollment," or "startup"
- **-user=**: Short username
- **-identifier=**: Profile identifier
- **-path=**: File path
- **-uuid=**: Profile UUID
- **-enrolledUser=**: Enrolled username
- **-verbose**: Enable verbose mode
- **-forced**: When removing profiles, automatically confirms requests
- **-all**: Select all profiles
- **-quiet**: Enable quiet mode

Now that we've covered the verbs and options, let's put some together. In the next section, we'll step you through some basic tasks using the profiles command.

Using the Profiles Command

Mac administrators want the ability to manage everything through the command line. The ability to script tasks gives us the ability to make the lives of our users better. One shell script that saves 5 clicks amplified across 10,000 computers can save 50,000 clicks and valuable time our coworkers could be using to perform their jobs. But while this ease of use in automation is valuable, it's not at the risk of violating the privacy of those

10,000 humans who use those computers. So not everything is available using the profiles command – but a lot is!

Before managing profiles, you'll want to know what profiles are on a device. Configuration profiles are assigned to users or Macs. To the user profiles on a system, use the **list** option:

```
/usr/bin/profiles list
```

A common step when troubleshooting is to remove all profiles from a computer, thus zeroing out policies to see if a symptom is related to a profile. This can be done using the **remove -all** option (and once the symptom is cured, you can put the profiles back programmatically as we'll cover in a bit):

```
/usr/bin/profiles remove -all
```

The better way to troubleshoot an issue is to remove profiles in order to get to the source of which is causing a problem. The **remove** option removes individual profiles. Use **-path** to indicate its source is a file. To remove a profile called apress.mobileconfig that was at /tmp/apress.mobileconfig:

```
/usr/bin/profiles remove -path /tmp/apress.mobileconfig
```

On macOS Catalina and earlier versions of macOS, installing a profile through an agent is a quick way to get settings on a device. For the relevant versions of macOS, the **install** option installs profiles. For example, the following command installs apress.mobileconfig that has been placed in the /tmp directory:

```
/usr/bin/profiles install -path /tmp/apress.mobileconfig
```

Profiles can also be installed at the next reboot on macOS Catalina and earlier. This is because you might want to give a user a dialog, indicating you're changing some settings at the next boot rather than freaking them out by having things on their device change. Use the **-type** option to define a startup profile. The profile attempts to install at each reboot until installed. Use the profiles command with the **-type** option and the **-path** option for the profile. For example, the following will set up a profile named /startupprofile.mobileconfig to be installed at the next boot:

```
profiles install -type startup -path /startupprofile.
mobileconfig -forced
```

The option to install profiles using the **profiles** tool, either at reboot or on demand using the **profiles install** option, was removed in macOS Big Sur and later versions of macOS.

Other options include **-verbose** which displays additional information about a profile, **-password** to define a removal password, and **-output** to export a file path so that we can then remove that profile.

Note You cannot remove individual configuration profiles that are deployed by an MDM solution.

It's possible to see what some of these profiles are doing through MCX, which we'll cover in the next section of this chapter.

MCX Profile Extensions

As we've mentioned, many of the underlying interpretations of profile options are handled through what's otherwise referred to as the "legacy" MCX framework. The dscl command has extensions for dealing with profiles to see what's been interpreted as well. These include the available MCX Profile Extensions:

```
-profileimport -profiledelete -profilelist [optArgs]
-profileexport -profilehelp
```

To list all profiles from an Open Directory object, use -profilelist. To run, follow the dscl command with -u to specify a user, -P to specify the password for the user, then the IP address of the OD server (or name of the AD object), then the profilelist verb, and finally the relative path. Assuming a username of diradmin for the directory, a password of scarlett, and then charlesedge as a user:

```
dscl -u diradmin -P scarlett 192.168.100.2 profilelist
/LDAPv3/127.0.0.1/Users/charlesedge
```

To delete that information for the given user, swap the profilelist extension with profiledelete:

```
dscl -u diradmin -P scarlett 192.168.100.2 profiledelete
/LDAPv3/127.0.0.1/Users/charlesedge
```

To export all information to a directory called ProfileExports on the root of the drive:

```
dscl -u diradmin -P scarlett 192.168.100.2 profileexport . all -o
/ProfileExports
```

Note Provisioning profiles can also be managed, frequently using the lowercase variant of installation and removal (e.g., -i to install, -r to remove, -c to list, and -d to delete all provisioning profiles). Provisioning profiles can also come with a -u option to show the uuid. Finally, the -V option verifies a provisioning.

Profiles can also perform actions. As an example, running the following command with root privileges will rerun the Apple Device Enrollment (ADE) enrollment process on a Mac, allowing you to quickly and efficiently move Mac devices between MDM servers in a manner not available for iOS or tvOS:

```
profiles renew -type enrollment
```

There are also a number of other tools including libimobiledevice, the command-line utilities bundled with Apple Configurator, AEiOS, and Ground Control. These provide additional automations, occasionally using private APIs to get deeper into a device. For more on those, see Chapter 6.

Summary

Apple has made it clear that profiles are the future of managing Apple devices, with iOS and tvOS leading the way and macOS catching up rapidly. Profiles provide a unified, easy, streamlined methodology to implement settings and restrictions on devices - and they do so in a manner that preserves the privacy of a user in a transparent manner. While it is not currently possible to manage all settings on macOS using profiles, it is increasingly possible to be able to write one profile and use it on multiple Apple platforms to manage settings, which is more efficient and less work for Apple admins.

Profiles can't be used to manage everything. But Apple has been quickly closing the gap of what can and what can't be managed using a profile (or an MDM action).

Now that we have some profiles, let's spend some time doing a deep dive into how those profiles can be implemented in a more dynamic and automated way in Chapter 4.

CHAPTER 4

MDM Internals

Mobile Device Management, or MDM, is a device management software that comes built into tvOS, macOS, iPadOS, and iOS. MDM allows an administrator to control and secure devices by establishing policies and monitoring the adherence of a device to those policies. MDM is often referred to as "agentless" technology. There is no such thing as "agentless" management, and so in this chapter, we go through what the built-in agents on these devices are, how they work, and why some of those weird requirements for MDM to communicate are... requirements.

MDM is the culmination of a number of different technologies developed by Apple and other vendors over the past 15 years. The great part about MDM is that it provides a common management technique for macOS, iOS, and tvOS. At its most basic responsibility, an MDM server implements the MDM and check-in protocols, defined by Apple to send MDM commands to devices, which are interpreted by the devices using that built-in agent to perform commands, such as lock a device, wipe a device, push an app to a device, or install a profile (for more on profiles, see Chapter 3).

Setting up MDM once required accounts in three to five separate Apple portals, but over the past couple of years, Apple has unified all of those accounts under one hood, according to the type of organization. Before setting up an MDM service, users will therefore need an Apple Business Manager account or Apple School Manager account.

C. Edge and R. Trouton, *Apple Device Management*,
https://doi.org/10.1007/978-1-4842-9156-6_4

What MDM Can Access

Apple can't see the information sent to devices through MDM (unless Apple's MDM called Apple Business Essentials is used and then in a compliant fashion). But always concerned about privacy, Apple engineers want administrators to have access to be able to manage devices and not access to potentially private data that might be stored on devices (e.g., no one wants the IT professional in a company accused of reading someone's email). So by default, an MDM server has access to the name and serial number of a device, as well as the phone number, model, how much space is available on the device, the version number of the operating system installed, and the apps installed on the device.

For Bring Your Own Device, or BYOD, Apple also began to provide new enrollment types in iOS 13 and macOS 10.16, which further limits what data is accessible by the MDM (and so the administrators who run the MDM). The thought here is again that private devices should be even more private. So a user will have a separate volume to store data, and things like the serial number of a device won't be transmitted through the MDM protocol for those types of enrollments.

Additionally, and we'll cover this later in the chapter, User Approved MDM (UAMDM) is a feature introduced in iOS 12 and macOS Sierra that prompts users to accept enrollment. This is similar to the transparency provided for agents described in Chapter 2. If users do accept the MDM enrollment, the MDM server can have increased controls on a device, such as the ability to accept certain settings for apps based on a Bundle Identifier.

The MDM doesn't have access to the location of a device, although a third-party app that had been granted access to Location Services would have access to the GPS coordinates of a device. The MDM protocol doesn't allow for app usage information, although on a Mac you can load an agent that can access that information. Things like Safari history, FaceTime history, call history, SMS/iMessages messages, mail, calendars, contacts, data inside apps, the score of your games in Game Center, and what content is on the device are all private and not accessible via MDM, although some vendors have used private frameworks to get that information through an app that's loaded on a device.

Apple Business Manager and Apple School Manager

The foundational technologies that we'll cover in this chapter are those that enable MDM to function properly and to be the most beneficial for most organizations. These include APNs, Automated Device Enrollment (or ADE - previously called the Device Enrollment Program), iCloud, and Volume Purchasing (or VPP). We'll cover these later in the chapter, but for now, know that aspects of each are configured in a central portal called Apple Business Manager, for companies with a DUNS number, or Apple School Manager, for educational institutions.

The two look similar, although there are a few specific features in Apple School Manager to enable the use of the Schoolwork and Apple Classroom apps, which we don't cover at length in this chapter. The primary focus for this chapter is to get the components to make MDM function configured in order to cover how MDM works. For that, an APNs Token for an MDM server is required (to support the ability to push messages to devices). A DEP token (to support automated enrollment) and a VPP token (to support app distribution) are also required for those options to work. These make up the Apple Enrollment Programs, now made simpler with Apple Business Manager and Apple School Manager.

To get started, log in to Apple Business Manager or Apple School Manager, located at business.apple.com or school.apple.com. This is where a .csr is exchanged for an APNs token and Automated Enrollment (also known as DEP) is configured. It's also where apps and other content can be purchased in volume for centralized distribution.

To define the MDM server to be used for automated enrollment (as seen in Figure 4-1), simply log in and click the username in the lower-left corner of the screen, click Preferences, and click MDM Server Assignment. This shows a list of MDM servers available for the organization. If the organization is enrolled in the Apple MDM service, Apple Business Essentials will be shown. Click the Add button to see the setup screen for a third-party MDM.

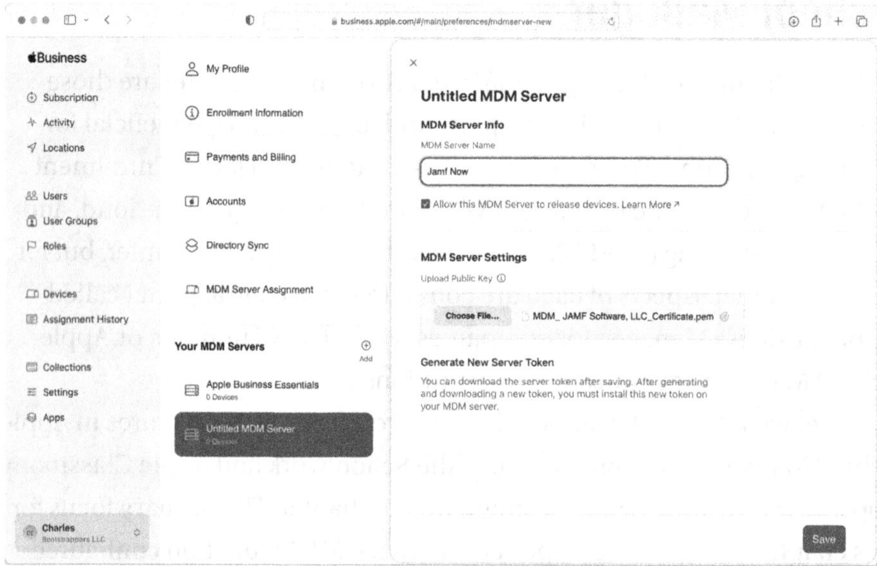

***Figure 4-1.** Apple device management portals*

At the entry for the new MDM server, provide a name for the server (this is just for you tracking it) and click save (Figure 4-2). You can then do the APNs key exchange that we will describe later in this chapter - where the .pem to make automated enrollment is downloaded from the MDM server (see Figure 4-2).

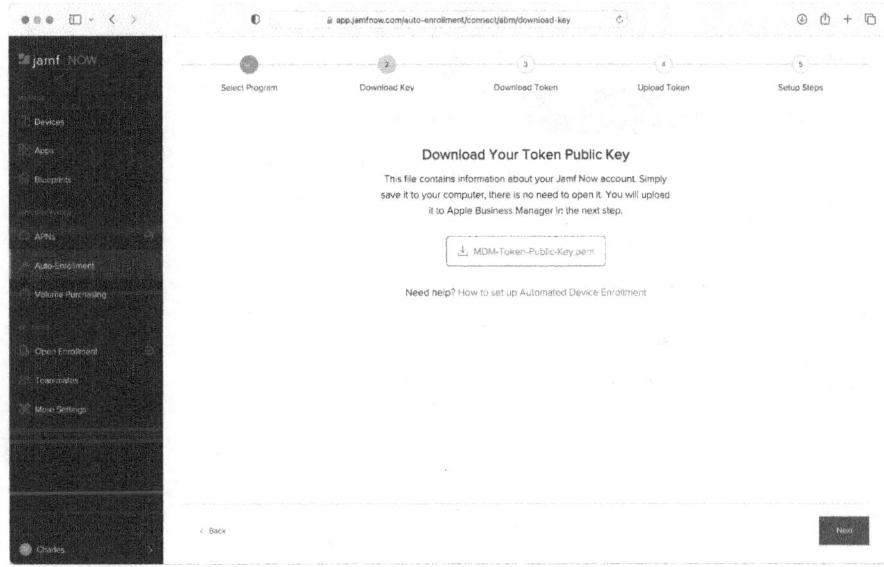

Figure 4-2. *Download the .pem from the MDM server or service*

Automated Device Enrollment (the artist formerly known as DEP) uses serial numbers to do the automatic setup. Without them, users will enroll manually, and you will have less management available for those devices once enrolled. To configure them, click Device Assignments from the main Apple Business Manager or Apple School Manager screen.

Any devices that were purchased linked to an Apple Customer Number can appear in Apple Business Manager or Apple School Manager. That number can be obtained either through the Apple reseller or Apple team that sold the devices. The number is configured in the Enrollment Information section (note that it's hidden in Figure 4-3, but if not present, there is only an option to enter it).

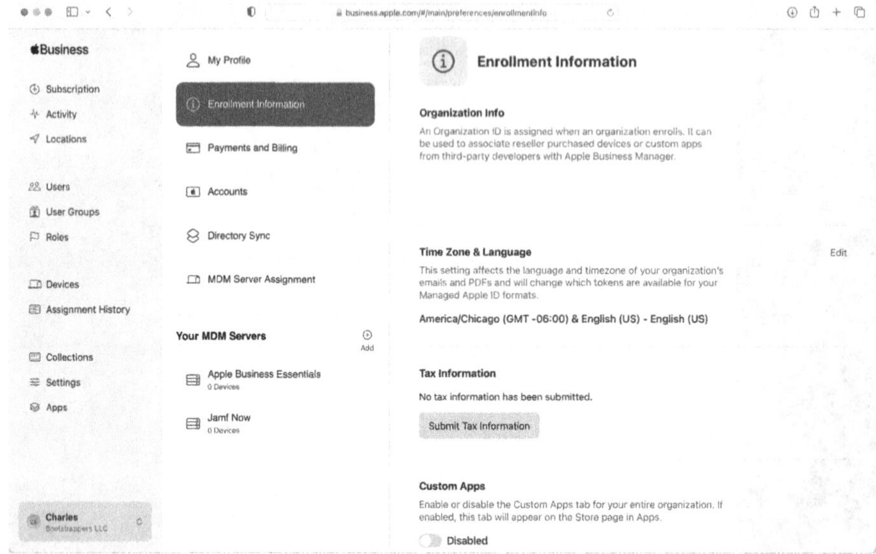

***Figure 4-3.** Configure the Apple Customer Number to link organization info in Enrollment Information*

Next, download a DEP token, once the server is added. According to the type of MDM in use, there will be a different screen to configure all of these. As an example using an MDM called XenMobile, once the DEP server token has been exported, click Add in this screen in XenMobile to complete the setup (Figure 4-4).

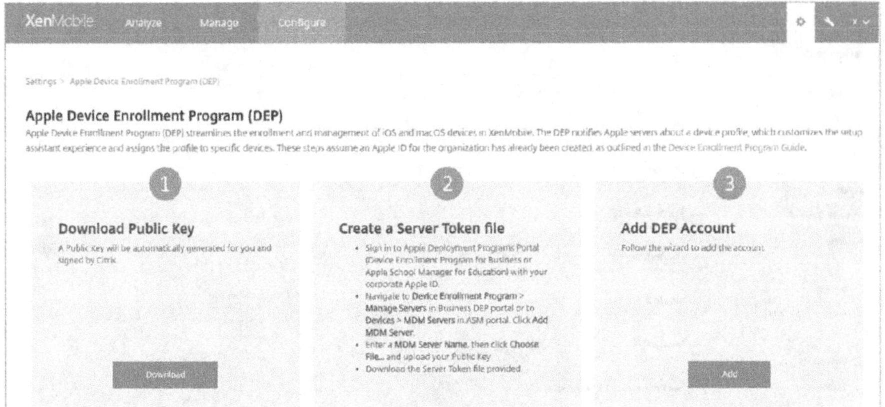

Figure 4-4. *XenMobile DEP interface*

Once devices are linked with the Apple Customer Number, Automated Enrollment can be configured to Apple Business Essentials or a third-party device management solution. Multiple of these can also be used (e.g., one for iOS and one for macOS or one for various suborganizations or teams in an organization). Once the customer numbers are linked, users see a list of each device that can be managed by clicking Devices in the left sidebar, as seen in Figure 4-5.

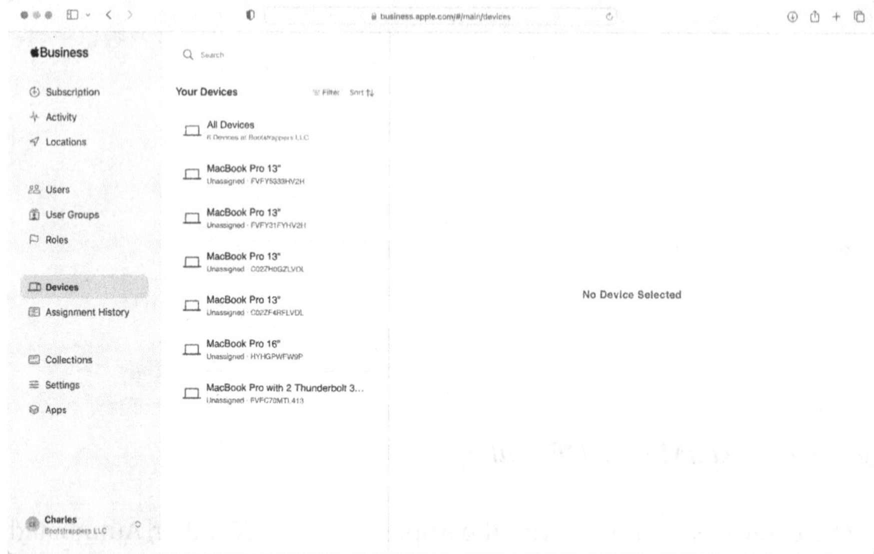

Figure 4-5. *List of devices purchased through Apple programs*

Any devices that don't appear might not be properly linked. These can be linked with Apple Configurator, which is covered later in the book, or with a support case with Apple. Once devices are populated, it's possible to configure which MDM server new devices are assigned to. Further, existing devices have an "Edit MDM Server" option when clicked, to assign them that way. To configure how new devices will be handled, click the username in the lower-left corner of the screen and click Preferences. Click MDM Server Assignment in the list of options. Device types can then be configured to be the default (or automatic) MDM server for each device type as seen in Figure 4-6.

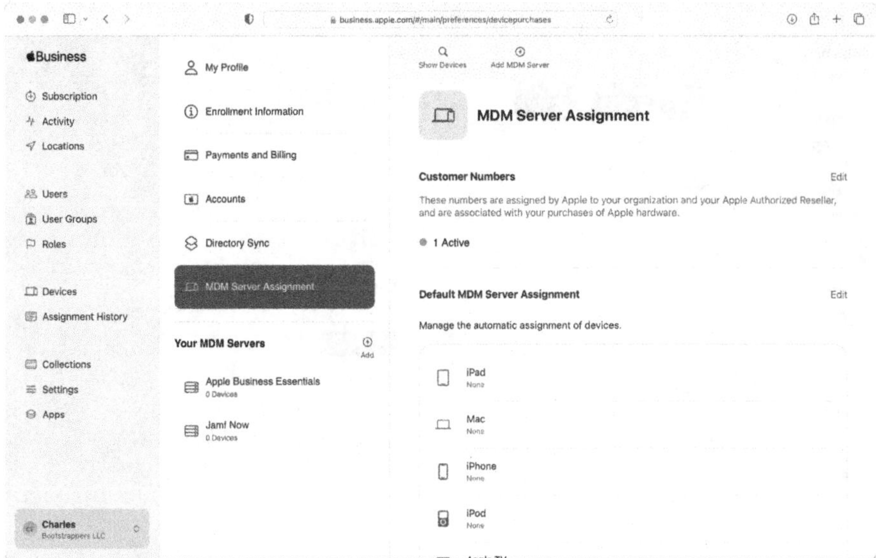

Figure 4-6. *Configure default MDM servers for each device type*

Once devices boot for the first time, they look for the MDM server they were assigned to. Configuration profiles from the server and apps are then installed as defined on that server. Some apps are still packaged as standard software packages, but most for the Mac, iPhone, and iPad now get installed via the App Store. The volume purchasing of apps was once done in a dedicated portal, but that has since been moved to Apple Business Manager and Apple School Manager as well.

Buy Apps to Distribute with MDM

Organizations can purchase up to 25,000 licenses a day (some are "purchases" of free seats of apps). To purchase apps, click Apps in the left sidebar and then click View Store, as seen in Figure 4-7.

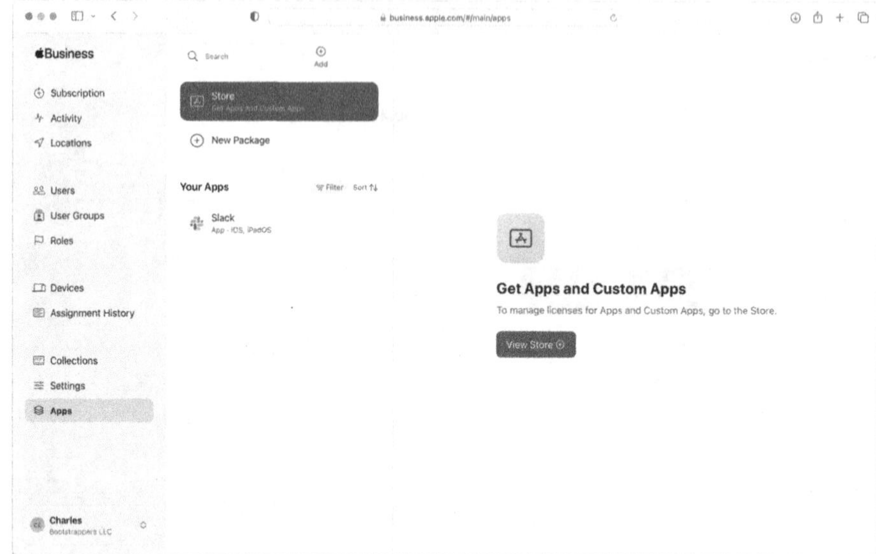

Figure 4-7. Buy apps in Apple's Business and School programs

Click the Add button to search for an app. Figure 4-8 shows searching for the Microsoft Teams app and then acquiring licenses for distribution.

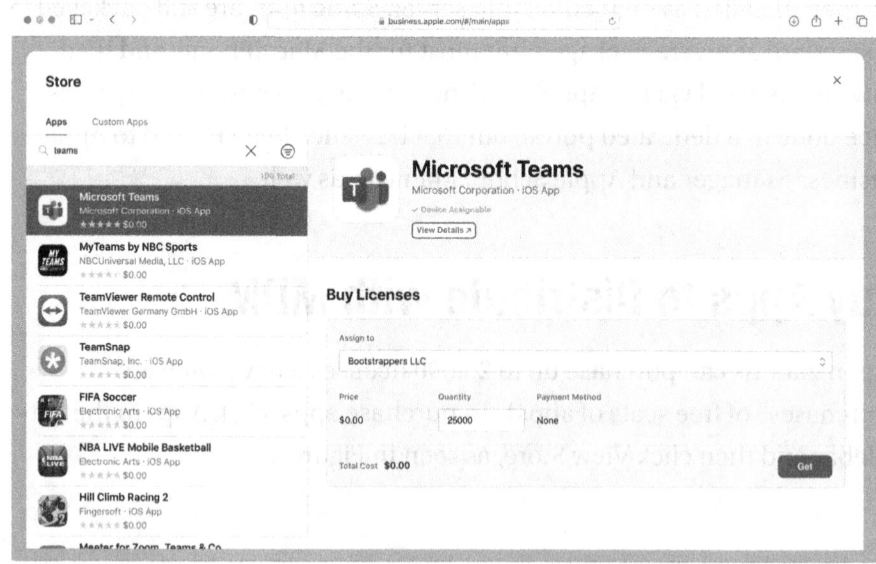

Figure 4-8. Buy an app for distribution

More apps can be purchased (developers have a choice whether to make an app available in volume) and distributed as needed. However, to distribute apps with a third-party MDM, a token needs to be uploaded from the Apple Business or Apple School portal to a third-party MDM. To do so, click the username in the lower-left corner of the screen and then click Preferences. Click Payments and Billing and then click the Apps and Books tab.

Toward the bottom of the screen is a section for Server Tokens. Click the server token, and it will download to the local computer, as seen in Figure 4-9.

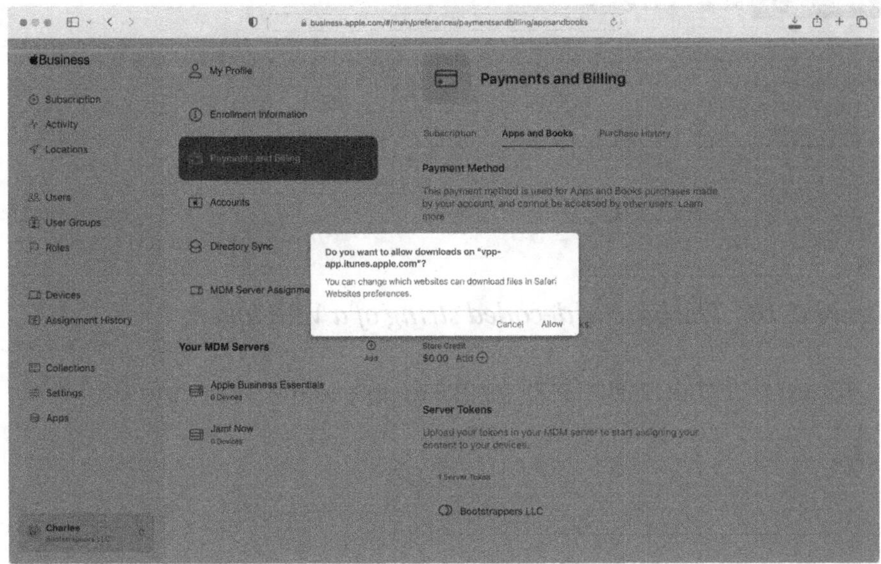

Figure 4-9. *Export the tokens*

Once the token is downloaded, log in to an MDM. We've gone through a few different MDMs at this point to show how things are different, and yet the wording is typically the same as a token is a token is a token. To be specific, the token is base64 encoded json with a token and some metadata, as seen in Figure 4-10.

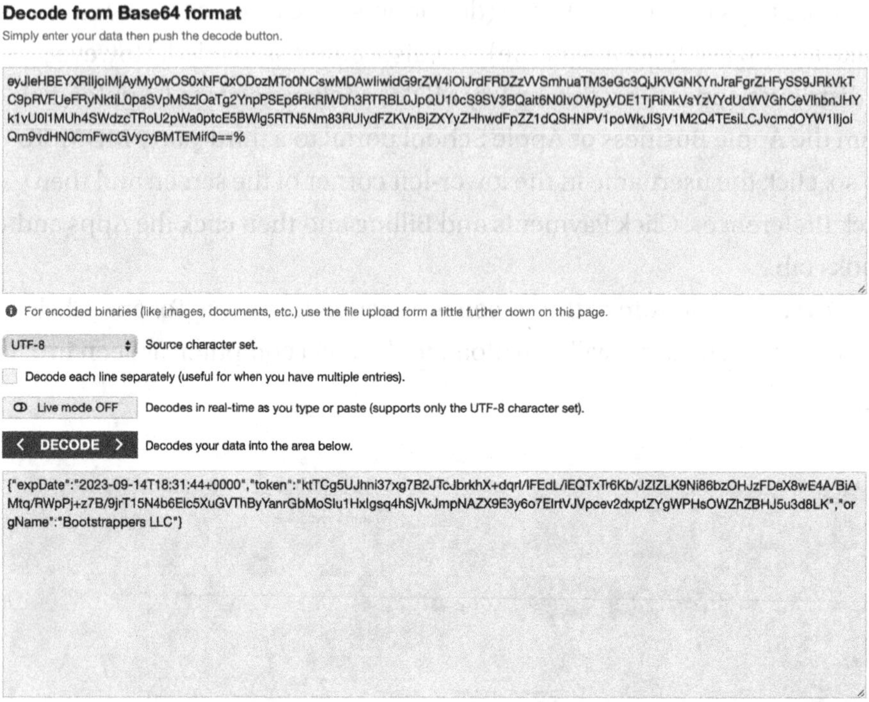

Decode from Base64 format

Simply enter your data then push the decode button.

eyJleHBEYXRlIjoiMjAyMy0wOS0xNFQxODozMTo0NCswMDAwIiwidG9rZW4iOiJrdFRDZzVVSmhuaTM3eGc3QjJKVGNKYnJraFgrZHFySS9JRkVkT
C9pRVFUeFRyNktiL0paSVpMSzlOaTg2YnpPSEp6RkRlWDh3RTRBL0JpQU10cS9SV3BQait6N0IvOWpyVDE1TjRiNkVsYzVYdUdWVGhCeVlhbnJHY
k1vU0l1MUh4SWdzcTRoU2pWa0ptcE5BWlg5RTN5Nm83RUlydFZKVnBjZXYyZHhwdFpZZ1dQSHNPV1poWkJISjV1M2Q4TEsiLCJvcmdOYW1lIjoi
Qm9vdHN0cmFwcGVycyBMTEMifQ==%

For encoded binaries (like images, documents, etc.) use the file upload form a little further down on this page.

UTF-8 Source character set.

Decode each line separately (useful for when you have multiple entries).

Live mode OFF Decodes in real-time as you type or paste (supports only the UTF-8 character set).

< DECODE > Decodes your data into the area below.

{"expDate":"2023-09-14T18:31:44+0000","token":"ktTCg5UJhni37xg7B2JTcJbrkhX+dqrI/IFEdL/iEQTxTr6Kb/JZIZLK9Ni86bzOHJzFDeX8wE4A/BiA
Mtq/RWpPj+z7B/9jrT15N4b6Elc5XuGVThByYanrGbMoSIu1HxIgsq4hSjVkJmpNAZX9E3y6o7EIrtVJVpcev2dxptZYgWPHsOWZhZBHJ5u3d8LK","or
gName":"Bootstrappers LLC"}

***Figure 4-10.** The base64 decoded string of a VPP token*

Figure 4-11 shows what it looks like to upload the token into Jamf Now.

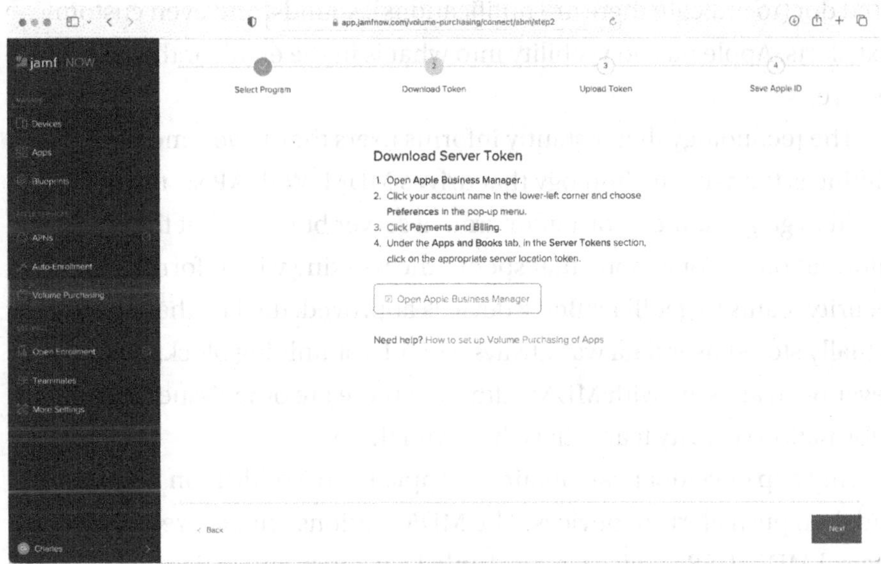

Figure 4-11. *Add the token to an MDM*

Now that we've got all of these keys to link Automated Enrollment and volume app purchases to an MDM solution, let's move to looking at how APNs fits into the MDM picture. This is handled for administrators by default with Apple Business Essentials, but we see more of how the certificates allow servers to trust one another with third-party solutions. That begins with Apple Push Notifications.

Apple Push Notifications

Apple Push Notifications (or APNs for short) is a platform developed in 2009 to enable third-party vendors or Apple to send notifications to mobile devices. Web services or apps trigger a device to check into the server via APNs. That notification data is what causes a different badge to appear for an app, including a number (the number of notifications the app has), a red dot (to indicate there are notifications), sounds, and even custom text alerts. Apple has no visibility into what is in the email or the text you receive.

The technology that instantly informs users they have a message waiting is the same technology that drives MDM. With APNs, the device is told to go get some information from a server but not what that information is. For anyone that spent time working with information security teams to get BlackBerry devices approved, the fact that BlackBerry actually stored user data was always a bit of a stumbling block. This has never been an issue with MDM, although there are other issues that information security teams have here and there.

Any app developer can obtain an Apple Push Notification certificate and then push alerts to devices. The MDM options, though, require a special MDM CSR service via the Apple Developer Enterprise portal. Most MDM vendors will have this certificate and then provide customers with the ability to generate a CSR via Apple and issue a new certificate based on that, in order to push the fact that there are management commands waiting for devices. While most vendors will have an account with the Developer Enterprise portal and provide the necessary links, anyone can sign up for an account for $299 per year.

In Chapter 2, when we looked at agents, each client registered with an agent, often performing a certificate exchange and/or caching a hashed value of some kind in order to verify its identity to the server and in order to check in with the server automatically. MDM is no different; a client device will "enroll" in the server, which establishes such a key exchange and passes shared secrets between devices and servers so the device can securely authenticate back into the server to retrieve instructions. Much of that key exchange is handled by Simple Certificate Enrollment Protocol, or SCEP for short.

Check-Ins: Device Enrollment

Notice that the term enroll is derived from SCEP. This is because the client device performs a Certificate Signing Request (CSR) and submits it to the server. The server then issues a certificate to the device that only that device can install due to a PKCS#7 certificate with a challenge password from the original CSR. This certificate is anchored by a certificate issued by Apple. That transaction is handled in Apple Business Manager, Apple School Manager, or using the developer portal. Each MDM vendor allows you to generate a CSR that you then upload to Apple as can be seen in Figure 4-12 for Jamf Now.

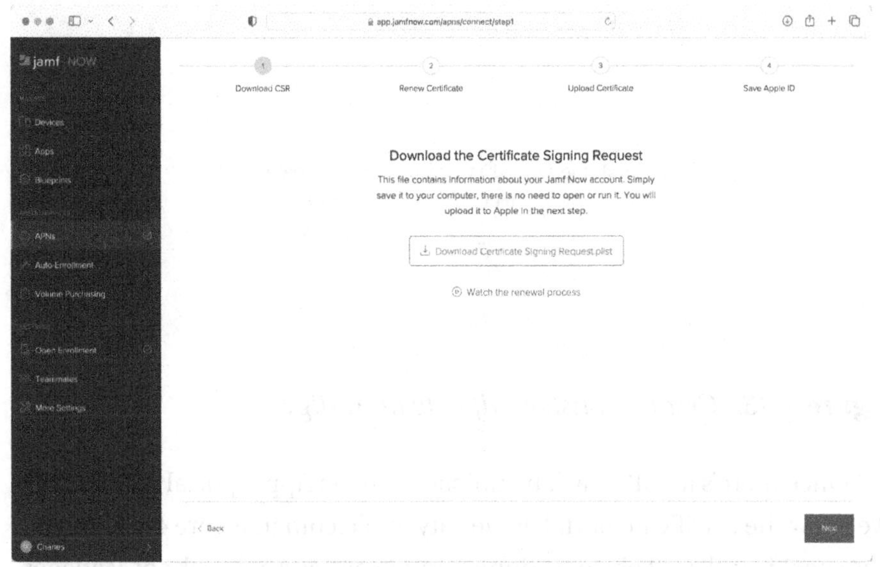

***Figure 4-12.** Download a CSR in Jamf Now*

Notice that this process will look similar with most vendors, with this option shown in Figure 4-13 for Addigy.

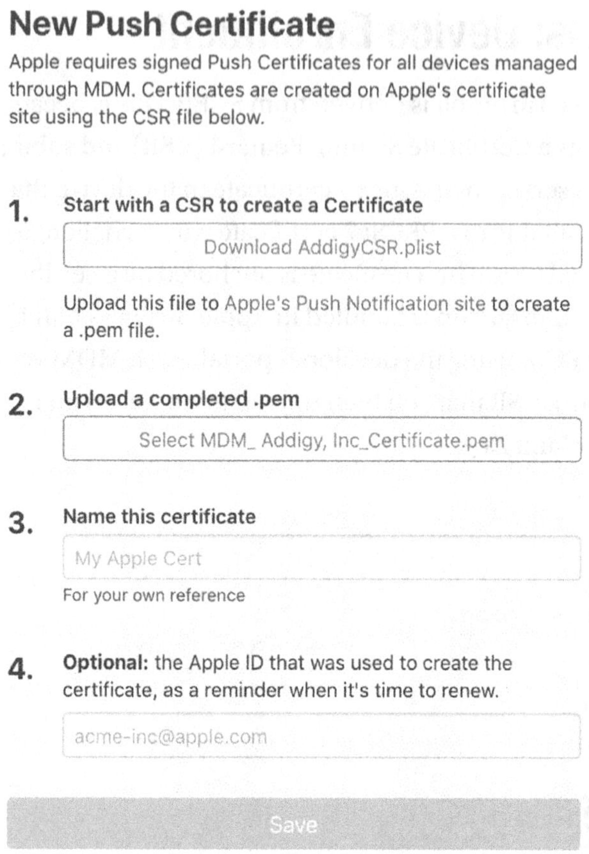

New Push Certificate

Apple requires signed Push Certificates for all devices managed through MDM. Certificates are created on Apple's certificate site using the CSR file below.

1. **Start with a CSR to create a Certificate**

Download AddigyCSR.plist

Upload this file to Apple's Push Notification site to create a .pem file.

2. **Upload a completed .pem**

Select MDM_ Addigy, Inc_Certificate.pem

3. **Name this certificate**

My Apple Cert

For your own reference

4. **Optional:** the Apple ID that was used to create the certificate, as a reminder when it's time to renew.

acme-inc@apple.com

Save

***Figure 4-13.** Create a push certificate in Addigy*

Once there's a CSR, it will be uploaded to the Apple portal you prefer. We show the certificate portal at identity.apple.com in Figure 4-14, but this specific task is likely to be done through either Apple School Manager or Apple Business Manager eventually as it puts all required tasks on Apple portals to configure MDM in one location. Click Create a Certificate once authenticated to identity.apple.com and then upload the file from the portal.

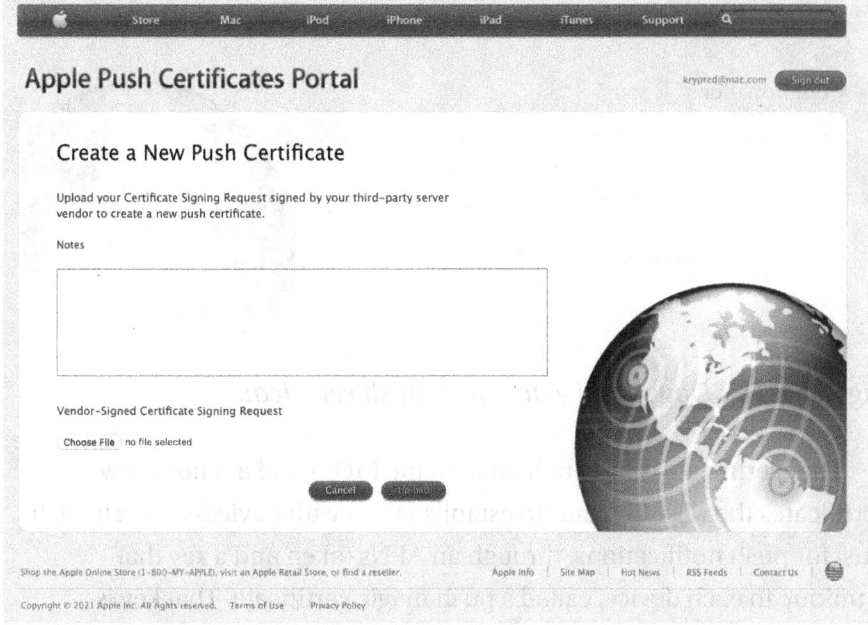

***Figure 4-14.** Provide the Signing Request in the push portal*

When you upload the CSR in a plist format, you then receive back a certificate and can use the portal you created the certificate to renew or perform subsequent downloads, as seen in Figure 4-15. That certificate is pinned to the hostname, and so once you start enrolling devices, you cannot change the certificate or the name of the server without breaking the ability for a device to communicate back to the server.

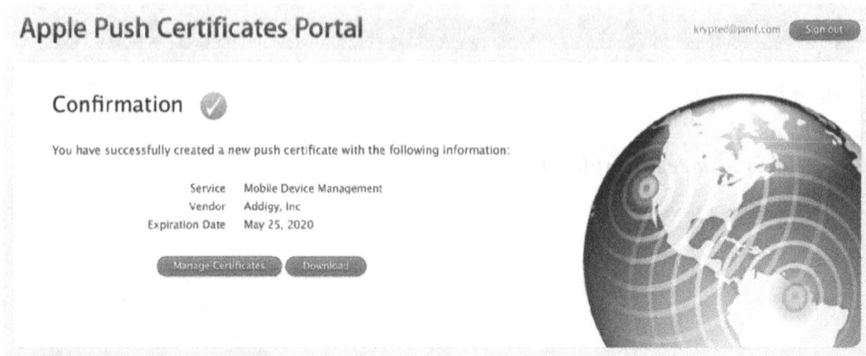

Figure 4-15. *Download your Apple push certificate*

That certificate is then uploaded to the MDM and anchors new certificates the MDM creates to establish trust with devices and establish trust for push notifications, through an APNs token and a key that is unique to each device, called a push magic certificate. That key is generated by a device and later used to prove authenticity of the device during TokenUpdate commands. Installation of the profile that starts this process can happen by opening an enrollment certificate, using Automated Enrollment (which will be covered further later in this chapter) or through Apple Configurator (covered more in Chapters 5 and 6).

Make sure not to let that certificate expire. As Jamf Now is alerting the administrator in Figure 4-16, when the push certificate expires, the devices must all be reenrolled. This is because a device can no longer communicate to the server to obtain a new certificate. Enrolling a fleet of 1000 or 100,000 is no fun task, given that with iOS devices, this process would be manual and so require a lot of tapping on device screens.

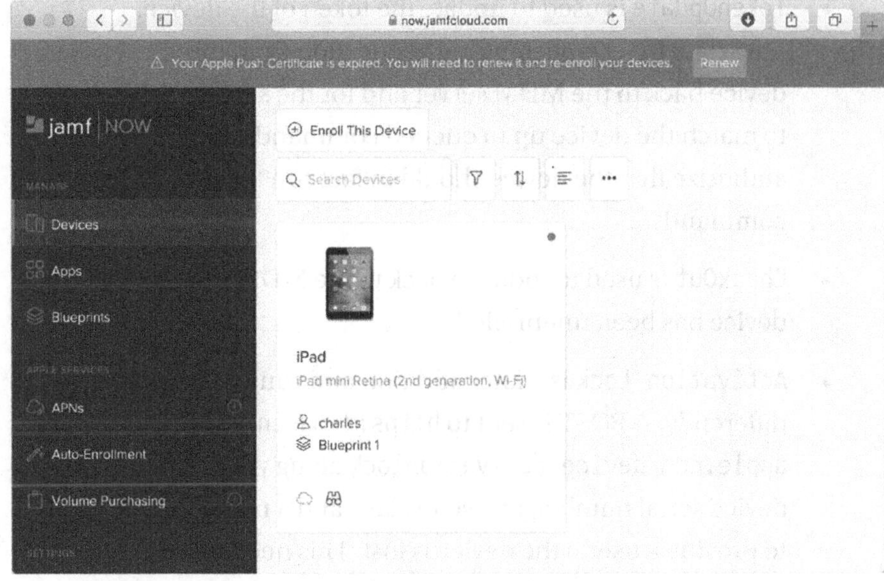

***Figure 4-16.** Jamf Now push certificate renewal*

When the MDM enrollment certificate is installed, the `mdmclient` agent will be called. The device's `mdmclient` then accesses a REST API with an MDM vendor using a `/checkin` endpoint. Commands are pulled from devices over HTTPS in plist-encoded dictionaries along with a UUID of each command with the MDM server pinned, thus establishing a secure connection from the client to the MDM vendor and a normalized communication language between the two. Upon receiving an APN to contact the server, which contains the topic of the server to check into, the device communicates with the MDM check-in protocol to verify the device can enroll, initialize a connection, and then update device tokens when needed. The check-in has a few supported commands, or `MessageTypes`, each submitted in a plist from the device:

- `Authenticate` is a property list with a MessageType of Authenticate, a topic (e.g., com.orgname.mdm), and the UDID of the device.

- `TokenUpdate` is used to update the token of the device. These are for establishing authentication from the device back to the MDM server and for the server to match the device up to queued commands and authorize that the device should in fact run those commands.
- `CheckOut` is used to indicate back to the MDM that a device has been unenrolled.
- `Activation Lock` is a later addition and runs differently. A POST is sent to `https://mdmenrollment.apple.com/device/activationlock` along with a device serial number, an escrow key, and a message to provide a user if the device is lost. This needs to be done prior to the device going through the setup assistant and so is done as a part of the check-in protocol rather than the MDM protocol, although some of the Activation Lock tasks are handled by the MDM protocol.

The MDM protocol runs all the device commands post-enrollment. The MDM endpoint is hard-coded into the enrollment profile at the time of enrollment and so, as with the check-in URL, cannot be changed post-enrollment without breaking the ability to communicate back to the server. All POSTs look to that endpoint to see what commands are waiting for the device. The URL for the check-in is immutable because the device is authorized to talk to that endpoint using the certificates exchanged at enrollment time, the `.csr` for which was submitted through SCEP at enrollment. When the device checks in, it picks up any commands, in dictionary form, waiting for the device. The check-in URL is not displayed in the MDM profile in the System Preferences pane, but the MDM URL is, as seen in Figure 4-17.

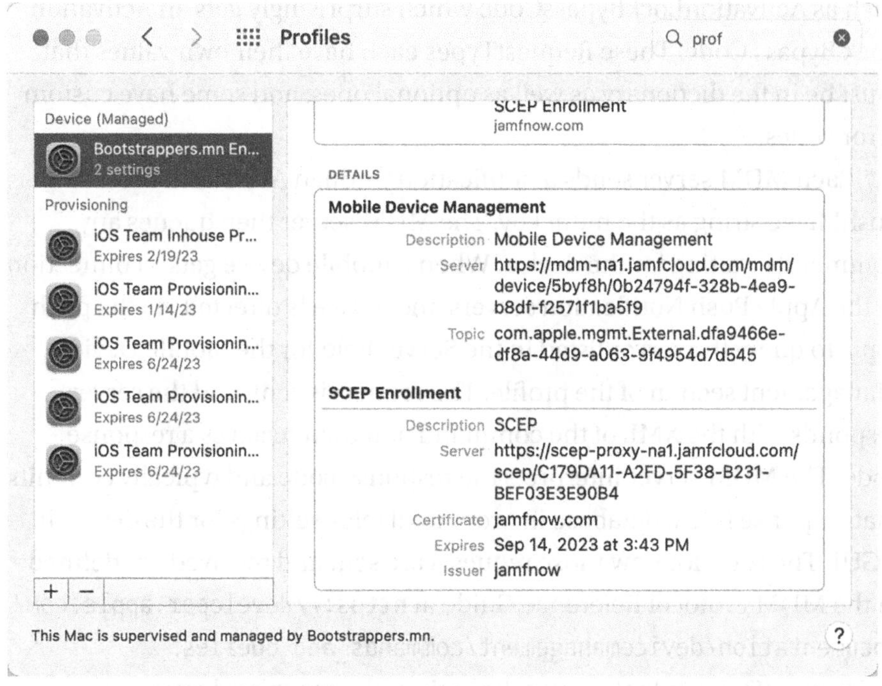

***Figure 4-17.** Profiles in System Preferences*

MDM: Device Management

The MDM Server, shown in the Mobile Device Management profile, shows the URL to the endpoint that the device sends a POST to (typically just called /mdm). That POST contains a standard dictionary with the device UDID in a plist, and the response to that POST includes a status message that there's no action to be performed, or there will be an MDM command, in the form of a dictionary.

The command dictionary includes a request type called RequestType and a RequestRequiresNetworkTether – which when set to true only allows the command to run when connected to a network (this is rarely used). The RequestType is going to include most of the MDM commands, such as ActivationLockBypassCode which surprisingly gets an Activation Lock Bypass Code. These RequestTypes each have their own values that must be in the dictionary as well as optional ones, and some have custom error codes.

Each MDM server sends a notification through APNs with the PushMagic string as the mdm key. The MDM server then queues any commands waiting for the device. When a mobile device gets a connection to the Apple Push Notification servers, the device is directed via the push topic to query the server listed in the Server field for the Mobile Device Management section of the profile. The request is sent, and the server responds with the XML of the command and then receives a response code. The MDM server interprets the response code and typically commits that response into a database in order to display settings for the device in a GUI. The rules for how those requests are sent and received are defined in the MDM Protocol Reference Guide at `https://developer.apple.com/documentation/devicemanagement/commands_and_queries`.

Each MDM vendor handles the logic of the command queue differently. Most vendors store each action and then interpret that into a log-on screen for administrators to view. Most vendors also deduplicate commands, so devices aren't told to install the same app five or six times because an administrator duplicated some groups. Most vendors also prioritize commands, so a wipe is sent as the highest priority command for a device. But these are all different for each vendor. Most vendors have built more and more logic as humans end up doing weird things to their software (humans are the worst).

Now that we've looked at how devices get enrolled into an MDM and how commands are queued up so the /mdm endpoint can respond appropriately to devices, let's look at what commands are available (we'll save the idea of declarative management for a future edition that has more widespread adoption of the features - but make sure to watch the video at `https://developer.apple.com/videos/play/wwdc2022/10046/` to see what the future of Apple Mobile Device Management is likely to entail).

Further, check out the KMFDDM project from Jesse Peterson to see a reference implementation of declarative management at `https://github.com/jessepeterson/kmfddm`.

MDM Commands

Each MDM command maps to a RequestType, and there are optional keys at the same level in a dictionary for some commands. Additionally, given that it's a dictionary, there are other attributes that can be sent along with a command. In some cases, there is only one, and in other cases, there are over a dozen keys that alter the behavior of a command. As you look at the list of commands, just imagine how these are displayed in the graphical interface of your favorite MDM. The MDM commands (a.k.a. RequestTypes) that are placed into those dictionaries include the following commands (as well as a few that get added each year as more functionality is added to the MDM specification):

1. `ActivationLockBypassCode`: Responds with a code used to unlock a device that has Activation Lock enabled (used if an Apple ID is not available).
2. `ProfileList`: Lists profiles on a device.
3. `InstallProfile`: Installs a profile on a device (see Chapter 3 for more information on profiles).
4. `RemoveProfile`: Deletes a profile from a device.
5. `ProvisioningProfileList`: Provisioning profiles link deploy signing certificates, App IDs, and a URIs to an App ID to install an app on a device, so this command lists those profiles deployed (and so the apps if they successfully installed).

6. `InstallProvisioningProfile`: Installs a provisioning profile to cause an app to be installed on a device.

7. `RemoveProvisioningProfile`: Removes a provisioning profile which causes an app installed based on the URL of the provisioning profile to be removed.

8. `CertificateList`: Lists identity certificates installed on a device.

9. `InstalledApplicationList`: Lists applications installed on a device.

10. `DeviceInformation`: Responds with metadata about a device, including UDID, the device ID, and the last iCloud backup date, if the device is in an AwaitingConfiguration state (to see if it has run the Setup Assistant).

11. `SecurityInfo`: Responds with security-centric metadata about a device, including if the device has a T2 chip (or M1 with similar functionality), has FileVault enabled, etc.

12. `DeviceLock`: Locks a device and optionally sets a PIN to unlock the device and a message for the user, presumably about why the device was locked or how to return it.

13. `RestartDevice`: Reboots a device.

14. `ShutDownDevice`: Shuts down a device.

15. `ClearPasscode`: Clears a passcode on a device.

16. `EraseDevice`: Remotely erases a device so it can be set up from scratch.

17. `RequestMirroring`: Begins an AirPlay mirroring session on the device, along with a destination to mirror the device to.

    a. `StopMirroring`: Stops any active mirroring session on a device.

18. `Restrictions`: Obtains a list of restrictions that have been configured on a device.

    a. `ClearRestrictionsPassword`: Clears a restrictions password in case that password has been forgotten.

19. `UserList` for Shared iPad: Responds with a list of users that have accounts on a device, along with some metadata about those users, such as name, full name, and UID.

    a. `UnlockUserAccount`: Unlocks an account that has been locked because a user provided an incorrect password too many times.

    b. `LogOutUser`: Logs out the active user.

    c. `DeleteUser`: Deletes a user indicated in the UserName key.

20. `EnableLostMode`: Sets a managed device into Lost Mode.

    a. `PlayLostModeSound`: Causes a device in Lost Mode to make an audible alert so you can find the device if it's lost in the office or classroom.

    b. `DisableLostMode`: Disables Lost Mode on devices that have that setting enabled.

   c. `DeviceLocation`: Returns with the GPS coordinates of a device that has been set in Lost Mode.

21. `InstallApplication`: Installs applications on devices from the app store or a URL and optionally sets the applications to "managed."

   a. `InstallEnterpriseApplication`: Installs software packages which can be pinned for additional security.

   b. `ApplyRedemptionCode`: Redeems an app from the App Store based on a redemption code (this software installation method isn't used that much anymore as redemption codes are not reusable).

   c. `ManagedApplicationList`: Returns with a list of all managed applications or applications installed by the MDM.

   d. `RemoveApplication`: Removes an application based on the identifier (easily obtained via ManagedApplicationList).

   e. `InviteToProgram`: Invites an Apple ID to join the VPP for per-user app assignments to the hash of an ID provided using a query to iTunesStoreAccountIsActive.

   f. `ValidateApplications`: Validates that apps installed with a provisioning profile are on a device.

22. `InstallMedia`: Installs a PDF, epub (in gzip), or iBooks Author media file (in gzip) into the Books app on a device.

   a. `ManagedMediaList`: Lists all documents installed using the InstallMedia command, along with the state of each (e.g., downloading).

   b. `RemoveMedia`: Removes any items returned by the ManagedMediaList command response.

23. `Settings`: Allows for enabling or disabling various supervised managed settings on a device, such as the device wallpaper, data roaming, and Bluetooth.

    a. `ManagedApplicationConfiguration`: Reports back a dictionary for each app that has been built for Managed App Config.

    b. `ApplicationConfiguration`: Sets Managed App Config dictionaries, sending NSUserDefaults into the app.

    c. `ManagedApplicationAttributes`: Queries attributes set via Managed App Config (from NSUserDefaults).

    d. `ManagedApplicationFeedback`: Provides a response to key-pairs.

24. `AccountConfiguration`: Creates a local administrative account on a Mac.

25. `SetFirmwarePassword`: Enables the firmware password on a device, provided one was not set before the device was enrolled into an MDM.

    a. `VerifyFirmwarePassword`: Sends a password to a device and verifies that the firmware password on the device matches the one sent as a part of the MDM command.

26. `SetAutoAdminPassword`: Sends a salted PBKDF2 SHA512 password hash to a GUID for a given local admin account.

27. `DeviceConfigured`: Bypasses DEP for devices currently set into an await configuration state.

28. `ScheduleOSUpdate`: Causes an iOS, iPadOS, and tvOS device to install product keys provided to the device.

    a. `ScheduleOSUpdateScan`: Boolean that causes a device to check for updates using Software Update.

    b. `AvailableOSUpdates`: Installs updates supplied in the dictionary or if none are present installs all pending operating system updates.

    c. `OSUpdateStatus`: Causes a device to check for the status of any updates pending for that device.

29. `ActiveNSExtensions`: Lists active NSExtensions for a user.

30. `NSExtensionMappings`: Manage NSExtension mappings.

31. `RotateFileVaultKey`: Rotates FileVault keys (e.g., if they're used by IT, they should be rotated).

Note For a more detailed description of commands, including the arguments available for each command, the minimum OS to run each command, and a description of each, see `https://developer.apple.com/documentation/devicemanagement#topics`.

New commands show up in every version of operating systems, so don't be surprised if new ones come around before this book goes to print. Keep in mind that the MDM server isn't sending these commands directly to the devices. They can't as they don't know the address of those devices. The MDM server is putting the property list into a queue, and when the device gets the notification, it will automatically check with the MDM server and perform the action the command is telling the device to perform. The commands then have response codes that are returned to the MDM server. Those are too numerous to put in this chapter, but they provide the MDM solution with the ability to interpret what information Apple MDM developers determined would be important for the MDM solution to have.

The simplest way to show how to send a custom command would be to do so. We'll use VMware Workspace ONE for this example. If you have a Workspace ONE account, to get to the custom command screen, to create and deploy a custom command, browse to a device in List View. Then check the box for the device, and under the More Actions dropdown, choose Custom Commands to see the dialog box to provide your dictionary.

As seen in Figure 4-18, administrators can provide the necessary XML code to run a command. This can be a bit dangerous, so make sure you know what you're doing.

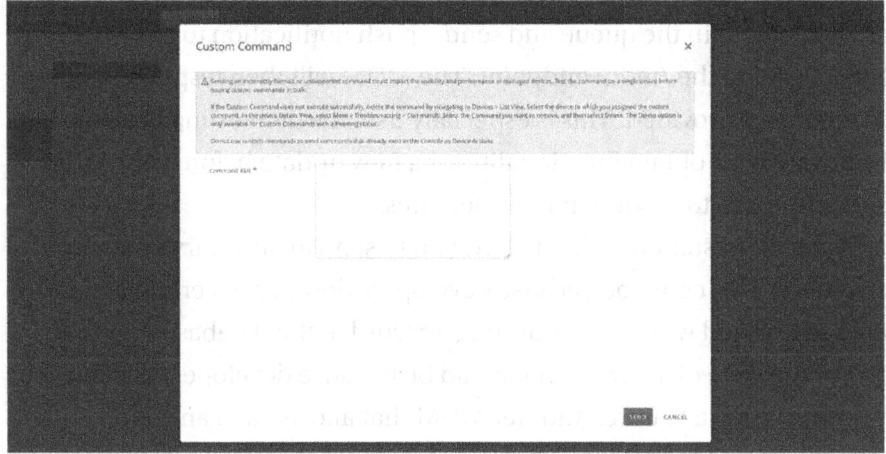

***Figure 4-18.** Running arbitrary MDM commands using VMware Workspace ONE*

In this example, we'll simply restart a device using the RestartDevice as the string for the RequestType key. Notice we don't need to send any other keys for this type of action:

```
<dict>
    <key>RequestType</key>
    <string>RestartDevice</string>
</dict>
```

Or to receive a list of certificates installed on a device, we might use this command:

```
<dict>
        <key>RequestType</key>
        <string>CertificateList</string>
</dict>
```

In both of the preceding examples, when we click the save button, we will put an item in the queue and send a push notification to the device to send a POST to the /mdm endpoint. The MDM will then respond with the command we provided. This is especially useful when testing beta versions of software or to obtain functionality for a new update before your MDM vendor updates to account for new features.

Most MDM solutions don't allow you to send an arbitrary command to a device. This could be because developers don't want certain actions being performed without committing a record to the database they use to track the state of a device, or it could be because developers haven't prioritized such a feature. Another MDM that allows such an action would be MicroMDM. MicroMDM is, as the name implies, a slimmed down MDM solution. MicroMDM allows an administrator to submit an MDM command using a standard POST to a command's endpoint. That endpoint will parse the command from a standardized json format where each key is an --arg that is followed by the value in the key.

In the following example, we'll send a more complicated command, InstallApplication. Here, we provide a UDID and a manifest_url as the first and second positional parameters sent into the script:

```
#!/bin/bash
        source $MICROMDM_ENV_PATH
        endpoint="v1/commands"
        jq -n \
          --arg request_type "InstallApplication" \
          --arg udid "$1" \
          --arg manifest_url "$2" \
          '.udid = $udid
          |.request_type = $request_type
          |.manifest_url = $manifest_url
          '|\
          curl $CURL_OPTS \
            -H "Content-Type: application/json" \
-u "micromdm:$API_TOKEN" "$SERVER_URL/$endpoint" -d@-
```

Upon receiving the action to the endpoint, MicroMDM routes a push notification message to the device; and when the device receives the push, it looks to the server for the dictionary that's waiting in the MicroMDM queue and then interprets the dictionary to perform the app installation. Luckily, the developers do much of the work, so you don't have to build your own server for the device to talk back to. But it is helpful to understand what is happening so you can deal with issues when they come up and in general be better informed about how you're managing devices.

Now that we've gone through what happens with standard MDM commands, we'll move into automating device enrollment.

Automated Enrollment, or DEP

One component of MDM is Automated Enrollment, which was formerly referred to as the Device Enrollment Program, or DEP for short. Automated Enrollment automatically enrolls a device into an MDM or at least configures a device to log in to an MDM server and enrolls the device if the server doesn't require a user to authenticate. This is useful for provisioning. An organization can ship a box to a user, and the user can open the box and configure their own device by simply joining a network and optionally providing credentials to complete the setup.

The DEP API provided by Apple is more modern, and messages are exchanged in standard JSON format rather than in plist-driven dictionaries. There are three primary APIs. The first is for resellers. When DEP was initially released, only devices sold directly by Apple could use DEP. Because a device is tied to uniquely identifying information such as a UDID and a serial number, Apple was able to direct devices to an MDM. But in order to support allowing DEP to work with devices sold by resellers, an API was created for resellers to submit data about which customer purchases each device.

The Reseller DEP API

The most important thing to keep in mind about how resellers interact with the Apple DEP program is that the reseller submits an order that contains an orderNumber, orderDate, orderType, customerId, poNumber, and then an array of deviceIds and assetTags. The deviceIds are the serial numbers of the devices, and the link between the deviceId and the customerId is created at this time and causes the devices for each organization to properly appear in their Apple Business Manager or Apple School Manager accounts. That json (stripped down for readability) would look something like the following:

```
"orders": [
      {
          "orderNumber": "ORDER1234",
          "orderDate": "2022-09-22T08:07:13X",
          "orderType": "OR",
          "customerId": "Charles",
          "poNumber": "12345",    {
      "deviceId": "SERIALNUMBER1",
      "assetTag": "MYASSETTAG1"
   },}
```

For more on the DEP APIs, see `https://applecareconnect.apple.com/api-docs/depuat/html/WSReference.html`. The second is an identity API used to authorize devices, which we won't be covering as there is no real public information available.

The Cloud Service DEP API

The important API for the context of this chapter is the cloud service API. This is available at `https://mdmenrollment.apple.com/account`. Here, MDM vendors pull records of what devices are meant to access servers they host. In exchange, those MDM vendors send back DEP profiles to Apple. Those profiles are then placed on the device, so it is trusted by the server and so it trusts the server back. These profiles contain the screens that a device should skip during the Setup Assistant, a server URL, and any certificates necessary for establishing a chain of trust to the URL being accessed. The MDM authenticates back to the cloud service API over OAuth 1.0 tokens.

The MDM will provide parameters for devices assigned to it in json to the Apple DEP servers. An example POST would look as follows (e.g., in Postman):

```
User-Agent:ProfileManager-1.0
X-Server-Protocol-Version:2
Content-Type: application/json;charset=UTF8
Content-Length: 350
X-ADM-Auth-Session: $SESSIONID
  {
     "profile_name": "krypted.com",
     "url":"https://mdm.krypted.com/getconfig",
     "is_supervised":false,
     "allow_pairing":true,
     "is_mandatory":false,
     "await_device_configured":false,
     "is_mdm_removable":false,
     "department": "Marketing",
     "org_magic": "$PUSHMAGIC",
     "support_phone_number": $PHONENUMBER,
     "support_email_address": $EMAILADDRESS,
     "anchor_certs,
     "supervising_host_certs:,
     "skip_setup_items":[
        "Location",
        "Restore",
        "Android",
        "AppleID",
        "TOS",
        "Siri",
        "Diagnostics",
        "Biometric",
        "Payment",
        "Zoom",
        "FileVault"
```

```
    ],
      "devices":["$SERIALNUMBER1", "$SERIALNUMBER2"]
}
```

Upon request, the MDM server then receives a list of devices from `https://mdmenrollment.apple.com/server/devices` - some of that data would likely appear in the interface of your MDM solution (the exact way these appear is a bit different in each vendor):

```
"serial_number" : "ABCD123AB1AB",
"model" : "IPAD",
"description" : "IPAD WI-FI 32GB",
"color" : "grey",
"profile_status" : "assigned",
"profile_uuid" : "12ab1a123abc1234a12a1a1234abc123",
"profile_assign_time" : "2022-08-01T00:00:00Z",
"device_assigned_date" : "2022-08-01T00:00:00Z",
"device_assigned_by" : "krypted@me.com"
```

Enrollment profiles from an MDM are not removable. When the device powers up, mobileactivationd sends a dictionary with a DeviceID, SerialNumber, UniqueDeviceID, as well as information about the Bridge OS (an embedded variant of watchOS that provides the interface to the T2 chip or an M1). If any of that information is altered, then Apple will reject the activation. More importantly for the purposes of this chapter, if the serial number is matched with one that's been linked in the preceding manner between the Apple Business Manager and Apple School Manager accounts, the device receives the settings from the first set of information provided to Apple from the MDM server to mdmenrollment.apple.com.

The device then uses the /getconfig URL (in Jamf, this is /cloudenroll, and in microMDM, it is just /enroll) to obtain an enrollment profile and responds based on the interpretation of that profile. If devices get wiped, they will continue to reach out to the MDM /getconfig endpoint to pull down a new enrollment profile. That /getconfig endpoint is different per provider - and some have handlers for objects in the URLs, but that setting is required in order for devices to know how they'll enroll.

Finally, there's an endpoint to unenroll devices and there's an endpoint to disown devices at `https://mdmenrollment.apple.com/devices/disown`. This endpoint is used to remove devices from the portal, so you can, for example, allow employees to purchase them when you remove them from production. Now that we've looked at how devices enroll and receive profiles and actions from the MDM server in response to their APNs instructions to look for those payloads in their queue, let's look at how the mdmclient that sits on devices interprets those.

mdmclient

The agent for MDM actions is mdmclient, which is the "app" that push notifications are sent to. Once enrollment profiles are installed on a Mac, mdmclient, a binary located in /usr/libexec, processes changes such as wiping a system that has been FileVaulted (note you need to FileVault if you want to wipe an OS X Lion client computer). This is started by the mdmclient daemons and agents at /System/Library/LaunchDaemons (com.apple.mdmclient.daemon.plist and com.apple.mdmclient.daemon.runatboot.plist) and /System/Library/LaunchAgents, which are used for computer and user commands, respectively. This, along with all of the operators, remains static from 10.10 and on, with small new functionality added with each new version.

The Volume Purchase Program, now a part of Apple School Manager and Apple Business Manager, also responds to requests through mdmclient. CommerceKit is a framework that mdmclient uses by calling CKMDMProcessManifestAtURL with a dictionary that contains any pinning certificates and optionally checks that the certificates haven't been revoked. This causes storeassetd to download the manifest and then place any specified assets to be downloaded in the queue using NSURLConnection. Then storedownloadd takes over and completes the download, installing packages when complete.

The mdmclient hands any profile transactions (the most common task most administrators use MDM to perform). To script profile deployment, administrators can add and remove configuration profiles using the new /usr/bin/profiles command. For more on scripting the profiles command, which is helpful in testing and automating tasks when there's no MDM present, see Chapter 3.

The UUID for a given enrolled user profile can be found at the following path, where * can be replaced by a given username:

```
defaults read /Library/Managed\ Preferences/*/com.apple.
systempolicy.managed.plist
```

The UUID would then be output as a PayloadUUID, as follows:

```
PayloadUUID = "CF4BCAA5-BCC6-4113-86D4-31A08C683770";
```

As usual, the Mac is a little different. You can see the directories to better understand what's happening under the hood using a jailbroken iOS device or using the simulator.

If you look at an iOS device in the simulator, you'll find com.apple.managedconfiguration.mdmd.plist and com.apple.managedconfiguration.profiled.plist in the LaunchDaemons for the simulator (and so /Library would be relative to / on a jailbroken device). These are the two agents that are the underlying MDM services. If you swap iPhoneOS.platform with AppleTVOS.platform or WatchOS.platform, then you will see the same for tvOS and watchOS, respectively.

When running commands, you can see that these are the agents that control settings for iOS, based on processes that get started and run:

- /Library/Managed Preferences/ce/com.apple.systempolicy.managed.plist
- /Library/Managed Preferences/com.apple.AssetCache.managed.plist
- /Library/Managed Preferences/com.apple.systempolicy.managed.plist
- /private/var/db/ConfigurationProfiles/Settings/com.apple.managed.PlugInKit.plist

Much of the management in the future is likely to be handled using the newer ManagedConfiguration.framework, with teslad invoked as a LaunchDaemon by /System/Library/LaunchDaemons/com.apple.managedconfiguration.teslad.plist (via /System/Library/PrivateFrameworks/ManagedConfiguration.framework/Versions/Current). Teslad has entries for a number of enrollment options, and while, at the time this book is printed, it isn't used much on the Mac, this framework has started managing a number of other management tasks. The fact that there's a new framework for the Mac indicates that more options otherwise reserved for supervised devices are likely to be made available to the Mac in subsequent releases.

Device Supervision

Employees at Apple and engineers in the broader community that supports Apple devices have always been proud of the beautiful, curated user experience on devices. No one ever wants to limit functionality when possible. But in some cases, doing so is necessary. No one wants their credit card numbers, social security numbers, or any private information leaked.

There was a split in how engineers at Apple felt about managing iOS devices. Everyone wanted to give administrators more and more control. But many wanted to only do so if a device was owned by an organization. The concept of Bring Your Own Device (or BYOD for short) has always been the tip of the spear for Apple to get into the enterprise. But enterprises began buying lots and lots and lots of iPads and iPhones for staff.

The compromise was the ability to supervise a device. Devices enrolled through Automated Enrollment (DEP) are usually set as supervised. The MDM can choose to not set a device to supervised based on settings (whether exposed to administrators or not). You can also retroactively supervise iOS devices using Apple Configurator, as shown in Chapter 5.

Since the maturity of device supervision, most new iOS management commands have required device supervision in order to work. The T2 chipset (and M1 being rolled out throughout Apple's product line) is now making true device supervision for the Mac a possibility and likely indicates that commands reserved for supervised devices will start finding their way to the Mac, including Managed Open-In functionality. One aspect of Automated Enrollment and the ability to more granularly control settings is the amount of clicking and tapping we want to allow our users to avoid during the initial provisioning of devices. One aspect of where users can get click fatigue with all the new privacy options is UAMDM.

UAMDM

For iOS, Apple has had device supervision to act as the bright dividing line between "this is a personal iOS device" and "this is a work-owned iOS device." On Macs running macOS Sierra and earlier, the line was less clear as there weren't MDM functions that would not run equally well on personally owned Macs and Macs owned by a company, school, or institution. To address this, Apple introduced User-Approved

Mobile Device Management (UAMDM) as part of macOS High Sierra 10.13.2. UAMDM grants Mobile Device Management (MDM) additional management privileges, beyond what is allowed for macOS MDM enrollments which have not been "user approved."

There are two ways to mark a Mac as being user approved. The first is to have the Mac enrolled in Apple's Device Enrollment Program. This is a process where Apple explicitly sets the Mac as belonging to a company, school, or institution and enrolls it with a specific MDM service. Since the Mac is not a personally owned device, it gets UAMDM automatically. The second is to have a human being click a button on the MDM profile issued by an MDM server which supports UAMDM. To click the button, you would use the following process:

1. Open System Settings and go to the **Privacy & Security** preference pane.
2. Click Profiles toward the bottom of the list of options.
3. Click the MDM profile (Figure 4-19).

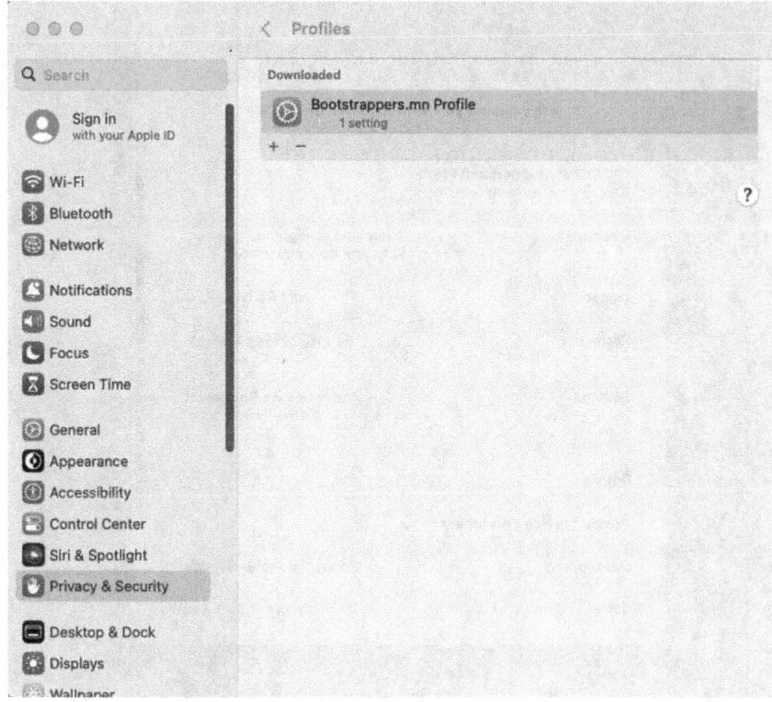

Figure 4-19. *The MDM profile*

4. Click the **Install** button.
5. Click the ***Install*** button in the confirmation window which appears (Figure 4-20).

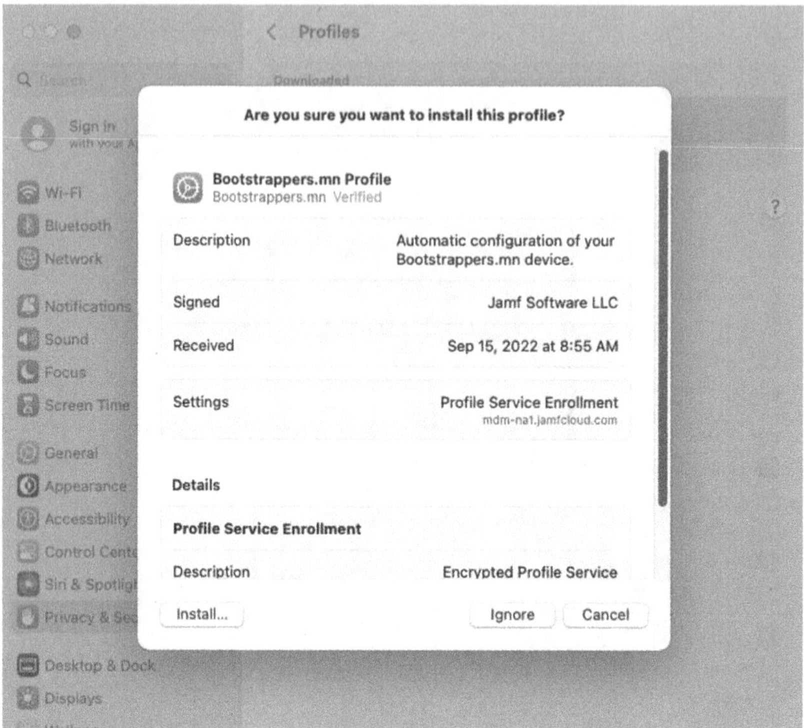

Figure 4-20. *Approving the UAMDM profile*

Once that is done, the Mac is now enabled for UAMDM, and the managing MDM can now use the additional management options which are only available for UAMDM-enabled Macs. The rights the MDM server has are outlined in the profile, as seen in Figure 4-21.

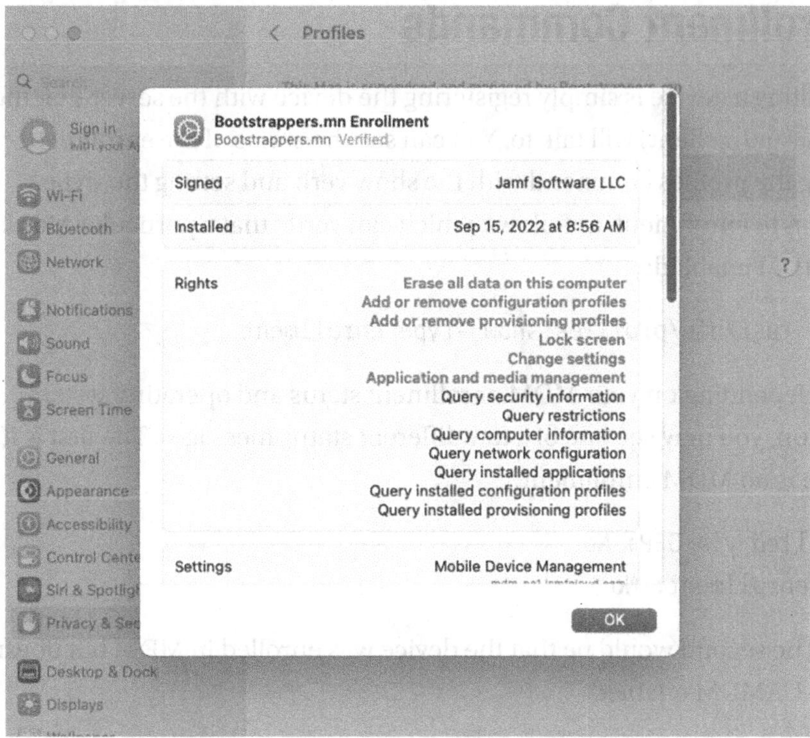

***Figure 4-21.** The MDM profile, once approved*

Something to be aware of is that Apple has taken some pains to block automated ways to enable UAMDM, so clicking this button cannot be performed via remote screen sharing or through the use of tools which would normally help automate the clicking of a button. These protections against machine-based enabling are to help make sure that a human being has approved enabling UAMDM.

Enrollment Commands

Enrolling a device is simply registering the device with the server that the agent (mdmclient) will talk to. You can see the status of the enrollment using the profiles command with the show verb and setting the -type option to enrollment, as follows, which can verify that a particular Mac is UAMDM enabled:

```
sudo /usr/bin/profiles show -type enrollment
```

Depending on your MDM enrollment status and operating system version, you may see one of a few different status messages. The first is if there is no MDM enrollment:

```
Enrolled via DEP: No
MDM enrollment: No
```

The second would be that the device was enrolled in MDM but doesn't have UAMDM enabled:

```
Enrolled via DEP: No
MDM enrollment: Yes
```

The third output is that the device was enrolled manually *and* the user chose to accept the MDM enrollment options, which indicates (User Approved)

```
Enrolled via DEP: No
MDM enrollment: Yes (User Approved)
```

The fourth output is that the device was enrolled via Automated Enrollment (DEP) *and* the user chose to accept the MDM enrollment options, which indicates (User Approved)

```
Enrolled via DEP: Yes
MDM enrollment: Yes (User Approved)
```

Some machines may also show an error that reads

```
Error fetching Device Enrollment configuration: Client is not
DEP enabled.
```

User Accepted MDM enrollment is likely to become more and more important as the focus from Apple engineering teams seems to be around protecting privacy at the cost of management options. This focus on privacy is one of the reasons many choose an Apple device and increasingly core to the Apple ethos. Now that we've reviewed how to see the enrollment type, let's move to what happens when UAMDM has been accepted.

The Impact of UAMDM

There are certain management privileges associated with UAMDM, which otherwise can't be centrally managed. As of macOS 10.14, those management privileges include

- Centralized approval of third-party kernel extension loading
- Centralized approval of application requests to access privacy-protected data

Having UAMDM enabled allows a UAMDM-compatible MDM service to deploy management profiles which can approve the following:

- Automatic loading of specified third-party kernel extensions
- Automatic approval for specific actions by applications, where those actions are accessing data protected by macOS's privacy controls

Third-Party Kernel Extension Management

Starting with macOS 10.13.4, Apple introduced its first management privilege exclusively associated with UAMDM. This was the ability to deploy a profile which provides a whitelist for third-party kernel extensions. This profile allows a company, school, or institution to avoid the need to have individual users approve the running of approved software.

Without the profile, the third party will need to be approved through the User-Approved Kernel Extension Loading (UAKEL) process. Apple later moved to block kernel extensions in general in favor of more specific extensions based on new frameworks and APIs Apple released to do what the previous kernel extensions had done. For example, rather than use a kernel extension to perform virus scans, Apple provided the Endpoint Security framework. These extensions often require entitlements similar to how UAKEL functioned.

When a request is made to the OS to load a third-party extension which the user has not yet approved, the load request must be manually approved to protect the user's privacy. Otherwise, it is denied and macOS presents an alert to the user. The alert tells the user how to approve the loading of the kernel extension signed by a particular developer or vendor, by following this procedure. The user can then see extensions in a similar way to how profiles are viewed:

A. Open System Preferences.

B. Go to the **Privacy & Security** preference pane.

C. Click the **Extensions** button (Figure 4-22).

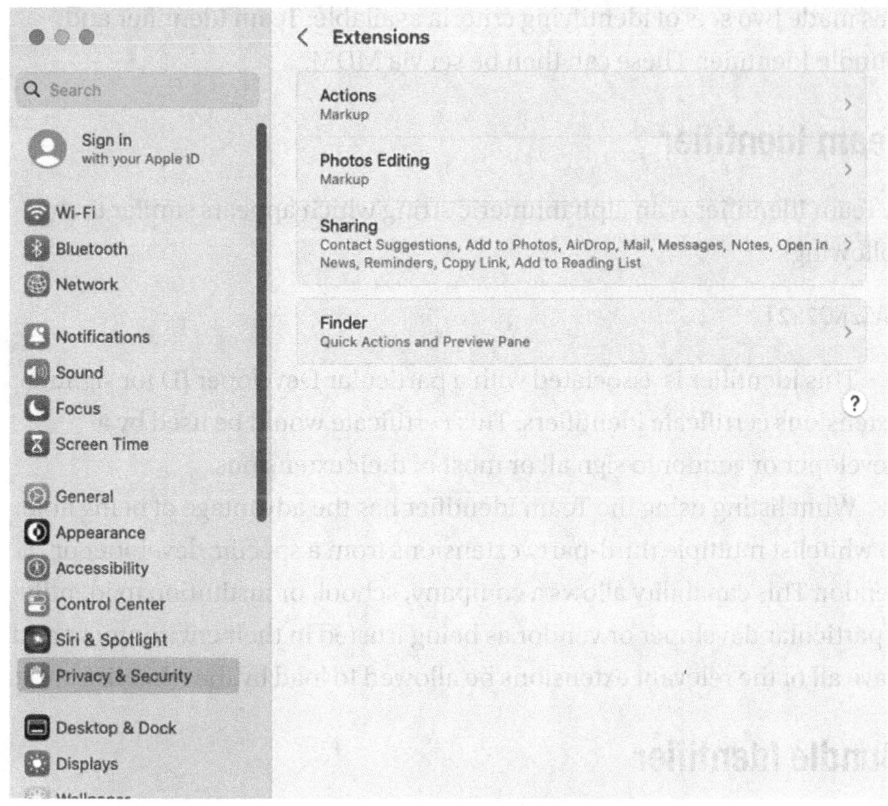

***Figure 4-22.** Click into an extension to see where it's active*

While waiting for kernel extensions to be approved, a copy of the kernel extension was made by the operating system and stored in /**Library/StagedExtensions**. This persists with system extensions in apps, and once approved, the extension is made and allowed to load.

This process is relatively easy for an individual to manage on their own computer, but it can be very difficult to manage when dealing with more than a handful of Macs. To help manage a company, school, or institution, Apple provided the option of using a management profile to centrally approve specified third-party system extensions. To help whitelist all extensions from a particular vendor or whitelist only specific ones, Apple has made two sets of identifying criteria available: Team Identifier and Bundle Identifier. These can then be set via MDM.

Team Identifier

A Team Identifier is an alphanumeric string which appears similar to the following:

```
7AGZNQ2S2T
```

This identifier is associated with a particular Developer ID for signing extensions certificate identifiers. This certificate would be used by a developer or vendor to sign all or most of their extensions.

Whitelisting using the Team Identifier has the advantage of being able to whitelist multiple third-party extensions from a specific developer or vendor. This capability allows a company, school, or institution to identify a particular developer or vendor as being trusted in their environment and have all of the relevant extensions be allowed to load by the whitelist.

Bundle Identifier

The Bundle Identifier is specific to a particular kernel extension. It is contained in the **Info.plist** file and is stored inside each extension. Whitelisting using the Bundle Identifier allows a company, school, or institution to get very granular about which kernel extensions from a specific developer or vendor are approved and which are not. If using the Bundle Identifier as part of the whitelist, both the Team Identifier and the Bundle Identifier need to be specified in the profile.

Using Team Identifier by Itself in a Third-Party Extension Profile

If you want to use only the Team Identifier when whitelisting kernel extensions, the profile can be viewed from Terminal. Here, you'll see the keys that show the UUID, the name, and much more that isn't displayed in System Preferences, as shown in Figure 4-23.

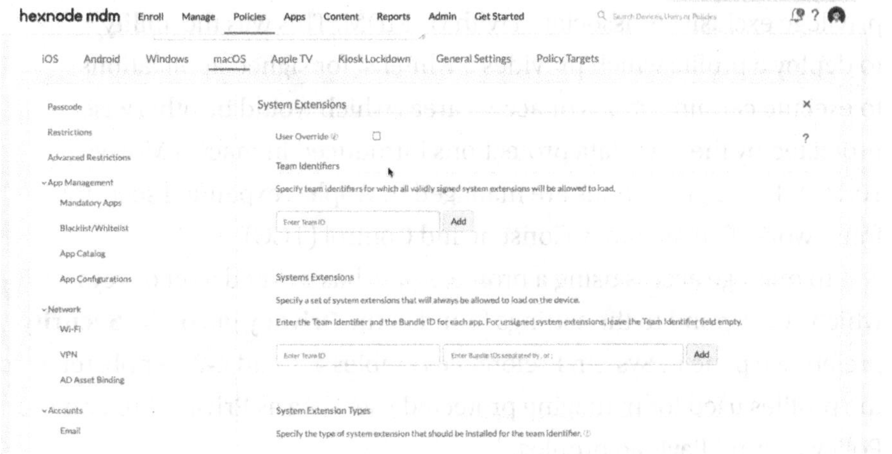

Figure 4-23. *The contents of the Approved Extension profile*

On the Macs which receive the profile, it will show as Approved Extensions with the green Verified option. Under the hood, these are sent to /var/db/SystemPolicyConfiguration/KextPolicy or ExecPolicy (at the same path), which are sqlite databases. You can log in and see both manually created kext policies and those pushed into SystemPolicyConfiguration via mdm. To see manual entries (from within sqlite) and then to see MDM-derived entries:

```
SELECT * FROM kext_policy;
SELECT * FROM kext_policy_mdm;
```

Based on the output, note that kext_policy shows a bundleID whereas kext_policy_mdm only shows generated IDs. While kexts aren't used as much any longer, the same still rings true for system extensions.

Privacy Control Management

Starting with macOS 10.14.0, Apple introduced its second management privilege exclusively associated with UAMDM. This was the ability to deploy a profile which provides a whitelist for signed applications to execute certain actions or access areas which would be otherwise protected by the user data protections introduced in macOS Mojave 10.14.0. These protections are managed by Apple's expanded security framework, Transparency Consent and Control (TCC).

To manage access using a profile, Apple has defined a set of keys which correspond to the settings found in the **Privacy** tab of the **Security** preference pane in System Preferences (Tables 4-1 and 4-2). Apple refers to the profiles used for managing protected user data as Privacy Preferences Policy Control Payload profiles.

Table 4-1. *Privacy Service Dictionary Keys*

Key	Type	Value
AddressBook	Array of Identity Dictionaries	Contact information managed by Apple's Contacts.app.
Calendar	Array of Identity Dictionaries	Calendar information managed by Apple's Calendar.app.
Reminders	Array of Identity Dictionaries	Reminders information managed by Apple's Reminders.app.
Photos	Array of Identity Dictionaries	Pictures managed by Apple's Photos. app, where the picture data is stored in the following location: **~/Pictures/.photoslibrary**

(continued)

Table 4-1. (*continued*)

Key	Type	Value
Camera	Array of Identity Dictionaries	A system camera. Access to the camera can only be denied. There is no way to automatically grant access.
Microphone	Array of Identity Dictionaries	A system microphone. Access to the microphone can only be denied. There is no way to automatically grant access.
Accessibility	Array of Identity Dictionaries	Control the application via the **Accessibility** subsystem.
PostEvent	Array of Identity Dictionaries	Allows the application to use CoreGraphics APIs to send CGEvents to the system event stream.
SystemPolicyAllFiles	Array of Identity Dictionaries	Allows the application access to all protected files.
SystemPolicySysAdminFiles	Array of Identity Dictionaries	Allows the application access to some files used in system administration.
AppleEvents	Array of Identity Dictionaries	Allows the application to send a restricted AppleEvent to another process.

Table 4-2. *Identity Dictionary Keys*

Key	Type	Value
Identifier	String	The bundle ID or installation path of the binary.
IdentifierType	String	The type of Identifier value. Must be either bundle ID or path. Application bundles should be identified by bundle ID. Nonbundled binaries must be identified by installation path. Helper tools embedded within an application bundle will automatically inherit the permissions of their enclosing app bundle.
CodeRequirement	String	Digital signature of the binary. The digital signature is acquired via running the following command: **codesign--display-r-/path/to/binary/here**.
StaticCode	Boolean	If set to **true**, statically validate the code requirement. Used only if the process invalidates its dynamic code signature. Defaults to false. **Optional**.
Allowed	Boolean	If set to **true**, access is granted. Any other value denies access.

(*continued*)

Table 4-2. (*continued*)

Key	Type	Value
AEReceiverIdentifier	String	The identifier of the process receiving an AppleEvent sent by the Identifier process. Required for AppleEvents service; not valid for other services. **Optional**.
AEReceiverIdentifierType	String	The type of **AEReceiverIdentifier** value. Must be either bundle ID or path. Required for AppleEvents service; not valid for other services. **Optional**.
AEReceiverCodeRequirement	String	Code requirement for the receiving binary. Required for AppleEvents service; not valid for other services. **Optional**.
Comment	String	Used to provide information in the profile about what is being managed. **Optional**.

These are more thoroughly documented at `https://developer.apple.com/documentation/devicemanagement/privacypreferencespolicycontrol`. In the case of an application which needs access to all data in a user's home folder, a profile would need to be created which does the following:

- Identifies the application by its bundle ID and code signature
- Allows it access to all protected areas using the **SystemPolicyAllFiles** payload key

On the Macs which receive the profile, it should appear similar to the one shown in Figure 4-24.

Slack PPPC
Verified
Description Whitelisting the pop-up for access to Downloads folder
Signed JSS Built-In Signing Certificate
Installed Mar 15, 2022 at 3:20 PM
Settings Privacy Preferences Policy Control
DETAILS
Privacy Preferences Policy Control
Description Privacy Preferences Policy Control
Access the User's Downloads folder - Allowed

Figure 4-24. *Privacy Preferences Policy Control profile*

With all of these moving pieces, a lot can go wrong, especially for newer administrators. Learning to troubleshoot and debug can make it easier to get your devices into the hands of users without going crazy.

Enable APNs Debug Logging

Nearly every issue can be solved by looking at logs. Troubleshooting MDM communications can be a bit of a tricky. Push notification communications between macOS Server or another MDM and Apple Push Notification are basically the same as troubleshooting the apsd client on macOS. To facilitate troubleshooting, put the APNs daemon, apsd, into debug mode.

To enable APNs debug logging, first set the log level:

```
sudo defaults write /Library/Preferences/com.apple.apsd
APSLogLevel -int 7
```

Then set an APSWriteLogs key to true to actually start writing these entries out:

```
sudo defaults write /Library/Preferences/com.apple.apsd
APSWriteLogs -bool TRUE
```

Then simply restart the daemon:

```
sudo killall apsd
```

Now that you're capturing logs, use tail with the -f option to watch the apsd.log file at /Library/Logs/apsd.log. Be wary, as this can fill up your system:

```
tail -f /Library/Logs/apsd.log
```

So to disable, use these commands, which undo everything we just did:

```
sudo defaults write /Library/Preferences/com.apple.apsd
APSWriteLogs -bool FALSE
sudo defaults delete /Library/Preferences/com.apple.apsd
APSLogLevel
sudo killall apsd
```

Another aspect of troubleshooting APNs and mdm commands would be to check that all of the necessary ports are open. A useful tool for this would be Push Diagnostics available on the Mac app store at `https://apps.apple.com/us/app/push-diagnostics/id689859502`. Once installed, simply open the app and click Start. As seen in Figure 4-25, if all communications flow properly there is a green light for each category. Hover over any that do not work properly to see the status of that one specifically.

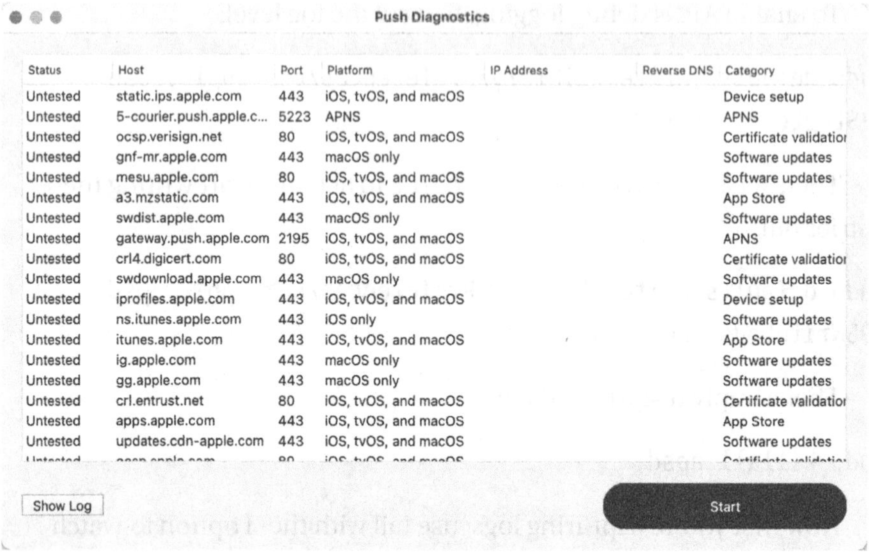

Push Diagnostics

Status	Host	Port	Platform	IP Address	Reverse DNS	Category
Untested	static.ips.apple.com	443	iOS, tvOS, and macOS			Device setup
Untested	5-courier.push.apple.c...	5223	APNS			APNS
Untested	ocsp.verisign.net	80	iOS, tvOS, and macOS			Certificate validatior
Untested	gnf-mr.apple.com	443	macOS only			Software updates
Untested	mesu.apple.com	80	iOS, tvOS, and macOS			Software updates
Untested	a3.mzstatic.com	443	iOS, tvOS, and macOS			App Store
Untested	swdist.apple.com	443	macOS only			Software updates
Untested	gateway.push.apple.com	2195	iOS, tvOS, and macOS			APNS
Untested	crl4.digicert.com	80	iOS, tvOS, and macOS			Certificate validatior
Untested	swdownload.apple.com	443	macOS only			Software updates
Untested	iprofiles.apple.com	443	iOS, tvOS, and macOS			Device setup
Untested	ns.itunes.apple.com	443	iOS only			Software updates
Untested	itunes.apple.com	443	iOS, tvOS, and macOS			App Store
Untested	ig.apple.com	443	macOS only			Software updates
Untested	gg.apple.com	443	macOS only			Software updates
Untested	crl.entrust.net	80	iOS, tvOS, and macOS			Certificate validatior
Untested	apps.apple.com	443	iOS, tvOS, and macOS			App Store
Untested	updates.cdn-apple.com	443	iOS, tvOS, and macOS			Software updates

Show Log   Start

Figure 4-25. *Running Push Diagnostics*

You can also see a more detailed log of what worked and what didn't. As you can see in Figure 4-26, all communications are working as intended.

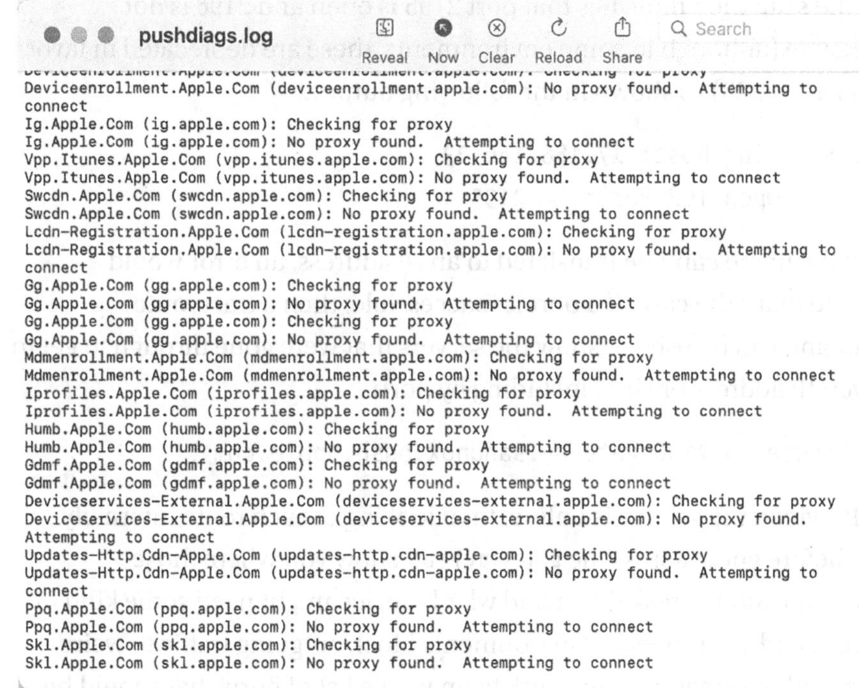

Figure 4-26. *Push Diagnostic logs*

If those communications were not working as they should, you would see a failure in the logs. In that event, there are some techniques for verifying a failure and then possibly isolating where in the communications that the failure occurs. Luckily, macOS comes with a built-in port scanner. So you can use this command, nested inside the Network Utility app, to interrogate a given port manually:

```
/System/Library/CoreServices/Applications/Network\ Utility.
app/Contents/Resources/stroke gateway.sandbox.push.apple.com
2195 2196
```

The scan then indicates that port 2195 is open and 2196 is not accessible (although in some environments, these are deprecated in favor of 443 and 5223) as shown in the following output:

```
Port Scanning host: 17.188.166.23
        Open TCP Port:    2195
```

If the name can't be translated to an IP address, an error would indicate that's the case. If a port is inaccessible, then a traceroute command can be used to show the servers that were gone through to get to a given IP address or URL, including by port:

```
traceroute -p 2196 gateway.sandbox.push.apple.com
```

Provided the service is online, then looking at each route internally (e.g., before going across the gateway) can show you where those communications break down and which device might need some kind of port opened. A number of environments block outgoing traffic to weird ports, and so providing a network team with a list of ports that should be opened to Apple is sometimes necessary.

Sometimes, in testing you find that the Apple services that are foundational for device management are offline. This is why Apple, and any responsible vendor, provides a few locations to find information about the status of hosted services. The two primary locations to look would be

- **System Status**: `www.apple.com/support/systemstatus/` for information on Apple Business Manager, Apple School Manager, App Store, Device Enrollment Program, iCloud, Screen Time, Software Update, and Volume Purchase Program endpoints
- **Developer System Status**: Apple Push Notification services, TestFlight, App Verification, App Store Connect (used by many vendors to look up metadata about apps), `https://developer.apple.com/system-status/`

According to how the developer of any third-party products that you might use for MDM and other related services has integrated those services into their software, if any of these services is down, it might cause other services not to work. Many vendors try not to create service dependencies where possible, but they do happen and can cause services to be unavailable to devices or cause weird artifacts to appear in the software you use to manage devices.

To get more detailed information, many of these services can be contacted directly, for example:

```
curl -v -X POST https://tbsc.apple.com/ucrt/vend2
```

Other troubleshooting options include using the sysdiagnose command and reviewing the log output of that. Now that we've looked at troubleshooting some of the push communications required for devices to receive commands, let's move into one of the more valuable commands: app deployment.

App Deployment

The App Store changed the world of software distribution. First, the App Store came to the iPhone and then the iPad and the Mac. While many developers avoid those stores, it's much simpler to deploy apps through the stores than using the various other mechanisms Apple provides, making management simpler and more secure. Additionally, the cost of each app plummeted since the introduction of the App Store. A number of services have also now moved to a subscription model.

This began before the App Store, with a number of vendors moving to subscriptions for hardware firmware, etc. Apple just did a better job than anyone else at it, turning the services division of the company into a cash cow. But organizations needed to deploy apps to a lot of devices – and so the Volume Purchase Program (VPP) was born. To best understand VPP, it helps to look at how it evolved. In the beginning, teachers were given gift cards. This violated so many basic concepts around financial responsibility in schools and companies, and so Apple engineers started looking at ways to deploy applications to devices that didn't include a gift card.

Gift and VPP Codes

The first stab at large-scale app deployment was using a gift code, which leveraged existing functionality that already existed for the App Store. Basically, you can buy an app or other media on the app store for someone else. You do this by using the Gift This button in the Apple Music Store (not the streaming service) as seen in Figure 4-27.

	NAME	ARTIST	TIME	POPULARITY	PRICE
	Counting Backwards	Throwing Muses	3:15		$1.29
2.	Him Dancing	Throwing Muses	1:10		$1.29
3.	Red Shoes	Throwing Muses	3:33		$1.29
4.	Graffiti	Throwing Muses	2:37		$1.29
5.	Golden Thing	Throwing Muses	2:25		$1.29
6.	Ellen West	Throwing Muses	2:49		$1.29

Gift This Song
Add to Wish List
Tell a Friend
Share On Twitter
Share On Facebook
Copy Link

Figure 4-27. *Gifting an Apple Music asset creates a code*

When you do, the Apple Music Store services sends a gift code to the person you purchased it for. When the link is clicked, iTunes is opened, and you are directed to associate that code to your iTunes account. Rather than associating a code, you can instead harvest those gift codes and deploy a link to buy an app with the gift codes embedded into a buy.itunes.apple.com URL, where 12345678 is replaced with a code:

```
https://buy.itunes.apple.com/WebObjects/MZFinance.woa/wa/com.
apple.jingle.app.finance.DirectAction/freeProductCodeWizard?app
=itunes&code=12345678
```

When the link is used, the gift code is marked as consumed and is no longer able to be used to buy another app. Early versions of VPP were a web service that would track these gift codes and assign them to a device dynamically by deploying the link to the device. The user needed a unique Apple ID on the device, and new codes were added to VPP using a csv that was basically the same thing as the codes as shown in the preceding link. Later, they could be pulled back rather than just deployed. They could also be taken out and added to a csv file.

Volume Purchase Program

The csv with gift codes could also be loaded into Apple Configurator or an MDM that supported that deployment type to deploy the apps (some still do in a hybrid model for backward compatibility). This method consumed codes upon device setup and so was short-lived. But the concept was similar. The fact that most users used personal Apple IDs and once an app was assigned, the ownership was assigned permanently, even when the user left the organization, caused Apple to move to a user assignment service. This is a collection of API services, available at `https://vpp.itunes.apple.com/WebObjects/MZFinance.woa/wa/<serviceName>` (where <servicename> is one of the following):

- **registerVPPUserSrv**: Creates a user in VPP and sends the user an invitation, or if it's a Managed Apple ID, links the Apple ID to the instance. Accounts then use a GUID (clientUserIdStr) for tracking information about the accounts.
- **getVPPUserSrv**: Checks the clientUserIdStr to get the associated itsIdHash or the hash of the Apple ID. This is important philosophically because the MDM server should not know the Apple ID for non-Managed Apple IDs.

- **getVPPUsersSrv**: Responds with a list of users, including those retired, so the MDM can track its own information about those users internally.
- **GetVPPLicensesSrv**: Responds with a list of licenses (adamIds) and the users (in the form of clientUserIdStr) to link which user is consuming which licenses and the remaining license counts.
- **GetVPPAssetsSrv**: Returns adamIds, whether an app is revocable, how it is licensed, and consumption of the available assignments of the licenses owned.
- **retireVPPUserSrv**: Unlinks a user (clientUserIdStr) from the VPP account.
- **manageVPPLicensesByAdamIdSrv**: Associates licenses for apps and other content to the users who will need them and then removes the assignments of that content when needed.
- **editVPPUserSrv**: Used to edit Managed Apple ID information.
- **VPPClientConfigSrv**: Allows organizational information to be pulled from the server.
- **VPPServiceConfigSrv**: contentMetadataLookupUrl a response for obtaining metadata about an app, which includes most things you see on the iTunes or App Store pages for content and apps

The preceding commands can change and are documented at `https://developer.apple.com/documentation/devicemanagement/client_configuration`. Most administrators won't have to interact with these commands directly, although it helps to know what is happening as you're using tools to analyze network traffic when troubleshooting or looking at a device while working on app distribution issues. Most of the preceding commands need to have an sToken. An MDM solution is integrated with that service using a VPP token. The token creates a connection between an MDM solution (e.g., Bushel, Apple's Profile Manager, Casper, etc.) and apps you purchase through the VPP portal. But what's in a token? The VPP token is a base64 encoded file. You can cat the file, and it will show you a bunch of garbly-gook (technical term):

```
base64 --decode /Users/charlesedge/Desktop/kryptedcom.vpptoken
```

This was shown in a screenshot earlier in the chapter, but there's more to it than all that. Once the vpptoken is decoded, this file can display improperly; if it fails, use the following command:

```
echo `cat /Users/charlesedge/Desktop/kryptedcom.vpptoken` |
base64 --decode
```

The contents of the file are then displayed, as follows:


```
{"token":"AbCDe1f2gh3DImSB1DhbLTWviabcgz3y7wkDLbnVA2AIrj9gc1h11
vViMDJ11qoF6Jhqzncw5hW3cV8z1/Yk7A==","expDate":"2022-09-03T08:
30:47-0700","orgName":"Krypted.com"}
```


This is a comma-separated set of keys, including token, expDate, and orgName. Once the sToken is downloaded and installed into your MDM, the token establishes the trust until the expiration date (which should give you plenty of time to renew by). The orgName is what you entered in the VPP portal when you set up the account and is also escaped and then used as the filename, as we covered earlier. Once the sToken is installed, administrators then purchase apps using the VPP store or, if they've moved their sTokens to Apple Business Manager, through the Apple Business Manager front end to the VPP store.

The content purchase experience is pretty straightforward as shown earlier in the chapter. Once you hit purchase, the MDM uses the preview services to keep the purchase history in sync with the vpp endpoints at `https://vpp.itunes.apple.com/WebObjects/MZFinance.woa/wa`. VPP is one of the more challenging services to develop around on the MDM side. Keeping all of that metadata in sync with Apple and dealing with failed API calls when servers aren't responsive can be a challenge. Additionally, for non-Managed Apple IDs, the MDM server is constantly polling the VPP service to see if they have registered with VPP or unregistered.

There are also a lot of flows to how you build VPP into a product, which means there are different interpretations that make it challenging to plan around as an administrator who is a customer of an MDM vendor. One of the more important of these is whether you have supervised or unsupervised devices. You can deploy apps to a supervised device through device-based VPP without the consent of a user. You can deploy apps to a user via an invitation, and they may or may not ever accept your invitation. You can deploy apps to Managed Apple IDs that then appear in the purchase history.

The interactions between VPP and end users are at times challenging to manage. When a user is prompted with various account types, they can change between iOS and macOS versions, as Apple improves the experience with managing how apps get managed on devices. And different vendors implement some of the workflows differently. Therefore, work with each MDM vendor to plan the best workflow for each specific environment.

Managed Open-In

Managed Open-In is a feature that allows organizations to protect the information on devices they provide to employees. When an app is deployed, you can select whether the content that is obtained via the app is managed. If you manage this content, then any data that is provided via the MDM is then no longer accessible outside of other tools provided by that

MDM. For example, if an MDM solution is used to deliver email settings and apps, the users on those devices will only be able to open attachments in the apps that the MDM delivered and cannot use a share sheet to transfer data to an app they loaded themselves. This keeps organizational data out of your user's personal Dropbox account and hopefully makes it easier to remove the organizational data from a device without impacting the rest of the data on the device, such as photos people took of their kids.

The Managed Open-In feature requires Apple's Volume Purchase Program (VPP) for app distribution. For more on this technology, see `www.apple.com/business/resources/docs/Managing_Devices_and_Corporate_Data_on_iOS.pdf`.

Host an .ipa on a Web Server

You can also manually install an app on iOS devices without the use of the app store. This provides a little insight into what's happening behind the scenes of the VPP services. To do so, you'll need to sign the app in Xcode, which is outside the scope of this book. The resulting asset you'll get is an .ipa file (the application bundle) signed by your organization's distribution certificate. The .ipa file can then be loaded into Apple Configurator for distribution or distributed through a web server.

By default, most web servers do have a handler that tells them what to do in the event that a call attempts to access one of these files. Therefore, in order to support downloading those files properly, you need to teach the server how to handle them.

We'll start by obtaining the MIME type from the Mac file command in Terminal. To do so, run the file with the, big surprise, -mime-type option and then the path to the file:

```
file --mime-type /Users/ce/Downloads/enrollmentProfile.
mobileconfig
```

The output would be as follows, indicating that a file with the .mobileconfig extension has the application/octet-stream extension:

```
/Users/ce/Downloads/enrollmentProfile.mobileconfig:
application/octet-stream
```

Since more and more apps are deep linking a plist into the app, we'll also add a plist. The output on a Mac for the various file types is

- .mobileconfig: text/xml or application/octet-stream if signed
- .mobileprovisioning: text/xml or application/octet-stream if signed
- .ipa: application/x-ios-app
- .plist: text/xml or application/octet-stream if a binary plist

In the preceding outputs, note that a signed mobileconfig, a signed mobile provisioning, and a binary plist are basically interpreted as binary files. This means that when possible, use signed mobileconfig and mobileprovisioning files so you have a consistent handler.

We'll start defining those with Apache. Handlers are managed in Apache's global configuration file, often located at /etc/httpd.d/httpd.conf, and you would paste the following toward the bottom of the file where you see the media types (note that each AddType is teaching the web server what type of file each file extension indicates):

```
AddType application/octet-stream .ipa
AddType text/plain .plist
AddType application/octet-stream .mobileconfig
```

In the preceding example, we set a plist to plain in order to show that sometimes it is, given that many an app developer does things differently. Alternatively (or additively if you need to host both binary and flat plist files), you could create an .htaccess file in the directory with the files (e.g., if you don't have root access to change the httpd.conf), by adding something similar (the # is indicating a commented line):

```
# Apps
AddType application/octet-stream .ipa
AddType application/octet-stream .plist
AddType application/octet-stream .mobileconfig
```

For IIS, you would instead go into IIS Manager and right-click the name of the server, select Properties, and click New... in order to create new MIME types. Then add each using the preceding types.

To add a MIME type on nginx, edit the mime.types file in the conf directory for nginx. This is often found in /etc/nginx or /opt/nginx but ymmv. Once found, in mime.types look for a types section wrapped in curly braces {}:

```
types { application/octet-stream mobileprovision; application/
octet-stream mobileconfig; application/octet-stream plist;
application/octet-stream ipa; }
```

Note In some cases, you might find that "application/x-apple-aspen-config" and in others text/plain or text/xml work better for .mobileconfig MIME types. For more on this, see the official Apple documentation at `https://developer.apple.com/documentation/devicemanagement/account_configuration`.

If you have failures, you can use a proxy to check it. Here, you'd probably want to use a unique port number to make calls easier to use. If you use Charles Proxy, you'd configure the proxy in the Wi-Fi settings of an iOS device and then open the link in a browser and watch for any failures. You can create app provisioning profiles in Xcode at the time the app is built.

Sign and Resign macOS Applications

The codesign command-line tool is used to sign applications and packages. If you have an .app, then you'll need to first load a certificate that can be used to sign an app onto the Mac being used and then point it at the app to be signed. Any time you alter an .app, you'll want to do this, and before doing so, you'll want to make sure that the certificate you're using to sign the app is either from a public CA or has been distributed to client computers.

As an example, let's use the codesign command to sign the Microsoft Word application using a certificate called pretendcocert that's been loaded in your keychain. Here, we'd use the codesign command followed by the -s option to sign and then the name of the cert followed by an escaped (or quoted) path to the app bundle, as follows:

```
codesign -s mycert /Applications/Microsoft\ Office\ 2021/
Microsoft\ Word.app
```

This has become more of a challenge since Apple implemented various controls to validate the authenticity of software as a part of App Notarization, covered in the next section - especially for software that's submitted to the App Store. However, the codesign command is capable of much more, but isn't the only tool that administrators need to learn to distribute applications. You could then perform similar operations on iOS using techniques similar to those described: `https://docs.microsoft.com/en-us/intune/app-wrapper-prepare-ios`.

App Notarization

As of 10.14.5, Apple requires that all software be notarized (and signed) by Apple. This is referred to as App Notarization. In order for Apple to sign software, they check the software to make sure it's safe, and for new apps, developers will require that all software be notarized, including apps and extensions (most will have dylibs disabled for further protection). Submitting an app for notarization is easy. We'll cover using the xcrun command-line tool with the altool verb to do so. But first, there are some requirements you should know about:

- The notarization service uses an automated scan that usually takes about 20 minutes and requires at least the 10.9 macOS SDK.
- Before submitting, make sure code signing has been enabled for all executables and that you enabled the Hardened Runtime option.
- Find a workaround if you're setting com.apple.security.get-task-allow to true for any reason.
- Make sure to use an Apple Developer ID instead of a local cert from Xcode for apps and kexts. And make sure all code signing certs have a timestamp when running your distribution workflows in Xcode, or if using codesign, make sure to add –timestamp.

Now we'll need to use xcrun with the altool. Here, we'll use the –notarize-app option and then define the bundle. This is done using the reverse naming convention you've always used for the –primary-bundle-id option and then the username and password from your Apple ID linked to your Developer ID and finally the –file which is the zipped output from Xcode:

```
#!/bin/bash
/usr/bin/xcrun altool --notarize-app --primary-bundle-
id "com.myorg.myproduct" --username "krypted@myorg.com"
--password "icky_passwords" --file "/Users/krypted/Documents/
myproduct.zip"
```

You can use any tools to build this into your development pipeline. In this example, we'll use the open source Bamboo solution as the postflight from our xcrun workflow. We'll start by naming our script /usr/bambooscripts/notarize.sh and then follow these tasks to get the build automation step in place (Figure 4-28):

- Open the Tasks configuration tab for a job (or default job in a new plan).
- Click Add Task.
- Add a Task Description, which is just how the task is described in the Bamboo interface.
- Uncheck the box to "Disable this task."
- Provide a path to the command executable, which in this case will be a simple bash script that we'll call /usr/bambooscripts/notarize.sh. If you're stringing workflows together, you might add other scripts as well (e.g., a per-product script as opposed to a generic script that takes positional parameters for arguments).
- Provide any necessary arguments. In this case, it'll just be a simple job, but you can reduce the work by adding arguments for processing paths of different products.
- Provide any necessary environment variables. We won't use any in this project.

- Provide any necessary "Working Sub Directory" settings, which is an alternative directory, rather than using a relative path. If you don't provide a working subdirectory, note that Bamboo looks for build files in the root directory.
- Click the Save button (as you can see in Figure 4-28).

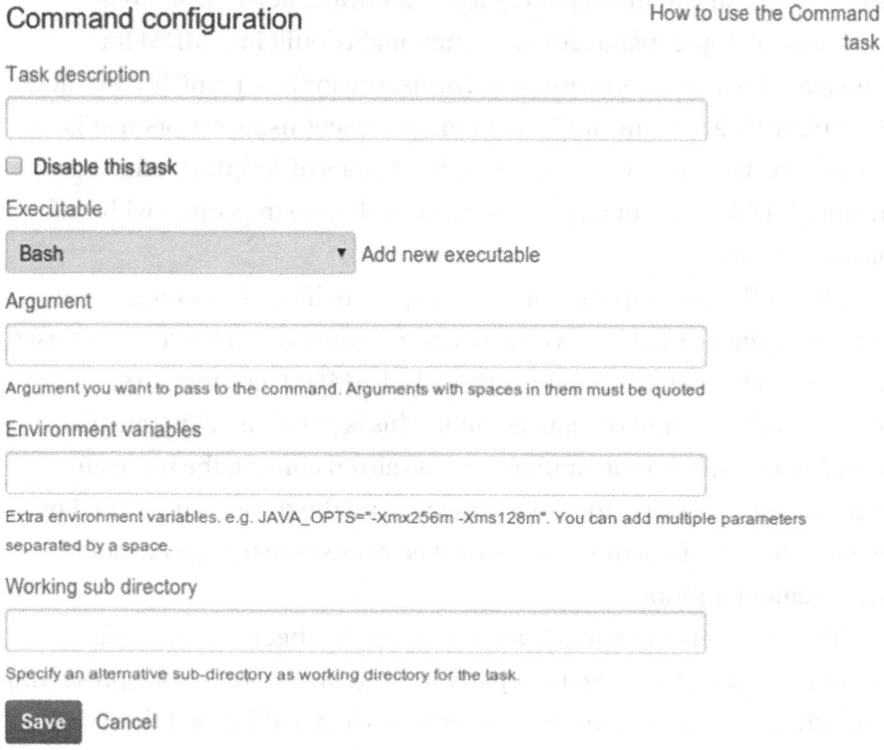

***Figure 4-28.** Automate Bamboo tasks*

As you can see, the actual notarization process with Apple isn't that big of a deal. What can be more challenging is to resolve any issues Apple may find with software before it can pass the notarization checks and to deal with latency issues. This type of code change is based on the app you might be developing (or resigning) and therefore beyond the scope of this book. We do pick up more on app distribution and automation in Chapter 9.

Summary

MDM is the built-in management agent for Apple devices. MDM is the future of Apple management. Functionality built into MDM for management increases every year. This is true for iOS, iPadOS, tvOS, and macOS. For macOS, the ability to manage devices using scripts seems to conversely decrease every year (and the options of scripting languages), making MDM-based management more and more important with each passing release.

The addition of supervision allows Apple to limit the management options available on devices a given organization doesn't own. Supervised devices can be managed more granularly. UAMDM also increases or decreases the amount of management. This is part of a deliberate plan from Apple to allow more and more centralized control, the more an organization can prove they own a device and the device isn't owned by an employee, and the more the employee chooses to opt into various management options.

iOS device management is simple. Apple has been able to scale offerings (especially using third-party management tools) while preserving that privacy of the humans that use their devices. iOS has led the way, but the Mac is quickly catching up. As an example, it's easy to imagine a time when apps on a Mac will only be self-contained .app bundles and when the only deployment method for those apps in large organizations will be via the App Store or MDM. The installation package has been around for a long time and gives software developers the ability to distribute a number of different kinds of files, fonts, and automation scripts to run when an app is installed. But Apple has been locking down all of those technologies for a long time. There's no reason to think MDM won't be the only real way to manage an Apple device in a few years (although we said that in the first edition of this book as well).

Volume distribution of applications is another place where Apple takes great care to put a line in the sand between institutional data and personal data. The device management tools don't know the Apple ID of a user unless it's a Managed Apple ID. The device management tools can't install an app on a device without a user's approval unless it is a supervised device. In macOS 10.15, Apple also added a whole new enrollment type, putting all data from a Managed Apple ID onto a separate partition on a computer. This attention to detail is one of the reasons that people want Apple devices, but the lack of programmatic management here and there certainly seems to chafe some administrators.

Now that we've pulled back the covers a bit to expose what's going on behind the scenes with Apple device management, let's look to get devices into the hands of our coworkers, starting with iOS Provisioning, in Chapter 5.

CHAPTER 5

iOS Provisioning

Imaging. We used to say that we "imaged" computers. An image was a perfect representation of a device that was ready to go into the hands of a user. The images were often monolithic or later packages that created an end result that still appeared like one completed monolith. But then came iOS and then iPadOS. Administrators didn't "image" iOS or iPadOS devices as much as they "prepared" them, or at least that's what the buttons in the software said at the time. These days, preparing a device to go into the hands of an end user is more about provisioning the device to a user than it is about imaging the device.

Eventually, the content of Chapters 4 and 5 will be merged as the technology itself converges to tell a similar management story for all Apple platforms. Until then, we will use the same process to prepare an iPhone, iPad, or Mac. For some environments, this might have already happened ever since the M1 Macs began to ship. But imaging never entered into the vernacular for iOS. You could restore a signed operating system to a device in the form of exploding the files from a compressed file of the iOS operating system, which is distributed as an ipsw file provided by Apple that can't be altered. That's now possible on an M1 Mac. This would be expanded onto the disk of an iPhone or iPad. And you could deploy a profile to enroll the device into a Mobile Device Management, or MDM, solution, using a tool like Apple's Profile Manager (or Apple Business Essentials for newer entrants into the Mac Admin community), until the Device Enrollment Program, or DEP, made that unnecessary. This is another example of how the technology from iOS benefits the Mac.

C. Edge and R. Trouton, *Apple Device Management*,
https://doi.org/10.1007/978-1-4842-9156-6_5

When we say "imaging" a Mac, we typically think of erasing a device and putting new bits on the device in the form of a fully functional operating system on the filesystem of the device. This gives the device everything a user needs to get their work done - and doing so by restoring a monolithic "image" to the device is the simplest step when deploying a device for the first time. First, we moved from monolithic imaging to package-based imaging. Then we moved from package-based imaging to restoring a "thin" image or one with just the operating system and an agent. Then Apple gave us the Device Enrollment Program (or DEP for short), and we went to skipping that step and taking devices out of the box with the default operating system. This allowed users to do the imaging on the fly that many large organizations used to pay $20–$40 per device to have done off-site. Automated Device Enrollment automatically enrolls the device into MDM, puts apps on the device, and puts the agent on the device through MDM. There are less options, but the process has never been so streamlined with such a small amount of work.

Shipping devices directly to a user makes people feel like they're getting the new device they were always getting. That "new device feel" is special. Once administrators had everything necessary to provision a device out of the box, Apple released the APFS filesystem (or Apple Filesystem), and the native restrictions for restoring became common on the Mac. It was a learning curve but ultimately one that makes our lives better. Opening the plastic on a device also makes the users feel more empowered to care for the device, like they would if they went to the Apple store and paid for it.

Operating system updates for iOS were always free (except that one time early on, but we don't need to go into that). Mac updates became free and simplified the distribution process while allowing users to always run the latest operating system. By making the operating system free, Apple was then able to simplify the options for reinstalling macOS.

There are certainly differences still, though. Therefore, this chapter covers the items specific to iOS. It's also useful for those who work with the Mac exclusively, as the Mac has been trending toward iOS when it comes to deployment for years (especially with regard to how Apple Configurator is used).

iOS Provisioning

As mentioned, in a perfect world, administrators can send a device to a user directly from Apple or a reseller, the user opens the device, and all of the magic happens to put that device into a state where it just works with the organization's environment. Behind the scenes, a lot goes into how admins can make that happen. We've discussed many of those building blocks. In Chapter 3, we covered Profiles. In Chapter 4, we covered MDM. There are still some gaps; and many are more logistical than they are technical. There are times when automated enrollment doesn't do everything an organization might need.

For starters, you have to get on a Wi-Fi network in order to be able to enroll an iOS device into MDM, even with Automated Device Enrollment. This means a user has to join the network, and so if you use 802.1x or need an agent to be able to enroll, there's a chicken and egg situation. Some organizations use Ethernet adapters for iPads to get those certificates going and to kickstart those communications. Others need a completely over-the-air workflow assuming users are never in the office. Most environments are somewhere in the middle, so we'll cover the options available for provisioning iOS devices in this section, starting with doing so using Apple Configurator.

Prepare an iOS Device Using Apple Configurator

In Chapter 3, we used Apple Configurator to create profiles, but it can be used for much, much more. In this chapter, we'll build out a workflow to get certificates on devices (also using profiles), but just as importantly we'll take some actions on those devices to provide a consistent user experience.

One theme of this book is that in the Apple world, we don't like to be heavy-handed with management (unless necessary in high-security environments). But we do like to ensure devices meet our requirements in order to join networks, and we like to make the experience of getting a new device as frictionless as possible, so the people who use them don't avoid making eye contact in the hallways! Apple Configurator gives us a lot of the tools to do just that. Because not all devices are handled the same, we typically begin by grouping our workflows into what are known as Blueprints. In the next section, we'll install Apple Configurator and create our first Blueprints.

Install Apple Configurator

Apple Configurator is available on the App Store. It can be run from iOS or Mac. For the purposes of this chapter, we'll use it on a Mac. To download it, simply go to the App Store and search for Configurator and then click or tap Install. Once installed, open Configurator, agree to the licensing terms, and at the Get Started screen (Figure 5-1), click Get Started.

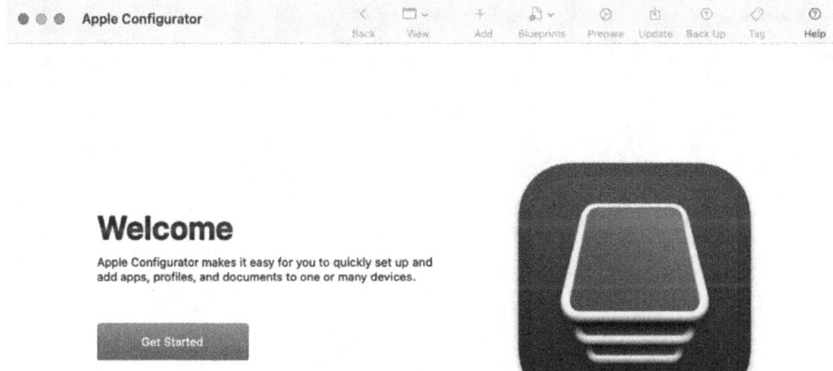

Figure 5-1. *Create a blueprint*

The Configurator screen will then look a little lonely because the initial screen has no settings yet (Figure 5-2). The main tasks the tool is used for are to back up, to "restore" a device backup, add content (apps, documents, or profiles), remove content, modify the look of a device (e.g., wallpapers), and associate devices with Automated Enrollment that weren't properly associated at the time of purchase.

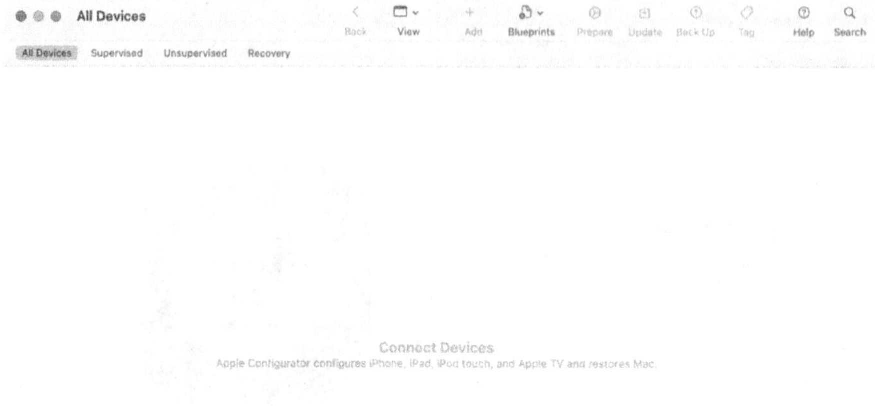

***Figure 5-2.** Configurator is full of promise, but has no devices yet*

Most of the things that we'll use Configurator for will require an Apple ID for the organization (like the one associated with the MDM) to be used with it. To sign in, click Account and then Sign In (Figure 5-3). When prompted, provide the credentials for the organization and select a location if applicable (both of these are from Apple Business Manager or Apple School Manager and covered in Chapter 3).

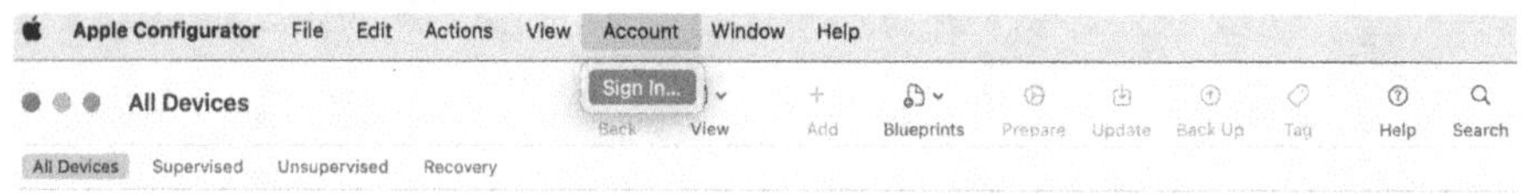

***Figure 5-3.** Sign in to an admin Apple ID for the organization*

Provide a second factor for authentication if prompted, and then it's time to create the first blueprints.

Create Blueprints

Blueprints allow administrators to configure a template of settings, options, apps, and operating systems. Blueprints are applied to an iOS device, which represents a predefined workflow. For example, if you have 1000 iOS devices, you can create a blueprint with a restore item, an enrollment profile, or a default wallpaper. You can also skip all of the activation steps, install four apps, and then enable encrypted backups. The blueprint provides all of these features to any device that the blueprint is applied to.

Note In the following sections, we'll look at a lot of different options. They're all optional, according to what it is your organization needs to accomplish.

Keep in mind that they're called Blueprints because you're not dynamically making changes to devices over the air or grouping devices. Instead, you're making changes to devices when you apply that blueprint or workflow to the device. To get started, open Apple Configurator and click the Blueprints button and then click Edit Blueprints. Notice that when working on Blueprints, you'll always have a blue bar toward the bottom of the screen. Figure 5-4 shows a blank slate so you can start building workflows. Once created, Blueprints are tiled on the screen, although as you get more and more of them, you can view them in a list.

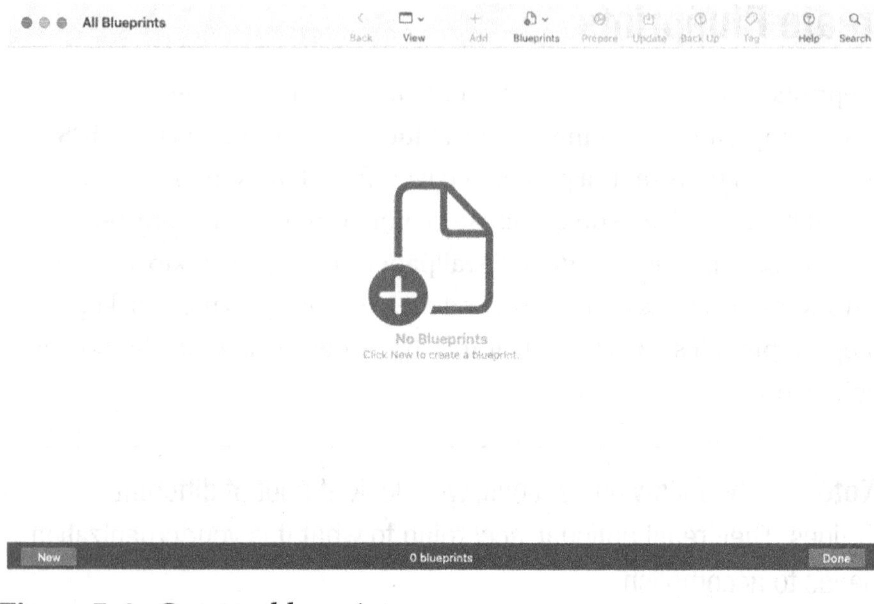

Figure 5-4. *Create a blueprint*

Click the New button to create the first blueprint. Here, give it a name and then double-click it once created. You'll have a number of options which we'll describe later in this chapter including

- Install or remove apps and documents.
- Change the name of devices en masse, using variables.
- For supervised devices, you can change the wallpaper of devices and modify the layout of apps.
- Update software.
- Install or remove profiles.
- Back up and restore saved backups onto devices.
- Perform some actions, such as caching an unlock token so you can reset passcodes, putting devices into kiosk mode, and wiping devices.

You can also configure automated enrollment. But for an increasing number of environments, before we can enroll, we need to get a certificate to join a wireless network.

Manage Content

We can manage files on disks. Configuration files are stored in what are known as profiles or xml files (as covered in Chapter 3). These can be used to distribute apps, to install certificates, and to deploy content to devices.

Add Certificates for 802.1x with Profiles to Blueprints

One of the tasks you'll need to perform in Apple Configurator is to assign Profiles to iOS devices in order to set them up with features or restrict the device from using certain features. Adding a certificate to a device and configuring the device to join a wireless network is pretty common and a fairly simple workflow. To get started, open a Blueprint or create a new Blueprint. Then follow along with these steps:

1. From the screen for that Blueprint, click Profiles in the sidebar (Figure 5-5).
2. If you're working with a new Blueprint and creating a new profile, click the File menu and click New Profile.
3. Next, provide a name for the profile in the Name field. In this example, we just called the profile 802.1x.
4. Leave the identifier in the Identifier field.

5. Click in the Organization field and provide the name of your organization.

6. Click Description and provide a brief explanation of what the profile is meant to do (this is nice for the next person who needs to manage what you're working on).

7. Consent is rarely required with Apple Configurator-based workflows, but you can provide a message that an end user has to tap at the time of the deployment. Apple Configurator is often used to reduce taps, not increase them, so this is not likely to be necessary.

8. Optionally, if you want users to be able to remove the profile, leave the Security option set to Always. You can also set it to Never so the profile can only be removed through Apple Configurator or with Authorization, which requires a passcode to remove the profile.

9. Use Automatically Remove Profile if you want the profile removed at a certain date or amount of time.

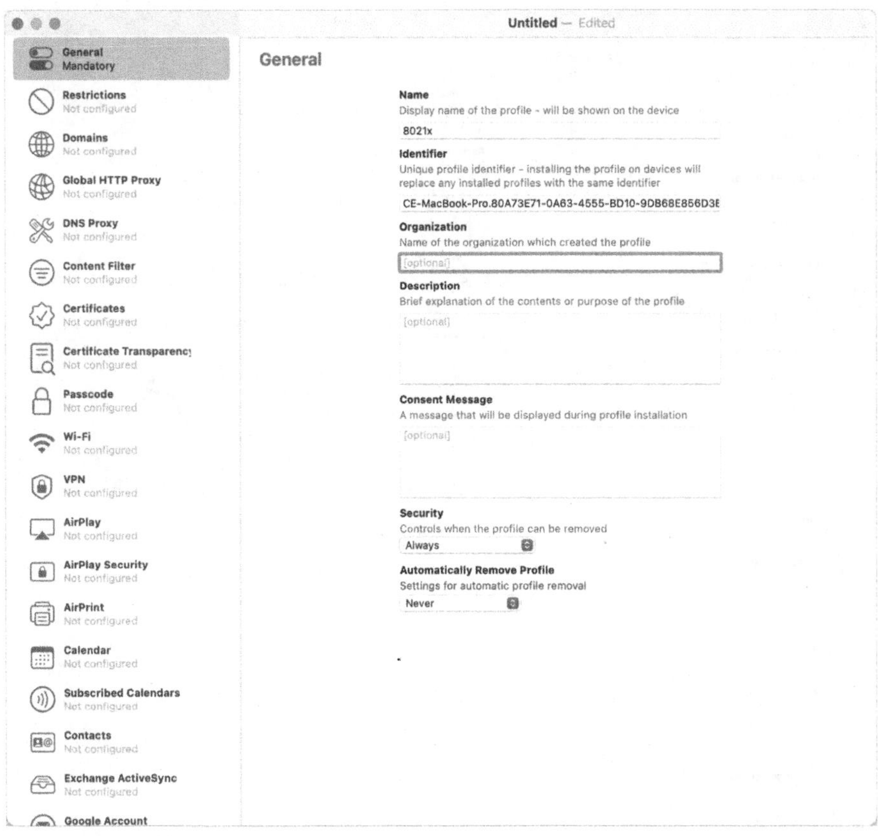

Figure 5-5. *Naming your profile*

10. Next, click the Certificates profile in the sidebar and click Configure.

11. When prompted, select a .p12 file and click OK.

12. At the Certificates screen, provide the password required to open the p12 (Figure 5-6).

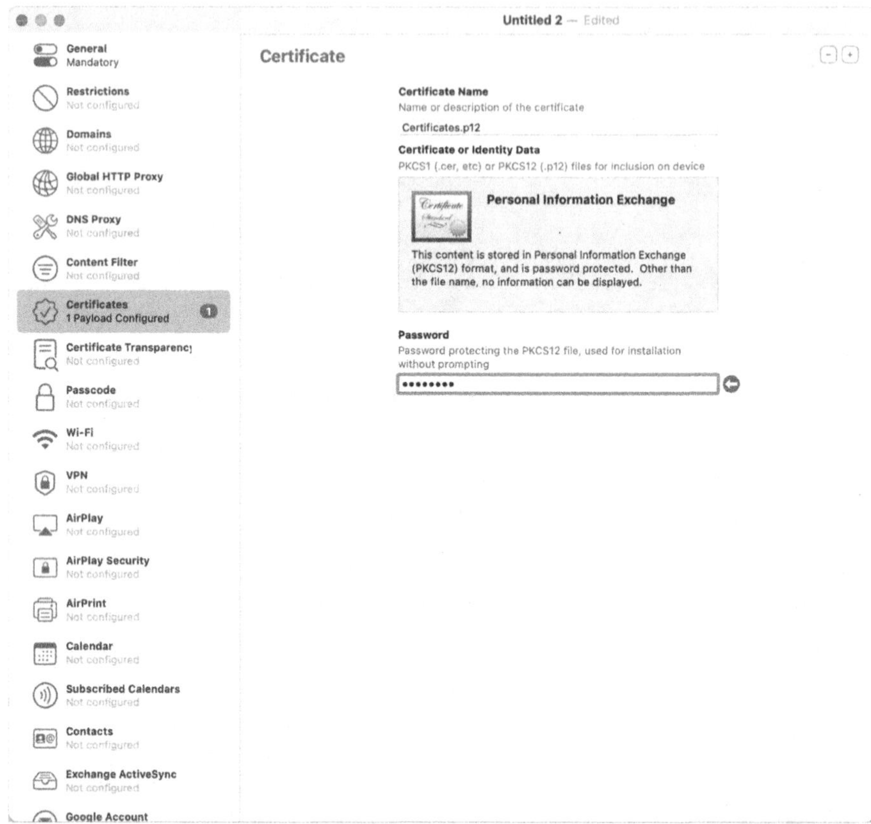

Figure 5-6. *Select your certificate to use with the profile*

13. Click Wi-Fi and click Configure.
14. Provide the name of the wireless network in the "Service Set Identifier (SSD)" field.
15. If the network name is suppressed, check the box for Hidden Network.
16. If you want the device to automatically join the network, check the box for Auto Join. You likely want that box checked any time you're using Apple Configurator as, again, you're trying to minimize the number of taps on devices.

17. If a proxy server is required, configure those settings using the Proxy Setup options.
18. Set the Security Type (in Figure 5-7, we're using TLS, so we'll select "WPA/WPA2 Enterprise" and then check the box for TLS), but a lot of environments use a lot of different settings, so work with a network administrator if needed.

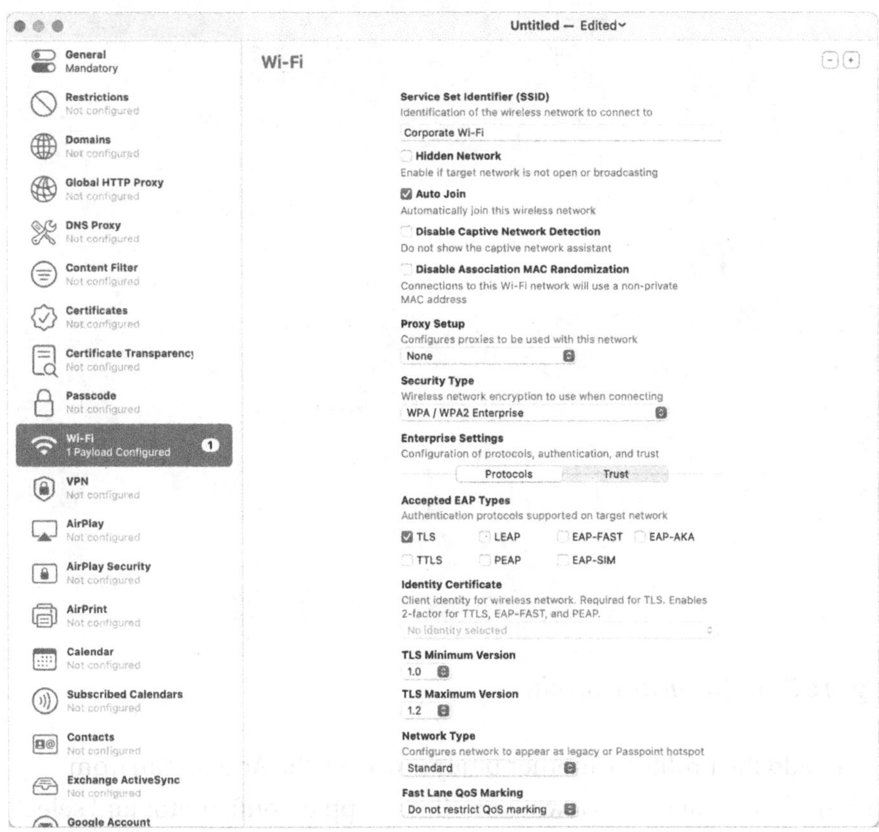

***Figure 5-7.** Change the Security Type to see more options*

Once you've configured the profile, click the close button (the red jelly marked with an x in the upper-left corner of the screen). When prompted, provide a name and location for the profile, as you can see in Figure 5-8.

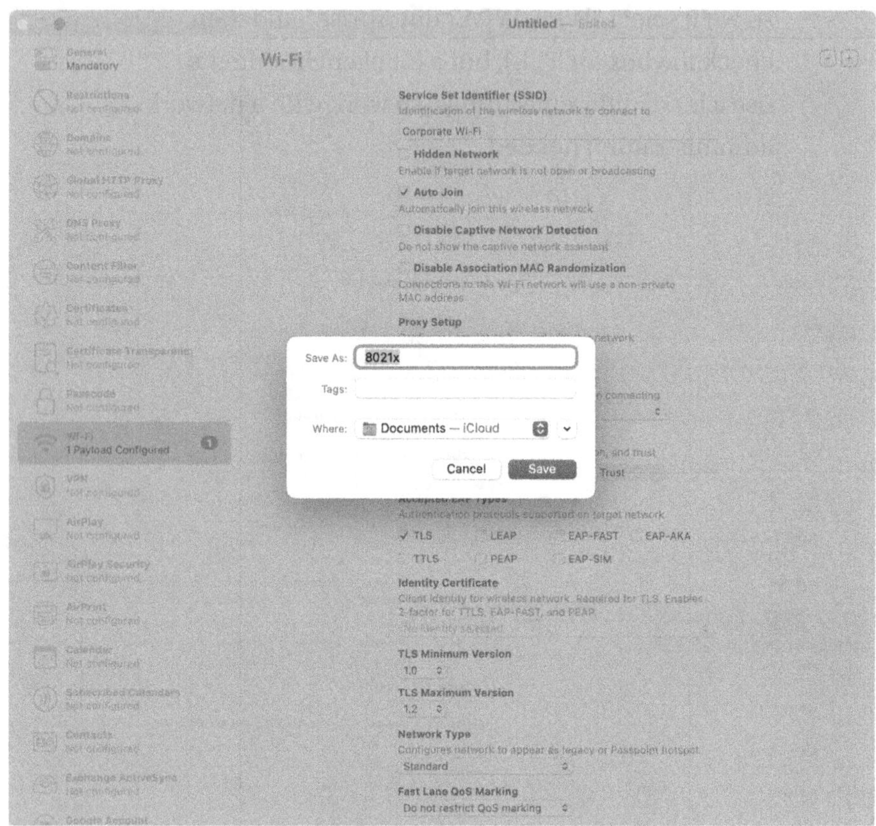

***Figure 5-8.** Name the profile*

To add the profile to another blueprint, click the Add button from within a blueprint when viewing profiles in Apple Configurator and select the file location. You can also add a profile that you export from your MDM solution by simply copying it to a secure location on the computer and doing that last step. This will help keep you from doing duplicate work in two different tools. Now that we can add profiles to prepare a device for distribution, let's look at getting apps on the device - but keep in mind that when you have the option to push an app from Apple Configurator or an MDM, use the MDM so that it can be managed dynamically once deployed.

Install Apps with Apple Configurator

One reason to use Apple Configurator to push an app to a device is if there are 10 or 20 gigs of apps (which could be 10 or 100 apps) to install, as that data transfer might go faster over a USB cable than it will over the air from the App Store, especially if you're preparing a lot of devices at once. In this section, we'll look at a basic app deployment using Apple Configurator, which can be added to the Wi-Fi and certificates payloads we prepared previously.

To get started, first make sure an Apple ID that is an administrator of the Apple Business Manager or Apple School Manager portal is logged in to Apple Configurator. Then, open a Blueprint, click Apps, and click Add Apps... (Figure 5-9).

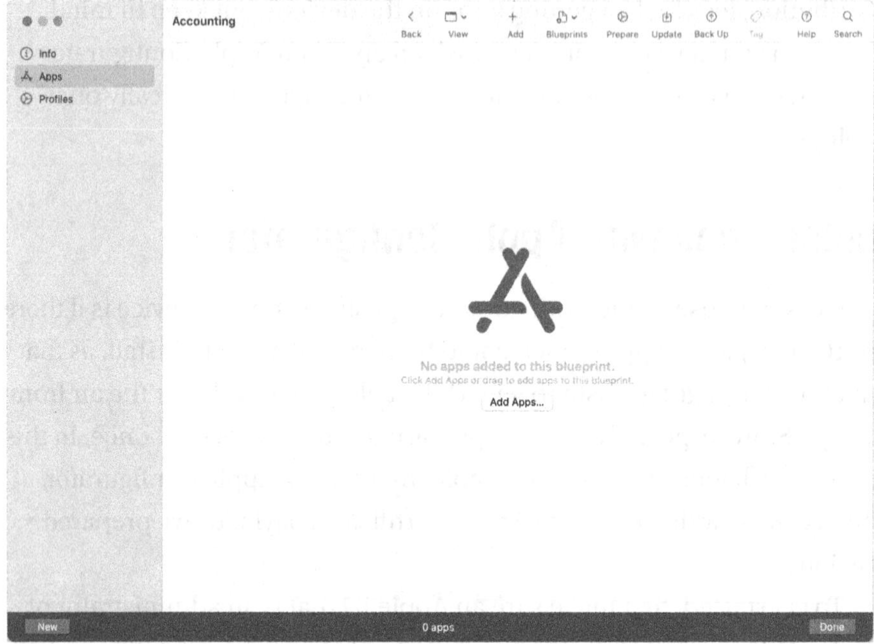

***Figure 5-9.** Add Apps to a Blueprint*

Next, view the apps that were acquired with the volume purchase App Store account setup for the organization in Chapter 4. Optionally, enter the name of the app in the search dialog. Click the app and then click Add (Figure 5-10).

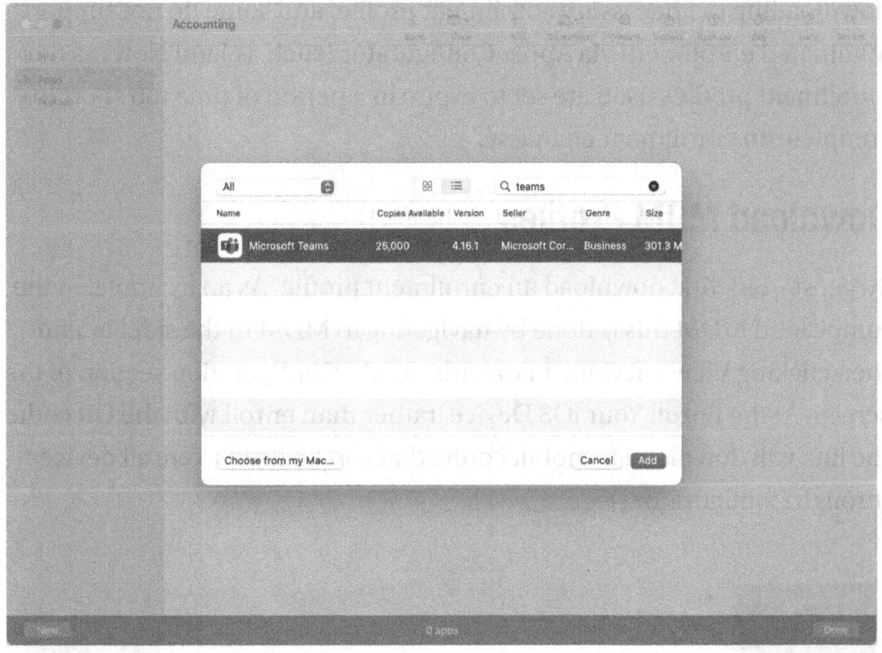

Figure 5-10. *Select the App*

Once the app has been added, any device the blueprint is applied to then receives the app. You can also assign an app to a device manually. To do so, control-click (or right-click) a device and then use Add to choose the Apps... option. Next, we'll configure automatic enrollment, so the device gets added to the MDM server used in your environment when being prepared.

Automate Enrollment with Apple Configurator

When doing larger deployments, the initial enrollment process can be automated so that devices are automatically enrolled into an MDM when set up using an enrollment profile. We won't focus on getting the enrollment profile in this section as much as how to add it to Apple Configurator, given that each MDM vendor provides a different way of downloading the necessary enrollment profile, and some do not support automated enrollment via Apple Configurator (such as Jamf Now) as the enrollment profiles used are set to expire in a period of time too short to complete an enrollment en masse.

Download MDM Profiles

To get started, first download an enrollment profile. As an example, in the JumpCloud MDM this is done by navigating to MDM in the sidebar and then clicking View QR Code in the Admin iOS Configuration section of the screen. At the Enroll Your iOS Device, rather than enroll with the QR code, the link will download a .mobileconfig that can be used to enroll devices through Configurator (Figure 5-11).

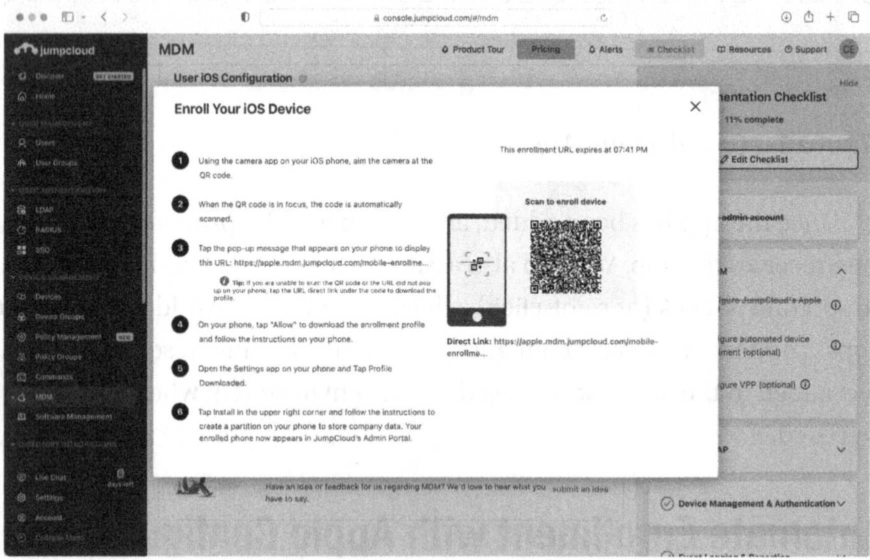

Figure 5-11. Download the JumpCloud MDM profile

If using Jamf Pro, there's an option to download the Enrollment Profile in the sidebar of the Devices screen as well (Figure 5-12).

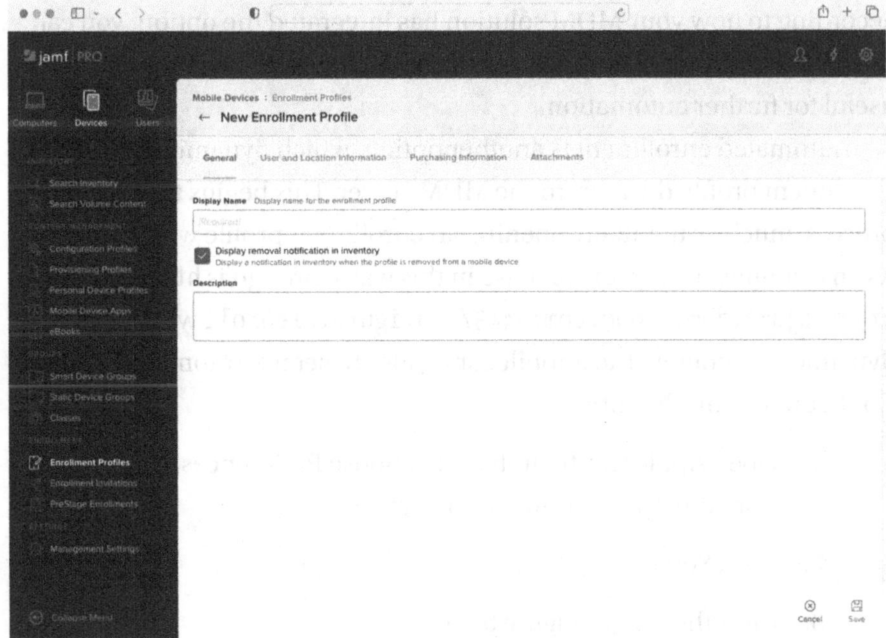

Figure 5-12. *Download the Jamf MDM profile*

Additionally, a certificate from the CA of an MDM server can be needed if the certificate is not included in the profile and the device doesn't trust the server, an option available as a checkbox in the setup. This is a good reason to use certificates from a valid CA rather than using self-signed certificates. Once you have the enrollment profile (a .mobileconfig file), then it's time to configure automated enrollment as a part of your blueprint (just make sure the profile doesn't expire too quickly). To do so, simply add the enrollment profile to the profiles options as we did in the previous section of this chapter.

Configure Automated Enrollment in Apple Configurator

Automated enrollment requires less work on the administrative side, but according to how your MDM solution has integrated the option, you can associate a number of metadata attributes in the MDM server that can be useful for further automation.

Automated enrollment is another option, which dynamically pulls the enrollment profile down from the MDM server. This begins the enrollment process, much as manually opening an enrollment profile would do. As an example, the server we'll use in this walk-through is `https://kryptedjamf.jamfcloud.com:8443/configuratorenroll` which can dynamically generate the .mobileconfig file. To set up Automated Apple Configurator Enrollment:

1. Open Apple Configurator and choose Preferences from the Apple Configurator 2 menu.
2. Click Servers.
3. Click the + sign (Figure 5-13).

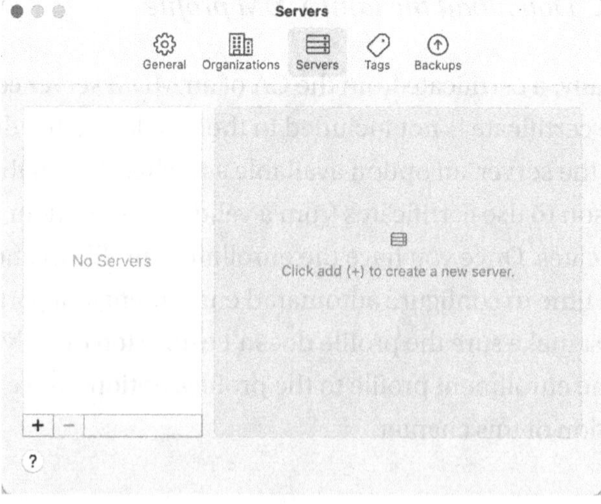

Figure 5-13. *Add a server for automated enrollment*

4. At the Define an MDM Server screen, click Next.
5. At the next screen, in the Name field provide a name, such as “My MDM Server.”
6. Complete the “Host Name or URL” field as seen in Figure 5-14.

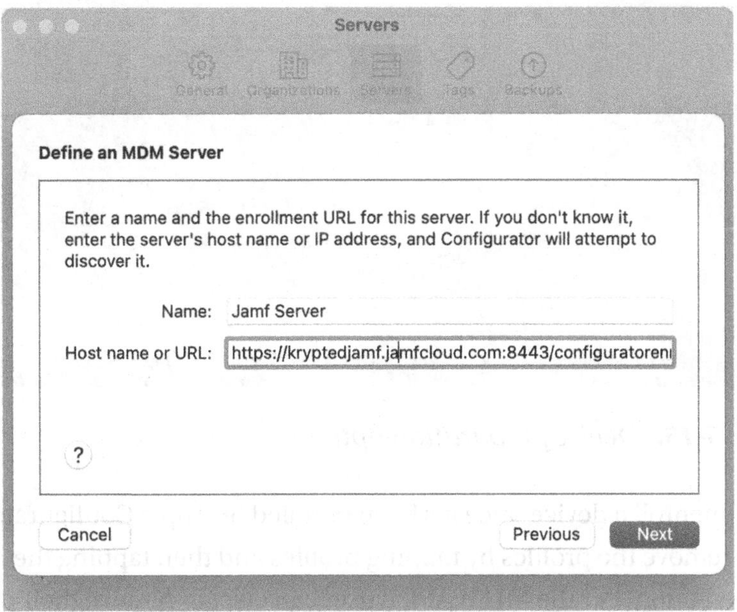

***Figure 5-14.** Provide the URL to your MDM Server to use for automated enrollment*

7. Apple Configurator will then download any required trust certificates, and the “Define an MDM Server” wizard will complete. Once you see your MDM server listed, the process is complete.

We won’t cover preparing devices just yet, but Automated Enrollment will then be an option when you go to prepare (Figure 5-15).

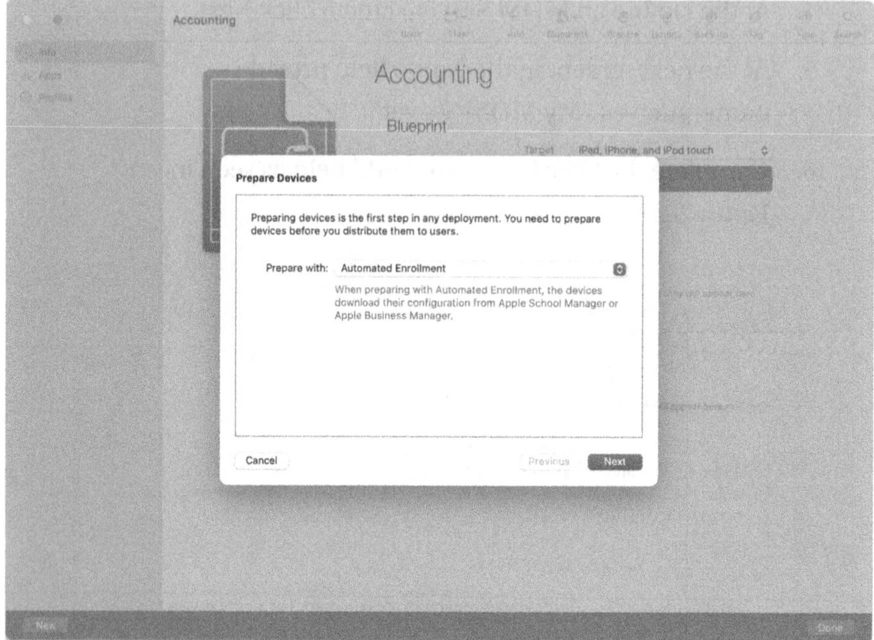

Figure 5-15. *Device preparation options*

To unenroll a device once it's been enrolled by Apple Configurator, simply remove the profiles by tapping profiles and then tapping the Remove button. Per the MDM API, a user can elect to remove their device from management at any point unless the device is supervised, so expect this will happen occasionally, even if only by accident.

Now that we've looked at automating MDM enrollment, let's move to customizing each device, starting with naming them so it's easier to manage devices once they're in the hands of a user (or 1000 users).

Change Device Names Using Apple Configurator

Apple Configurator can also rename iOS devices. This is done in an automated fashion when devices are prepared (or when the workflow provided in a blueprint is implemented on the device). This is important because a device name can be used to implement further automations once enrolled in an MDM solution, or it can be used to quickly identify devices when troubleshooting.

To use Apple Configurator to rename a device, plug it into a Mac running Apple Configurator and then right-click the device and choose Device Name... from the Modify menu. More importantly, to associate a rename action in the preparation of a device, follow these steps:

1. Open a blueprint.
2. Select Device Name under the Modify submenu of Actions.
3. At the Rename device menu, shown in Figure 5-16, provide the name you want a device to have, followed by a variable, available using the + menu.

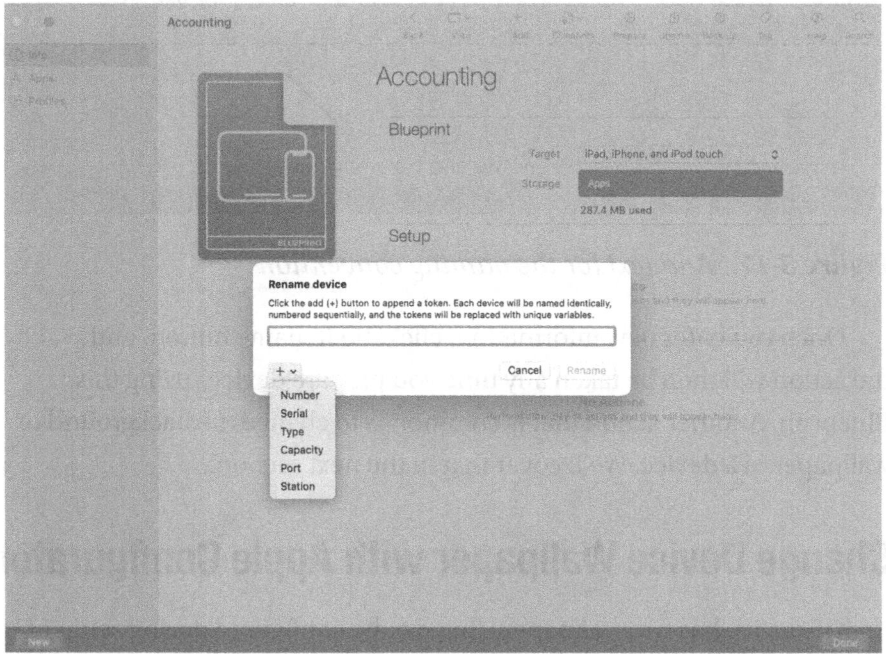

***Figure 5-16.** Select Serial Number for a naming convention*

4. In Figure 5-17, we used Accounting since we're mass configuring Accounting devices, followed by Serial, so if a device has a serial number of 123abc, then the name of the device would be "Accounting-abc123."

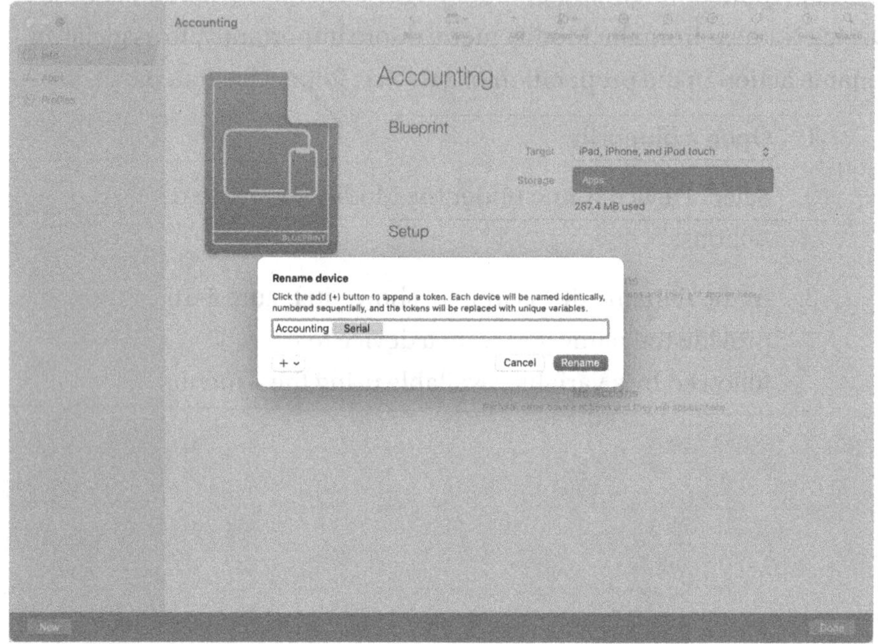

***Figure 5-17.** Add text for the naming convention*

Once you enter new information, click the Rename button, and the action will then be taken any time you prepare devices using this Blueprint. Another action that is common is to change the background or wallpaper of a device. We'll cover that in the next section.

Change Device Wallpaper with Apple Configurator

An iOS device has two wallpapers that can be configured during setup of devices: home screen and lock screen. The home screen is the image that you see with apps on top of it. This should be simple so as not to distract from finding the app a user is looking for. In this example, we'll apply a Sales background to the lock screen so we can easily identify the sales devices when handing them out to sellers.

Before you begin, save the image or images to a local directory on the computer running Apple Configurator. Then follow this process to set wallpapers:

1. Right-click the device and choose the Modify menu and then Wallpapers... from the Modify submenu.

2. When prompted, use the Choose image... button (Figure 5-18) to set the lock screen (the screen that is displayed when the device is locked).

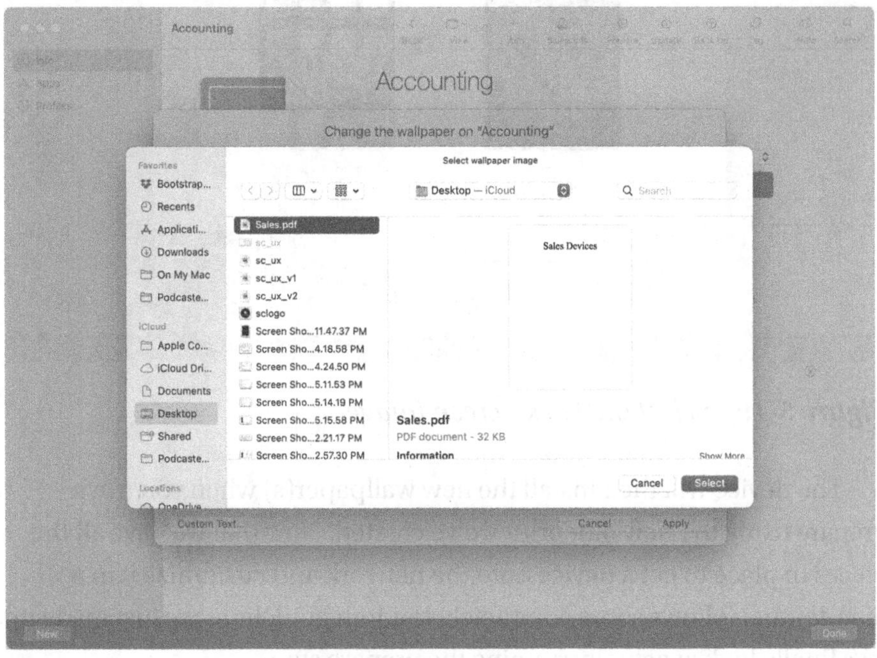

Figure 5-18. Select your wallpaper image

3. Repeat that process to set the home screen (the background behind all your icons on each screen of the iPhone or iPad).

4. Once you have chosen the appropriate images, click the Apply button (Figure 5-19).

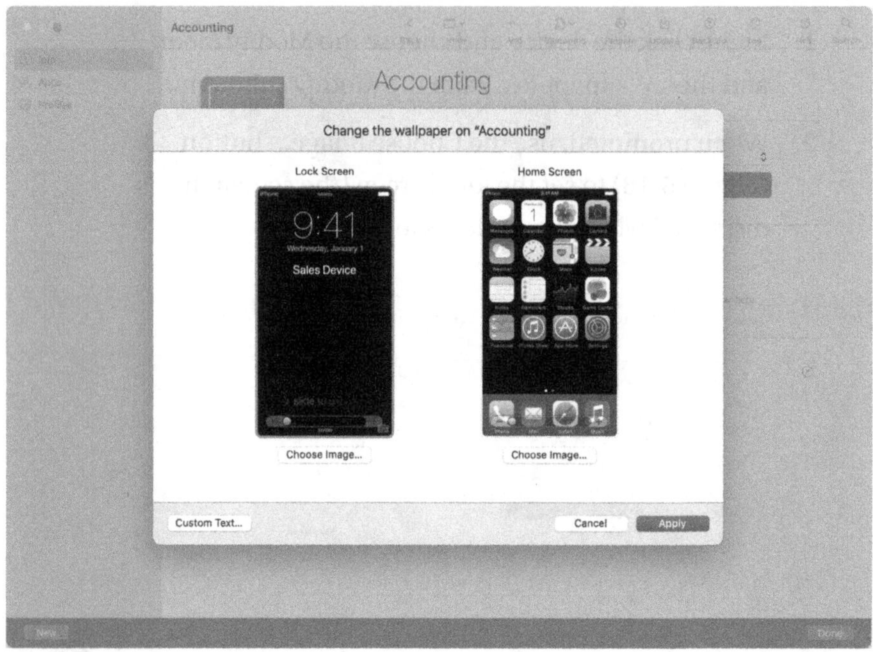

Figure 5-19. *Select the Lock Screen image*

The device will then install the new wallpaper(s) when you run a prepare using the new blueprint we've created. Now that we have all the pieces in place to get a device onto the network and customize it in a manner that follows some completely random guidelines we just made up, let's finally look at actually running the prepare step.

Prepare a Device

Device preparation is the act of running a workflow on a device. This isn't a preset as you're meant to configure the steps to run each time you run a new session of Apple Configurator. This is to say you run a wizard to configure the setups in preparing devices each time. This is why we put as much logic into the blueprint as possible. Preparing also requires the computer running Apple Configurator to be run while online (e.g., in order to access the App Store and any certificate stores or MDMs to enroll as possible).

Note Keep in mind that if you are erasing devices as part of your preparing them for deployment, any device plugged into the Apple Configurator can be wiped, and so don't accidentally plug your own phone or iPad into it.

To prepare devices using our Blueprint:

- Open Apple Configurator.
- Click Blueprints.
- Control-click your Blueprint and select Prepare (Figure 5-20).

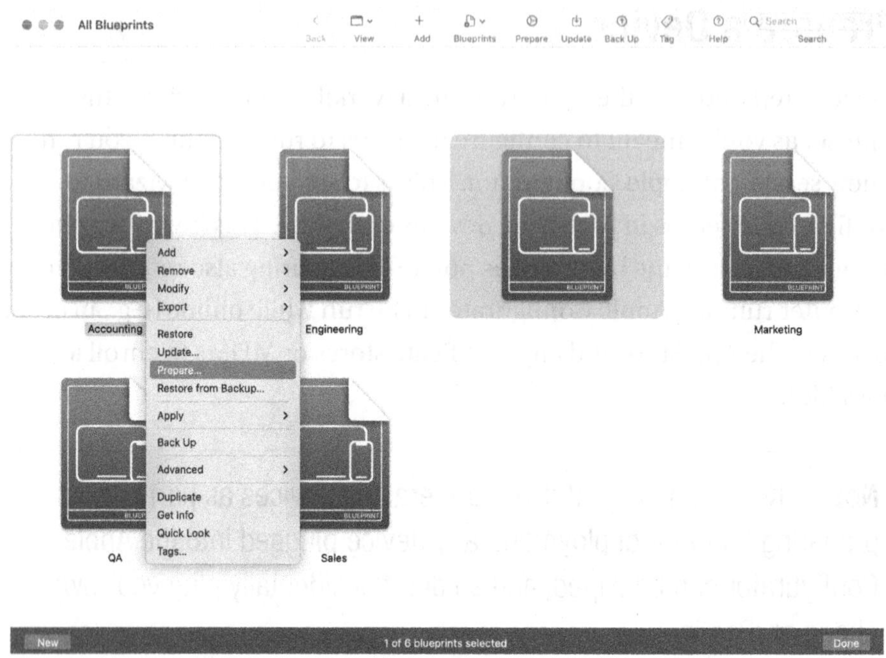

Figure 5-20. *Run Prepare to start your Blueprint*

- At the Prepare Devices wizard, select whether you will be running a Manual Configuration (Figure 5-21) or Automated Enrollment.

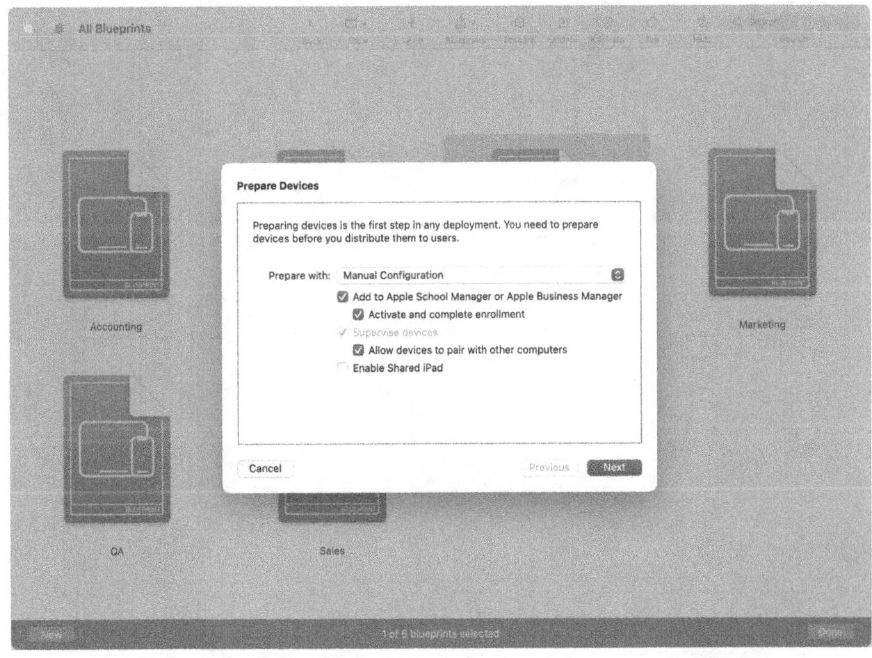

***Figure 5-21.** Configure the steps in your Prepare workflow*

The devices we'll be working with in this workflow are DEP enabled, so we'll select Automated Enrollment (Figure 5-22) and then click Next.

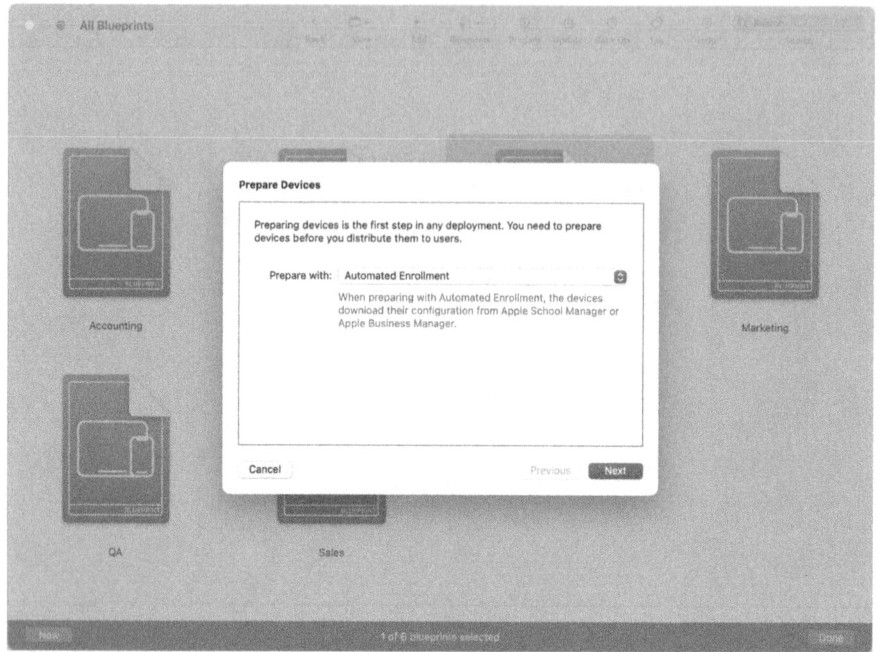

Figure 5-22. *Configure the device to use Automated Enrollment*

- At the Choose Network Profile screen of the wizard, we select the profile created previously, so the device can join the network and enroll into the DEP instance (Figure 5-23).

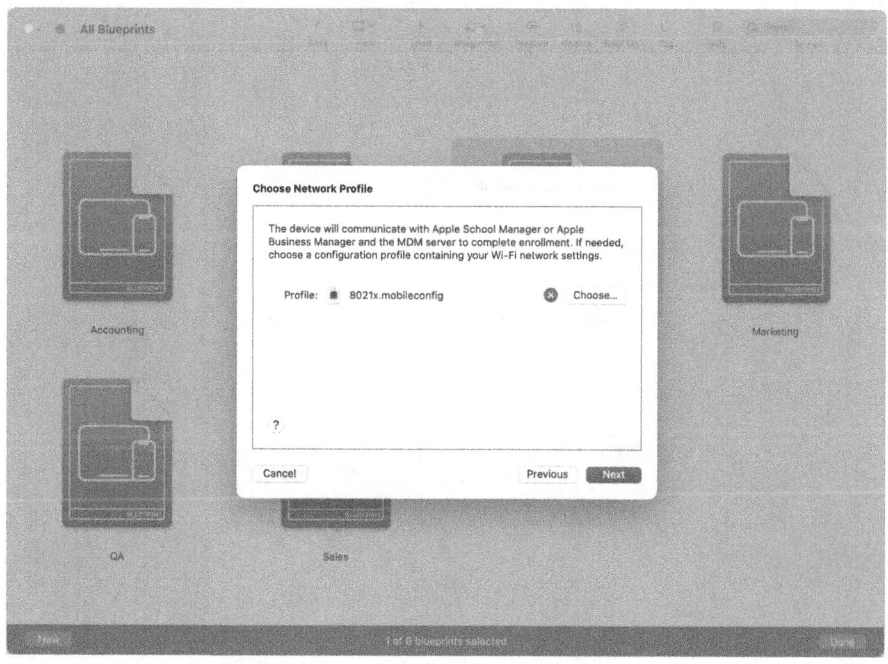

***Figure 5-23.** Select the 802.1x Profile we created earlier*

- Given that the MDM instance requires authentication, at the Automated Enrollment Credentials screen, we'll provide credentials that can be used to authenticate to the MDM provider (Figure 5-24). DEP is somewhat insecure without authentication, and so you should always do authentication when possible. See the Black Hat talk from Jesse Endahl for more information on why: `www.blackhat.com/us-18/speakers/Jesse-Endahl.html`.

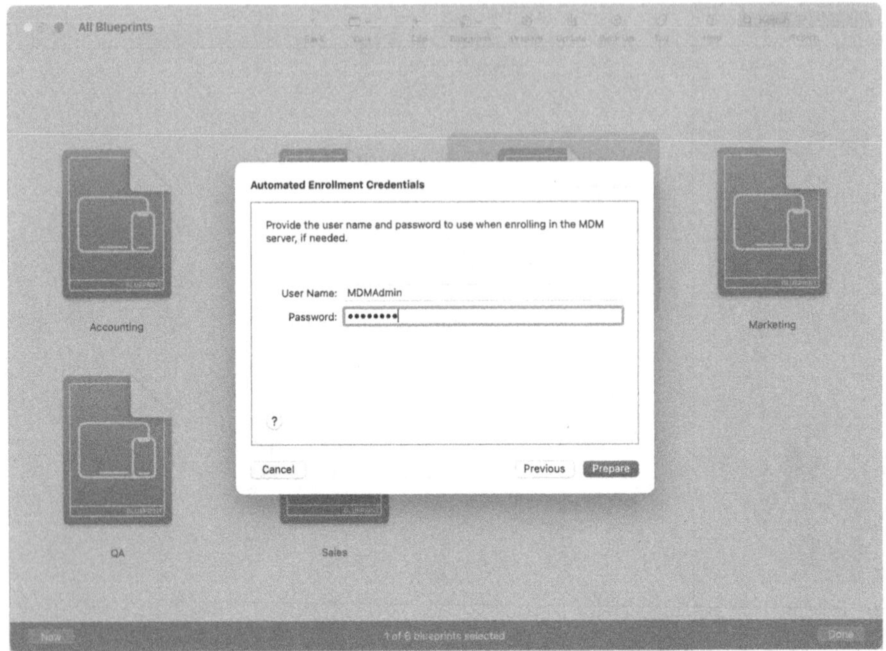

***Figure 5-24.** Provide authentication credentials to your MDM solution*

Click the Prepare button, and any devices that are plugged in will be set up to run the workflows laid out in the Blueprint! If you were not doing DEP/automated enrollment, then you'd also see the Configure iOS Setup Assistant screen (Figure 5-25). This screen is used to suppress the startup screens in iOS, allowing you to get all the closer to the magical zero-touch setup. If you're using DEP, then the Apple Configurator workflows assume that you are using MDM to suppress those screens.

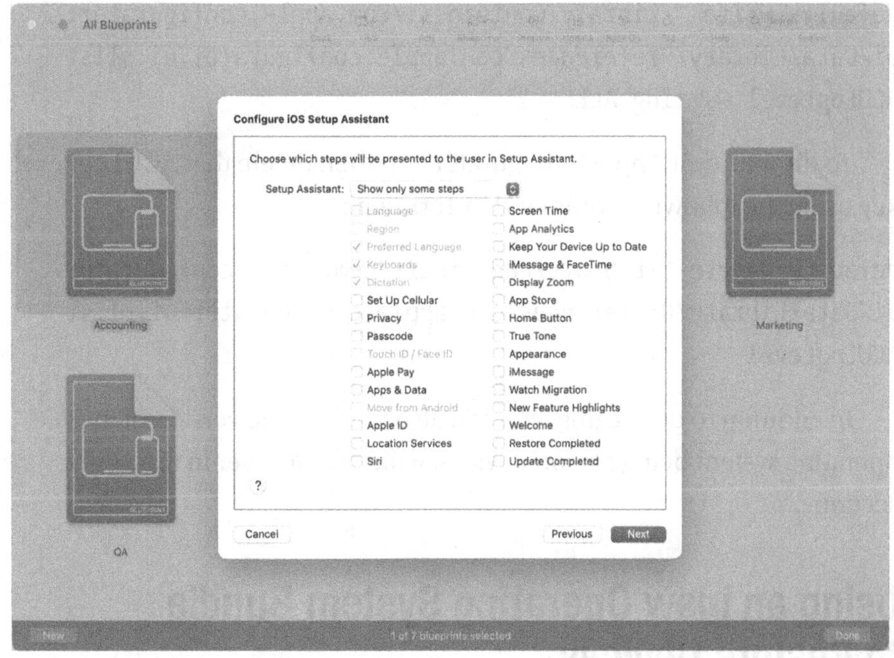

Figure 5-25. *Configure the screens to skip during setup*

Now that we've used Apple Configurator to set up devices, it's time to move to using Configurator as a debugging tool.

Debugging Apple Configurator Logs

Apple Configurator is a great tool. But you need to debug things from time to time. This might mean that a profile is misconfigured and not installing or that a device can't perform a task you are sending it to be performed. This is about the time that you need to enable some debug logs.

To do so, quit Apple Configurator and then use Terminal to write a string of ALL into the ACULogLevel key in ~/Library/Containers/com.apple.configurator.ui/Data/Library/Preferences/com.apple.configurator.ui.plist by using the following command:

```
defaults write ~/Library/Containers/com.apple.configurator.
ui/Data/Library/Preferences/com.apple.configurator.ui.plist
ACULogLevel -string ALL
```

To disable, quit Apple Configurator and then delete that ACULogLevel key using the following command in Terminal:

```
defaults delete ~/Library/Containers/com.apple.configurator.
ui/Data/Library/Preferences/com.apple.configurator.ui.plist
ACULogLevel
```

In addition to debugging, you can also manage the version of the operating system being run on devices, which we'll cover in the next section.

Using an ipsw Operating System Bundle to Restore Devices

Apple Configurator allows you to run a specific version of iOS on a device. This might mean an older version for testing or to deploy an operating system that hasn't been released into the wild yet as part of testing for future versions using the betas you have access to from the Developer or Seed programs.

An iOS operating system is a bundle of files, as with many other things in the Apple-verse. This particular bundle is an ipsw file. The .ipsw must be signed and unadulterated in order to be restored to an iOS device. They can be downloaded from the Downloads section of developer.apple.com, where each operating system will have a separate installer file (Figure 5-26).

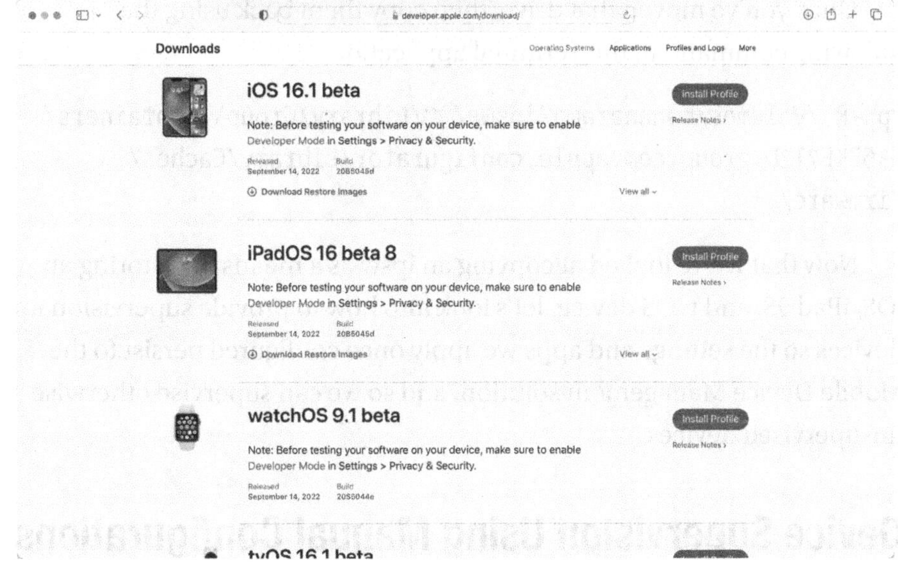

Figure 5-26. *The Downloads page on developer.apple.com*

If you have a bunch of Apple Configurator workstations, and you are running a training session or attempting to run beta software for standard software testing, this can get infinitely more annoying. In these types of lab environments, you're in luck. If you have an ipsw (the iOS OS update file), you can copy the file from ~/Library/Group\ Containers/K36BKF7T3D.group.com.apple.configurator/Library/Caches/Firmware/ onto another machine. To copy them onto a USB drive called bananarama, for example, use the following Terminal command:

```
cp -R ~/Library/Library/Group\ Containers/K26BKF7T3D.group.
com.apple.configurator/Library/Caches/Firmware/ /Volumes/
bananarama/ipsws/
```

Once you've moved that drive, then copy them back using the following command in the Terminal application:

```
cp -R /Volumes/bananarama/ipsws/ ~/Library/Group\ Containers/
K36BKF7T3D.group.com.apple.configurator/Library/Caches/
Firmware/
```

Now that we've looked at copying an ipsw as a means of restoring an iOS, iPadOS, and tvOS device, let's look into how to provide supervision for devices so the settings and apps we apply once configured persist to the Mobile Device Management solution, and so we can supervise otherwise unsupervised devices.

Device Supervision Using Manual Configurations

When using Apple Configurator, you can supervise devices that purchased outside of an organizational PO or Apple Management program. This allows you to assign an existing supervision identity to be used with devices you place into supervision or to supervise random devices. These need to be wiped in order to apply the appropriate level of permissions to prove they are owned by an organization.

This was done earlier in the chapter to some degree, but now it's for a specific purpose. The organization must be linked so a sign-on to the Apple Business Manager or Apple School Manager instance is required. This doesn't piggyback off the sign-in established when we initially installed Apple Configurator earlier in the chapter, so to get started, first open Apple Configurator and click Organizations (Figure 5-27).

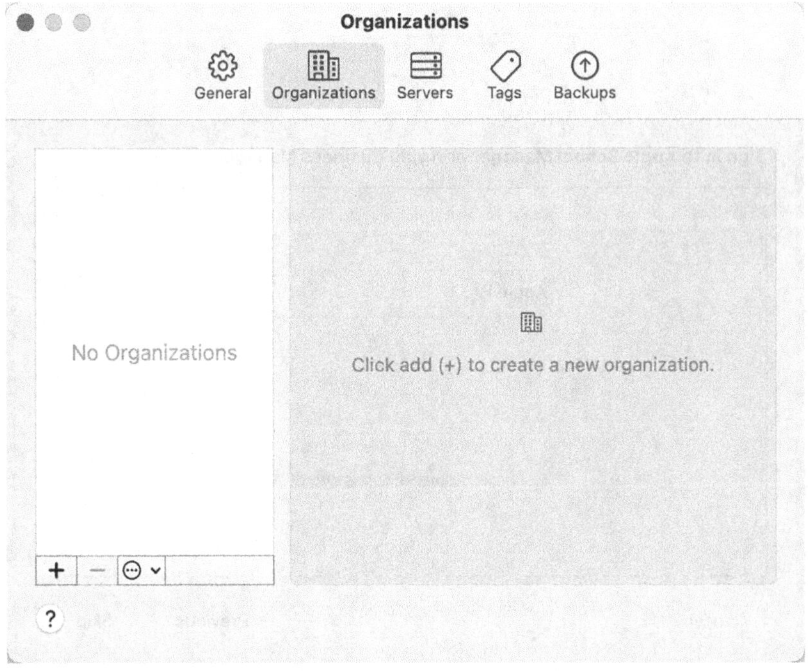

Figure 5-27. *Create an organization*

From Organizations, click the plus sign ("+") to set up a supervision profile and then click Next at the first Create an Organization screen. When prompted, provide a username and password to the Apple Business Manager or Apple School Manager portal for the organization as seen in Figure 5-28.

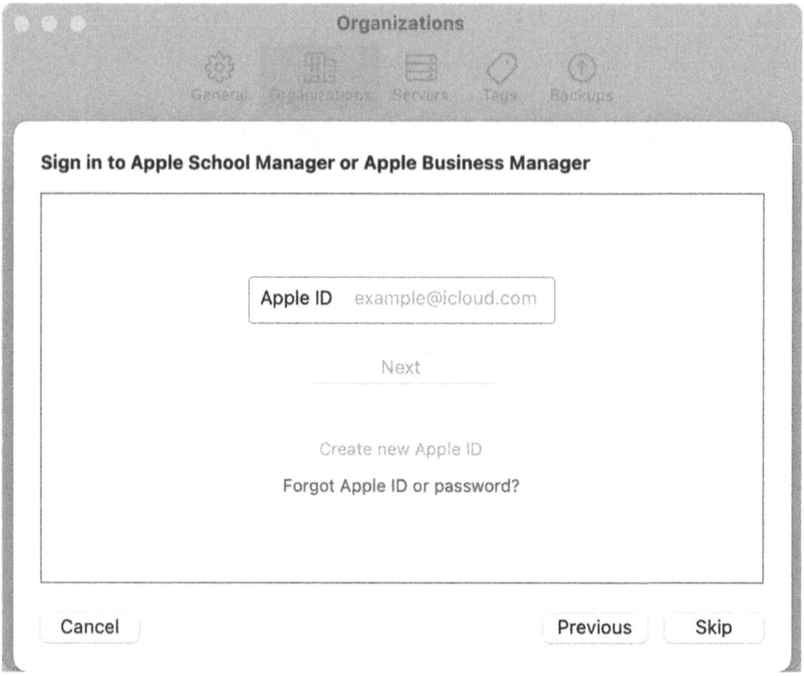

Figure 5-28. *Authenticate to the appropriate Apple ID*

If importing an identity, select "Choose an existing supervision identity" and click Next (Figure 5-29).

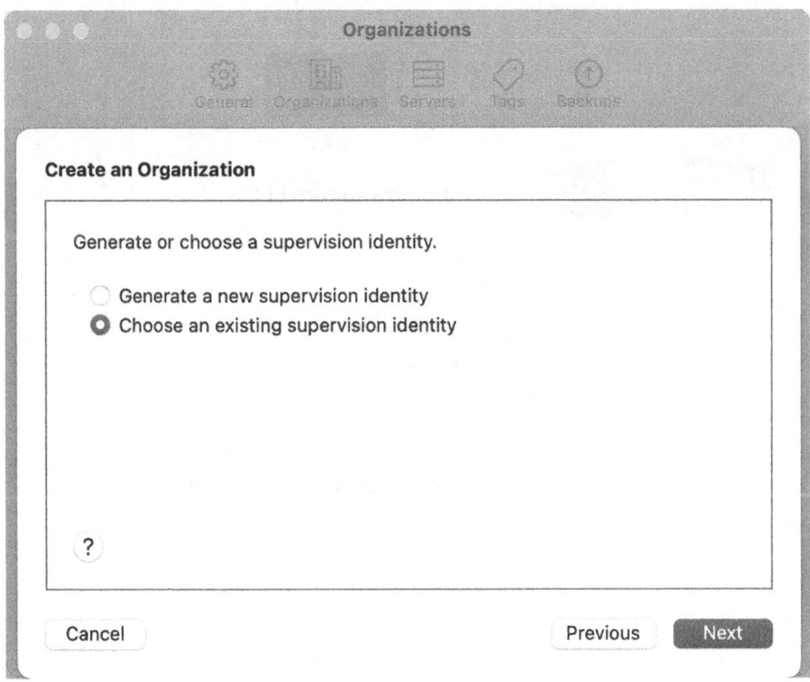

Figure 5-29. *Create a supervision identity*

When prompted, click Choose to select the identity to use or allow the certificate to be imported automatically, as seen in Figure 5-30. These are pulled from the list of certificates found in Keychain. As an example, if you promote a server to a Profile Manage server, when Open Directory is installed, a certificate will also be installed. This certificate can then be used here. Or you can download one from a CA on a third-party MDM solution.

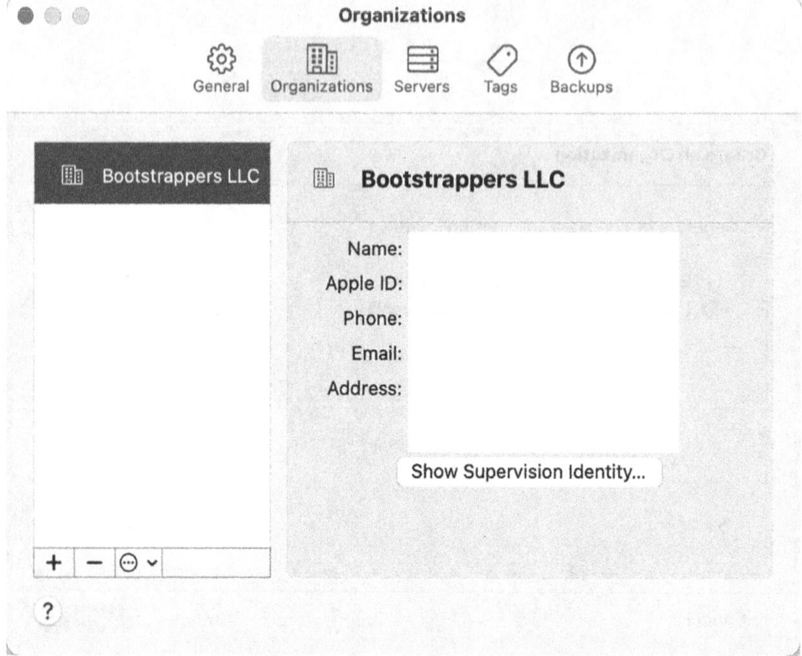

Figure 5-30. *Select a certificate*

If manually importing, click **Choose** when you've highlighted the appropriate certificate and then click Done. You now have the appropriate identities (certificates) to supervise previously unsupervisable devices, thus obtaining more options for tasks you can deploy on those devices. When configured, the Supervision Private Key is a signing identity using an exportable DER that can be migrated to another Apple Configurator host and authenticates a Mac to be able to supervise a device. This is required when running various actions that Apple developers deem should be able to be run on a device even without a passcode because the organization has proven that they own a device and not the person using the device. This includes commands like resetting a passcode without wiping a device.

Now that we've done a number of tasks manually using Apple Configurator, let's turn toward automating tasks using various scripting tools.

Automating iOS Actions

There are a few tools for automating tasks on iOS, iPadOS, and tvOS devices that we'll cover in the next few sections. These allow you to string together complex workflows. For example, when a device is plugged in, you could automatically back up the device, erase it, supervise it, restore the backup, and then run a shell script that provides details about the series of tasks into a standard support tool like ServiceNow. Or a user could trigger an action in a device management solution using the APIs of one of those.

Luckily, you have a few options around automating such a workflow. These include the following tools:

- **AEiOS**: `https://github.com/univ-of-utah-marriott-library-apple/aeios`
- **GroundControl from Imprivata**: `www.groundctl.com`
- **Libimobiledevice**: `https://libimobiledevice.org/`

GroundControl is a solution available at `www.groundctl.com`. It allows you to do some of what Apple Configurator does, but much more. GroundControl can set up devices, manage MDM and Wi-Fi settings, take configuration information from a SaaS login environment, and assign roles to devices using GroundControl, which automatically sets various configuration options including some that aren't available through any of the other tools that we reference in this chapter, because it uses private frameworks to edit devices.

GroundControl has a number of features that appeal to various use cases:

- Integration with USB hubs to enable and disable LED lights when a device is in a given state.
- Self-Heal reimages devices on the fly so they can be put back in the hands of users when the devices aren't working properly.
- APIs and webhooks (for more on these, see Chapter 11) provide additional automation, and rather than running these from a Mac running Apple Configurator, the automations are run from a cloud solution so they are always available.
- Run on Microsoft Windows either running on a full computer or using an Intel Compute Stick with a USB hub attached to the device.
- Tap & Go (sold as an add-on) comes with a Locker app that integrates with your MDM and tracks who uses each iOS or iPadOS device. GroundControl integrates with VMware Workspace ONE as a federated identity provider (via SAML 2.0) and automatically logs devices out of apps when events trigger GroundControl to do so.

If you have the ability to license a tool, it's worth doing so just for the support. But since not everyone can, the remainder of the tools we'll look at in this section are free and/or open source automation tools.

The Apple Configurator Command-Line Tools

Apple Configurator has an optional command that can be installed to automate a number of the tasks we've done throughout this chapter. Don't let the fact that it's a command-line tool fool you – in some cases, a well-structured command-line tool is easier to use than a tool with hidden or nested options in a graphical interface. The Apple Configurator command line is such a tool, and you should be a master within about half an hour tinkering with it.

Before using the command-line options to automate tasks, you need to install it. To do so, open Apple Configurator 2 and then click the Apple Configurator 2 menu. Select Install Automation Tools from the menu, and you'll be prompted with the Install Automation Tools dialog (as you can see in Figure 5-31). Click Install and provide local administrative credentials if you are prompted to do so.

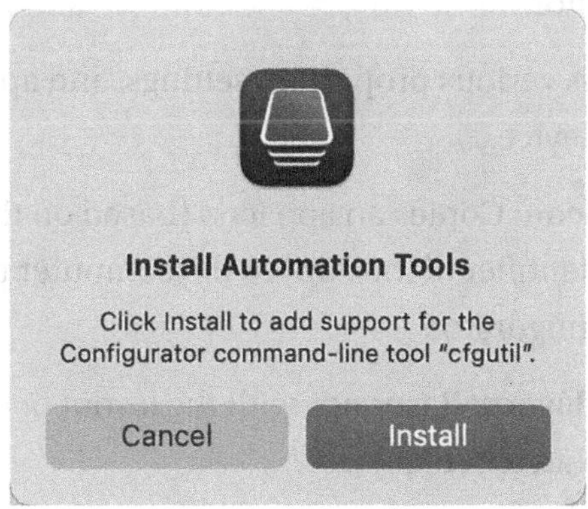

Figure 5-31. *Install the Apple Configurator command-line tools*

Once installed, you'll find a binary called cfgutil at /Applications/Apple Configurator 2.app/Contents/MacOS/cfgutil. The cfgutil command has a number of verbs you can see by running the command followed by the help verb, as follows:

```
/Applications/Apple\ Configurator\ 2.app/Contents/MacOS/
cfgutil help
```

The following is a list of officially supported verbs:

- **activate**: Activates iOS and iPadOS devices.
- **add-tags**: Adds a tag for iOS and iPadOS devices.

- **backup**: Creates a backup of an iOS or iPadOS device the Configurator computer has prepared.
- **clear-passcode**: Clears the passcode of a supervised iOS or iPadOS device.
- **erase**: Erases any content and settings configured on any supervised iOS and iPadOS devices.
- **exec**: Runs scripts when iOS and iPadOS devices connect or detach from the computer running Apple Configurator.
- **get**: Shows various properties, settings, and apps that are on a device.
- **get-app-icon**: Copies an app icon (based on the Bundle Identifier of the app) to the computer running Apple Configurator.
- **get-icon-layout**: Responds with the layout of the home screen on attached devices.
- **get-unlock-token**: Responds with the unlock token of a device provided Apple Configurator has the appropriate supervision identity.
- **help**: Displays how to use commands or a list of commands.
- **install-app**: Pushes an app (e.g., via an ipa file) to attached iOS and iPadOS devices.
- **install-doc**: Pushes a document to an attached iOS or iPadOS device.
- **install-profile**: Installs profiles saved to a file path on the Apple Configurator workstation onto attached devices.

- **list**: Shows a list of all devices attached to the computer.
- **list-backups**: Provides a list of the backups stored locally on the Apple Configurator computer where the command is being run.
- **pair**: Sends the device pairing command to a device, which requires someone unlock a device and click Trust on the device so further automations can run.
- **prepare**: Runs a prepare workflow, similar to what we did previously in this chapter in the preparation section.
- **remove-app**: Deletes an app from a device, based on the Bundle Identifier.
- **remove-profile**: Deletes a profile from a device, based on the profile identifier.
- **remove-tags**: Deletes any tags that were applied to a device.
- **rename**: Configures the name on attached devices.
- **restart**: Restarts any attached and supervised devices.
- **restore**: Wipes the device and installs the latest available operating system (will cache the ipsw file if it's not already cached).
- **restore-backup**: Restores a backup to an iOS device.
- **revive**: If a device is in recovery mode, attempts to remove that setting from the device so it works again as normal (if this fails, the device may need to be wiped to do so).

- **set-backup-password**: Configures backup password settings on attached devices.
- **set-icon-layout**: Configures the home screen - for more on how to send data to the command, look at the output of get-icon-layout.
- **set-wallpaper**: Configures background images on supervised iOS and iPadOS devices that are attached.
- **shut-down**: Turns off any supervised devices that are attached.
- **syslog**: Displays the syslog of the device in Terminal.
- **unpair**: Disables the pairing for attached devices, making it impossible to run the rest of the commands in this list.
- **version**: Outputs with the version of the cfgutil command (e.g., 2.15.1).

These are mostly features available in the graphical interface of Apple Configurator, many we've shown throughout this chapter. Let's start by listing devices currently attached to the Configurator workstation. First, we'll open the Terminal app, and then we'll run the cfgutil command from within the Apple Configurator app bundle. Showing verbs is done using the list verb, as follows:

```
cfgutil list
```

One of the most important aspects of automating Apple Configurator is to be able to run a script when a device is plugged into the Apple Configurator workstation. This is done using the exec verb along with either a -a or a -b option, which will run the script you provide either when a device is connected (-a) or when the device is disconnected (-b). In the following example, we will run a simple cfgutil command followed by the exec verb and then a -a so that the connected.sh script will be run when devices are connected to the computer running as the Apple Configurator workstation:

```
cfgutil exec -a connected.sh
```

The results from the preceding command would simply be the output of the connected.sh script, which is a custom script that shows all devices connected to the instance. We won't spend the rest of the book going through all of the verbs available here as there are other tools to be covered, but suffice it to say that you can script most anything you can do in Apple Configurator 2. Next, let's move on to alternatives that provide even more techniques, using open source tools for scripting iOS management.

Use libimobiledevice to Automate Device Management

Xcode, Apple Configurator, and other tools can be used to view logs on iOS devices and automate actions as we've shown throughout this chapter. One of those other tools is libimobiledevice. It's usually a good idea to install libimobiledevice using homebrew, a popular package management tool. Homebrew makes installers of potentially otherwise difficult open source tools simpler by scripting the installation of the tool and any required dependencies that can be a little annoying when compiling and working with the tool manually. To install homebrew if you haven't already, run the following command from the Terminal application:

```
ruby -e "$(curl -fsSL https://raw.githubusercontent.com/
Homebrew/install/master/install)"
```

Once run, follow the prompts to complete the installation. Once homebrew is installed, run the following brew command to download the required components and then libimobiledevice:

```
brew install -v --devel automake autoconf libtool wget
libimobiledevice
```

Then run ideviceinstaller:

```
brew install -v --HEAD --build-from-source ideviceinstaller
```

Use Basic libimobiledevice Options

Once these are installed, you can plug in a paired device, unlock it, and use the following command to view the logs on the screen: idevicesyslog. This is akin to running a tail against the device. Again, the device must be paired. You can use the command line (e.g., if running this on Linux) to view the logs, but if you're not paired, you'll need to use idevicepair to pair your device, followed by the pair verb (which is very different from the pear verb):

```
idevicepair pair
```

The screen will then show that the device is paired. You can also unpair using the unpair verb:

```
idevicepair unpair
```

When pairing and unpairing, you should see the appropriate entries in /var/db/lockdown. The final option to cover in this section is the date (very useful when scripting unit tests using this suite). To obtain this, use the idevicedate command, no operators or verbs required:

```
idevicedate
```

You can also use a number of other commands that come bundled with the tool.

Dig in with Additional Management Commands

The first command we'll use is idevicedate, which simply returns with the date and timestamp currently on the device: /usr/local/bin/idevicedate. The response would simply include the date. Next, let's check the apps installed on a device. We can do this with the ideviceinstaller command (also part of the libimobiledevice suite of tools). Here, we'll use the -l option to just list what's installed:

```
/usr/local/bin/ideviceinstaller -l
```

The output would show the app, along with the version of the app at rest on the device:

```
com.apple.Pages - Pages 1716
```

To uninstall one of the listed apps, use the –uninstall option:ideviceinstaller --uninstall com.protogeo.Moves. You can also install apps provided you've cached the ipa file (e.g., via iTunes).

```
ideviceinstaller --install /Users/charlesedge/Music/iTunes/
iTunes\ Media/Mobile\ Applications/Box.ipa
```

When run against a device, you can then open apps provided the Apple ID owns the app. There's also a command for ideviceprovision, which can be used to view provisioning profiles, when run with the list verb, which would appear as follows:

```
/usr/local/bin/ideviceprovision list
```

The ideviceprovision command can also form the basis of a tool like wirelurker by allowing you to install a provisioning profile:

```
/usr/local/bin/ideviceprovision install angrybirds.
mobileprovision
```

You can also remove this, by feeding in the UUID of the provisioning profile (obtained using the list verb but replacing MYUUID from the following code block):

```
/usr/local/bin/ideviceprovision remove MYUUID
```

Or you could do something more substantial, like put a device into recovery mode, so it would need to be plugged into a computer running iTunes and get a new ipsw installed, which is as simple as feeding the udid into ideviceenterrecovery:

```
/usr/local/bin/ideviceenterrecovery
af36e5d7065d4ad666bf047b6e4de26dd144578c
```

This brings up an interesting question: How would you get the udid? You can use ideviceinfo to view the output, which shows more information that I knew you could actually get about a device previously. You can also grep for the UniqueDeviceID and then parse the output to return just the value you're looking for, making it easy to build much more complicated workflows or output the command into other tools using APIs:

```
ideviceinfo | grep UniqueDeviceID | awk '{ print $2}'
```

This would just return with the UDID. Since that's blank when there's no device connected, you can run a loop that waits a few seconds when empty and then uses that UDID as a $1 in some script. Of course, it's much easier to use a command they built for this called idevice_id:

```
idevice_id -l
```

A number of commands make troubleshooting devices on networks or code simpler, which we'll look at in the next section.

Troubleshooting Commands

Next, you can use idevicediagnostics, which has debugging information in the output, to obtain some information about the current state of the device:

```
idevicediagnostics diagnostics All -u
af36e5d7065d4ad666bf047b6e4de26dd1445789
```

Or query the IOreg of the device to see what's connected:

```
idevicediagnostics ioreg IODeviceTree -u
af36e5d7065d4ad666bf047b6e4de26dd1445789
```

The output is way too long to paste in here, but interesting (kinda). The idevicediagnostics command can also do some basic tasks such as restart, sleep, and shutdown (each sent as a verb without a required UDID):

```
idevicediagnostics restart
```

The crash reports on a device (which include reports for uninstalled apps, forensically providing a glimpse into what apps were removed from a device and when) can all be extracted from a paired device as well, using idevicecrashreport:

```
idevicecrashreport -e /test
```

You can then view the logs or grep through them for specific pieces of information: cat /Test/Baseband/log-bb-2019-06-06-stats.plist. The last command we're going to cover in this article is idevicebackup2, used to back up devices. Here, we're going to feed it the udid which we're lazily using the idevice_id command from earlier in backticks to grab the udid and backing up into that /test directory.idevicebackup2 -u `idevice_id -l` backup /test. Here, we've backed up whatever device is plugged in, to the / test directory. Subsequent backups will be incrementals.

As you can see in the preceding examples, libimobiledevice is capable of managing a number of features on iOS devices. Many of these are unavailable in other tools. It's an important component of many large iOS and iPadOS deployments with implications to how provisioning, device replacement, device maintenance tasks, and of course troubleshooting are handled throughout the entire life cycle of a deployment. Next, we'll look at one of the more recent entrants into the iOS and iPadOS device management world, another open source tool called AEiOS.

Using AEiOS to Create Workflows

AEiOS is a python library that uses the cfgutil command-line tool installed as a part of the Apple Configurator 2 command-line tools. This makes installing Apple Configurator 2 and the command-line tools that we covered earlier in this chapter a requirement before getting started with AEiOS. What AEiOS adds to that mix is the ability to string together a workflow that can be saved in a configuration and then called on a Mac to check devices out or provision them, without having to teach a support representative (or librarian, nurse, etc.) how to maintain and start an instance of Apple Configurator.

This also cuts down on human error that can easily cause support tickets to a service desk. The beauty of managing devices programmatically is that you have a certain level of... well, certainty into the outcome of the processes you put into place. The beauty of the AEiOS script is that it's python, so it's easy to follow along with what the developer is doing when various incantations of the scripts are run.

To get started with AEiOS, first let's install the Apple Configurator command-line tools, covered earlier in this chapter. Then, download AEiOS from `https://github.com/univ-of-utah-marriott-library-apple/aeios/releases` (it downloads as a .dmg file). Once downloaded, extract the .dmg file and run the installer. The aeiosutil python script is the primary way you interface with the tool. This is installed in /usr/local/bin/, and the python scripts that aeiosutil calls are installed in the /Library/Python/2.7/site-packages/aeios directory.

The aeiosutil command is fairly straightforward to use, providing a simple wrapper to the standard Apple Configurator command-line options. We covered setting up a supervision identity in Apple Configurator earlier. Many of the workflows for aeios will also require you to use a supervision identity. To import unencrypted supervision identity certificates, use the add verb, followed by the identity option and then the identity. Also provide the required certificates using --certs followed by the path to your certificates directory. In the following command, we'll do that, using the /Users/cedge/Documents/aeioscerts directory as where to import those certificates from:

```
/usr/local/bin/aeiosutil add identity --certs /Users/cedge/
Documents/aeioscerts
```

A common task for multiuser devices is to add a background image. To do so with aeiosutil, run the add verb again, followed by image and then --background, as the type of background to add. We'll store that in our home directory as well, as follows:

```
/usr/local/bin/aeiosutil add image --background /Users/cedge/
Documents/aeiosimages/background.png
```

Other image options include the alert image and the lock image, which are --alert and –lock, respectively. The devices we're setting up will also need to access a standard Wi-Fi network. To add a Wi-Fi profile, first create the .mobileconfig file (e.g., using Apple Configurator). Then use the add verb, followed by the Wi-Fi option and then the path to the mobileconfig file, as you can see as follows:

```
/usr/local/bin/aeiosutil add wifi /Users/cedge/Documents/
aeiosprofiles/mathdept.mobileconfig
```

Apps that Apple Configurator can access can be installed as a part of the running workflow, based on name. Simply use the add verb, followed by app and then the name of the app (as it appears in Apple Configurator). For example, let's tell the device to install the most important app ever published to the app store, Sudoku:

```
/usr/local/bin/aeiosutil add app "Sodoku"
```

There are also settings for how aeiosutil behaves. Let's say you want the workflow to post to Slack when something happens; there's an integration for that. Admins can then take all of these configurations that were created and start aeiosutil waiting for devices; simply call the command followed by the start verb:

```
/usr/local/bin/aeiosutil start
```

You can also remove the settings that we added in the preceding examples using the remove verb. You can also remove that profile, using

```
/usr/local/bin/aeiosutil remove identity
/usr/local/bin/aeiosutil remove wifi
/usr/local/bin/aeiosutil remove app "Soduku"
/usr/local/bin/aeiosutil remove image
```

Slack is a popular messaging tool used in IT departments. One really cool feature of aeios that you might want to take use of is the ability to post to Slack, with certain changes. This is done by sending a webhook to a Slack listener. To set up a webhook for your slack instance, see `https://api.slack.com/incoming-webhooks`. As you can see, you can post to that webhook manually by sending a post to the endpoint you set up using the steps in the Slack API. Let's say that endpoint was `https://hooks.slack.com/services/ABC123/123456789`. Then the POST would look like this:

```
POST
https://hooks.slack.com/services/ABC123/123456789
Content-type: application/json
{
    "text": "There's a new app in aeios"
}
```

The preceding post is sent by aeios. The aeios tools wrap alerts into this type of framework and can configure the sender automatically using the configure verb followed by slack as the service to configure and then the URL to the endpoint, followed by a channel name (which in this case is simply #helpdesk). It can be configured via

```
aeiosutil configure slack "https:// https://hooks.slack.com/
services/ABC123/123456789" "#helpdesk"
```

Once run, you'll see an update in the indicated Slack channel when the workflow is run. As we've shown throughout the previous few sections, there are a number of automation frameworks that can help you to manage iOS and iPadOS devices en masse. A companion service that most organizations with more than a dozen or so devices will likely take a lot of value in is caching, which allows devices on a network to download assets from other devices rather than relying on a connection to Apple, which we'll cover in the next section.

Caching Services

The Caching service can be run on a Mac and caches content from Apple. The Caching service provides (through a local cache) updates to iOS, iPadOS, Mac, tvOS, and the "content" destined for those devices and therefore cuts down your Internet data usage and accelerates downloads on the operating system and other Apple-provided tools dramatically. In this section, we'll look at how to configure this critical system. First, let's look at what type of data is cached so we can make sure a caching server (or a few of them) makes sense for your organization.

What's Cached?

The Caching service was moved out of macOS Server and into the client macOS in High Sierra where it remains as of 10.15. This means administrators no longer need to run the Server app on caching servers. Given the fact that the Caching service only stores volatile data easily recreated by caching updates again, there's no need to back the service up, and it doesn't interact with users or groups.

The type of content cached includes, but is not limited to, the following:

- App Store apps for iOS, iPadOS, macOS, and tvOS, including on-demand resources for those apps and app updates
- Apple Books content for iOS, iPadOS, and macOS
- Apple Configurator content (e.g., ipsw updates)
- Downloads in the GarageBand app
- iCloud photos and documents on iOS and macOS
- Content for all supported platforms
- Language dictionaries
- Legacy macOS printer drivers
- Over-the-air iOS, iPadOS, macOS, and tvOS software updates
- Siri voices

Caching Service Configuration

And the setup of the Caching service has never been easier. The Caching service requires you to install no third-party or additional components. To enable caching, first open System Settings and search for the **Sharing** pane and then click the checkbox for Content Caching to start the service. Click the icon next to the service to see available options for what's cached (All Content, Shared Content, or iCloud Content), as seen in Figure 5-32.

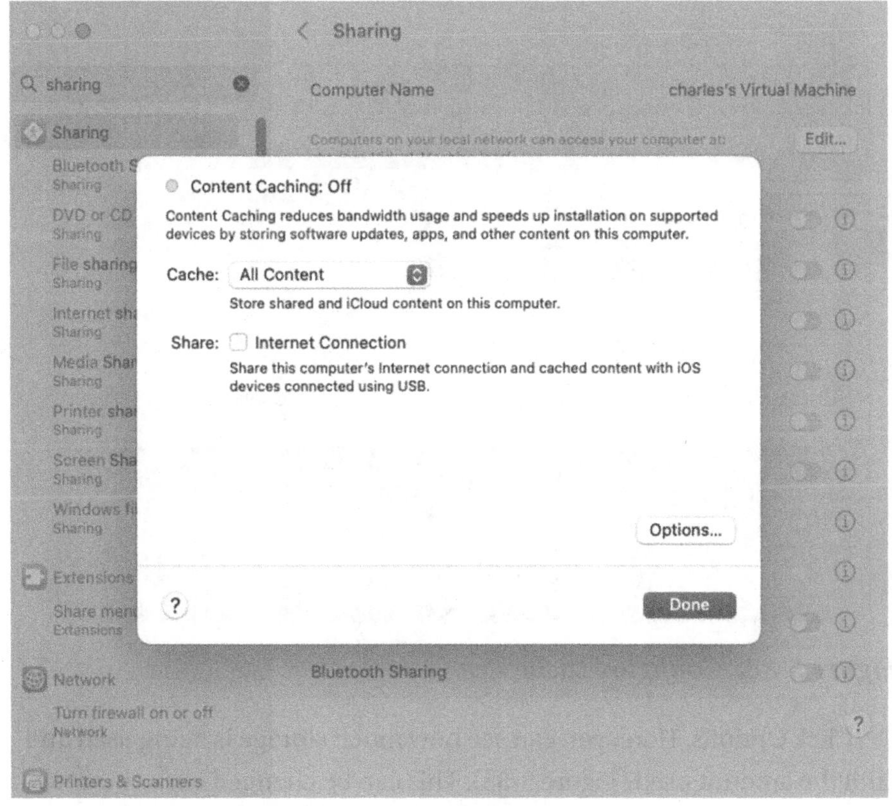

***Figure 5-32.** The Sharing System preference pane*

At the Content Caching panel, the service will say "Content Caching: On" once it's running. Here, you can disable the "Cache iCloud content" option, which will disable the caching of user data supplied for iCloud (everything in here is encrypted, by the way). You can also choose to share the Internet connection, which will create a wireless network that iOS devices can join to pull content.

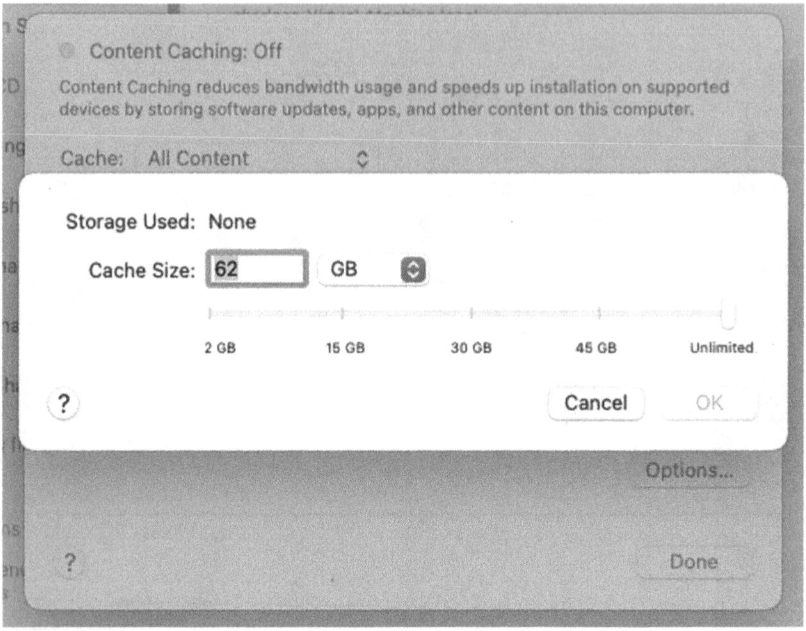

Figure 5-33. *Configure cache size*

Click Options. Here, you can see how much storage is being used and limit the amount used (Figure 5-33). This can be changed here or through /Library/Preferences/com.apple.AssetCache.plist. Digging into other options, it's worth noting that nothing was removed from the time that the Caching service was migrated from macOS Server to macOS. This means that all those settings that you used to see in the GUI are still there, you just access them via the command line, by sending defaults commands. For example, we can write a limit on the amount of data that a server can cache using a standard defaults command, but writing an integer into CacheLimit of com.apple.AssetCache.plist, as follows:

```
defaults write /Library/Preferences/com.apple.AssetCache.plist
CacheLimit -int 20000000000
```

The caching server has a status verb, so you can see a number of details about how it's functioning:

```
AssetCacheManagerUtil status
```

This returns something similar to the following:

```
2022-09-11 11:49:37.427 AssetCacheManagerUtil[23957:564981]
Built-in caching server status: {
Activated = 1;
Active = 1;
CacheDetails = {
iCloud = 4958643;
"iOS Software" = 936182434;};
CacheFree = 472585174016;
CacheLimit = 0;
CacheStatus = OK;
CacheUsed = 941141077;
Parents = ();
Peers = ();
PersonalCacheFree = 472585174016;
PersonalCacheLimit = 0;
PersonalCacheUsed = 4958643;
Port = 56452;
PrivateAddresses = ("192.168.104.196");
PublicAddress = "18.126.164.226";
RegistrationStatus = 1;
RestrictedMedia = 0;
StartupStatus = OK;
TotalBytesDropped = 0;
TotalBytesImported = 4958643;
TotalBytesReturnedToChildren = 0;
TotalBytesReturnedToClients = 166627405;
```

```
TotalBytesReturnedToPeers = 0;
TotalBytesStoredFromOrigin = 166627405;
TotalBytesStoredFromParents = 0;
TotalBytesStoredFromPeers = 0;
```

You can also use AssetCacheManagerUtil to manage tasks previously built into the Server app. To see the available options, simply run the command:

```
/usr/bin/AssetCacheManagerUtil
```

One of the first tasks most administrators would need to do would be to enable the server:

```
/usr/bin/AssetCacheManagerUtil activate
```

To disable the server, use the deactivate verb, which disassociates the service from the main Apple update services:

```
/usr/bin/AssetCacheManagerUtil deactivate
```

To check if the server can be activated, use the canActivate verb, which performs an activation dry run:

```
/usr/bin/AssetCacheManagerUtil canActivate
```

To flush the cache of assets on the server, thus manually cleaning out any old updates and freeing up some valuable disk space on the server:

```
/usr/bin/AssetCacheManagerUtil flushCache
```

To reload settings, which would be necessary if making any changes to the property lists manually:

```
/usr/bin/AssetCacheManagerUtil reloadSettings
```

To move the database manually, which then relinks all assets (e.g., if you're moving the database off of an internal drive and onto some kind of direct attached storage, or DAS for short), use the moveCacheTo verb followed by the target path (which is quoted in the following example command):

```
/usr/bin/AssetCacheManagerUtil moveCacheTo "/Volumes/SONY/
Library/Application Support/Apple/AssetCache/Data"
```

Finally, if you'd like to see the caching server your client system is using, run the AssetCacheLocatorUtil – the information following that is simply to parse out all the extraneous information you likely don't need:

```
/usr/bin/AssetCacheLocatorUtil 2>&1 | grep guid | awk
'{print$4}' | sed 's/^\(.*\):.*$/\1/' | uniq
```

Nearly every organization can benefit from a caching server. As is hopefully obvious in the previously mentioned commands, it's fairly straightforward to script a caching server to provide assets to your Apple devices, and it's much more efficient on a number of levels from running a standard caching proxy. Now that we've covered a lot of different automation and provisioning options for iOS and iPadOS devices, let's step through a less mature but in many ways more complicated setup process: that of the Mac.

Summary

Imaging is dead. Then it isn't. Other words like restoring devices, provisioning, and reinstalling operating systems are all very much alive. They're just different than they were for the past 20 years, especially for iOS.

As we've shown in this chapter, you can plug an iOS device into Apple Configurator (or one of the other tools designed for more specific use cases) and provision operating system updates, wireless networking, enrollment, and for the most part get a device configured and ready to put into the hands of a coworker without ever touching it. Or even better, ship the device directly to them, so they can get that new Apple device smell (and sticker) and feel empowered, not conquered by their IT department. The way it should be.

From a high level, Mac and iOS devices appear to provision similarly. But under the hood, they are quite a bit different. For all the additional automation features available for the Mac, the devices are only easier to configure once the startup screens have been cleared. Given all these differences, we'll cover the Mac further next, in Chapter 6.

CHAPTER 6

Mac Provisioning

Imaging. We used to say that we imaged computers. But then came Apple File System (APFS) and the need for Macs to have specific firmware installed to support APFS's capabilities. These days, preparing a device to go into the hands of an end user is more about provisioning the Mac for use by installing an OS and then configuring it for a person's use than it is about creating a disk image and applying it to a Mac to prepare it for someone to use.

When we say "imaging" a Mac, we typically think of erasing a device and putting new bits on the device so the device has everything a user needs to get their work done. At first, this was done by creating a "monolithic" image, where the disk image was taken from a Mac which had been set up with everything needed. That monolithic image was then applied to other Macs to make them exact clones of that first Mac. But that lacked flexibility, so we moved from monolithic imaging to package-based imaging, where we installed an image just containing the OS and then applied a series of installer packages to set up the Mac. Then we moved from package-based imaging to restoring a "thin" image, or one with just the operating system and an agent, where the agent would set up the Mac using settings and software pulled down from a management server. Then Apple gave us the Automated Device Enrollment program (or ADE for short), formerly known as the Device Enrollment Program (DEP), and we skipped doing any predelivery setup work altogether and started just providing a fresh-out-of-the-box Mac to our non-IT colleagues. Once they started the Mac for the first time, Apple's Setup Assistant and the follow-up

C. Edge and R. Trouton, *Apple Device Management*,
https://doi.org/10.1007/978-1-4842-9156-6_6

configuration workflows enabled our colleagues to set up their own Macs without anyone else's assistance. This saves many large organizations the $20–$40 per device cost that they used to pay to have Macs set up prior to delivering them. ADE automatically enrolls the device into a Mobile Device Management (MDM) solution, puts apps on the device, and puts the agent on the device through MDM. There are less options, but the process has never been so streamlined with such a small amount of work.

Shipping devices directly to a user makes them feel like they're getting the new device they were always getting. Once administrators had everything necessary to provision a device out of the box. However, with the release and general adoption of Apple's Apple File System (APFS) filesystem, traditional imaging became much more difficult. In its place, Apple has recommended installing the operating system and using MDM profile, scripts, and installer packages to configure the operating system for use. These changes introduced a learning curve for many Mac admins, but ultimately this change is one for the better.

macOS Startup Modifier Keys

To aid with provisioning and other functions, Apple has always allowed you to boot a computer while holding down a given keystroke in order to invoke a specific startup sequence.

With the introduction of Apple Silicon Macs in addition to Macs with Intel processors, those keystrokes (otherwise known as Startup Modifiers) are going to be different between Apple Silicon and Intel Macs.

Macs with Apple Silicon Processors

Power key (hold down for ten or more seconds)	Boots into the Startup Options screen, which allows you to select which volume you want to boot to, choose to boot into Safe Mode or choose to boot into the Recovery environment.

Macs with Intel Processors

Alt or Option key	Boots into the Startup Manager, which allows you to select a wireless network and then choose which volume you want to boot to.
C key	Boots into volumes on a CD, DVD, or USB drive.
Command-Option-P-R keys	Resets the parameter RAM (or PRAM for short).
Command-R keys	Boots into the macOS recovery mode, useful when doing an Internet restore or using Disk Utility to repair a volume.
Command-Option-R keys	Boots into Apple's cloud-hosted recovery mode.
Command-S keys	Boots into single-user mode.
Command-V keys	Boots into verbose mode, so you see a log of everything during the startup process.
D key	Boots into diagnostics, used for checking the hardware of your system. Depending on Mac model, this will load either Apple Hardware Test (for Mac models introduced before June 2013) or Apple Diagnostics (for Mac models introduced in June 2013 or later).
Option-D keys	Boots into Apple's cloud-hosted Diagnostics.
Eject key, F12 key, or mouse/trackpad button	Ejects any removable media inserted into the Mac.
N key	On NetBoot-capable Macs, boots to a NetBoot volume. (Macs equipped with T2 chips are not capable of NetBooting.)
Option-N keys	On NetBoot-capable Macs, boots to the default NetBoot volume on a particular network.

(*continued*)

Shift key	Boots into Safe Boot mode. Safe Boot verifies the startup disk and repairs directory issues, disables user fonts, and clears the cache for them, only loads required kernel extensions and clears the cache for them, clears system caches, and disables startup and login items.
T key	Boots into Target Disk Mode (TDM). TDM sets the system as a disk which can be mounted on another system as an external drive.
X key	Boots to a macOS startup disk when otherwise booting to a Windows partition or startup manager.

macOS Provisioning with ADE

Apple's ADE program does include some prerequisites before you can use it:

1. You must have an Apple School Manager (ASM) or Apple Business Manager (ABM) instance set up for your company, school, or institution.

    - If you're a school or other educational institution, you will be using Apple School Manager.
    - If you're not a school or other educational institution, you will be using Apple Business Manager.

    From the ADE point of view, both ASM and ABM offer equivalent functionality.

2. You must have a Mobile Device Management (MDM) solution, and that MDM solution must be capable of working with ASM/ABM.

3. The Mac being set up must be registered with your company, school, or institution's ASM/ABM instance.

Once these prerequisites are fulfilled, you can use ADE to set up your Macs. In your ASM/ABM instance, you can set your registered Macs to be automatically enrolled with your MDM. This automated enrollment means that the Macs will automatically check in with your MDM when the Mac is going through the initial setup process for macOS. The MDM can in turn provide an automated setup workflow for that Mac to run through.

For Macs registered with ABM/ASM instances, Mac admins can take advantage of ADE's automatic enrollment into an MDM to automate the setup of Macs. The basic workflow looks like this:

1. Assign a Mac's serial number to a particular MDM server.
2. Install a fresh copy of macOS onto the Mac.
3. On boot, the Mac will be automatically enrolled in the MDM server, and Apple's Setup Assistant can be managed to set up the Mac with a desired configuration.
4. If desired, the MDM can also install software and profiles to further configure the Mac.

For the additional software and profile installation options, there are several tools available to help automate the post-Setup Assistant installation actions. One well-known free and open source solution is DEPNotify (Figure 6-1). This tool provides a user-facing interface that allows the new Mac's user to see the following:

- The Mac is being set up.
- Provide status information about where the Mac is in the setup process.

- Provide any additional information that the system administrator may choose to provide as part of the setup process.
- The other important function provided by this tool is that they prevent the user from making any changes to the Mac before the setup workflow has completed its task of setting up the Mac with its required set of software and settings.

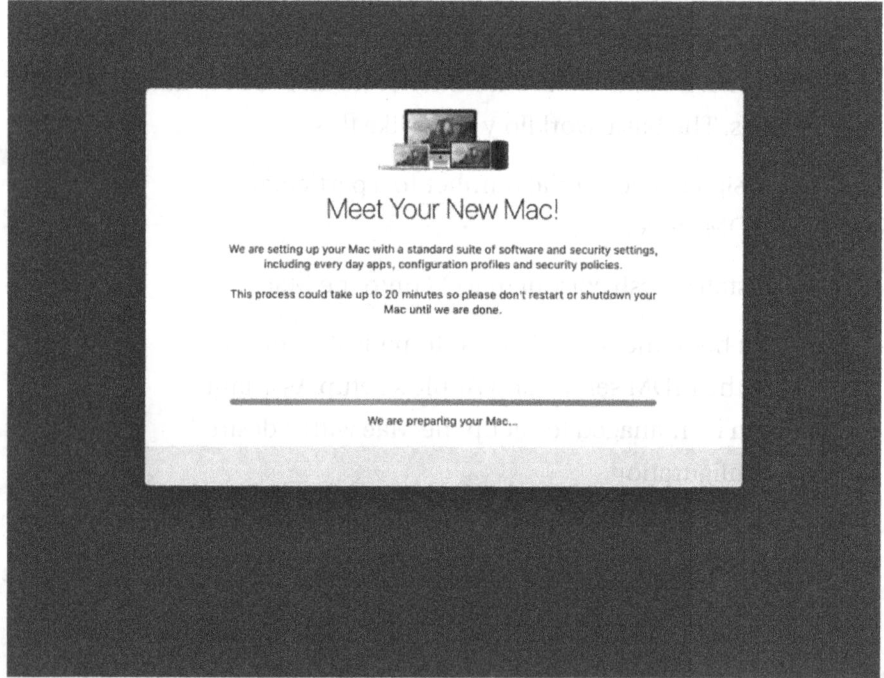

***Figure 6-1.** DEPNotify running an automated setup workflow*

A commercial tool with similar functionality is Octory from Amaris Consulting. This tool provides a user-facing interface that allows the new Mac's user to see the following.

DEPNotify

Site: `https://gitlab.com/Mactroll/DEPNotify`

Octory

Site: `www.octory.io`

macOS Provisioning Without ADE

ADE is a great deployment solution, but being able to use it requires Apple School Manager (ASM) or Apple Business Manager (ABM), an MDM solution, and also having the Mac registered with the appropriate ASM or ABM instance. For some environments, one or more of those components aren't available, but Macs still need to be set up and configured.

One solution to this problem is a tool called Mac Deploy Stick (MDS) from Twocanoes Software. MDS makes it easy to wipe and reinstall a Mac quickly the same way you can with Apple Configurator for iOS and iPadOS. The reason you need a tool like Mac Deploy Stick is that Apple gives users the ability to reinstall the operating system from the recovery partition, but that installer has to get downloaded during a very manual process. MDS creates those resources locally (e.g., on a USB stick or other external media) instead and organizes them into workflows, which can be deployed more quickly - and come with a simple setup so Macs can be set up faster. An optional Arduino can become a Mac Deploy Stick Automation, which inserts keystrokes during boot time so administrators don't have to hold down Command-R during the boot process (see more on Startup Modifier Keys in the next section of this chapter).

Installation

To get started, download MDS from `http://twocanoes.com/products/mac/mac-deploy-stick/`. Then run the installer package. Once installed, open the MDS app from your Applications directory, and provided it opens, it's time to create your first workflow.

Create a Workflow

MDS calls a workflow a list of automations the computer will perform during a setup. This includes an operating system installation, packages to deploy to create a workflow, packages or profiles that simply provide a description, optionally provide a description of the workflow as well, and click OK (Figure 6-2).

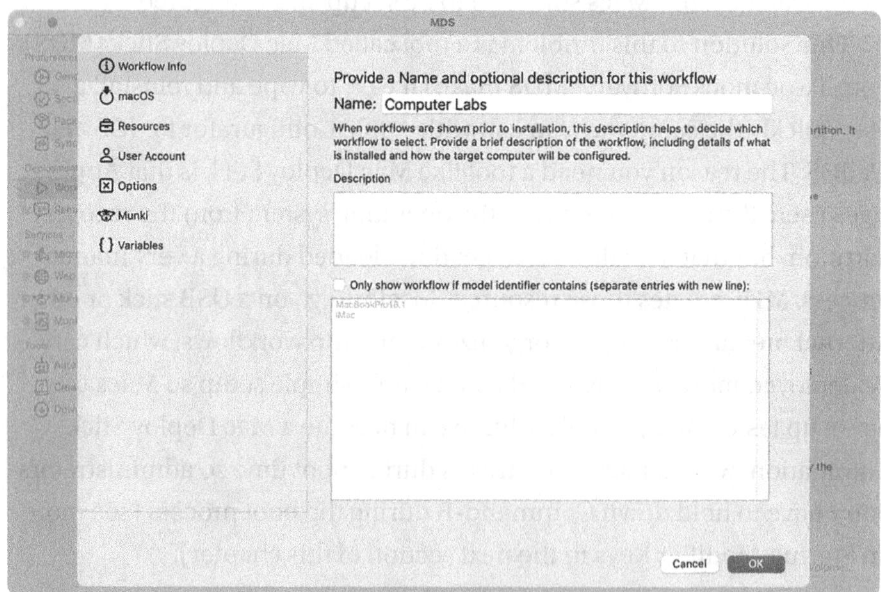

Figure 6-2. Entering a name for the MDS workflow

At the macOS screen, click "Install macOS" and then choose the installation media to generate the installer from (this will use installESD inside that bundle). Optionally, choose whether to erase the volume and then if you want the volume renamed. Click OK to proceed, as seen in Figure 6-3.

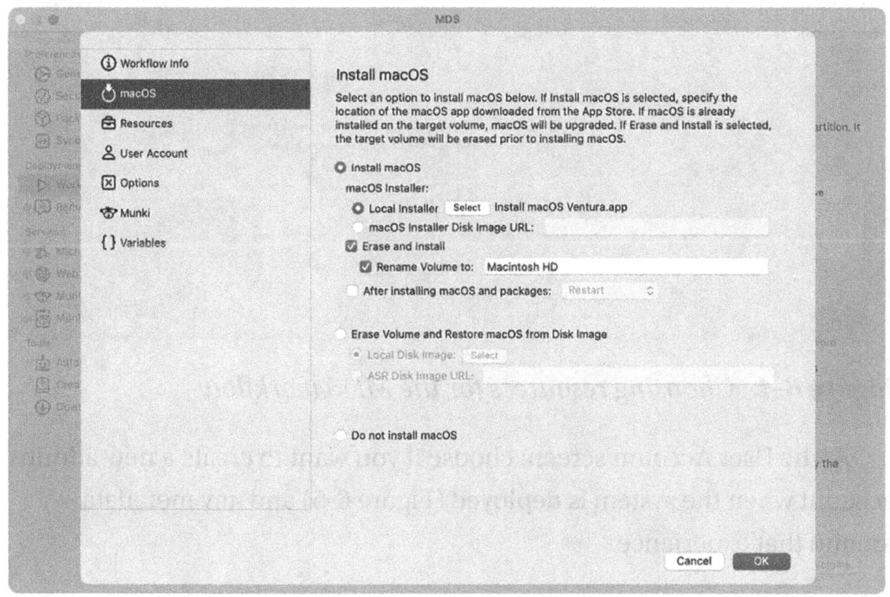

***Figure 6-3.** Choosing a macOS installer for the MDS workflow*

At the Resources screen, add the directory that contains scripts, packages, and other resources to be deployed to the client. This is an interesting approach and doesn't provide for manually selecting what order packages, apps, scripts, and policies get laid down on devices. I've had hit-or-miss luck with doing so by numbering assets in those folders. I recommend creating a directory for each type of asset in an MDS directory for that workflow prior to doing this step. Once you've bundled all of them up and selected the appropriate directory, click OK (Figure 6-4).

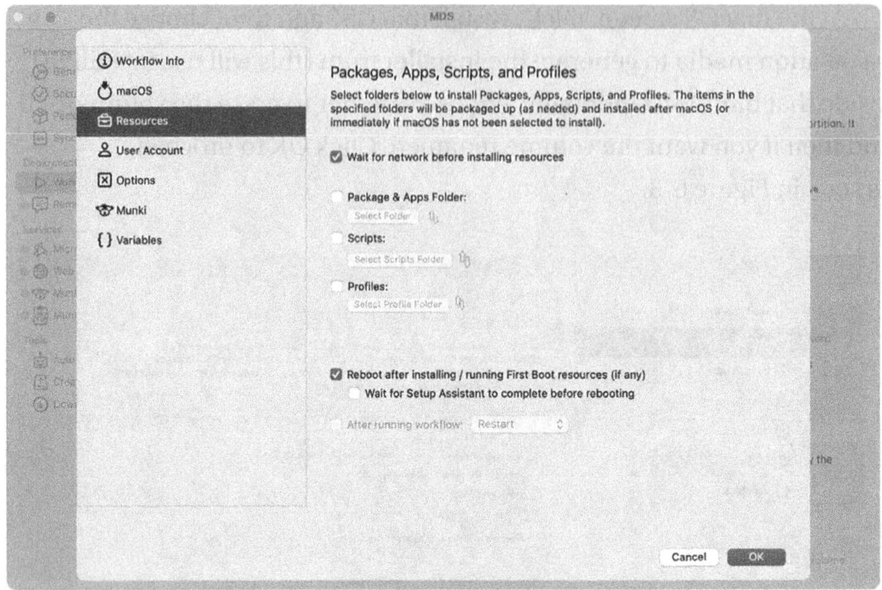

Figure 6-4. *Choosing resources for the MDS workflow*

At the User Account screen, choose if you want to create a new admin account when the system is deployed (Figure 6-5) and any metadata around that experience.

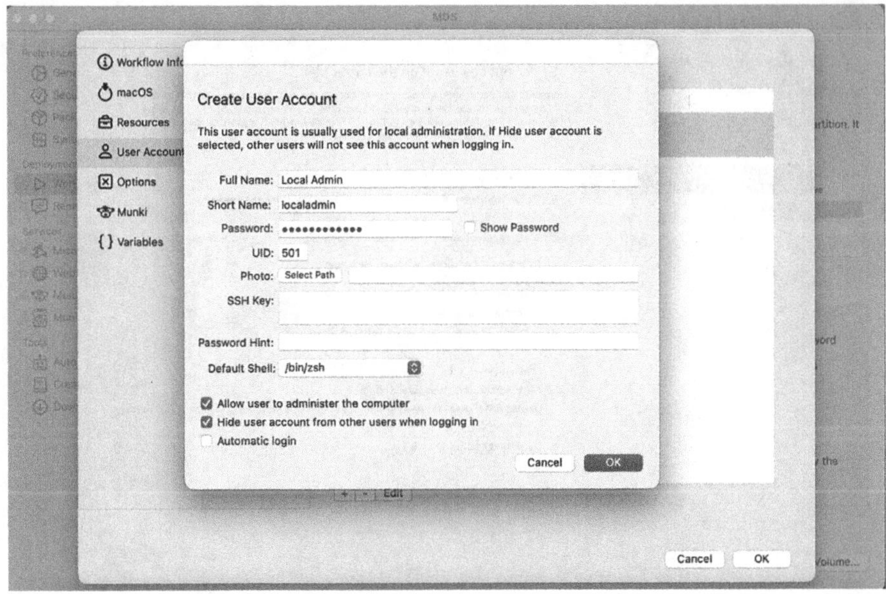

Figure 6-5. *Creating a local admin user for the MDS workflow*

At the Options screen, choose whether to automatically join a Wi-Fi network, if the computer should be renamed based on serial number, if SSH should be enabled, and if the setup assistant should be skipped. Once all options have been configured as desired, click OK as seen in Figure 6-6.

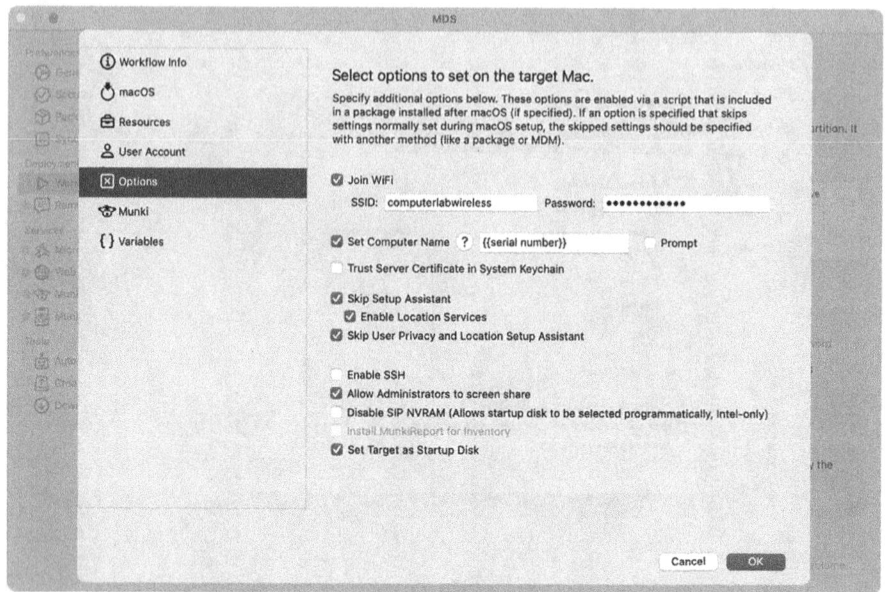

***Figure 6-6.** Defining additional options for the MDS workflow*

MDS has multiple hooks that make Munki easier to deploy on devices. Click OK as shown in Figure 6-7.

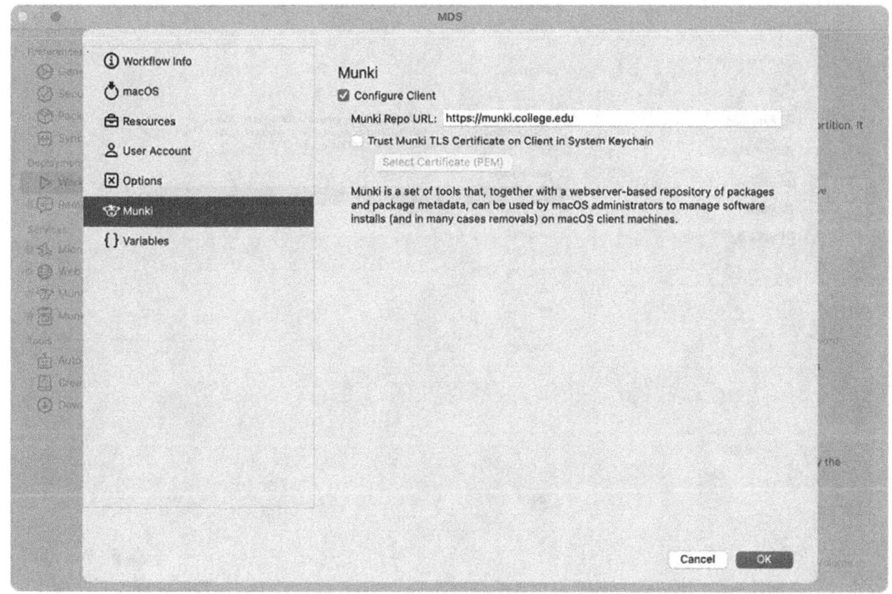

***Figure 6-7.** Configuring Munki options for the MDS workflow*

At the Variables screen (Figure 6-8), provide variables you can then call in shell scripts. These are similar to how we used to fill ARD fields (which is still an option). Sending a $1 from a shell script into these provides a little more flexibility around renaming scripts, binding operators, etc. Click OK (Figure 6-9).

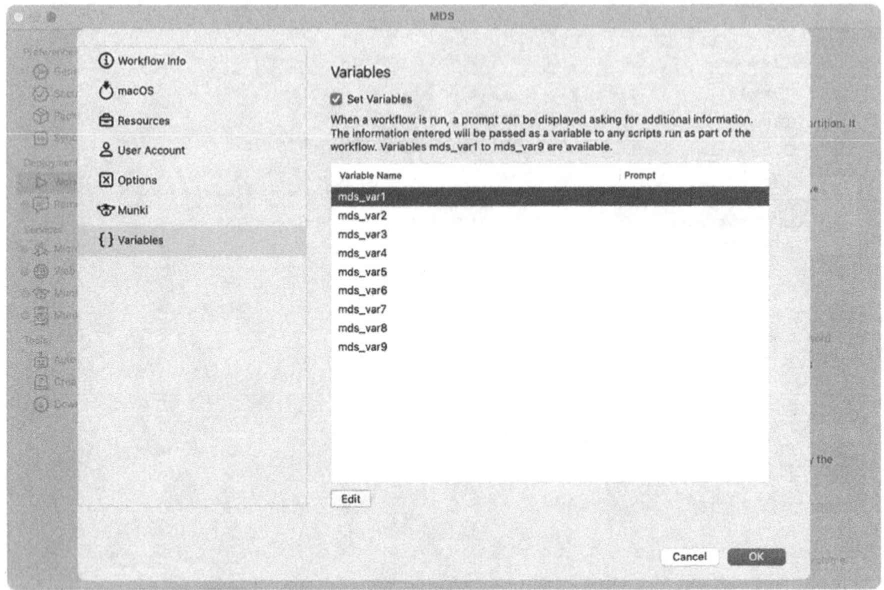

***Figure 6-8.** Defining shell script variable options for the MDS workflow*

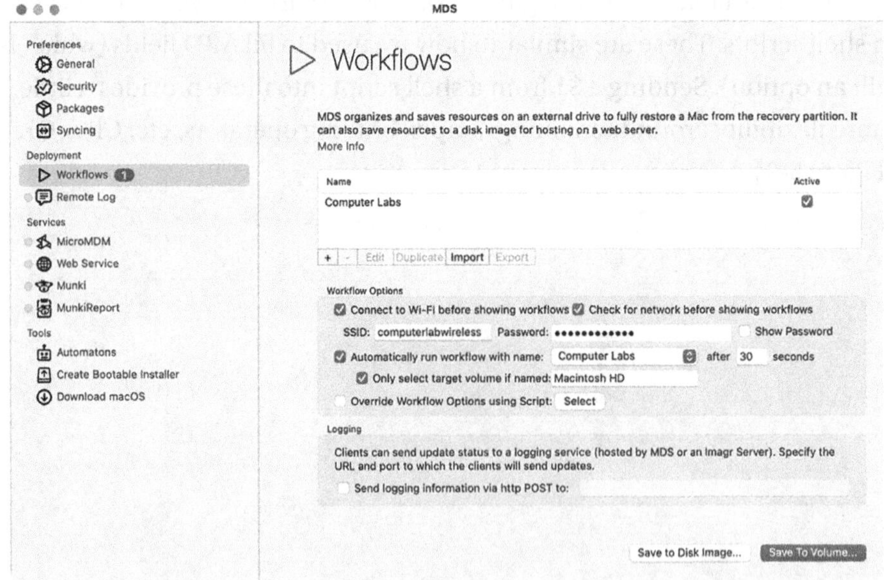

***Figure 6-9.** MDS main configuration window*

Once done, it's time to run the workflow. To do so, boot a Mac into recovery mode, and then from Terminal, run the following command (shown in Figure 6-10)

```
/Volumes/mdsresources/run
```

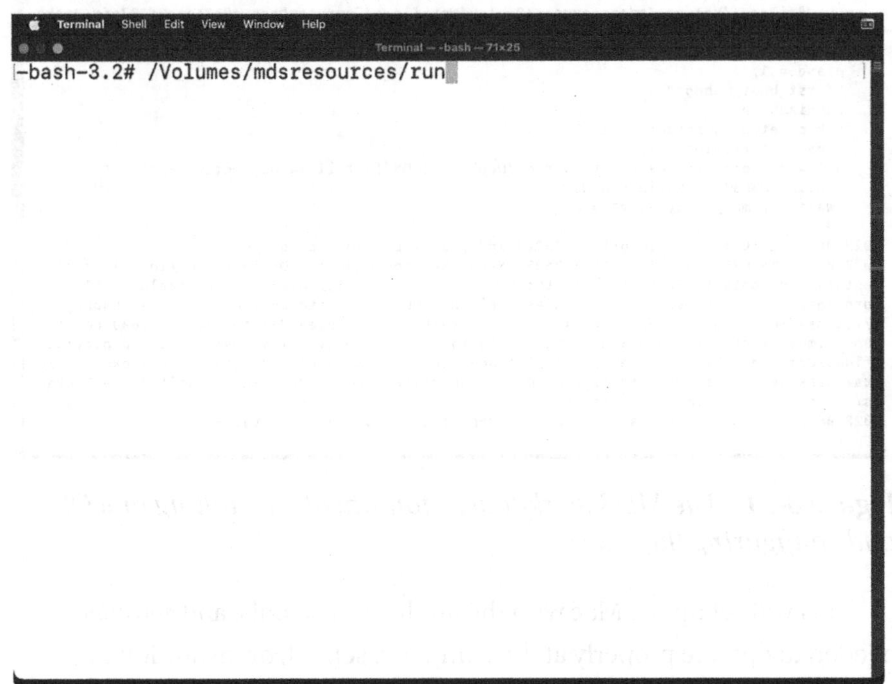

***Figure 6-10.** Launching the MDS workflow from the Recovery environment*

The configuration you created in the previous step will then be run and the output similar to that in Figure 6-11.

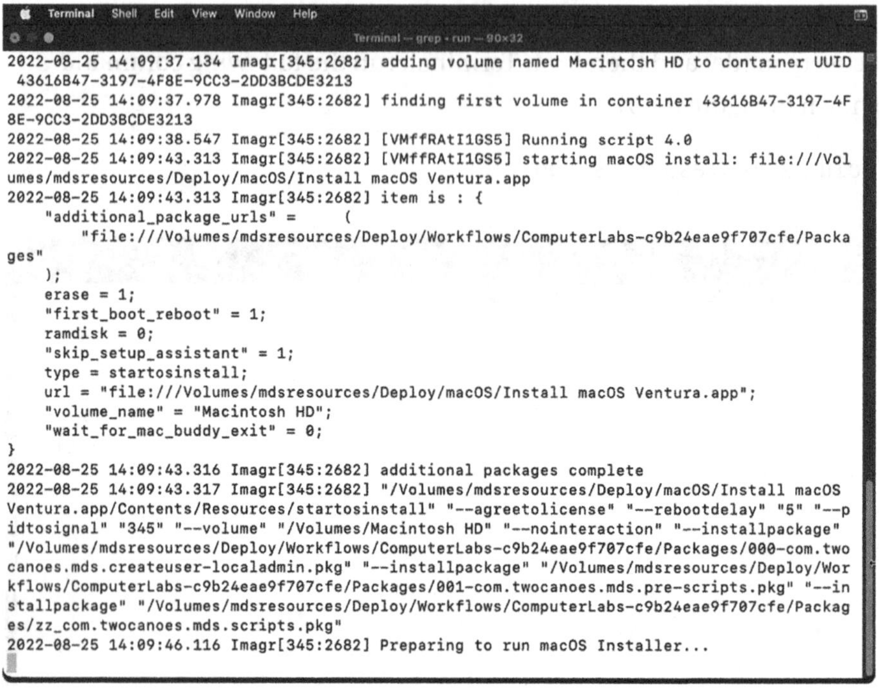

```
Terminal  Shell  Edit  View  Window  Help
Terminal — grep · run — 90×32
2022-08-25 14:09:37.134 Imagr[345:2682] adding volume named Macintosh HD to container UUID
 43616B47-3197-4F8E-9CC3-2DD3BCDE3213
2022-08-25 14:09:37.978 Imagr[345:2682] finding first volume in container 43616B47-3197-4F
8E-9CC3-2DD3BCDE3213
2022-08-25 14:09:38.547 Imagr[345:2682] [VMffRAtI1GS5] Running script 4.0
2022-08-25 14:09:43.313 Imagr[345:2682] [VMffRAtI1GS5] starting macOS install: file:///Vol
umes/mdsresources/Deploy/macOS/Install macOS Ventura.app
2022-08-25 14:09:43.313 Imagr[345:2682] item is : {
    "additional_package_urls" =     (
        "file:///Volumes/mdsresources/Deploy/Workflows/ComputerLabs-c9b24eae9f707cfe/Packa
ges"
    );
    erase = 1;
    "first_boot_reboot" = 1;
    ramdisk = 0;
    "skip_setup_assistant" = 1;
    type = startosinstall;
    url = "file:///Volumes/mdsresources/Deploy/macOS/Install macOS Ventura.app";
    "volume_name" = "Macintosh HD";
    "wait_for_mac_buddy_exit" = 0;
}
2022-08-25 14:09:43.316 Imagr[345:2682] additional packages complete
2022-08-25 14:09:43.317 Imagr[345:2682] "/Volumes/mdsresources/Deploy/macOS/Install macOS
Ventura.app/Contents/Resources/startosinstall" "--agreetolicense" "--rebootdelay" "5" "--p
idtosignal" "345" "--volume" "/Volumes/Macintosh HD" "--nointeraction" "--installpackage"
"/Volumes/mdsresources/Deploy/Workflows/ComputerLabs-c9b24eae9f707cfe/Packages/000-com.two
canoes.mds.createuser-localadmin.pkg" "--installpackage" "/Volumes/mdsresources/Deploy/Wor
kflows/ComputerLabs-c9b24eae9f707cfe/Packages/001-com.twocanoes.mds.pre-scripts.pkg" "--in
stallpackage" "/Volumes/mdsresources/Deploy/Workflows/ComputerLabs-c9b24eae9f707cfe/Packag
es/zz_com.twocanoes.mds.scripts.pkg"
2022-08-25 14:09:46.116 Imagr[345:2682] Preparing to run macOS Installer...
```

***Figure 6-11.** The MDS workflow automatically installing macOS and configuring the Mac*

This will set up the Mac with the applications, tools, and settings needed to operate properly at the company, school, or institution in question.

There are a lot more workflows than just this one, so to learn more about MDS, go to `https://twocanoes.com/knowledge-base/mds-4-guide/`.

One of the important components of MDS when used on Intel Macs is an open source project known as Imagr, developed by Graham Gilbert. Imagr is a community project that runs not only on macOS but on Linux as well. While Imagr was originally developed for use with NetInstall and a web server, Twocanoes built on the existing Imagr project to provide MDS's ability to provision Macs.

Imagr

Site: `https://github.com/grahamgilbert/imagr/`

Purpose: Imaging and deployment for Mac systems

For Apple Silicon Macs, Twocanoes has developed a counterpart solution called MDS Deploy. MDS will detect which kind of processor the Mac is using and automatically use Imagr or MDS Deploy as needed.

Upgrades and Installations

You install or upgrade the macOS operating system using an installer provided by Apple. This used to be an installer which required an Apple ID to access, but beginning with macOS Sierra, Apple made operating system installer free for all Mac users and even began pushing the installer for new OS versions shortly after the new OS's release date. The installer itself appears as an application normally stored in the **Applications** directory (shown in Figure 6-12).

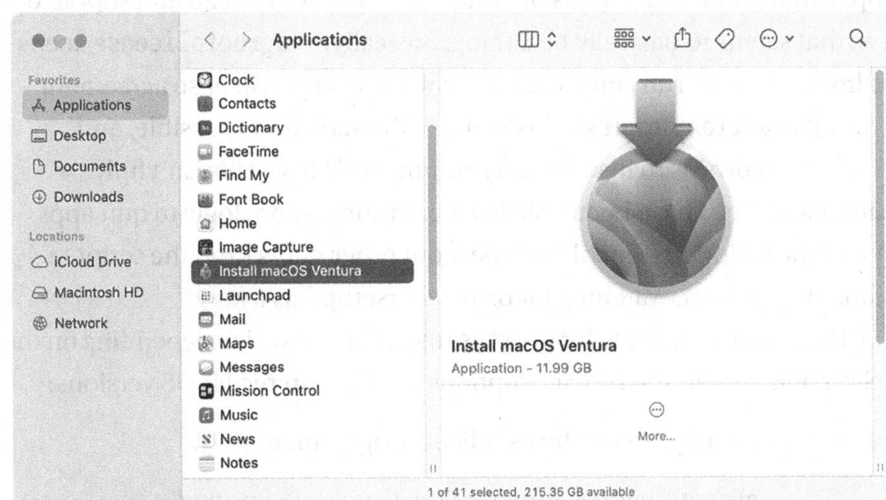

***Figure 6-12.** The macOS Ventura installer application in the **Applications** directory*

Running the OS installer on an individual Mac requires administrator rights, but otherwise is an easy experience where you double-click to launch the installer application and follow the prompts.

Automating OS installations is going to eventually be about as easy on macOS as it is in iOS, but we're not there yet. At present, the automation tool provided by Apple these days is the `startosinstall` command. This tool first shipped with OS X El Capitan and so should work with that operating system or any that have been distributed since then. To use the `startosinstall` command, you will need to open Terminal and run commands similar to the one shown as follows:

```
sudo "/Applications/Install macOS Ventura.app/Contents/
Resources/startosinstall" --applicationpath "/Applications/
Install macOS Ventura.app" --agreetolicense --nointeraction
--volume "/Volumes/Macintosh HD"
```

In the preceding command, we've already loaded the "Install macOS Ventura.app" on a machine. While you'd guess that it would find the application path based on its own surname, we went ahead and supplied it as that seems to basically be a thing. Basically, `--agreetolicense` keeps us from having to run some expect scripts to accept a license agreement, `--nointeraction` suppresses as many of the screens as possible, and `--volume` allows us to install to any volume we'd like. This isn't fully automated, but I have been able to layer in some more logic to quit apps before the script fires and then expect out other items from the script to automate a restart, watching for osinstallersetupd as a key.

The options available for `startosinstall` have varied depending on the OS version, but here's the list of options available in recent OS versions:

--license: Prints the user license agreement only.

--agreetolicense: Agrees to the license you printed with --license.

--rebootdelay: How long to delay the reboot at the end of preparing. This delay is in seconds and has a maximum of 300 (5 minutes).

--pidtosignal: Specifies a PID to which to send SIGUSR1 upon completion of the prepare phase. To bypass "rebootdelay," send SIGUSR1 back to startosinstall.

--installpackage: The path of a package (built with productbuild(1)) to install after the OS installation is complete; this option can be specified multiple times.

--eraseinstall: (Requires APFS) Erases all volumes and installs to a new one. Optionally specify the name of the new volume with --newvolumename.

--newvolumename: The name of the volume to be created with --eraseinstall.

--preservecontainer: Preserves other volumes in your APFS container when using --eraseinstall.

--usage: Provides the list of startosinstall options.

--nointeraction: Suppresses a number of screens where a human would be asked to make choices.

--volume: Allows startosinstall to run the installation process on a drive other than the boot drive.

One particularly useful function is the `--installpackage` function, which allows one or more packages stored on the Mac in question to be installed following the upgrade. Something to be aware of is that if you want to add any additional packages, they must all be signed or unsigned distribution-style flat packages. This is a requirement that Apple first introduced for the OS X Yosemite installer, and it still applies to the latest versions of macOS.

You can convert a nondistribution package to be a distribution-style flat package by running the following command:

```
productbuild -package /path/to/original.pkg /path/to/
distribution.pkg
```

To run an automated upgrade to macOS Ventura, where two distribution-style flat packages stored in /Users/Shared are installed following the upgrade, please run the command shown as follows with root privileges:

```
"/Applications/Install macOS Ventura.app/Contents/Resources/
startosinstall" --applicationpath "/Applications/Install macOS
Ventura.app" --agreetolicense --installpackage /Users/Shared/
installer_one.pkg --installpackage /Users/Shared/installer_two.
pkg --nointeraction
```

This is all a bit bulkier than just using something like createOSXinstallPkg, a tool available for building OS installers which was compatible with Mac OS X Lion through macOS Sierra, but it's important to mention that there are a number of system components that are allowed for in SIP that use osinstallersetupd, and so this blessed mechanism is likely the future until you can trigger an OS upgrade (and update I suppose) using an MDM command.

Reprovisioning a Mac

Most organizations will take an iOS device out of service, erase the device, and hand it to the next user. Administrators of Macs have long wanted a similar feature, and it arrived as of macOS Monterey with the **Erase All Content and Settings** feature for Apple Silicon Macs and Intel Macs equipped with the T2 security chip.

To use the **Erase All Content and Settings** feature on macOS, open System Settings and then select **General**. From there, you will see an entry for **Transfer or Reset** preference pane (Figure 6-13).

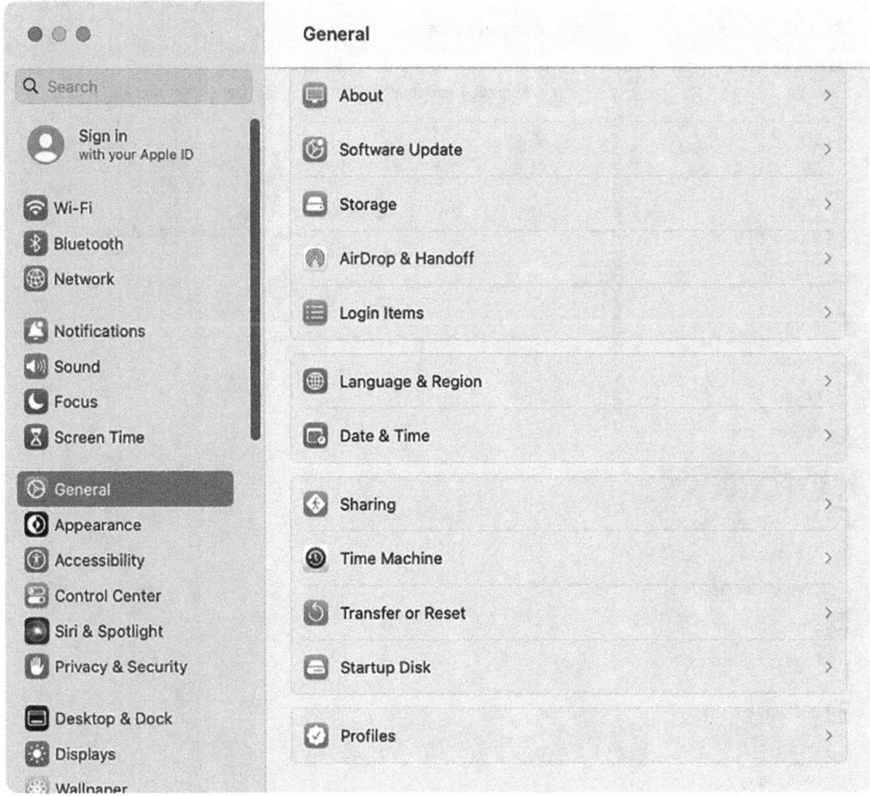

Figure 6-13. *The **Transfer or Reset** preference pane in System Settings*

Selecting the **Transfer or Reset** preference will provide access to the **Erase All Content and Settings** button.

Clicking the **Erase All Content and Settings** button (Figure 6-14) will prompt for administrator credentials before opening the Erase Assistant app (Figure 6-15).

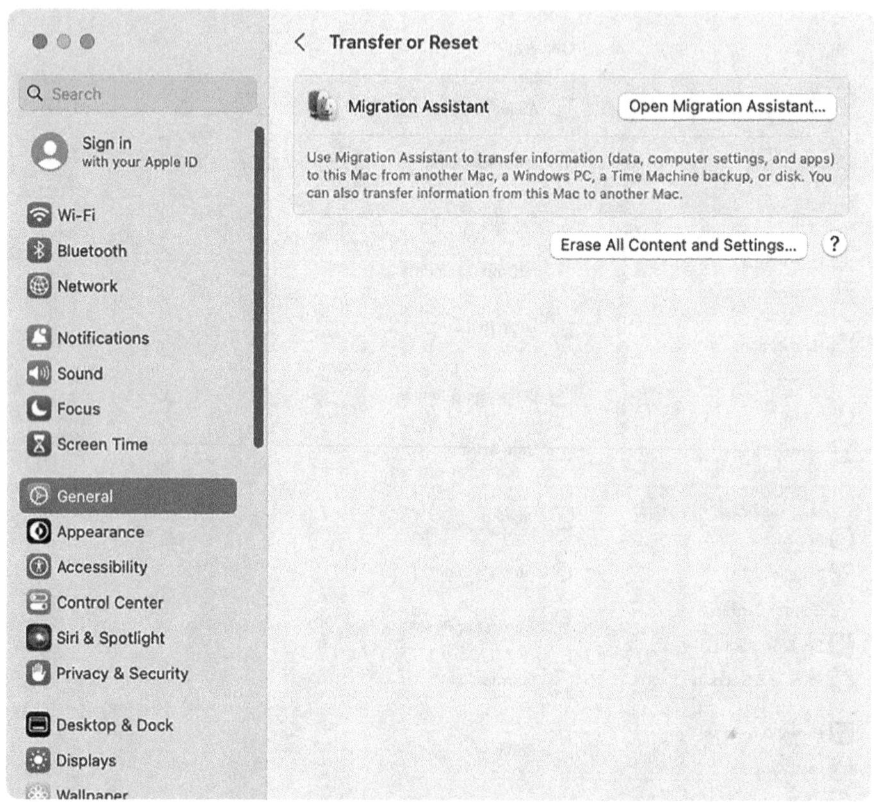

Figure 6-14. *The **Erase All Content and Settings** button in System Settings' **Transfer or Reset** preference pane*

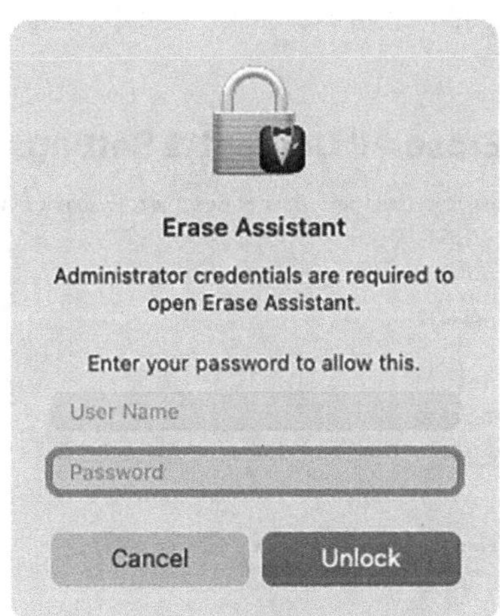

Figure 6-15. *Requesting administrator credentials before opening the Erase Assistant application*

The Erase Assistant will display a summary of what's being removed, along with a **Continue** button (Figure 6-16).

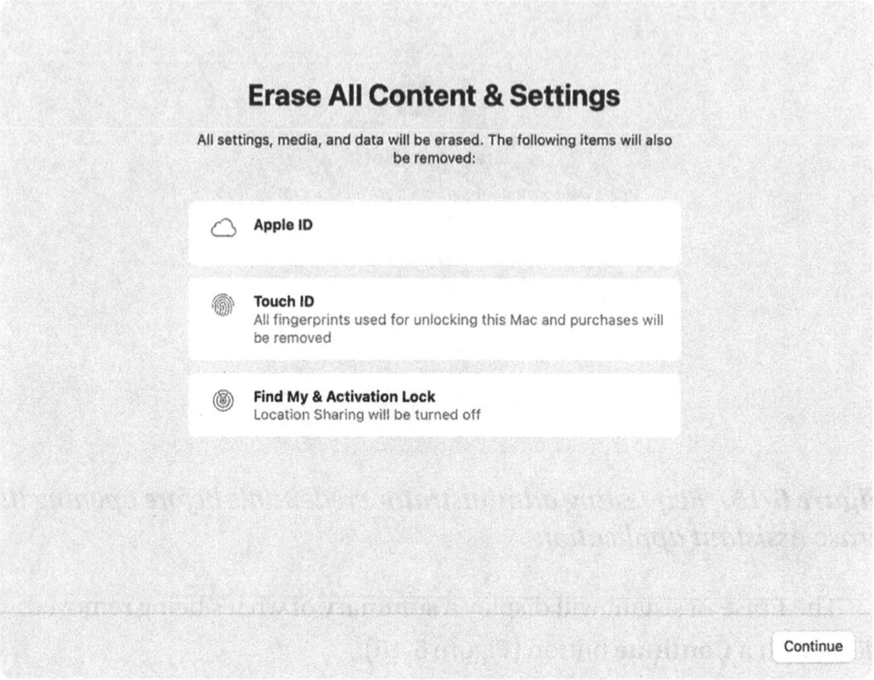

Figure 6-16. *The Erase Assistant app displaying a summary of the data which will be removed from the Mac*

Clicking **Continue** will wipe the encryption keys used to protect the data on the Mac, along with all other data which is not part of the operating system. The end result will be that the Mac will be returned to a factory-default configuration with an unconfigured macOS installation.

Once the Mac is back to having only an unconfigured copy of macOS installed, it can now be set up for use with whatever provisioning tool works best for the Mac admin in question.

Virtual Machines

Virtual machines running macOS as their OS can be provisioned for deployment using the same tools used for physical Mac hardware. The main limitations stem from virtual machines being software constructs and not actual hardware. Here are some of the major ones:

- **Anything involving having an Apple-registered hardware serial number/sending hardware serial number back to Apple**: This includes iCloud services like Find My Mac and Messages. It also applies to getting hardware-specific OS installers via Recovery HD.
    - Depending on the virtual machine software being used, it may be possible to get around some of the limitations by assigning an actual Mac's model and serial number to the virtual machine.
- **Most things involving EFI**: Functions like Apple Internet Recovery or holding down the Option key to get a list of bootable volumes will not work. However, some things involving EFI work specifically because VMware made them work. For example, both NetBoot and FileVault 2 work fine in a VMware VM.
- **Wireless connections**: Virtual machines don't have a Wi-Fi card, though it may talk to a network via your Mac's Wi-Fi connection. You can test in a VM to make sure that your Wi-Fi settings apply; you can't test to verify that they work.

There are a number of virtualization solutions available which support running macOS virtual machines. Several well-known ones are listed as follows.

Parallels

Site: `www.parallels.com/products/desktop/`

UTM

Site: `https://mac.getutm.app`

Summary

Imaging's death has been widely reported, but workflows for restoring devices, provisioning, and reinstalling operating systems are all very much alive. With ADE, it's now possible to provide a user-centric setup experience for both macOS and iOS where it's possible that IT's only involvement is making sure that the device was delivered to the right person. On macOS in particular, tools like DEPNotify or Octory allow IT to enable a great user experience by providing a guided setup process for a Mac.

Meanwhile, for those companies, schools, or institutions that as of yet can't take advantage of ADE, tools like Mac Deploy Stick enable automated provisioning workflows which demand the bare minimum of IT intervention required.

In the end, Mac admins need to choose the setup and provisioning workflows which work best for them, but wise use of these tools will help conserve the most precious resource a Mac admin has: time.

CHAPTER 7

Endpoint Encryption

The data stored on your computer or mobile device is important to at least one person, and that is the person using the device. Along with it being important, there is always at least some data that you would prefer other people not see. This data could include passwords, financial data, browser history, or that text conversation between you and your significant other which is really just for your eyes only. Encryption helps protect that data from being accessed by others, and Apple has invested considerable effort to make sure that the encryption available to both iOS and macOS is not only strong enough to fend off both casual interlopers and investigators with the resources of nation states behind them.

iOS Encryption Overview

Modern iOS devices which can use Touch ID or Face ID use a combination of hardware encryption and filesystem encryption to protect data stored on the device. The hardware encryption includes the Secure Enclave coprocessor and a dedicated AES-256 cryptography engine which sits between system memory and the flash storage used to store data.

The Secure Enclave is its own self-contained processor within an iOS device. It runs its own OS, which is not directly accessible by either iOS or any of the apps running on your iOS device. The Secure Enclave's purpose is to store 256-bit elliptic curve cryptographic private keys, which are used by iOS and apps to encrypt and decrypt data stored on the iOS device. It's

C. Edge and R. Trouton, *Apple Device Management*,
https://doi.org/10.1007/978-1-4842-9156-6_7

noteworthy that neither iOS nor the apps ever get to see these private keys. Instead, the Secure Enclave is asked to encrypt and decrypt data for the operating system and apps. The private keys stored in the Secure Enclave are also unique to the device and never leave the Secure Enclave. This makes data stored on a particular iOS device incredibly difficult to decrypt on any other device because the private keys used to encrypt and decrypt data essentially work unseen and are forever locked to that one iOS device. The Secure Enclave is also responsible for processing the fingerprint and face data which comes in from the Touch ID and Face ID sensors and determining if there's a match.

This alone would help secure an iOS device, but Apple also leverages filesystem encryption technology known as Data Protection to further secure data. Data Protection constructs and manages a hierarchy of cryptographic keys and controls data by assigning each file on the iOS device's flash storage to a particular class. Access to that data is then determined by whether that class's keys have been unlocked. With Apple's introduction of Apple File System (APFS), cryptographic keys can be assigned on a per-extent basis. Since files can have multiple extents, this means that portions of a file can now be assigned different cryptographic keys.

How it all works is that every time a new file is created, Data Protection creates a new cryptographic key for the file. This key is given to the AES-256 cryptography engine, which uses that key to encrypt the file as it's being written to the flash storage used to store data. The per-file key is then wrapped with a class key, depending on the circumstances under which the file should be accessible, and the wrapped per-file encryption key is stored in the file's metadata. This metadata is itself encrypted using a different filesystem key, which is used to protect the metadata of each file. This filesystem key is also used in part to help generate the class keys and per-file keys.

The combination of keys means there are a minimum of three different filesystem-level cryptographic keys which are protecting a particular file:

- **Filesystem key**: Protects the file metadata
- **Class key**: Governs file accessibility
- **Per-file key**: Protects the file

Combine that with the fact that all the keys are being generated by the Secure Enclave, which manages all of these keys but which isn't even directly accessible by either the hardware doing the encrypting or the files being encrypted, and it becomes clear that Apple has done its legwork on protecting user data.

So how do you enable this protection? Enable a passcode. Data Protection is automatically enabled when a passcode is set up for an iOS device. As of iOS 16, iOS supports the following kinds of passcodes:

- Four digits
- Six digits
- Alphanumeric passcodes of arbitrary length

In addition to unlocking the device, the passcode provides entropy for certain cryptographic keys, including the filesystem key. Entropy is another way of saying "randomness," which means that the filesystem key is always different every time it is generated. The reason why this is important is that the hardware encryption fundamentals can't change, they're hardwired into the iOS device. By ensuring that the filesystem key can and will change every time the device is wiped and restored, Apple helps ensure that the encryption keys used on the device are also completely unique to the device.

The filesystem key is created when an iOS device is wiped and set up as new. Once the filesystem key is generated, it is stored in what's known as Effaceable Storage. Effaceable Storage is a dedicated area of flash memory used to store cryptographic keys, and it is different from the regular flash storage in two respects:

- It does not use wear leveling.
- It can be erased completely and leave no trace of original data.

Flash storage has a finite number of times it can be written to. Wear leveling is used to prolong the life of flash storage by spreading out writes evenly across the flash storage. While this helps prolong the life of the flash storage in question, it also makes it harder to securely erase data because traces of old data may be found on random blocks long after the original data was erased.

In contrast, Effaceable Storage's flash storage can be completely erased, and no data can be recovered from it. Apple leverages this capability with the **Erase All Content and Settings** option in iOS's Settings to destroy all of the cryptographic keys stored in Effaceable Storage. This key destruction instantly makes all of the user data files stored on the iOS device inaccessible by making it impossible to unlock the encryption on the files. The files themselves are still there, but there's now no way to access their contents. As an added benefit, wiping out the keys in Effaceable Storage instead of erasing the files themselves saves wear on the user data's flash storage and helps it to last longer.

What if a passcode isn't enabled? All of the encryption is still there. However, when the iOS device starts up, the needed encryption keys to unlock the encryption are automatically provided by the Secure Enclave. This is why turning on Data Protection is instant when the passcode option is enabled. The only change is for the Secure Enclave to stop automatically providing the unlock keys.

Enabling Encryption on iOS

To enforce encryption on multiple iOS devices, the simplest method is to use configuration profiles deployed through your MDM server solution. You can use Apple Configurator to create the configuration profile:

1. Open Apple Configurator.
2. Select **File: New Profile**.

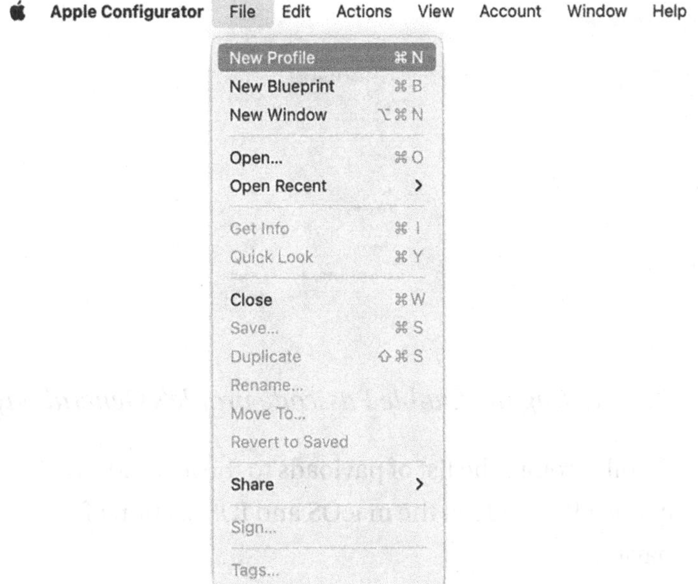

Figure 7-1. *Creating a management profile in Apple Configurator*

3. A new profile creation window should open, with Configurator defaulting to showing the **General** section.
4. Complete the information in the General payload of the new configuration profile. Set the Security drop-down menu to Never to prevent removal of the profile.

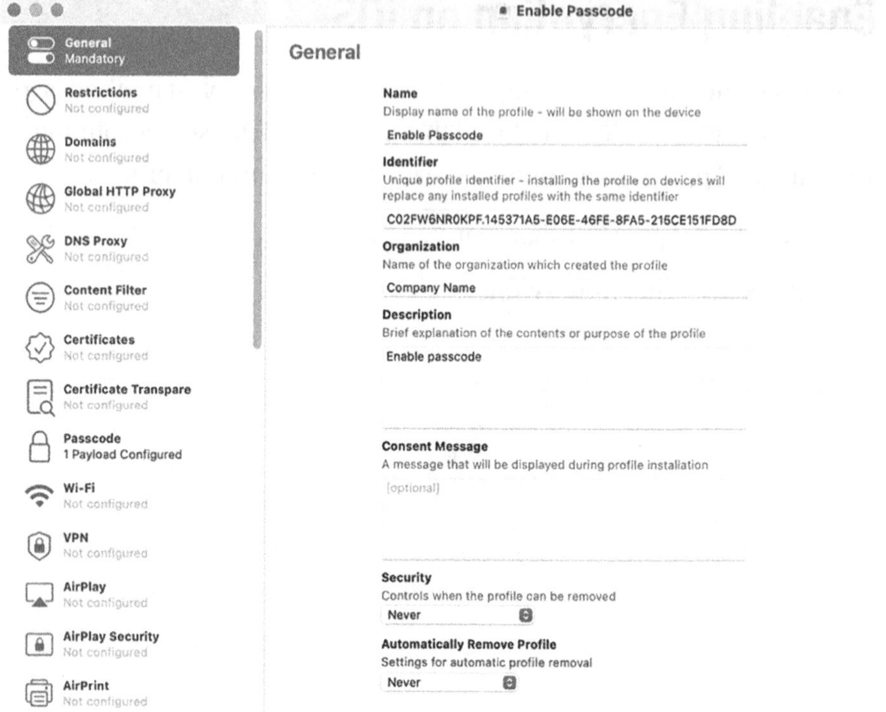

***Figure 7-2.** Creating the Enable Passcode profile's General payload*

5. Scroll through the list of payloads to the left and choose Passcode in the macOS and IOS section of payloads.

6. Configure passcode settings as desired.

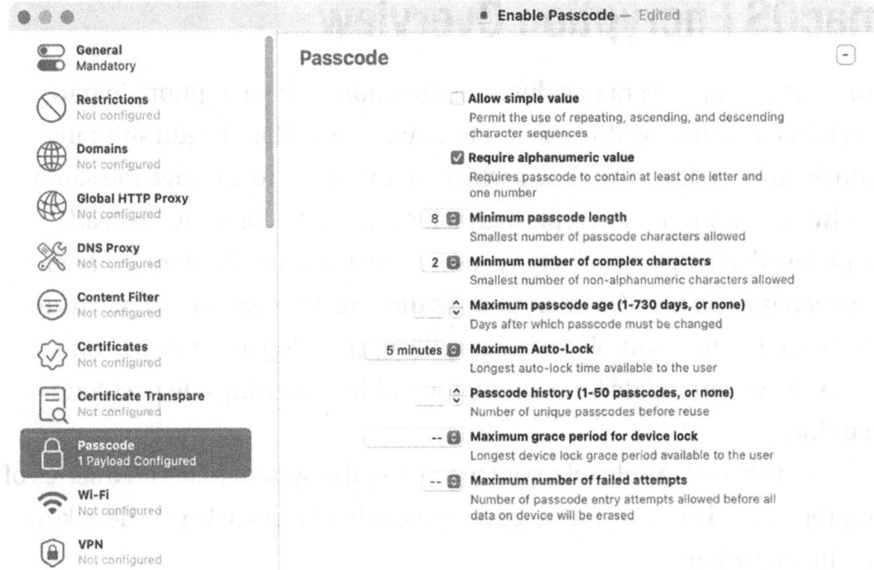

Figure 7-3. *Creating the Enable Passcode profile's Passcode payload*

7. Click the OK button when done configuring the profile.

8. Select **Save** under the **File** menu to save the new Enable Passcode configuration profile.

9. Email or download this .mobileconfig file to a test iOS device and double-tap it to install.

10. Verify that you are now being asked to set a passcode with the desired settings.

After successful testing, upload the profile to your MDM server. Once completed, scope the profile to the desired mobile devices enrolled in your MDM and use its push capabilities to deploy the profile.

macOS Encryption Overview

For macOS, Apple went in a different direction with encryption. In part, this is because only within the last few years have Macs begun shipping with Secure Enclave processors which enable them to leverage the same hardware support for encryption that iOS has had for a while. Instead, Apple needed to handle all encryption using software. Another difference between macOS and iOS encryption is that macOS's encryption needs to be able to handle multiple cryptographic users to log in, while iOS only needs to accommodate for one cryptographic user using one passcode to unlock.

On Macs with Apple File System (APFS), the system relies on a series of cryptographic keys granting access to two other layers of keys. These keys are the following:

- Derived encryption key
- Key encryption key
- Volume encryption key

To examine them from the filesystem level upward, let's first look at the volume encryption key (VEK). This is the key that is interacting with the APFS volume that the FileVault 2 encryption process has created. All cryptographic operations on an encrypted APFS volume are unique to that volume because a different volume encryption key is randomly generated for each volume. This is the key that is actually unlocking the encrypted volume, and it's also the key that's deleted when a wipe command is sent to a FileVault 2-encrypted Mac.

On the next level up, there's the key encryption key (KEK) which is otherwise known as a Secure Token. This key is generated when FileVault 2 encryption is initialized on a particular volume. It is used to unlock the volume encryption key one layer down and acts as the middleman between the volume encryption key and the derived keys. This middle layer allows the derived keys to change without affecting the derived keys' ability to unlock the encrypted volume. One thing that's important to know on APFS volumes is that Apple has set up the KEK/Secure Token so that user accounts need to be enabled for Secure Token access and that it's possible to have user accounts which are not Secure Token enabled. If an account is not Secure Token enabled, it's not possible for that account to unlock FileVault's encryption. Secure Token has caused a lot of confusion for Mac admins, so there will be further discussion of it later in this chapter.

On the top layer, there's the derived encryption keys. These keys begin the chain reaction of unlocking the other keys below it, resulting in the unlocking or decryption of the encrypted volume. Any derived key can be independently changed without affecting its ability to unlock the other two layers of keys.

Any given APFS volume must be able to support multiple cryptographic users, each with their own derived key which is able to unlock the encryption. This is important because it means that there can be multiple ways to access the encrypted volume. In the case of FileVault 2's encryption, it means that multiple-user accounts can be enabled to unlock an encrypted Mac at the preboot login screen. Derived keys are also used for the FileVault 2 recovery keys, which we'll be covering in more detail later.

For those Macs which have the Secure Enclave processor, how does the Secure Enclave fit into this model? Just like it does on iOS. The overall macOS encryption model remains the same, but Secure Enclave–equipped Macs are always encrypted. Period. Even if FileVault is not enabled.

How this works is that the solid-state drives which ship with these Macs have built-in hardware encryption support, and the Secure Enclave processor stores the keys needed to unlock the encrypted storage. If FileVault isn't turned on, the Secure Enclave automatically provides the unlock keys when the Mac boots. Once FileVault is turned on, the Secure Enclave stops providing the unlock keys on boot and now requires authentication by a Secure Token–enabled account in order to unlock the encryption. This allows FileVault to be instantly turned on and off, just as you can instantly turn on and off encryption on iOS using the passcode settings.

On Macs that don't have a Secure Enclave processor, the lack of hardware support means that the APFS volume must be encrypted using the filesystem's native encryption capabilities. This is usually a slower process than "instant," with time to encrypt varying depending on the speed of the storage in use, size of the storage volume, and speed of the processor.

For Apple Silicon Macs, Apple has also implemented Data Protection (discussed earlier in the iOS encryption section) to bring file-level encryption to macOS. This extra level of protection is not available for Macs with Intel processors.

However, Data Protection on macOS is a hybrid implementation which is different from the iOS implementation of Data Protection. To understand how, let's first look at how Data Protection is implemented on iOS.

iOS's Data Protection implementation includes the following classes:

a. **Class A - Complete Protection**: The class key is protected with a key derived from the user passcode and the device UID. Shortly after the user locks a device (10 seconds, if the Require Password setting is Immediately), the decrypted class key is discarded, rendering all data in this class inaccessible until the user enters the passcode again or unlocks (logs in to) the device using Face ID or Touch ID.

b. **Class B - Protected Unless Open**: Some files may need to be written while the device is locked or the user is logged out. To protect them, the file is protected by a wrapped per-file key which is generated by the Protected Unless Open class's private key and an ephemeral public key. The per-file key is then wiped from memory when the file is closed. When the file is reopened, the process repeats.

c. **Class C - Protected Until First User Authentication**: This behaves the same as Class A (Complete Protection) with the exception that the decrypted class key stays in memory when the device is locked or the user is logged out. This is the default class for all third-party app data which is not otherwise assigned to a Data Protection class.

d. **Class D - No Protection**: This class key is protected only with the UID, and the key itself is stored in Effaceable Storage. All the keys needed to decrypt files in this class are stored on the device, so this class doesn't afford any real protection to files aside from having its keys deleted as part of a fast remote wipe.

On Apple Silicon Macs, macOS uses the same Data Protection classes, with the following differences:

1. Class D (No Protection) is not supported.
2. The default Class C (Protected Until First User Authentication) uses a volume key and acts like FileVault does on an Intel Mac.

Other important differences for Data Protection on macOS include the following:

1. **Class A - Complete Protection**: On macOS, the decrypted class key is discarded shortly after the last user is logged out. This makes all data in this class inaccessible until a user enters their password again or logs in to the device using Touch ID.
2. **Class B - Protected Unless Open**: On macOS, the private part of the Protected Unless Open class is accessible as long as any users on the system are logged in or are authenticated.

Secure Token

As mentioned previously, Secure Token is the key encryption key (KEK) which acts as the middleman between the derived encryption keys and the encrypted volume's volume encryption key (VEK). The KEK has been around as long as FileVault 2 has, but access to it on an APFS volume requires that an account be enabled for it. Moreover, an account can only be enabled for Secure Token by another account with Secure Token.

There is one exception to this rule: to help make sure that at least one account has been enabled for Secure Token, the first account to log in to the OS login window on a particular Mac is automatically enabled for Secure Token.

Once an account has been enabled for Secure Token, it can then create other accounts which will in turn automatically be enabled for Secure Token. For those who use Apple's Setup Assistant to set up their Macs, this usually takes the following form:

1. Secure Token is automatically enabled for the user account created by Apple's Setup Assistant.
2. The Setup Assistant–created user account with Secure Token enabled then creates other users via the Users & Groups preference pane in System Preferences. Those accounts get enabled for Secure Token automatically.

The reason this works is that the original user account is able to use their account's derived key, which is authorized to add additional keys to the list of keys able to access the KEK, to enable the additional accounts' own derived keys to the KEK's access list.

However, user accounts created using command-line tools may not be automatically enabled for Secure Token because they were created by the root account, which is **not** a Secure Token–enabled account. If these accounts are not later enabled for Secure Token by an account which does have Secure Token enabled for it, it won't be possible to enable these accounts to work with FileVault 2 because they won't have access to the KEK and thus have no access to the encrypted volume's VEK.

Bootstrap Token

To help ensure that user accounts are granted secure tokens on Macs managed by an MDM server, bootstrap tokens are used to help with granting a secure token to accounts which need them. These tokens are only available if the Mac meets the following requirements:

- Managed by an MDM server
- Using Apple device supervision

On macOS Catalina, bootstrap tokens can be used to grant a secure token to both mobile accounts and to the managed administrator accounts created by Apple's Automated Device Enrollment (ADE).

On macOS Big Sur and later, this capability to grant secure tokens is extended to grant a secure token to any user account logging in, including local user accounts.

Bootstrap tokens have additional functionality on Apple Silicon Macs. On macOS Big Sur and later, bootstrap tokens can be used by an MDM server to authorize the following on Apple Silicon Macs:

- Installation of kernel extensions
- Software updates

On macOS Monterey and later, the bootstrap token is also used to silently authorize Erase All Contents and Settings commands when those commands are sent by the MDM used to manage the Mac.

Enabling Encryption on macOS

There are several ways to enable FileVault 2, but let's first look at the simplest method using System Preferences.

To enable FileVault 2 on a Mac using System Settings:

1. Open the Privacy & Security pane in System Settings and scroll down to the FileVault section.
2. Click the Turn On... button.

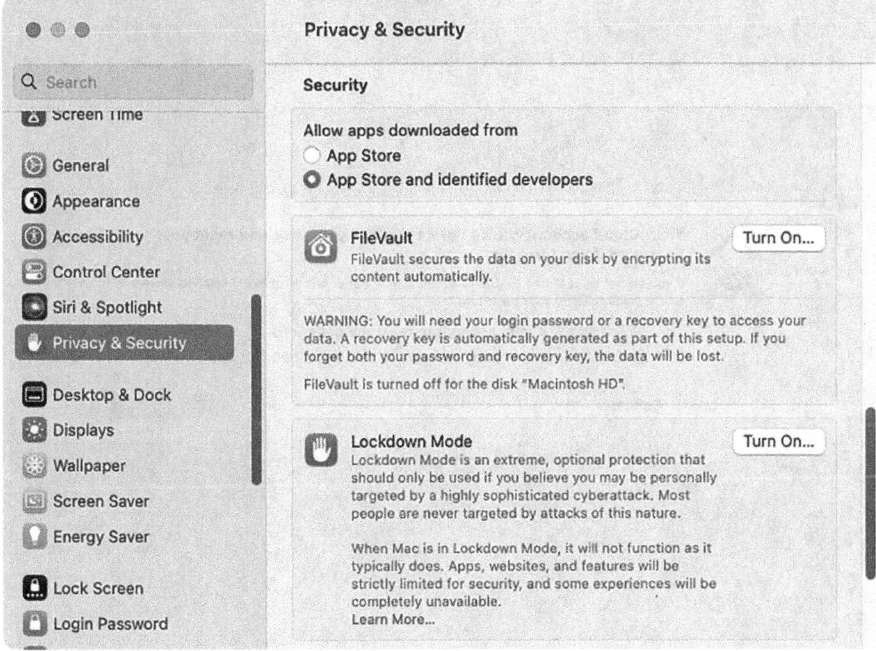

***Figure 7-4.** Accessing the FileVault controls in the Privacy & Security preference pane in System Settings*

3. Authenticate when prompted.

4. Choose “Create a recovery key and do not use my iCloud account” and click the Continue button.

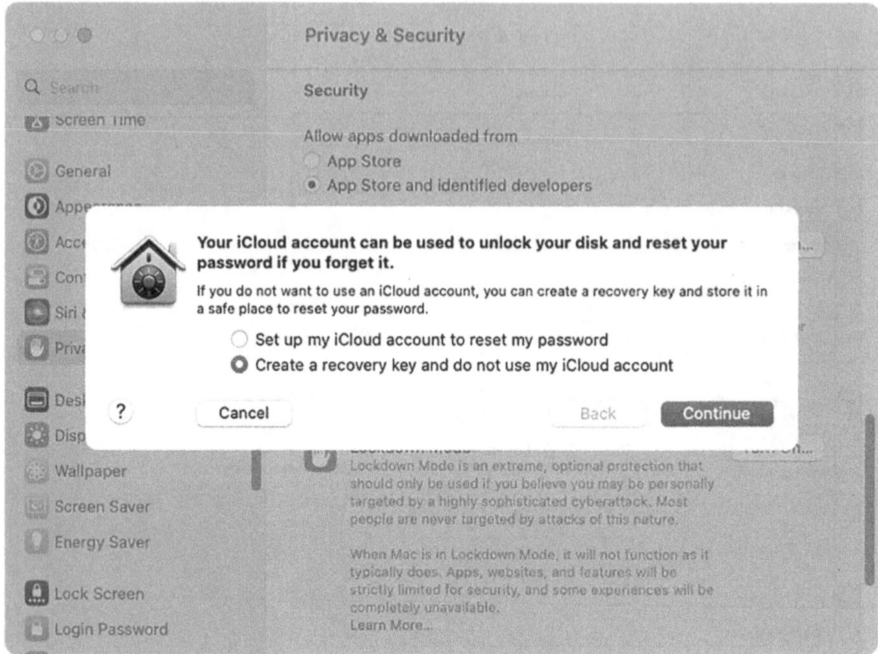

Figure 7-5. *Creating a recovery key*

Carefully document the recovery key. Preferably, use macOS's screen capture tools to take a screenshot of the window and copy the file to a secure location. If any user forgets their password or that user leaves the organization, an administrator will only have this recovery key as an option for unlocking the protected boot volume and recovering data. Click the Continue button to begin the encryption process.

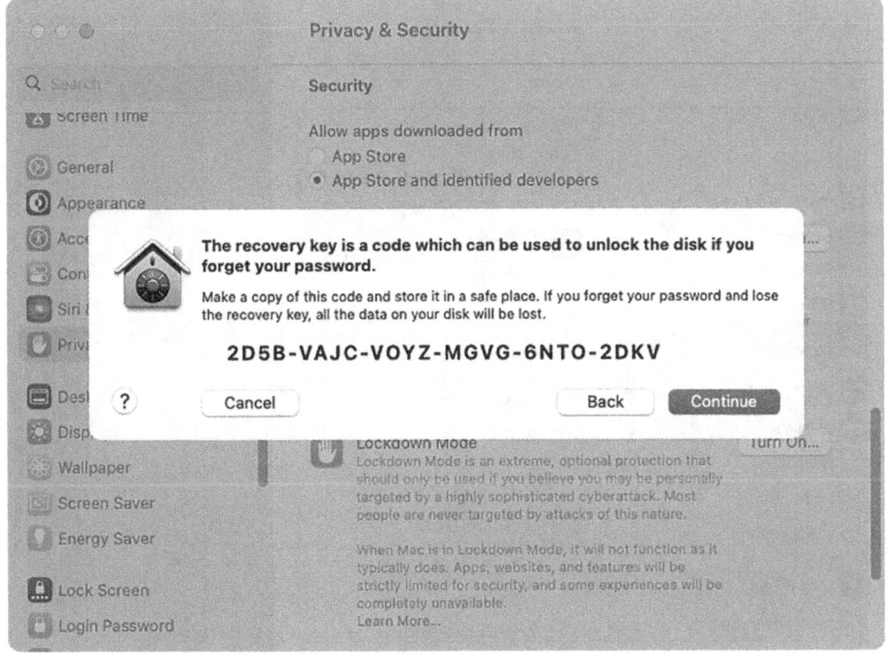

***Figure 7-6.** Displaying a recovery key*

5. The encryption process can be monitored by opening the Privacy & Security pane in System Preferences and clicking the FileVault tab.

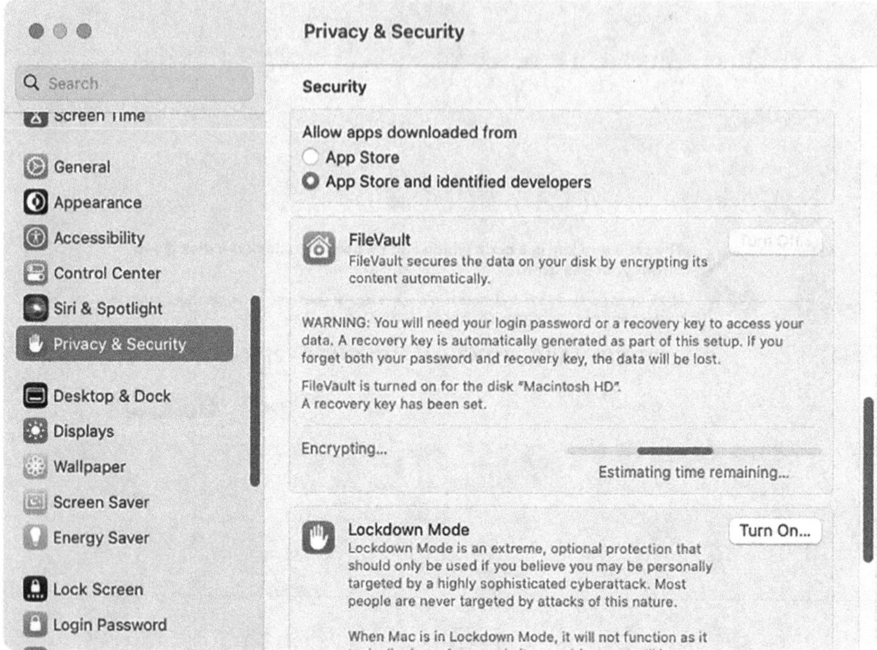

***Figure 7-7.** Monitoring encryption progress*

FileVault Recovery Keys

We briefly discussed FileVault 2's recovery keys earlier, but not why they're important. These recovery keys are derived keys and act as a backup method to unlock FileVault 2's encryption in the event that the usual method of logging using a user's account password is not available.

There are two main types of recovery keys available:

1. **Personal recovery keys**: These are recovery keys that are automatically generated at the time of encryption. These keys are generated as an alphanumeric string and are unique to the machine being encrypted. In the event that an encrypted Mac is decrypted and then reencrypted, the existing

personal recovery key would be invalidated, and a new personal recovery key would be created as part of the encryption process.

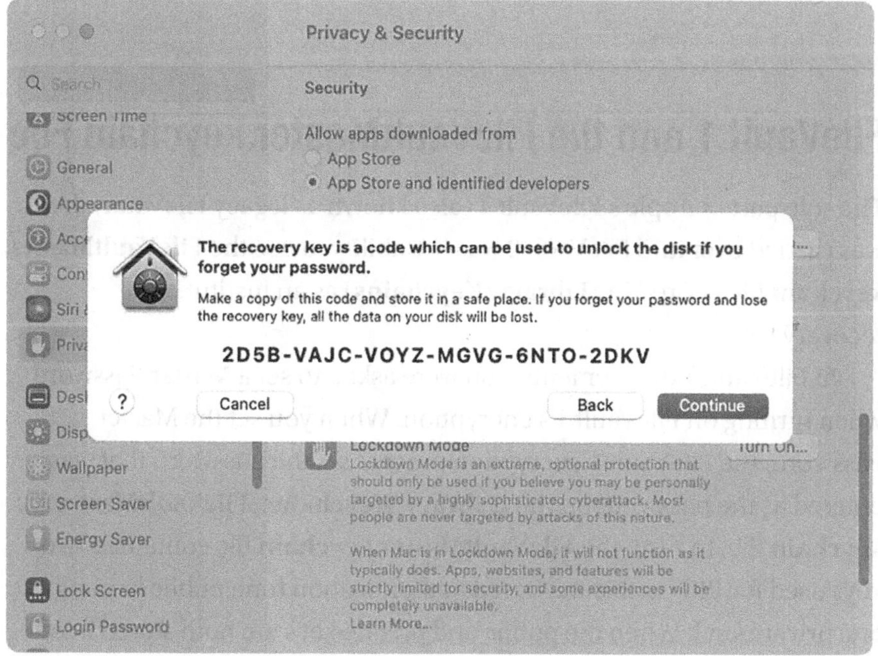

***Figure 7-8.** Personal recovery key displayed in the FileVault preference pane*

2. **Institutional recovery keys**: These are premade recovery keys that can be installed on a system prior to encryption and most often used by a company, school, or institution to have one common recovery key that can unlock their managed encrypted systems.

Institutional keys are not automatically created and will need to be properly generated before they can be used. To help understand why, here's some historical background on institutional recovery keys and how they came to be used in FileVault 2.

FileVault 1 and the FileVaultMaster.keychain File

The sole part of Apple's FileVault 1 (also known as legacy FileVault) that was carried over into FileVault 2 was the ability to use the **FileVaultMaster.keychain** file (stored in **/Library/Keychains**) as an institutional recovery key.

In FileVault 1 deployments, you were asked to set a Master Password when turning on FileVault 1's encryption. When you set the Master Password, the FileVault 1 encryption process set the password that was entered as the password on the **/Library/Keychains/FileVaultMaster.keychain** file. In turn, the **FileVaultMaster.keychain** file contained two keys used for PKI certificate-based authentication (one public key and one private key). When the public and private keys are both stored in one keychain, the keychain can be used to unlock your FileVault 1-encrypted home folder in the event that the password to open it was lost or forgotten. The Master Password only unlocked the keychain and allowed the system to access those two PKI keys. This is the reason why you needed to set the Master Password before encrypting and why it was also important to use the same **FileVaultMaster.keychain** file across the machines where you wanted to make sure that the same recovery key was being used.

If you were deploying the same recovery key for your FileVault-encrypted Macs, Apple consistently recommended that you go into the **FileVaultMaster.keychain** file, remove the PKI private key, put the private key somewhere secure, and deploy the **FileVaultMaster.keychain** file with only the public key inside. The reason was that, in the event that the password to the **FileVaultMaster.keychain** file was compromised, all the compromiser got was one half of the keypair (the public key half.) The private key would not be on the machine and thus not available to compromise the FileVault 1-encrypted homes on the machine. However, FileVault 1 would work with both the public and private keys in **/Library/Keychains/FileVaultMaster.keychain.**

In FileVault 2, Apple changed removing the private key from being a suggested best practice to being a technical requirement. If you want to use an institutional recovery key, your **FileVaultMaster.keychain** file needs to have just the public key in it. If both public and private keys are stored in the **/Library/Keychains/FileVaultMaster.keychain** file on a Mac, FileVault 2 will ignore the keychain and not use it as an institutional recovery key. In this case, enabling FileVault 2 encryption will automatically generate a personal recovery key.

Note As of macOS Monterey and later, Apple is no longer recommending the use of institutional recovery keys on macOS. The reasons are the following:

A. The only environment in which institutional recovery keys can be used to unlock or decrypt a FileVault 2-encrypted Mac is the Recovery environment. If user accounts are set up in macOS, Apple has implemented the need to authenticate using an administrator account's password in order to access the Recovery environment, and an institutional recovery key cannot be used to provide authentication for that process.

B. Target Disk Mode is not available on Apple Silicon Macs, so it is not possible to boot an Apple Silicon Mac into Target Disk Mode and then connect it to another Mac to unlock the Apple Silicon Mac's encrypted drive.

While institutional recovery keys can still be created and will work to unlock FileVault-encrypted drives, these limitations mean that you may not be able to successfully use an institutional recovery key in all circumstances when you need to unlock or decrypt an encrypted drive.

Creating an Institutional Recovery Key

If you want to use an institutional recovery key on FileVault 2-encrypted Macs, you will need to create and configure a **FileVaultMaster** keychain. Apple has provided a way to create this keychain by using the **security** command's **create-filevaultmaster-keychain** function. To create a **FileVaultMaster.keychain** file, run the following command:

```
security create-filevaultmaster-keychain /path/to/
FileVaultMaster.keychain
```

You'll be prompted for a password for the keychain. When provided, the keychain will be created and will contain both the private and public keys needed for recovering a FileVault 2-encrypted drive that uses this institutional recovery key. Make copies of the keychain and store them in a safe place. Also make sure to securely store copies of the password you used to create the keychain.

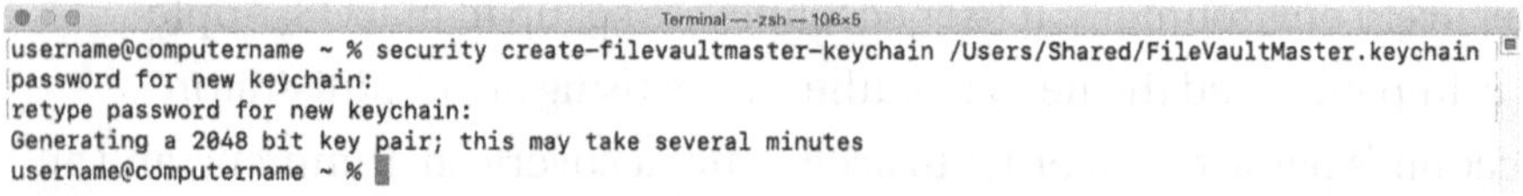

```
Terminal — -zsh — 106×5
username@computername ~ % security create-filevaultmaster-keychain /Users/Shared/FileVaultMaster.keychain
password for new keychain:
retype password for new keychain:
Generating a 2048 bit key pair; this may take several minutes
username@computername ~ %
```

Figure 7-9. *Using **security create-filevaultmaster-keychain** to create an institutional recovery key*

If you want to create the **FileVaultMaster** keychain in its proper place, run the security command with root privileges and use **/Library/Keychains** for the destination path.

```
Terminal — -zsh — 116×6
username@computername ~ % sudo security create-filevaultmaster-keychain /Library/Keychains/FileVaultMaster.keychain
Password:
password for new keychain:
retype password for new keychain:
Generating a 2048 bit key pair; this may take several minutes
username@computername ~ %
```

Figure 7-10. *Running **security create-filevaultmaster-keychain** with root privileges to create an institutional recovery key in **/Library/Keychains***

Once you've made your copies, make another copy and remove the private key from that copy of the keychain. Once the private key is removed, the **FileVaultMaster.keychain** file is ready to be used for encrypting Macs with FileVault 2 with the institutional recovery key.

It doesn't appear that the **security** main page includes information about the **create-filevaultmaster-keychain** function, but you can see what it does by running the **security help** command in Terminal and checking at the bottom of the list that appears.

```
Terminal — -zsh — 108×14
    authorize                         Perform authorization operations.
    authorizationdb                   Make changes to the authorization policy database.
    execute-with-privileges           Execute tool with privileges.
    leaks                             Run /usr/bin/leaks on this process.
    error                             Display a descriptive message for the given error code(s).
    create-filevaultmaster-keychain   Create a keychain containing a key pair for FileVault recovery use.
    smartcards                        Enable, disable or list disabled smartcard tokens.
    translocate-create                Create a translocation point for the provided path
    translocate-policy-check          Check whether a path would be translocated.
    translocate-status-check          Check whether a path is translocated.
    translocate-original-path         Find the original path for a translocated path.
    requirement-evaluate              Evaluate a requirement against a cert chain.
    filevault                         Handles FileVault specific settings and overrides.
username@computername ~ %
```

Figure 7-11. *Using security help to display information about the security tool's **create-filevaultmaster-keychain** function*

A way to modify **/Library/Keychains/FileVaultMaster.keychain** so that it only has the public key inside would be to do the following:

1. Create the **FileVaultMaster.keychain** file using the **security** command.

2. Next, make several copies of the **FileVaultMaster.keychain** file that you just created and store the copies separately in secure locations. A locked safe would be a good place, or in an encrypted disk image that is on an access-restricted file share.

3. Next, unlock the newly created **FileVaultMaster.keychain** file by running the following command and entering the keychain's password when prompted for the password:

```
security unlock-keychain /Library/Keychains/
FileVaultMaster.keychain
```

```
Terminal — -zsh — 95×5
username@computername ~ % security unlock-keychain /Library/Keychains/FileVaultMaster.keychain
password to unlock /Library/Keychains/FileVaultMaster.keychain:
username@computername ~ %
```

***Figure 7-12.** Using the security tool's unlock-keychain function to unlock the **FileVaultMaster** keychain for editing*

Note The **FileVaultMaster** keychain will need to be unlocked from the command line as the keychain will not unlock in Keychain Access by clicking the lock.

---

4. If it succeeds, you'll get the next system prompt. If not, get another copy of the **FileVaultMaster.keychain** file and try again. A **FileVaultMaster.keychain** file with an unknown password should

not be used because there is no way to use it for recovery purposes without first knowing the keychain's current password.

5. Once you've unlocked the **FileVaultMaster. keychain** file, open the **Keychain Access** application from **/Applications/Utilities/**.

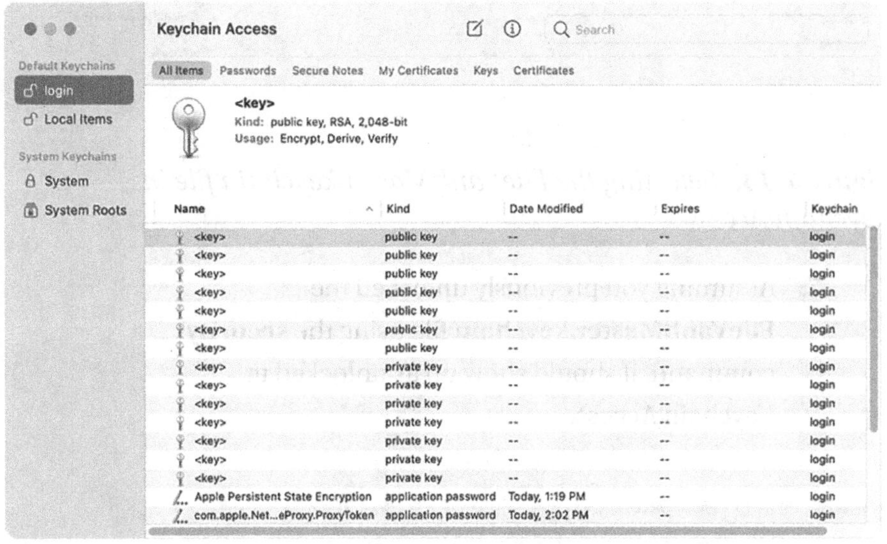

***Figure 7-13.** Looking at Keychain Access prior to adding FileVaultMaster.keychain*

6. In Keychain Access, go to **File: Add Keychain...** and add **/Library/Keychains/FileVaultMaster. keychain**.

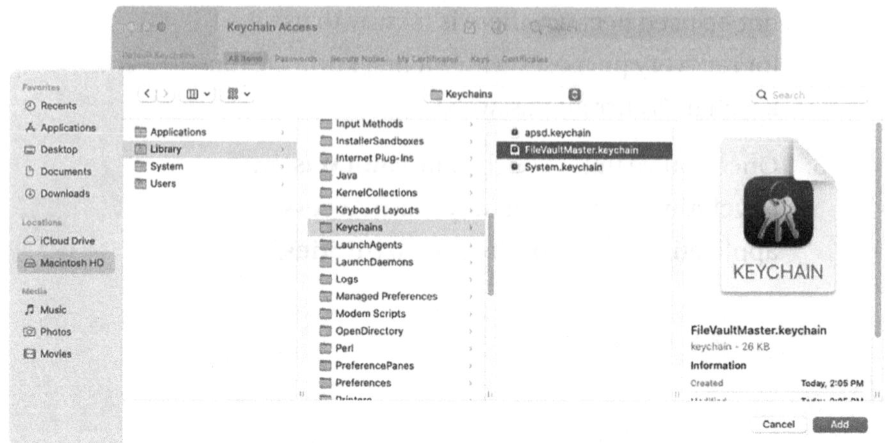

***Figure 7-14.** Selecting the FileVaultMaster.keychain file in Keychain Access*

7. Assuming you previously unlocked the **FileVaultMaster.keychain** file using the **security** command, it should show up as unlocked in Keychain Access.

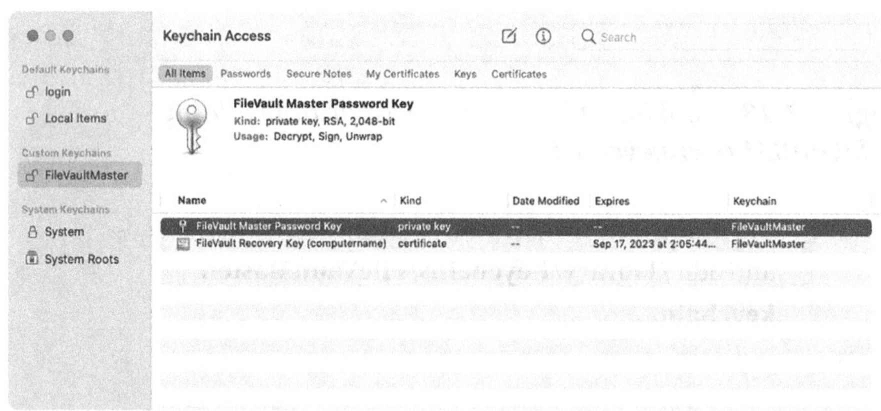

***Figure 7-15.** What the **FileVaultMaster** keychain's private key looks like in Keychain Access*

8. Go into the **FileVaultMaster** keychain and remove the private key. (It should be called **FileVault Master Password Key**, and its kind should be listed as **private key**.)

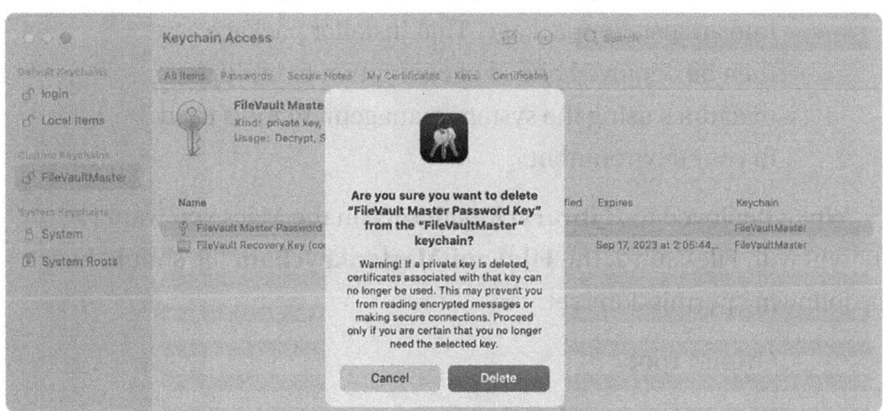

***Figure 7-16.** Removing the private key from the **FileVaultMaster** keychain in Keychain Access*

9. Relock the **FileVaultMaster** keychain.

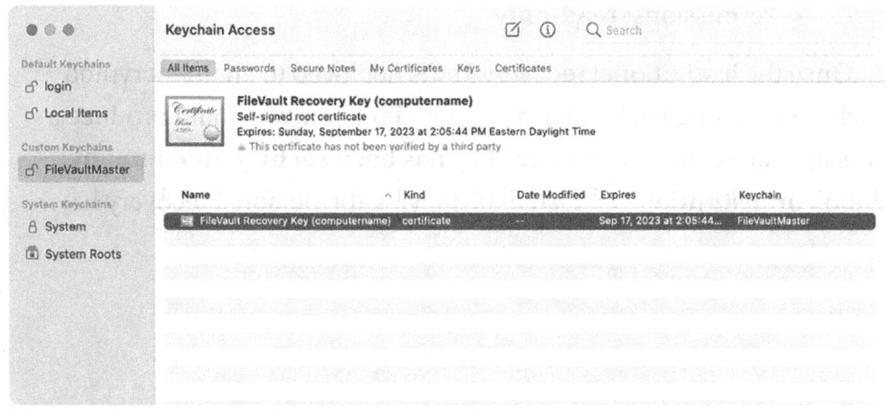

***Figure 7-17.** How the **FileVaultMaster** keychain should look with only the public key inside*

10. Copy the modified **FileVaultMaster.keychain** file (now with only the public key inside) to the / **Library/Keychains** directory of the Macs you want to encrypt with FileVault 2. For ease of deployment, you can package the **FileVaultMaster.keychain** file into an installer package. That installer package can then be deployed ahead of encryption to multiple machines using the system management tools used in your environment.

When deployed to **/Library/Keychains** on the Macs you want to encrypt with FileVault 2, the **FileVaultMaster.keychain** file should have the following permissions set:

Owner: **root**

Permissions: **read and write**

Group: **wheel**

Permissions: **read only**

Everyone

Permissions: **read-only**

Once the institutional recovery key is deployed to an unencrypted machine, enabling FileVault 2 via System Preferences should produce a message stating that "**A recovery key has been set by your company, school, or institution**" instead of displaying the personal recovery key.

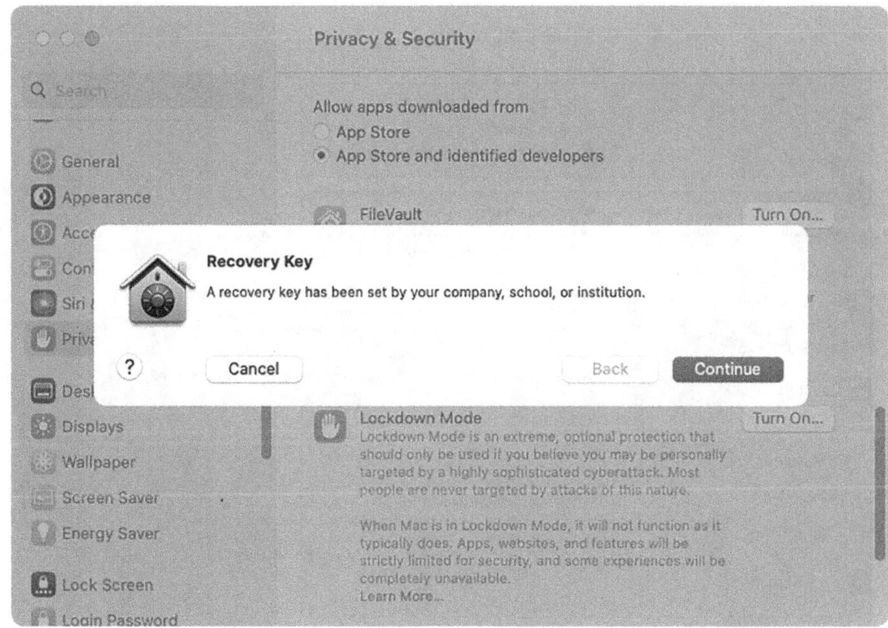

Figure 7-18. *Message indicating that a properly configured FileVaultMaster.keychain is being used as an institutional recovery key*

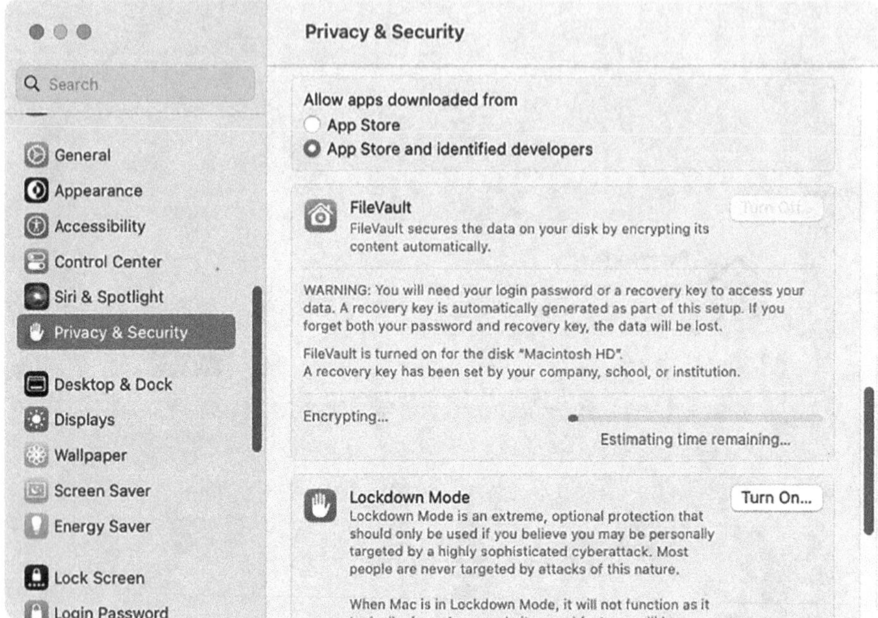

***Figure 7-19.** FileVault 2 encrypting the boot drive using an institutional recovery key*

For mass FileVault 2 management, use Apple's command-line tool `fdesetup` for enabling and managing encryption and escrowing recovery keys.

`fdesetup` gives Mac administrators the following command-line abilities:

- Enable or disable FileVault 2 encryption on a particular Mac.
- Use a personal recovery key, an institutional recovery key, or both kinds of recovery key.
- Enable one or multiple user accounts at the time of encryption.

- Get a list of FileVault 2-enabled users on a particular machine.
- Add additional users after FileVault has been enabled.
- Remove users from the list of FileVault-enabled accounts.
- Add, change, or remove individual and institutional recovery keys.
- Report which recovery keys are in use.
- Perform a one-time reboot that bypasses the FileVault preboot login.
- Report on the status of FileVault 2 encryption or decryption.

Enabling FileVault 2 Encryption for One or Multiple Users

`fdesetup` is amazingly flexible when it comes to enabling FileVault 2 encryption from the command line. To start with the simplest method, run the following command with root privileges to enable FileVault 2 encryption:

```
fdesetup enable
```

You'll be prompted for the username and password of the primary user, which is the account you will work with at the FileVault 2 preboot login screen once the encryption is turned on.

If everything's working properly, FileVault will enable, and you'll be given an alphanumeric personal recovery.

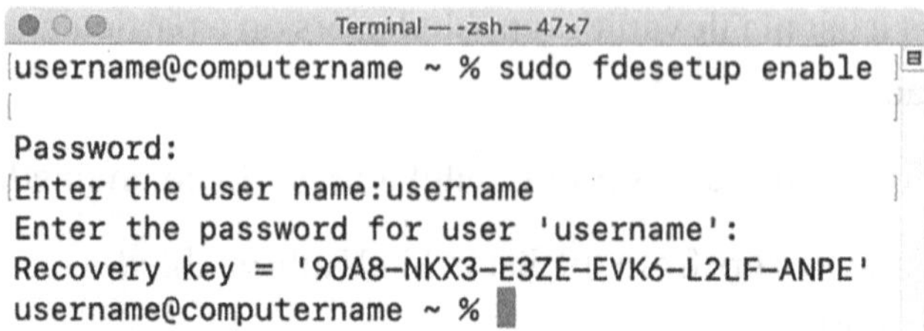
```
username@computername ~ % sudo fdesetup enable

Password:
Enter the user name:username
Enter the password for user 'username':
Recovery key = '90A8-NKX3-E3ZE-EVK6-L2LF-ANPE'
username@computername ~ %
```

Figure 7-20. *Running fdesetup enable to enable FileVault 2 encryption*

Very Important The fdesetup-generated personal recovery key is not saved anywhere outside the machine. Make a record of it or you will not have a recovery key available to help unlock your Mac's encryption in case of a problem.

You can also enable additional user accounts at the time of encryption, as long as the accounts are either local or mobile accounts on the Mac being encrypted. Run the following command with root privileges to enable FileVault 2 and specify the accounts you want:

```
fdesetup enable -user username -usertoadd other_username
-usertoadd yet_another_username
```

You'll be prompted for the passwords of the accounts specified. After that, you'll be given an alphanumeric personal recovery key, and FileVault will turn on. All of the accounts specified should appear at the FileVault 2 preboot login screen.

```
username@computername ~ % sudo fdesetup enable -user username -usertoadd otheruser
Password:
Enter the password for user 'username':
Enter the password for the added user 'otheruser':
Recovery key = 'LG8R-P54P-UNP3-UFZQ-DQZW-APYH'
username@computername ~ %
```

***Figure 7-21.** Running fdesetup enable to enable FileVault 2 for multiple accounts*

For those who want to automate the process, `fdesetup` also supports importing a properly formatted plist via a standard input stream (stdin). The plist needs to follow the format shown in Figure 7-22.

```
<?xml version="1.0" encoding="UTF-8"?>
<!DOCTYPE plist PUBLIC "-//Apple//DTD PLIST 1.0//EN" "http://www.apple.com/DTDs/PropertyList-1.0.dtd">
<plist version="1.0">
<dict>
<key>Username</key>
<string>localadmin</string>
<key>Password</key>
<string>password</string>
<key>AdditionalUsers</key>
<array>
    <dict>
        <key>Username</key>
        <string>tom</string>
        <key>Password</key>
        <string>password</string>
    </dict>
    <dict>
        <key>Username</key>
        <string>harry</string>
        <key>Password</key>
        <string>password</string>
    </dict>
</array>
</dict>
</plist>
```

***Figure 7-22.** Plist format for fdesetup enable*

Additional users can be included as needed by adding additional user information under the **AdditionalUsers** plist key.

Note All account passwords need to be supplied in clear text.

Once the plist has been set up and properly formatted, run the following command with root privileges to enable FileVault 2 encryption and reference the account information in the plist file:

```
fdesetup enable -inputplist < /path/to/filename.plist
```

Since the accounts and passwords are in the plist file, `fdesetup` does not need to prompt for passwords. Instead, the alphanumeric personal recovery key is displayed, and FileVault turns on. All of the accounts specified in the plist file should appear at the FileVault 2 preboot login screen.

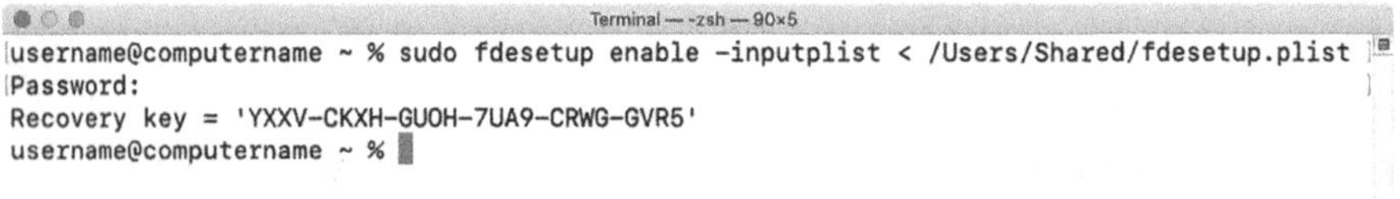

```
Terminal — -zsh — 90×5
username@computername ~ % sudo fdesetup enable -inputplist < /Users/Shared/fdesetup.plist
Password:
Recovery key = 'YXXV-CKXH-GUOH-7UA9-CRWG-GVR5'
username@computername ~ %
```

Figure 7-23. *Using fdesetup enable with plist to enable FileVault 2 for multiple accounts*

To avoid the need to enter a password, `fdesetup` also has a **-defer** flag that can be used with the "enable" command option to delay enabling FileVault 2 until after the current (or next) user logs out. With the **-defer** flag, the user will be prompted for their password at their next logout or restart. The recovery key information is not generated until the user password is obtained, so the **-defer** option requires a file location where this information will be written to as a plist file.

The property list file will be created as a root-only readable file and contain information similar to what's shown in Figure 7-24.

```
<?xml version="1.0" encoding="UTF-8"?>
<!DOCTYPE plist PUBLIC "-//Apple//DTD PLIST 1.0//EN" "http://www.apple.com/DTDs/PropertyList-1.0.dtd">
<plist version="1.0">
<dict>
    <key>EnabledDate</key>
    <string>2022-09-17 13:33:23 -0400</string>
    <key>EnabledUser</key>
    <string>username</string>
    <key>HardwareUUID</key>
    <string>0F2E600C-A252-51FE-8483-FA0C041A2A47</string>
    <key>RecoveryKey</key>
    <string>EK6W-MOCA-GQT3-GT3R-6P9F-8JZK</string>
    <key>SerialNumber</key>
    <string>ZPHF92VJ61</string>
</dict>
</plist>
```

Figure 7-24. *fdesetup enable -defer recovery information plist format*

Note For security reasons, the plist file with the recovery key information should not stay on the encrypted system. Please copy it to a safe location and then securely delete this plist file from the encrypted system.

Run the following command with root privileges to defer enabling FileVault 2 and specify the account you want, as seen in Figure 7-25:

```
fdesetup enable -user username -defer /path/to/filename.plist
```

```
Terminal — -zsh — 99×5
username@computername ~ % sudo fdesetup enable -user username -defer /Users/Shared/recovery.plist
Password:
username@computername ~ %
```

Figure 7-25. *Using fdesetup enable -defer with specified user to enable FileVault 2*

If there is no user account specified with the **-user** option, then the current logged-in user will be enabled for FileVault 2. If there is no user specified and no users are logged in when the command is run, then the next user that logs in will be chosen and enabled.

If you don't want to specify the account, run the following command with root privileges (Figure 7-26):

```
fdesetup enable -defer /path/to/filename.plist
```

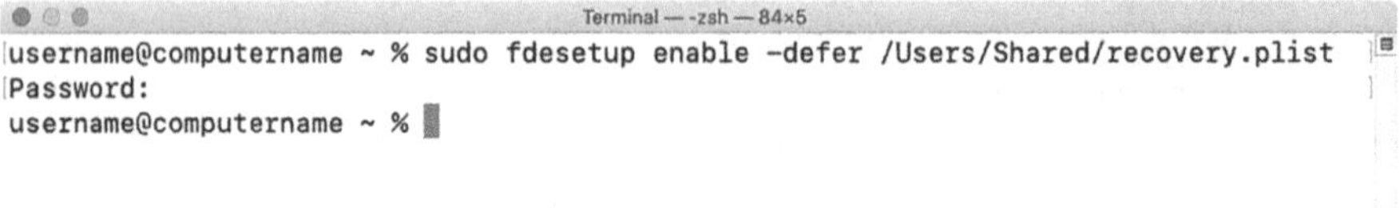

```
Terminal — -zsh — 84×5
username@computername ~ % sudo fdesetup enable -defer /Users/Shared/recovery.plist
Password:
username@computername ~ %
```

***Figure 7-26.** Using fdesetup enable -defer without specified user to enable FileVault 2*

On logout, the user will be prompted to enter their account password in a screen similar to that of Figure 7-27.

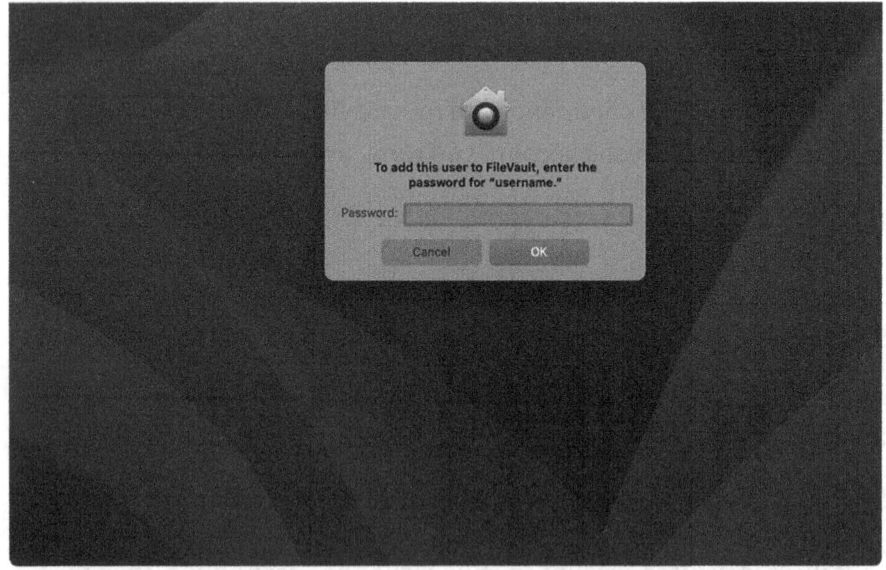

***Figure 7-27.** User being prompted to enter password at logout for deferred enabling of FileVault 2*

Once entered, FileVault 2 will be enabled, and the recovery information plist file will be created. Once the enabling process is complete (the indicator shown in Figure 7-28), the Mac will restart.

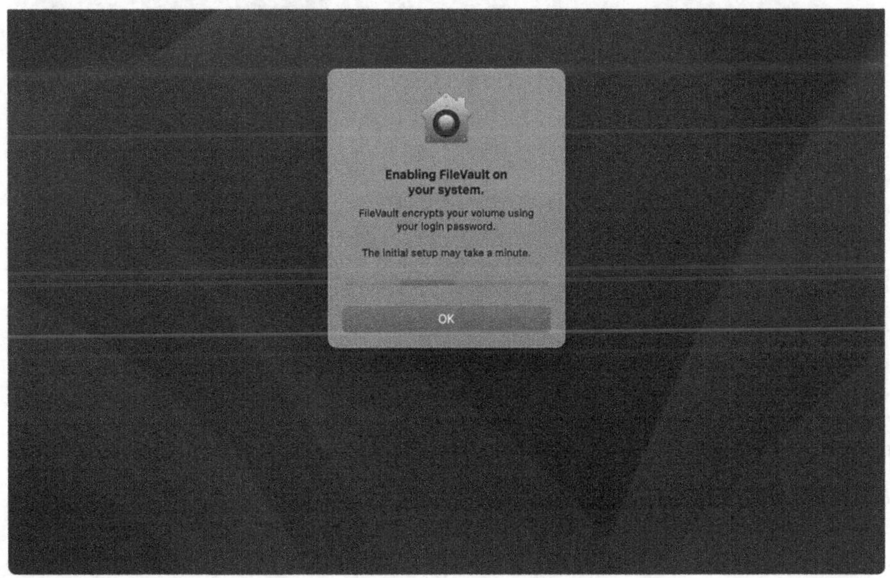

Figure 7-28. *FileVault 2 deferred enabling process*

In addition to enabling FileVault 2 as part of the logout process, Apple provided the ability to set a deferred enablement at login. This means that Mac admins can set a deferred enablement with the following options, which prompts the user with the screen shown in Figure 7-29:

1. Enforce FileVault 2 enablement at logout.
2. Enforce FileVault 2 enablement at login.
3. Enforce FileVault 2 enablement at both login and logout.

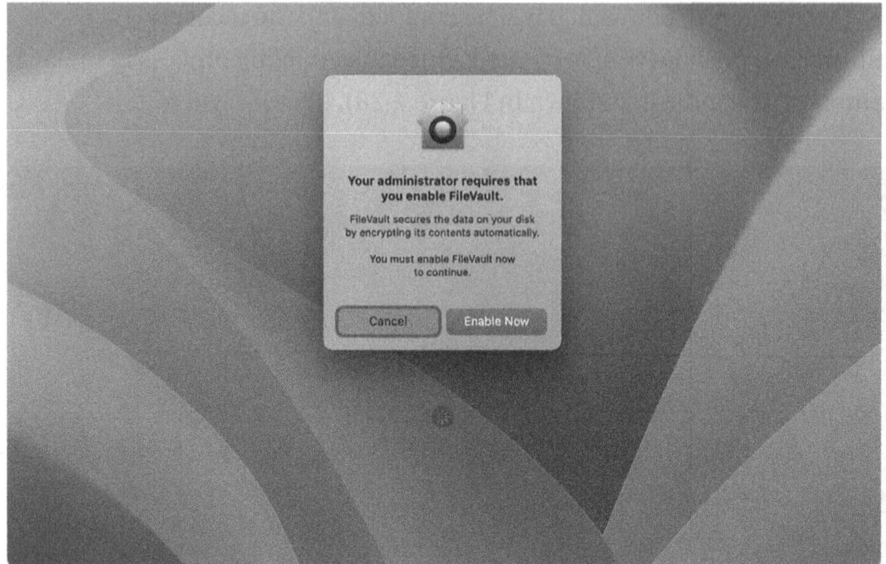

Figure 7-29. *User being prompted to enter password at login for deferred enabling of FileVault 2*

To set a deferred enablement at login, the following options may be added to `fdesetup` 's **-defer** flag:

- **-forceatlogin** *max_cancel_attempts*
- **-dontaskatlogout**

These additional options allow a deferred FileVault 2 enablement to be enforced at the login window, rather than waiting for a logout or restart of the Mac in question.

The **-forceatlogin** option must be set with an accompanying numerical value, shown in Figure 7-30. This numerical value governs how many times the account being enabled can choose to defer having the FileVault 2 encryption process begin. For example, running the following command with root privileges will set a maximum number of ten deferral opportunities:

```
fdesetup enable -defer /path/to/filename.plist -forceatlogin 10
```

```
Terminal — -zsh — 101x5
username@computername ~ % sudo fdesetup enable -defer /Users/Shared/recovery.plist -forceatlogin 10
Password:
username@computername ~ %
```

Figure 7-30. *Using fdesetup enable -defer -forceatlogin to permit deferred enablement of FileVault 2*

If the user chooses to defer, they will need to select the **Don't Enable** button in the dialog window when it appears, seen in Figure 7-31. They will also be informed of how many more times they can log in before FileVault 2 encryption must be enabled.

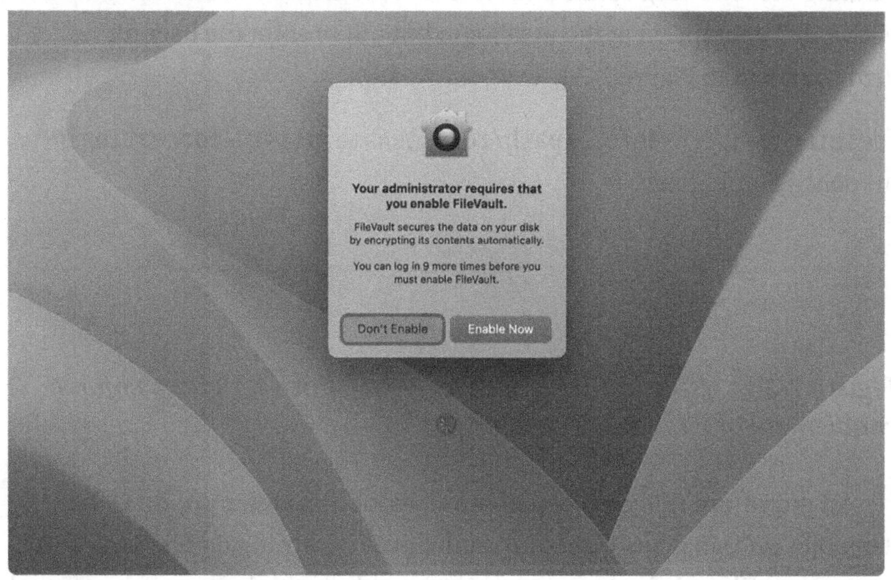

Figure 7-31. *User being given the option to defer FileVault 2 encryption*

If immediate enforcement is desired, setting a value of zero will enforce FileVault 2 encryption at the next login. To do this, run the following command with root privileges, shown in Figure 7-32:

```
fdesetup enable -defer /path/to/filename.plist -forceatlogin 0
```

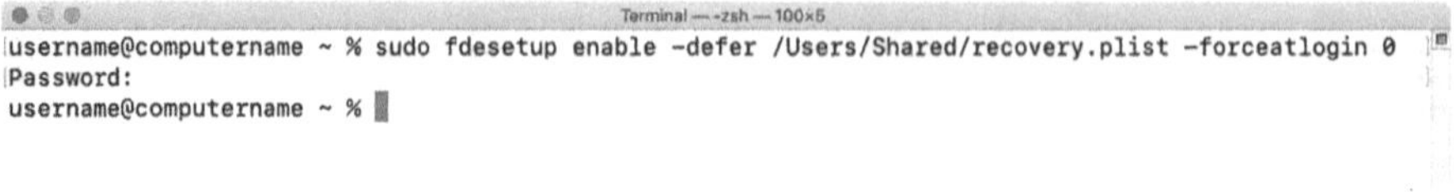

```
Terminal — -zsh — 100×5
username@computername ~ % sudo fdesetup enable -defer /Users/Shared/recovery.plist -forceatlogin 0
Password:
username@computername ~ %
```

Figure 7-32. *Using fdesetup enable -defer -forceatlogin to enforce enablement of FileVault 2*

The `fdesetup` commands shown earlier will enforce FileVault 2 enablement at both login and logout. If only enforcement at login is desired, the **-dontaskatlogout** option can be used. This will prevent a deferred FileVault 2 enablement to be enforced at logout. For example, running the following command with root privileges will enforce FileVault 2 encryption at the next login but not prompt the user on logout, shown in Figure 7-33:

```
fdesetup enable -defer /path/to/filename.plist -forceatlogin
0 -dontaskatlogout
```

```
Terminal — -zsh — 117×5
username@computername ~ % sudo fdesetup enable -defer /Users/Shared/recovery.plist -forceatlogin 0 -dontaskatlogout
Password:
username@computername ~ %
```

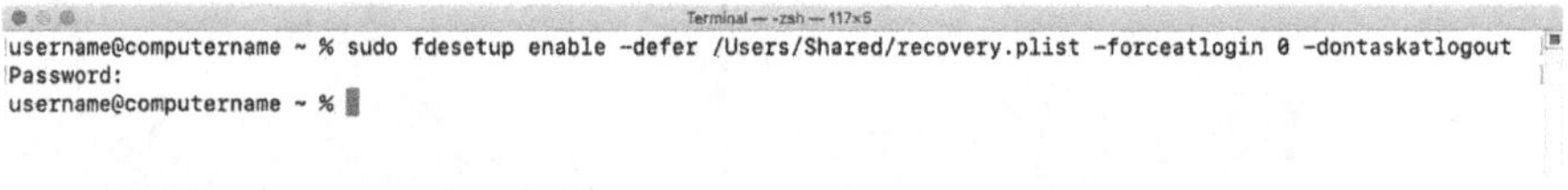

Figure 7-33. *Using fdesetup enable -defer -forceatlogin to enforce enablement of FileVault 2 at login*

An important thing to keep in mind about the **-defer** option is that it enables one single user account at the time of turning on FileVault 2 encryption. The **-defer** option does not enable multiple user accounts and cannot be used to enable accounts once FileVault 2 encryption has been turned on.

Enabling FileVault 2 Encryption Using One or Multiple Recovery Keys

Another capability of FileVault 2 is the ability to use the alphanumeric personal recovery key, an institutional recovery key using **/Library/Keychains/FileVaultMaster.keychain**, or both kinds of recovery key at the same time.

As seen in the earlier examples, `fdesetup` will provide the alphanumeric personal recovery key by default. To use the institutional recovery key, the **-keychain** flag needs to be used when enabling encryption, shown in Figure 7-34:

```
fdesetup enable -keychain
```

```
Terminal — -zsh — 57×6
username@computername ~ % sudo fdesetup enable -keychain
Password:
Enter the user name:username
Enter the password for user 'username':
Recovery key = 'JDDD-8N23-P437-6GHO-HOFG-2TCZ'
username@computername ~ %
```

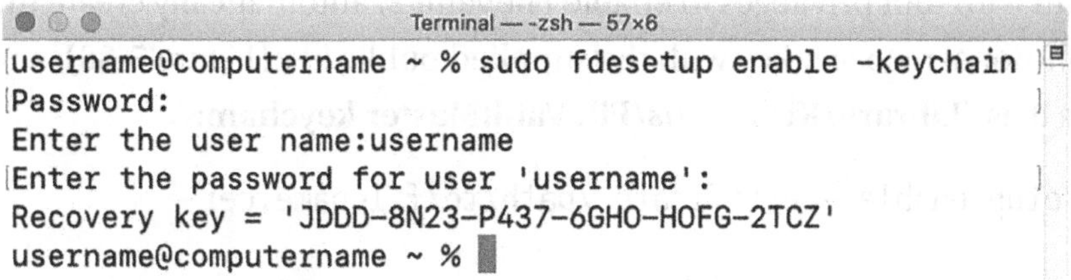

Figure 7-34. *Using fdesetup enable -keychain to enable encryption with both recovery key types*

The alphanumeric personal recovery key is displayed, but the encryption will also use the **/Library/Keychains/FileVaultMaster.keychain** institutional recovery key. In case recovery is needed, either recovery key will work to unlock or decrypt the encrypted drive.

If you want to specify that only the **FileVaultMaster.keychain** institutional recovery key be used, both the **-keychain** and **-norecoverykey** flags need to be used when enabling encryption, shown in Figure 7-35:

```
fdesetup enable -keychain -norecoverykey
```

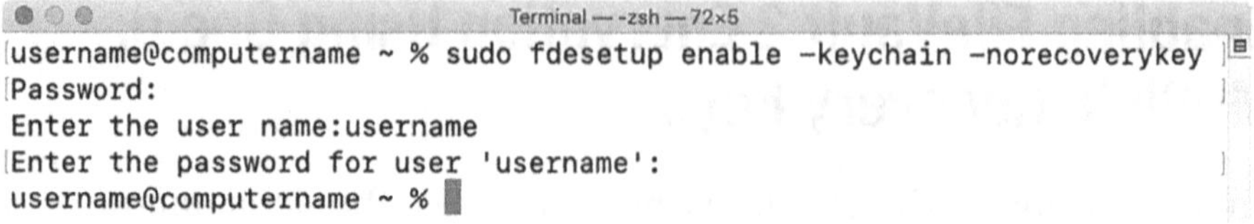

```
Terminal — -zsh — 72×5
username@computername ~ % sudo fdesetup enable -keychain -norecoverykey
Password:
Enter the user name:username
Enter the password for user 'username':
username@computername ~ %
```

***Figure 7-35.** Using fdesetup enable -keychain -norecoverykey to enable encryption with only the institutional recovery key*

`fdesetup` is also capable of creating an institutional recovery key, using the **-certificate** flag to import an existing FileVault 2 public key. Once imported, `fdesetup` will automatically create a **FileVaultMaster.keychain** file to store the public key and save the keychain to **/Library/Keychains**.

The public key will need to be available as a DER-encoded **.cer** certificate file. Once the certificate is available, the following command can be run with root privileges to enable FileVault 2, automatically create the institutional recovery key with the supplied public key (Figure 7-36), and store it as **/Library/Keychains/FileVaultMaster.keychain**:

```
fdesetup enable -certificate /path/to/filename.cer
```

```
Terminal — -zsh — 88×6
username@computername ~ % sudo fdesetup enable -certificate /Users/Shared/filevault.cer
Password:
Enter the user name:username
Enter the password for user 'username':
Recovery key = 'NTUM-LMBL-UTQ6-EMKU-KT2D-F69Y'
username@computername ~ %
```

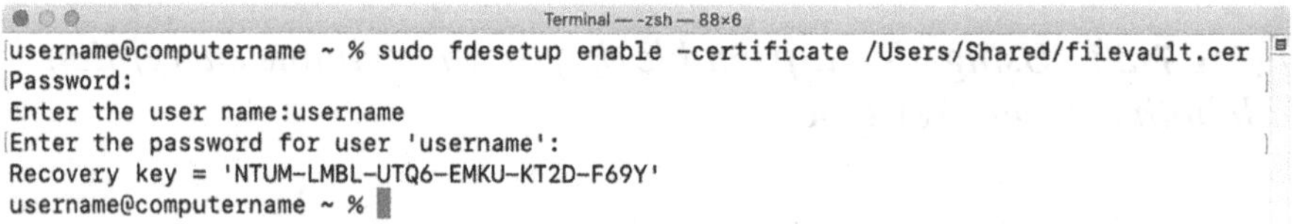

***Figure 7-36.** Using fdesetup enable -certificate to enable encryption with an imported certificate*

To specify that only the **FileVaultMaster.keychain** institutional recovery key be used, add the **-norecoverykey** flag to the command, shown in Figure 7-37:

```
fdesetup enable -certificate /path/to/filename.cer -
norecoverykey
```

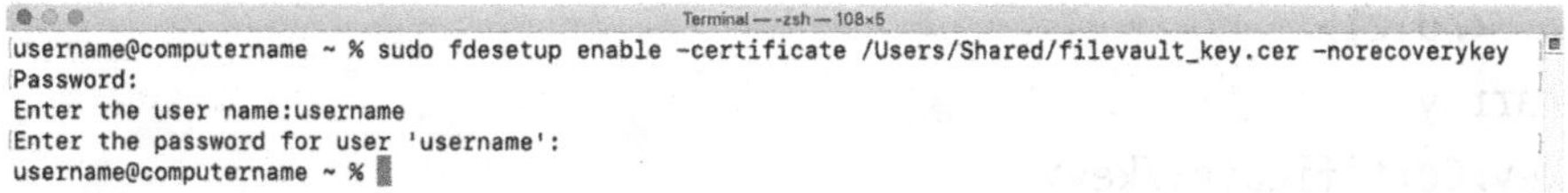

```
username@computername ~ % sudo fdesetup enable -certificate /Users/Shared/filevault_key.cer -norecoverykey
Password:
Enter the user name:username
Enter the password for user 'username':
username@computername ~ %
```

Figure 7-37. *Using fdesetup enable -certificate -norecoverykey to enable encryption with only the imported certificate*

It is also possible to include the public key data in a plist file, which allows the use of a plist to set up the institutional recovery key. The plist needs to follow this format:

```
<?xml version="1.0" encoding="UTF-8"?>
<!DOCTYPE plist PUBLIC "-//Apple//DTD PLIST 1.0//EN" "http://
www.apple.com/DTDs/PropertyList-1.0.dtd">
<plist version="1.0">
<dict>
<key>Username</key>
<string>username</string>
<key>Password</key>
<string>password</string>
<key>AdditionalUsers</key>
<array>
    <dict>
        <key>Username</key>
        <string>username</string>
        <key>Password</key>
        <string>password</string>
    </dict>
    <dict>
        <key>Username</key>
        <string>username</string>
        <key>Password</key>
        <string>password</string>
```

```
    </dict>
</array>
<key>Certificate</key>
<data>
(Certificate data goes here...)
</data>
</dict>
</plist>
```

Using the public key's DER-encoded certificate file, the public key data for the plist can be obtained using the **base64** tool by using the following command:

```
base64 /path/to/filename.cer > /path/to/filename.txt
```

At this point, you would copy the data string contained in the text file and place it into the **Certificate *<data></data>*** value area of the plist file. You would store either the password of an existing FileVault 2-enabled user or (if available) an existing personal recovery key in the **Password** key in the plist, as seen in Figure 7-38.

```
<?xml version="1.0" encoding="UTF-8"?>
<!DOCTYPE plist PUBLIC "-//Apple//DTD PLIST 1.0//EN" "http://www.apple.com/DTDs/PropertyList-1.0.dtd">
<plist version="1.0">
<dict>
<key>Username</key>
<string>username</string>
<key>Password</key>
<string>pass123</string>
<key>AdditionalUsers</key>
<array>
    <dict>
        <key>Username</key>
        <string>tom</string>
        <key>Password</key>
        <string>password</string>
    </dict>
    <dict>
        <key>Username</key>
        <string>harry</string>
        <key>Password</key>
        <string>password</string>
    </dict>
</array>
<key>Certificate</key>
<data>
MIIDLjCCAhagAwIBAgIENsqyWTALBgkqhkiG9w0BAQUwSTEfMB0GA1UEAwwWRmlsZVZhdWx0IFJlY292ZXJ5IEtleTEmMCQGA1UE
DQwddHJvdXRvbnQtdm0zLnRhb21lY2h3b3Jrcy5uZXQwHhcNMTMwODI0MjEzNTI1WhcNMTQwODI0MjEzNTI1WjBJMR8wHQYDVQQD
DBZGaWxlVmF1bHQgUmVjb3ZlcnkgS2V5MSYwJAYDVQQNDB10cm91dG9udC12bTMudGFvbWVjaHdvcmtzLm5ldDCCASIwDQYJKoZI
hvcNAQEBBQADggEPADCCAQoCggEBAMJpO4TYyH8HC3H4WWV0FPV48I1cdRjhBGi9OYJX8cQrgWb72FTDCNbU+fD1ce1++
KALheMNCmhOIwPshQtbUuU9ngpfRYI/L6KIgIaUW4bpUksHXZ0CIwSvfqD6+
np06wniS48KNPmnyHqxNeYyfU20wAITPznP7w0VjU7pMbvvJra03gNDxxLc44Rj5YdHxn7U7gIUNc08RxntNgC6hPSMuZVIgz8AU
FcOYuBYML9fXrHytNoaZ0JXS2djGRdwRT0V3OtK2qDFh8+vVr9vTBt3xmk6hPREXfB9odRDH6ZP9mn6R2vLLzF4ANwklha0L4+
mwbPtdfVOSs3wdkoUFF8CAwEAAaMgMB4wCwYDVR0PBAQDAgK0MA8GA1UdEwEB/wQFMAMBAQAwDQYJKoZIhvcNAQEFBQADggEBAJ+
5ZaqzQmnVDrIQBkxiBXql/
aRbQpetu5jLsJtHDxRd1d2YiEFJHwy4jnUefrvTUf7648oCQ5FtOjYL5lYn7QQ3MjvsFKzBh2wVlqJJAhjjjwbzMoVdRxfY8Aftc
ler9Tw/WvxiECvdgxBA37iA+EGVTrRUGuCytY+GhawIKQMR5Ac2XBpfgPatbV9xAtCo4+M9I4jqhSxOGMwLjRHs4yELyH71w/
Au3VlTYezf+dqof0aZ8c4wBOK3T4VeoWMJjjwDe9Q3/j3sf/CjxvNhm1yYRUqUieZx7Vdf2+
oKKqMczyAVz0Y8UX26lMnpMQn4Fv9b5mOvo5U2/ZgpiQ8cHxM=
</data>
</dict>
</plist>
```


Figure 7-38. *Plist format with institutional public key data*

Disabling FileVault 2 Encryption

In contrast to all of the various options available for enabling FileVault 2 using `fdesetup`, the command to turn off FileVault 2 encryption is the following (Figure 7-39):

```
fdesetup disable
```

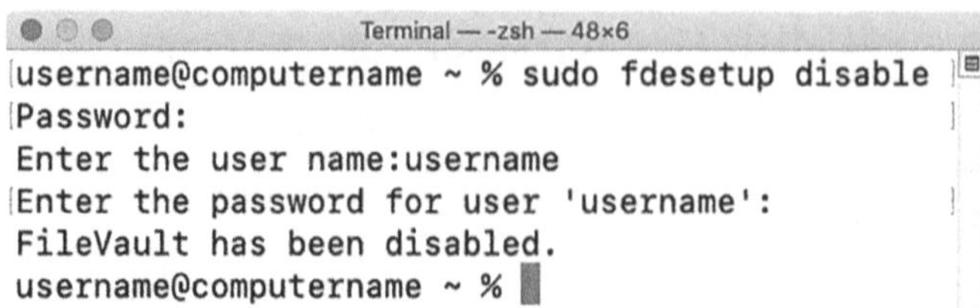

Figure 7-39. *Using fdesetup disable to turn off FileVault 2's encryption*

ADDING ADDITIONAL USERS AFTER FILEVAULT 2 HAS BEEN ENABLED

Once FileVault 2 has been enabled, you can add additional users using `fdesetup`. To do so, you will need to (a) wait until the FileVault 2 encryption has completed and (b) provide both the username and password of a previously enabled account as well as the password of the account you want to add. The following command (Figure 7-40) run with root privileges will enable a user account named **otheruser**:

```
fdesetup add -usertoadd otheruser
```

```
Terminal — -zsh — 65×6
username@computername ~ % sudo fdesetup add -usertoadd otheruser
Password:
Enter the user name:username
Enter the password for user 'username':
Enter the password for the added user 'otheruser':
username@computername ~ %
```

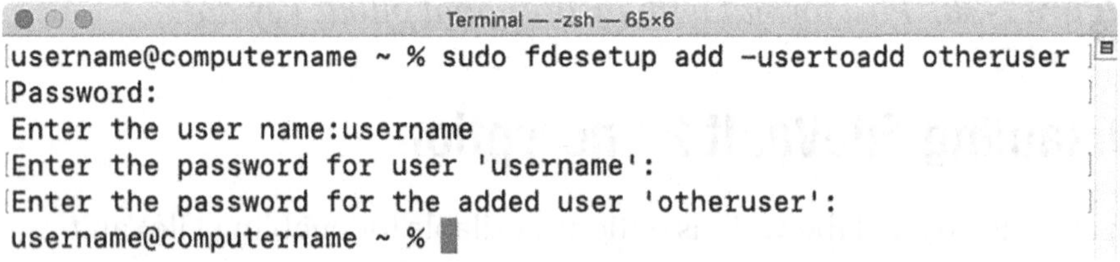

Figure 7-40. *Using fdesetup add -usertoadd to enable additional accounts*

For those who want to automate the process, `fdesetup` also supports importing a properly formatted plist via a standard input stream (stdin). The plist needs to follow this format:

```
<?xml version="1.0" encoding="UTF-8"?>
<!DOCTYPE plist PUBLIC "-//Apple//DTD PLIST 1.0//EN" "http://
www.apple.com/DTDs/PropertyList-1.0.dtd">
<plist version="1.0">
<dict>
<key>Username</key>
<string>username</string>
<key>Password</key>
<string>password</string>
<key>AdditionalUsers</key>
<array>
    <dict>
        <key>Username</key>
        <string>username</string>
        <key>Password</key>
        <string>password</string>
    </dict>
    <dict>
        <key>Username</key>
        <string>username</string>
        <key>Password</key>
        <string>password</string>
    </dict>
</array>
</dict>
</plist>
```

When adding additional users using a plist file, the top-level **Username** key is ignored, and the **Password** key value should either be an existing FileVault user's password or the recovery key. Additional users can be added as needed by adding additional user information under the **AdditionalUsers** plist key (Figure 7-41).

```
<?xml version="1.0" encoding="UTF-8"?>
<!DOCTYPE plist PUBLIC "-//Apple//DTD PLIST 1.0//EN" "http://www.apple.com/DTDs/PropertyList-1.0.dtd">
<plist version="1.0">
<dict>
<key>Username</key>
<string>rtrouton</string>
<key>Password</key>
<string>password</string>
<key>AdditionalUsers</key>
<array>
    <dict>
        <key>Username</key>
        <string>fcheeryble</string>
        <key>Password</key>
        <string>password</string>
    </dict>
    <dict>
        <key>Username</key>
        <string>nnickleby</string>
        <key>Password</key>
        <string>password</string>
    </dict>
</array>
</dict>
</plist>
```

Figure 7-41. *Plist format for fdesetup add*

Note All account passwords need to be supplied in clear text.

Once the plist has been set up and properly formatted, run the following command with root privileges to add additional users by referencing the account information in the plist file (Figure 7-42):

```
fdesetup add -inputplist < /path/to/filename.plist
```

```
Terminal — -zsh — 89×5
username@computername ~ % sudo fdesetup add -inputplist < /Users/Shared/userstoadd.plist
Password:
username@computername ~ %
```

Figure 7-42. *Using fdesetup add -inputplist to enable accounts*

Listing Current FileVault 2 Users

To list all accounts enabled for FileVault 2, run the following command with root privileges:

```
fdesetup list
```

All accounts will be listed with both the accounts' username and UUID, as seen in Figure 7-43.

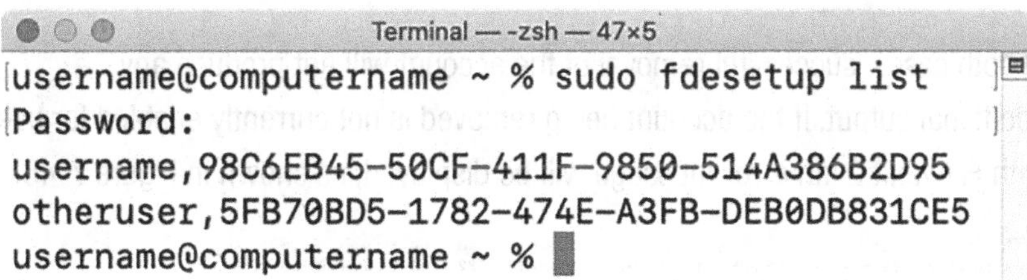

Figure 7-43. *Using fdesetup list to show enabled accounts*

REMOVING USERS FROM THE LIST OF FILEVAULT 2–ENABLED ACCOUNTS

You can remove users from the list of FileVault-enabled accounts by using either their username or the account's UUID. To remove the account using the username, run the following command with root privileges (Figure 7-44):

```
fdesetup remove -user username_goes_here
```

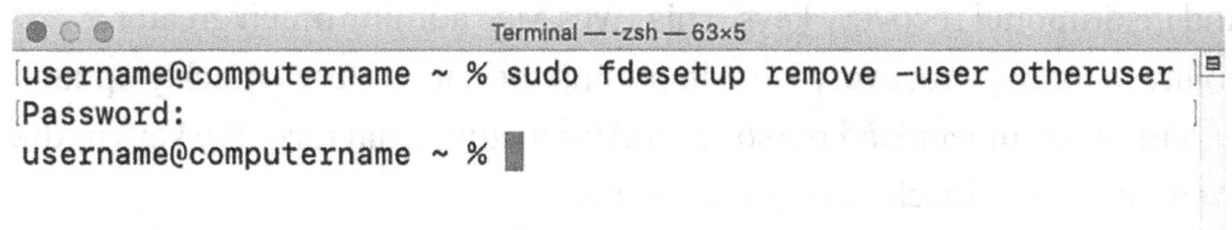

Figure 7-44. *Using fdesetup remove with username*

To remove the account using the account's UUID, run the following command (Figure 7-45) with root privileges:

```
fdesetup remove -uuid UUID_here
```

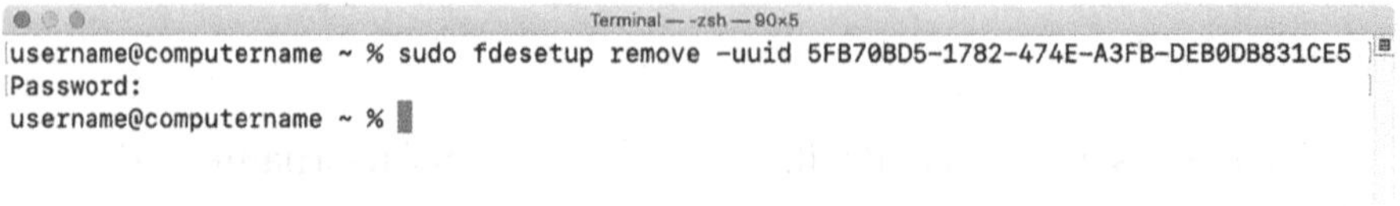

```
username@computername ~ % sudo fdesetup remove -uuid 5FB70BD5-1782-474E-A3FB-DEB0DB831CE5
Password:
username@computername ~ %
```

***Figure 7-45.** Using fdesetup remove with UUID*

In both cases, successful removal of the account will not produce any additional output. If the account being removed is not currently enabled for use with FileVault 2, an error message will be displayed, as shown in Figure 7-46.

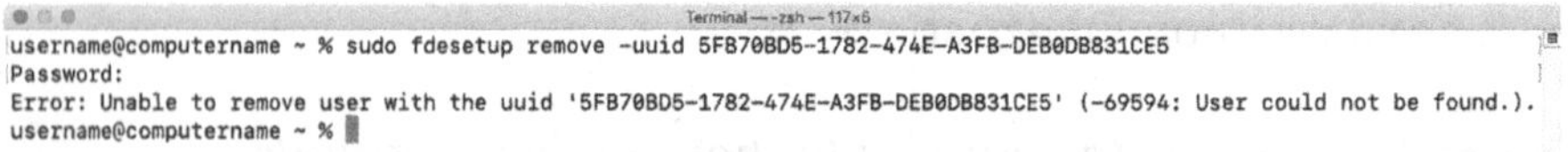

```
username@computername ~ % sudo fdesetup remove -uuid 5FB70BD5-1782-474E-A3FB-DEB0DB831CE5
Password:
Error: Unable to remove user with the uuid '5FB70BD5-1782-474E-A3FB-DEB0DB831CE5' (-69594: User could not be found.).
username@computername ~ %
```

***Figure 7-46.** -fdesetup remove error when specified account is not FileVault 2 enabled*

Managing Individual and Institutional Recovery Keys

`fdesetup` includes the ability to change, add, and remove both personal and institutional recovery keys. This gives Mac admins much greater ability to manage recovery keys, including the capability to quickly update or remove compromised personal and/or institutional recovery keys in the event of a data breach or other problems.

You can add or change recovery keys using **fdesetup changerecovery**. To change to a new personal key, run the following command with root privileges:

```
fdesetup changerecovery -personal
```

You'll be prompted for the password of an existing FileVault 2-enabled user or the existing personal recovery key. Once entered, a new personal recovery key will be generated and displayed, as can be seen in Figure 7-47. The former personal recovery key will no longer work.

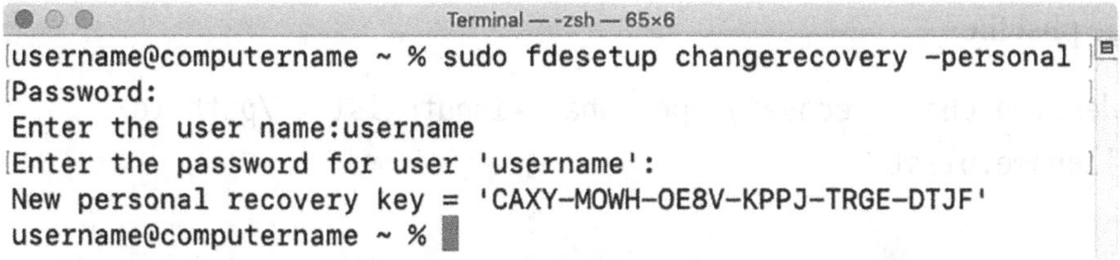

Terminal — -zsh — 65×6

```
username@computername ~ % sudo fdesetup changerecovery -personal
Password:
Enter the user name:username
Enter the password for user 'username':
New personal recovery key = 'CAXY-MOWH-OE8V-KPPJ-TRGE-DTJF'
username@computername ~ %
```

Figure 7-47. *Using fdesetup changerecovery to change to a new personal recovery key*

For those who want to automate the process, fdesetup also supports importing a properly formatted plist via a standard input stream (stdin). The plist needs to follow the format displayed in Figure 7-48, this format:

```
<?xml version="1.0" encoding="UTF-8"?>
<!DOCTYPE plist PUBLIC "-//Apple//DTD PLIST 1.0//EN" "http://
www.apple.com/DTDs/PropertyList-1.0.dtd">
<plist version="1.0">
<dict>
<key>Password</key>
<string>password</string>
</dict>
</plist>
```

```
<!DOCTYPE plist PUBLIC "-//Apple//DTD PLIST 1.0//EN" "http://www.apple.com/DTDs/PropertyList-1.0.dtd">
<plist version="1.0">
<dict>
<key>Password</key>
<string>password</string>
</dict>
</plist>
```

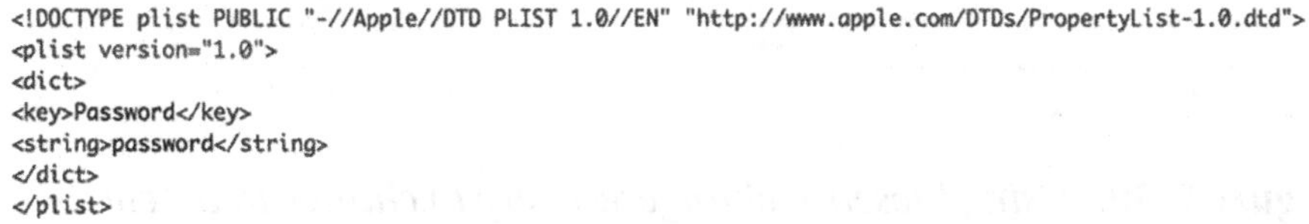

Figure 7-48. *Plist format for fdesetup changerecovery -personal*

You would store either the password of an existing FileVault 2–enabled user or the existing personal recovery key in the **Password** key in the plist.

Once the plist has been set up and properly formatted, run the following command with root privileges to change to a new personal recovery key (Figure 7-49) and reference the password or recovery key in the plist file:

```
fdesetup changerecovery -personal -inputplist < /path/to/
filename.plist
```

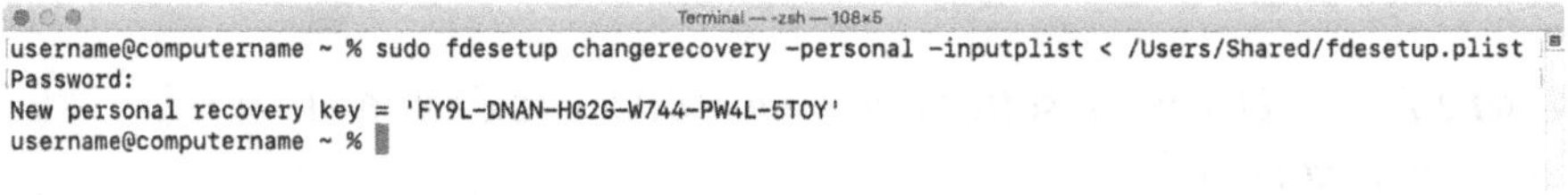

```
Terminal — -zsh — 108×5
username@computername ~ % sudo fdesetup changerecovery -personal -inputplist < /Users/Shared/fdesetup.plist
Password:
New personal recovery key = 'FY9L-DNAN-HG2G-W744-PW4L-5TOY'
username@computername ~ %
```

Figure 7-49. *Using fdesetup changerecovery -personal with -inputplist*

In the event that the Mac in question does not have a personal recovery key, running the preceding commands will add a personal recovery key instead of changing an existing one.

To change to a new institutional recovery key, you will need to have the new public key available. If you have a new institutional public key available as a DER-encoded certificate file, you can run the following command with root privileges, as done in Figure 7-50, to replace the current institutional key:

```
fdesetup changerecovery -institutional -keychain -certificate /
path/to/filename.cer
```

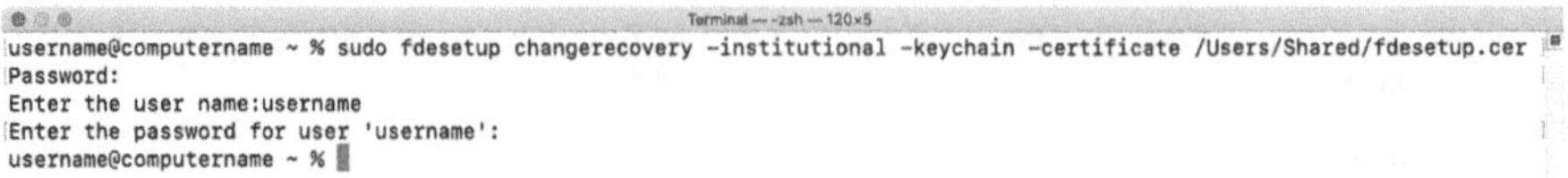

```
Terminal — -zsh — 120×5
username@computername ~ % sudo fdesetup changerecovery -institutional -keychain -certificate /Users/Shared/fdesetup.cer
Password:
Enter the user name:username
Enter the password for user 'username':
username@computername ~ %
```

Figure 7-50. *Using fdesetup changerecovery to change to a new institutional key*

If an institutional keychain is being used on this Mac, you will see a message that an existing FileVault Master keychain was found and moved (Figure 7-51). The reason for this is that, as part of this process, the current institutional key's **/Library/Keychains/FileVaultMaster.keychain** file is replaced with a new **/Library/Keychains/FileVaultMaster.keychain** file that includes the new institutional recovery key's public key.

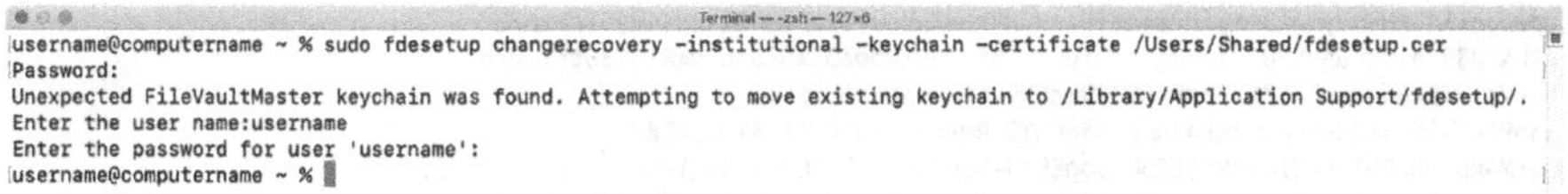

```
username@computername ~ % sudo fdesetup changerecovery -institutional -keychain -certificate /Users/Shared/fdesetup.cer
Password:
Unexpected FileVaultMaster keychain was found. Attempting to move existing keychain to /Library/Application Support/fdesetup/.
Enter the user name:username
Enter the password for user 'username':
username@computername ~ %
```

Figure 7-51. *fdesetup changerecovery warning that an existing keychain has been found and moved*

While the former institutional key's **/Library/Keychains/FileVaultMaster.keychain** was moved and not deleted, the former institutional recovery key will no longer work.

For those who want to automate the process, **fdesetup** also supports importing a properly formatted plist via a standard input stream (stdin). The plist needs to follow this format (shown in Figure 7-52 as well):

```
<?xml version="1.0" encoding="UTF-8"?>
<!DOCTYPE plist PUBLIC "-//Apple//DTD PLIST 1.0//EN" "http://
www.apple.com/DTDs/PropertyList-1.0.dtd">
<plist version="1.0">
<dict>
<key>Password</key>
<string>password</string>
<key>Certificate</key>
<data>
(Certificate data goes here...)
</data>
</dict>
</plist>
```

```
<!DOCTYPE plist PUBLIC "-//Apple//DTD PLIST 1.0//EN" "http://www.apple.com/DTDs/PropertyList-1.0.dtd">
<plist version="1.0">
<dict>
<key>Password</key>
<string>password</string>
<key>Certificate</key>
<data>
MIIDLjCCAhagAwIBAgIENsqyWTALBgkqhkiG9w0BAQUwSTEfMB0GA1UEAwwWRmlsZVZhdWx0
IFJlY292ZXJ5IEtleTEmMCQGA1UEDQwddHJvdXRvbnQtdm0zLnRhb21lY2h3b3Jrcy5uZXQw
HhcNMTMwODI0MjEzNTI1WhcNMTQwODI0MjEzNTI1WjBJMR8wHQYDVQQDDBZGaWxlVmF1bHQg
UmVjb3ZlcnkgS2V5MSYwJAYDVQQNDB10cm91dG9udC12bTMudGFvbWVjaHdvcmtzLm5ldDCC
ASIwDQYJKoZIhvcNAQEBBQADggEPADCCAQoCggEBAMJpO4TYyH8HC3H4WWV0FPV48I1cdRjh
BGi9OYJX8cQrgWb72FTDCNbU+fD1ce1++KALheMNCmhOIwPshQtbUuU9ngpfRYI/
L6KIgIaUW4bpUksHXZ0CIwSvfqD6+
np06wniS48KNPmnyHqxNeYyfU20wAITPznP7w0VjU7pMbvvJra03gNDxxLc44Rj5YdHxn7U7
gIUNc08RxntNgC6hPSMuZVIgz8AUFcOYuBYML9fXrHytNoaZ0JXS2djGRdwRT0V3OtK2qDFh
8+vVr9vTBt3xmk6hPREXfB9odRDH6ZP9mn6R2vLLzF4ANwklha0L4+
mwbPtdfVOSs3wdkoUFF8CAwEAAaMgMB4wCwYDVR0PBAQDAgK0MA8GA1UdEwEB/
wQFMAMBAQAwDQYJKoZIhvcNAQEFBQADggEBAJ+5ZaqzQmnVDrIQBkxiBXql/
aRbQpetu5jLsJtHDxRd1d2YiEFJHwy4jnUefrvTUf7648oCQ5FtOjYL5lYn7QQ3MjvsFKzBh
2wVlqJJAhjjjwbzMoVdRxfY8Aftcler9Tw/WvxiECvdgxBA37iA+EGVTrRUGuCytY+
GhawIKQMR5Ac2XBpfgPatbV9xAtCo4+M9I4jqhSxOGMwLjRHs4yELyH71w/Au3VlTYezf+
dqofOaZ8c4wBOK3T4VeoWMJjjwDe9Q3/j3sf/CjxvNhm1yYRUqUieZx7Vdf2+
oKKqMczyAVz0Y8UX26lMnpMQn4Fv9b5mOvo5U2/ZgpiQ8cHxM=
</data>
</dict>
</plist>
```

Figure 7-52. *Plist format for fdesetup changerecovery -institutional*

```
fdesetup changerecovery -institutional -keychain -inputplist <
/path/to/filename.plist
```

In the event that the Mac in question does not have an institutional recovery key, running the preceding commands will add an institutional recovery key instead of changing an existing one.

Removing Individual and Institutional Recovery Keys

You can remove recovery keys using `fdesetup`. To remove the current personal recovery key, run the following command with root privileges:

```
fdesetup removerecovery -personal
```

You'll be prompted (Figure 7-53) for the password of an existing FileVault 2-enabled user or the existing personal recovery key. Once entered, the personal recovery key will be removed from the system. The former personal recovery key will no longer work.

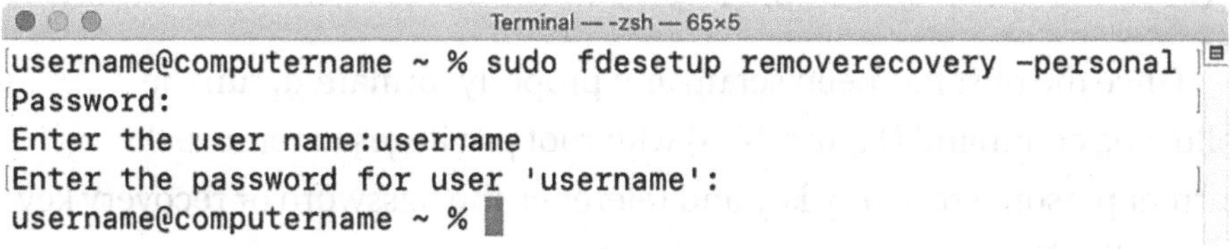

```
Terminal — -zsh — 65×5
username@computername ~ % sudo fdesetup removerecovery -personal
Password:
Enter the user name:username
Enter the password for user 'username':
username@computername ~ %
```

Figure 7-53. *Using fdesetup removerecovery to remove a personal recovery key*

For those who want to automate the process, `fdesetup` also supports importing a properly formatted plist via a standard input stream (stdin). The plist needs to follow this format:

```
<?xml version="1.0" encoding="UTF-8"?>
<!DOCTYPE plist PUBLIC "-//Apple//DTD PLIST 1.0//EN" "http://
www.apple.com/DTDs/PropertyList-1.0.dtd">
<plist version="1.0">
<dict>
<key>Password</key>
<string>password</string>
</dict>
</plist>
```

You would store either the password of an existing FileVault 2-enabled user or the existing personal recovery key in the **Password** key in the plist (Figure 7-54).

```
<!DOCTYPE plist PUBLIC "-//Apple//DTD PLIST 1.0//EN" "http://www.apple.com/DTDs/PropertyList-1.0.dtd">
<plist version="1.0">
<dict>
<key>Password</key>
<string>password</string>
</dict>
</plist>
```

Figure 7-54. *Plist format for fdesetup removerecovery*

Once the plist has been set up and properly formatted, run the following command (Figure 7-55) with root privileges to remove the current personal recovery key and reference the password or recovery key in the plist file:

```
fdesetup removerecovery -personal -inputplist < /path/to/
filename.plist
```

```
username@computername ~ % sudo fdesetup removerecovery -personal -inputplist < /Users/Shared/fdesetup.plist
Password:
username@computername ~ %
```

Figure 7-55. *Using fdesetup removerecovery -personal with -inputplist*

To remove institutional recovery keys, run the following command with root privileges:

```
fdesetup removerecovery -institutional
```

You'll be prompted for the password of an existing FileVault 2-enabled user or a personal recovery key if one is available (Figure 7-56). Once entered, the institutional recovery key will be removed from the system and will no longer work.

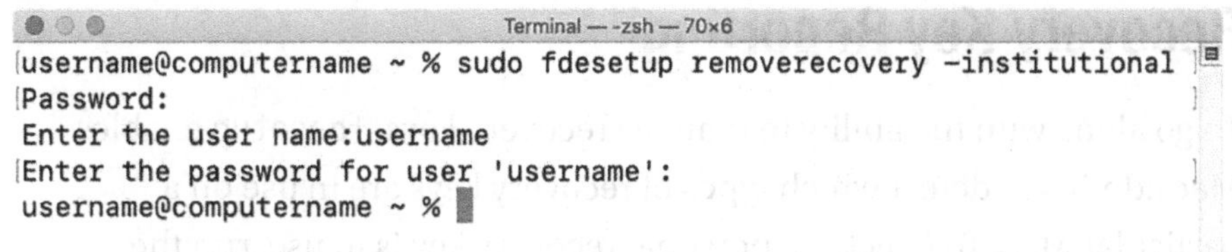

***Figure 7-56.** Using fdesetup removerecovery to remove an institutional recovery key*

The removal of the institutional key can also be automated using a properly formatted plist via a standard input stream (stdin). The plist is the same as the one used for removing the personal key.

Once the plist has been set up and properly formatted, run the following command (Figure 7-57) with root privileges to remove the institutional recovery key and reference the password or recovery key in the plist file:

```
fdesetup removerecovery -institutional -inputplist < /path/to/
filename.plist
```

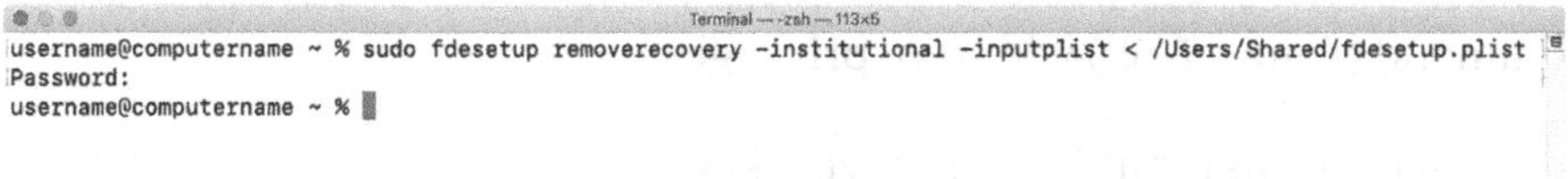

```
username@computername ~ % sudo fdesetup removerecovery -institutional -inputplist < /Users/Shared/fdesetup.plist
Password:
username@computername ~ %
```

***Figure 7-57.** Using fdesetup removerecovery -institutional with -inputplist*

It is possible to use `fdesetup` to remove one or both recovery keys on a particular Mac. Once the recovery keys are removed, the only way to unlock the FileVault 2 encryption is by using the password of an enabled account. That said, you could use `fdesetup's` **changerecovery** function to add one or both types of recovery keys back to the encrypted Mac.

Recovery Key Reporting

To go along with the ability to manage recovery keys, `fdesetup` enables Mac admins to detect which types of recovery keys are in use on a particular Mac. To check if a personal recovery key is in use, run the following command with root privileges:

```
fdesetup haspersonalrecoverykey
```

If FileVault 2 is using a personal recovery key, this command will return **true**. This can be seen in Figure 7-58. Otherwise, it will return **false**.

```
Terminal — -zsh — 63×5
username@computername ~ % sudo fdesetup haspersonalrecoverykey
Password:
true
username@computername ~ %
```

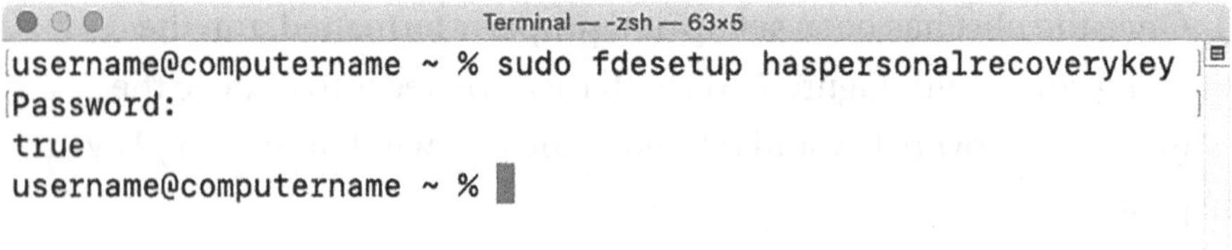

Figure 7-58. *Using fdesetup haspersonalrecoverykey*

To check if an institutional recovery key is in use, run the following command (Figure 7-59) with root privileges:

```
fdesetup hasinstitutionalrecoverykey
```

```
Terminal — -zsh — 68×5
username@computername ~ % sudo fdesetup hasinstitutionalrecoverykey
Password:
true
username@computername ~ %
```

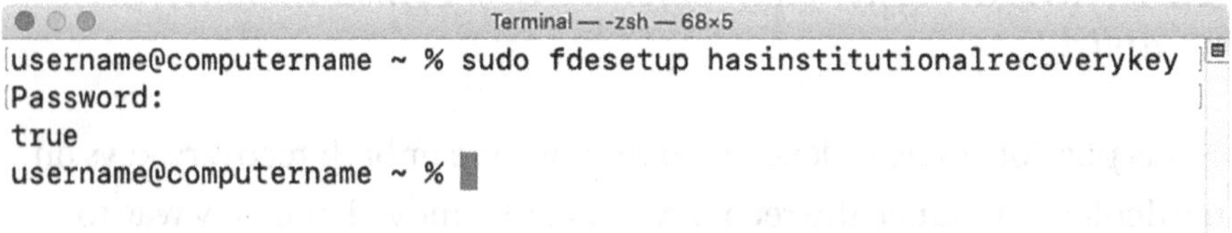

Figure 7-59. *Using fdesetup hasinstitutionalrecoverykey*

If FileVault 2 is using an institutional recovery key, this command will return **true**. Otherwise, it will return **false**.

ONE-TIME FILEVAULT 2 ENCRYPTION BYPASS

`fdesetup` has the **authrestart** verb, which allows a FileVault 2–encrypted Mac to restart, bypass the FileVault 2 preboot login screen, and go straight to the OS login window.

To restart and bypass the FileVault 2 preboot login screen, run the following command with root privileges:

```
fdesetup authrestart
```

When you run the **fdesetup authrestart** command, it asks for the password of an existing FileVault 2–enabled user or a personal recovery key (Figure 7-60).

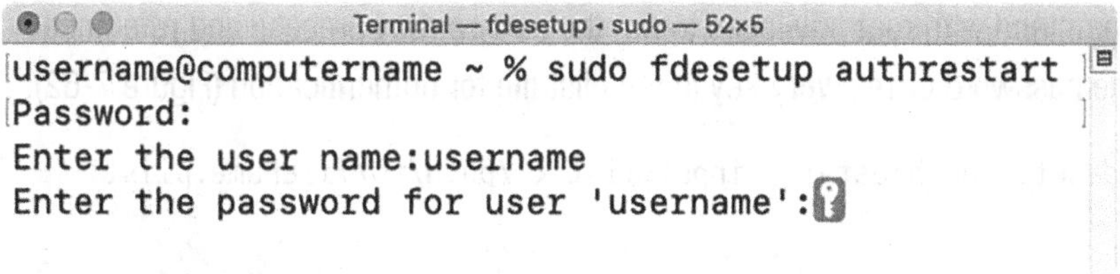

```
Terminal — fdesetup • sudo — 52×5
username@computername ~ % sudo fdesetup authrestart
Password:
Enter the user name:username
Enter the password for user 'username':
```

Figure 7-60. *Using fdesetup authrestart*

Once authenticated, the **authrestart** process puts an unlock key in system memory and reboots. On reboot, the reboot process automatically clears the unlock key from memory.

It's also possible to automate this process by importing the authentication via a properly formatted plist. The plist needs to follow the format shown in Figure 7-61 (and seen below):

```
<?xml version="1.0" encoding="UTF-8"?>
<!DOCTYPE plist PUBLIC "-//Apple//DTD PLIST 1.0//EN" "http://
www.apple.com/DTDs/PropertyList-1.0.dtd">
<plist version="1.0">
<dict>
<key>Password</key>
```

```
<string>password</string>
</dict>
</plist>
```

```
<!DOCTYPE plist PUBLIC "-//Apple//DTD PLIST 1.0//EN" "http://www.apple.com/DTDs/PropertyList-1.0.dtd">
<plist version="1.0">
<dict>
<key>Password</key>
<string>password</string>
</dict>
</plist>
```

Figure 7-61. *Plist format for fdesetup authrestart*

You would store either the password of an existing FileVault 2–enabled user or a personal recovery key in the **Password** key in the plist.

Once the plist has been set up and properly formatted, use the following command with root privileges to run the **authrestart** process and reference the password or recovery key in the plist file for authentication (Figure 7-62):

```
fdesetup authrestart -inputplist < /path/to/filename.plist
```

```
Terminal — sudo — 95×5
username@computername ~ % sudo fdesetup authrestart -inputplist < /Users/Shared/fdesetup.plist
Password:
```

Figure 7-62. *Using fdesetup authrestart with -inputplist*

`fdesetup`'s **authrestart** functionality is not supported by all Macs. To verify if a specific Mac supports **authrestart**, run the following command with root privileges:

```
fdesetup supportsauthrestart
```

If the Mac supports using **authrestart**, this command will return **true** as seen in Figure 7-63. Otherwise, it will return **false**.

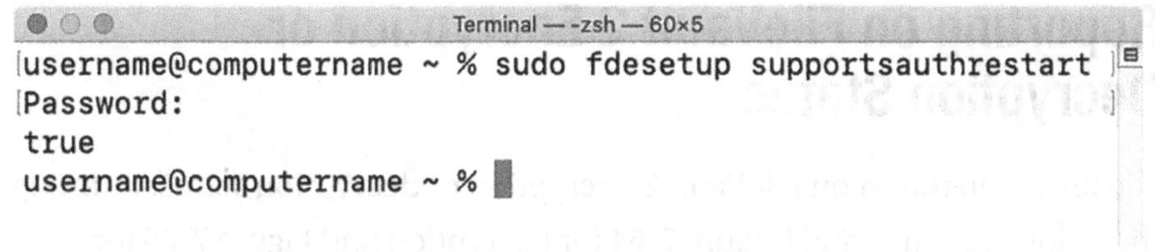

Terminal — -zsh — 60×5
username@computername ~ % sudo fdesetup supportsauthrestart
Password:
true
username@computername ~ %

Figure 7-63. *Using fdesetup supportsauthrestart*

Note The **authrestart** functionality works on both Intel and Apple Silicon Macs, but Apple Silicon Macs do not have a preboot login screen like Intel Macs have.

On Intel Macs, Apple is dependent on using the EFI login environment for the FileVault 2 login screen. This is a very limited environment in terms of functionality and is used in the FileVault 2 context to provide a way to boot the Mac while the main boot volume is locked by FileVault's encryption. Once EFI has booted the Mac, the Mac then uses authentication from the user and the tools stored on the unencrypted preboot volume to unlock the much larger encrypted boot volume.

Apple Silicon Macs have a unified login screen experience where the Mac boots to the OS login window without unlocking the encrypted disk storage. FileVault-enabled accounts can log in at the OS login window and unlock the encrypted storage. On an Apple Silicon Mac, using fdesetup's **authrestart** functionality effectively only reboots the Mac without providing additional benefits.

Reporting on FileVault 2 Encryption or Decryption Status

fdesetup can report on FileVault 2 encryption or decryption status. Running the following command (Figure 7-64 for decryption and Figure 7-65 for encryption) with root privileges will display the current state (Figure 7-66 shows the output for the completed process and Figure 7-67 shows a fully decrypted state):

```
fdesetup status
```

```
Terminal — -zsh — 50×6
username@computername ~ % sudo fdesetup status
Password:
FileVault is On.
FileVault master keychain appears to be installed.
Decryption in progress: Percent completed = 9
username@computername ~ %
```

***Figure 7-64.** fdesetup status reporting decryption status*

```
Terminal — -zsh — 47×5
username@computername ~ % sudo fdesetup status
Password:
FileVault is On.
Encryption in progress: Percent completed = 11
username@computername ~ %
```

***Figure 7-65.** fdesetup status reporting encryption status*

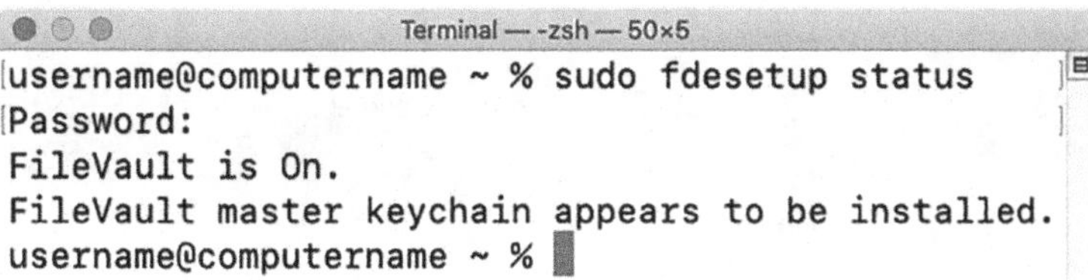

Figure 7-66. *fdesetup status reporting encryption is enabled*

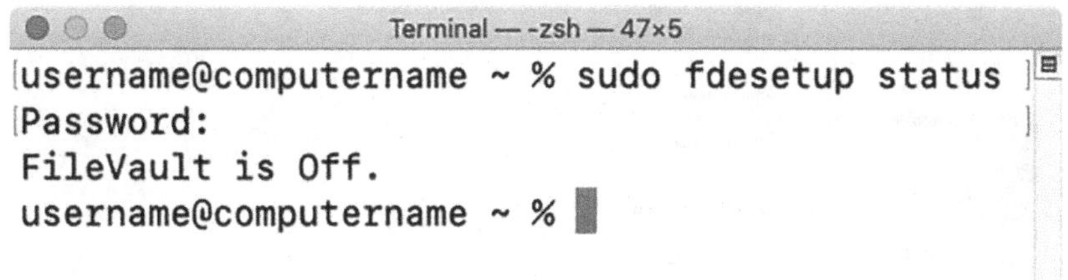

Figure 7-67. *fdesetup status reporting encryption is disabled*

You can also enable FileVault 2 using configuration profiles deployed through your MDM server solution. You can use various tools to create a FileVault 2 management profile, but for the illustrations in this example, DigiDNA's iMazing Profile Editor is being used:

1. Open the profile creation tool.
2. Complete the information in the General payload of the new configuration profile (Figure 7-68).

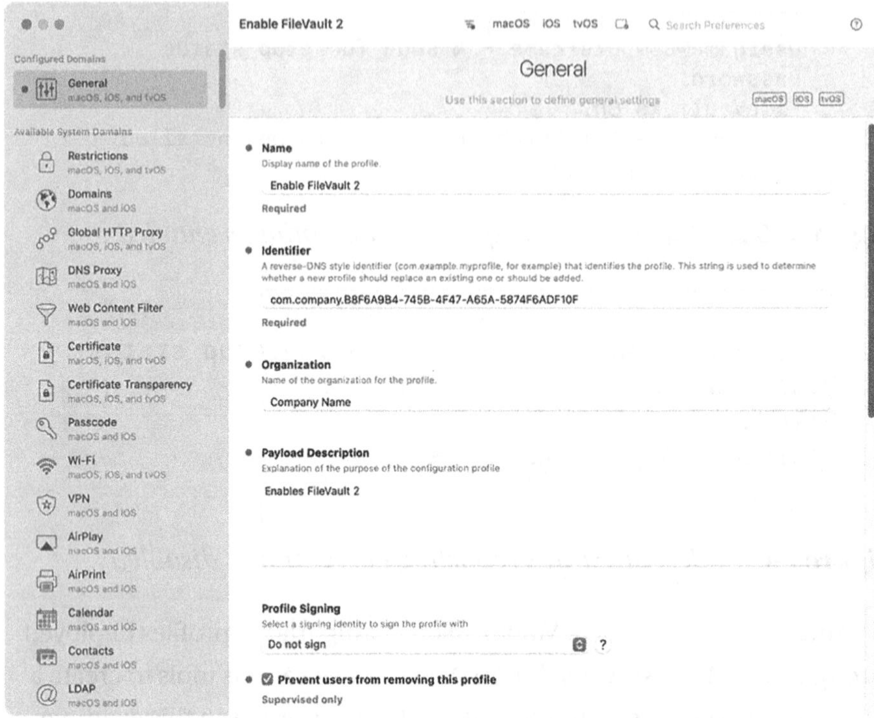

Figure 7-68. *Creating the Enable FileVault 2 profile's General payload*

3. Scroll through the list of payloads to the left and choose the relevant FileVault 2 payload option.

4. Set Enable FileVault to On (Figure 7-69).

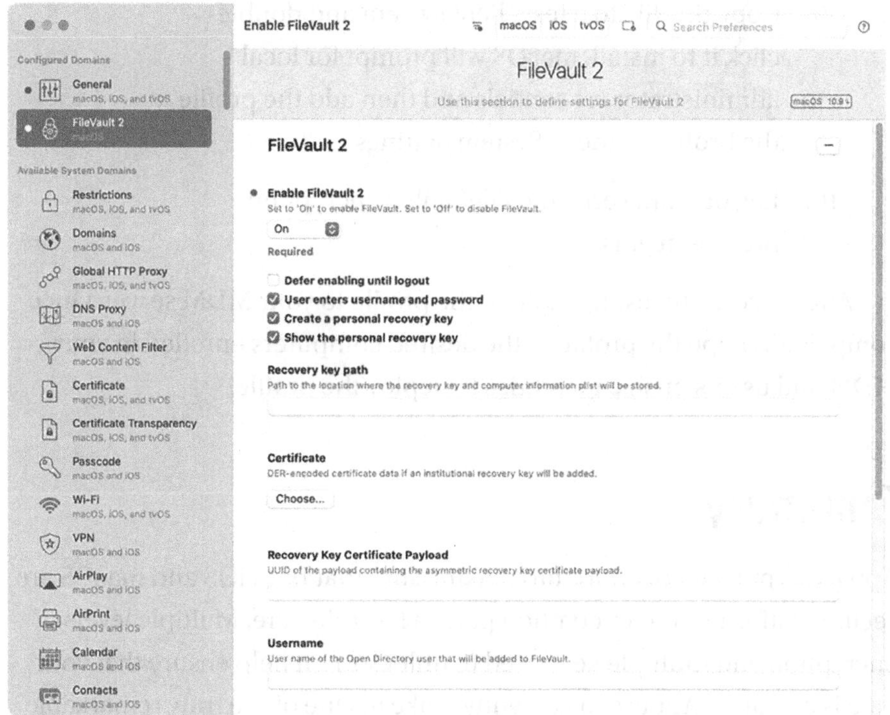

***Figure 7-69.** Creating the Enable FileVault 2 profile's payload settings*

5. Choose to create a personal recovery key.

6. Enable other settings as desired.

7. When finished configuring the desired payload options, save the new Enable FileVault 2 configuration profile.

8. To test the new configuration profile, click the Download button to download a .mobileconfig file.

9. Copy this file to a test client system and double-click it to install. macOS will prompt for local administrator credentials and then add the profile to the Profiles pane of System Settings.
10. Log out and verify the FileVault 2 encryption process begins.

After successful testing, upload the profile to your MDM server. Once completed, scope the profile to the desired computers enrolled in your MDM and use its push capabilities to deploy the profile.

Summary

Apple has put a lot of effort into making sure that both iOS and macOS are secure platforms, and encryption plays a key role here. Multiple levels of encryption and multiple keys used to unlock them help ensure that your data is as safe as Apple can currently make it. One of the truly remarkable things about this protection is how little the average person needs to think about it. Apple has built an easy-to-use security model where enabling a passcode on iOS or enabling FileVault 2 on macOS is simple enough for anyone to do, but where those acts enable unrivaled protection for that person's data.

That said, the weak link in Apple's protection is that ultimately human beings are the ones choosing whether to enable the encryption and picking the unlock codes. Your Mac or iOS device is only going to be as secure as you make it. Enabling encryption and choosing strong passwords or passcodes will go a long way toward making sure that your data remains for your eyes only.

CHAPTER 8

Securing Your Fleet

What's really a threat on an Apple device? That's often according to who you ask. But in order for Apple devices to be allowed on corporate networks, there's a few criteria that must be met, and rarely have I seen an auditor who is willing to budge on these requirements. If you disagree that something is necessary, then you should absolutely speak up; however, a second or third effort is really just likely to make them dig into their position and trust you less. And sometimes, they're right.

2018 was one of the roughest years for Mac security. You can find a rundown of the vulnerabilities and malware introduced at `https://digitasecurity.com/blog/2019/01/01/malware2018/` which indicates OSX.MAMI, OSX.CrossRAT, and OSX.CreativeUpdate, among others. It hasn't been smooth sailing since then either. Suffice it to say that given that security researchers are only beginning to scratch the surface of attacking the platform, there's going to be more ahead of us than behind us. Given the closed nature of iOS, there's just less to attack, and so expect fewer vulnerabilities there and maybe expect the Mac to trend in that direction as well. So more of this chapter is dedicated to the Mac than iOS, starting with securing the Mac.

Securing the Platform

Compliance is a thing. In this book, we have covered (and continue to cover) how to get devices into a compliant state. But compliance means different things for different teams and different platforms. While the

C. Edge and R. Trouton, *Apple Device Management*,
https://doi.org/10.1007/978-1-4842-9156-6_8

Apple platforms are similar, what you can do on iOS is much more limited and so the security threats are as well. As an example, this means you don't use antivirus on iOS but can on macOS. In general, mobile devices are treated differently in organizations: you don't assume they're always on your network, you don't expect access to the filesystem on the device so you plan workflows that are app driven, and on Apple platforms, you leverage MDM to do much of the heavy lifting to secure devices.

The Mac is very different. You can do practically anything you want on the device. In many ways, the Mac is becoming more iOS-like, but you can still disable SIP (System Integration Protection), which has been covered throughout this book, and do anything you want on a device. Apple produces a great guide to macOS security at `www.apple.com/business/resources/docs/macOS_Security_Overview.pdf`, and this chapter is meant as a technical journey through the basic security measures required by most organizations. This starts with the operating system but quickly becomes as much about apps and content as hardened systems that follow guidelines, like those issued by the National Institute of Standards and Technology in the United States, or NIST. NIST has made their compliance work open source at `https://github.com/usnistgov/macos_security` with assistance from agencies like NASA and the Pentagon.

With both Mac and iOS, many assume any software that goes through the App Store is safe. This is because Apple scans software to indicate that it is indeed safe. Now with App Notarization, Apple is scanning apps for security flaws. This service is currently optional (except for kernel extensions, or kexts), and if an app has been certified by Apple and signing matches Apple's database, then Gatekeeper (described further later in this chapter) provides a special icon that the software is clean. As we cover later in the chapter, this is good for many, but not all, organizations.

Security is a trade-off. In general, the more secure a fleet of devices becomes, the less features are available on devices and/or the slower the device will run. For example, removing the ability to use iCloud is interpreted as some environments as improving security; however, without iCloud, many services work suboptimally. Most classic Apple users and administrators think "Apple has me covered" when it comes to security. Most classic IT departments think "we must lock down everything that makes anything cool." And according to the type of data being stored on a computer, they may be correct. The answer for how much security is required to protect a device is somewhere in the middle and is entirely based on the security posture of any given organization.

Many organizations have anywhere between three and eight LaunchAgents and/or LaunchDaemons that run on a Mac. Given the types and number of vulnerabilities on the Mac as well as what frameworks are allowed to touch on the Mac, it is unimaginable that a customer would actually need to deploy all of those agents given that each can have an expensive load on system resources, with some taking up 10–30% of the CPU or memory on a computer. One is usually too few, four is too many. None should touch the kernel (and therefore should not be kernel extensions) because doing so can lead to unbootable devices, and most existing products do not provide for zero-day support.

Mac Security

The Mac includes a number of built-in security features, on both the system level and the user level. Two major components of these security features are the signed system volume and System Integrity Protection (SIP).

Signed System Volume

As of macOS Big Sur and later, Apple has moved the parts of the OS it can make immutable by moving them to the system volume of the boot drive. This volume is mounted as read-only at boot by macOS, and all files stored in the volume on it now have a SHA-256 cryptographic hash which is stored in the filesystem. This allows macOS to check each file's current hash against the stored hash at boot time, to verify that the file hasn't been tampered with or damaged.

In addition, further hashing is used in the filesystem metadata itself. This additional hashing covers all directories from the deepest nested directories to the root level. This additional hashing is referred to as a cryptographic seal and covers the entire system volume, its directory structure, and all the data contained inside. This seal is verified every time the Mac starts up, though the behavior is slightly different between Apple Silicon Macs and Intel Macs equipped with T2 security chips:

- **Apple Silicon Macs**: Bootloader verifies the seal before transferring control to macOS's kernel.
- **Intel Macs with T2 security chips**: Bootloader forwards seal measurement and signature to macOS's kernel. The kernel verifies the seal before mounting the root filesystem.

If this seal verification fails, the macOS boot process halts at that point, and the user is prompted to reinstall macOS.

System Integrity Protection

Once the Mac is booted and running, System Integrity Protection (SIP) provides a security layer designed to limit the power of the **root** account on macOS.

The **root** account is the superuser for a Unix system, and the Unix permissions model is designed around the assumption that the **root** account has access to everything. To limit what the superuser can do and add another layer to the macOS security model, Apple developed System Integrity Protection (SIP) and first deployed it as part of OS X El Capitan. SIP is designed to limit the power of root and to protect the system, even from its own root user.

SIP is an overall security policy with the goal of preventing system files and processes from being modified by third parties. To achieve this, it has the following concepts:

- Filesystem protection
- Runtime protection
- Kernel extension protection

SIP prevents parties other than Apple from adding, deleting, or modifying directories and files stored in certain directories, including the following:

/bin

/sbin

/usr

/System

The preceding directories are required for the computer to boot properly, and not allowing users to alter them keeps the operating system safe. Because the software you install needs to go somewhere on the system, Apple has indicated that the following directories are available for developers to access:

/usr/local

/Applications

/Library

~/Library

All directories in **/usr** except for **/usr/local** are protected by SIP, and third-party developers should not write to protected locations. It is possible to add, remove, or change SIP-protected files and directories via an installer package which is signed by Apple's own certificate authority.

This allows Apple to make changes to SIP-protected parts of the OS without needing to change the existing SIP protections (Figure 8-1).

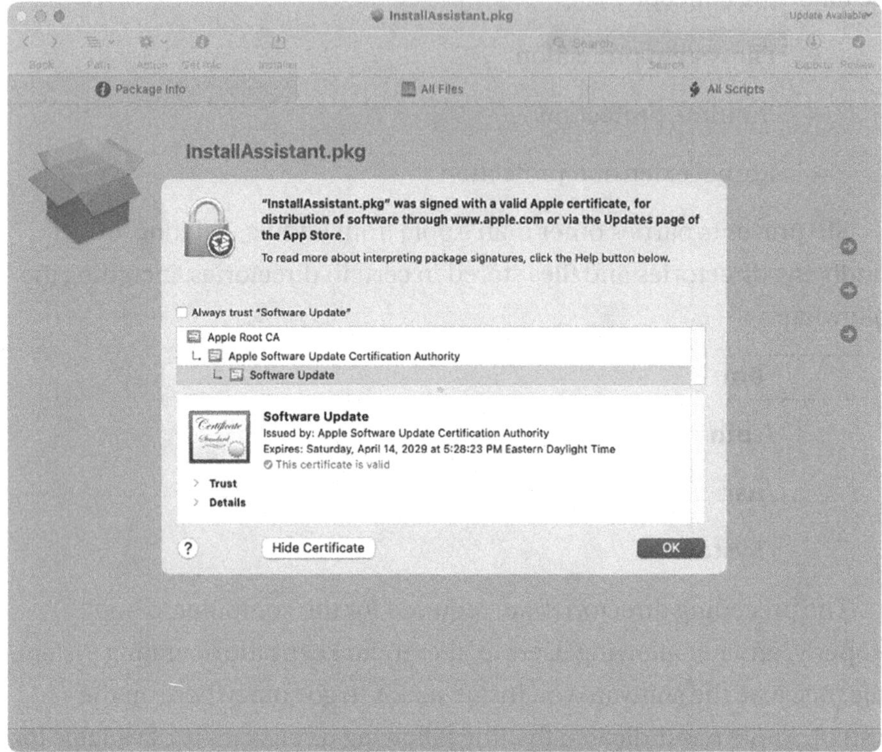

Figure 8-1. *Suspicious package showing signing information for an Apple installer which uses Apple's signing certificate*

The certificate authority in question is reserved by Apple for their own use; Developer ID–signed installer packages are not able to alter SIP-protected files or directories. To define which directories are protected, Apple has currently defined a configuration file, which is **/System/Library/Sandbox/rootless.conf**. This file is controlled exclusively by Apple and lists all the applications and top-level directories which SIP is protecting (Figure 8-2).

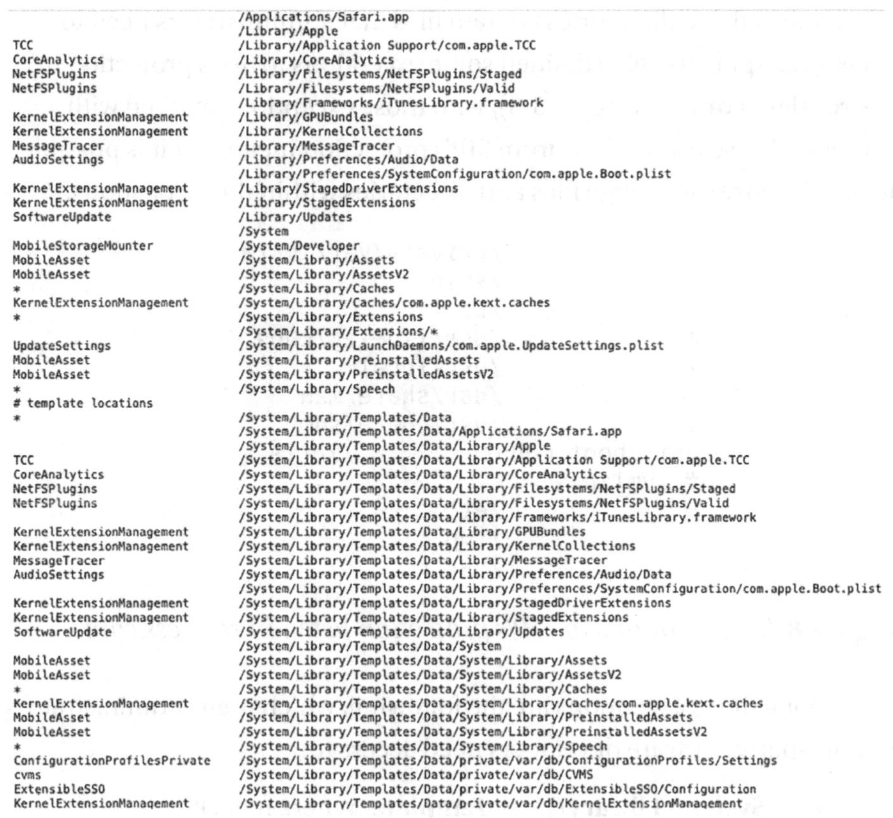

```
                                /Applications/Safari.app
                                /Library/Apple
TCC                             /Library/Application Support/com.apple.TCC
CoreAnalytics                   /Library/CoreAnalytics
NetFSPlugins                    /Library/Filesystems/NetFSPlugins/Staged
NetFSPlugins                    /Library/Filesystems/NetFSPlugins/Valid
                                /Library/Frameworks/iTunesLibrary.framework
KernelExtensionManagement       /Library/GPUBundles
KernelExtensionManagement       /Library/KernelCollections
MessageTracer                   /Library/MessageTracer
AudioSettings                   /Library/Preferences/Audio/Data
                                /Library/Preferences/SystemConfiguration/com.apple.Boot.plist
KernelExtensionManagement       /Library/StagedDriverExtensions
KernelExtensionManagement       /Library/StagedExtensions
SoftwareUpdate                  /Library/Updates
                                /System
MobileStorageMounter            /System/Developer
MobileAsset                     /System/Library/Assets
MobileAsset                     /System/Library/AssetsV2
*                               /System/Library/Caches
KernelExtensionManagement       /System/Library/Caches/com.apple.kext.caches
*                               /System/Library/Extensions
                                /System/Library/Extensions/*
UpdateSettings                  /System/Library/LaunchDaemons/com.apple.UpdateSettings.plist
MobileAsset                     /System/Library/PreinstalledAssets
MobileAsset                     /System/Library/PreinstalledAssetsV2
*                               /System/Library/Speech
# template locations
*                               /System/Library/Templates/Data
                                /System/Library/Templates/Data/Applications/Safari.app
                                /System/Library/Templates/Data/Library/Apple
TCC                             /System/Library/Templates/Data/Library/Application Support/com.apple.TCC
CoreAnalytics                   /System/Library/Templates/Data/Library/CoreAnalytics
NetFSPlugins                    /System/Library/Templates/Data/Library/Filesystems/NetFSPlugins/Staged
NetFSPlugins                    /System/Library/Templates/Data/Library/Filesystems/NetFSPlugins/Valid
                                /System/Library/Templates/Data/Library/Frameworks/iTunesLibrary.framework
KernelExtensionManagement       /System/Library/Templates/Data/Library/GPUBundles
KernelExtensionManagement       /System/Library/Templates/Data/Library/KernelCollections
MessageTracer                   /System/Library/Templates/Data/Library/MessageTracer
AudioSettings                   /System/Library/Templates/Data/Library/Preferences/Audio/Data
                                /System/Library/Templates/Data/Library/Preferences/SystemConfiguration/com.apple.Boot.plist
KernelExtensionManagement       /System/Library/Templates/Data/Library/StagedDriverExtensions
KernelExtensionManagement       /System/Library/Templates/Data/Library/StagedExtensions
SoftwareUpdate                  /System/Library/Templates/Data/Library/Updates
                                /System/Library/Templates/Data/System
MobileAsset                     /System/Library/Templates/Data/System/Library/Assets
MobileAsset                     /System/Library/Templates/Data/System/Library/AssetsV2
*                               /System/Library/Templates/Data/System/Library/Caches
KernelExtensionManagement       /System/Library/Templates/Data/System/Library/Caches/com.apple.kext.caches
MobileAsset                     /System/Library/Templates/Data/System/Library/PreinstalledAssets
MobileAsset                     /System/Library/Templates/Data/System/Library/PreinstalledAssetsV2
*                               /System/Library/Templates/Data/System/Library/Speech
ConfigurationProfilesPrivate    /System/Library/Templates/Data/private/var/db/ConfigurationProfiles/Settings
cvms                            /System/Library/Templates/Data/private/var/db/CVMS
ExtensibleSSO                   /System/Library/Templates/Data/private/var/db/ExtensibleSSO/Configuration
KernelExtensionManagement       /System/Library/Templates/Data/private/var/db/KernelExtensionManagement
```

Figure 8-2. *Partial listing of SIP-protected paths in the /System/Library/Sandbox/rootless.conf file*

SIP-Protected Directories

SIP is also protecting a number of directories and symlinks outside of /**Applications**. Many of those directories contain frameworks, binaries brought in from other projects, and binaries that have always been a part of the Mac, since the inception of Mac OS X.

Some of those directories contain files that administrators need to access. So Apple has also defined some exceptions to SIP's protection in the **rootless.conf** file (Figure 8-3), with those exceptions marked with asterisks. These exemptions from SIP's protection mean that it is possible to add, remove, or change files and directories within those locations.

```
                        /private/var/install
                        /sbin
                        /usr
*                       /usr/libexec/cups
*                       /usr/local
*                       /usr/share/man
*                       /usr/share/snmp
apfs_boot_mount                  /xarts
# symlinks
                        /etc
                        /tmp
                        /var
```

Figure 8-3. *Exceptions to SIP's protection listed in rootless.conf*

Among those exceptions are the following, which many administrators or third-party software developers need access to:

- **/System/Library/User Template**: Where macOS stores the files and directories it uses when creating home folders for new accounts.
- **/usr/libexec/cups**: Where macOS stores printer configuration information.
- **/usr/share/man**: A number of third-party software developers and open source projects will write a man file so you can have a manual of what the software does.

View SIP Protections Interactively

To see which files and directories have been protected by SIP, use the **ls** command with the capital **O** flag in Terminal:

```
ls -O
```

As you can see in Figure 8-4, the output will list SIP-protected files and directories as **restricted**. This is a common troubleshooting step you'll get used to if you have a lot of scripts that touch these folders, and you need to resolve issues that come up with them due to not being able to write to objects in those directories or remove them.

```
username — -zsh — 120×24
username@computername ~ % ls -laO /
total 9
drwxr-xr-x   20 root  wheel  sunlnk              640 Sep 16 03:34 .
drwxr-xr-x   20 root  wheel  sunlnk              640 Sep 16 03:34 ..
lrwxr-xr-x    1 root  admin  -                    36 Sep 16 03:34 .VolumeIcon.icns -> System/Volumes/Data/.VolumeIcon.icns
----------    1 root  admin  -                     0 Sep 16 03:34 .file
drwxr-xr-x    2 root  wheel  hidden               64 Sep 16 03:34 .vol
drwxrwxr-x    8 root  admin  sunlnk              256 Sep 21 18:04 Applications
drwxr-xr-x   66 root  wheel  sunlnk             2112 Sep 21 18:03 Library
drwxr-xr-x@  10 root  wheel  restricted          320 Sep 16 03:34 System
drwxr-xr-x    7 root  admin  sunlnk              224 Sep 22 07:52 Users
drwxr-xr-x    3 root  wheel  hidden               96 Sep 23 14:54 Volumes
drwxr-xr-x@  39 root  wheel  restricted,hidden  1248 Sep 16 03:34 bin
drwxr-xr-x    2 root  wheel  hidden               64 Sep 16 02:34 cores
dr-xr-xr-x    3 root  wheel  hidden             4552 Sep 23 14:54 dev
lrwxr-xr-x@   1 root  wheel  restricted,hidden    11 Sep 16 03:34 etc -> private/etc
lrwxr-xr-x    1 root  wheel  hidden               25 Sep 23 09:05 home -> /System/Volumes/Data/home
drwxr-xr-x    2 root  wheel  hidden               64 Sep 16 02:34 opt
drwxr-xr-x    6 root  wheel  sunlnk,hidden       192 Sep 23 14:54 private
drwxr-xr-x@  64 root  wheel  restricted,hidden  2048 Sep 16 03:34 sbin
lrwxr-xr-x@   1 root  wheel  restricted,hidden    11 Sep 16 03:34 tmp -> private/tmp
drwxr-xr-x@  11 root  wheel  restricted,hidden   352 Sep 16 03:34 usr
lrwxr-xr-x@   1 root  wheel  restricted,hidden    11 Sep 16 03:34 var -> private/var
username@computername ~ %
```

Figure 8-4. *Using the ls command to display SIP-protected root-level directories*

An important thing to note is that even if a symlink (a symbolic link acts as a shortcut of sorts) is protected by SIP, that does not necessarily mean that the directory it's linking to is being protected by SIP. For example, the root level of a macOS boot drive contains several SIP-protected symlinks pointing to directories inside the root-level directory named **private**. Usually, this means that if one of those symlinks were removed, it would cause problems with the device.

However, when the contents of the **private** directory are examined (Figure 8-5), the directories to which those SIP-protected symlinks point are not themselves protected by SIP, meaning those directories and their included files can indeed be moved, edited, or changed by processes using root privileges.

```
username — -zsh — 68×9
username@computername ~ % ls -laO /private
total 0
drwxr-xr-x   6 root  wheel  sunlnk,hidden  192 Sep 23 14:54 .
drwxr-xr-x  20 root  wheel  sunlnk         640 Sep 16 03:34 ..
drwxr-xr-x  79 root  wheel  -             2528 Sep 23 09:05 etc
drwxr-xr-x   2 root  wheel  -               64 Sep 16 02:34 tftpboot
drwxrwxrwt   4 root  wheel  -              128 Sep 23 14:56 tmp
drwxr-xr-x  33 root  wheel  sunlnk        1056 Sep 23 14:54 var
username@computername ~ %
```

Figure 8-5. *Using the ls command to display directories inside the private directory*

Runtime Protections

As mentioned, SIP's protections are not limited to protecting the system from filesystem changes. There are also system calls which are now restricted in their functionality, including the following, which are more for developers and debugging:

- **task_for_pid()/processor_set_tasks()** fail with EPERM.
- Mach special ports are reset on **exec(2)**.
- dyld environment variables are ignored.
- DTrace probes are unavailable.

Of the preceding list, DTrace is probably the most problematic for a Mac administrator. If you need DTrace to troubleshoot, then you will need to disable SIP while troubleshooting. If you are a developer rather than an administrator, SIP does not block inspection by the developer of their own applications while they're being developed, so instrumentation tools are still available. Xcode's tools will continue to allow apps to be inspected and debugged during the development process.

Kernel Extension Protections

The third type of protection that SIP proxies is for kernel extensions. While the use of kernel extensions has been reduced by the introduction of system extensions, SIP blocks the installation of unsigned kernel extensions as well as those that haven't been notarized using Apple's Notarization service. In order to install a kernel extension on macOS with SIP enabled, a kernel extension must

- Install into **/Library/Extensions**.
- Be signed with a Developer ID for Signing Kexts certificate.
- Be notarized using the Apple Notarization service, which is described in more depth in Chapter 5.

For the purposes of this chapter, be aware of what kexts are running. A good tool for this is KextViewr available at `https://objective-see.com/products/kextviewr.html`.

If installing an unsigned kernel extension, SIP will need to be disabled first. However, SIP should only be disabled temporarily. Any time you start managing the settings for SIP by rebooting a machine into recovery mode, think long and hard about whether you should touch anything before you do so. You have plenty of time to do so, because the process is a bit slower than we might want.

Managing System Integrity Protection

To ensure that third parties will not be able to disable these protections, SIP's configuration is stored in NVRAM (Non-volatile random-access memory) rather than in the filesystem itself and is only configurable if the Mac is booted into one of two environments:

- The macOS Installer environment
- The macOS Recovery environment

Note The macOS Installer and macOS Recovery environments are in fact the same environment from macOS's perspective. The main difference between the two is that the macOS Installer environment contains a copy of the installation files for macOS and the Recovery environment does not.

Because SIP's configuration is stored in NVRAM, these settings will apply to the entire machine and will persist even if the OS is reinstalled. SIP can be managed to the extent of turning it on, turning it off, adding and removing IP addresses into a NetBoot whitelist, and reporting on whether SIP is enabled or disabled. All changes to SIP's configuration settings also require a reboot before they take effect, and performing the changes without physically touching the computers will not be possible (and so you won't be doing this en masse).

The tool used to manage SIP is **/usr/bin/csrutil**. **csrutil** is able to work with SIP because it has a unique application entitlement assigned to it by Apple. This entitlement is viewable using the codesign command shown in the following:

```
codesign -d --entitlements - /usr/bin/csrutil
```

The response to the command includes the com.apple.private.iokit.nvram-csr key as shown in Figure 8-6.

```
username@computername ~ % codesign -d --entitlements - /usr/bin/csrutil
Executable=/usr/bin/csrutil
[Dict]
        [Key] com.apple.private.bootability
        [Value]
                [Bool] true
        [Key] com.apple.private.iokit.nvram-csr
        [Value]
                [Bool] true
        [Key] com.apple.rootless.volume.Preboot
        [Value]
                [Bool] true
        [Key] com.apple.rootless.volume.Recovery
        [Value]
                [Bool] true
        [Key] com.apple.rootless.volume.iSCPreboot
        [Value]
                [Bool] true
        [Key] com.apple.private.security.bootpolicy
        [Value]
                [Bool] true
        [Key] com.apple.rootless.volume.iSCRecovery
        [Value]
                [Bool] true
        [Key] com.apple.private.IASInstallerAuthAgent
        [Value]
                [Bool] true
        [Key] com.apple.private.CoreAuthentication.SPI
        [Value]
                [Bool] true
        [Key] com.apple.private.iokit.system-nvram-allow
        [Value]
                [Bool] true
        [Key] com.apple.private.applecredentialmanager.allow
        [Value]
                [Bool] true
username@computername ~ %
```

Figure 8-6. *Displaying csrutil's application entitlement*

When you run **csrutil** without any associated commands, Terminal will respond with the help page. Here, you'll see any options get guidance on how to use the available commands, as you can see in Figure 8-7.

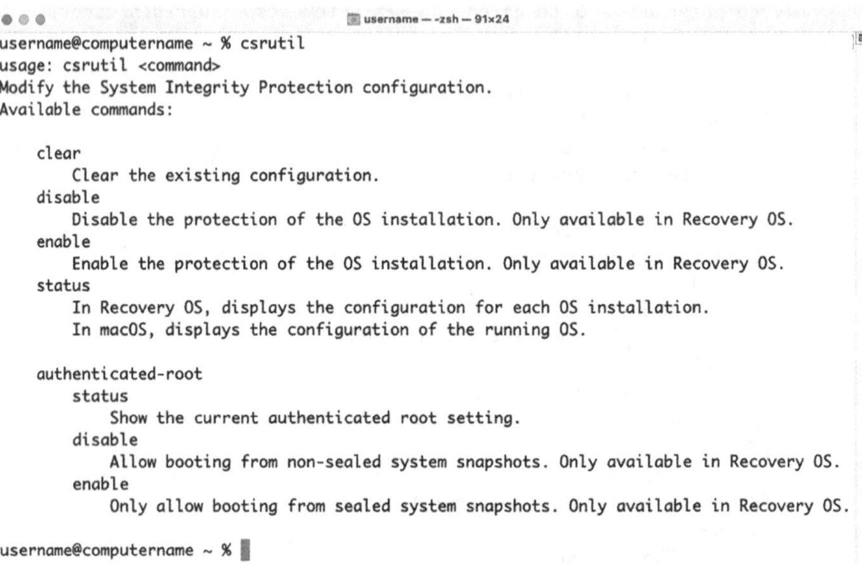

username — -zsh — 91×24
username@computername ~ % csrutil
usage: csrutil <command>
Modify the System Integrity Protection configuration.
Available commands:
clear
Clear the existing configuration.
disable
Disable the protection of the OS installation. Only available in Recovery OS.
enable
Enable the protection of the OS installation. Only available in Recovery OS.
status
In Recovery OS, displays the configuration for each OS installation.
In macOS, displays the configuration of the running OS.
authenticated-root
status
Show the current authenticated root setting.
disable
Allow booting from non-sealed system snapshots. Only available in Recovery OS.
enable
Only allow booting from sealed system snapshots. Only available in Recovery OS.
username@computername ~ %

***Figure 8-7.** Displaying csrutil's help page*

When booted from the Recovery environment, the command used to enable SIP is simply csrutil with the enable verb:

```
csrutil enable
```

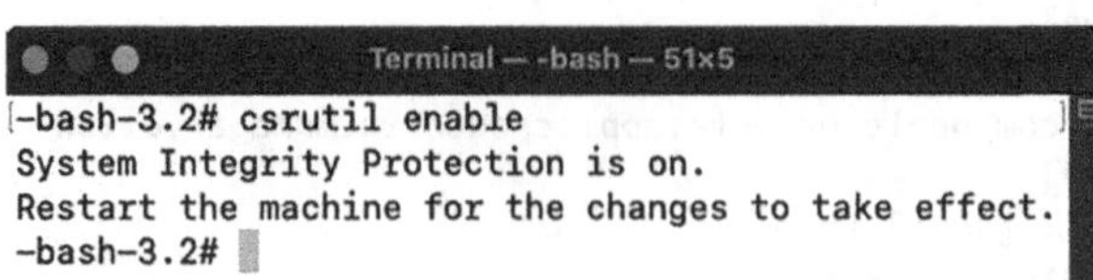

***Figure 8-8.** Running csrutil enable from the Recovery environment*

When run, you'll receive a message that SIP was enabled, as seen in Figure 8-8.

When booted from the Recovery environment, simply replace the enable with a disable in order to turn SIP off so you can perform some of the actions that would otherwise be unavailable to an administrator:

```
csrutil disable
```

The message is almost identical, but states disabled instead of enabled (Figure 8-9).

```
Terminal — -bash — 51×5
-bash-3.2# csrutil disable
System Integrity Protection is off.
Restart the machine for the changes to take effect.
-bash-3.2#
```

***Figure 8-9.** Running csrutil disable from the Recovery environment*

You can also reset the configuration for SIP by running the clear command. This simply returns the state to the factory-installed state:

```
csrutil clear
```

The resultant message doesn't indicate that SIP is disabled or enabled, only that the state was cleared, as you can see in Figure 8-10.

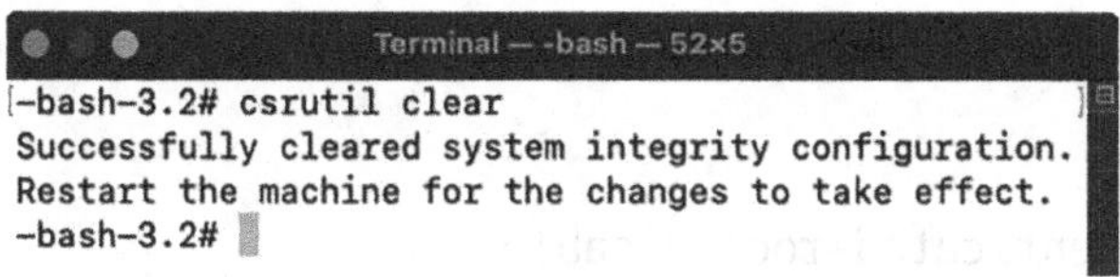
Terminal — -bash — 52×5
-bash-3.2# csrutil clear
Successfully cleared system integrity configuration.
Restart the machine for the changes to take effect.
-bash-3.2#

***Figure 8-10.** Running csrutil clear from the Recovery environment*

When **csrutil clear** is run, SIP goes back to its factory-default settings. That means SIP is enabled if it was disabled previously and any custom configuration is cleared out.

Signed System Volume and csrutil

As of macOS Big Sur and later, Apple has moved the parts of the OS it can make immutable by moving them to the system volume of the boot drive. As discussed earlier, this volume is cryptographically sealed, and the seal is verified against tampering every time the Mac starts up. The **csrutil** command can report whether this seal verification process is enabled or not and also turn this verification process on or off from the Recovery environment.

To enable the seal verification, run the following command as seen in Figure 8-11:

```
csrutil authenticated-root enable
```

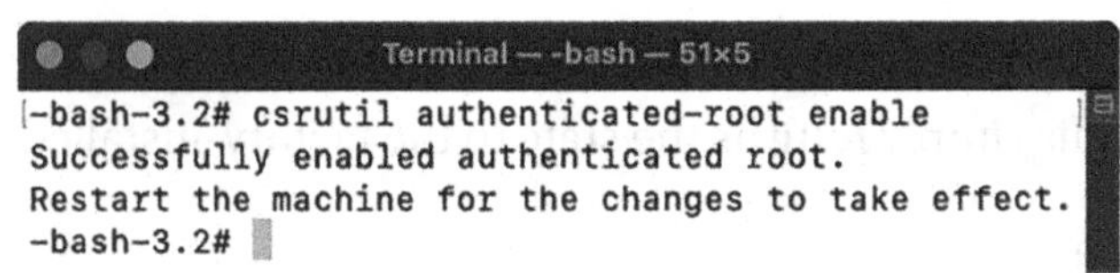

Figure 8-11. *Running csrutil authenticated-root enable from the Recovery environment*

To disable the seal verification, run the following command as seen in Figure 8-12:

```
csrutil authenticated-root disable
```

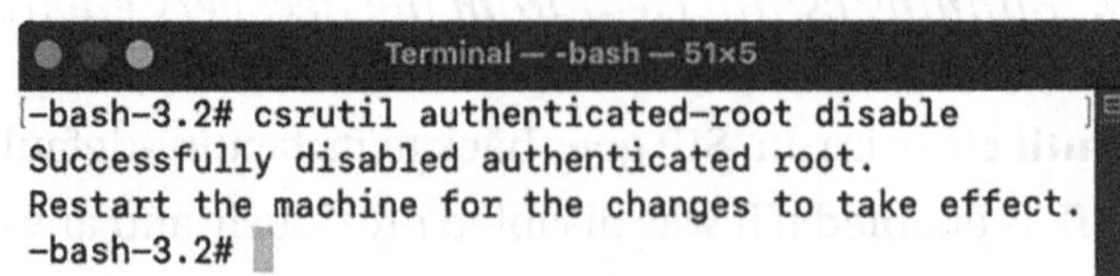

Figure 8-12. *Running csrutil authenticated-root disable from the Recovery environment*

Running csrutil Outside of the Recovery Environment

If you run the **csrutil enable** and **csrutil disable** commands when you aren't booted into the Recovery OS environment, you will receive a message that these commands need to be run from the Recovery OS. The current SIP configuration will remain unchanged, as you can see in Figure 8-13.

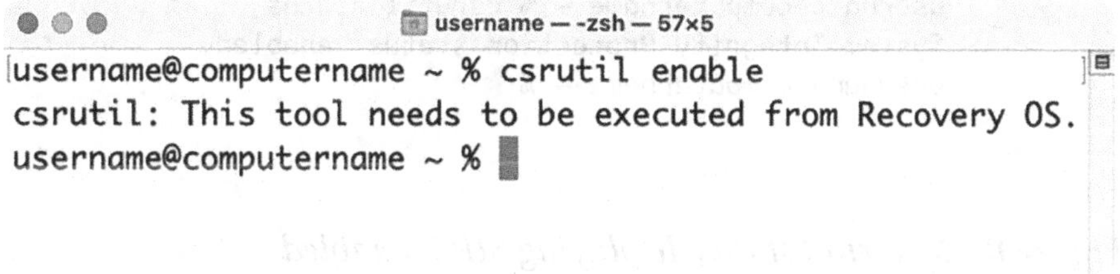

```
username — -zsh — 57×5
username@computername ~ % csrutil enable
csrutil: This tool needs to be executed from Recovery OS.
username@computername ~ %
```

***Figure 8-13.** Running csrutil enable outside the Recovery environment*

Likewise, if you try to run the **csrutil authenticated-root enable** and **csrutil authenticated-root disable** commands while booted from a regular boot drive, you will receive a message that these commands need to be run from the Recovery OS (Figure 8-14).

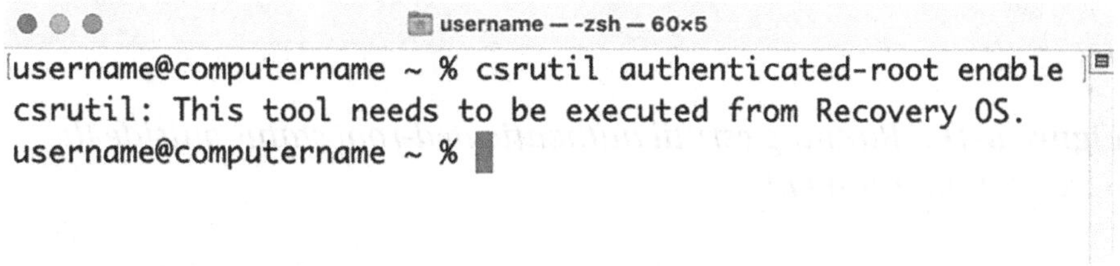

```
username — -zsh — 60×5
username@computername ~ % csrutil authenticated-root enable
csrutil: This tool needs to be executed from Recovery OS.
username@computername ~ %
```

***Figure 8-14.** Running csrutil authenticated-root to enable outside the Recovery environment*

What can be run while outside the Recovery environment are **csrutil**'s reporting functions. For example, to learn if SIP is enabled or disabled, run the following command:

```
csrutil status
```

This command can be run without root privileges and will display if SIP is enabled or disabled, as you'll note in Figure 8-15.

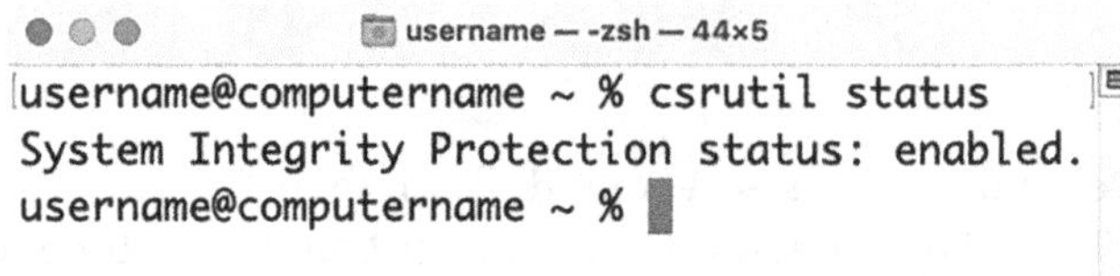

***Figure 8-15.** csrutil status displaying SIP is enabled*

Similarly, **csrutil authenticated-root status** can be run to report on the status of the system volume seal's verification check, as you can see in Figure 8-16.

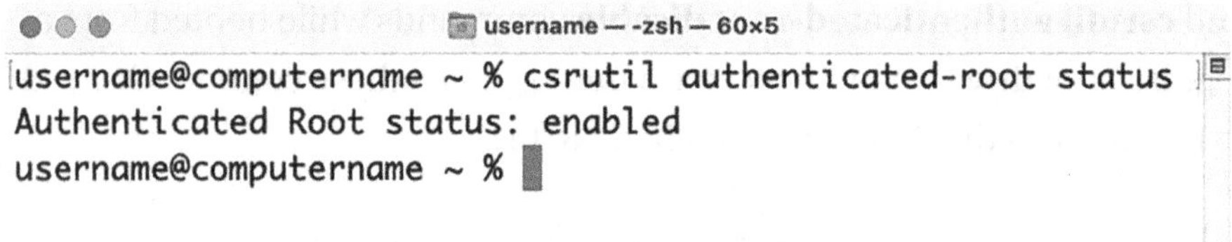

***Figure 8-16.** Running csrutil authenticated-root status outside the Recovery environment*

So you can programmatically derive information about SIP, but you can't augment SIP when booted to the standard operating system. Now that we've covered getting SIP turned on and off, it's worth noting that the enable options have more granular settings, usually invoked with a -- in the command.

Custom System Integrity Protection Configuration Options

It is possible to enable SIP protections and selectively disable aspects of it, by adding one or more flags to the **csrutil enable** command. All the following examples require being booted from Recovery in order to successfully configure.

To enable SIP and allow installation of unsigned kernel extensions, run the `csrutil` command with the enable verb, but then use the `--without` option and use the kext selection for what to disable:

```
csrutil enable --without kext
```

When this option is enabled, running **csrutil status** outside the Recovery environment should produce output similar to this, indicating that Kext Signing is disabled, as you can see in Figure 8-17. This isn't to say that signed kexts can't be run but instead that forcing signed kexts in order to run a kext has been disabled.

```
username — -zsh — 111x14
username@computername ~ % csrutil status
System Integrity Protection status: unknown (Custom Configuration).

Configuration:
        Apple Internal: disabled
        Kext Signing: disabled
        Filesystem Protections: enabled
        Debugging Restrictions: enabled
        DTrace Restrictions: enabled
        NVRAM Protections: enabled
        BaseSystem Verification: enabled

This is an unsupported configuration, likely to break in the future and leave your machine in an unknown state.
username@computername ~ %
```

Figure 8-17. *csrutil status displaying SIP is enabled with kext protections disabled*

If you need to write to those protected directories we reviewed earlier in the chapter (whether you *need* to is very arguable), then you'll need to disable Filesystem Protection. To enable SIP and disable Filesystem Protections, run the enable option for csrutil, with the --without option again, and then indicate fs instead of kext:

```
csrutil enable --without fs
```

When this option is enabled, running **csrutil status** should produce output similar to Figure 8-17 but with the Filesystem Protections set to disabled. You can also disable the debugging restrictions. To keep SIP enabled but disable debugging restrictions, run the same command as before but use debug as your option:

```
csrutil enable --without debug
```

When this option is enabled, running **csrutil status** will show Debugging Restrictions set to disabled. A common task is to disable DTrace restrictions so you can run dtrace commands and scripts. To leave SIP enabled but disable the DTrace enforcement, run the same command but use dtrace as the option to start SIP without, as follows:

```
csrutil enable --without dtrace
```

When this option is enabled, running **csrutil status** should produce a similar output but with the DTrace Restrictions listed as disabled. Many administrators will want to customize NVRAM options (e.g., to bless NetBoot servers). To enable SIP and disable restrictions on writing to NVRAM, run the same command but use the nvram option:

```
csrutil enable --without nvram
```

When this option is enabled, running **csrutil status** should produce output similar to the previous few iterations of the command, but with NVRAM Protections showing as Disabled. To enable SIP and disable basesystem verification, which will allow the use of a modified disk image to install macOS, run the command again but use basesystem as the exclusion:

```
csrutil enable --without basesystem
```

When this option is enabled, running **csrutil status** should produce a similar output but showing BaseSystem Verification set to disabled. These commands allow you to access specific options while still leaving SIP enabled. If you have to access those, try to do so granularly so the deployment still makes use of the added security features from running with SIP enabled on the fleet, and do so only for machines you have to. For example, try to only disable the nvram protections if you have a lab that you'd like to run with the option to boot into a NetBoot environment.

System Integrity Protection and Resetting NVRAM

As mentioned previously, SIP stores its active security configuration in NVRAM. This allows SIP's configuration to persist across OS installs, but this design choice also means that resetting NVRAM will cause SIP's configuration to reset as well. In my testing, a NVRAM reset will result in the following SIP configuration:

- SIP will be enabled with all protections in place.
- No entries will be set in the NetBoot whitelist.

Resetting the NVRAM, otherwise known as a PRAM reset or PRAM zap, has been a standard part of the Mac troubleshooting toolkit for a long time, but the process is different depending on if you're using an Intel Mac or an Apple Silicon Mac.

For Intel Macs, a PRAM reset is performed by pressing and holding down the **Option**, **Command** (⌘), **P**, and **R** keyboard keys at startup (Figure 8-18). You can verify this worked because the startup tone will change.

Figure 8-18. Apple keyboard with PRAM reset keys indicated

For Apple Silicon Macs, you will need to boot to the Recovery environment. When booted from the Recovery environment, run the following command as shown in Figure 8-19.

```
nvram -c
```

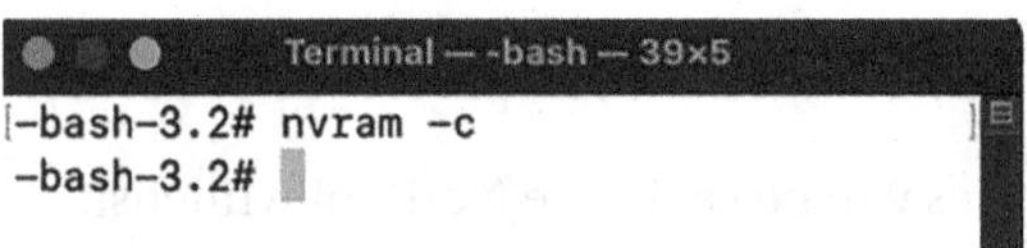

Figure 8-19. Running the nvram -c command from the Recovery environment

For environments that do not plan to change SIP's default configuration, NVRAM resets should not affect normal operations. However, for those environments where custom SIP configurations need to be maintained, be advised how this change affects SIP configuration in your environment.

User-Level Protections

The final type of protection we'll cover is user-level protections. Introduced as a part of the entitlement framework in macOS Mojave, these protections are managed by Apple's expanded security framework, Transparency Consent and Control (TCC). These new protections are primarily focused on protecting data within a user's home folder, but also affect access to the Mac's built-in camera and microphone.

To summarize the protection, applications will now be required to request user approval before they'll be able to access specific application data. If access is not granted, the application will not be able to access that data, and whatever function the application was trying to run may fail. Apple has not documented which files and directories inside an account's home folder are affected by the user data protections, but in our research and testing, these are the affected areas we know of today:

~/Library/Application Support/CallHistoryTransactions

~/Library/Application Support/com.apple.TCC

~/Library/Application Support/AddressBook

~/Library/Application Support/CallHistoryDB

~/Library/IdentityServices

~/Library/Calendars

~/Library/Preferences/com.apple.AddressBook.plist

~/Library/Messages

~/Library/Mail

~/Library/Safari

~/Library/Suggestions

~/Library/Containers/com.apple.Safari

~/Library/PersonalizationPortrait

~/Library/Metadata/CoreSpotlight

~/Library/Cookies

~/Library/Caches/CloudKit/com.apple.Safari

/private/var/db/dslocal/nodes/

In order for applications to be able to access those protected areas, they must be approved either manually or by using a management profile. For more information on using a profile to manage privacy protections, please see Chapter 4. To show an example of an application which would legitimately need access to protected areas would be a backup solution. To manually approve a backup application to access all data stored in an account's home folder, including protected data, the following procedure is used on macOS Mojave:

1. Open System Settings.
2. Select the **Privacy & Security** preferences.
3. Click the **Full Disk Access** settings.
4. Add the application to the **Full Disk Access** section as you can see in Figure 8-20.

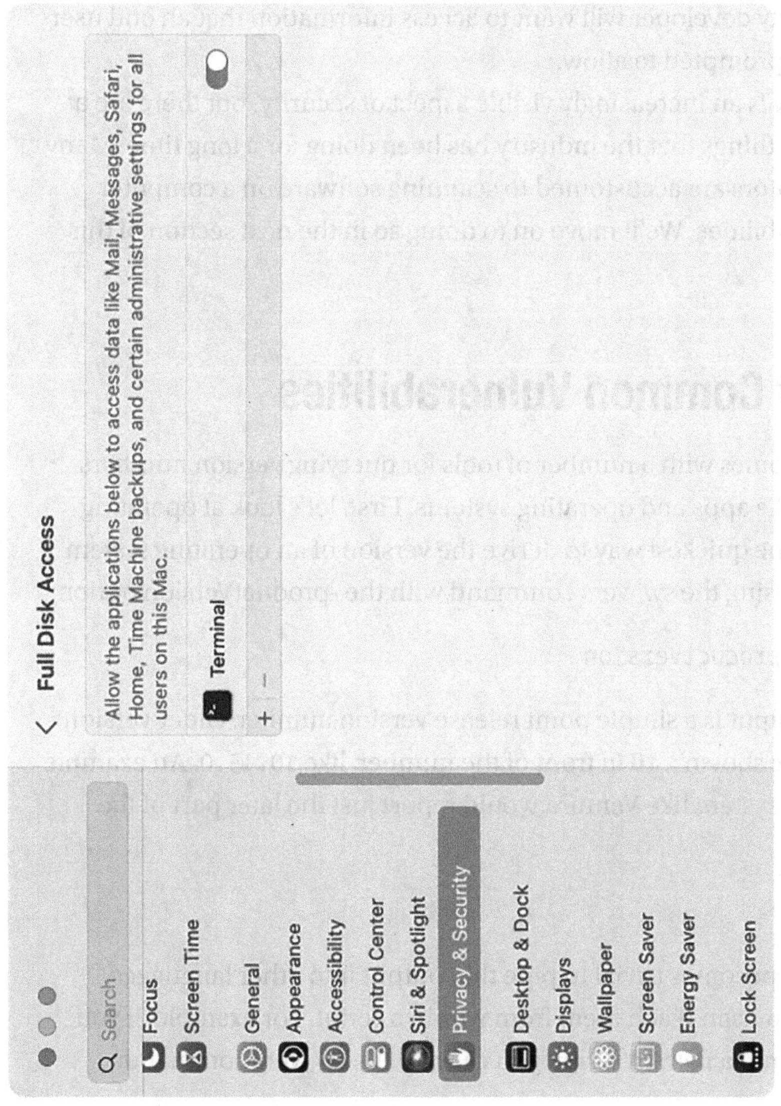

***Figure 8-20.** Allowing Terminal.app to have Full Disk Access*

The Location Services, Contacts, Calendars, Photos, Camera, Microsoft, and other items that are covered by the privacy controls are configured in the same manner and represent the most likely places where a third-party developer will want to access information that an end user should be prompted to allow.

Privacy is an increasingly visible aspect of security, but there are a number of things that the industry has been doing for a long time. Many administrators are accustomed to scanning software on a computer for vulnerabilities. We'll move on to doing so in the next section of this chapter.

Detect Common Vulnerabilities

The Mac comes with a number of tools for querying version numbers of things like apps and operating systems. First, let's look at operating systems. The quickest way to derive the version of an operating system would be using the sw_vers command with the -productVersion option:

```
sw_vers -productVersion
```

The output is a simple point release version number. Older versions would have shown a 10 in front of the number, like `10.15.0`. An example of a newer system like Ventura would report just the later part of the numbers:

```
13.0
```

It then becomes trivial to pipe that output into other languages, provided you can reach them from within a script. For example, if you import os into a python script, you can use the sw_vers command:

```
import os
os.system('sw_vers -productVersion')
```

Or to grab the version of the OS, you could import a function just for that:

```
version = platform.mac_ver()
```

So in the following example, this is in a python script that lists any available Common Vulnerabilities and Exposures, or CVEs, for a given macOS operating system, using cve.circl.lu, a public repository of CVEs copied from `https://cve.mitre.org` and with a REST API put in front of the database:

```
maccvecheck.py
#!/usr/bin/python import sys, urllib, json, platform
if len(sys.argv) > 1: url = 'https://cve.circl.lu/api/search/
apple/mac_os_x:{}'.format(sys.argv[1])
print([j['id'] for j in json.loads(urllib.urlopen(url).read().
decode('utf-8'))])
else:
version = platform.mac_ver() url = 'https://cve.circl.lu/api/
search/apple/mac_os_x:{}'.format(version[0])
print([j['id'] for j in json.loads(urllib.urlopen(url).read().
decode('utf-8'))])
```

Rather than typing all of that should you need this, copy it from `https://github.com/krypted/maccvecheck`.

The operating system isn't all we might want to keep updated, the script can be used to check for other software on the computer as well. You can also read the index of an app using mdls, a command to query the Spotlight index on a Mac. To use the command, we'll use the -name option and the kMDItemVersion attribute, as follows for Zoom:

```
mdls -name kMDItemVersion /Applications/zoom.us.app
```

And then you can look that up in the CVE database as well using a simple call to the same database:

```
curl https://cve.circl.lu/api/search/apple/itunes:12.5
```

Adding a bit more logic, you could then build a similar script that checks all items in /Applications. Ultimately, Apple has a number of products that are tracked in the cve database, and a library of each could easily be built and parsed to produce all cve hits encountered on a Mac. The number of products you would need to scan seems to go down every year. Obviously, you might not want to trust some random site from Luxembourg, and you can do this directly against the zip from Mitre or create your own microservice that responds similarly to this site. For the purposes of this book, we used the public-facing API, so we didn't need to parse the json files distributed by Mitre. Now that we've looked into vulnerability scanning, another common practice (and therefore a checkbox in your security assessment forms) is managing the firewall.

Manage the macOS Firewall

macOS comes with an Application Layer Firewall (we'll call it ALF for short), which is what is configured from the Security System Preference pane. You can enable the firewall simply enough by using the defaults command to augment the /Library/Preferences/com.apple.alf.plist file, setting the globalstate key to an integer of 1:

```
sudo defaults write /Library/Preferences/com.apple.alf
globalstate -int 1
```

You can also configure the firewall from the command line. Stopping and starting ALF is easy enough, whether the global state has been set to zero or one, done using launchd. To stop:

```
launchctl unload /System/Library/LaunchAgents/com.apple.alf.
useragent.plist launchctl unload /System/Library/LaunchDaemons/
com.apple.alf.agent.plist
```

To start:

```
launchctl load /System/Library/LaunchDaemons/com.apple.alf.
agent.plist launchctl load /System/Library/LaunchAgents/com.
apple.alf.useragent.plist
```

These will start and stop the firewall daemon (aptly named firewall) located in the /usr/libexec/ApplicationFirewall directory. As you can imagine, the settings for ALF can be configured from the command line as well. The socketfilterfw command, in this same directory, is the command that actually allows you to manage ALF. ALF works not by the simple Boolean means of allowing or not allowing access to a port but instead by limiting access by specific applications, more along the lines of Mandatory Access Controls. When an application is allowed to open or accept a network socket, it's known as a trusted application – and ALF keeps a list of all of the trusted applications. You can view trusted applications using socketfilterfw with the -l option, although the output can be difficult to read, and so you can constrain it using grep for TRUSTEDAPPS as follows:

```
sudo /usr/libexec/ApplicationFirewall/socketfilterfw -l | grep
TRUSTEDAPPS
```

You can also use the command line to add a trusted application using the -t option for older versions of macOS or –blockapp or –unblockapp followed by a path to the binary of an app. For example, to unblock FileMaker Pro, we'd point to the FileMaker binary:

```
sudo /usr/libexec/ApplicationFirewall/socketfilterfw -blockapp
"/Applications/FileMaker Pro 19/FileMaker Pro.app/Contents/
MacOS/FileMaker Pro"
```

To see a list of apps the firewall has been configured to work with, use the –listapps option. You can also use the socketfilterfw command to sign applications, verify signatures, and enable debugging. Finally, there are a number of global preferences for the firewall that can be configured using the /usr/libexec/ApplicationFirewall/com.apple.alf.plist preferences file. You might be looking at the path to this file and think that it looks odd and it should really be in /Library/Preferences. And you might be right. Some keys in this file that might be of interest include globalstate (0 disables the firewall, 1 configs for specific services, and 2 is for essential services - as in the GUI), stealthenabled, and loggingenabled. All are integers and fairly self-explanatory vs. GUI settings from the System Preference pane.

Firewalls are one layer of security; the next we'll cover is malware.

Combat Malware on macOS

One of the security requirements handed down by many an information security team that has seemed controversial since before macOS even is antivirus. In previous books, we tried to explore what the difference is between a virus, trojan, logic bomb, worm, backdoor, zombie, retrovirus, macrovirus, rootkits, etc. But here, we'll just call it all malware. It's something bad on the computer, and we need to scan for it routinely and correct it when found. Most malware that gets on an Apple device can't actually hurt the device; instead, the device ends up sending infected files to other computers that the malware can actually affect. Or at least that was the perception in previous decades and is mostly still true for iOS.

Mac malware can be dangerous though. When it is, you'll need a way to limit the impact and remediate. There are tons of great options to buy mature antivirus tools on the market. Apple has also provided a number of built-in tools, and for some, those will suffice to satisfy a CISO. We'll start by covering XProtect.

XProtect and Gatekeeper

Gatekeeper is often used as a term to cover a number of different technologies. The first we'll cover is XProtect, a tool built into macOS that is meant to protect the operating system by detecting various viral signatures and reacting to them by blacklisting that signature. Apple doesn't add items to this list often, as there aren't a lot of things that need to be added. If your organization requires the use of an antivirus tool, the first question you should answer is "will XProtect be sufficient?" The answer will often be no, but it's worth understanding what XProtect is and how it works.

The signatures that are installed by default can be found in the /System/Library/CoreServices/CoreTypes.bundle/Contents/Resources/Xprotect.plist property list, which includes a wonderful list of malware items that Apple has automatically decided you should not run on your computer. This allows other developers to extend signatures by adding more items into the XProtect.plist in Security Updates, or Apple may choose to deploy more items in subsequent software updates.

The great thing about XProtect is that it's already running on the Mac and covers a number of different threats to the system by scanning files as they're opened and then identifying those deemed dangerous. This means you're not creating additional load on a computer during traditional antivirus scans, and you're not going to hold up the deployment of new operating systems while testing if something works. XProtect is configured using Gatekeeper, a System Preference used to configure a few basic security options. To view and configure Gatekeeper settings, use the Privacy & Security System Settings pane, scroll down to the Security section, and choose whether your device will only allow App Store apps or whether to allow those from the "App Store and identified developers" as seen in Figure 8-21.

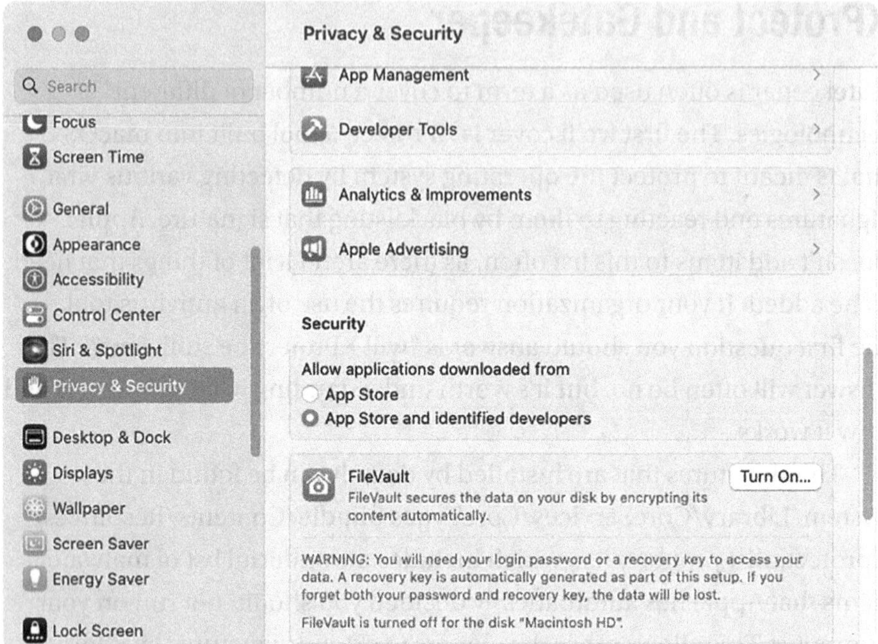

***Figure 8-21.** Gatekeeper settings in System Settings*

Gatekeeper is enabled by default, and configuring Gatekeeper is as easy as selecting one of these options. There's much more that can be done under the hood. The state of Gatekeeper is kept in /var/db/SystemPolicy--prefs.plist. There's only one option there, though: enabled. You can run defaults to manage the status of Gatekeeper with the command line via the spctl binary. To enable:

```
sudo spctl -master-enable
```

Or to use --master-disable to disable Gatekeeper:

```
spctl --master-disable
```

Whether Gatekeeper (assessments) is enabled or disabled can be returned using the --status option:

```
spctl --status
```

The -a option is used to assess an application to see if it will open or not:

```
spctl -a /Applications/GitHub.app
```

If an application passes and has a rule available, then you'll get no response. If there's no rule for the application, you'll get a response that

```
/Applications/GarageBuy.app: unknown error 99999=1869f
```

You don't want users to just start clicking to accept screens, so, when possible, add the rules on behalf of users. To add rules about apps, use the --add option. Each app gets a label, defined with the –label option. For example, to add GitHub:

```
spctl --add --label "GitHub" /Applications/GitHub.app
```

To then enable access to GitHub:

```
spctl --enable --label "GitHub"
```

Or to disable an app:

```
spctl --disable --label "GitHub"
```

As with most things, there's actually a rub: spctl doesn't always work. There have been more than a few issues with getting the labels to apply properly. Sometimes, the -a will report back that an app is rejected and yet the app will still open, so build some sanity checking into any scripts when managing app labels. When you encounter problems with spctl, file a radar with Apple. Gatekeeper is more fully documented at `https://support.apple.com/en-us/HT201940`. To understand some of the underpinnings though, we'll look at lsquarantine in the next section of this chapter.

lsquarantine

Gatekeeper works by scanning files that have been downloaded from the Internet, as we mentioned in the previous section. Deciding what files are allowed to be opened and what aren't, as well as prompting users is handled using lsquarantine, Spotlight works very quickly because it maintains an index of metadata attributes. The lsquarantine tool works similarly. There is a set of attributes attached to any files downloaded from the Internet, and on opening a special screen appears, which can be seen in Figure 8-22.

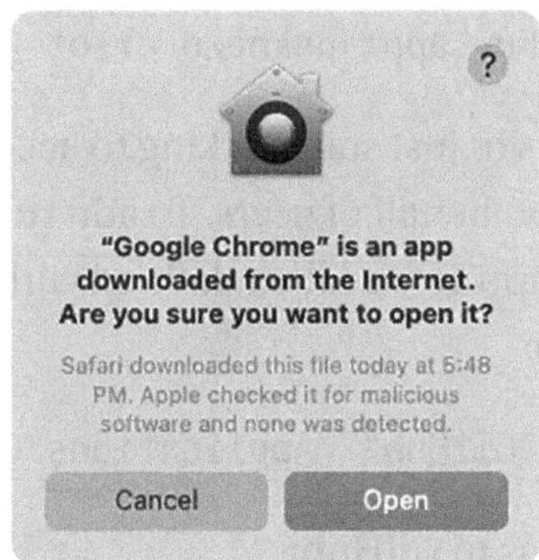

Figure 8-22. *Prompt for quarantined apps*

Any file downloaded from external sources (such as email attachments) attaches quarantine attributes, including Safari, Messages, HipChat, etc. These attributes include date, time, and a record of where the file was downloaded from. When you open a file received through a quarantine-aware application, macOS warns you where the file came from. You receive an alert asking, "Are you sure you want to open it?"

For more on how lsquarantine works under the hood, see `https://developer.apple.com/documentation/foundation/urlresourcevalues/1792021-quarantineproperties`. But let's look at those attributes, given how important they are.

Xattr has a lot of different uses; you can programmatically manage Finder tags with it (Finder tags aren't just used for security, so for more on Finder tags, see `http://krypted.com/mac-os-x/command-line-finder-tags/`). To see the full xattr dump on a given file, use the -l option as follows:

```
xattr -l com.apple.quarantine MyAppImage.dmg
```

The output is as follows:

```
xattr: No such file: com.apple.quarantine MyAppImage.dmg:
com.apple.metadata:kMDItemDownloadedDate: 00000000 62 70 6C
69 73 74 30 30 A1 01 33 41 BE 31 0B A5 |bplist00..3A.1..|
00000010 70 D4 56 08 0A 00 00 00 00 00 00 01 01 00 00 00
|p.V.............| 00000020 00 00 00 00 02 00 00 00 00 00 00
00 00 00 00 |................| 00000030 00 00 00 00 13 |.....|
00000035 MyAppImage.dmg: com.apple.metadata:kMDItemWhereFroms:
00000000 62 70 6C 69 73 74 30 30 A1 01 5F 10 22 63 69 64
|bplist00.._."cid| 00000010 3A 69 6D 61 67 65 30 30 31 2E 70 6E
67 40 30 31 |:myappimage.dmg@01| 00000020 44 32 36 46 46 44 2E
35 37 31 30 37 30 46 30 08 |D26FFD.571070F0.| 00000030 0A 00
00 00 00 00 00 01 01 00 00 00 00 00 00 00 |................|
00000040 02 00 00 00 00 00 00 00 00 00 00 00 00 00 00 00
|................| 00000050 2F |/| 00000051
```

This could be helpful when troubleshooting and/or scripting. If you're an application developer, check out the new API for App Translocation in the 10.12 SDK for <Security/SecTranslocate.h>. I guess one way to think of this is... Apple doesn't want you running software this way anymore. And traditionally they lock things down further, not less, so probably best to find alternatives to running apps out of images, from a strategy standpoint. To remove the com.apple.quarantine bit, use xattr along with the -r option (given that Mac apps are bundles of files we need to do so recursively) and then the -d option for delete, followed by the bit being deleted and then the path to the app, as follows:

```
xattr -r -d com.apple.quarantine /Volumes/MyApp/MyAppImage.app
```

If you have multiple user accounts on your Mac, the user account that downloaded the file is the only user account that can remove the quarantine attribute on a file. All other user accounts can open a quarantined file, but they are still presented with an alert asking, "Are you sure you want to open it?" every time they open the file.

While a lot of focus is put on malware and privacy, the most substantial risk to most computers is a binary running persistently. Most malware will want to run in such a way. A lot of services run on a Mac and most are built by Apple, so can be identified as com.apple.something. We cover kexts, LaunchAgents, and LaunchDaemons in this book. But in the next section, we'll look at manipulating the Launch Services database to find and isolate a foreign persistent service based on it being registered to open a given file type.

Using lsregister to Manipulate the Launch Services Database

The `lsregister` command is used to query and manage the Launch Services database, or the database that is used to determine the default application used to open files of various types. lsregister is part of Core Services and stored in /System/Library/Frameworks/CoreServices.framework/Versions/A/Frameworks/LaunchServices.framework/Versions/A/Support. To see the options available to lsregister, run the command with no operators:

```
/System/Library/Frameworks/CoreServices.framework/Versions/A/
Frameworks/LaunchServices.framework/Versions/A/Support/
lsregister
```

You can dump the database to the screen using the -dump option:

```
/System/Library/Frameworks/CoreServices.framework/Versions/A/
Frameworks/LaunchServices.framework/Versions/A/Support/
lsregister -dump
```

You can then grep the database or redirect the output into a text file for parsing:

```
/System/Library/Frameworks/CoreServices.framework/Versions/A/
Frameworks/LaunchServices.framework/Versions/A/Support/
lsregister -dump > dump.txt
```

The dump of the database is really just meant to parse in other tools if you have security requirements to do so. Sometimes, applications don't open with a given file type. When this happens, you can quickly and easily check if the problem has to do with the launchservices database. To do so, run the open command and define the application (using the -a option) followed by the app and then the file. For example, to open an XML file called krypted.xml in TextWrangler (assuming your working directory contains krypted.xml):

```
open -a TextWrangler.app krypted.xml
```

A full scan of apps can be run to repopulate the database with the --seed option:

```
/System/Library/Frameworks/CoreServices.framework/Versions/A/
Frameworks/LaunchServices.framework/Versions/A/Support/
lsregister -seed
```

You can force an application to reregister file types for that application using the -f option followed by the application path. For example, to reregister Xcode:

```
/System/Library/Frameworks/CoreServices.framework/Versions/A/
Frameworks/LaunchServices.framework/Versions/A/Support/
lsregister -R -f /Applications/TextPlus.app
```

You can also unregister a specific application using the -u option. To unregister Xcode, you would use the -u option:

```
/System/Library/Frameworks/CoreServices.framework/Versions/A/
Frameworks/LaunchServices.framework/Versions/A/Support/
lsregister -u /Applications/Xcode.app
```

One of the most important aspects of lsregister is to look for changes that indicate an app has registered to handle a given file type. An example of a security threat would be an app that registers to open a file type and then each time that file type is run opens and then opens the legitimate app for the file type. This would allow malware to run without being detected.

The launchservices database can get unwieldy. There are applications registered in the local domain, system domain, and each user's domain. These can be cleared with the following command, which also recursively rebuilds based on the output of a -lint option:

```
/System/Library/Frameworks/CoreServices.framework/Versions/A/
Frameworks/LaunchServices.framework/Versions/A/Support/
lsregister -kill -r -domain local -domain system -domain user
```

To check the progress:

```
/System/Library/Frameworks/CoreServices.framework/Versions/A/
Frameworks/LaunchServices.framework/Versions/A/Support/
lsregister -v
```

Changing File Handlers

To set a specific application to open a file type, use the Get Info dialog (Command-I when clicked on the file type). This dialog has a section for "Open with:" as seen in Figure 8-23.

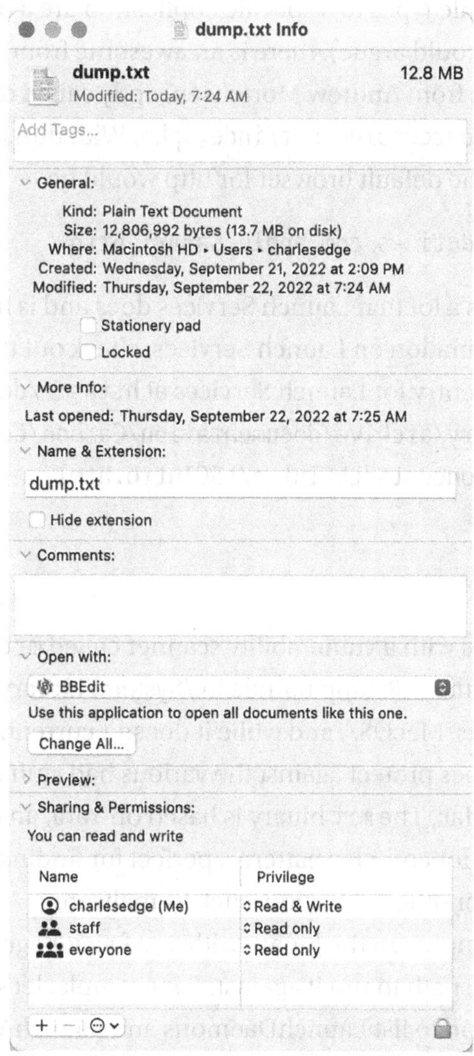

Figure 8-23. *Use Get Info to change how files are handled*

Click the option list for opening the file and then use the Change All button to set the behavior from just that instance of the file type to all instances of the file type. You can also set the default application for a network protocol (e.g., smb://, rdp://, vnc://, http://, and https://). Because the options for lsregister leave one wanting in some ways (the commands to set file types to a specific application are a bit overly complicated one could argue), there is an awesome front-end app for older operating systems from Andrew Mortensen, aptly called duti, available at `http://duti.sourceforge.net/index.php`. With duti installed, the command to set the default browser for http would be

```
/usr/local/bin/duti -s com.apple.safari http
```

Finally, there's a lot that Launch Services does and is involved in. For more information on Launch Services, check out the Apple developer library entry for Launch Services at `https://developer.apple.com/library/archive/documentation/Carbon/Conceptual/LaunchServicesConcepts/LSCIntro/LSCIntro.html`.

MRT

macOS also comes with a vulnerability scanner called `mrt`. The `mrt` binary is installed inside the MRT.app bundle in /System/Library/CoreServices/MRT.app/Contents/MacOS/, and while it doesn't currently have a lot that it can do, it does protect against the various bad stuff that is actually available for the Mac. The `mrt` binary is based on Yara, an open source tool that searches for complex patterns, perfect for finding files that meet a known signature or other condition, such as malware.

To use mrt, simply run the binary with a -a flag for agent and then a -r flag along with the path to run it against. For example, let's say you run a launchctl command to list LaunchDaemons and LaunchAgents running:

```
launchctl list
```

The list is a long listing of every LaunchAgent and LaunchDaemon running. Let's say there's something that starts with com.abc. Be assured that nothing should ever start with that. So it can easily be scanned with the following command:

```
/Library/Apple/System/Library/CoreServices/MRT.app/Contents/
MacOS/MRT -a -r ~/Library/LaunchAgents/com.abc.123.
c1e71c3d22039f57527c52d467e06612af4fdc9A.plist
```

The preceding command works for Big Sur and above, but previous versions might use

```
sudo /System/Library/CoreServices/MRT.app/Contents/
MacOS/mrt -a -r ~/Library/LaunchAgents/com.abc.123.
c1e71c3d22039f57527c52d467e06612af4fdc9A.plist
```

What happens next is that the potentially bad thing to scan will be checked to see if it matches a known hash from MRT or from /private/var/db/SystemPolicyConfiguration/XProtect.bundle/Contents/Resources/XProtect.yara, and the file will be removed if so. A clean output will look like the following:

```
2018.09-24 21:19:32.036 mrt[48924:4256323] Running as agent
2018.09-24 21:19:32.136 mrt[48924:4256323] Agent finished.
2018.09-24 21:19:32.136 mrt[48924:4256323] Finished MRT run
```

Yara rules are documented at `https://yara.readthedocs.io/en/v3.8.0/`. For a brief explanation of the json you see in those yara rules, see `https://yara.readthedocs.io/en/v3.5.0/writingrules.html`. Apple can update the yara rules silently.

A user would have had a username and password for most malware to run properly. XProtect with mrt protects against hundreds of file hashes that include over 100 variants of threats. Those are threats that Apple has effectively publicly acknowledged for the Mac based on their inclusion in Apple-supplied files. Most malware is a numbers game. The attacker needs to get enough people to click on a phishing email (e.g., one that looks very legitimate about their iTunes account), and the attacker can start sending things from their computers to further the cause provided they can make the message seem credible enough to accept.

The mrt binary runs somewhat resource intensive at the moment, and a common troubleshooting step is simply moving the binary out of the MRT.app directory, a heavy-handed way to disable mrt. All of this leads to Gatekeeper, XProtect, and mrt not covering the possible threats a third-party tool might cover. However, there are some tools that wrap mrt into graphical interfaces. One is DetectX from Phil Stokes of SentinelOne (Figure 8-24).

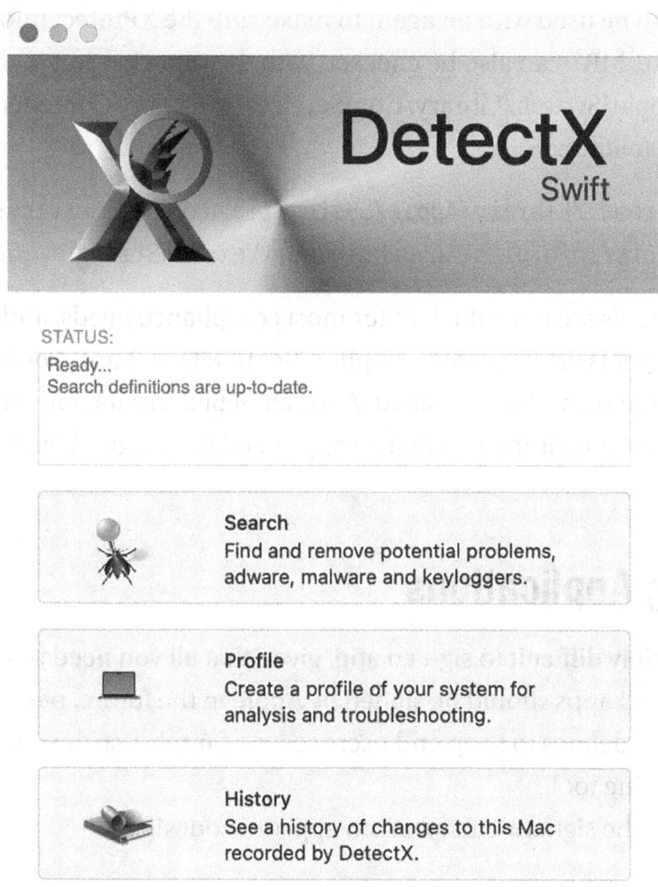
DetectX
Swift
STATUS:
Ready...
Search definitions are up-to-date.
Search
Find and remove potential problems, adware, malware and keyloggers.
Profile
Create a profile of your system for analysis and troubleshooting.
History
See a history of changes to this Mac recorded by DetectX.

Figure 8-24. *DetectX*

The XProtect and bundle information is stored in the CFBundleShortVersionString field in /Library/Apple/System/Library/CoreServices/XProtect.bundle/Contents/Info.plist and can be checked with the defaults command as follows:

```
defaults read /Library/Apple/System/Library/CoreServices/
XProtect.bundle/Contents/Info.plist CFBundleShortVersionString
```

This can be used with an agent to make sure the XProtect information is up to date. MRT can also be checked with the same key but in the /Library/Apple/System/Library/CoreServices/MRT.app/Contents/Info.plist file as follows:

```
defaults read /Library/Apple/System/Library/CoreServices/MRT.
app/Contents/Info.plist CFBundleShortVersionString
```

These tools are not sufficient for most compliance needs, and so third-party tools like Symantec, Sophos, SentinelOne, Jamf Protect, and others are often employed instead. Another default protection on the Mac that we've covered is the fact that all apps need to be signed (and many notarized).

Signing Applications

It's not terribly difficult to sign an app, given that all you need is a signing certificate. All apps should be signed by Apple in the future, per Apple's changing guidelines to keep end users secure. Simply use the codesign command-line tool.

To view the signature used on an app, use codesign:

```
codesign -dv MyAwesome.app
```

The same would be true for a package, which is equally as dangerous when provided with an administrative account:

```
productbuild --distribution mycoolpackage.dist --sign
MYSUPERSECRETIDENTITY mycoolpackage.pkg
```

And some files are distributed in disk images (.dmg files). To sign a dmg:

```
codesign -s MYSUPERSECRETIDENTITY mycooldmg.dmg
```

So codesign is used to manage signatures and sign, but spctl only checks things with valid Developer IDs, and spctl checks items downloaded from the App Store. None of these allow for validating a file that has been brought into the computer otherwise (e.g., through a file share). These help to keep binaries from running on machines as persistent threats that might, for example, subvert a traditional malware defense infrastructure.

ClamAV

ClamAV is an antivirus application that is among the easiest to use. It is available at `www.clamxav.com` in a variety of languages. Although ClamAV lacks many of the features available in some of the commercial packages that are centrally manageable, it is a great and accessible tool that can be used as a first-line-of-defense warning system against malware. The underlying code is actually developed and distributed by the open source community as part of the ClamAV project. The GUI tools that ClamXAV brings to the table can then be distributed to large numbers of users to help administrators discover virus outbreaks and perform quarantine measures on infected files.

ClamXAV is a front end for ClamAV, which provides a nice graphical interface to ClamAV for a nominal cost. Other third-party antivirus solutions include Carbon Black, Cisco AMP, Malwarebytes, Panda Security, Sophos, Symantec, Trend Micro, Webroot, and now even Microsoft. For more, see Appendix A.

There are a number of ways to install ClamAV. For this example, just to get it done quickly, we'll use homebrew which is simply brew with the install verb and clamav as the recipe to be brewed:

```
brew install clamav
```

This places the configuration files in /usr/local/etc/clamav, and these cannot be used as those supplied by default are simply sample configurations. Because the .sample files have a line that indicates they are an "Example," they cannot be used. So we'll copy the sample configuration files for freshclam.conf and clamd.conf (the demonized version) and then remove the Example line using the following two lines:

```
cp /usr/local/etc/clamav/freshclam.conf.sample /usr/local/etc/
clamav/freshclam.conf; sed -ie 's/^Example/#Example/g'/usr/
local/etc/clamav/freshclam.conf
cp /usr/local/etc/clamav/clamd.conf.sample /usr/local/etc/
clamav/clamd.conf; sed -ie 's/^Example/#Example/g'/usr/local/
etc/clamav/clamd.conf
```

Next, we'll need to update the virus definitions for clamav. This can be run without the fully qualified file path, but we are going to go ahead and include it as some computers might have another version installed (e.g., via macOS Server):

```
freshclam -v
```

The initial scan should cover the full hard drive and can be run as clamscan:

```
sudo /usr/local/bin/clamscan -r – bell -i /
```

Your routinely run jobs should be set up to a quarantine location. Because all users should be able to see their data that was quarantined, we would write this to /Users/Shared/Quarantine. We can then use a standard clamscan to scan the system and then "move" quarantined items to that location and log those transactions to /Users/Shared/Quarantine/Quarantine.txt.

```
sudo mkdir /Users/Shared/Quarantine
sudo clamscan -r – scan-pdf=yes -l /Users/Shared/Quarantine/
Quarantine.txt – move=/Users/Shared/Quarantine//
```

You can then use an Extension Attribute to read the Quarantine.txt file (the following is an example of using a Jamf Extension Attribute to do so):

```
#!/bin/bash
#Read Quarantine
result = `cat /Users/Shared/Quarantine/Quarantine.txt`
#Echo Quarantine into EA
echo"<result>$result</result>"
```

The clamdscan binary is multithreaded and hence runs a lot faster than a clamscan call. You can easily daemonize ClamAV by using this repo, which has a plist that automatically runs on-demand clamdscan on a schedule: `https://github.com/essandess/macOS-clamAV`.

Every environment is different. When combined with standard mrt scans using the built-in malware removal tool for macOS, ClamAV can provide a routine added protection to isolate and help you remediate infections. You can easily run this nightly and parse the quarantine.txt file prior to picking it up with the Extension Attribute routinely in order to provide an additional layer of defense against potential threats to the Mac. Putting all of this into a software package would be rudimentary and could benefit many organizations without putting our coworkers through the performance hit that many a commercial antivirus (or more importantly full malware prevention or threat hunting) solution brings with it.

Threat Management on iOS

There are plenty of threats of any kind of device; however, iOS is more secure than most. As with securing a Mac, start with the Apple security guide at `www.apple.com/business/resources/docs/iOS_Security_Overview.pdf` and determine what gaps your organization might have. For the most part, keeping devices running the latest operating system, make sure to have a passcode on devices (or Touch ID or Face ID) and make sure your servers encrypt communication to and from devices. Some organizations will also look to containerization technologies and restricting features of devices. Make sure to go through each restriction available with an information security team and check which correspond to an organization's security posture. This will keep you from starting to think that iOS is immune from any external threats.

YiSpecter was the first iOS malware to infect jailbroken and nonjailbroken phones by abusing private APIs in the iOS system. The malware spread via hijacked traffic from nationwide ISPs within China and Taiwan, an SNS worm on Windows, and an offline app installation and community promotion. YiSpecter contains four components signed with enterprise certificates. Abusing the APIs allows these components to download from a server and install on a targeted iOS device. Three of these components hide their icons, preventing the user from finding and deleting them. After infection occurs, iOS apps can be downloaded, installed, and launched; existing apps can be replaced with other apps; apps can be hijacked to display advertisements; Safari's default search engine can be changed; and device information can be sent to the C2 server. YiSpecter is capable of maintaining persistence on the device and can defeat attempts to delete it. Abusing private APIs allows even iOS users who only download apps from the official App Store to be infected with YiSpecter.

The landscape is very different on iOS than most any other platform – yet another reason macOS continues to move in the direction of iOS. Most security solutions available to mobile devices such as an iOS device try to protect against the following types of attacks:

- **Rogue AP**: A wireless access point that is made to look like a legitimate network in order to perform man-in-the-middle attacks.

- **Man-in-the-middle**: Intercepts insecure communication between a server and a client by pretending to be the intended server.
- **SSL strip**: Replaces encrypted HTTPS version of a web page with an HTTP version so the unencrypted traffic can be captured.
- **Femtocell**: A fake antenna is used to intercept traffic on a cellular network.

All of these are basically about intercepting communication and not attacking an actual device. There have been small attacks that involved brute forcing the device when plugged into a computer, but nothing very successful. Many organizations will not need a tool for their iOS deployments. If you do, start the hunt for a vendor that does real things at Zimperium and Cylance and do a thorough review of what protections each provider offers as compared to those your organizational security posture requires. Things to look for might be a demo of them blocking a real-world example of an exploit.

Additionally, phishing is one of the top threats for the iOS and iPadOS devices. This is where ZTNA and other zero-trust solutions become important for most environments. These are often provided by companies like Palo Alto, the Citrix Zscalar, and Cisco. There are some that are fairly Apple-centric, like Jamf Private Access and Jamf Threat Defense, which was built based on Jamf's acquisition of Wandera. All of these tools require routing data from a device to a server like how proxies and VPNs work. These protect network access but don't typically help with binaries that can run on devices, which is more an issue with the Mac.

macOS Binary Whitelisting

By default, only binaries loaded through the App Store or installed via an ipsw can be opened on an iOS device and Apple TV. The Mac is much more open, even though it has been closing down more and more in the past few years. Of the binaries that can be opened on a Mac, you can limit them using what is known as binary whitelisting or binary blacklisting.

There are a few techniques for managing which binaries can be opened on Apple devices. The original technique to manage binaries, which still mostly works, but is actively being deprecated, was using MCX, or Managed Client Extensions. The easiest way to describe how this worked was with the now defunct Workgroup Manager, seen in Figure 8-25. More modern techniques include

- Gatekeeper, which was covered earlier in this chapter, which can be managed through the command line, through a Privacy & Security configuration profile manually, or via MDM
- Editing the permissions to remove access to an app either manually through the Finder or using a script
- Using a Restrictions profile through MDM or installed manually (only covers certain Apple apps)
- Using a third-party LaunchDaemon or agent that can terminate apps which have been blacklisted
- Blocking the installation of a given application, as is done with Munki (`https://github.com/munki/munki/wiki/Blocking-Applications`)

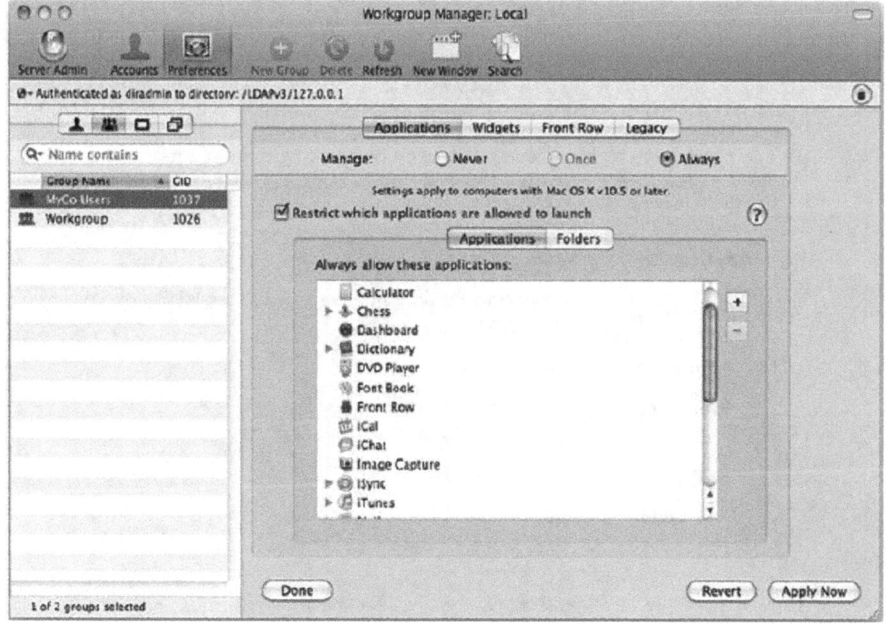

Figure 8-25. *MCX in Workgroup Manager*

As seen in the preceding screen, it's possible to whitelist only the Applications a given user should be able to launch. If this is something you need to do and you want to do so sanely, then consider Google Santa. Available at `https://github.com/google/santa`, Santa is a project that uses a kernel extension to monitor for the execution of a blocked binary and then terminates it.

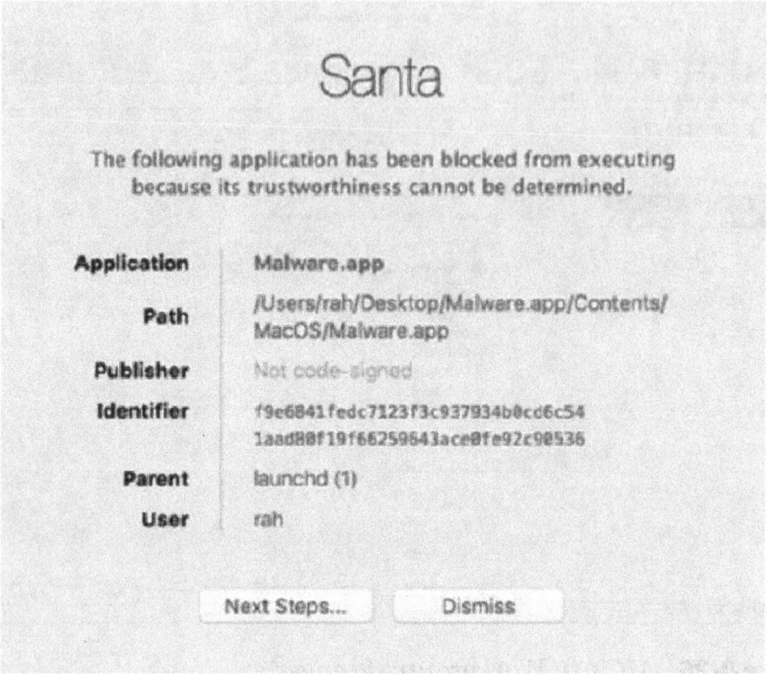

Figure 8-26. *Google Santa*

This is one of those rare places where a kernel extension is necessary to shut down a binary before it could potentially do harm to a system or the network environment a system is in. As can be seen in Figure 8-26, Santa reacts so quickly that a notice can be displayed indicating that access to an application has been blocked.

The reason we said "sanely" is because a large user base is likely to run a lot of software you don't know about. So prior to deploying a tool like Santa, you'll likely define all of the software allowed to be run on your fleet only to end up having to pull back your spiffy new whitelisting solution because users are angry about it. Upvote is another Google tool available at `https://github.com/google/upvote` that allows users to submit apps to be whitelisted, and then when an app has had enough votes, the app is whitelisted. This allows users to self-manage what software is allowed en masse.

Compliance

Sometimes, it seems like every organization has a different interpretation of what compliance is. Not only are there dozens of compliances (from SOC2 to CIS to FedRAMP), but there is an interpretation to each of their components that is left to the attorneys at a given organization. And then as engineers, we often tighten various areas where we feel confident and smile and nod in areas we don't.

There is remedial compliance checking in a number of device management solutions. Workspace ONE and Jamf both have the ability to check devices for compliance. These are configuration management solutions. Additionally, there are a number of third-party solutions dedicated to scanning a device for compliance against known frameworks, such as Qualis or Lynis, which can be found at `https://cisofy.com/lynis/`.

One of the most common guidelines for compliance today is the CIS Benchmarks, put out by the Center for Internet Security and available freely at `www.cisecurity.org/cis-benchmarks/`. An example of scanning to check if a computer meets those guidelines would be using the extension attributes and remediation scripts available at `https://github.com/jamf/CIS-for-macOS-High-Sierra-CP`, which is written to work with Jamf Pro but can be conformed to other tools if need be as was done with the NIST macOS Security Compliance project (`https://github.com/usnistgov/macos_security`). Beyond checking to see if a device is in compliance, a number of organizations also need to review logs to check for unapproved or anomalous security events. In the next section, we'll review the logging API in macOS.

Note Logs are not available in the graphical interface of an iOS device but can be viewed using the Console app on a Mac.

Centralized Log Capture and Analysis

Apple has a number of different logging APIs. For the past few releases, Apple has tried to capture everything possible in logs, creating what many administrators and developers might consider to be a lot of chatter. As such, an entirely new interface needed to be developed to categorize and filter messages sent into system logs.

Writing Logs

The logger command is used to create entries in system logs. However, if you are then using tail to view /var/log/system.log, then you will notice that you no longer see your entry being written. This is because as the logs being created in macOS have gotten more complex, the tools to read and write those logs have gotten more complicated as well. Let's take a simple log entry. In the following example, we'll write the string "Hello Logs" into the system log.

To do so, use the -i option to put the process ID of the logger process and -s to write to the system log, as well as to stderr. To make the entry easier, we'll tag it with -t followed by the string of the tag. And finally, we'll quote the entry we want written into the log. This is basically the simplest form of an entry:

```
logger -is -t krypted "Hello Logs"
```

Once written, use the log command to read new entries. If you are developing scripting tools, you will need to note that all of the legacy APIs you might be using, which include asl_log_message, NSLog, and syslog, have been redirected to the new Unified Logging system, provided you build software for 10.12 (you can still build as before for 10.11, iOS 9, tvOS 10, and watchOS 3 and below). These are replaced with the os_log, os_log_info, os_log_debug, os_log_error, os_log_fault, and os_log_create APIs (which correspond to various levels of logs that are written).

Reading Logs

Logs are now stored in the tracev3 formatted files in /var/db/diagnostics, which is a compressed binary format. As with all binary files, you'll need new tools to read the files. Console has been updated with a new hierarchical capability and the ability to watch activities, subsystems, etc.

The log command provides another means of reading those spiffy new logs. To get started, first check out the man page: (using the man log command). The log command can be used to easily view logs using the "log show" command. In the following example, we'll just run a scan of the last three minutes, using the -last option, and then provide a -predicate. We'll explain those a bit later, but think of it as query parameters - here, we'll specify to look for "Hello Logs" in eventMessage:

```
log show --predicate 'eventMessage contains "Hello Logs"'
--last 3m
```

Filtering the log data using `"eventMessage CONTAINS "Hello Logs""` shows us that our entry appears as follows:

```
Timestamp                           Thread     Type
Activity              PID 2022.08-23 23:51:05.236542-0500
0x4b83bb   Default     0x0                    88294  logger:
Hello Logs ————————————————————————————————————— Log -
Default:          1, Info:                 0, Debug:
0, Error:          0, Fault:           0 Activity - Create:
0, Transition:           0, Actions:          0
```

How do you find out what to use where? Here's an example where I'm going to try to find all invalid login attempts. First, I'm just going to watch the logs. Many will prefer the "log stream" command. I'm actually going to just use show again, because I like the way it looks more. I'm also going to use log with the syslog –style so it's easier to read (for me at least), and then here I'm just looking at everything by specifying a space instead of an actual search term:

```
log show --style syslog --predicate 'eventMessage contains " "'
--info --last 24h
```

Looking at the output, you can see an entry similar to the following:

```
2022.08-23 14:01:43.953929-0500  localhost
authorizationhost[82865]: Failed to authenticate user <admin>
(error: 9).
```

Just search for "Failed to authenticate user," and I'll be able to count invalid login attempts. To then take this and place it into a command that, for example, I could build an extension attribute using, I can then just find each entry in eventMessage that contains the string, as follows:

```
log show --style syslog --predicate 'eventMessage contains
"Failed to authenticate user"' --info --last 1d
```

As with many tools, once you have a couple of basic incantations, they become infinitely simpler to understand. These few commands basically get you back to where you were with tailing logs. If you want to get that –f functionality from tail, to watch the logs live, just swap show with stream. The most basic incantation of this would just be "`log stream`" without bothering to constrain the `output:log stream`. Running this is going to spew so much data into your terminal session. So to narrow down what you're looking for, let's look at events for Twitter: log stream --predicate 'eventMessage contains "Twitter"'. You can also view other logs and archives by calling a filename:

```
log show system_logs.logarchive
```

Now that you can browse logs, in the next section, we'll cover how they're organized and classified starting with Subsystems.

Organization and Classification

The logging format also comes with Subsystems. If you're a developer, you'll be able to file your messages into, for example, a `com.yourname.whatevers` domain space, so you can easily find your log messages. You can also build categories and of course, as we noted previously, tag. So there are about as many ways to find log entries as you can possibly ask for. Apple has a number of subsystems built into macOS. We put together a list of Apple subsystems into a class that you should be able to throw into your python projects at `https://gist.github.com/krypted/495e48a995b2c08d25dc4f67358d1983`.

You also have different logging levels. These include the basic levels of Default, Info, and Debug. You also have two special levels available: Fault and Error. All of this is to add hierarchical logs (which makes tracing events a much more lovely experience) and protect privacy of end users (think sandbox for logs). I'd recommend watching the WWDC session where Unified Logging was introduced at `https://developer.apple.com/videos/play/wwdc2016/721` if interested in learning more about these types of things, especially if you'll be building software that makes use of these new logging features.

The one thing that's worth mentioning for the Mac Techs out there is how you would go about switching between logging levels for each subsystem. This is done with the "log config" command. Here, I'll use the –mode option to set the level to debug and then define the subsystem to do so with the –subsystem option: log config --mode "level:debug" --subsystem com.krypted. If you have a particularly dastardly app, this might just help you troubleshoot a bit. As mentioned earlier, we also have these predicates, which you can think of as metadata in the searching context. These include the following:

- **category**: Category of a log entry.
- **eventMessage**: Searches the activity or message.

- **eventType**: Type of events that created the entry (e.g., logEvent, traceEvent).
- **messageType**: Type or level of a log entry.
- **processImagePath**: Name of the process that logged the event.
- **senderImagePath**: Not all entries are created by processes, so this also includes libraries and executables.
- **subsystem**: The name of the subsystem that logged an event.

Comparisons and Searches

Let's make things just a tad bit more complicated. We'll do this by stringing together search parameters. Here, we have a number of operators available to us, similar to what you see in SQL. These include the following:

- && or AND indicates two matches.
- || or OR indicates one of the patterns matches.
- ! or NOT searches for items that the patterns don't match for, which is useful for filtering out false positives in scripts.
- = indicates that one search matches a pattern or is equal to.
- != indicates that the search is not equal to.
- > is greater than.
- < is less than.
- => means greater than or equal to.

- =< means less than or equal to.
- CONTAINS indicates a string matches a given pattern with case sensitivity.
- CONTAINS[c] indicates a string matches a given pattern without case sensitivity.
- BEGINSWITH indicates a string begins with a given pattern.
- ENDSWITH indicates that a string ends with a given pattern.
- LIKE indicates a pattern is similar to what you're searching for.
- MATCHES indicates that two text strings match.
- ANY, SOME, NONE, IN are used for pattern matching in arrays.
- NULL indicates a NULL response (e.g., you see "with error (NULL)" in logs a lot).

To put these into context, let's use one in an example. Thus far, my most common use case has been a compound search, so in this example we'll be matching both patterns. Here, we'll look at the WirelessProximity subsystem for Bluetooth, and we'll look at how often it's scanning for new devices, keeping both patterns to match inside their own parentheses, with all patterns stored inside single quotes, as follows: log show --style syslog --predicate '(subsystem == "com.apple.bluetooth.WirelessProximity") && (eventMessage CONTAINS[c] "scanning")' --info --last 1h. Developers and systems administrators will find the Apple guide on predicate programming, available at `https://developer.apple.com/library/prerelease/content/documentation/Cocoa/Conceptual/Predicates/AdditionalChapters/Introduction.html`, to be pretty useful if you're doing lots of this kind of work.

Simply run the log command with the show verb. I'm including -last to only look at the last couple of minutes and then using -predicate to define that the processImagePath contains the word Slack, the app I'm searching for:

```
log show --last 120s --predicate 'processImagePath CONTAINS[c]
"Slack"'
```

Note sysdiagnose, a tool long used for capture diagnostics information to include in bug reports, is still functional and now includes Unified Logging information, so Apple developers can get a complete picture of what's going on in systems.

Ultimately, the new Unified Logging is a bit more complicated than the previous options for both creating and reading logs. But once you get used to it, you'll log it – I mean, love it.

The built-in logging facilities in macOS provide logging for a number of tasks, mostly those app developers choose to log events for. But you can get deeper with Apple's implementation of Sun's Basic Security Module, or OpenBSM.

OpenBSM

OpenBSM is a subsystem that has been installed on the Mac for some time. While deprecated as of macOS Big Sur and replaced with the Endpoint Security API for system extensions, OpenBSM provides the ability to create and read audit logs based on the Common Criteria standards. By default, OpenBSM is not enabled, so we'll go through checking what is being audited, enabling, and reviewing those logs.

Audit Logs

OpenBSM stores information about security events in audit logs. The quick and easy way to see what OpenBSM is auditing is to cat the /etc/security/audit_control file, as follows:

```
cat /etc/security/audit_control
```

The output displays the directory of audit logs, as well as what is currently being audited. By default, the configuration is as follows:

```
#
# $P4: //depot/projects/trustedbsd/openbsm/etc/audit_
control#8 $
#
dir:/var/audit
flags:lo,aa
minfree:5
naflags:lo,aa
policy:cnt,argv
filesz:2M
expire-after:10M
superuser-set-sflags-mask:has_authenticated,has_console_access
superuser-clear-sflags-mask:has_authenticated,has_
console_access
member-set-sflags-mask:
member-clear-sflags-mask:has_authenticated
```

You can then see all of the files in your audit log, using a standard ls of those:

```
ls /var/audit
```

As you can see, the files are then stored with a date/timestamp naming convention:

```
2220119012009.crash_recovery 20220407065646.20180407065716
20220407073931.20220407074018
20220119022233.crash_recovery 20220407065716.20180407065747
20220407074018.20220407074050
20220119043338.crash_recovery 20220407065748.20180407065822
20220407074050.20220511030725
20220119134354.crash_recovery
20220407065822.20180407065853
```

The files are binary and so cannot be read properly without the use of a tool to interpret the output. In the next section, we will review how to read the logs.

Using praudit

Binary files aren't easy to read. Using the praudit binary, you can dump audit logs into XML using the -x flag followed by the path of the log. For example, the following command would read a given log in the preceding /var/audit example directory:

```
praudit -x 20180407065748.20180407065822
```

One record of the output would begin as follows:

```
record version="11" event="session start" modifier="0"
time="Sat Aug  7 01:58:22 2022" msec=" + 28 msec" >
<argument arg-num="1" value="0x0" desc="sflags" />
<argument arg-num="2" value="0x0" desc="am_success" />
<argument arg-num="3" value="0x0" desc="am_failure" />
<subject audit-uid="-1" uid="root" gid="wheel" ruid="root"
rgid="wheel" pid="0" sid="100645" tid="0 0.0.0.0" />
<return errval="success" retval="0" />
</record>
```

In the preceding output, find the time that an event was logged, as well as the type of event. This could be parsed for specific events and, as an example, just dump the time and event in a simple json or xml for tracking in another tool, for example, if you're doing statistical analysis for how many times privileges were escalated as a means of detecting a bad actor on a system.

You can also use the auditreduce command to filter records. Once filtered, results are still in binary and must be converted using praudit. You can also stream OpenBSM output over a tool formerly called cmdReporter and now a part of Jamf. A tool like this is helpful to get logging data to what's known commonly as a SIEM, or Security Information and Even Management system, such as Splunk. Of course, the ability to have an event that violates an organization's policies assumes users actually have permissions to perform some of those tasks (although logging failures is common as well). We're not going to go in depth on editing the Authorization Database on a Mac, a journey that begins at /System/Library/Security/authorization.plist. The database is a SQLite database stored at /var/db/auth.db which can easily be viewed using the

```
security authorizationdb read admin
```

The default values change, but for older operating systems, these can be seen at `http://krypted.com/utilities/authorizationdb-defaults-macos-10-14` or historically at `www.dssw.co.uk/reference/authorization-rights/`. For more on scripting changes to the database to provide more granular access, see `https://scriptingosx.com/2018/05/demystifying-root-on-macos-part-4-the-authorization-database/`.

Given that many organizations will not have the time, skills, or inclination for such granular permissions management, tools like Avecto Defendpoint alter the database on behalf of administrators using a least privilege model. This is important as in high-security environments, Mac users can work without needing admin rights yet remain on task and not calling the service desk every time they need to reset a printer queue.

How do you know what privileges they need or what to look for in logs, or what a system is actually doing? This is one of the hardest parts of information security and, once you get started, the most fun: reverse engineering.

Reverse Engineering

The documentation provided by any vendor about their software only goes so far. Apple has some pretty solid documentation, but when it comes to security research, the ability to decompile, disassemble, and trace signals sent by software is important. There are entire books on these topics - and most of the techniques are similar enough between Windows, Linux, and macOS. And therefore, some of the tools are easily used, or ported, between the platforms, especially the open source tools.

As an example of these low-level similarities, most computers use a 64-bit version of x86 architecture, and most mobile devices use a variation of ARMv8. Different implementations of ARM and x86 have their own modes and formats, but in general reverse engineering is done using similar tools (if not the same tools). macOS seems more and more built for software developers with every passing year.

There are a number of these tools that are well documented, including the following:

- Class-dump is a tool used to view Objective-C runtime information stored in Mach-O files. Seeing class declarations and headers provides you with a lot of information about what a file is doing. Class-dump can be found at `http://stevenygard.com/projects/class-dump/` and represents one of the better tools to locate private APIs in macOS.

- **codesign**: Command-line tool built into macOS that outputs extremely granular information about signatures used to sign code and installation packages.
- **dtrace**: Short for dynamic tracing, dtrace (built into macOS) can show anything you can build a program to access using the D programming language. For example, you can get as finely grained as a script that outputs the arguments used calling a function. You can only do this with SIP disabled, but then, you can only do reverse engineering on an iOS device if you've jailbroken the device.
- Hopper Disassembler (Figure 8-27) is a solid tool for translating machine language into assembly. Hopper isn't going to show you the raw code for compiled files, but can help you find files and information that points you in the right direction during research.
- IDA is short for Interactive Disassembler and should be reserved for highly complex research tasks. IDA is available at `www.hex-rays.com/products/ida/`.
- **lldb**: Built-in macOS lldb debugger library interface (if you call one of these tools a debugger or a reverse engineering tool is really determined based on your profession).
- Lulu (`https://objective-see.com/products/lulu.html`) and Little Snitch (`www.obdev.at/products/littlesnitch`) both prompt and provide information about egress and ingress network connections.

- MachOView provides a view into Mach-O files using a GUI but hasn't been updated for some time so suffers from stability issues. To download the latest version, see `https://github.com/gdbinit/MachOView`.
- **nm**: Built-in tool for viewing names and symbols in Mach-O executables.
- **otool**: Command-line tool built into macOS that shows dependencies (based on what frameworks were included in a piece of software which can be seen using the -L option) and allows you to view raw Mach-O executables. To find all apps dependent on a given binary, see `https://github.com/krypted/looto`.
- **Task Explorer**: Free tool to receive really detailed information about processes running on a Mac, `https://objective-see.com/products/taskexplorer.html`.

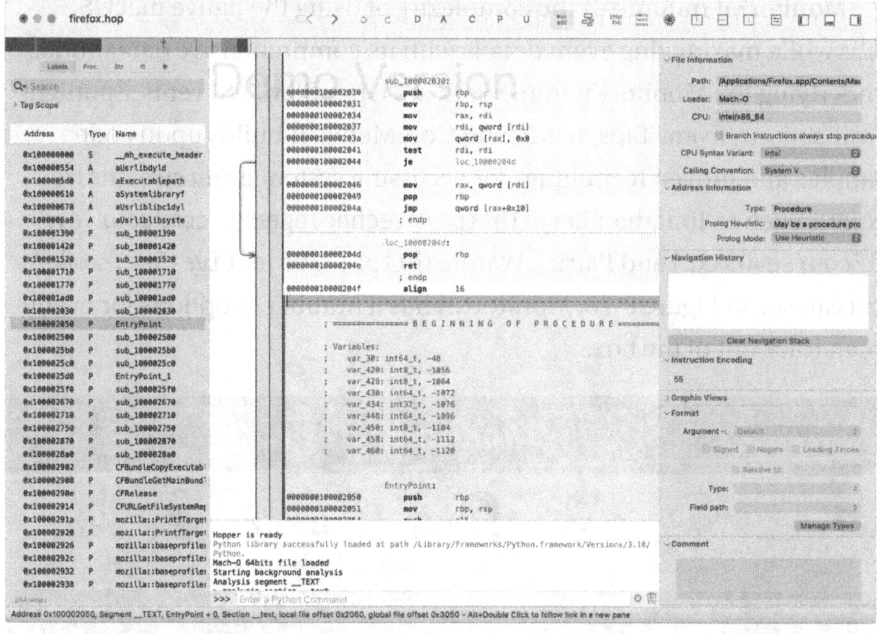

Figure 8-27. Hopper Disassembler

Perhaps we'll write a book about reverse engineering someday because we used so many more tools and products to write this book, but the best way to get started would be to download some of these tools and start playing around or try to answer a specific question, like installing some malware (you can find plenty of samples to play with at `https://objective-see.com/malware.html`) on a virtual machine and start trying to figure out what it's trying to do, by reading source code, taking it apart, and watching signals.

Beyond reverse engineering, there's an emerging discipline for iOS known as threat hunting. This is the act of looking for malware or other threats on the Mac. MonitorKit, from Digita Security (`https://digitasecurity.com`) is an event-driven macOS monitoring framework, written in Swift (compatible with Objective-C), that gives developers easy-to-use access to a wide array of native macOS monitoring capabilities.

MonitorKit minimizes the complexity of using the native macOS APIs while maximizing event details with its comprehensive data model. Underlying the MonitorKit framework are OpenBSM, FSEvents, Spotlight Notifications, Event Taps, IOKit, and CoreMedia. It builds upon code samples and proven techniques for accessing system event streams from experts such as Jonathan Levin (`http://technologeeks.com/course.jl?course=OSXRE`) and Patrick Wardle (`https://Objective-See.com`). As you can see in Figure 8-28, MonitorKit has a number of options for events it can track out of the box.

Figure 8-28. *MonitorKit*

Jamf Protect is Endpoint Detection and Response (EDR) tailor-made for macOS, built on top of MonitorKit, among other tools. Through on-device analysis of macOS system events, Jamf Protect (originally called GamePlan) creates unprecedented telemetry and provides enterprise security teams with the insights they require for behavioral detections and threat hunting. With its streaming insights and KEXT-less design, Protect extends Apple's security and privacy model to an enterprise while upholding the Apple user experience and never delaying an OS upgrade.

There are a number of other tools, many of which are provided by large technology companies that are happy to sell software that works on the Mac, but often don't work as well as we'd like. This isn't to say there isn't merit in them, and there are tools out there evolving at a rapid pace.

And, of course, there are environments that see no need for any security solutions whatsoever, relying entirely on their own automations using built-in frameworks in macOS.

Administrator Rights on macOS

An important topic from both an operational and security standpoint is how to manage administrator rights for the user accounts used on the fleet. Before delving into that, first some backstory on how administrator rights came to exist on macOS.

Apple currently has five platforms available:

- iOS
- iPadOS
- macOS
- tvOS
- watchOS

Most of these Apple platforms do not have the concept of multiple users. There's just one user state in play by default. iOS and iPadOS do include authentication, but there is still usually only one user context which is in scope.

iPadOS does have the concept of multiple user accounts via supporting user sessions for multiple Managed Apple IDs, but that's a special configuration option for when sharing an iPad between multiple people is necessary. All of the Managed Apple ID user accounts are equal in terms of what they can do on the iPad, so the idea of standard user vs. admin user doesn't come into play. Instead, the user paradigm is equal user rights with separation of documents and data for each user.

It's only on macOS that the paradigm of multiple user accounts and those accounts having different permissions for access and actions exists. The Macs haven't always had it though. If you look at the various versions of the original Mac OS between System One's introduction and Mac OS 9, you see a similar user paradigm to what you see on Apple's other platforms. By default, there was only one user context, and the operating system would boot into it automatically.

So if the paradigm we use today didn't come from the original Mac OS, where did it come from?

It comes from NeXT Computers and more specifically the Unix-based NeXTSTEP operating system developed by NeXT. When Apple bought NeXT in 1996, it began using NeXTSTEP's foundations to build what would eventually become Mac OS X. This included building a Unix-based operating system, which included multiple user accounts. More importantly for this topic, NeXTSTEP included the paradigm of an account named root which is a superuser account. On NeXTSTEP, root can do anything. It has read/write access to the entire local filesystem and can run any command.

Apple had previously built Unix-based operating systems with superuser accounts for specialized purposes, but with this change, Apple began mainstreaming the paradigm for its main operating system of both multiple user accounts and a superuser account which has more access and privileges than other user accounts.

However, there's only one root user in Unix and only one password to that account. Sharing passwords is a security issue. Apple's solution was to introduce a new set of superuser privileges for Mac OS X, which they designated an admin account. These privileges could then be applied to multiple accounts.

Management of which accounts have admin rights is handled by membership in a local group on the Mac named **admin**, shown in Figure 8-29. However, membership in this group only handles admin rights for the Mac OS X graphical user interface.

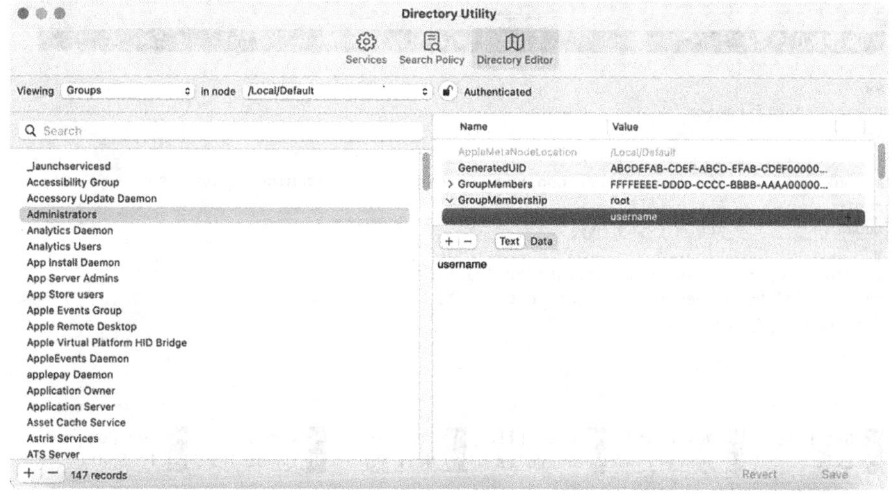

***Figure 8-29.** Accessing the admin group in Directory Utility.app*

To provide administrative rights on the command line, Apple uses the **sudo** command-line tool. This tool enables authorized user accounts to run commands as root or another user. As part of the OS installation process, Apple installs a configuration file for **sudo** that grants members of the admin group all the privileges that the **sudo** tool can grant. In turn, this means that members of the admin group have the same ability as the root account to run all commands and functions with the root account's privileges (Figure 8-30).

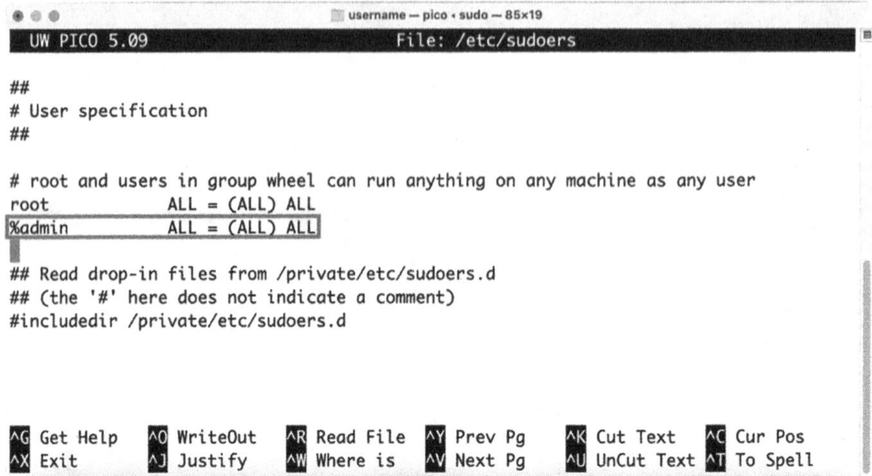

***Figure 8-30.** Default sudo configuration for macOS with admin group's permissions highlighted*

With regard to the actual root user, Apple put some controls in place to limit the root user account's abilities and permissions. These controls include disabling the root account by default, discouraging its use, and providing ways to access elevated or root privileges using other means.

This paradigm of multiple user accounts, a superuser account whose use is discouraged, special accounts (referred to as administrator accounts) which have more access and privileges than other user accounts, and nonspecial accounts (referred to as standard accounts) has been used in all versions of the Mac operating system from Mac OS X 10.0 Cheetah through to today's version of macOS.

Administrator and standard accounts have different access and privileges, as described as follows:

Administrator Account	Standard Account
Install software	Install software*
Change their own account's settings and system settings	Change their own account's settings
Add or manage user accounts	

** Standard accounts can install software into areas of the filesystem where the standard account has read and write permissions, like the standard account's home folder. It is also possible for standard accounts to install software in situations where Apple makes it possible, like installing software from the App Store on macOS or running software updates using Software Update in System Settings.*

Note Why does it matter if an account has admin rights or not? Because anything the root account on macOS can do, an account with administrator rights can do.

Giving admin rights to a user account on the current version of macOS means they now have all the powers that the root account has. That said, as discussed earlier in this chapter, the power of the root account is constrained by the following security measures built into macOS:

- Signed system volume
- System Integrity Protection
- User-level privacy protections

With these protections in place to contain the power of the root account, where large sections of the filesystem can't be written to or altered and user data requires permission to access, let's reexamine the statement about root as it relates to administrator rights. It remains true that anything root can do, an account with admin rights can do, but what root can do on macOS is significantly contained compared to other Unix-based OSs. With the lowered capability also comes lowered risk.

Now that we've examined how admin rights work and their capabilities, let's look at managing them. As discussed earlier, Apple has enabled an account to have admin rights in two locations:

- **Admin rights in the graphical user interface**: Adding the user account to the **admin** group
- **Admin rights for the command line**: Apple installing a configuration file for the **sudo** tool which grants all available privileges to the admin group

With these rights being managed in two locations, this leaves open the possibility that admin rights in the macOS graphical user interface and the command line can be managed separately. If desired, you could assign admin rights in the GUI but not to the command line or vice versa by editing the sudo configuration file to change it from Apple's default settings.

Note sudo configuration options are available via the sudo documentation: `www.sudo.ws/docs/man/1.8.17/sudoers.man/`.

Assuming that you choose to manage admin rights, there's three states of management to consider for your accounts:

- Permanent admin rights
- No admin rights
- Admin rights allowed on a nonpermanent basis

Permanent admin rights can be granted to an account by adding the account in question to the **admin** group and not removing it. With Apple's default configuration for **sudo**, this should grant the account administrator rights for both the graphical user interface and the command line.

Not granting administrator rights to an account means making sure that the account is not a member of the **admin** group. Assuming Apple's default configuration for **sudo**, keeping the account out of the **admin** group should ensure it only has the rights granted to a standard user account.

Granting administrator rights on a nonpermanent basis to an account usually means that there is a mechanism in place to enable the account to be added and removed from the **admin** group as needed.

Is there a one best way for deciding how to manage admin rights? Unfortunately, not. There are a number of factors which affect this decision, which may include legal requirements, complying with the requirements of an external standard that your business has committed to complying with, internally created policy requirements of your company, school, or institution, or operational requirements in your environment.

No matter what other factors exist, the key question which must be answered is going to be if you can trust your users with admin rights while also remaining in compliance with your other requirements. If you can, then (in this author's opinion) they should have them. If you can't, then they shouldn't.

If you make the choice to grant admin rights on a nonpermanent basis, as mentioned earlier, you will likely need a mechanism in place which can enable accounts to be added and removed from the **admin** group as needed. A tool for enabling this is the Privileges app (Figure 8-31), an application developed and open sourced by SAP, which allows a user account which is logged in to macOS's graphical user interface to grant and remove administrator rights.

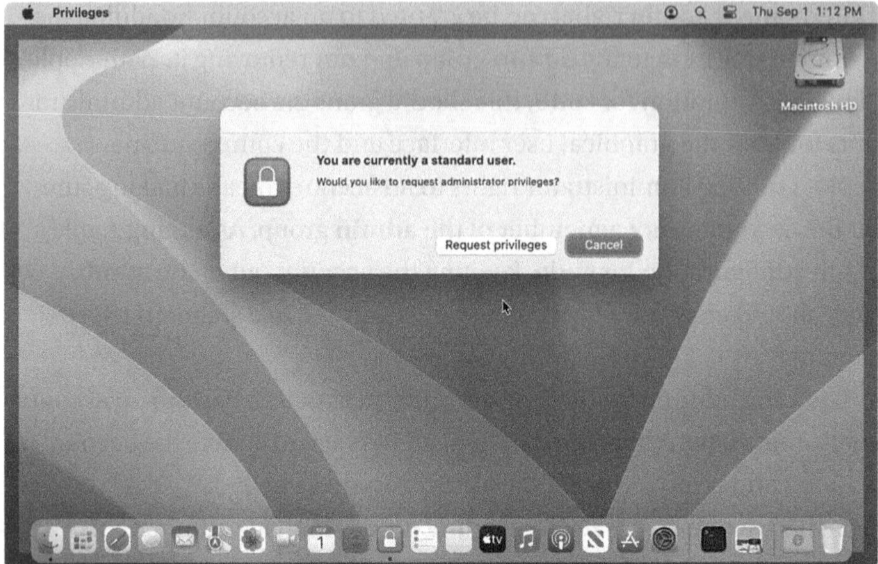

Figure 8-31. *Privileges app granting administrator rights to an account*

Note The Privileges app and configuration documentation are both available on GitHub: `https://github.com/SAP/macOS-enterprise-privileges`.

Summary

The Mac is still very much treated as a computer by most corporate IT departments. Therefore, they will expect the same full complement of tools to be used on the Mac so it is an equal citizen to Windows. You may disagree that you need a tool to perform various tasks, but that doesn't mean that you always have the option to choose whether to run these tools or not. iOS is very different. You can't run an agent on iOS. But you can check that the device meets certain criteria and look for threats on the device.

You have to implement these tools, settings, or procedures so the device is compliant with the policies required to be able to get on the network of most organizations. Doing so may require two to three agents. But the alternative is likely that you can't let devices access the network.

Ultimately, the Mac team at most organizations will start off by integrating solutions the larger Windows population of devices already leverage. For example, if you're using Symantec products for other platforms, you probably already have licensing and so will just use those same tools to secure the Mac. However, as your deployment matures and grows, you will end up with the political capital to go to your CISO and argue for the tools that work best for the platform (see Appendix A) or to explain why those tools are irrelevant for the platform your team manages.

Some of the more talented administrators might read this chapter and be surprised that something wasn't covered. We included the links to Apple's security documents and didn't want to duplicate any of the content covered there. Some aspects of securing devices simply couldn't be covered as they're moving targets, though. Security might be the fastest changing landscape in technology.

Now that you're starting to get a number of different tools running on devices throughout your enterprise, let's shift our attention toward testing, so you can make sure everything works when Apple accelerates the rate of change in their systems even faster in the years to come.

CHAPTER 9

A Culture of Automation and Continuous Testing

Apple is on an annual release cycle for operating systems. Apple now has a new point release in beta at all times. There's also a new version of Firefox released every 18 minutes (or what seems like 18 minutes). This means that the next thing is always around the corner. To compound problems, rather than push updates to computers and iOS devices, updates are now automatic, which means new ways to validate when updates were run can be required. With a major OS release and three or more point releases per year, it's time to get a solid plan for how to always be testing together, if you haven't already.

This chapter can be a career path as much as it can be a guide. Once you get comfortable with the command-line parts of this chapter, there's the automation. Once you've gotten comfortable with the automation, there's the more specific DevOps types of automations. Once you're comfortable with that, you can work at most any startup on those same solutions. This process can take thousands of hours with all the various ways software and operating systems are used.

C. Edge and R. Trouton, *Apple Device Management*,
https://doi.org/10.1007/978-1-4842-9156-6_9

Malcolm Gladwell claimed it takes 10,000 hours with a topic to master it, in his book *Outliers*. Once there, administrators can make a deliberate decision about the future of a given career, given that your skillset will be equally if not more valuable to software development companies who always need more help in that confluence between development and IT operations (or if you mash it up, DevOps).

From Manual to Automated Testing

The scripting options available on the Mac allow access to be able to do almost anything you want on a device. Those have been reduced here and there in recent years with the advent of the sandbox or technology that blocks automations and other apps from doing things those processes aren't entitled to do. But scripting and automating events on the Mac and on the management tools you use to orchestrate events on Mac and iOS is still a critical skillset and one that has the potential to save your organization massive amounts of labor as deployments grow.

There's a maturity scale that usually works in testing. The first phase is manual testing. You build a list of what you want to test and then add things that failed as you go. This allows organizations to run through those tests with each update and try to catch errors before they appear on client computers. Administrators can hold updates back where possible in order to prevent frustrations with the people that use systems (and so reduce calls to a help desk).

The second phase is often to start automating those tests. Here, you pull a tool or set of tools into the workflow and either look for a setting (e.g., a defaults domain) or a state that a system should be in. We typically refer to this as automated testing, and while there are a lot of tools out there to help with automated testing, not all work on the Mac, or those that do aren't as mature as similar tools for other platforms.

The third phase usually coincides with bringing on teams to build apps that help organizations close gaps in workflows. Here, we move from the automated testing of the state of a device to the automated testing of how an app performs. This is a very mature industry with lots of competing products and processes.

This chapter takes us through those phases and then provides a little information on how to streamline the build operations using common tools so people across your organization can have visibility into what stage each update is in. Not that people look at that information usually, but it's good to provide transparency where possible. As a side effect, you get automation into task or service management systems for free when doing so!

Scripting and the Command Line

One of the greatest strengths of macOS is the abundance of scripting languages supported out of the box. Many of these languages are interpreted by a host program rather than run directly as lower-level machine code, and thus they are text files with human-readable syntax. Because such languages are translated into machine code at runtime, interpreted programs are sometimes much slower than their compiled equivalents. However, because you can edit these programs and then run them immediately, they are common tools used by system administrators to automate tasks.

Some interpreters are specifically made to run code such as Python, Perl, or Ruby, while others are more interactive and meant for day-to-day use, facilitating most of the command-line administration tasks covered in this book. Typically, this interactive interpreter component is referred to as a *shell*. The primary purpose of a shell is to translate commands typed at a terminal into some kind of system action or to send a command. In other words, the shell is a program through which other programs are invoked.

There are several different UNIX shells, including the C shell (`csh`), the Bourne shell (`sh`), and their more modern equivalents, `tcsh` and `Bash`. In the most recent versions of OS X, new users are assigned the Bash shell as the default shell. In early versions of Mac OS X, the default user shell was `tcsh`, perhaps due to the presence of Wilfredo Sanchez on Apple's team. He served as the former lead engineer for macOS but was also a developer of the `tcsh` shell. However, Bash has proliferated through the various Linux distributions and has become one of the most prominent shell programs in use today. Perhaps recognizing this, Apple switched the default shell to Bash in Mac OS X 10.3 Panther, and it remains as such today in OS X 10.14 Mojave. Given new security options, the default shell will move to zsh in macOS 10.15.

While the choice of a shell and its resultant scripting language can be difficult, we recommend you learn at least the basics of the Z shell (zsh) before moving onto any other shell and language that may be better suited to your higher-level tasks. This is because, unlike with languages such as Python or Perl that are more strictly used for scripting, you will typically use the Bash shell every time you open a terminal to run any command. The more comfortable you become with Bash/zsh scripting, the more you may find yourself writing one-line scripts that allow you to automate even basic operations.

In this chapter, we present some basic building blocks required to build complex automations. In the process, we attempt to show some real-world syntax examples of scripting in action. Hopefully by the end of this chapter, you'll be armed with enough knowledge to tackle the problems you face in your environment (or at a minimum read open source projects found on GitHub).

We'd like to make a strong point at the outset: while you do not have to use the command line to be a good system administrator, most good system administrators do. This is because a simple operation, such as creating a series of folders, can be done using basic scripts, and in using these scripts, you will find your administration becomes not only more efficient but also (and importantly in large environments) more consistent.

This chapter is not intended to provide in-depth coverage of all shells; that could be a book unto itself. This chapter will introduce you to scripting with zsh and bash and then supply some information on Perl for those who begin to outgrow the standard command-line environment. We will walk through the basic constructs and control statements, providing a decent foundation for you to build on. Due to its default support in the latter iterations of macOS, we will focus primarily on the zsh shell syntax.

Command-Line Basics

Every shell has some built-in functions that it performs directly, but most commands entered cause the shell to execute programs that are external to the shell. This sets the shell apart from other command interpreters, as its primary mechanism for invoking functionality is largely dependent upon other programs. That's not to say that shells don't have built-in capabilities. They do; they can read, create, and append files and manipulate data through globbing and variable mangling, and they can utilize looping constructs. However, the ability to parse and extend that data will often require external calls. This chapter seeks to arm you with the ability to fully utilize the Bash shell's internal functions, as well as introduce pertinent external functions that will help you to fully employ the power of the command line.

The first step toward learning the shell is firing it up and getting your feet wet, preferably on a nonproduction box. In macOS, this is done simply by opening up the Terminal application on your system. When the application opens, provided your user account has the default shell assigned, you will be presented with a zsh prompt, something like

```
krypted@CE-MacBook-Pro ~$
```

The default prompt consists of the following template:

```
username@devicename directory $
```

In this example, the current directory is ~. The tilde represents a user's home directory. Thus, for any respective user, ~ expands to `/Users/username`. The tilde can be used when specifying paths for commands. You can always reference your own home directory via ~, and you can even reference other users' home directories as well:

```
krypted@CE-MacBook-Pro ~$ cd ~/emerald
krypted@CE-MacBook-Pro ~$ pwd
/Users/emerald
```

In this text, we are issuing the `cd` command to change directories and passing `~emerald` as an argument. We can see at the shell prompt that our new directory is `emerald`. We then issue the `pwd` command, which outputs our current path. In this case, it's Emerald's home directory at /Users/emerald.

Note Pathnames can be passed to commands in two different forms. An absolute path contains every folder and element relative to the root (/) of the drive. A relative path contains items relative to the current directory. For instance, if we run the command `cd /Users`, we have provided cd with an absolute path to the Users directory. Next, we run the command `ls emerald`, providing a path `emerald`, relative to our current directory, `/Users`. Alternatively, we can run the command using an absolute path `ls /Users/emerald` and net the same results regardless of the current directory.

Basic Shell Commands

You'll want to become familiar with the basic commands that are normally used for administration. Here's a very small list of some of the most common ones used for basic Mac administration:

- `cd`: Change directory. This command takes a single argument - a path to a directory. You can use `cd ..` to change to the parent directory.
- `pwd`: Lists the current directory. `Pwd` accepts no arguments.
- `ls`: Lists the contents of the current directory. `ls` has numerous options. A common set of arguments `-hal` will show all items in list form (by default, any file beginning with a period is invisible) with human-readable file sizes. Optionally, a directory or file can be provided, and ls will output either the file's information or a directory list. For instance, `ls -hal /Users` will output a detailed list of files and folders present in the directory `/Users`.
- `cat`: Displays the contents of a file or concatenates files.
- `more`: Displays the contents of a file page by page and allows you to scroll down to see the rest. Useful with large files when `cat` shows too much information to see on the screen.
- `less`: Similar to the **more** command but displays the contents of a file page by page and allows you to scroll up to see the rest.

- `tail`: Views the end of a file. Very useful when used with the -f option, as you can watch the end of a log file and view on the screen new lines as they're written to the file.
- `rm`: Deletes a file or directory. `rm` offers several options. It can be passed a file or directory for deletion. If a directory is passed, the `-r` flag must be used to recursively delete all contents. For instance, the command `rm -r /Users` would delete the entire /Users folder (probably best to avoid that one).
- `pico`: A very basic text editor for editing files from the command line. `pico (nano)` uses `emacs`-style keyboard shortcuts, supports arrow keys for navigation, and is pretty basic. It accepts a path to a file as an argument. When you're finished editing, type Ctrl+o to save and Ctrl+x to exit the document. (Another common text editor is `vi`, but that utility, though rewarding, is much more difficult to learn.)
- `sudo`: Executes a command with root privileges. By default, this command can only be run by administrators. It has numerous options, but in its most basic form, it can simply be prefixed to any command to execute that command with root privileges.
- `defaults`: Shows or changes the behavior of a preference on a Mac.
- `history`: Shows the last commands completed from a command line. The `history` command requires no other parameters or options.

- `whatis`: Searches the `whatis` database, handy for determining the appropriate command to run. For instance, by using the command `whatis "change owner"`, you can determine that the `chown` command may be what you're looking for. You can then use the `man` command, discussed next, to determine the capabilities of the `chown` command.
- `which`: Shows the location of a command.
- `man`: Used to access manual pages for the hundreds of command-line programs that come with your computer, so it may well be the most important command to know. For instance, you can type `man hier` to see information on OS X's directory structure, while `man chown` brings up the manual page for the `chown` command, giving you the syntax and functionality of that command. `man` even has its own manual. Explore how to use it: `man man`.
- `find`: Lets you search for a file or directory by name. `Find` is a fairly complex command and has a lot of utility. In its most basic form, it can be used for a simple directory search. For example, if you were trying to hunt down .DS_Store files on a network share mounted at /Volumes/MyCoolNetworkFolder, you could run the command `find /Volumes/MyCoolNetworkFolder -name ".DS_Store"`. Pretty nifty. Even better, `find` lets you take the output and act on it. Say you want to delete all .DS_Store files. To do this, run the command: `find /Volumes/MyCoolNetworkFolder -name ".DS_Store" -delete`.

- `echo`: Used to output text to the stdout data stream (discussed later in the section "Standard Streams and Pipelines"). When writing scripts, the `echo` command is a great way to ensure that your script gives proper feedback to the user.
- `grep`: Used in combination with piping to filter a command's output (piping is discussed later in the section "Standard Streams and Pipelines"). For instance, the command `ls /Users | grep -i admin` would filter the output of `ls /Users`, outputting only user home folders that match the admin criteria, using a substring match so that user home "admin" would match, as would "mycoadmin." The `-i` flag means that `grep` will ignore capitalization. In another form, `grep` can be used to search files for strings. The command `sudo grep -r http://www2.krypted.com /etc/apache2` would search the directory `/etc/apache2` and output the filenames containing the string `http://www2.krypted.com`. The `-r` flag tells `grep` to recursively search through a directory. You can omit the `-r` flag and search across a single file if necessary. You can prefix the `sudo` command to ensure that the `grep` search has access to all necessary files.
- `ps`: Lists running processes. This command has numerous arguments. One common iteration is `ps auxww`. The flags `auxww` result in the output of all running processes across all users on the system. You can use piping to filter this list: the command `ps auxww | grep httpd` will determine if the Apache daemon (`httpd`) is running. If `httpd` is found, the command will display the running process ID (the PID column), as well as CPU and memory utilization.

- `chmod`, `chown`: Can be used respectively to change permissions and ownership on a file or group of files. Both commands utilize the `-R` flag to recurse across all children of a directory. In the following example, `chown` changes the owner of the folder `/Users/cedge` to cedge and changes the group to `admin`. We then utilize `chmod` to ensure that the owner (`o`) has both read and write (`rw`) access:

```
chown -R cedge:admin /Users/cedge
chmod -R o+rw /Users/cedge
```

- `kill`: Terminate a running process. This command has a few optional arguments, but in its most basic form, it is simply given the process ID of a running process to terminate. A process's ID can be determined through the `ps` output, as discussed earlier. The `kill` command must be run with root privileges via `sudo` in order to terminate a process running as root. Other common flags include `-HUP`, which can be used to restart a process. Alternatively, the infamous `-9` argument, equivalent to `-KILL`, can be used to forcibly terminate a process without prejudice regardless of state or any pending activity.

- `curl`: Communicates with a web server to download assets. This command can be used to download files from a web server but also has flags for placing information into a header, usually necessary for interacting with a REST interface to an API.

These are merely a small selection of the most useful commands for many to navigate and manipulate objects in a shell. If you know a few commands that, when executed, will complete a larger overall task, you can then combine them to make a program, which we call a script. This is how most people start to learn shell scripting.

Note The command-line interpreter (e.g., the bash shell or zsh shell) has the ability to search back through your history file. Press Ctrl+r to do a "reverse" search through the history file by typing some or all of the original command or its arguments. Continue to press Ctrl+r to cycle through previous incarnations.

To switch between shells, you need only type the name of the shell you desire to use. For example, to switch to the sh shell:

```
sh
```

As you alternate between shells, you'll notice that the appearance of the screen and the area where you input text appears slightly different.

Shell Scripting

The makings of a typical script begin with a line describing the shell, often called a shebang line. This appears as follows:

```
#!/bin/zsh
```

Next come variable declarations `"declare FOO=BAR"` and optionally command variable declarations. This is all we need to create a static script. We will cover these terms more in depth in the following section, as well as explore the logical constructs that make a script such a powerful wrapper for the command-line tools OS X provides. To put these into a single script, we would simply create a file with those lines and then a third to echo the results:

```
#!/bin/zsh
"declare FOO=BAR"
echo $FOO
```

The preceding example creates a variable called FOO and then populates it with the string BAR and echos out (or writes to the screen) the result (BAR).

The Bash shell is based on the Bourne shell (`sh`) and is syntactically backward-compatible. In fact, the b and a in BASH stand for Bourne Again, a tribute to sh and its author Stephen Bourne. The Bash shell is very capable and has support for numerous control statements. This includes support for standard control statements: `if/elif/else` constructs, `case` statements, as well as `for`, `while`, and `until` loop statements.

A control statement in a programming or scripting environment provides ways for a programmer to control the execution of code. These statements provide the means to perform basic tests on data, which will then define the flow of execution, all based upon the criteria we design. Through the use of `if/else` and `case` control statements, we can control whether or not code gets executed at all. These functions are referred to as branching statements, as they control specific paths of code execution. Looping statements, such as `for`, `while`, and `until`, are control statements that allow for reuse of code through iteration. Shell scripts provide looping statements in the form of "for," "until," and "while" loops. Each of these looping statements provides capabilities to help you manage highly repetitive tasks. Control statements serve as the fundamental tools for logical execution of code, shown later in this chapter.

Shells also include some internal data manipulation routines, provided via globbing and variable mangling, though for any advanced parsing, such as regular expressions, you'll be much better off with an external program that is suited for the purpose. That being said, we'll walk you through some of the commonly used constructs, which will bestow upon you the building blocks toward implementing your own automations.

Note On many systems, `/bin/sh` is linked to the Bash or zsh installation. However, be aware that with Bash built upon the basic `sh` constructs, language like "declare" will not work when called from an `sh` script. We will show you how to set the shebang to specify that your script runs in Bash; you can add the code at the top of your script `[ -z "$BASH" ] && exit 1` to check for this as well.

Declaring Variables

Variables are the single most important concept of scripting in relation to automating administrative tasks. While other languages have relative benefits, most admins typically end up using Bash for basic day-to-day administration, where many tasks can be accomplished by very simple scripts or even a single line of chained commands ("one-liners"). A one-line script could look something like this:

```
systemsetup -setnetworktimeserver my.pretendco.com
```

In the preceding script, we have called the `systemsetup` command along with an option to set a network time server and then the name of the time server. But perhaps you are in a Windows Active Directory environment, and the server you use for time is also your authentication server. Your script may have "my.server.com" listed 10–20 times by the time you are finished if you didn't use a variable. This is because you often need sanity checks or loops as a script matures, and you find reasons it may have failed when run. Now imagine you need to change that code later on. You could cut and paste all 20 lines, but if you use variables, you can declare the server once and then retrieve this value over and over again in your script. You can even then use it to echo output as well.

Each variable has a name that uniquely identifies it within scope. Variable names need to begin with an alphabetic character and cannot contain a period. In other words, if you work for a company called 318, you'd often need to declare variables called, for example, "THREE18" to avoid starting with a number. Variables can't be longer than 255 characters. Even for your one-liner scripts, using variables will allow them to grow over time and cut down on the number of typos, as you have just one line rather than 20 to check when you have a problem.

```
#!/bin/zsh
declare TIME_SERVER="my.pretendco.com"
systemsetup -setnetworktimeserver "$TIME_SERVER"
echo "Time Server: $TIME_SERVER has been set"
```

When a variable is used in a script, the script "expands" the variable to its respective value (in this case, `$TIME_SERVER` becomes "`my.pretendco.com`"). However, a variable may not always contain string data, which is why you can have a dynamic error message using the simple echo command. Because of this, it is important to always double quote variables. Expansion works within double quotation marks, not single quotes. Double quotes also help when working with filesystem paths that have spaces, often the cause of issues with novice users. When in doubt, quote. If you want to see variable expansion as it occurs (often helpful for debugging a script), add -x to the shebang, like this: "`#!/bin/zsh -x`".

In traditional programming languages, you must declare a variable and the kind of information that will go into it before using the variable (in other words, you tell the script what's going into a variable before you actually "put" something in it). In modern scripting languages, this is usually considered good practice (and great for readability), but it's not required. In the Bash shell, the command to declare a variable is `declare`.

When you declare a variable, you can then call it multiple times, adding and removing data from it, augmenting it, or just reading it for reference.

For example, in Bash, the two following statements are equal to one another or produce the same output:

```
#!/bin/zsh
declare -i CUSTOM_PORT=8088
echo "My web server is running on port $CUSTOM_PORT."
# Example script 2
CUSTOM_PORT="8088"
echo "My web server is running on port $CUSTOM_PORT."
```

In the first example, we are explicitly defining the variable CUSTOM_PORT as an integer and setting it to 8088. In the second, typecasting in Bash automatically determines the type of data that a variable contains. Typecasting occurs when a variable is set to a certain type (such as an integer) and then used to store a different data type (say the string "Hello World"). In this case, there is a type conversion from integer to string. While both of the preceding examples work, relying on automatic typecasting can present problems in certain circumstances; if your script logic is expecting a numeric (integer) value and is passed a string instead, your script will die with a fatal error. The following script shows how this works:

```
#!/bin/bash
# A simple script that checks if a console user is active
# We will cover the "who | grep 'console' -c" portion later
# for now just know that this test will return "1" if a user
# is logged in and nothing if no one is logged in
declare -i CONSOLE_USERS="`who | grep 'console' -c`"
# The command above returns nothing if no users are logged in.
# However, when declared as an integer, if this variable is
# set to a null / nothing string, it will convert that to the
```

```
# number zero; that way the result of the command
doesn't matter.
# We can always rely of the result being a numerical value,
# which we can then numerically test against, using the greater
# than or equal to syntax -ge. This type of test expects
# CONSOLE_USERS to expand to a numerical value
# If we did not use -i, then any numeric tests on
$CONSOLE_USERS
# would fail if there were no users logged in. The script would
# expand CONSOLE_USERS to nothing instead of 0
# You can test this by changing the declare line above to
# declare CONSOLE_USERS=
# which will simulate the command returning nothing
# and without the use of the -i, it will stay just
that: nothing
# which will cause the test below to fail with the error:
# "line 17: [: -ge: unary operator expected"
if [ $CONSOLE_USERS -ge 1 ] ; then
       echo "Console user logged in, exiting..."
       exit 1
else
       echo "No console users, we can go to town..."
       # Your code goes here
Fi
```

This script uses comments to explain the flow of the script; these are covered later in this chapter. For now, be aware that any line that starts with a # (except for line 1) is a comment, and the script will not "run" that text. This is a best practice, and you should always comment all of your code, adding notes to explain your script's logic and activity. The more complicated a script gets, the more important that commenting becomes. If you do not comment the script effectively, you will not be able to trace your own steps at some point, much less have anyone else be able to take over your work when you, say, get a promotion to Senior Deity of Computer Operations for integrating 10,000 Macs into your enterprise in a week.

Expanding on Z Shell

The default shell changed to zsh from bash in macOS 10.15. Most scripts that existed prior to macOS 10.15 are likely to work fine, but there are some differences between these shells, which we'll cover in this section.

To quickly see which you're using (e.g., when testing a new release), use $0:

```
echo $0
```

Z Shell or zsh for short was written by Princeton University student Paul Falstad in 1990. Most shells are just extensions of the Bourne shell (including bash) and work similarly, but there are minor differences here and there. Yes, Z Shell comes with a control-R reverse incremental search, but that's not a good reason to make this kind of change. Z Shell is more modern (e.g., more customizable autocompletion, use Alt + . to put parameters from the previous command into your next command, slicker tabbed autocomplete), considered by some to be more secure (not considered as such by others). One of the most visible of these features for Apple administrators will be file globbing. This is where you use an asterisk (∗) to list file contents. To step through this example, we'll declare the Contents variable in bash and echo the contents:

```
Apps=*
```

Then let's read the contents of that $Contents variable:

```
echo $Apps
```

The output would be as follows, a basic list of files (assuming the directory you ran it in is /Applications):

About This Mac.app Archive Utility.app DVD Player.app Directory Utility.app Feedback Assistant.app Folder Actions Setup.app Network Utility.app RAID Utility.app Screen Sharing.app Storage Management.app System Image Utility. app Wireless Diagnostics.app

Now let's do the same operation in zsh. The output shows that the * was accepted literally:

```
*
```

To get the same result, wrap the globs in a () as follows (which includes two to trap for hidden directories):

```
Apps=(*(N))
```

The security benefit here is that you don't accidentally include something you're not supposed to while getting more options for dealing with expansion. If this doesn't work because you have a lot of scripts deployed and are in the midst of an upgrade, you can do this the same old way by enabling globsubst with the default shell or simply include bash in the shebang of any scripts you're running.

Another difference would be the way directory aliases are handled. The alias command in zsh allows for expanded aliases anywhere in a line. To put this in context, let's grep output to something with an alias:

```
alias -g GS="| grep something"
```

Then cat that output:

```
cat somefile GS
```

Another change includes environment scripts. These are

- `zlogin`: Sets environment variables and commands that won't change often, as you have to reinvoke the login for the changes to take effect.
- `zlogout`: Clears out terminals and resources set by zlogin, in order to release any resources being taken up unnecessarily.
- `zprofile`: Similar to .zlogin except that it's sourced before .zshrc instead of after .zlogin. The two shouldn't be used concurrently.
- `zshenv`: Sets the search path and environment variables unless a -f is provided to start a session.
- `zshrc`: Sets up aliases, functions, key bindings, shell options, and hosts for autocompletion. This is used for interactive shells.

Other areas where zsh is different (some of these will be lesser used, but should benefit more advanced administrators):

- Don't set BASH_ENV (obviously), ENV, or SHELL to be the same.
- exec changes (see `http://zsh.sourceforge.net/Doc/Release/Shell-Builtin-Commands.html` for more on how zsh does this).
- Native hashed data structure support in zsh using typeset.
- The zsh interpreter doesn't have an -x option like in bash.
- Remove any PROMPT_COMMAND entries.

- Replace any calls to getopts with zparseopts.
- SHELLOPTS isn't run at startup, although zshrc, zlogin, and zprofile can be run at different times during the startup of the shell.
- Use zcalc for all the maths including floating-point support not present in bash natively: autoload -Uz zcalc.
- -norc doesn't skip anything.
- -rcfile calls.
- Spelling corrections.
- There is no restricted mode (--restricted) in zsh.
- There is no posix mode (-o posix) in zsh.
- You can autoload extensions like zmv in zsh.

Another reason Apple engineering picked zsh is that it's modular. This means you can load modules that help provide things like additional file manipulation commands (zsh/files), use posix regex (zsh/regex), or deal with sockets (zsh/net/socket). To check out a list of plug-ins that are available, see `https://github.com/unixorn/awesome-zsh-plugins`. In general, zsh is a more secure and modern shell environment, and despite the transition period for administrators, it's easy to understand why Apple engineers felt it a better option leaving bash as the default shell.

Altering Variables (Mangling)

The various shells have several facilities for internally altering data in variables. This is referred to as "variable mangling," and there are numerous string operators to be applied to a variable that will filter its value. Mangling uses curly brackets {} that enclose the variable name prepended to a number of possible special operator characters.

One common use of variable mangling is to perform pattern matching on a variable, both left to right (specified by the hash (#) character) and right to left (specified by the percent (%) character):

```
MY_VAR="the value of a variable"
echo ${MY_VAR#the}
```

The preceding example returns

```
"value of a variable"
```

Now let's change the echo statement:

```
echo ${MY_VAR%a *}
```

Now the return echoes the following to the screen:

```
"the value of"
```

This can be handy for grabbing filenames or extensions explicitly:

```
MY_FILE=songname.m4a
echo "Filename: ${MY_FILE%.*} extension: ${MY_FILE##*.}"
```

The return is then as follows:

```
Filename: songname extension: m4a
```

Notice the use of the greedy string operator (##); this ensures that even if the file has additional periods in its name, the only one we consider the extension (and thereby exclude from our filter) is everything past the last dot. The ability to remove file extensions this way is very handy. For instance, the Apple `defaults` command used to require you pass in the filename without the .plist extension (no longer the case today). In the following script, we utilized this method to isolate the file extension when needed, allowing us to perform our operations. The commands here are not as important as the concept – that now we can use the same variable for both operations and have the extension automatically removed for commands that require it.

```
#!/bin/zsh
declare -i TIME_OUT=5
# This sets the timeout of the AD plug-in in 10.5+
declare PLIST_FILE=\
"/Library/Preferences/DirectoryService/ActiveDirectory.plist"
# The path of the plist \ is used to continue the command on
the next line
# Note that the path has a .plist extension, which normally
would cause
# The defaults command to fail. However, with variable
mangling we can
# remove the .plist extension of the PLIST_FILE value when
we use it
# with defaults and then call it normally when we use a
command that
# requires a more standard path with file extensions
like plutil.
if [ -w "$PLIST_FILE" ] ; then

defaults write "${PLIST_FILE%.plist}" 'LDAP Connection Timeout'
$TIME_OUT
        plutil -convert xml1 "$PLIST_FILE"
else
        echo "File is not writable try sudo $0"
fi
```

Note We use a variable that is automatically set by the shell, $0 here. This is the full path to the script, and it's good for making dynamic usage error messages match your script path and name automatically.

Another form of variable mangling provided by Bash is substitution, which uses four operators, `:-`, `:=`, `:+`, and `:?`. Suppose I use the command `echo ${MY_VAR:-hello}`. If the variable `MY_VAR` exists and isn't null, the command will output its value. If `MY_VAR` doesn't exist or has a null value, the string "hello" will not print out. The `:=` operator is very similar. The main distinction is that when `:=` is used, it will set the variable `$MY_VAR` to the value specified, in this case "hello." The `:+` operator is essentially the inverse of the `:-` operator. In the command echo `${MY_VAR:+hello}`, if `$MY_VAR` exists and is not null, then we return "hello." If it doesn't exist or is null, it will return a blank value. Lastly, the `:?` operator can be used to perform sanity checks. For instance, when used with the syntax echo `${MY_VAR:?my error}`, if the variable `$MY_VAR` is not set, the script will immediately terminate, printing the error message "my error." If no error is specified, a generic "parameter null or not set" error is output, along with the variable name. Use of the `:?` operator is a great way to ensure that critical variables are set.

Note Scripts can be very damaging if certain operations are called with malformed data, so be extra diligent in using these string operators to verify that appropriate values are set.

All shells provide further capabilities for data substitution via the / and // operators. For instance, if `MY_VAR` has a value of Hello World, the command echo `${MY_VAR//Hello/Hi}` would output the text Hi World. The use of // vs. / simply denotes how greedy the matching is:

`echo #{MY_VAR/o/a}` would output Hella World, while the command `echo #{MY_VAR//o/a}` outputs Hella Warld. A real-world example of this follows (excuse the rather hacky use of AppleScript via osascript to get this MAC address value, but it's a simple way to get only your MAC address returned):

```
#!/bin/zsh
declare MAC_ADDRESS=`osascript -e 'primary Ethernet address of
(system info)'`
echo "Address with colons: $MAC_ADDRESS"
echo "Address without colons: ${MAC_ADDRESS//:/}"
```

The preceding examples are fairly simple scripts and wouldn't require much to make them much more interesting in terms of their capabilities. We'll keep providing a little more complexity to what we're doing and move into streams and pipes in the next section.

Standard Streams and Pipelines

In any *nix terminal environment, numerous information channels exist that control the flow of information between a process and its console session. The three primary data channels from a scripting perspective are standard input (stdin), standard output (stdout), and standard error (stderr). These data streams can be captured, evaluated, and redirected through scripting:

- Standard input, or `stdin`, represents data resulting from a read operation. This can be text input via keyboard or text that has been programmatically redirected.
- Standard output, or stdout, represents any data output by a program. The output will typically go to the current console session but can also be redirected to other programs or files.

- Standard error, or stderr, is a data channel that represents textual error information. For instance, if a program detects an error in one of its subroutines, it will typically spit the details of this error out to stderr. Understanding the use of these channels by any program you intend to script will help you to write your code more efficiently.

As mentioned, we can use pipelines or redirects to control the flow of data between separate programs. The most common use of pipelines is the practice of piping stdout from one script to stdin of another. For example, we call the command

```
ps auxww | grep -v "grep" | grep -c "Finder"
```

If you were to look up the man page for grep (`man grep`), you would find that the program takes optional flags and two arguments, a string pattern and a path to a file. However, in this context, we are simply calling `grep` with only one argument. How does that work? Well, the answer is due to our implementation of command pipes `|`. As mentioned, the pipe is used explicitly for passing data between programs. In this case, we are passing data from the `ps` command out to `grep`. The `grep` command recognizes that it is being passed data over stdin and utilizes this data as its second argument. After filtering this data and removing any occurrences of the term `grep`, it outputs the modified data to stdout, which is piped to yet another instance of `grep`. This program is responsible for outputting a numeric count for the number of times the term Finder appeared in data passed to it through stdout. In a command pipeline, the resulting text output will be that parsed by the final command in the chain.

In many cases, you may want to redirect the flow of data to a file. To do this, you use data stream redirectors. In Bash, the most common implementation of redirectors is through the `>>` and `>` operators:

```
ps auxww > ~/process_list.txt
```

In this example, we are redirecting stdout of the ps program to the file located at `~/process_list.txt`. The use of the > operator means it will overwrite any data that previously existed with the file. Thus, every time the preceding command is run, the file will contain only data from the most recent operation. The >> operator in contrast is an append operation; any data previously will simply have our latest data added to it. This is a less destructive redirect and is desirable in many scenarios.

It is also possible to redirect the data streams themselves. For instance, perhaps we want to set a variable to the output of the `ls` command:

```
lsTxt=$(ls /Applications)
```

This syntax will capture the output of the `ls` program's stdout as a single string. However, if `ls` is passed a nonexistent path, it will output its text to stderr, which will never be passed to our `lsTxt` variable. To address this issue, we can use data stream redirects once again. To pull this off, we want to redirect the stderr channel (in ∗nix systems channel 2) to stdout channel, channel 1:

```
lsTxt=$(ls /Applications 2>&1)
```

This way, `lsTxt` will contain either the file listing or any subsequent errors. It is also possible to perform two redirects:

```
ls /Applications >> ~/lsLog.txt 2>&1
```

In this context, we are redirecting stdout to append our file found at `/lsLog.txt`. However, we are also redirecting stderr to stdout. This command will output the results of both data streams into the file. This becomes a handy way to log all activity reported by a process, rather than just merely relying on stdout.

If and Case Statements

If/else and case statements serve primarily as traffic routers. Both facilities are specifically referred to as branching statements; their purpose is to directly affect the flow of code. For instance, perhaps there is a VIP user on the network who needs VIP treatment. If this user logs in to a computer, we need to ensure they have a "Deep Thoughts" folder on their desktop, and then perhaps we need to prune this folder for old files, sweeping them away into a "Stale Thoughts" folder. In the end, the specific task doesn't really matter, it is only important that we recognize that all of this activity represents a "branch" of code - a full path of activity initiated by the evaluation of an initial `if` statement. That `if` statement represents a test - is this user my VIP? If they are, the next step is a flurry of activity. Otherwise (`else`), skip the code and proceed as usual.

Note When coding or scripting in any language, the general rule of thumb when implementing branching statements is to organize your code so that the most commonly executed branch is in the first block.

For basic string comparison, both if/else and case statements are similar, though lengthy case statements tend to be easier to read than lengthy if/else statements. Here is the syntax to implement each (note: the `USER` variable is set automatically by the shell and expands to the username of the user running the script):

```
# Check to see if our user is "jdoe"
if [ "$USER" = "jdoe" ]; then
       echo "My name is John"
       exit 0
elif [ "$USER" = "janedoe" ]; then
       echo "My name is Jane"
       exit 1
```

```
elif [ "$USER" = "jsmith" ] ; then
       echo "My name is jsmith"
       exit 1
else
       echo "Failed over to catch all…"
       exit 192
fi
# While the above works, it's rather ugly, so a case statement
normally is much more readable
## case statement
case $USER in
r"jdoe")
               echo "My name is John";
               exit 0;;
       "jsmith" )
               echo "My name is jsmith" ;
               exit 1;;
       "janedoe")
               echo "My name is Jane";
               exit 1;;
        *)
       echo "Failed over to catch all...";
       exit 192 ;;
esac
```

Note When using case, specify each entry with a ;; following the line, and then when all possible matches have been specified, you will use esac (end of case) to close out the case statement.

We have introduced a few new concepts here. First are the test brackets `[ ]`. The use of brackets represents a conditional expression, which will ultimately evaluate to true or false. In Bash, test brackets are used with conditional operators to form tests. One example of this is in the previous example's `if` statement:

```
if [ $CONSOLE_USERS -eq 1 ] ; then
\
```

This logic in English would translate as follows: if the string variable $USER is equal to the string "jdoe," execute the following code. In this case, "is equal to" is syntactically denoted by a string comparison operator, =, which compares two arguments (referred to as a binary operator) and returns true if they have equal string values. Its antithesis != will return true if the two given arguments are not the same. In our case statement, the variable $USER is tested in a similar fashion (=) against each of our possible matches, each denoted by the values specified prior to the closing parenthesis. When a match occurs, the respective code block is executed until it reaches the break specifier `;;`. In the case statement, the last line *) represents a wildcard and is the equivalent to an else block in an `if` statement; its execution is dependent on all prior matches failing.

Caution Not all languages, such as PHP and Python, regard the symbol = as a comparison operator and will actually interpret it as a value assignment. In many cases, it is best to use the == operator to do string comparison to prevent alteration of your variable's value. The == comparison operator is fully supported by Bash.

In addition to these two binary operators (= and !=), there are several arithmetic-based binary operators:

- `-eq`: arg1 equals arg2.
- `-ne`: arg1 does not equal arg2.
- `-lt`: arg1 is less than arg2.
- `-le`: arg1 is less than or equal to arg2.
- `-gt`: arg1 is greater than arg2.
- `-ge`: arg1 is greater than or equal to arg2.

Besides binary operators, the test facility provides many valuable unary operators (to test against a single argument). Unary operators are usually used to perform tests against filesystem objects. Two of the most common unary operators are `-f` and `-d`, which respectively test for the presence of a file or directory.

```
if [ -d /System/Library/CoreServices/Finder.app ]; then
        echo 'Finder was Found!'
fi
```

This code will print the text "Finder was found!" if a directory exists at the path /System/Library/CoreServices/Finder.app (which is true in any OS X system because the Application bundle "Finder" is in fact a directory like almost all modern apps). There are numerous unary operators, most easily found by consulting the man page for test, using `man test`. Here are some that are notable:

- `-f string`: True if string is the path to a regular file
- `-d string`: True if string is the path to a directory
- `-r/-w/-x string`: True if string is a file that is readable, writable, or executable (respectively)

`-L string`: True if string is a path to a symbolic link

`-z/-n string`: True if string is zero or nonzero length (respectively)

Note You can also run these checks directly using the test command (although you might have to wrap the test condition into quotes or double parentheses depending on exactly what you're attempting to test), like so:

```
test -d /Users/ && echo "directory exists"
```

```
#!/bin/bash
if ( [ "$USER" == "janedoe" ] || [ "$USER" ="jsmith" ] ); then
echo "User is jane or john"
else
        echo "User is not jane or john"
fi
```

In the `if/elif` example, we also demonstrate the use of the logical OR operator `||`:

```
if ( [ "$USER" ="janedoe" ] || [ "$USER" ="jsmith" ] ); then
```

The logical OR operator and its partner the logical AND operator (&&), often referred to as Boolean operators, are used to test against multiple expressions. In the implementation earlier, we are using the logical OR operator to test against two possible usernames, janedoe and jsmith. We want to know if a user is *either* of these usernames, so we need to be able to run both tests. In this example, if we used && instead of ||, the end result would always evaluate to false, as the $USER variable will never be equal to both values. When using logical operators && and || to combine expressions, execution of the control statement will terminate immediately after it evaluates to false or true, respectively. Thus, in the preceding example, if the username is janedoe, the test will never be executed against "jsmith." In similar spirit, if we used && in that statement, the test against "jsmith" will only ever get tested if the first expression is true (the username is "janedoe"). Understanding this becomes very important to writing clean, effective code. Recognizing this, we can take the previous example:

```
if [ -d /System/Library/CoreServices/Finder.app ]; then
        echo 'Finder Found!'
fi
```

Next, let's slim it down to a single "one-liner":

```
[ -d /System/Library/CoreServices/Finder.app ] && echo
'Finder found!'
```

As covered earlier, if our expression returns false (in this case because the Finder.app directory could not be found), then the test will abort and the `printf` statement will never fire. In this iteration, we are also omitting our `if` control statement, as our branching code (`printf "Finder found!\n"`) can easily fit onto a single line.

In our previous example, the case statement, as you may have deduced, also uses a logical `OR` operator, implemented by supplying multiple matches in a single test block:

```
case "$USER" in
"janedoe")
        echo "My name is Jane Doe";;
"jsmith")
        echo "My name is John Smith";;
*)
        echo "Remember Sammy Jenkins…";;
esac
```

In this example, by placing both "janedoe" and "jsmith" together, we are implying a logical OR between the two values. A case statement will then perform a string comparison of $USER to the string "janedoe" and, if no match is found, will test against "jsmith" and so on. Once a match is found, it will execute any preceding lines of code until it runs against our break specifier (;;). In the case of janedoe or jsmith, a match would result solely in the execution of the code: echo "My name is Jane Doe". Case statements, unlike if/else statements, do not have access to the more advanced unary or binary operators provided by Bash. They are pretty much limited to string comparisons and thus provide only limited (but important) functionality.

For, While, and Until Statements

So, at this point, we have learned how to define the flow of our program through the use of branching statements, expressions, and conditional operators. Automation, however, is rarely about performing an operation once; the benefits of automation lie in the ability to scale production as needed with minimal investment. Automation is particularly well suited for boring, repetitive tasks that will result in hundreds, thousands, or even millions of iterations. To harness the ability of repetition and iteration, Bash provides three looping statements: `for`, `while`, and `until`. The `for` loop is usually for iterating over basic items.

```
declare plistbuddy="/usr/libexec/PlistBuddy"
declare python="/usr/bin/python"
REQUIRED_COMMANDS="$plistbuddy $python"
for COMMAND in $REQUIRED_COMMANDS; do
       if [ -x  $COMMAND ] ; then
```

```
            echo "Command: $COMMAND is installed"
        else
            echo "Command: $COMMAND is missing"
        fi
done
```

Every element of this script is native to the shell and would output the text:

```
Command: /usr/libexec/PlistBuddy is installed
Command: /usr/bin/python is installed
```

Note To determine if a command will result in the execution of an external program, use `type` followed by the name of the function. If the process is external to the shell, it will specify the absolute path to the binary (as found in $PATH). For example, `type echo` returns `echo is a shell builtin`, meaning that Bash will use its internal echo ability rather than the external command `/bin/echo` when the echo command is called in a script.

The `while` and `until` statements are used for building more customized looping structures. The -ge operator allows us to loop while certain criteria are met:

```
while [ $( ps aux | grep -v "grep" | grep -c "Finder" )
-ge 1 ];
do
        echo "Finder is still running"
        sleep 15
done
```

In this example, there are a few new concepts. First and foremost, whenever we use expressions, they are primarily expecting string arguments. If we want to call an external program inside of an expression, we must designate that the text not be treated as a string, but rather as an external process. To do this, we wrap the entire command pipeline inside of `$()`. This wrapper tells the shell to evaluate the contents of the entire pipeline in a subshell. This same behavior applies if we want to assign the output of a command to a variable. The following syntax is used to set the value of variable `$psTxt` to the output of our `ps` command chain (this time, we will use `grep` with pipes to accomplish the same count):

```
psTxt=$( ps aux | grep -v "grep" | grep -c "Finder" )
```

Examining this command chain, we see that we are utilizing the external programs `ps` and `grep`. The `ps` command lists running processes, and `grep` is a basic filtering tool. Because `grep` is a program, it will sometimes be found in the `ps` process list, so we must first filter out our own `grep` line, using the `-v` flag. Then we do a search for the string "Finder." The `-c` flag specifies that we will output the number of matches. If we find one or more processes, we will proceed through our loop. Next, we output a simple text line stating that the program is running, then we sleep for 15 seconds. At this point, the end of our loop has been reached, and we will once again test for our criteria. If the criteria match, we will proceed through our loop again, indefinitely, until our criteria fail to match.

The `until` loop represents a different utility. In Bash, it does not represent true trailing logic (as it does in C), but rather serves as an inverse of the `while` loop. Because of this, it is of rather limited use. For example, we can easily replicate the logic of the preceding while loop, simply inversing our conditional logic:

```
until [ $(ps aux | grep -v "grep" | grep -c "Finder" ) -lt 1 ];
do
      printf "Finder is Running\n"
      sleep 15
done
```

Note Bash, like most languages, provides control statements for managing individual loop iterations. For instance, the control statement `continue` will instruct a loop to terminate the execution for that particular instance, at which point it will return to its evaluation statement (or the next iterated item in the case of a `for` loop), and continue through the loop. The `break` statement will instruct a loop to terminate completely.

Arrays

An array, sometimes known as a vector, is one of the simplest data structures. Arrays hold a collection of values, generally of the same data type. Each element uses a consecutive range of numbers (integers) to retrieve and store the values. Bash has basic support for one-dimensional arrays. Creating a basic array in Bash is pretty simple:

```
## set the variable MY_APPS to an array populated with a
directory listing of /Applications
declare -a MY_APPS=(/Applications/*.app)
```

You can then iterate through these items with a `for` loop:

```
for APP in "${MY_APPS[@]}"; do
      echo "Application: $APP"
done
```

There are a few things to note in this code. In our `for` statement, we quote the array string `${MY_APPS[@]}` to ensure that individual items with spaces or tabs in the data are escaped. When accessing a specific index in an array, the curly braces are always needed, and the index number specified inside them. For instance, here's how to access the first item list in our applications:

```
${MY_APPS[1]}.
```

You can also assign arrays using numeric methodology:

```
declare -a USER_NAME[501]=krypted
declare -i USER_UID=501
echo ${USER_NAME[501]}
        returns: "krypted"
echo ${USER_NAME[$USER_UID]}
       returns  "krypted"
```

Arrays are very handy for collating and organizing data. However, their support in shell programming is a bit limited compared to more robust programming environments. Also be aware that one of the major limitations of an array is that their scope is downward only, meaning you can't export an array between scripts or functions of a script. Basically, arrays are going to only work in your main body of code and not in subprocesses you launch. In practice, this is a major limitation to consider before trying to use Bash arrays in a complicated fashion.

Exit Codes

Command-line applications, when implemented properly, will provide what is called an exit code or return code after execution. This exit code is internally defined in the program and is used to signal proper execution or perhaps a specific error code. When a UNIX command-line utility executes successfully, it should return an integer value of zero, which indicates successful operation. Any nonzero value will represent an error condition in the code, and this is a handy way to determine whether a program properly executed. Exit codes vary from application to application and are often referenced in the commands' documentation (192 is also a common error status). To check the exit code of a process, you can test against the special variable `$?` immediately after the command has executed:

```
rsync -avu /Folder1/ /Folder2/
if [ $? = 0 ]; then
      echo "The Rsync finished without an error!"
else
      echo "The rsync had problems!!"
fi
```

Alternatively, do the same thing on one line:

```
rsync -avu /Folder1/ /Folder2/ && ( echo "Rsync Finished" ||
echo "Rsync had problems" )
```

When writing scripts, it is important to follow good practice and properly report the script's status. Do so with the `exit` statement in the code, followed by an integer value defining the proper state, remembering to `exit 0` on proper execution, and use an arbitrary value of one or greater on error. If your script is primarily a wrapper for a different program, it may not be a bad idea to mirror its exit code by referencing the `$?` variable immediately following the execution of your command. Because `$?` will change with each process that is run, you will want to save the `$?` value into a separate variable for later reference in the script, allowing your script to exit with the same value of the original command that you are wrapping your logic around (such as an `if` or `for` statement):

```
rsync -avu /Folder1/ /Folder2/
```

```
declare -i RSYNC_CODE=$?
if [ $RSYNC_CODE =0 ]; then
       echo "The Rsync finished without an error!"
else
       echo "The rsync had problems!!"
fi
exit $RSYNC_CODE
```

More Advanced Shell Script Logic

To be properly processed by a shell, a UNIX executable script must specify which interpreter the shell should use to parse and execute its contained shell code. This information is provided via a shebang or hash-bang (`#!`) specifier, which should always be at line 1 of the script and should precede the absolute path to the file's interpreter. To specify the zsh interpreter, we use the following shebang specifier at the start of the script:

```
#!/bin/zsh
```

Note You can add an `-x` to the interpreter line of Bash scripts to assist with debugging. This will echo the expanded variables and actual runtime code in addition to the more common output vectors like the `echo` command, for example, `#!/bin/zsh -x`.

Using this syntax, you can also specify atypical shell interpreters, such as Perl (`#!/usr/bin/perl`), Python (`#!/usr/bin/python`), or Ruby (`#!/usr/bin/ruby`); the list goes on. For the most part, OS X and most *nix variants all utilize the same directory to store interactive user shells in the `/bin/` folder. This folder is defined by BSD as housing: "user utilities fundamental to both single-user and multi-user environments." This folder is very common among the *nix variants and can usually be trusted to contain at least the Bourne shell (sh) and, on most modern systems, the Bash shell. However, nonshell interpreters, such as Python, Perl, or Ruby, are going to vary greatly from OS to OS and can change if Xcode or a manual implementation isn't installed. Because of this, if we want our shell to be portable (which these languages provide), then providing a static path is not going to provide much utility on nonconforming systems. If portability is your goal (and certainly it's never a bad one), you may want to forgo specifying an absolute path and instead let the parent shell dynamically determine its location. To do this, utilize the following shebang specifier:

```
#!/usr/bin/env python
```

The key thing to know here is that /usr/bin/env is a very commonly supported binary and will cause the shell to search through its $PATH to locate the Python executable. If that's found in our path, this executable will be used as the interpreter for the script. The $PATH variable is an environmental variable used by nearly all shells and specifies a number of directories that should be consulted when searching for a binary. This variable contains a colon-delimited string of directories and will search through them in order of preference from left to right. For instance, if I run the command echo $PATH, I will see all of the directories in my path:

```
echo $PATH
/usr/bin:/bin:/usr/sbin:/sbin
```

Thus, if I were to run the command ifconfig, my shell would first look for the binary ifconfig in the /usr/bin folder, then in /bin, /usr/sbin, and so on until it ultimately finds the command (in this case, in the /sbin directory). If the command is not found after searching the entire path, the shell will terminate execution of the script with an error. On top of this, the PATH variable becomes a good way for a user to inject their own versions of a binary in place of a system binary. For instance, Mr. Joebob Poweruser always likes to have the latest, greatest version of Perl on his system, dutifully installed at `/usr/local/bin/perl`. However, with a default PATH variable, when Joebob runs the command `perl`, he will be treated to our localization's binary stored at `/usr/bin/perl`. To change this, Joebob will want to modify his `~/.profile` file, adding the line

```
export PATH="/usr/local/bin:$PATH"
```

After doing this, when the user starts a shell, the path `/usr/local/bin` will be the first folder searched in his path. Knowing all of this, it is easy to see how utilizing the `/usr/bin/env` in your shebang line can provide benefits if your script will have a wide audience.

Note With all the variants of Linux and UNIX systems out there, it certainly can be a mental exercise to remember each one's folder hierarchy. For this purpose, many such systems provide documentation as to their particular folder eccentricities. On such systems, you can access this documentation via the `hier` man page by running the command `man hier` at your Terminal prompt.

With the shebang out of the way, we can now start writing our script. Typically, at this point in the script, we will do what is referred to as *initialization*. That is, we will define the variables to be utilized by the script. Initializing all of your variables at the beginning of the script provides many benefits. Primarily, it serves as a blueprint for your script. Assuming you adopt good naming conventions for your variables, the general utility and configurability of a script can often be deduced by scanning the variables, at least to an extent. To assign a variable in the shell, simply specify the variable name, followed by an equal sign, and then the value, for instance, in the following line:

```
USER_NAME="charles"
```

With this line, we are assigning the global variable USER_NAME the value of charles. Variables in Bash can be uppercase and can contain underscores such as PLIST_FILE and can even be camel case – plistFileNumberThree. The choice is up to you – just be consistent. Notice that during assignment, we do not prepend the variable name with a $ specifier, unlike Perl. However, utilizing the global scope in Bash will ultimately make your code less extensible. For instance, if you were to refactor the code into a function, you could have issues with scope conflict. To address this, you can utilize the declare statement, which will initialize the variable only in the local context:

```
declare USER_NAME="charles"
# Charles is available only to the local context
declare -x USER_NAME="bill"
# Bill is only available to the local and sub shells
export USER_NAME="emerald"
# Emerald is available to the local sub shells and
parent shells
# (but no type assignment such as array "-a" or "-i" integer)
```

Any local declares will not export to subprocesses or script functions, but stay within the current scope of code running. If you use declare in a function, once the function is complete, the variable will no longer be active. This may be advantageous if, for instance, you have a function that contains a password as a variable. If you want to keep a function's variable around after the function is complete, you can use `export`, as shown in this example:

```
#!/bin/zsh
# This is a basic function
littleFunction(){
      declare LITTLE_VAR="local"
      export BIG_VAR="global"
```

```
        echo "$FUNCNAME: LITTLE_VAR: $LITTLE_VAR"
        echo "$FUNCNAME: BIG_VAR: $BIG_VAR"
}
littleFunction # This is how we run a function
echo "$0: BIG_VAR: $BIG_VAR"
echo "$0: LITTLE_VAR: ${LITTLE_VAR:?}" # This should error out
$ ./bigscript
littleFunction: LITTLE_VAR: local
littleFunction: BIG_VAR: global
./bigscript: BIG_VAR: global
./ bigscript: line 16: LITTLE_VAR: parameter null or not set
```

While not always necessary, it is a good idea to get in the habit of using declare statements with shell programming. It will save time and headaches down the road as code gets repurposed.

One mistake rookie coders make is that they rely heavily on utilizing PATH resolution in shell scripts. That is, instead of typing the command

```
/usr/sbin/networksetup -getdnsservers "Airport"
```

the command can be typed as follows:

```
networksetup -getdnsservers "Airport"
```

This won't necessarily prove to be an issue, as networksetup resides in the default path at /usr/sbin. The main problem with this methodology is that PATH variables can be manipulated rather easily. If this script were ever to get called with the sudo command, which escalates privileges to uid 0, then we could potentially compromise a machine simply by injecting our own path variable into the user environment. This way, instead of the system calling networksetup, someone could call our own program identically named networksetup, which might install goodies all over the machine. Modifying a user's PATH is rather trivial to do once a user account has been compromised and can then be used for local privilege escalation and to ultimately control the box. Several OS X escalation vulnerabilities have been found due to failure to sanitize PATH exploits.

To combat this issue, we have a few options. The first option is to manually specify the PATH variable in our script. This way, we can utilize the dynamic lookup capabilities of scripts and still provide our own known-good paths. To do this, we simply declare PATH in the global scope of the script:

```
#!/bin/zsh
PATH="/usr/local/bin:/usr/bin:/bin:/usr/sbin:/sbin
```

By specifying the PATH variable, we are in essence designating trusted paths. Because we are doing this, it is important that we ensure proper restrictions are applied to these paths. We want to make sure that all specified paths are locked down from modification, restricted only to admin users. For instance, the Bash `/usr/local/bin` does not exist by default, so it could theoretically be possible for a user to create this directory, inject their own executables, and then interject those executables into our script. To prevent this, we utilize filesystem permissions. In the case of `/usr/local/bin`, a user would first have to create both the `local/bin` branch. Thus, that user would need to be able to modify the directory at `/usr`. Luckily, filesystem privileges are locked down such that a user would need root access to alter any of the specified directories. If they can alter these system paths, we have bigger issues to worry about.

Specifying a PATH for our shell script doesn't solve all issues. For instance, what if the user installs a copy of a command, which is syntactically incompatible with the options specified in our script? Perhaps only part of what we utilize the utility for in our script actually works with the user's app. In such case, our script would certainly execute abnormally, at best merely failing to execute, but in a worst-case scenario, the side effects could certainly prove to be damaging. For this reason, you may want to allow only a specific binary to be utilized for the context of your script. The standard methodology to implement this is to declare full commands as variables and then call that variable instead of the command. Also, you can use the -x test to see if the command is executable:

```
#!/bin/zsh
declare networksetup =" /usr/sbin/networksetup "
if [ -x $networksetup ] ; then
       $networksetup -setv6off "Airport"
else
       echo "$networksetup is missing, is this Tiger(10.4)?"
fi
```

This practice certainly has its benefits. First, we ensure that all binary paths are hard-coded to the system defaults. Of course, ensuring that the system's default software has not been altered is outside of our control. We could certainly calculate md5 sums or check binary version output, but the risk/effort rewards really aren't there; it is perfectly sensible for our script to assume a stock software package, particularly in the context of this chapter.

The second benefit to declaring our commands is that we now have a nice list of all external commands utilized by the script, which is a great way to show our users what we are using to make our script work.

Passing Arguments to Shell Scripts

When a script is called, it can have options, much like the options present in commands you run in OS X. These commands are programmatically stored in a predefined variable called a *positional parameter*. The positional parameters are easily identified because they are $1, $2, $3, and so on, with each position the area between a space and the next input.

For example, to send a command called `foo` a variable called `bar`, you would use the command `foo bar`, which would result in being able to use the variable `$1` in the script. In the following script, we declare a number of variables and even put the target of the script and the information to change within the script; this is an example postflight script in a package installer. Apple's installer will pass these parameters to a script automatically, but you can simulate them with the following command:

```
sudo /path/to/this_script 1 2 /Volumes/Macintosh\ HD  /Volumes/
Macintosh\ HD
sudo /path/to/this_script 1 2 /Volumes/ /
```

Note We put the placeholders `1` and `2` here to stand in for what would really be passed during an install. In this case, because we don't use $1 or $2, any value here would do, just to make sure the count was right. This is a common way of testing scripts that are destined for Apple package installers.

```
#!/bin/bash
# This script removes the time machine prompt from newly
created users
# $1 and $2 are not used in this script
declare -x DSTROOT="$3"
# Installation Volume of mount point.
declare -x SYSROOT="$4"
declare defaults="/usr/bin/defaults"
"$defaults" write "$PLIST" 'DoNotOfferNewDisksForBackup' -bool
'YES' &&
echo "$PLIST updated successfully"
exit 0
```

Many do some of these tasks in profiles now, but it's good to understand how they might be done both at a shell and with a profile. The shell environment and some of the other included scripting languages such as perl, python, and ruby provide a great environment for automating tasks in macOS. These tasks are useful for setting up systems as well as testing that various configurations that were set up work once the setup has been complete. Earlier in the book, we looked at automating tasks through agents, Mobile Device Management (MDM), automated software deployment, configuration management, and automated provisioning. A little bit of testing that these configurations are as intended will go a long way in making sure that the devices work as intended. This keeps the total cost of ownership of systems low by thwarting troublesome service desk tickets and keeps users happy knowing that their administrators have their backs.

Now that we've looked at some basic shell scripting, we'll turn our attention to testing. While we will get into more automated testing, we'll start with manual testing and documenting what you will test.

Manual Testing

Organizations typically start testing programs when they grow to a few dozen devices. At this point, there's usually one person with access to a spare machine who tests new stuff when it's released. As the organization (or Apple team within the organization) grows and as people in that organization get bit by bad upgrades, you will invariably need more maturity prior to releasing major releases and then point releases and app updates than randomly clicking around and seeing if you broke something.

Build a Test Matrix

The first and easiest step is to start with a spreadsheet. The spreadsheet starts simple but usually gets much more complex. To save time, the spreadsheet is a cost-effective means of documenting what tests you will run and providing some metadata around those tests. These are some columns to consider putting in your spreadsheet:

- **Test**: A name for you to easily identify the test being run, often something like "Verify device can print to the nearest printer."
- **Category**: A group for test. Examples might include Wi-Fi, Accessibility, application titles, preferences, Dock, etc.
- **Date**: Identify when the test was run for that version being tested.
- **Impact**: The impact is how many people are impacted should a release go out with a defect. A 1 to 5 value is usually sufficient. If you have 10,000 users and all would be impacted in the case that the given test has a defect, then the impact score should be a 5. If 2 people might be impacted, then the impact score might be a 1 (unless it's your boss).
- **Risk**: Risk is usually a numeric value. It's a good idea to keep the number with smaller increments like one through five, and the risk is based on the likelihood something will go wrong.
- **Priority**: This would usually be another 1 to 5 score, but the priority should set the order you resolve issues.

- **Steps**: This is important as it will feed your automated testing some day when you can do that. The steps are a detailed list of steps to recreate the desired result. This could be a numbered list, and it's a good idea to make them so simple an intern can do them, mostly because you'll probably want to hire an intern to do them when you can move on to automated testing.
- **Model columns**: Here, you list each model supported. Not every environment can have dedicated testing equipment for each model, but it's important to note that.
- **Status**: Based on all the rows, does the test pass or fail? This can be a Boolean or the words "pass" and "fail".
- **Tester**: Some organizations with larger testing teams also have each person doing the test add their name or initials to each test they run.
- **Notes**: If a test failed, notes would help go back and investigate later (especially in teams where one person is testing and another is doing the work to resolve issues that are encountered).

Not all columns are required for everyone. You might start with just a name, steps, status, and notes. Keep it simple at first and don't spend too much time doing unnecessary data entry where you don't have to. The primary objective is to be methodical.

The most important part is to outline the tests as simple walk-throughs. An example of how to structure one would be

- Open Microsoft Word.
- Click the Font selection in the toolbar.

- Select the "Copperplate" font.
- Make sure text appears in the Copperplate when typing.

Another example would be to check that the device can get on the Internet without configuring any network settings, that the correct default browser is configured, and that the correct default home page loads:

- Open Safari.
- Verify that the wireless SSID is set to ACME.
- Verify that `www.krypted.com` loads.
- Verify you aren't prompted to set the default browser.
- Check that the browser history is empty.

Yes, we added to check the browser history. The preceding test is testing a number of things. By validating the SSID and connectivity on that SSID, we also make sure that 802.1x is correctly configured, that certificates are obtained properly, that the automation to set the default home page is functioning, that installing a second and third browser hasn't changed the default browser, and that there's no cruft in the browser history. The fewer paths to check, the more efficient the testing.

The manual testing spreadsheet then grows over time. Every time there's a failure, a row is likely to be added to the spreadsheet. No environment will have a 100% coverage for manual testing but expect support incidents to drop as you build out more and more tests. And the very act of building a matrix is likely to force you to plan time in each update to do testing and keep the well-being of the people who have to use the systems you build front and center.

If you're doing it right, at some point, the tests will take too long. That's when you know it was time to start building out an automated testing environment a while ago.

Automated Testing

When creating a large number of images, MDM configurations, app integration options, and other custom configurations, testing each one can be critical to verifying a successful deployment. Each of these is a regression of a build that you will deploy to users. If you prompt your users with one dialog box in one of those builds, you might get 200 phone calls (true story). If you notice the dialog box and don't prompt users, that's a lot of calls you won't need to take, and a lot of unhappy users you won't have to deal with.

Graphical-Based Testing

Automated testing comes in a few forms. The most straightforward (or least technical) form of testing is going through the process manually and seeing what happens when you try to do a number of predefined tasks. Doing so requires having a testing system that you can reimage as needed. But manually testing images may give only a fraction of what can be done in the same amount of time if the process is automated. If you have a well-regimented image and software deployment environment, the results of testing against specific known configurations typically provide an early warning sign of problems in the image or a specific build of a package.

There are a few different solutions for macOS that can be used for regression testing. Two that we recommend are Eggplant Functional and Sikuli. Eggplant is primarily used to test software applications during development but can also be used for this purpose. Regression testing is mostly useful in larger environments, with a large number of builds. Not only can it be used to qualify combinations of different settings applied to a system, but regression testing can also be leveraged to qualify updates for release. By automating various testing tasks, you can often quickly reduce the change and release management times for new software and operating systems. Eggplant is a tool available at `www.Eggplant.com`.

Eggplant uses VNC to run checks on the remote systems and then recognizes events based on known, predefined patterns. If the pattern is a match, then the test is a pass; if not, it is a fail. Because Eggplant uses VNC, it comes with the VINE server, although you can use ARD as well if you've enabled VNC in your ARD configuration. Eggplant is pretty straightforward once you get started, allowing you to define visual patterns in the form of screenshots and letting Eggplant click those for an expected result.

You can also use a tool like Sikuli, which is a free alternative to Eggplant and doesn't have as many features. Sikuli is available at `http://sikuli.org`. Sikuli can do the same but doesn't require VNC. Sikuli uses jython (a mix of Java and Python) to provide a rich framework for scripting regression testing. For example, you can have Sikuli or Eggplant open Word and check to see whether those specific fonts from our earlier examples are in the list of available fonts. In addition to verifying that fonts load, you can test pretty much anything else you might want. And you can run these tests without touching a system, allowing you to define test cases and then perform quality assurance (QA) on your image prior to deploying that image to client computers en masse.

There are several tools that can be used for automated testing, some of which can even be used with a fairly high amount of regression testing. Before you get overly committed to any single tool, test each and think through the cost vs. the amount of time you feel each could save you:

- **Squish**: `www.froglogic.com/squish/`
- **Eggplant**: `https://Eggplant.io`
- **Sikuli**: `http://sikulix.com`
- **Selenium browser automation**: `www.seleniumhq.org`

It's worth mentioning that the Observer Effect is real in automated QA testing. In order to run tests through Eggplant, you need to install a VNC server. In order to run Sikuli tests, you need to install a runtime. These are changes on systems and we've seen them alter the outcome of tests. It's better than nothing, but it's a real thing to consider when planning your automated testing environment. And it sure beats not noticing a screen when manual testing and feeling like crap when a bunch of people can't log in to their computer.

Now that we've covered some basics around automated testing, let's build an actual test using one of these tools, starting with Sikuli.

Sikuli

Sikuli uses actions taken via screenshots to run automated tests. To use Sikuli, first download it from `https://raiman.github.io/SikuliX1/downloads.html` and then open the .jar file. Also download the Jython.jar and the Jruby.jar. These all need to be put into the same directory before you open the sikulix.jar. Opening Sikuli can then be done by simply double-clicking the file or using the command line as follows:

```
java -jar path-to/sikulix.jar
```

There may be a version number in the name of the .jar file. Additionally, add Sikuli to the Accessibility and Screen Recording list of apps in the Privacy & Security System Settings pane.

Sikuli then prompts to open. Once Sikuli opens, it looks like a typical (although simple) IDE, but without a ton of features as with a tool like IntelliJ. What you do have that you don't see in a lot of other IDEs is the ability to "Take screenshots" as seen in Figure 9-1.

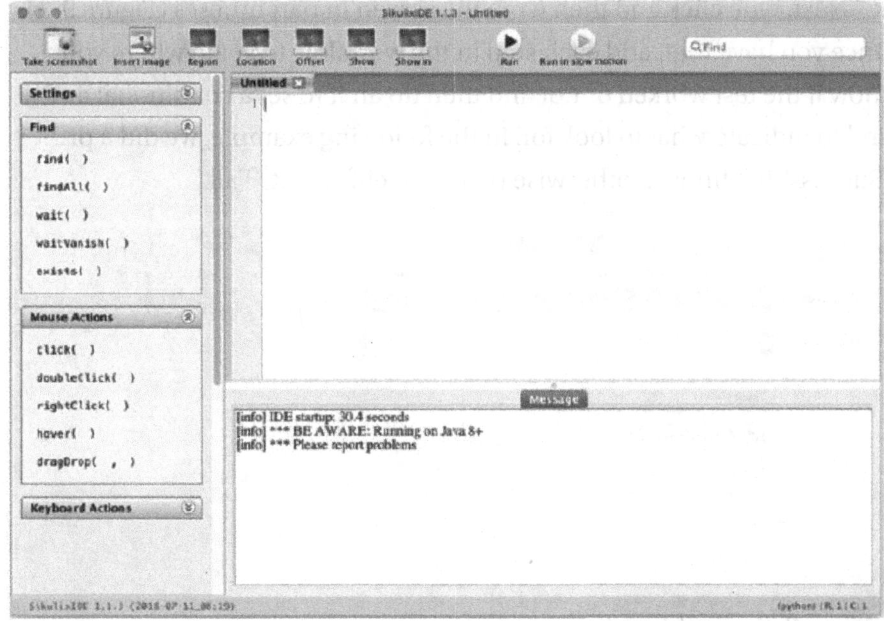

***Figure 9-1.** Start your Sikuli script*

To create our first test, click Take screenshot and make a screenshot of the area to click (Figure 9-2).

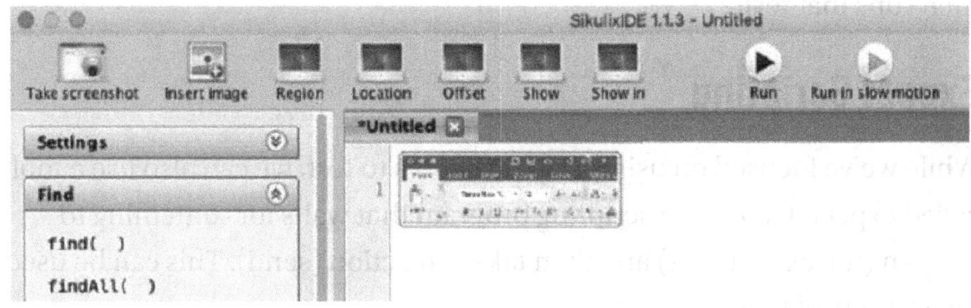

***Figure 9-2.** Import an image*

Next, type click and then wrap the screen in parentheses (Figure 9-3). Once you have that, add each step in the workflow to get to where you know if the test worked or not and then do an if to set a conditional and a find to indicate what to look for. In the following example, we did a print "Success" if it finds it; otherwise (using an elif) print "Fail."

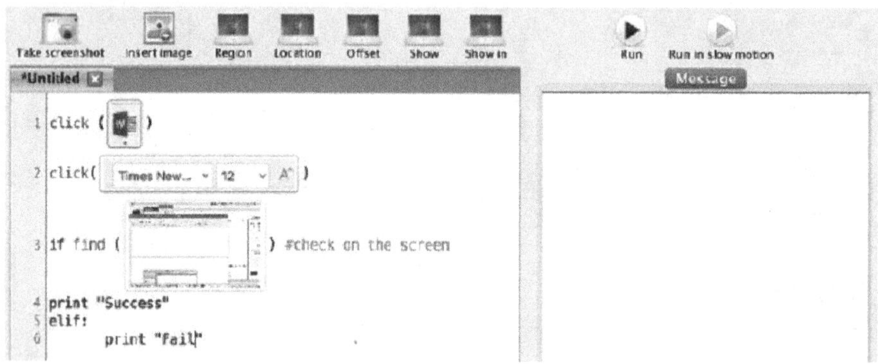

***Figure 9-3.** Building the script*

The script can then be called directly, and each test can be set up as a basic script. One nice way of tracking these is to have a column in your manual testing matrix with the file location or name of each script that then runs that test.

Expect Scripting

While we've focused on using graphical tools to test, we can also use a tool called expect. Expect is a scripting program that waits for something to happen (the expect part) and then takes an action (send). This can be used for a variety of tasks.

In this example, we're connecting to a remote server using SSH and running a command which doesn't need root privileges. As part of the SSH login, we must provide the password to the account via an interactive prompt. The following script will gather the server address, username, password, and the remote command and run the desired actions using an expect block. Expect will watch for the password prompt to appear and then automatically provide the account's password when that prompt appears:

```
#!/bin/bash

# Set the SSH address.
read -p "Please enter the address of the remote server you want
to connect to : " ssh_address
# Set the SSH username
read -p "Please enter your user account : " ssh_user
# Set the SSH password
read -p "Please enter the password for the $ssh_user account:"
-s ssh_password

# At the prompt, enter the command that
# you want to run on the remote machine.
echo ""
read -p "Enter the command you want to run on the remote
server: " ssh_command

sshpassword=${ssh_password} expect -c "
    spawn -noecho ssh ${ssh_user}@${ssh_address} ${ssh_command}
    expect \"*assword*\"
    send \$env(sshpassword)\r
    expect eof
"
```

This script assumes that all information was entered correctly, or you may see failures. When scripting automation for any platform, one should test all scripts – especially if you aren't specifically invoking them through /bin/bash. Many of these changes won't be very impactful. Maybe you'll have to get used to something working just a tiny bit differently when you're interactively navigating through the shell; no big deal. But for scripting, definitely consider the globbing whatnot as something to look out for and know that if it breaks a script, rather than just calling bash to run, think about moving it over to the new default shell, because it's this way for a reason. And that reason probably isn't just that some developer didn't like the story or acting in *The Bourne Legacy* (although it might have been that bad).

Posting Issues to Ticketing Systems

If any tests fail, you can automatically create tickets to resolve any issues found. To do so, we'll use the command line to create Jira tickets (although many organizations use different ticketing systems). In the following one-liner, we're going to bring in some standard json and create a ticket. We'll use curl and use -u to define a username and password, then -X to define a POST, and –data to define the contents of the post, wrapped in the following single quotes. Then -H defines the content type as json and a URL to your Jira rest endpoint, "Issues" in the following code:

```
curl -D- -u krypted:MySuperSecretPassword -X POST --data
'{"fields":{"project":{"key": "TESTING"},"summary":
"Make my feature better.","description": "Going to make
everything better ever ever ever by doing things and
by things I mean allll the things","customfield_001":"
Testing testing","issuetype": {"name": "Story"}{"time
tracking":{originalEstimate": "2d 4h"}}}' -H "Content-
Type: application/json" https://krypted.atlassian.net/rest/
api/2/issue/
```

We'll cover other curl examples later in this chapter. You can swap out the json here with input to a script or a file. That json can look prettier than it looks in the preceding single line:

```
{
 "fields":{
   "project":
   {
    "key": "TESTING"
   },
   "summary": "Make my feature better.",
"description": "Going to make everything better ever ever ever
by doing things and by things I mean allll the things",
   "customfield_001":"Testing testing",
   "issuetype": {
    "name": "Story"
   }
   {
    "time tracking":{
    originalEstimate": "2d 4h"
   }
  }
}
```

As you can see, we're creating an issue in the TESTING project (which could also say ISSUE_RESOLUTION or whatever was generated when you created the project you're putting this issue into). We're then adding a "summary" and "description" as I don't think you can really create one without that information. Then we're adding information for a custom field our organization created and finally an estimate for how long the task should take, with those being optional.

Any other fields available can also be created (including custom Jira fields). Just add them to the correct part of the json with the correct label and inputs to accept. By automating as much of the build train as possible, you can then repeat your tests numerous times and deploy builds with maximum test coverage and a minimum of human interaction.

You can also link your device management platform up to Jira. AirWatch comes with a built-in connector (per `https://docs.vmware.com/en/VMware-AirWatch/9.3/vmware-airwatch-guides-93/GUID-AW93-MF_CG_Add_Connectors.html`), and one can be manually configured to work with Jamf Pro (see `http://krypted.com/jamf/node-plugin-embed-device-details-jamf-pro-jira-service-desk/`). In fact, now that computers are so easy to fix and even many large-scale deployment concerns are known quantities, the ability to string workflows together across vendors is likely one of the most exciting parts of the IT industry. Because we want to test against as many regressions as possible, we'll look at simulating environments with tools built into Xcode in the next section.

Simulating iOS Environments with the Xcode Simulator

The iOS simulator is a great way to test watchOS, tvOS, and iOS apps while writing them. The easiest way to work with the simulator is through Xcode. But you can also use simctl for interacting with it, helpful in automating QA operations when possible. The simctl binary is located at /Applications/Xcode.app/Contents/Developer/usr/bin/simctl and typically accessed as a verb from the /usr/bin/xcrun command.

First, let's list all the simulators, done using the list command, called by simply running xcrun followed by simctl for the type of operation to be run and then the list command:

```
/usr/bin/xcrun simctl list
```

The output shows a lot of device types, runtimes, and devices. The help subcommand shows all of the verbs available:

```
/usr/bin/xcrun simctl help
```

Notice there are a lot of verbs for simctl. These include the following:

- `addmedia`: Add photos and videos to a device's library.
- `boot`: Start a device.
- `create`: Create a new device.
- `clone`: Clone an existing device.
- `upgrade`: Upgrade a device to a newer runtime.
- `delete`: Delete a device or all unavailable devices.
- `pair`: Create a new watch and phone pair.
- `unpair`: Unpair a watch and phone pair.
- `pair_activate`: Set a given pair as active.
- `erase`: Erase a device's contents and settings.
- `shutdown`: Shut down a device.
- `rename`: Rename a device.
- `getenv`: Print an environment variable from a running device.
- `openurl`: Open a URL in a device.
- `install`: Install an app on a device.
- `uninstall`: Uninstall an app from a device.
- `get_app_container`: Print the path of the installed app's container.
- `launch`: Launch an application by identifier on a device.

- `terminate`: Terminate an application by identifier on a device.
- `spawn`: Spawn a process by executing a given executable on a device.
- `list`: List available devices, device types, runtimes, or device pairs.
- `icloud_sync`: Trigger iCloud sync on a device.
- `pbsync`: Sync the pasteboard content from one pasteboard to another.
- `pbcopy`: Copy standard input onto the device pasteboard.
- `pbpaste`: Print the contents of the device's pasteboard to standard output.
- `help`: Print the usage for a given subcommand.
- `io`: Set up a device IO operation.
- `diagnose`: Collect diagnostic information and logs.
- `logverbose`: Enable or disable verbose logging for a device.

Managing Simulated Devices

Before you can start simulating operations, a simulated device is required. Let's boot a fresh new spiffy simulator of iPhone 13. To do so, we'll use the UUID string for the listing that includes iPhone 13 after the boot option:

```
/usr/bin/xcrun simctl boot A2F29921-785A-4AD8-8353-D3C64C6C2F91
```

The output includes a UUID such as the following. That can then be used to track further interactions with the simulation:

```
A2F29921-785A-4AD8-8353-D3C64C6C2F91
```

The most common tasks would be booting, shutting down, erasing, and opening simulations. To shut that same simulator down, use the shutdown verb:

```
/usr/bin/xcrun simctl shutdown A2F29921-785A-4AD8-8353-
D3C64C6C2F91
```

Neither of these commands provide any output on success, but do error on failure. Once you've run tests, I like to erase my simulator and start fresh. To do so, simply use the erase command:

```
/usr/bin/xcrun simctl erase A2F29921-785A-4AD8-8353-
D3C64C6C2F91
```

To open the simulator you loaded, you can use the open Simulator.app:

```
open /Applications/Xcode.app/Contents/Developer/Applications/
Simulator.app/
```

Copy Content into the Simulator

macOS comes with a handy tool to interact with the clipboard (a.k.a. pasteboard) on a Mac called pbcopy. You can redirect information from a file into your clipboard using the pbcopy command.

Here, we'll simply call pbcopy and then a file path:

```
pbcopy ~/Desktop/transfer.txt
```

You can then redirect your text into simctl by doing a pbpaste into

```
xcrun simctl pbpaste booted
```

Once the data is copied, clean up the transfer file:

```
rm ~/Desktop/transfer.txt
```

It's also possible to pull text out. Write data into the clipboard (e.g., during instrumentation) so it can be extracted from that pasteboard with the simctl subcommand pbcopy as follows:

```
xcrun simctl pbcopy booted
```

We could also install apps, run instrumentation tests, view information coming from the device, view detailed logs, sync a device with iCloud, and more. iOS can be difficult to run various tests. But given the number of automations we've gone through in this section, if you need to test deployments, you should have plenty of tools at your disposal. Many an automation build train needs to test functionality at scale or across more regressions than what you might be able to test with what a simulator can do when run in Xcode. There are some other, fairly accessible tools that can be used to simulate and even delve deeper into iOS including Corellium.

API Orchestration

Orchestrating events with APIs starts with API documentation. In this example, we'll be working with the ZuluDesk API, and we'll start by reading `http://api.zuludesk.com/docs/` to better understand how to work with the API. Each tool you use will have API documentation, hopefully automatically generated as each build of their software is generated – making it straightforward to watch their URLs to know when changes might break automations you build.

Use cURL to Work with APIs

Using information from the API documentation, we'll go ahead and use a basic tool like curl to learn some basic uses of that API. The curl command can be used to authenticate to an API using a variety of authentication types such as Bearer, OAuth, Token, and of course Basic. To authenticate to the ZuluDesk API, first create an API token. This is done by logging in to ZuluDesk, clicking Organization, then Settings, then API, and then clicking the Add API Key button. Once you have your API key, your header will look as follows:

```
GET /users HTTP/1.1 User-Agent: curl/7.24.0 X-Server-Protocol-
Version: 2 Authorization: Basic YOURTOKENHERExxx000111222==
Content-Length: 0
```

The curl command can do this, would simply convert these into separate values in the -H or header. The URL provided will do a GET against devices, displaying a list of devices in json:

```
curl -S -i -k -H "Content-Length: 0" "User-Agent: curl/7.24.0"
X-Server-Protocol-Version: 2" "Authorization: Basic
YOURAPITOKENxx000111222==" https://apiv6.zuludesk.com/devices/
```

Once you have the "serialNumber," you can programmatically perform a number of other tasks using a POST. Another example would be obtaining a list of apps, done using the /apps/ endpoint:

```
curl -S -i -k -H "Content-Length: 0" "User-Agent: curl/7.24.0"
X-Server-Protocol-Version: 2" "Authorization: Basic
YOURAPITOKENxx000111222" https://apiv6.zuludesk.com/apps/
```

You can also run a POST in the same fashion. In the following, we'll do that, sending a simple delete command to the group 505:

```
curl -X DELETE -S -i -k -H "Content-Length: 0" "User-Agent:
curl/7.24.0" X-Server-Protocol-Version: 2" "Authorization:
Basic YOURAPITOKENxx000111222" https://apiv6.zuludesk.com/
users/groups/:505
```

Use Postman to Work with APIs

Postman is a tool that is a must-have for people who work with APIs these days. Given that more and more development work is basically working with REST APIs, Postman has gotten popular enough to warrant a $50,000,000 investment shortly before the release of this book. Despite the investment money, the tasks we'll use Postman for in this section are free, and organizations likely don't need to cut a check to the company unless they're doing much more than an individual would do.

To get started with Postman, download the app at `www.getpostman.com/downloads/`. Once downloaded, extract the zip file, drag the app to /Applications, and open it. You'll then see a screen that shows a number of options. As you can see in Figure 9-4, the left sidebar provides a history of API commands you've run, collections of APIs you've created (or downloaded from a vendor who published their collection), and APIs (a beta feature that allows you to sync your collections into the Postman cloud).

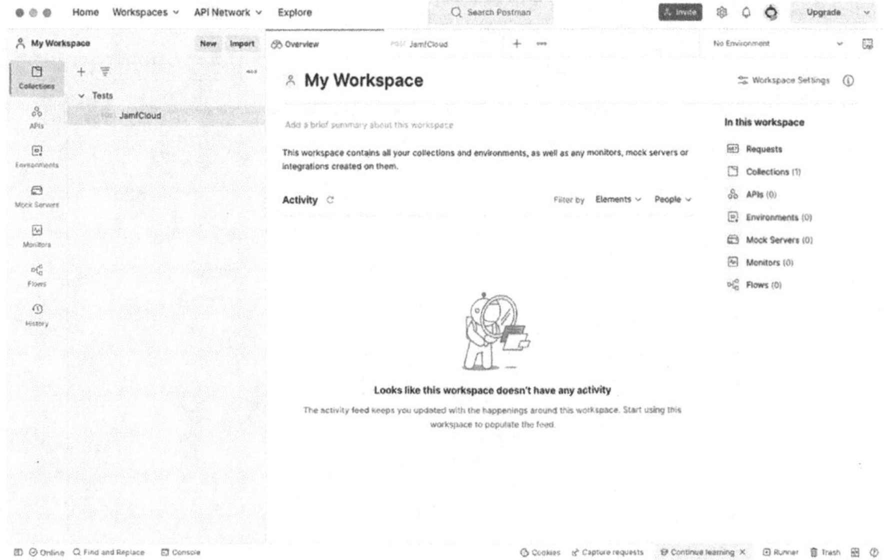

Figure 9-4. *Postman*

Think of the right side as a single API command, where you are defining which CRUD operation you are performing (GET, POST, PUT, DELETE, or other HTTP verbs supported by your API). Select a type of operation to perform and then provide a URL. If you are just retrieving information from an API you don't need to authenticate to, then you can just hit Send and see the response, usually in JSON.

Below that, you have tabs for Parameters, Authentication, Headers, Body, etc. Each of these is defining the various parts of that operation you are performing. First, let's click Authentication. As you can see in Figure 9-5, if the API you are connecting to supports basic authentication, this can be as simple as providing a username and password. However, many support more modern authentication types such as JWT, bearer tokens, and OAuth. For this specific API, we'll just use that username and password.

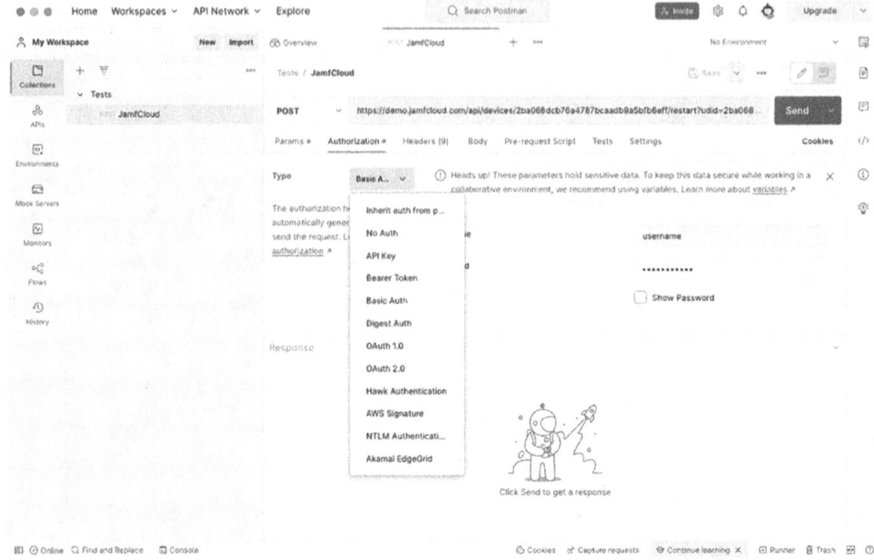

Figure 9-5. *Authenticating to a REST endpoint*

Click the Params tab to configure parameters you'll send to the device. Next, we're going to clear the passcode of a device. Because we're taking an action rather than just getting information (e.g., using a GET), the type of CRUD operation we're running against the URL of this command has changed to a POST. The URL includes the URL to that specific device and then a restart endpoint. Anything after the ? in that URL is a parameter, and we'll define a udid and clearPasscode. The reason for the udid is that per API documentation we know that any time you issue a wipe command on an iOS device, you also have to specify if you also want to clear the passcode of that device (Figure 9-6).

Figure 9-6. Parameters in a POST

One of the best parts of Postman is being able to trade collections with people at work or find them on the Internet. Postman has a network of API collections that are produced by the vendors you might want to automate tasks with. These are available at `www.getpostman.com/api-network/`. Additionally, you can find postman collections for a number of other vendors fairly easily. Some common integrations you might want to build off of are as follows:

- **Ping Identity**: `https://apidocs.pingidentity.com/pingone/customer/v1/api/guide/p1_sampleApps`
- **Jamf Pro**: `https://github.com/jamf/Classic-API-Postman-Collection`
- **Okta**: `https://developer.okta.com/docs/reference/postman-collections/`
- **MobileIron**: `http://downloads.skypeshield.com/downloads/Utils/Postman/MobileIron.zip`
- **BlackBerry**: `http://downloads.skypeshield.com/downloads/Utils/Postman/Blackberry.zip`

- **VMware**: https://blogs.vmware.com/management/2017/05/vrealize-automation-api-samples-for-postman.html
- **Box**: https://developer.box.com/docs/box-postman-collection
- **IBM MobileFirst**: https://mobilefirstplatform.ibmcloud.com/tutorials/en/foundation/8.0/adapters/testing-and-debugging-adapters/
- **Jira Service Cloud**: https://developer.atlassian.com/cloud/jira/service-desk/rest/
- **Confluence**: https://developer.atlassian.com/cloud/confluence/rest/

If you use a tool that has a standard RESTful API, and they don't have a Postman collection for it, then I'm sure they'd be happy to work with you to build one. This book isn't meant to go through hooking automations up between all of the APIs for every vendor you might use. Now that you see how developers communicate between one another when building integrations, hopefully you realize that every single task you need to perform routinely can be automated and consistent.

Release Management

The reason we're doing all this testing and automated testing is so that when we're done with our scripts and automations, we want to be able to make changes on hundreds or thousands or hundreds of thousands of devices at the same time. Release management is referred to as the processes to schedule, plan, manage, and control the release of software through different stages and environments. The first of those environments is when that software is being developed. Most of the rest of this book is about what to do with that software in an organization that consumes the technology once it goes to market. Understanding earlier parts of that build train is useful, especially if you want to future-proof parts of your deployment as various scripty bits get removed from macOS.

These days, we think of the word "release" a little less. Instead, we're moving into a world of continuous integration and continuous delivery (yet another industry acronym as CICD). Tools like Jira allow you to integrate with other tools that complete the automation of your testing matrix. Yes, it's a whole domino of workflows that's just one REST call after another. There are tons of great books on CICD and release management. Most are specific to a given technology stack, with some including

- **Travis**: `https://travis-ci.org/`
- **Jenkins**: `www.jenkins.io`
- **Atlassian's Bamboo**: `www.atlassian.com/software/bamboo`
- **Harness**: `http://harness.io/`
- **Shippable**: `www.shippable.com/` (now a part of JFrog)
- **Spinnaker**: `www.spinnaker.io/`
- **AWS CodePipeline**: `https://aws.amazon.com/codepipeline`
- **Fastlane**: `https://fastlane.tools`
- **GitLab CI/CD**: `https://about.gitlab.com/direction/cicd/`

A number of vendors also offer interfaces to their tools with git. This makes it simple to hook workflows together that result in journaled, approval-driven business processes that make managing devices look a little more like managing code. Tools like Munki are built from the ground up using these kinds of techniques, as you can see at `https://github.com/munki/munki/wiki/Munki-With-Git`. Other tools require a bit more finessing, and you won't likely have full coverage of everything the product can do. The git2jss (`https://github.com/badstreff/git2jss`) would be an example of that kind of situation, given not everything the creators want to do is supported by the APIs they work with.

Another aspect of automation is making sure that everything a build requires is where it needs to be. There are a number of tools that aid in this endeavor, which include one of the more popular repository managers, Artifactory from JFrog (`https://jfrog.com/artifactory/`). Gathering all of those dependencies, especially given how frequently many tools update, can be a bear, although the transition from tools like Carthage to Swift packages can make it far simpler for Apple developers.

Summary

Ultimately, the most important takeaway from this chapter would be to get comfortable using the command line to troubleshoot issues on your devices and then to introduce a testing program at your organization. Testing programs should start simple to garner quick wins. Until a team grows to the point that not having an appropriate level of processes and procedures starts to become a problem, do not get bogged down with unnecessary dogma and technology. If a spreadsheet works for you and an intern is cheaper than the combination of the cost of buying software and the cost of spending the time to build a QA infrastructure, use an intern.

More important than the techniques and tools we looked at in this chapter is the concept and the understanding that you will be continuously testing. Apple has gotten very, very efficient at developing and pushing out changes using the existing build train. A list of tests provides a pretty good idea of how much automation work might be required to move to automated testing while taking immediate value from the ability to be organized about your test cases.

The matrix of required tests will grow over time and occasionally require a little pruning. Pruning can be done when features are retired. Once you have that matrix, building tests to prove that a device is in a state you want the device in is according to what you're testing. If you're an app developer, then you even have customized tools just for your specific needs (and here Apple admins can learn a lot from app developers). Given the maturity of large application development organizations, you can even anchor your build train, whether that uses GitHub or a device management solution, to a vast ecosystem of REST endpoints that tickle one another across the globe.

Focusing on the full process, you want to get to a place where an app or package is built automatically using a tool like AutoPkg, then automated tests are completed, and then manual tests are completed. Once those are done, you can automate your release cycle, making it possible for more and more users to have their own regressions without sending you to retirement early - or at least, until Apple blocks all synthetic clicking and scripts. But that's pretty far out in the future, right?

Now that we've covered testing, let's look at how we get a user authenticated into computers in Chapter 10, when we start that journey with directory services.

CHAPTER 10

Directory Services

A directory service is a centralized service used to locate and access resources on a network. For the purposes of this chapter, a directory service is used to authenticate to various resources on the network and authorize a user or device to access those resources. The most widely used directory service is Microsoft's Active Directory, so most of this chapter is dedicated to Active Directory.

The Mac can tie into standard Active Directory and LDAP environments easily. In previous books about integrating the Mac into directory services, environments easily occupied three to four chapters. But a few things have happened in the past few years:

- The platform has evolved. Apple has sorted out most of the issues connecting to Active Directory environments. Now the technology used to talk to Active Directory mostly just works out of the box, including via a profile, as mentioned later in this chapter.
- The Apple community has devoted considerable time and resources documenting how to identify and resolve known challenges to integrating Macs with various directory services.

C. Edge and R. Trouton, *Apple Device Management*,
https://doi.org/10.1007/978-1-4842-9156-6_10

- Open source and commercial middleware have been developed to resolve and automate common integration scenarios.
- Open Directory, Apple's LDAP directory service included with macOS Server, has been discontinued as of macOS Monterey along with macOS Server.
- Active Directory remains important in many enterprise environments, but the methods used to allow a Mac to communicate with it have changed.
- Cloud-based directory services have become easy to implement for companies with or without legacy on-premises directory service infrastructure.
- iOS devices don't bind to Active Directory, which strengthens the argument that you should focus on integrating services and apps instead of integrating the entire device.
- People gave up the dream of having a network home folder that's accessible from any device.

Even with the changes of the past few years though, it may still be necessary to bind Macs to an Active Directory domain for a variety of reasons. These reasons may include

- Compliance with corporate policies
- Ensuring access to needed data
- Allowing multiple users to use one Mac

Let's take a look at several ways to accomplish this goal.

Manually Bind to Active Directory

The Active Directory plug-in is the easiest way to initiate a bind. When you bind, you establish a trusted relationship between your Mac and the Active Directory domain. An Active Directory account with the appropriate privileges is used to create a computer record in Active Directory and establish trust between the servers and the client. The local administrative account on the Mac creates an account on the local system and pulls down any attributes from the server as needed.

Each Mac contains a unique preshared key used to authenticate that machine to the directory. This individualistic nature is an important aspect to consider when looking at automating the process. If you are not automating this step, you will need to supply the person doing the bind with both local and directory administrator credentials.

You can provide local desktop admins with accounts that only have access to bind computers into the domain. You can also provide non-administrators with access to edit local configurations by modifying the authorization right "system.services.directory.configure" in /etc/authorization. Through the modification of this right, you can grant access to change directory settings to your non-admin users. The content of this file is considerable and goes through the specific rights of each subsystem.

Bind the Easy Way

Provided you have the appropriate credentials to bind, open the Users & Groups System Settings pane from within System Settings. Click the Users & Groups System Settings pane, as shown in Figure 10-1.

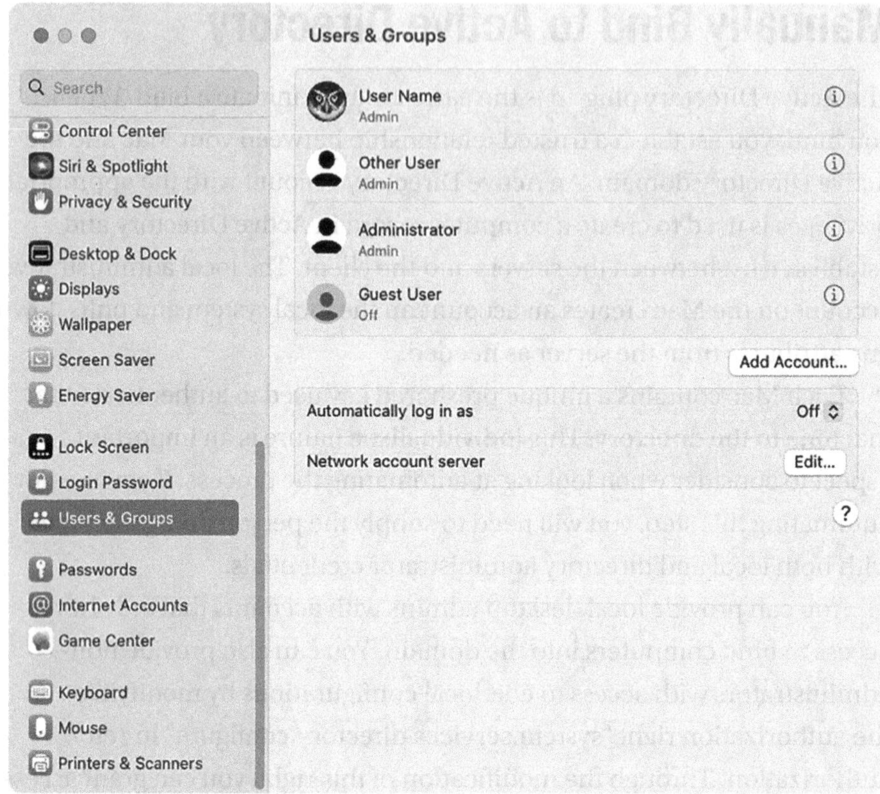

***Figure 10-1.** Click the **Edit...** button to initiate a bind*

Click the **Edit...** button beside **Network Account Server**, as seen in Figure 10-1.

This will bring up a pop-up screen that will have no servers listed. Clicking the plus button (+) will provide a field which you can use to enter an Active Directory domain name into, as seen in Figure 10-2.

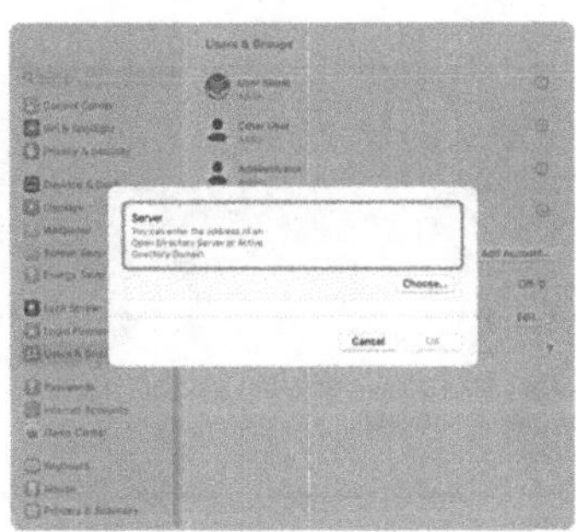

***Figure 10-2.** Enter the Active Directory domain name into the Server: field as part of the bind process*

Provided the domain name can be reached, the screen will expand. Enter the ID that the computer you are binding will have once it joins Active Directory (a.k.a. the name that will appear in the list of Computers). Also provide a username from Active Directory that can create a record in Active Directory in the AD Admin User field and the password for that account in the AD Admin Password field and hit OK (Figure 10-3).

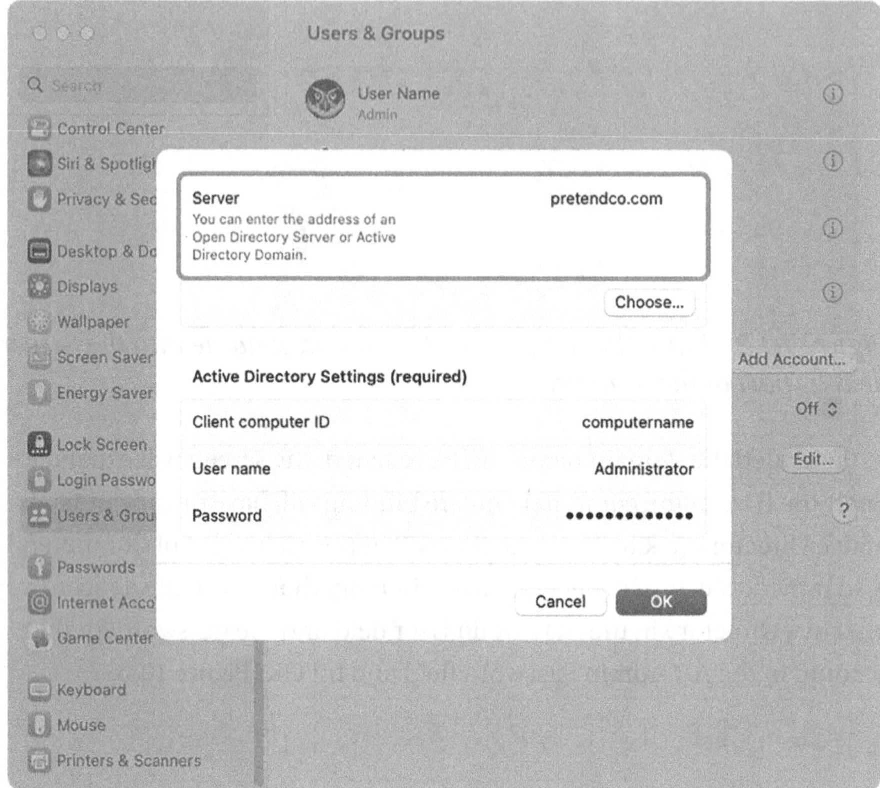

Figure 10-3. *Providing domain admin credentials as part of the bind process*

Bind with the Directory Utility

You can only bind with this simple experience if the client computer can enumerate the domain and if you don't need to leverage any of the more granular settings provided during the initial bind process. If you need either of those two, click the Open Directory Utility... button, unlock the tool, and click Services in the toolbar, as seen in Figure 10-4.

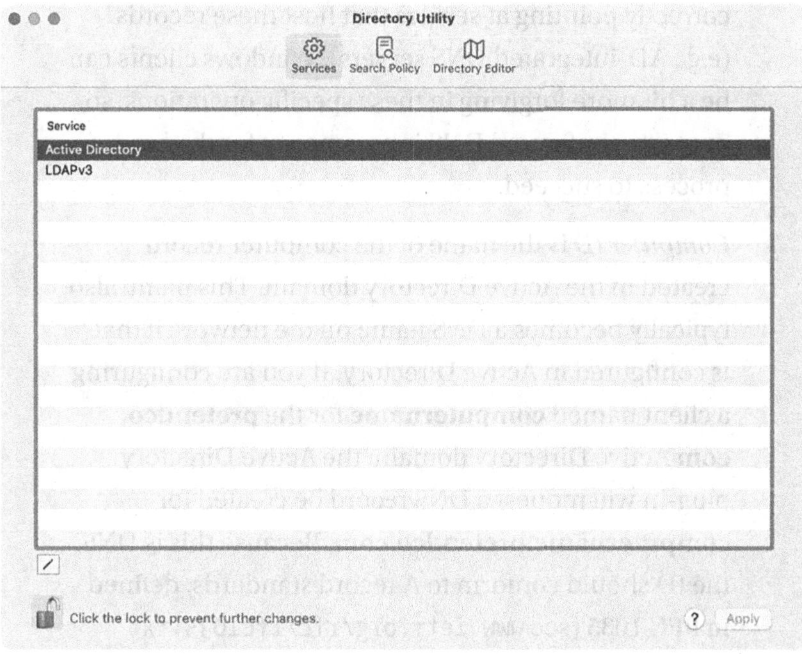

***Figure 10-4.** Services listing in Directory Utility*

Use the lock in the lower-left corner of the screen to authenticate so you can make changes and double-click the entry for Active Directory. You will then be prompted with three fields by default, which are also shown in Figure 10-5:

- *Active Directory Forest* is a setting configured automatically based on the domain name. If multiforest support is required, we will cover that in the command-line options available through dsconfigad.
- *Active Directory Domain* is the domain the active directory plug-in will use to look up the appropriate service records (SRV) to find the closest servers and complete the bind process. This relies on the client's DNS servers (usually provided by DHCP) to be

correctly pointing at servers that host these records (e.g., AD-integrated DNS servers). Windows clients can be a bit more forgiving in these specific operations, so properly configured DNS is paramount for the bind process to succeed.

- *Computer ID* is the name of the computer record created in the Active Directory domain. This name also typically becomes a DNS name on the network if that is configured in Active Directory. If you are configuring a client named **computername** for the **pretendco.com** Active Directory domain, the Active Directory plug-in will request a DNS record be created for **computername.pretendco.com**. Because this is DNS, the ID should conform to A record standards, defined in RFC 1035 (see `www.ietf.org/rfc/rfc1035.txt` for more).

Note For best results, keep computer names under 15 total characters in length. The reason for the 15-character limitation is that, on the Windows platform, NetBIOS names cannot be longer than 15 characters, and Apple's AD plug-in uses that same limitation to maximize compatibility.

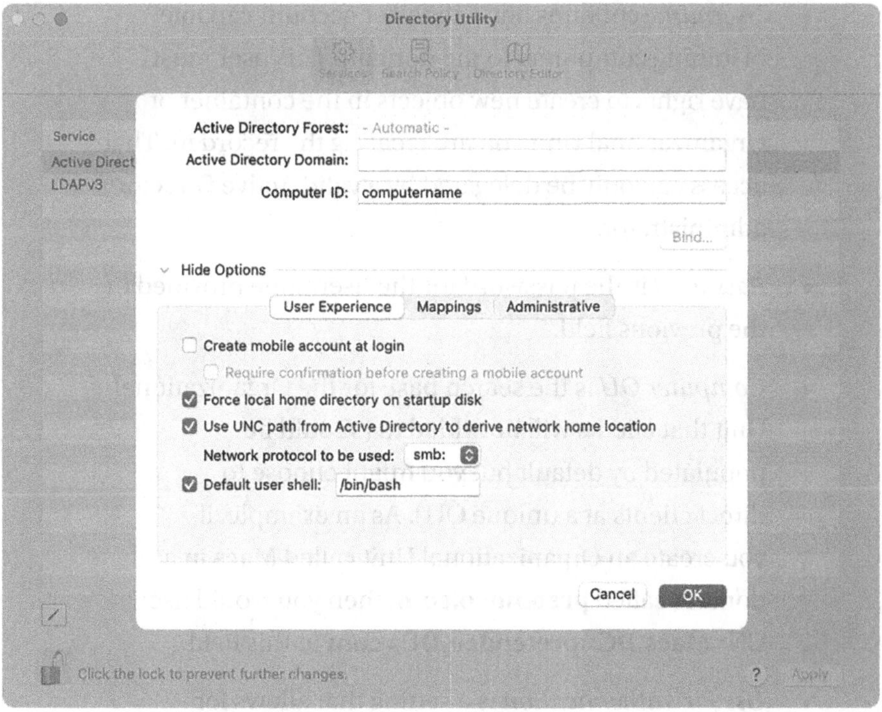

***Figure 10-5.** Bind using Directory Utility*

Note Since the computer name populates the Client ID, try to follow the LDH rule: use only ASCII alphabetic and numeric characters and a hyphen (-), but no other punctuation or characters. And don't use names with all numbers or that start with numbers when possible.

Next, click the Bind button, and you will be asked to authenticate into the Active Directory domain using the following fields, as you can see in Figure 10-6:

- *Username* contains any valid user account capable of joining computers to the domain. This user must have rights to create new objects in the container or Organizational Unit you are creating the record in. That access can only be delegated by a valid Active Directory administrator.
- *Password* is the password for the username provided in the previous field.
- *Computer OU* is the search base for the Organizational Unit that clients will be added to (should be populated by default but you might choose to direct clients at a unique OU). As an example, if you create an Organizational Unit called **Macs** in a domain called **pretendco.com**, then you would use **CN=Macs,DC=pretendco,DC=com** in this field.
- *Use for authentication* is a setting that allows for authenticating into the Mac at the login window using a valid Active Directory username and password.
- *Use for contacts* allows for searching for contacts using Address Book.

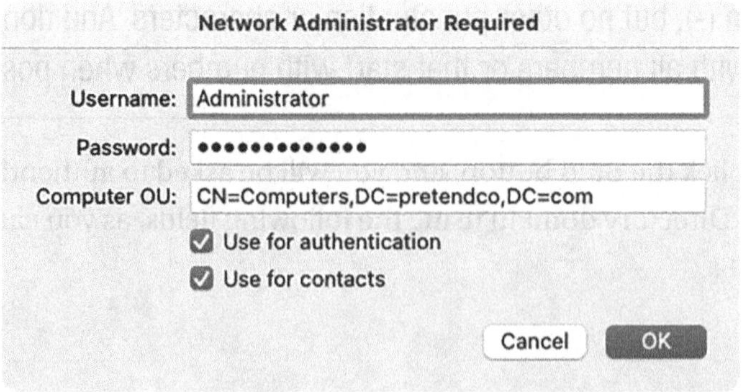

Figure 10-6. *Binding to Active Directory using Directory Utility*

The most common binding problem with Active Directory environments is with the Active Directory domain's DNS having an incomplete set of service records. If we had a nickel for every time a Windows admin swore up and down that there were no problems on their servers, only to have all problems resolved by a quick and dirty fix, we probably wouldn't be writing books. For example, an ipconfig /rebuilddns command run from a domain controller hosting the Active Directory integrated DNS to rebuild service records.

If you have not prepopulated the computer record, your computer account will be placed in the default OU, Computers. To continue with the previous **pretendco.com** example, Organizational Units are these containers, which are accessed using a convention, whereas the container is a CN followed by a DC for each part of a fully qualified domain name. Therefore, if you were to enter the **Computers** container of **mydomain.com** instead of **pretendco.com** from our previous example, you would use **cn=Computers,dc=mydomain,dc=com**.

Test Your Connection with the id Command

Once you have bound to Active Directory, it's time to test the connection. To get started, verify the light is green beside the Active Directory service listed in Directory Utility. You can also simply log in to the Mac as a user from Active Directory.

When automating, you will also need to verify binding from the command line (and should test it either way). As previously referenced, an integral part of logging in on macOS is a user account's UniqueID attribute. You can verify that user resolution is happening and view the UniqueID using the id command. To do so from a command-line environment, enter the **id** command followed by the username of a directory account:

```
id charles.edge
```

The response should appear as follows:

```
uid=1767690311(charles.edge) gid=703907591(PRETENDCO\
domain users) groups=338867591 (PRETENDCO\domain
users),5499333624(PRETENDCO\administrators)
```

The **id** command may fail with the following:

```
id: bob: no such user
```

If the command fails, verify it exists in the directory service and check the **Search Path** list in Directory Utility, which should show **Active Directory** as part of the list when everything is configured properly (Figure 10-7).

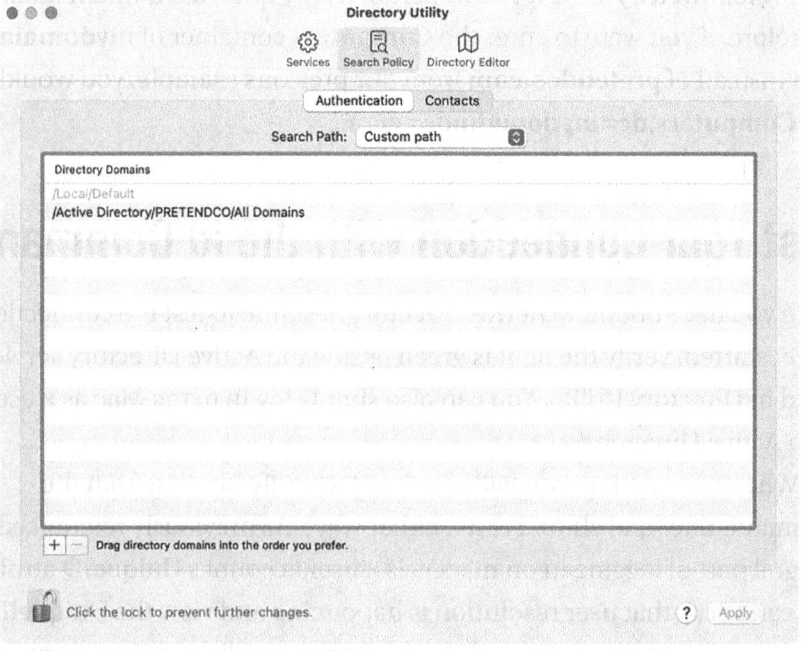

***Figure 10-7.** Check your search path listing in Directory Utility*

The Search Policy should automatically be configured during the bind process. However, if you are manually configuring or attempting to troubleshoot an automated binding, you can verify this configuration in Directory Utility. It's also possible to set the search path manually, by setting the Search Path to custom. This allows the search order to be changed and other alterations to be made as needed to the configuration. While **id** is probably the easiest tool used to check connectivity, **dscl** is a more robust tool for testing directory services.

Use dscl to Browse the Directory

The dscl command can be run interactively or from a script; we'll cover the interactive mode first. Simply run dscl to get started:

```
dscl
```

The output is a simple interactive shell:

```
Entering interactive mode... (type "help" for commands)
 >
```

The syntax for moving through the configured directory services is much like navigating around on the filesystem of a Mac from the command line. Once you have initiated your session, it will show an interactive prompt (>). Use the ls command to list the configured DirectoryService Plug-ins and then use cd to change your working directory into one.

If you do not see Active Directory listed, you are not yet bound. When you change directories with the cd command, you will need to quote in order to avoid any spaces, as follows:

```
cd 'Active Directory'
```

After you change directories into the Active Directory plug-in, you will see any domains and forests previously configured. You can only join one forest at a time.

The Apple Active Directory plug-in only allows you to configure one Active Directory forest at a time; the default behavior is to allow authentication from all domains within a forest on the local machine. This is an important note, as it means that depending on your organization's directory topology, you may not be able to see the users if you are in a separate forest. If you would like to restrict access to this computer (or server) to only one domain, you will need to uncheck the Allow authentication from any domain in the forest button in the Directory Utility or run the command dsconfigad -all domains disable, depending on your configuration. You will see either All Domains or your domain name, wallcity.org, when listing this value in dscl.

```
/Active Directory > ls
All Domains
```

To test that your binding worked correctly, you can change directory into the respective value and do an ls. You should see output similar to that shown as follows:

```
/Active Directory > cd 'All Domains'
/Active Directory/All Domains > ls
CertificateAuthorities
Computers
FileMakerServers
Groups
Mounts
People
Printers
Users
```

If you receive an error when changing directory, your Active Directory binding has most likely either failed or the current DirectoryService daemon has lost contact with your site's Domain Controller.

A common procedure used to verify connectivity is to use the dscl command along with the read verb to view the attributes associated with a given account. This will allow you to verify that user lookup is working within the Active Directory plug-in itself and look for any potential issues, such as a missing attribute. While you could ls Users, depending on the size of your organization, you may not receive all of the information that you are looking for. By default, the LDAP server in Active Directory will return a maximum of 1000 results. Although many more can be enumerated, this is just a limitation for how many are shown at once. Therefore, we will simply cd into the appropriate directory and then use read to view the attributes for a known good user account:

```
/Active Directory/All Domains > cd Users
/Active Directory/All Domains/Users > read CEDGE
dsAttrTypeNative:accountExpires: 456878888655687
dsAttrTypeNative:ADDomain: pretendco.com
dsAttrTypeNative:badPasswordTime: 0
dsAttrTypeNative:badPwdCount: 0
dsAttrTypeNative:cn:
Charles Edge
dsAttrTypeNative:codePage: 0
dsAttrTypeNative:countryCode: 0
dsAttrTypeNative:displayName:
Charles Edge
dsAttrTypeNative:distinguishedName:
CN=Charles Edge,CN=Users,DC=pretendco,DC=com
continued...
```

Caution The LDAP server in Active Directory by default will return a maximum of 1000 results. This limitation affects user, group, computer, and computer group listings in both dscl and Workgroup Manager and therefore may negatively affect any scripting automations derived from this information. This is a hard limit in Windows 2000 but can be adjusted in later versions, as instructed in the Microsoft Knowledge Base article found at `http://support.microsoft.com/kb/315071`.

One thing to keep in mind is that while viewing data from the Active Directory plug-in directly (by changing directories into it), you can verify that you have a connection to your organization's directory services. However, simply being able to view the raw directory service data does not in fact mean that you can authenticate against it. As with dsconfigldap in Chapter 2, the final step is to use the information gathered about your test user and verify that your user matches in the /Search path as well:

```
/Active Directory/All Domains/Users > read /Search/Users/cedge
dsAttrTypeNative:accountExpires: 456878097655687
dsAttrTypeNative:ADDomain: pretendco.com
dsAttrTypeNative:badPasswordTime: 0
dsAttrTypeNative:badPwdCount: 0
dsAttrTypeNative:cn:
Charles Edge
dsAttrTypeNative:codePage: 0
dsAttrTypeNative:countryCode: 0
dsAttrTypeNative:displayName:
Zack Smith
dsAttrTypeNative:distinguishedName:
CN=Charles Edge,CN=Users,DC=pretendco,DC=com
continued...
```

If the two read commands return different results, you have namespace collision, which could possibly be resolved by altering your search path. In some cases, it may be necessary to simply delete the conflicting user account. You can view the current search path with dscl along with a read verb, the path, and the attribute to display (in this case, /Search SearchPath).

```
/Active Directory > read /Search SearchPath
SearchPath:
/Local/Default
/BSD/local
/Active Directory/All Domains
/Active Directory >
```

Once you have verified that the user result is functional from the DirectoryService daemon, you can verify that authentication is correctly happening (so far, we have only verified that user resolution is possible). Type exit to end your interactive dscl session for the localhost:

```
/Active Directory/All Domains/Users > exit
Goodbye
```

Once you are bound to Active Directory, simply log in as an Active Directory user in order to test authentication. If the screen shakes and prompts you to log in again, then one of the following conditions may apply:

- The account credentials are incorrect.
- The account does not have permissions to log in to the Mac.
- The Active Directory binding is not correct.

Programmatically Binding to Active Directory

Most anything on a Mac can be managed using a command-line tool of some sort. And binding to Active Directory is certainly no different. A quick Google search is likely to net you about as many binding scripts as there are Mac Admins out there. But there are a few components that are important to understand. The first is simply checking the binding state of a Mac.

To see the Active Directory configuration on a Mac, use the **dsconfigad** command with the **-show** option:

```
dsconfigad -show
```

Here, you'll see a list of the options configured for any directories you've been bound to. To actually bind, use a command like the following (e.g., in a setup script):

```
dsconfigad -add $computername -u $username -ou "CN=Computers,
DC=pretendco,DC=com" -domain PRETENDCO -mobile enable
-mobileconfirm enable -localhome enable -useuncpath enable
-groups "Domain Admins,Enterprise Admins" -alldomains enable
```

Let's unpack the options used in the preceding command:

- **-add** adds the computer to the domain and uses the variable supplied to the script for $computername as the name for the computer that will appear in Active Directory.
- **-u** is the username of an Active Directory user with privileges to add a device into the Organizational Unit described.

- **-ou** defines the Organizational Unit the device will be placed in. If this setting is not included, then the device can still be enrolled but will be left in the default OU for your Active Directory environment.
- **-domain** defines the domain to join. In this case, that would be PRETENDCO.
- **-mobile** makes the account mobile or able to sign in when Active Directory can't be reached. This is important for laptops that will be out of the office frequently.
- **-mobileconfirm** skips the confirmation screen for Active Directory users when creating the mobile account.
- **-localhome** creates a local home directory for the user.
- **-useuncpath** sets a home directory to a path defined in Active Directory. This isn't used as much as it used to be given that devices don't sync mobile accounts to Active Directory using portable home directories like they once did.
- **-groups** defines the groups in Active Directory that are able to log in to the local computer with administrative privileges.
- **-alldomains** allows logins from any domain in the forest, if the forest has multiple domains.

Finally, you may find that you need to unbind at times. This can often be done with a simple **dsconfigad** command as well, with the following being the simplest incantation to achieve that goal (where $username and $password are variables that are variables to represent a valid local administrative username and password):

```
sudo dsconfigad -force -remove -u $username -p $password
```

You can also install a profile using a script, and the most common way that you bind Macs to Active Directory these days is using a profile. Provided your Active Directory deployment is healthy and not overly complicated, the next section will step you through how to configure a profile to bind to Active Directory.

Bind to Active Directory Using a Profile

As we've referenced throughout this book, always perform as much of the configuration on devices as possible using a profile.

Jamf Pro provides a setup similar to that used in most any management solution. The settings that you used in earlier sections, to bind to Active Directory, are now standardized and simplified in the following sections. If you can bind using the settings available via MDM, then you should, but also maybe you shouldn't do it the new way unless you know how to do it the hard way. Just in case.

To show how to bind using a profile, we'll show how to do so using Jamf Pro. This creates a standard profile that should be interpreted the same no matter which management solution you use. To get started, first open your Jamf environment and then browse to Computers and then Configuration Profiles.

Here, click Directory. At the Directory screen, you'll see a number of different settings, as seen in Figure 10-8. These include

- **Directory Type**: This section is about Active Directory so we'll select that, but you can also bind using other directory services, such as OpenLDAP.
- **Server Hostname**: The name of an Active Directory server in your domain. If you have problems connecting to a regular server, try one that has a global catalog role in the domain.

- **Username**: The name of an account in your Active Directory that has privileges to bind devices into an Active Directory domain.
- **Password**: The password to the account with privileges to bind devices.
- **Verify Password**: The password provided previously.
- **Client ID**: How the device will appear when viewing it in Active Directory.
- **Organizational Unit**: The Active Directory Organizational Unit the device will be added to when bound.

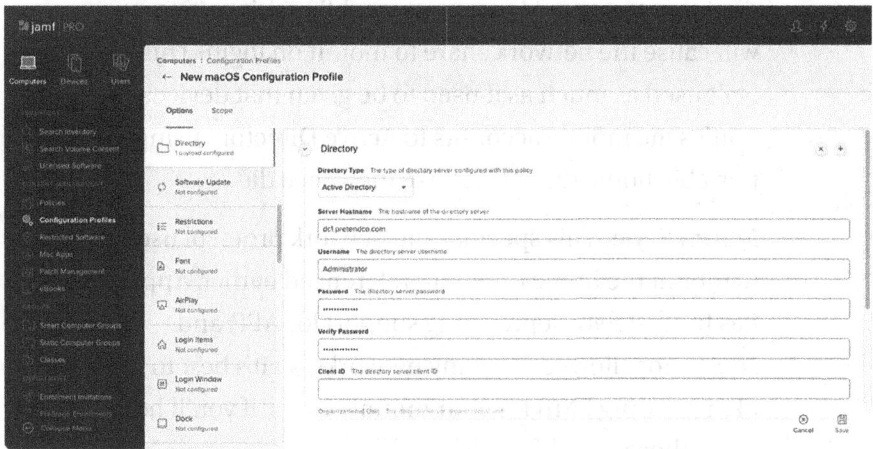

Figure 10-8. *Configuring a directory service configuration profile for macOS in Jamf Pro*

Those are the basic settings and will work for a pretty substantial percentage of environments where you're binding Macs to Active Directory. But there are some specific needs that many environments have. Next, scroll down so you can configure the more advanced options. Under the User Experience tab, you'll see the following options (Figure 10-9):

- **Create mobile account at login**: Creates an account where the login credentials are cached locally on the Mac, which enables the account to be able to log in to the Mac when Active Directory can't be reached. This is important for laptops that will be out of the office frequently.
- **Force local home directory on startup disk**: Skips the confirmation screen for Active Directory users when creating the mobile account.
- **Use UNC path from Active Directory to derive network home location**: If your account profile on the AD domain has a network share specified as a home directory for your AD account, enabling this setting will cause the network share to mount on login. This isn't used as much as it used to be given that devices don't sync mobile accounts to Active Directory using portable home directories like they once did.
- **Mount Style**: This specifies the network protocol used to mount the home directory referenced earlier. Apple has been slowly deprecating support for AFP, and NFS is not allowed on many networks, so it's best to plan on using SMB for your mount points, if you'll be using those.
- **Default User Shell**: It's usually best to leave this as is. The default setting in the profile for the user shell is /bin/bash, but can be changed to be /bin/zsh to match the default shell on macOS Catalina and later.

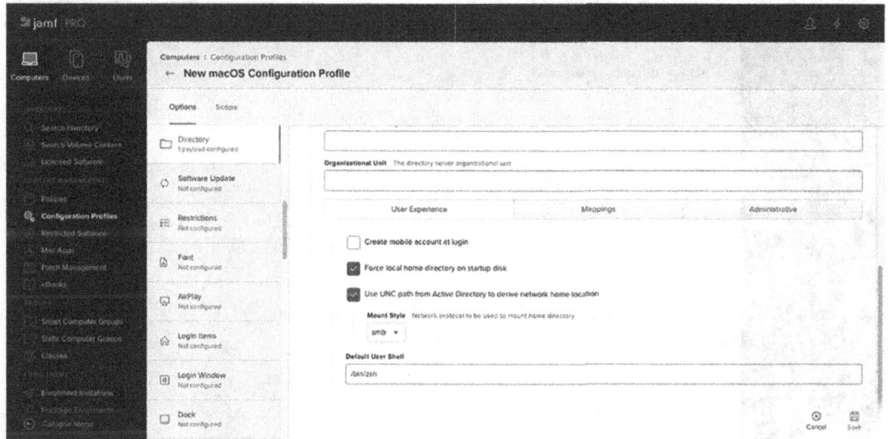

Figure 10-9. *Specifying the user experience settings for Active Directory in Jamf Pro for a directory service configuration profile for macOS*

The mappings are for more advanced scenarios and not frequently used anymore. Essentially, the unique identifiers for user accounts (or UIDs) and the generated identifiers for user and group accounts (GIDs) can be mapped to other attributes within a directory service, and these settings allow you to configure those, as you can see in Figure 10-10. These include the following:

- Map UID to attribute
- Map user GID to attribute
- Map group GID to attribute

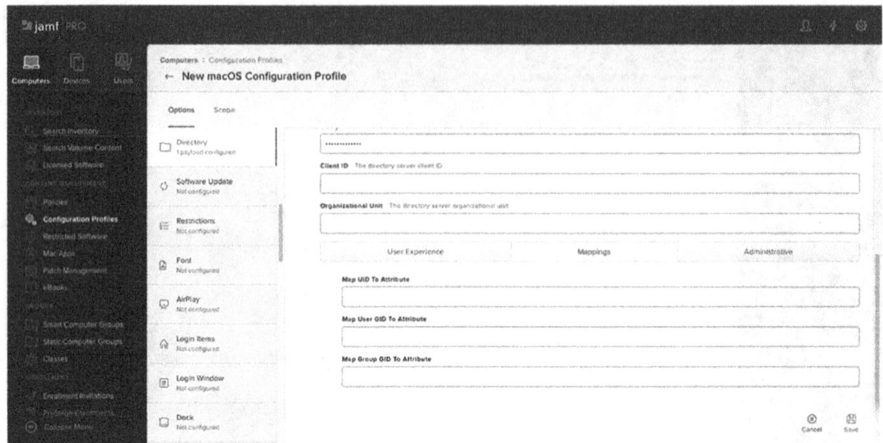

Figure 10-10. *Specifying the mapping settings for Active Directory in Jamf Pro for a directory service configuration profile for macOS*

Mappings aren't as common as they once were, but a number of administrative settings can be useful in a well-thought-out deployment. These include the following (Figure 10-11):

- Administrative
    - **Group**: An Active Directory Security Group whose members receive administrative access to devices.
    - **Allow authentication from any domain in the forest**: Allows intra-forest authentication.
    - **Namespace**: When set to forest, you have to include the domain name when authenticating.
    - **Packet signing**: Enables the packet signing option, blocking potential man-in-the-middle attacks.
    - **Packet Encryption**: When set to require, forces encryption, thus not allowing any weak settings in an Active Directory configuration to weaken the security of the Mac.

- **Restrict DDNS**: Restricts dynamic DNS registration into Active Directory–integrated DNS servers for certain interfaces (you don't typically want certain types of interfaces to register themselves into DNS, creating duplicate entries for a given computer name).
- **Password Trust Interval**: Computers can force a new computer password more frequently than might be configured in Active Directory. This setting allows you to specify a number of days to renew those passwords.

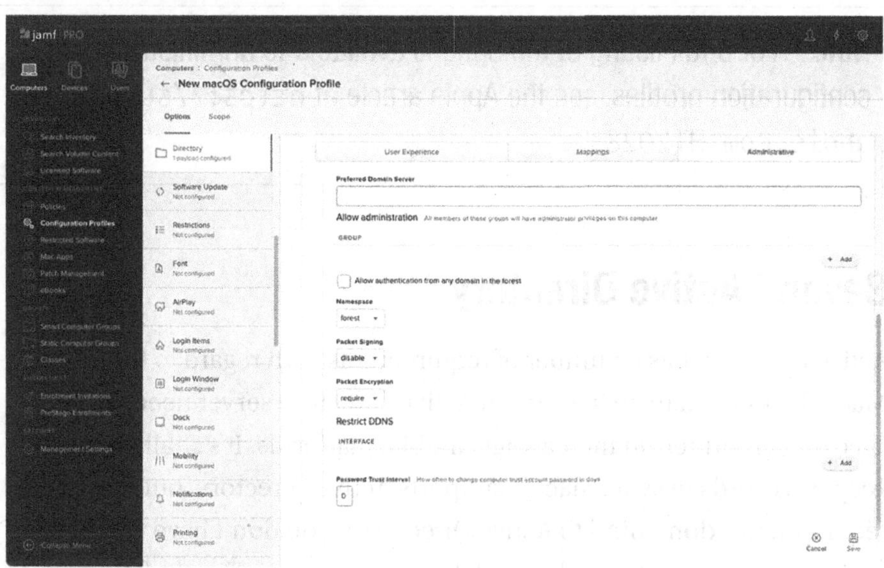

***Figure 10-11.** Specifying the administrative settings for Active Directory in Jamf Pro for a directory service configuration profile for macOS*

Once configured, click Save and then attempt to deploy the profile to client systems by scoping the profile using the Scope tab. You can scope different bind profiles to static groups, smart groups, or based on a number of other attributes, providing the ability to distribute different profiles to different sets of devices.

These options are pretty straightforward once you learn to bind client Macs from System Settings and definitely once you can use the command-line options available using dsconfigad. But now that we've mastered Active Directory, in the next sections, we'll dig into how to get away from using Active Directory in the first place, so you can move out of the 1990s and into the 2010s, just in time for 2023!

Note For a full listing of the options available to administrators in configuration profiles, see the Apple article at `https://support.apple.com/HT202834`.

Beyond Active Directory

Active Directory has a number of requirements with regard to the Mac. Clocks need to be in sync; an Active Directory server needs to be accessible routinely in increasingly mobile platforms. It's challenging to keep passwords in sync. macOS supports Active Directory, but due to the requirements, don't bind to Active Directory if you don't have to. There's a growing movement to go beyond directory services. Yes, we figured out how to do it as a community. But just when the process was perfected, we got smart. We learned that, yes, Apple devices can exist on enterprise networks as first-class citizens. But no, we don't have to. Just like Picasso had to master traditional art in his time, before he could think outside the box.

The use cases have also changed. Gone are the days when we were mostly managing stationary machines. We now manage primarily portable devices, and we've learned from our iOS fleets how to make them coexist in networks without binding. Still, some will need to. And for those who choose to try to go beyond binding to Active Directory and instead just use Active Directory accounts, there are tools available that can help you stop binding and start managing. An Apple-provided tool is the Kerberos SSO extension, available in macOS Catalina and later.

And there are organizations choosing to go even further. For those who want to ditch the entire directory service concept, there's a growing desire to actually leverage a third-party identity provider such as Okta, Microsoft Azure, and Ping Identity to access content online using a federated identity, which we'll cover further in Chapter 11.

All the Benefits of Binding Without the Bind

The early days of Mac management in enterprise settings involved a lot of scripting to get a Mac to bind to Active Directory reliably. This became such a large part of most new Apple customers that Apple built entire toolsets around binding, sanity checking, and automating joining an Active Directory environment.

Binding to Active Directory gave you authentication, authorization to log in to a device, single sign-on, and policies through what are known as Managed Client Extensions, or MCX. When profiles came along that could be deployed via MDM or command line (for more on this, see Chapter 2), Apple stopped supporting MCX, and with the scope of Active Directory reduced, the Apple platform management community was able to rethink how we deal with Active Directory.

So what really matters? We need an account to authenticate to, and we need to configure Kerberos for single sign-on. It was out of this rethinking that Apple's Kerberos SSO extension was born, based on the foundations of an earlier tool called Apple Enterprise Connect.

Apple Enterprise Connect

For macOS Mojave and earlier, Apple provides a toolset for connecting to an Active Directory domain without needing to bind, along with support and professional services, in the form of Apple Enterprise Connect. Given that Apple Enterprise Connect isn't available without paying Apple for it, this book is unable to go into detail around the offering. However, many of its capabilities are similar to Apple's Kerberos SSO extension.

Apple Kerberos SSO Extension

For macOS Catalina and later, Apple provides an SSO extension for connecting to an Active Directory domain without needing to bind. This extension allows local accounts to sync their password with the password of a selected account in an organization's Active Directory domain, as well as simplifying the process of acquiring a Kerberos ticket for the selected AD account. The Kerberos SSO extension also allows the password of the selected AD account to be changed, using the password rules set for the selected account, and also provides notification of when the selected account's password is about to expire.

The Kerberos SSO extension is configured by a profile, with a number of options being available for configuration. The profile can be deployed using any MDM solution, but Jamf Pro is being used for the example described as follows. To get started, first open your Jamf admin console and then browse to Computers and then Configuration Profiles.

Next, click Single Sign-On Extensions. At the Single Sign-On Extensions screen, you'll see a number of different settings, as seen in Figure 10-12.

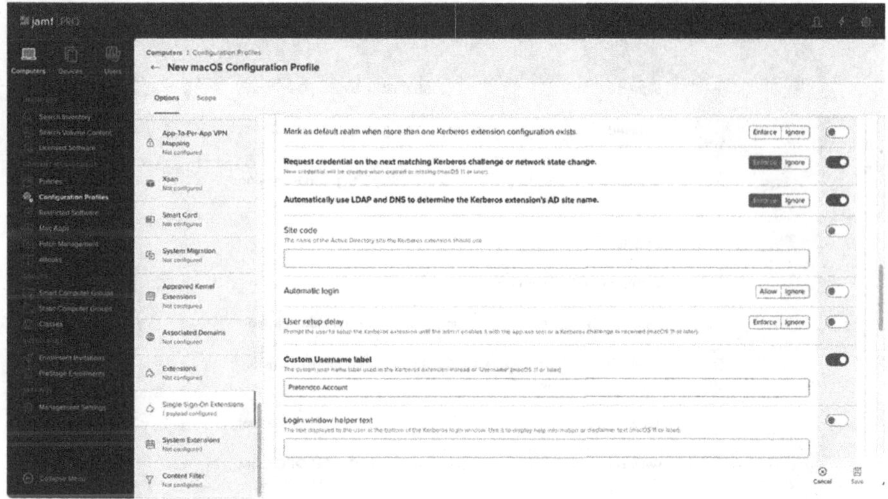

***Figure 10-12.** Configuring a Kerberos SSO extension configuration profile for macOS in Jamf Pro*

Note For a full listing of the options available to administrators in configuration profiles, see the Apple articles available via the following links:

`https://support.apple.com/guide/deployment/kerberos-single-sign-on-extension-depe6a1cda64/1/web/1.0`

`https://support.apple.com/guide/deployment/extensible-single-sign-kerberos-payload-dep13c5cfdf9/1/web/1.0`

Once you have the configuration profile created and deployed to your Macs, the Kerberos SSO extension profile should appear in your list of profiles as shown in Figure 10-13.

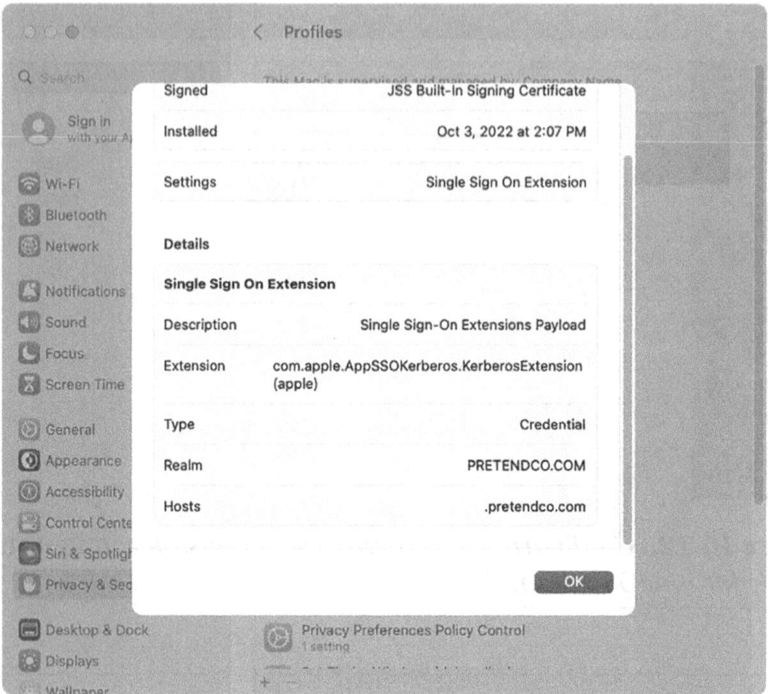

***Figure 10-13.** Kerberos SSO extension configuration profile deployed to a Mac*

Once the Kerberos SSO extension is able to verify a connection to a domain controller on the relevant AD domain, a key icon should appear as shown in Figure 10-14 in the Mac's menu bar (icon is circled for clarity).

***Figure 10-14.** Kerberos SSO extension menu bar icon in macOS*

In addition, a window should appear to prompt the user to sign in using their AD domain's username and password (Figure 10-15).

Figure 10-15. *Signing in to the Kerberos SSO extension using the username and password from the configured Active Directory domain*

Once signed in, the Kerberos SSO extension the menu bar item (Figure 10-16) should show the identity of the signed-in account, relevant information about the account, and an option to change the password of the Active Directory domain account.

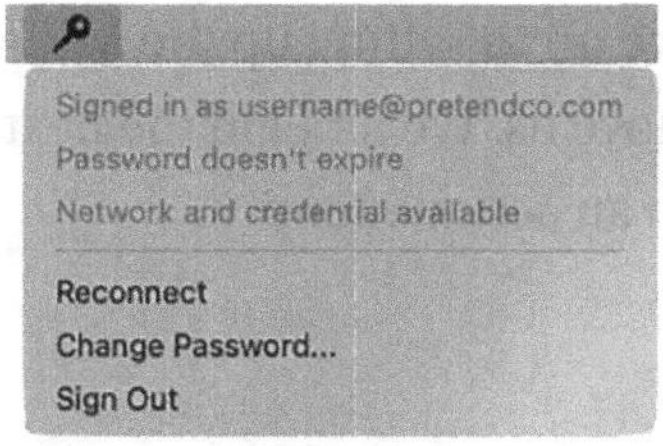

Figure 10-16. *Kerberos SSO extension menu bar item displaying information about the signed-in Active Directory domain account*

With a correctly configured Kerberos SSO extension active with a signed-in Active Directory user account, the Kerberos SSO extension should provide the logged-in user on macOS with the advantages of being able to get Kerberos and account credentials from an Active Directory domain while avoiding any drawbacks which may appear when using a traditional directory service bind to the domain.

Summary

In this chapter, we got devices configured to work with Active Directory, both with the built-in options as well as new options provided by open source alternatives. Active Directory should bring single sign-on to your devices when they're on the network that hosts the Kerberos Realm in Active Directory. But modern devices support SAML and other ways to do single sign-on that are far more flexible for use with SaaS (or web service providers) and when devices aren't on your network. Therefore, it's common for organizations to have a Federated Identity Provider, or IdP - and most work with SAML and OAuth these days.

Apple has limited support for SAML, though the introduction of Platform SSO in macOS Ventura shows that Apple's support for SAML is increasing. Given that SAML started as predominately web technology, Safari has long supported the protocol. An IdP then gives the ability to authenticate to a website and not subsequently get prompted for your credentials as you browse to other pages that are federated with the same provider. In the next chapter, we'll start customizing an identity with a SAML provider and move on to setting up the actual end-user experience, so you know, our users love us. We'll begin the next chapter by covering the move from a login to an actual identity.

CHAPTER 11

Customize the User Experience

Once you have secured and configured devices to work with your environment, it's time to turn your attention toward delighting your coworkers! This is where you go from just being another rude IT hack who's locking down devices to actually becoming a world-class awesome human (or at least someone with a tad bit of empathy) that people are genuinely excited to be in an elevator with. To begin this journey, try to always think of step 1 as thinking of your users as your coworkers, as our friend Emily from the Mac Admins Podcast says.

Therefore, when we like to think of customizing the user experience, we like to think of that experience as putting access to the resources our coworkers need to do their jobs front and center without putting any unnecessary obstacles in the way. We want to do so in an efficient way, where we automate as much as we can in order to delight our coworkers. We want to give freedom, but without putting people at risk. As we covered in the last chapter, each organization has a different posture when it comes to securing devices, but rarely will you hear people complain that you actually paid attention to what they thought.

If we do our job, the first thing most of our coworkers will do is take an Apple device out of a box, join a wireless network, and then get a bunch of stuff on their device. What happens next is still based on the platform and, in some cases, whether you're in a school or company.

C. Edge and R. Trouton, *Apple Device Management*,
https://doi.org/10.1007/978-1-4842-9156-6_11

Getting iOS and iPadOS Devices in the Hands of Users

iOS and iPadOS devices have a great setup experience that we're still trying to replicate on the Mac. Mobile devices can be automatically enrolled into an MDM using DEP, or the user can do a self-enrollment into the MDM service. From there, profiles, apps, and media can be pushed to the iOS and iPadOS device to configure the device in whatever manner is desired. The main difference in what's possible is going to be if the device is configured to be supervised or not.

- **Supervised**: The MDM is in total control of the management of the device, and the device cannot be unenrolled from the MDM. Push deployment of apps and media does not require the device's user to consent.
- **Unsupervised**: The MDM is managing the device, but the user is ultimately in charge because they can remove the MDM profile from the device and unenroll. While enrolled, push deployment of apps and media requires user consent.

For most companies, schools, and institutions, supervision of devices is the preferred method because it allows the mobile device to be completely managed without user consent. DEP makes this easy for those organizations by enabling devices to be automatically supervised once enrolled with the devices' associated MDM server. This can allow for a very streamlined process of getting the mobile device out of the shipping box and into the users' hands because the device can be set up with the desired configuration almost as soon as it powers on and communicates to a network for the first time.

For those organizations which can't use DEP for whatever reason, supervision is still possible by using tools like Apple Configurator to put iOS and iPadOS devices into supervised mode and enrolling them with the organization's MDM server. It's more work for that organization, but ultimately the same outcome: a mobile device which is completely managed by that organization's MDM.

macOS

For macOS, the process is a little more complicated. Supervision as its own management concept on macOS has only become possible starting with macOS Catalina, where all DEP-enrolled Macs are set as supervised by default, with refinement in macOS Big Sur and later, where all MDM-enrolled Macs are set as supervised by default. Meanwhile, it's possible to use means other than MDM to configure Macs, which is by itself unheard of in most mobile device environments. Instead, scripts, installer packages, and other means to deploy settings and files are available options on macOS. Let's take a look at how Mac admins can use MDM, configuration profiles, scripts, installer packages, and other means to build on Apple's work and provide an intuitive and customized user experience for their own environments.

Planning the macOS User Experience

Before you write a single script or build a solitary profile, think about what you want your users to experience. Many times, this experience will be set in part or wholly by the IT or legal policies of a company, school, or institution. A few items which may be included are

- Acceptable use policies that the user needs to agree to before using company equipment

- Branded desktop background image
- Branded word processing, presentation media, or spreadsheet templates
- Whether or not the user will have administrator privileges
- Organization-specific mail server settings for email clients
- Organization-specific bookmarks for web browsers

Other parts of the experience may be guided by feedback from the users themselves, based on what they want to have as part of their Mac's default experience. In general though, a wise Mac admin will try to change as little as possible from Apple's defaults. This is for two reasons:

1. Apple can make changes between OS versions which can make applying certain settings more difficult.
2. The more the user experience is governed by Apple's defaults, the less time that the Mac admin will need to spend on managing it.

In general, we recommend managing what's required and leaving everything else alone. Both your users and you will be better off for it.

Transparency Consent and Control Protections on User Home Folders

Something to keep in mind for macOS Mojave and later is that Apple has implemented protections on certain directories within the user folders. (Please see Chapter 8 for a deeper discussion of these user folder protections.) As of macOS Ventura, here's the list of directories within the user folder which appear to be covered by Apple's user-focused privacy protections:

```
~/Desktop
~/Documents
~/Downloads
~/Library/Application Support/CallHistoryTransactions
~/Library/Application Support/com.apple.TCC
~/Library/Application Support/AddressBook
~/Library/Application Support/CallHistoryDB
~/Library/IdentityServices
~/Library/Calendars
~/Library/Preferences/com.apple.AddressBook.plist
~/Library/Messages
~/Library/Mail
~/Library/Safari
~/Library/Suggestions
~/Library/Containers/com.apple.Safari
~/Library/PersonalizationPortrait
~/Library/Metadata/CoreSpotlight
~/Library/Cookies
~/Library/Caches/CloudKit/com.apple.Safari
~/.Trash
```

With these protections in place, it is not possible to write to these locations except with the following conditions:

A. You're logged in as the user in question.

B. The process or tool writing to the location has been allowlisted using a Privacy Preferences Policy Control profile. (More information on these profiles can be found in Chapter 4.)

This does not mean Mac admins won't be able to make changes to the user home directories, but it does mean that admins won't be able to just drop a file into place. Instead, alternate methods may need exploring.

Using Profiles to Manage User Settings

Using macOS configuration profiles is one method for configuring user settings which can be straightforward to set up and centrally manage from an MDM server. As an example, part of the mandated user experience at a particular organization may be that Safari's home page setting must always be set as the company's website (Figure 11-1). A profile like the one shown as follows can be applied to enable this:

```
<?xml version="1.0" encoding="UTF-8"?>
<!DOCTYPE plist PUBLIC "-//Apple//DTD PLIST 1.0//EN" "http://
www.apple.com/DTDs/PropertyList-1.0.dtd">
<plist version="1.0">
<dict>
      <key>PayloadContent</key>
      <array>
             <dict>
                   <key>HomePage</key>
                   <string>http://www.pretendco.com</string>
                   <key>PayloadDescription</key>
<string>Configures Safari configuration preferences</string>
                   <key>PayloadDisplayName</key>
                   <string>Safari</string>
                   <key>PayloadIdentifier</key>
<string>com.pretendco.com.apple.Safari. 39648B3BD130</string>
                   <key>PayloadOrganization</key>
                   <string></string>
```

```
                <key>PayloadType</key>
                <string>com.apple.Safari</string>
                <key>PayloadUUID</key>
<string>BA9D2B27-12F4-4AF9-B7B5-69E0FB3B6CB3</string>
                <key>PayloadVersion</key>
                <integer>1</integer>
            </dict>
        </array>
        <key>PayloadDescription</key>
<string>Set Safari's homepage to the company website
</string>
        <key>PayloadDisplayName</key>
        <string>Set Safari Homepage</string>
        <key>PayloadIdentifier</key>
<string>com.pretendco.D626B082-BDB1-476E-B34D-63DF10C08C39
</string>
        <key>PayloadOrganization</key>
        <string>Pretendco</string>
        <key>PayloadScope</key>
        <string>System</string>
        <key>PayloadType</key>
        <string>Configuration</string>
        <key>PayloadUUID</key>
        <string>D626B082-BDB1-476E-B34D-63DF10C08C39</string>
        <key>PayloadVersion</key>
        <integer>1</integer>
</dict>
</plist>
```

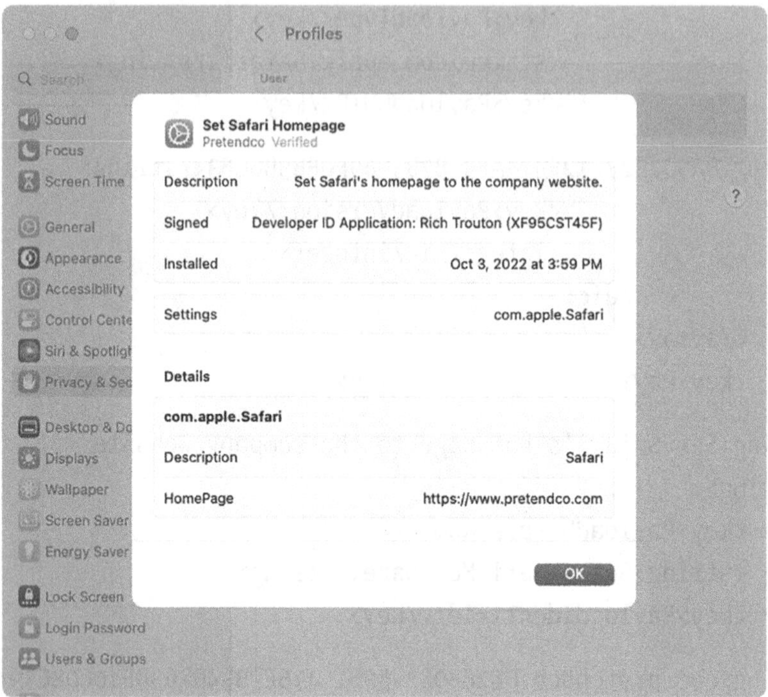

***Figure 11-1.** Profile managing the Safari home page settings*

The user experience of applying this profile is that the home page setting in Safari is filled in with the requested website. It is also grayed out to indicate that the setting cannot be changed (Figure 11-2).

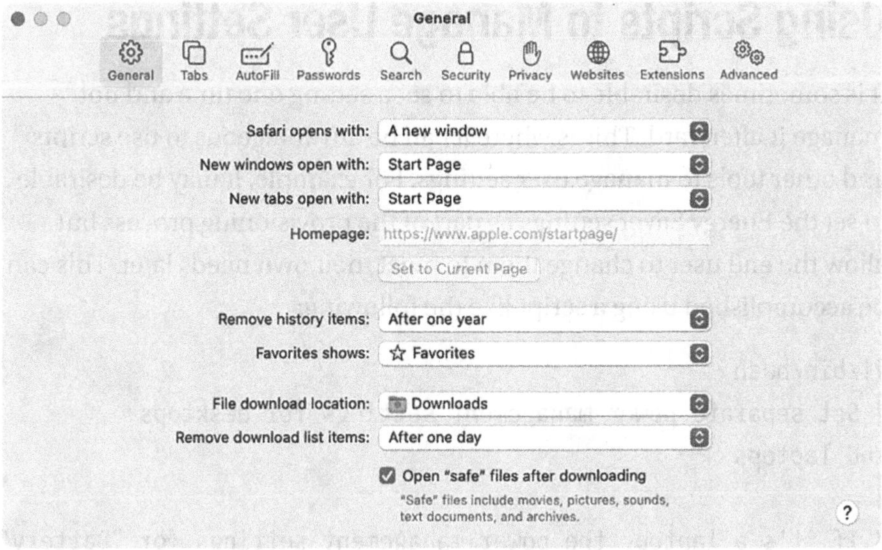

Figure 11-2. *The managed home page setting in Safari's preferences*

The fact that the end user can't change the Safari setting highlights one of the characteristics of profiles, which is that by default their settings are designed to be enforced and not allow the user to change them later. Depending on the requirements of your organization, this characteristic of profiles may be advantageous or be a drawback.

An advantageous characteristic of using profiles to manage settings is that they can be used to apply settings which would otherwise be blocked by the user-focused privacy protections. This is because profiles are using Apple's frameworks to apply these settings, rather than trying to write directly to a file stored in the user's home folder.

Using Scripts to Manage User Settings

It is sometimes desirable to be able to set a setting one time and not manage it afterward. This is where it can be advantageous to use scripts and other tools to manage user settings. For example, it may be desirable to set the Energy Saver settings as part of the provisioning process but allow the end user to change them to meet their own needs later. This can be accomplished using a script like the following:

```
#!/bin/bash
# Set separate power management settings for desktops
and laptops
#
# If it's a laptop, the power management settings for "Battery"
are set to have the
# computer sleep in 15 minutes, disk will spin down in 10
minutes, the display will
# sleep in 5 minutes and the display itself will dim to half-
brightness before
# sleeping.
# While plugged into the AC adapter, the power management
settings for "Charger" are
# set to have the computer never sleep, the disk doesn't
spin down,
# the display sleeps after 30 minutes and the display dims
before sleeping.
#
# If it's not a laptop (i.e. a desktop), the power management
settings are set to have
# the computer never sleep, the disk doesn't spin down, the
display sleeps after 30
# minutes and the display dims before sleeping.
```

```
# Detects if this Mac is a laptop or not by checking the
model ID
# for the word "Book" in the name.
IS_LAPTOP=$(/usr/sbin/system_profiler SPHardwareDataType | grep
"Model Identifier" | grep "Book")
if [ "$IS_LAPTOP" != "" ]; then
      pmset -b sleep 15 disksleep 10 displaysleep 5 halfdim 1
      pmset -c sleep 0 disksleep 0 displaysleep 30 halfdim 1
else
      pmset sleep 0 disksleep 0 displaysleep 30 halfdim 1
fi
```

Running this script as part of your provisioning process will ensure that the Mac will have the desired Energy Saver settings applied by the pmset command-line tool. However, unless the script is rerun later, the user won't be restricted from modifying the Energy Saver settings themselves.

Modifying the macOS Default User Template

Macs can have multiple accounts. Each new account gets a unique home directory, and so each user can have a different experience with a system. These home directories are created from a template directory provided by Apple, and it is possible to customize the template for new user home directories in order to provide a similar user experience to each new user account. The user templates are available at /System/Library/User Template on macOS Mojave and earlier and at /Library/User Template for macOS Catalina and later.

Note If you are considering altering the default user template, think long and hard about alternative ways to accomplish your goal.

For those not experienced with how permissions and settings work on macOS, modifying the user template directory can be a quick and effective way to give both you and your users weird and difficult to diagnose problems.

One circumstance where you may want to customize the user template is if you want to provide customized Word, Excel, or PowerPoint templates for the relevant Microsoft Office applications. As of Microsoft Office 2019 and later, the Office applications look for templates in the following location inside the home directory:

```
~/Library/Application Support/Microsoft/Office365/User Content.localized/Templates.localized
```

Everything past **`~/Library/Application Support`** does not exist by default in the User Template directory, but creating the missing directories inside the template and moving the Office template files into them would allow your users instant access to those templates.

Customize the Desktop

Another example of modifying the user experience would be to put a "Welcome to the Company" PDF on the desktop. Chances are your organization will have a bunch of forms and documents that new employees need to sign, agreeing not to abuse the Internet in your office or steal intellectual property. I like putting fun company facts up front and then at the end of that PDF maybe links to set up any accounts or eSign any forms at the bottom. This small way of crafting the onboarding experience can go a long way, and it's as simple as putting a PDF in the Desktop directory of the appropriate user template prior to creating user accounts.

Customize the User Preferences

User preferences are usually stored in a property list, or .plist, file. While you can customize the preferences stored in the user template directory, first try to customize the setting using a custom profile in the MDM of your choice. Once you've determined you can't customize settings in the way you want using MDM or via a script, an alternative approach is to configure the setting on your Mac and then find what preference file changed. Assuming it's a user setting stored in ~/Library/Preferences, you can then load the file into the Preferences directory of the appropriate user template to push it out to new user accounts.

This is a place where customizing the experience on an iOS device is substantially different from doing so on a Mac. We'll look at managing the home screen to provide an awesome user experience for iOS in the next section of this chapter.

Configure the iOS Home Screen

The home screen is how we interact with an iOS device. Pushing a specific home screen configuration allows you to customize that experience and make it easier for people to get at what they need.

Most MDM solutions will support customizing your home screen to make it easier to access your device data. To show how to customize the home screen, we'll use Apple Configurator. To start, open Apple Configurator and then click a device or a Blueprint. Then select the Home Screen Layout... option from the Actions menu, shown in Figure 11-3.

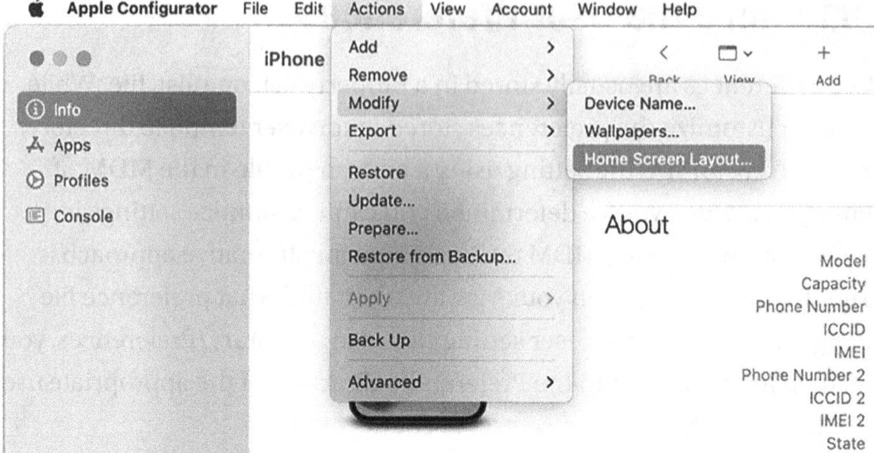

***Figure 11-3.** Modifying the iOS Home Screen Layout using Apple Configurator*

At the Modify screen, simply drag the icons to where you want them to be in order to best customize the layout for your environment, as seen in Figure 11-4. It's usually best to place apps on the screen based on frequency of use. The most common will go in the dock. This is often a mail app, a web browser, the phone app (for iPhones), and a corporate messaging app (like Slack or Teams).

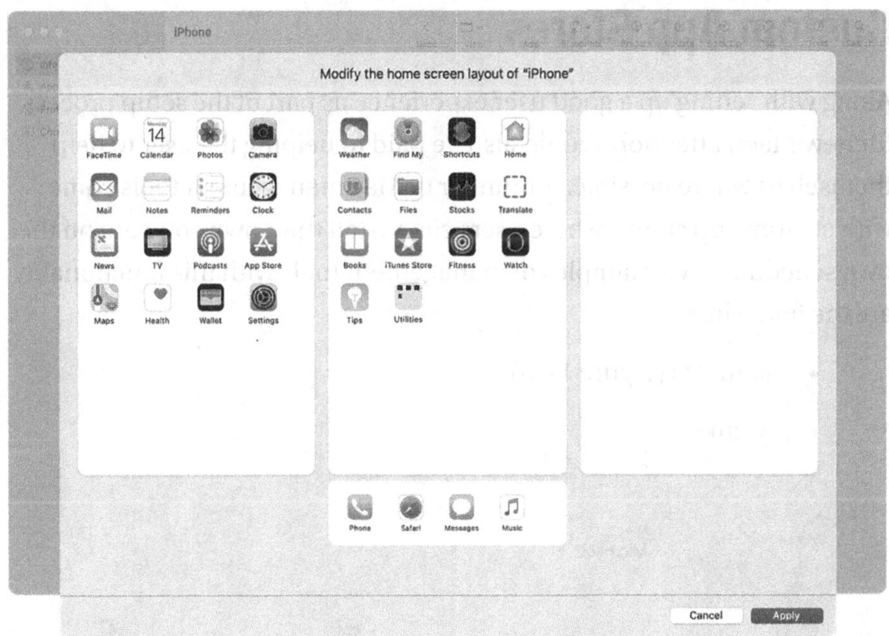

***Figure 11-4.** Adding apps to the iOS Home Screen Layout using Apple Configurator*

The right layout will be different for everyone. But usually you'll see an expense app, Maps, the camera, a line of business app like Salesforce, the Calendar app, an app to access your contacts, and any apps to access your organization's documents (e.g., Dropbox, OneDrive). Keep in mind that you want your coworkers to still like you and to have a great experience with their devices, so leaving some nonbusiness apps up front and center will help with that.

Once you've crafted the best experience for the humans who will be using your devices, click Apply to make the change and see your app badges move.

We reviewed how to do this with Apple Configurator, but most MDMs support similar functionality. The look and feel will be a little different, according to the device management tool you're using, but the experience usually looks similar to the one shown in this section.

Custom App Stores

Along with setting up a good user experience as part of the setup process for new Macs, attention should also be paid to helping the user to help themselves where possible. A number of Mac management tools come with custom app stores, where users can install their own software on their own schedule. Two examples of management tools with this functionality are the following:

- Jamf Pro (Figure 11-5)
- Munki

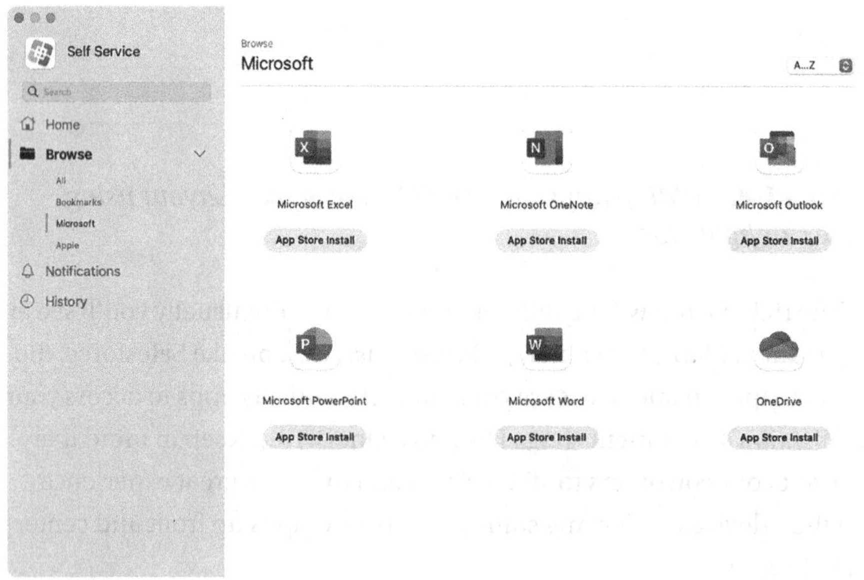

***Figure 11-5.** Jamf Pro's Self Service*

Most of these applications look and work in similar ways, where the user can launch the self-service application and make their own choices from what's available to either install an application or run a particular task.

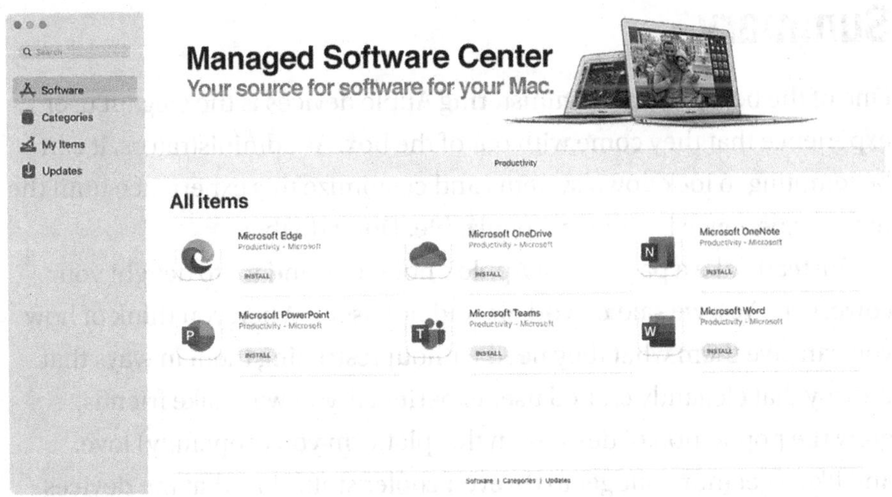

***Figure 11-6.** Munki's Managed Software Center*

In many cases, these self-service tools can also be branded with your company, school, or institution's official logo. This helps build trust in your user community for using the tool in question, since it is visually affiliated with your organization.

Test, Test, Test

In Chapter 3, we looked at building profiles, which can be used to customize settings on devices. In Chapter 4, we looked at pushing those profiles out through MDM. In Chapter 9, we talked about testing. But it's worth reiterating that you should be testing different regressions of tests. The information from Chapter 9 will help guide you to making sure that the desired state of devices after a test matches up with the state you actually end up with.

Summary

One of the best parts of administering Apple devices is the elegant user experience that they come with out of the box. As administrators, it can be tempting to lock down systems and customize this experience until the native experience is barely recognizable. Don't do that.

Instead, take a page out of Apple's notebook and try to delight your coworkers. Yes, we said coworkers and not users. When you think of how you can give them what they need without restricting them in ways that destroy that elegantly crafted user experience, you will make friends, grow the population of devices on this platform you (hopefully) love, and likely get more budget to do even cooler stuff. Now that the devices are in a secure and predictable state, we'll spend Chapter 12 reviewing how to customize the online experience and gate access to various SaaS services based on whether the device meets the security posture of your environment.

CHAPTER 12

Identity and Device Trust

Chapter 8 was about securing devices. Part of security is securing the connections between devices. Chapter 10 was about directory services. Most of the protocols for single sign-on for directory services were developed in a time when most of an organization's devices were on a single network and most resources were located behind a firewall. Today, devices are spread all around the world, and devices access multiple sites built by multiple Software as a Service vendors, who organizations want to use the same credentials to access their account as they use when those users are in the office.

The evolution of single sign-on has been toward thinking about those user accounts in a different way. We now use the term Identity and the engines that provide those identities as Identity Providers, or IdPs. Windows, Linux, and Apple are all developing technology in their operating systems to keep up with the rapidly changing pace of IdPs with new standards being developed on the fly to meet the needs of an increasingly global workforce.

We also looked at personalizing the user environment in Chapter 10. Part of that user environment now includes accounting for those identities and crafting a workflow as seamless as possible between the apps we run on devices and the sites we access as a routine part of doing our jobs. In this chapter, we'll look at what an IdP is, how Apple devices work with

C. Edge and R. Trouton, *Apple Device Management*,
https://doi.org/10.1007/978-1-4842-9156-6_12

IdPs, and what technologies can be put in place to make the lives of our coworkers better, starting with the fundamental technologies required to understand an IdP properly.

Use IdPs for User Identities

An IdP is a federated identity provider or a repository of records (identities) along with the metadata for those records such as the name and any keys necessary to unlock those records. The main vendors that an organization will use as an IdP include the following:

- Okta
- Ping Identity
- Microsoft Azure
- Google
- OneLogin
- VMware
- Salesforce Communities
- Duo Security

The real promise of an IdP is that by providing single sign-on services, an IdP removes the need for passwords. As usual, the IT industry can't just have one way of doing things, so most IdPs support two main protocols: OpenID Connect (built on top of OAuth 2.0) and SAML. As an example of working with both, `https://developer.okta.com/docs/api/resources/oidc` is the OpenID Connect documentation for Okta, and `www.okta.com/integrate/documentation/saml/` is the SAML documentation. Developers who decided to implement single sign-on into their web apps using either can then allow Okta to connect to them and federate customers who decide to use both services. Since much of the technology used in an IdP came out of the REST frameworks, we'll go in deeper with REST.

REST and Web Authentication

When you open a web page, a web browser once accessed a flat HTML file from a web server and then rendered what was on that web server in your web browser. As "the Web" matured, different pieces of data in those pages told browsers to do different things. At this point, most pages you view access a page that appears to be a flat HTML file, when it is in fact a dynamic representation of information created by dozens (if not thousands) of scripts. Those scripts are often lightweight pieces of code processed using Application Programming Interfaces, or APIs.

Some APIs are publicly accessible. Others require authentication and authorization. The authentication is usually sent in the header of a request for information from the API endpoint. The technology behind modern web authentication has been adopted to work with standard REST endpoints. REST, or representational state transfer, is a standard for communicating between websites. One of the easiest ways to send data to a REST endpoint is using the curl command through the macOS Terminal application.

In the following example, we'll simply use the cURL command to make a request to list the content of a file through a standard site:

```
curl https://raw.githubusercontent.com/krypted/jwttools/master/
README.md
```

The response is a bunch of text displayed in a fairly unstructured manner. This is great for showing flat information but can be more challenging if more structured data is required, such as username and password, or more appropriately for web authentication, a token – or even a key that is persistent only for a given session. You can run a curl command for any website to see that information converted into clear text. A RESTful endpoint will be a bit more structured – in the following example, we'll run a standard POST operation (we won't get into the differences between POST, GET, and DELETE):

```
curl -s -X POST -H 'Accept: application/json' -H 'Content-Type:
application/json' --data '{"userid":"{userid}","password":"{pas
sword}"}' https://www.krypted.com/flask/googlesyncscript
```

The output provides the data available at that endpoint the POST command is sent to. There are multiple types of web authentication that have become standard over the past few years. Once a session has been authenticated, most standard web applications now communicate by sending small pieces of data in a normalized JSON format, which we'll describe in the next section of this chapter.

JSON

Because we need more structure, we have various formats, such as SOAP (short for Simple Object Access Protocol) or the more modern JSON. JavaScript Object Notation (or json for short) is a lightweight format for exchanging data that has become a standard for the Web. Similar in origin to the XML used in a property list or SOAP, json removes the need for all the <> symbols and definitions, making it easier on the human eyes while still easy to parse and generate programmatically.

Because the Web continues to mature, you can also see authentication information as some of the fields, or metadata, transferred via JSON. In fact, we now have a standard that is built just for authenticating using information transmitted via json in a JWT. A JWT, or JSON Web Token, is an open standard for representing a claim between two entities. Defined in RFC 7519 at `https://tools.ietf.org/html/rfc7519`, JWT is one of a number of competing standards for authenticating over the Web. For example, the following JSON indicates that the token will be a JWT hashed using the HS256 algorithm:

```
{
  "alg": "HS256",
  "typ": "JWT"
}
```

Those claims submitted in a JWT are encoded in a json object, signed using a JWS or JSON Web Signature and encrypted using JWE (or JSON Web Encryption).

Use JWTs As Service Accounts

Everything that is old becomes new again. Much as RADIUS, an earlier authentication type for wireless networks and VPNs, used a preshared key to validate a party prior to decryption and much as Kerberos had clients submit a ticket granting ticket rather than a password, JWT is a modern evolution to that same type of transaction, complete with its own acronyms but without the trappings of 20–30 years of technical debt. In short, a JWT is a credential used to grant access to a resource.

Most of the time when you're making a transaction between two computers, that transaction is broken into three parts: a header, a payload, and a signature. The header defines rules about what's about to come, the payload it what you'll receive, and the signature. To see this put into motion, let's look at the header of a typical transaction:

```
{
 "alg": "HS256",
 "typ": "JWT"
}
```

In the preceding example, we're simply stating that the token will be cryptographically signed using HMAC-SHA256 (or HS256 for short) and that the grant type will be a JWT. If you wanted to, you could encode this using the following command:

```
echo -n '{"alg": "HS256","typ":"JWT"}' | openssl base64
```

You could also add more metadata, most notably the payload - or what command or API call you're sending between servers, for example, some personally identifiable information we maybe shouldn't send over the Web, but since everyone else does it, let's just go ahead:

```
{
"Email": "krypted@me.com",
"FirstName": "Charles",
"LastName": "Edge"
"iat": 1516239022
"exp": 2414245921
}
```

In the preceding example, we snuck something else in there: iat indicates the time the token was issued, and exp indicates the expiration time of the token. The signature is where it gets a bit more cryptographically challenging. To get the signature, you base64url encode the header (which we did by piping it into openssl, but next time adding the payload). You then concatenate the two using a period to indicate a field separator and then encrypt the whole thing with a secret key. The standard encryption algorithm in our experience seems to be HMAC-SHA256, but you can go as high as PS384 if you have the horsepower to do all that work on the fly for all the transactions that might come through.

Now it's starting to seem like we're getting really complicated (after all this isn't a book on cryptography), so let's look at JWT.io, a website where you can decode, verify, and generate a quick JWT. The important thing to note here is that you enter one of those pieces of information in an encoded form and get to see how it's decoded against the signature, shown in Figure 12-1.

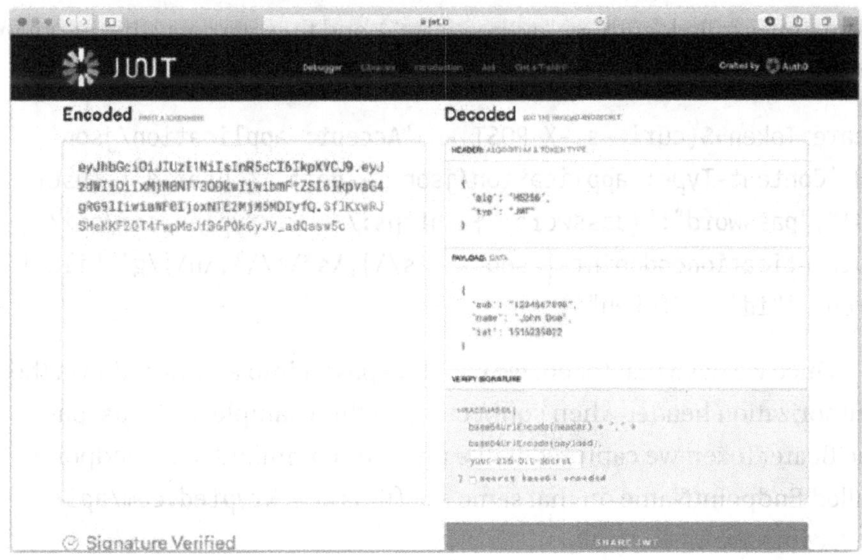

Figure 12-1. *JWT.io*

Another great project is jwtbuilder, which does much of the same but without hitting the website, at `http://jwtbuilder.jamiekurtz.com`. There are different schemas for JWTs, so you might see "Authorization: Bearer" in the header of a user agent (e.g., via Postman). We'll take a look at obtaining bearer tokens next.

Bearer Tokens

Web servers that host an endpoint usually allow you to submit some information. They then pass you a bearer token back, once it's done all that crypto-fun. In the following, we set a variable called BearerToken (which should look similar to the JWT shown from JWT.io) using a simple curl to the contents of a bearer token. We run a curl with data in the header for "userid" although sometimes we see this as just "user" or "username" and then a password (each rest endpoint can be different – such is the joy of working with "modern" technology). This hits an endpoint called authenticationendpoint (sometimes called "auth" or "authenticate"), and then we parse the output for a token field once we've parsed out the json symbols:

```
BearerToken=$(curl -s -X POST -H 'Accept: application/json'
-H 'Content-Type: application/json' --data '{"userid":"{user
id}","password":"{password}"}' https://www.krypted.com/api/
authenticationendpoint | sed -E 's/\},\s*\{/\},\n\{/g' File |
grep  '"id" : "token"')
```

Once we have that token, we can then pass it into another API via the Authorization header when connecting. In this example, we'll just pass the BearerToken we captured in the previous command to an endpoint called EndpointName on that same site (thus `www.krypted.com/api/EndpointName`):

```
curl -H 'Accept: application/json' -H "Authorization: Bearer
${BearerToken}" https://www.krypted.com/api/EndpointName
```

But if these tokens are used to connect between sites, who cares about how we create a Bearer Token, how might a rest endpoint give us one, and what that token is used for? Those tokens become the foundation of OAuth, which is suddenly where words like Facebook, Okta, Azure, Amazon, and Ping Identity start to come into play.

OAuth

OAuth is short for Open Authorization and per RFC 6749 (`https://tools.ietf.org/html/rfc6749`) is an open standard for using tokens to authenticate and authorize services, including use over public networks such as the Internet. It was invented by then lead developer at Twitter, Blaine Cook, in 2006 so other organizations could connect to another service using their Twitter account. OAuth continued to evolve over the next few years until 2012 when Oauth 2.0 was released, which added flows for web applications, mobile devices, IoT devices, and desktop apps, making it one of the most widely used authentication platforms today.

OAuth 2 allows those applications to obtain access in a way that is limited to only what an account needs to user accounts typically using standard REST endpoints. OAuth 2 delegates the actual user authentication to the service that hosts the user account, which can then change what an application is granted to access or have an account quickly disabled. OAuth 2.0 allows for account information to be traded between services via OAuth providers, which include organizations like Amazon, Box, Dropbox, Etsy, Facebook, GitHub, Google, Instagram, LinkedIn, Microsoft, PayPal, Reddit, Salesforce.com, Stack Exchange, Trello, Twitter, and Yahoo.

There are four roles in OAuth:

- **Resource Owner**: The Resource Owner is the user who allows (or authorizes) an application to access their account information. The Resource Owner can then identify what scope that service or application has, for example, when you authorize another site like OpenTable to use your Facebook account so you don't have to create yet another account. When you do that, you should see a list of the permissions that other site has. You are the Resource Owner, and those permissions are scopes.
- **Client**: The application that wants to access the information owned by the Resource Owner. In the preceding example, this would be OpenTable.

- **Resource Server and Authorization Server**: While defined separately, these are usually hosted in the same place and are the protected user accounts that should only have access delegated to by the Resource Owner. In the preceding example, this would be Facebook. At work, this might be Okta, Ping, OneLogin, or Azure AD.

What happens when you connect? You tap a button and the device goes to talk to an authorize API endpoint on an OAuth provider (the Resource Server):

```
https://www.randomoauthprovider.com/v1/oauth/
authorize?response_type=code&client_id=CLIENTID&redirect_
uri=CALLBACKURL&scope=read
```

In the preceding example, the & symbol separates fields to the request, so we're sending a response type, a client ID, a redirect URI, and a scope:

- **Client ID**: The unique identifier for that client.
- **Redirect URI**: The URL the authorization server calls once it's finished processing the login. This provides an extra layer of security because the response is sent from the server to a specific URL.
- **Response type**: Indicates that the authorization server provides an authorization code to clients which will then be used to get access tokens.
- **Scope**: What level of access or what accesses this specifies at a granular level, the "scope" of the access to the resource, that is, are we requesting authorization to read the resources, modify the resources, etc.?

The application requests authorization to access a resource (e.g., your name, email address, and authentication information) from the user. This is where an embedded Facebook screen in an app like OpenTable asks if you want to give access to the app that embedded it. Then if you want to grant access, you tap a button to allow that access, thus authorizing the application to receive an authorization grant. This would be a call to an API that looks something like this:

```
https://www.randomappredirect.com/callback?code=AUTHORIZATIONCODE
```

The application then authenticates and authorizes that the grant is valid from the Resource Server (e.g., by performing a standard API call against a REST endpoint hosted via the Facebook Graph API). The application that requests the resource – that metadata about you, and receives a token.

```
https://www.randomoauthprovider.com/v1/oauth/token?client_
id=CLIENT_ID&client_secret=CLIENT_SECRET&grant_
type=authorization_code&code=AUTHORIZATION_CODE&redirect_
uri=CALLBACK_URL
```

In the JWT example from earlier, that token would usually have a time when it expires, a Client ID, a Client Secret, and an Authorization Grant as well as any information that was provided such as the following:


```
{"access_token":" eyJhbGciOiAiSFMyNTYiLCJOeXAiOiJKV1QifQ.
eyJOYW1lIjogIkNoYXJsZXMiLCJOeXAiOiJKV1QifQ. iJKV1QifQ",token_
type":"bearer","expires_in":2414245921,"refresh_
token":"REFRESH_TOKEN","scope":"read","uid":667,"FirstName":
"Charles","LastName":"Edge","Email":"krypted@me.com"}
```


This is just standard json and that bearer token should look similar, just with additional metadata. A real-world example is the following. Here, you can see authenticating into Medium using Facebook for OAuth, including the redirect, client_id, scope, etc.:

```
https://www.facebook.com/v2.9/dialog/oauth?client_
id=542599123456789&redirect_uri=https%3A%2F%2Fmedium.com%2Fm%
2Fcallback%2Ffacebook&scope=public_profile%2Cemail&state=%7Ch
ttps%3A%2F%2Fmedium.com%3Fsource%3D-------------------------
post_free-%7Cregister%7C1ae249dc69bbb075abcdef123fcb369e&respon
se_type=token
```

At this point, you've used OAuth to communicate with the web service, and you can then access additional resources without reauthenticating. If we were still using the OpenTable analogy, we'd say it's time to go to dinner and talk about the services built on top of OAuth 2.0 and these standard token formats, which brings us to using an IdP to provide a user identity.

WebAuthn

The Web Authentication API (commonly referred to as WebAuthn) is an API specification for servers to register and authenticate a user using a public key instead of a password. WebAuthn allows servers to take use of the authentication built into a mobile device, like Apple Touch ID or Face ID, and then use a keypair from the device instead of a password when accessing a given server, such as those that host a website like Jamf Pro. The keypair is a common pair of keys with a public key as simply an identifier (kinda like a username) and the private key as a random or cryptographically generated representation of a password. Because we trust the local security of the device, we can then trust the key and a credential ID that is issued just for each server, with that pair representing an "identity." The web server only ever receives the public key, and so if compromised, the public key isn't useful.

WebAuthn was developed by the W3C and FIDO organizations, which added WebAuthn to FIDO2. WebAuthn is added to the Safari browsers from Apple, meaning support is now provided from Chrome, Firefox, and Microsoft Edge. Google, Mozilla, and Microsoft helped develop the standard and so released support for Chrome, Firefox, and Microsoft Edge early on. Apple first added WebAuthn support to Safari in a Technology Preview in 2018. Apple announced all Safari browsers would also support WebAuthn at WWDC in 2019. Apple further added WebAuthn functionality to Keychain to develop a feature they called Passkeys. To learn more about Passkeys, see the 2022 WWDC session introducing them: `https://developer.apple.com/videos/play/wwdc2022/10092/`.

OpenID Connect

OpenID Connect is a simple identity layer that sits on top of OAuth 2.0. OpenID Connect allows client devices and apps that run on those devices to verify the identity of users. This is done by authenticating to an authorization server and then receiving various pieces of metadata about the user in JSON. Those JWTs from earlier in this chapter are great for service accounts but not typically used by themselves for dynamic user authentication.

OpenID Connect is similar to the OAuth 2.0 flow we described earlier in this chapter. In addition, the authorization server (or endpoint) also provides an ID token (as well as a token endpoint) as a JWT in addition to the access token in a standard OAuth 2.0 flow. Additionally, because it's a hosted service specifically meant to provide identity information, there is a userinfo endpoint, a logout endpoint, a keys endpoint to view public keys, and a revoke endpoint so the user can disconnect their account. The authorize endpoint is also used to refresh tokens.

The id-token is the added piece in OpenID Connect, and the userinfo endpoint can provide additional information prior to authorization when needed. Now that we've covered OpenID Connect, let's look at SAML.

SAML

SAML, or Security Assertion Markup Language, uses similar signed and encrypted secure tokens for authentication and authorization data. SAML is a little older and so communicates over a standardized XML format.

While similar in nature to a JWT, SAML tokens are much longer when decoded. See Figure 12-2 to see the attributes in the XML schema for a SAML token at `http://samltool.io`. There will be x.509 certificate signatures, canonical naming to access resources, and a number of other items that are standardized and much more attuned to a more mature enterprise-class protocol. This doesn't make it better, just chattier.

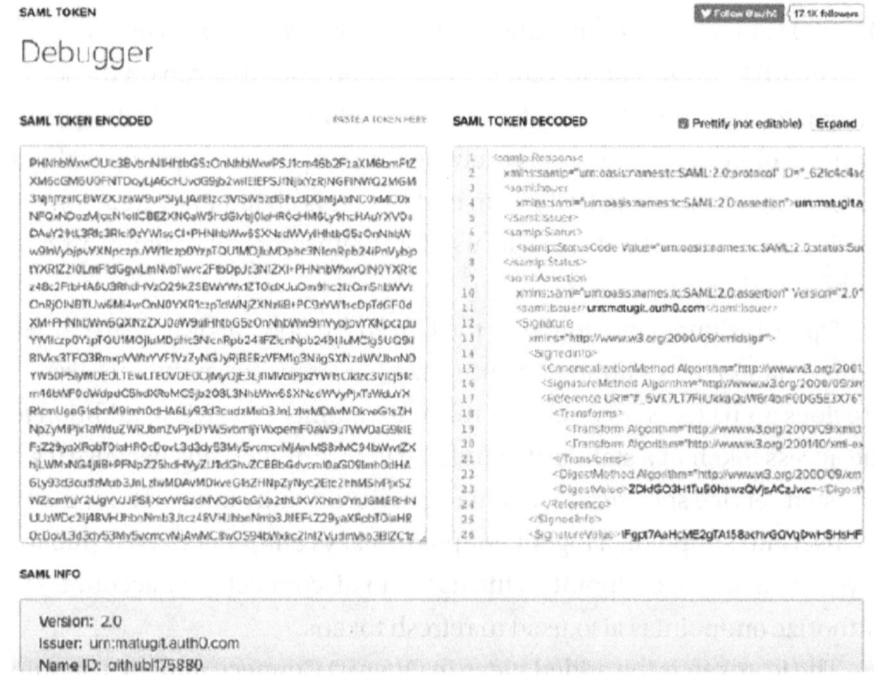

Figure 12-2. *samltool.io*

All that extra information you see in addition to what's in OpenID Connect though includes a lot of standardization. Those standards mean there are shared repositories of code that developers can use to quickly build features (such as a framework for iOS development or Spring Security for Java). This also means that in some cases it's easier for different vendors to work well with one another.

SAML also provides support for what's known as SCIM (System for Cross-domain Identity Management) and Just-in-Time (JIT) provisioning. These allow users to log in with enterprise credentials from a provider like Azure Active Directory or Google to log in using their credentials without the company getting billed for every user that could possibly use the service. SCIM syncs users and groups to the service, but JIT users are generated on the fly the first time they access a service using a SAML assertion. Each requires integration with a provider. For example, Just-in-Time provisioning then works by having the SAML identity provider pass user information to a Mobile Device Management solution the first time a user logs in during a DEP enrollment. Figure 12-3 shows how to link Kandji with a SCIM provider, and once configured, there will be an endpoint that Kandji would communicate with to import new users from the identity provider automatically.

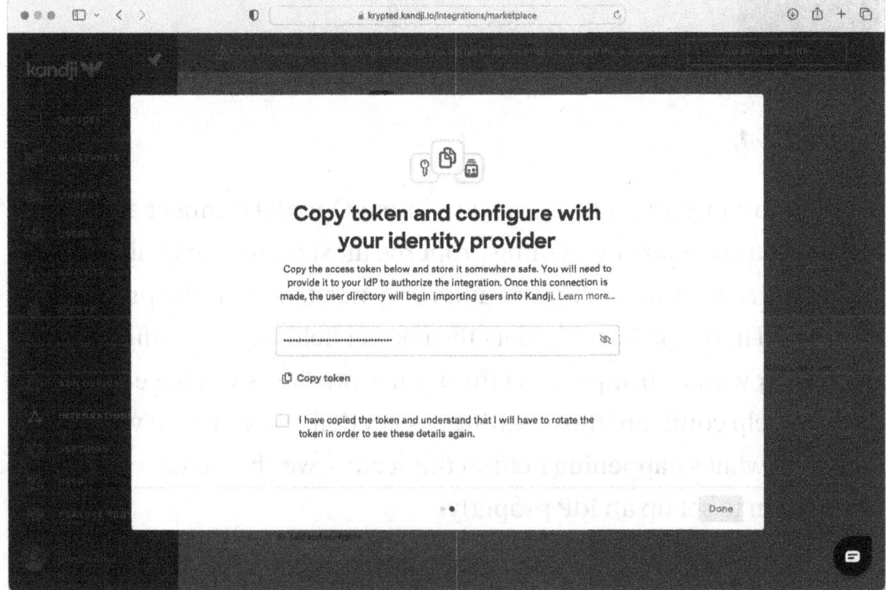

Figure 12-3. Configuring SCIM in Kandji

Once configured, many providers will also supply information for a Logout URL, certificate, authentication endpoint, and a name. We'll cover these more in the next few sections, but for perspective, Figure 12-4 shows how those endpoints are configured in JumpCloud. Other environments might install their own SCIM server based on a plethora of open source projects that do some of the heavy lifting to map attributes from various providers so they get passed into different tools properly.

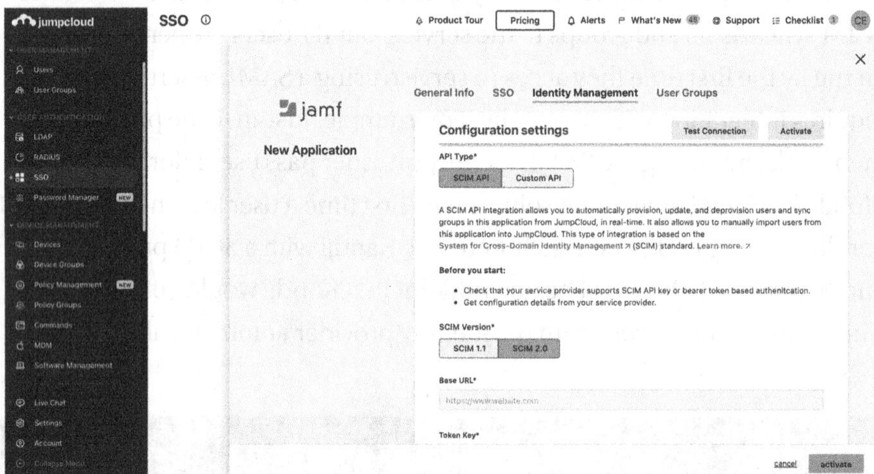

Figure 12-4.

The most important thing to know about OpenID Connect and SAML is that if you configure everything properly, most of the work will happen behind the scenes, and administrators only need to know the preceding terms to fill in the paths and select the correct fields when configuring an IdP to work with web apps. Most third-party providers will have support teams to help configure those settings as needed. Now that we've covered enough of what's happening behind the scenes, we should have enough information to set up an IdP properly.

Cookies

A cookie is a small amount of data that a website creates and stores on your computer using a special handler built into your web browser. Cookies can do a number of things, but the most common is to store login data, such as a username, or some kind of session tracking information. Cookies can also store preferences, a key to remember your identity, or a callback URL.

There are session and persistent cookies. Session cookies are deleted whenever you close a browser and often store information like shopping carts or callbacks. These are deleted when the browser closes. Persistent cookies still have an expiration date but are typically used to remember an identity, which is usually a key used to derive personal information on the server.

Cookies can get a bad rap because not all developers play with the information safely or because cookies can be shared between certain developers. As you can see in the Privacy pane of the Safari Preferences, Safari will show sites that are storing cookies in the browser (Figure 12-5).

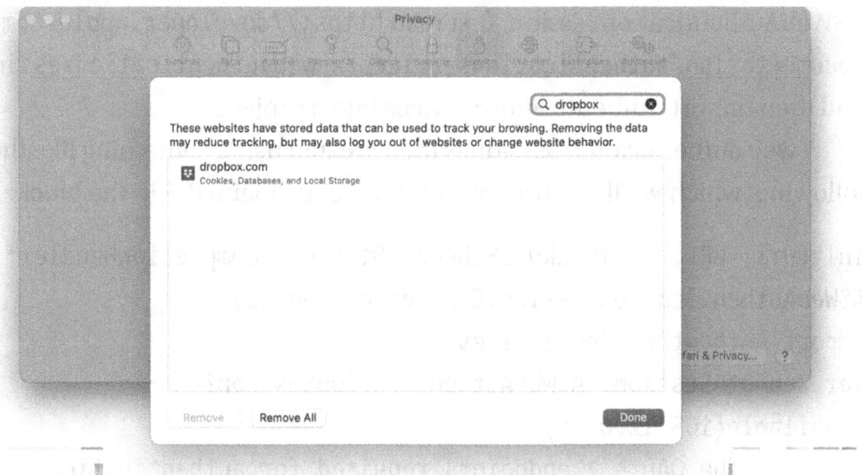

Figure 12-5. *Cookies in Safari*

In Safari, session cookies are stored in /Users/ce/Library/Caches/com.apple.Safari, and persistent cookies are stored in /Users/ce/Library/Cookies. These directories are protected, and so you cannot browse inside them. Since cookies are stored in a different location for each web browser, if you switch browsers, new cookies will need to be created. Apple has put cookies under privacy and made it difficult to access them. While disabling cookies does provide additional privacy, it can cause various websites to stop working as intended, especially those of identity providers.

ASWebAuthSession

ASWebAuthenticationSession is an API that launches a Safari View Controller for a sign-in URL, making it easier to authenticate users in a low-code scenario. That provides the user with an authentication dialog that allows a user to authenticate through a service, such as an OAuth provider. Upon a successful authentication, the OAuth service responds with an auth token and fires up a completion handler. To use ASWebAuthenticationSession, first read `https://developer.apple.com/documentation/authenticationservices/aswebauthenticationsession` and then import AuthenticationServices into a project.

A web authentication session is then created using something like the following, which we'll perform by populating the loginURL in the block:

```
init(url: URL, callbackURLScheme: String?, completionHandler:
ASWebAuthenticationSession.CompletionHandler)
Import AuthenticationServices
var webAuthSession: ASWebAuthenticationSession?
@available(iOS 12.0, *)
//Define the OAuth 2 endpoints required for authentication
func getOAuth2Token() {
let loginURL = URL(string: "https://account.krypted.com/idp/
login/oauth/authorize?client_id=<client_id>")
```

```
let callbackURLscheme = "https://account.krypted.com/idp/auth"
self.webAuthSession = ASWebAuthenticationSession.init(url:
loginURL!, callbackURLscheme: callbackURL, completionHandler:
{ (callBack:URL?, error:Error?) in
// Handler to receive the callback
guard error == nil, let WoohooURL = callBack else {
return
}
//Grab the token from the callback
let OAuth2Token = NSURLComponents(string: (WoohooURL.
absoluteString))?.queryItems?.filter({$0.name == "code"}).first
// Display the token or an error
print("You logged in and here is your token:" OAuth2Token ??
"No OAuth Token was received")
})
self.webAuthSession?.start()
}
```

This goes in the code wherever you want the login window to appear. All cookies that are accessed using ASWebAuthenticationSession other than session cookies can then be shared with the web browser. As we covered earlier in the chapter, according to the developer, those cookies can then be used to store different types of metadata.

There are much better and more thorough handlers out there such as `https://github.com/OAuthSwift/OAuthSwift/blob/master/Sources/OAuthSwiftURLHandlerType.swift`. The preceding code was really mostly meant to show the well-known endpoints for OAuth in use, how the token is passed, and the callback. The code to get much of this working is fairly straightforward for developers. It gets challenging though for developers to read between the lines of a rapidly changing ecosystem. Tools like Postman make it easier to spoof some of these methods of persistence and substantiation of new objects, but one wrong line of code could leak information or the ability to spoof a connection

Now that we better understand what the IdP is and how it works, let's actually look at how it works to configure aspects of an Apple deployment with a cloud provider. To show a standard identity provider in action, we'll log in to an existing Azure Active Directory account.

Work with Azure Active Directory

The first part of this chapter was about the underlying technology used for modern authentication. Previous chapters covered what we might call "legacy authentication," and solutions like Okta's Fastpass help bridge the gap (to set up Okta, see Appendix E).

Apple Business Manager and Apple School Manager allow administrators to create Managed Apple IDs. Similar to how supervised devices provide additional management options (see Chapter 4 for more on that), Managed Apple IDs allow administrators to do more with little or no interaction from users. Managed Apple IDs are owned by the organization and linked to (as of the time of this writing) Apple or Google as an identity provider. These are configured in Apple Business Manager or Apple School Manager. Log in to the appropriate portal, click the username in the bottom-left corner of the screen, and click Accounts. From the Accounts screen in Federated Authentication, click the Edit button as seen in Figure 12-6.

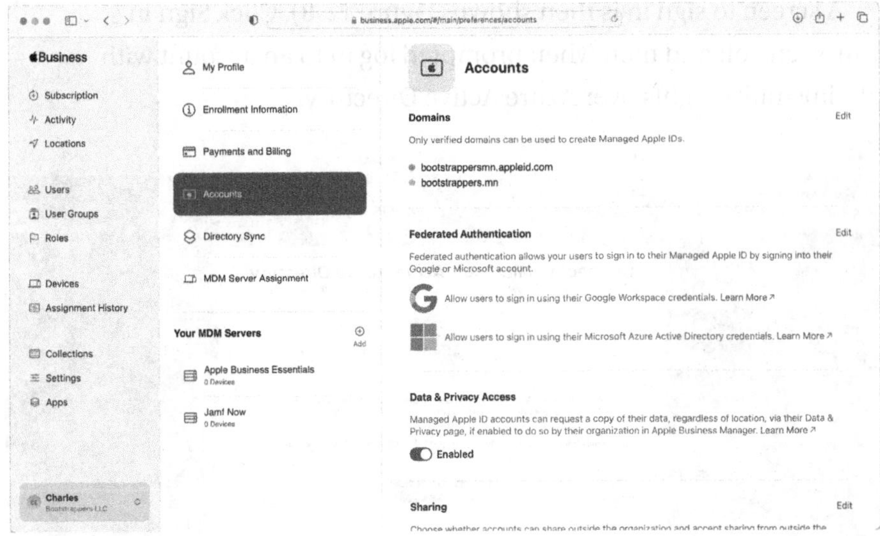

Figure 12-6. *Managed Apple ID setup in Apple Business Manager*

The Edit button brings up a modal to select between a Google Workspace and Azure Active Directory, as seen in Figure 12-7. Microsoft Azure Active Directory is used for this example.

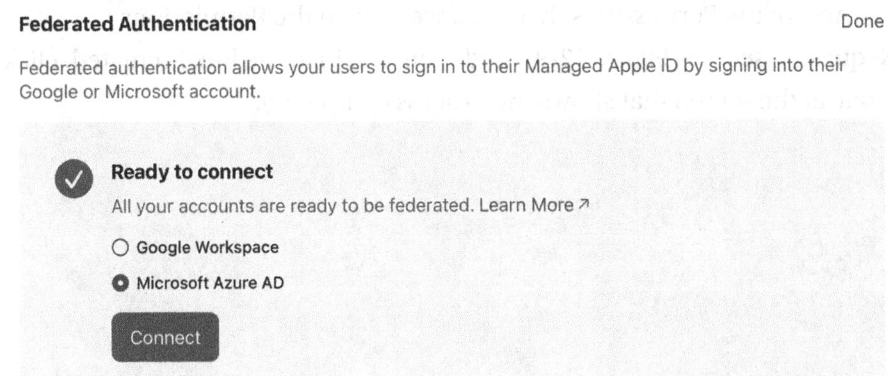

Figure 12-7. *Select between Google Workspace and Azure*

A screen to sign in is then shown (Figure 12-8). Click Sign in with Microsoft and then when prompted log in to an account with administrative rights over Azure Active Directory.

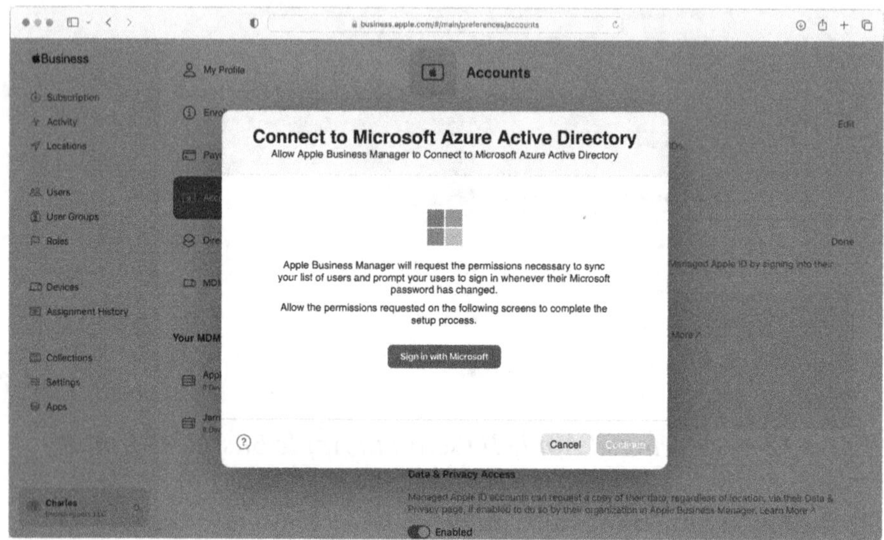

Figure 12-8. *Link accounts to the IdP*

Accept the Permissions that are necessary in the Permissions Requested screen (Figure 12-9), and then provided the link is created, click Done at the screen that shows the process completed.

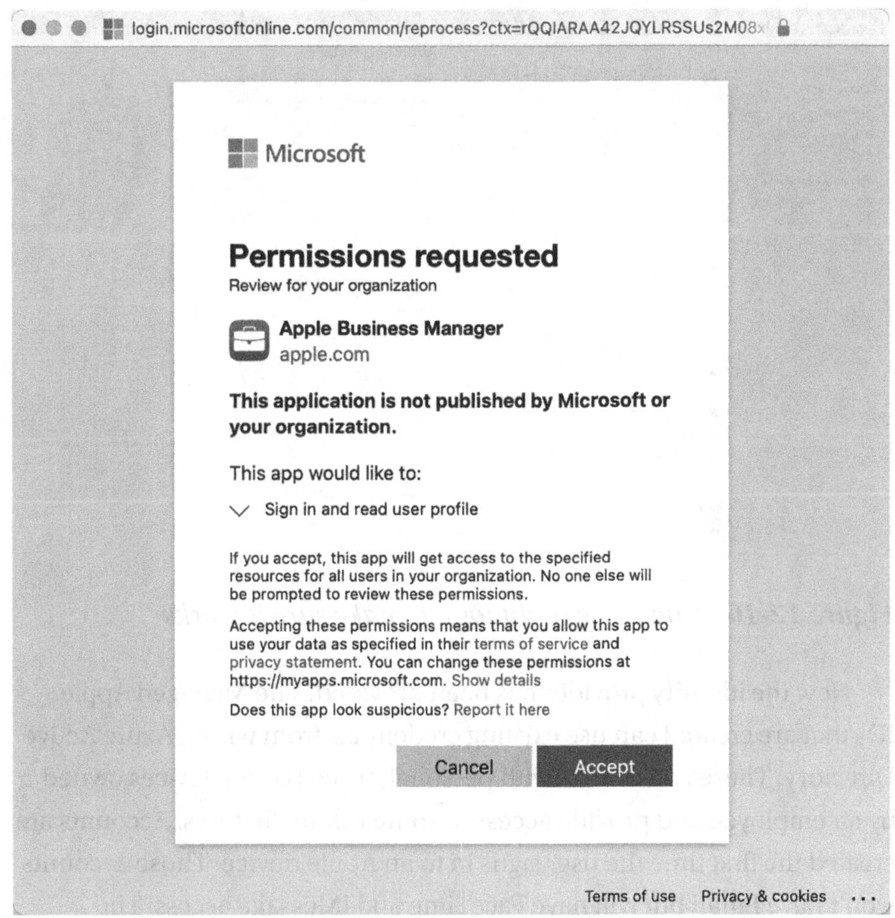

Figure 12-9. *Provide the necessary permissions*

Open the Azure Active Directory console and click the Audit Logs to verify the link was created successfully (as it was in Figure 12-10).

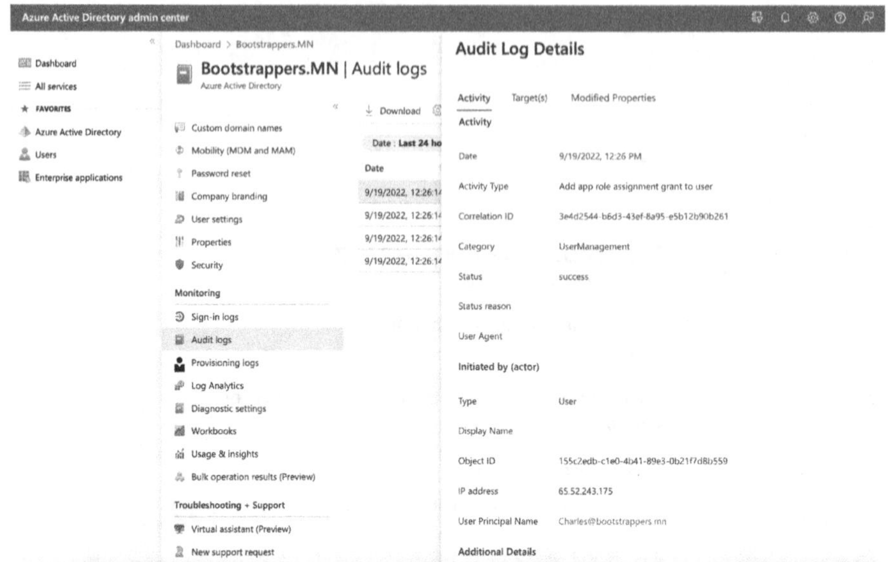

Figure 12-10. *Check the audit logs to make sure it works*

Now the identity provider has been provided. The Managed Apple IDs that are created can use existing credentials from within Azure Active Directory. These can coexist with personal Apple IDs on devices owned by an employee and provide access to some iCloud features. Accounts are created the first time the user signs in to an Apple device. Those accounts won't have Email but will have FaceTime and iMessage access. The accounts can collaborate with others who use iCloud apps and be disabled when the underlying Azure account is disabled. Some features like Apple Pay, Wallet, Find My, and iCloud Keychain will not work on these types of accounts as each of those is handled either by a personal Apple ID or by a feature within an MDM, like Lost Mode (compared to Find My).

The domain will need to be verified. This is done on the same screen, by creating a text record in the DNS for the domain registered. Any existing personal Apple IDs in the domain would then receive an email to change the email address so it doesn't use the TLD of the domain that was just configured. This can be tricky as most users who have used Apple devices in an organization, especially those that used older versions of VPP, likely have accounts. However, it's a process to start sooner rather than later. If there is an existing personal Apple ID in the domain, a Managed Apple ID will not be provisioned until that situation is resolved. Once the Azure tenant and Apple Business Manager are linked, it's time to set up SCIM.

Apple calls SCIM Directory Sync in Apple Business Manager. From Preferences, click Directory Sync to bring up the ability to configure SCIM. At the Directory Sync screen, click the Edit button (Figure 12-11).

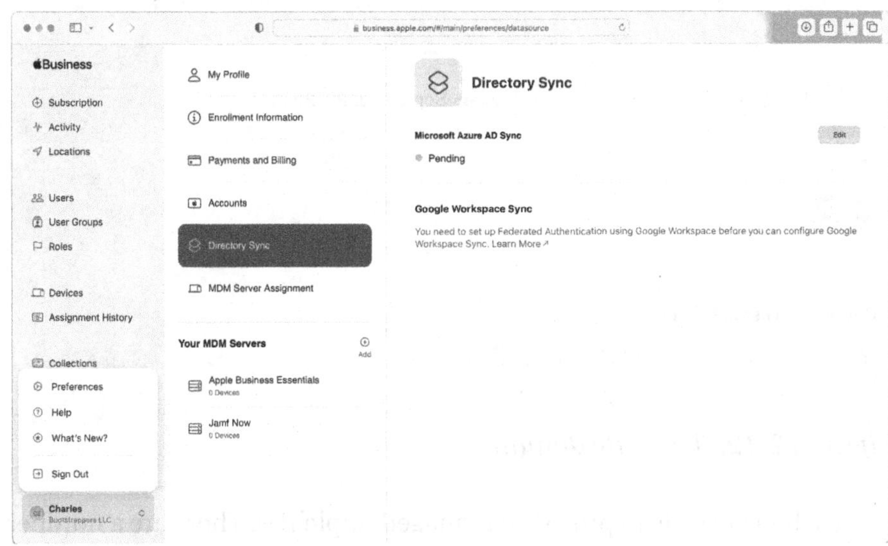

Figure 12-11. *Set up SCIM*

The domains now need to be federated, as the warning indicates (Figure 12-12). To do so, go back to the Azure AD tenant and follow the steps at `https://support.apple.com/guide/apple-business-manager/sync-users-from-azure-ad-axm3ec7b95ad/web` to configure an Enterprise Application (which federates the SAML connection to the token provided from Apple Business Manager). These screens are likely to change over time so we won't go through each, but plan for about an hour, usually.

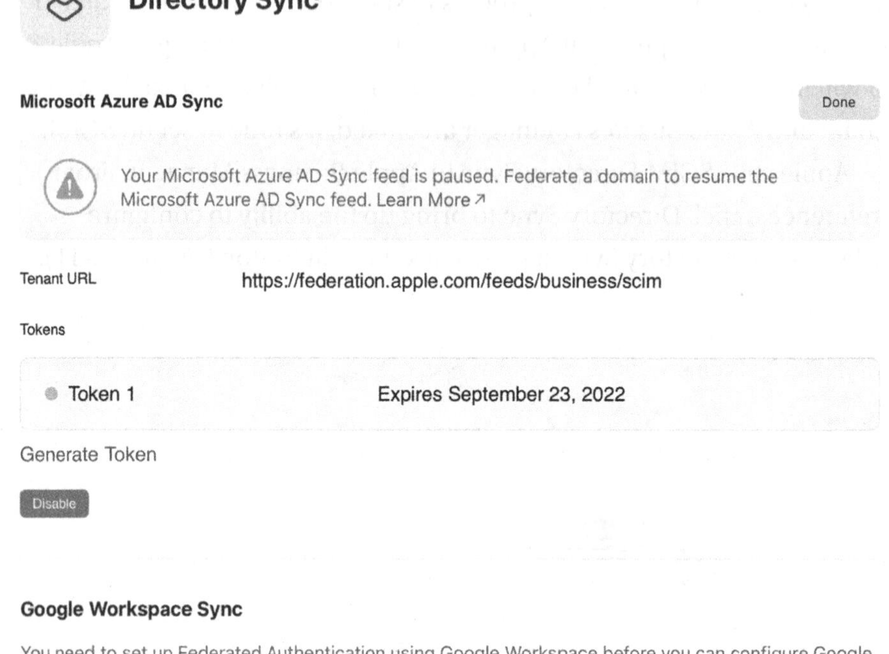

Figure 12-12. *Federate domains*

It's then possible to provision Managed Apple IDs. There are a number of other SAML, OIDC, and identity providers. We cover Okta in Appendix E, but there's also JumpCloud, Auth0, Ping Identity, and a host of others. Once Enterprise Applications are federated, users can see SAML responses from Apple, Microsoft, Google, and others.

View SAML Responses

SAML support was initially added to Safari a few years ago to help keep SharePoint users from having to provide credentials repeatedly. Since then, additional options for single sign-on solutions have been added as well. The Safari Web Inspector now has a feature to see the SAML response in action, an important tool when troubleshooting issues between federated sites. To do so

- Open Safari.
- From the Safari menu, click Preferences.
- Click the Advanced tab.
- Check the box for "Show Develop menu in the menu bar."
- Select Show Web Inspector from the newly displayed Develop menu.
- Select the Resources tab.
- Log in to a site.
- View the Requests by filtering for SAMLResponse.
- Decode the response from base64.

Chances are you won't be able to decipher much of the SAML response. This is by design, and as you get more accustomed to troubleshooting SAML responses, you'll pick up a few tricks here and there. One of our favorite would be SAML Tracer.

SAML Tracer is a plug-in for Firefox available at `https://addons.mozilla.org/en-US/firefox/addon/saml-tracer/`. Once installed, you'll be able to see a list of SAML requests as well as how the request was formatted and any SAML responses, decoded, as you can see in Figure 12-13.

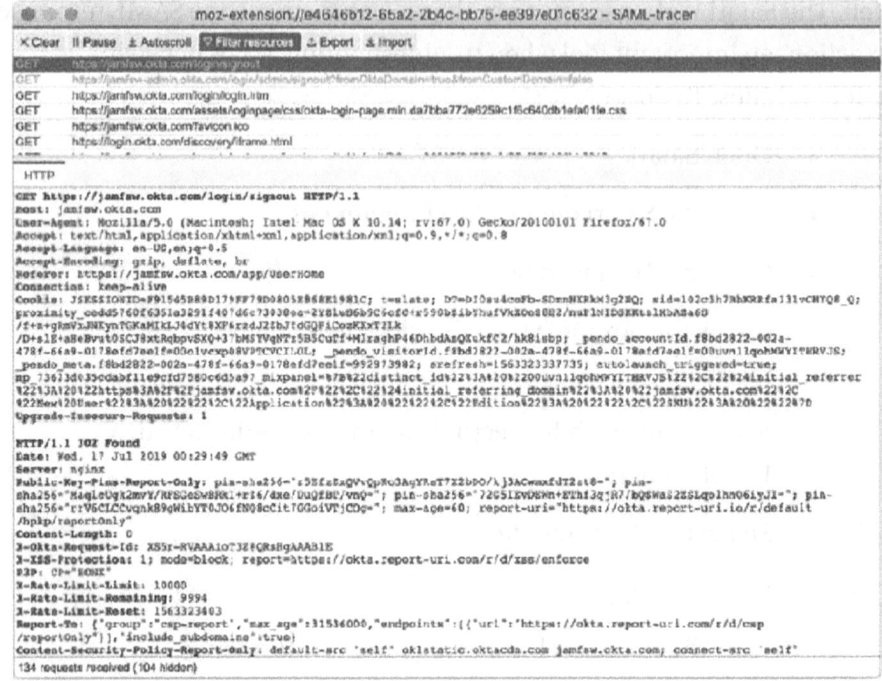

Figure 12-13. SAML Tracer

The same plug-in is available for Chrome browsers as well. Now that we've gotten used to SAML, let's look at OAuth, starting with using Jamf Connect for the Mac.

Use Jamf Connect to Authenticate to an IdP at the Login Window

Jamf Connect was the first app (as well as its original incarnation NoMAD Pro) is a bundle of three apps that provide access to a number of OpenID providers, including Google, Microsoft, and Yahoo!, at the login window for macOS. This includes a few tools (as seen in the installation package shown in Figure 12-14):

- **Jamf Connect Login**: Login window that helps administrators create accounts on machines and authenticates an end user to an identity provider.
- **Jamf Connect Verify**: Used for keeping the local account and web identity provider in sync. Then it handles the authentication and any following authorization for handling Kerberos tickets, linking legacy identity to more modern forms of identities.
- **Jamf Connect Sync**: Does the same as the preceding tool, but specifically for Okta.

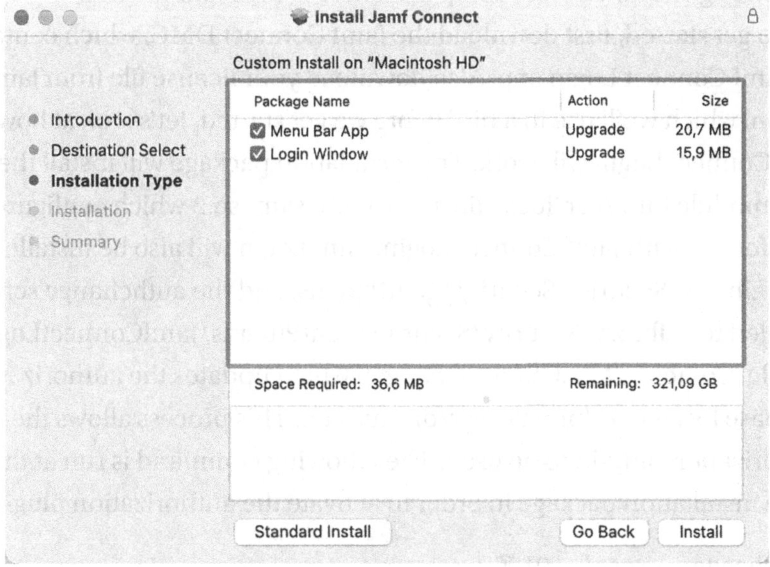

***Figure 12-14.** Jamf Connect installation*

The developers of Jamf Connect have indicated to the authors of this book that they plan to merge these into one app in the next year; however, understanding them as stand-alone apps helps keep the tasks being performed separate. We'll start with setting up Jamf Connect Login.

Configure Jamf Connect Login

The macOS login window is pluggable, meaning that developers can write tools that extend the functionality of the login window. Jamf Connect Login is an authorization plug-in for the login window, similar to a PAM module, or pluggable authentication module. There aren't a ton of PAM modules out there, and the technology has never been standardized, but Jamf Connect Login also comes with a PAM module in order to facilitate managing the login at a sudo prompt when using Terminal. But they have been around for a long time in variants of Unix and Linux and are commonly used to integrate authentication schemes between languages and through APIs. The API being used here is the login window.

To get started, first download the Jamf Connect DMG, which contains the Jamf Connect Login app. Also download your license file from Jamf Nation, which we'll use in a bit. Before we get started, let's look at how Jamf Connect Login will work. The installation package will install the PAM module into /usr/local/lib/pam/pam_saml.so.2 which configures sudo for use with Jamf Connect Login. Jamf Login will also be installed into /Library/Security/SecurityAgentPlugins, and the authchange script is installed to /Library/Security/SecurityAgentPlugins/JamfConnectLogin.bundle/Contents/MacOS/authchanger, which updates the authorization database located at /private/var/db/auth.db. This process allows the authorization plug-in to be used. The following command is run at the end of the installation package in order to activate the authorization plug-in:

```
authchanger -reset -OIDC
```

You don't need to do this manually, unless you're customizing the package that installs Jamf Connect Login for the client computer. Once run, to see your authorization database, simply run that authchanger command with the -print option:

```
authchanger -print
```

The authchanger command also supports a number of other flags such as -prelogin to provide a mechanism to use before the user interface shows up or -preAuth to give a mechanism to be used between the login interface and actual authentication (e.g., if you need to alter data prior to authentication. We won't get into more advanced preflight and postflight scripting to customize how things work, but know that these are options as your environment matures.

Now that we've covered how this works once installed, we'll customize the package for the specific identity provider and well-known URLs in use by your identity provider. To get started, customize the package for installation. We'll use Okta to continue on with the previous walk-throughs. Start by opening the Jamf Connect DMG available from Jamf. Then open the example plist in a text editor and provide the AuthServerpreference key.

Jamf Pro admins will also want to allow certificate-based and push notification access, as well as a PPPC profile for Connect (Figure 12-15, but for more on PPPC, see Chapter 4).

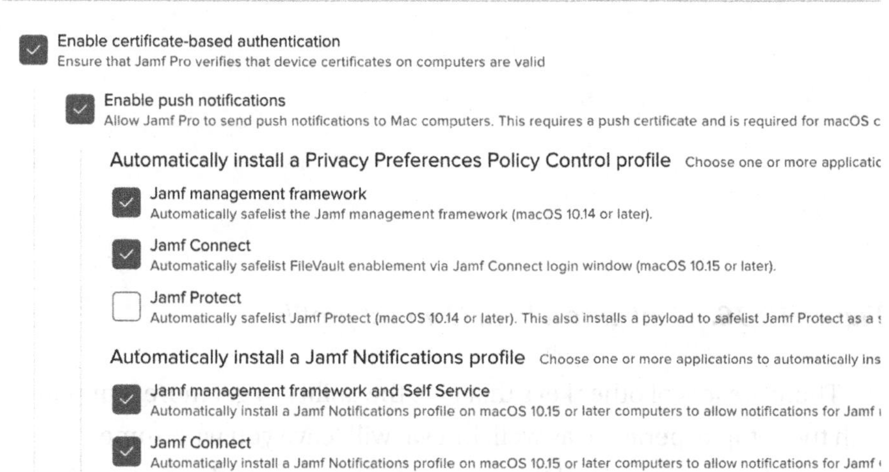

***Figure 12-15.** PPPC options for Jamf Connect*

Once satisfied with the changes to the Jamf Connect Login property list and other settings, it can be uploaded to an MDM solution for deployment. Jamf also makes some settings for Connect available (Figure 12-16) in the Applications & Custom Settings Payload options, which can also show a preview of the property list for use in other tools. Upload the provided license key configuration profile to your MDM solution.

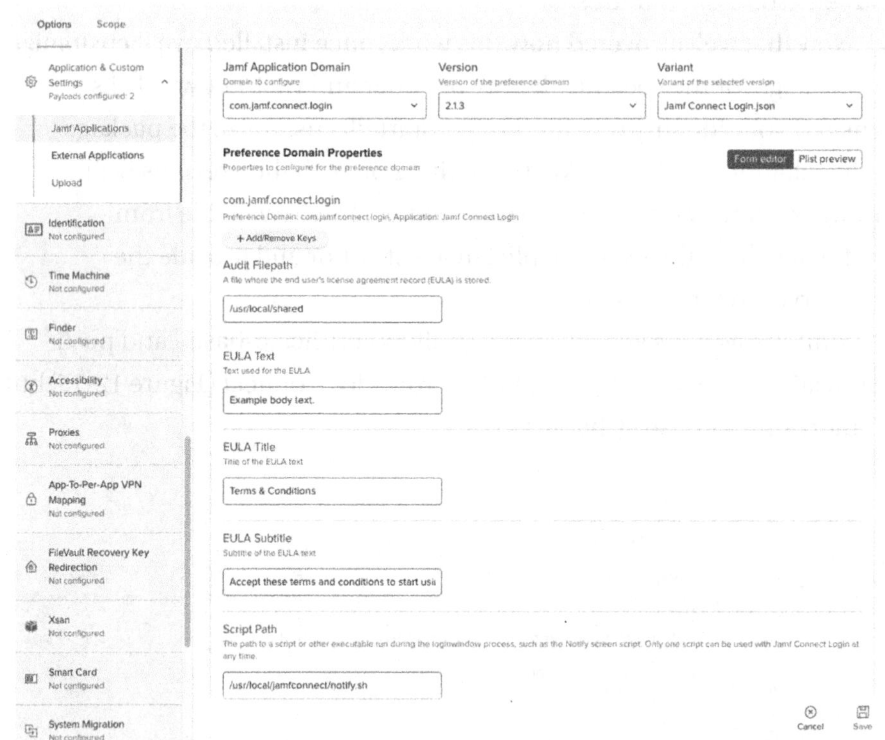

***Figure 12-16.** Configure a Jamf Connect profile*

There are lots of other keys that give the ability to get more granular with the setup experience as well, but we will leave you with some surprises for when you read the product manual. Once the package is installed and the preferences in place, it's time to test the first login!

To do so, first reboot the computer to make sure the experience matches what a user will see the first time they use their machine. At this point, you'll see the new Jamf Connect login screen (with branding, yours may appear different than that in Figure 12-17).

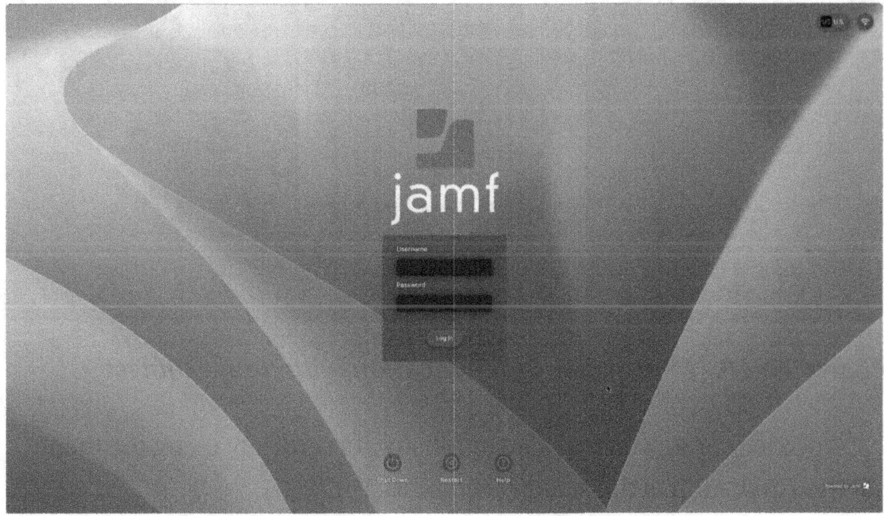

***Figure 12-17.** The Jamf Connect login window*

The federated identity service will then prompt for a login the first time you authenticate with that service, as seen in Figure 12-18, for Azure Active Directory. Provide the username and password using the screens, which also appear differently per vendor.

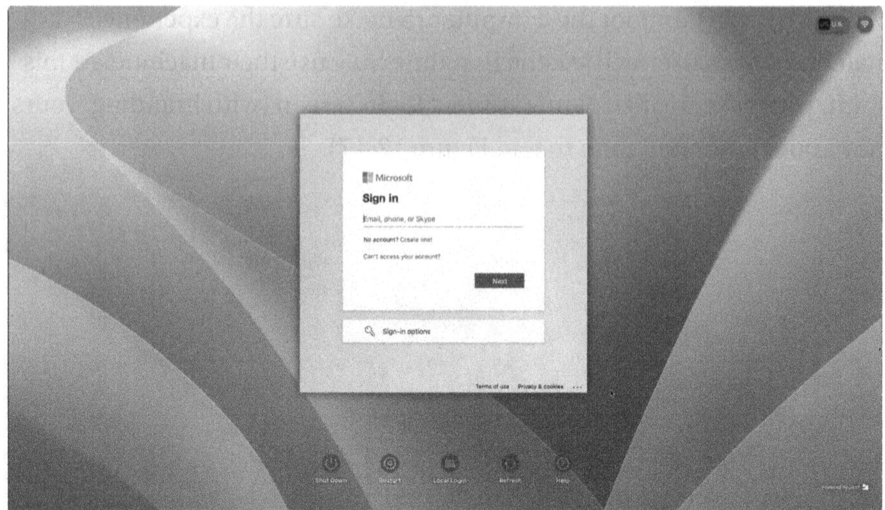

Figure 12-18. *Multifactor authentication with Jamf Connect*

Once logged in, you can also manually authenticate using the menu bar item at the top of the screen (Figure 12-19).

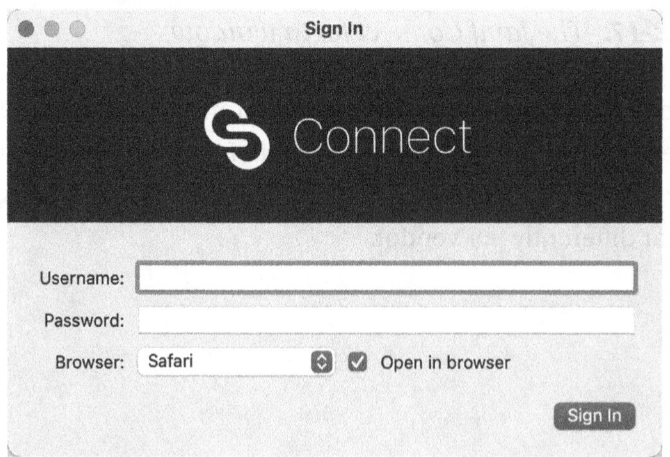

Figure 12-19. *Signing in with the Jamf Connect menu*

To see logs, open /private/tmp/jamf_login.log to see what was logged. You can also view debug logs by searching the log for com.jamf.connect.login as the predicate:

```
log stream --predicate 'subsystem == "com.jamf.connect.
login"' --debug
```

This gives you enough information to troubleshoot should you need to. If you so choose (and you should since you're paying for it), you can also get the passwords synchronized for Okta, using Jamf Connect Sync. Jamf Connect Sync is similar: a package and a profile that sends the AuthServer preference key to the com.jamf.connect.sync defaults domain. This is a string to your Okta instance. Once installed, the login window can be branded for your organization, have login policies, etc.

Jamf Connect for Mac can be useful in any Mac environment with an investment in an identity provider where Macs are used. Jamf Connect is an entirely different tool, and so we'll cover that in the following section.

Alternatives to Jamf Connect

Great ideas are meant to be copied, especially when some of the code from Jamf Connect is derived from the open source NoMAD project that existed before it became a Jamf product. Mosyle Auth, Kandji Passport (Figure 12-20), Addigy Identity, XCreds by Twocanoes (Figure 12-21 shows the configuration property list with lots of settings not found elsewhere as of the time of this writing), and others come with some of the same features as Jamf Connect but require less setup work with each of those solutions. Some also still use NoMAD, as we covered earlier in the book.

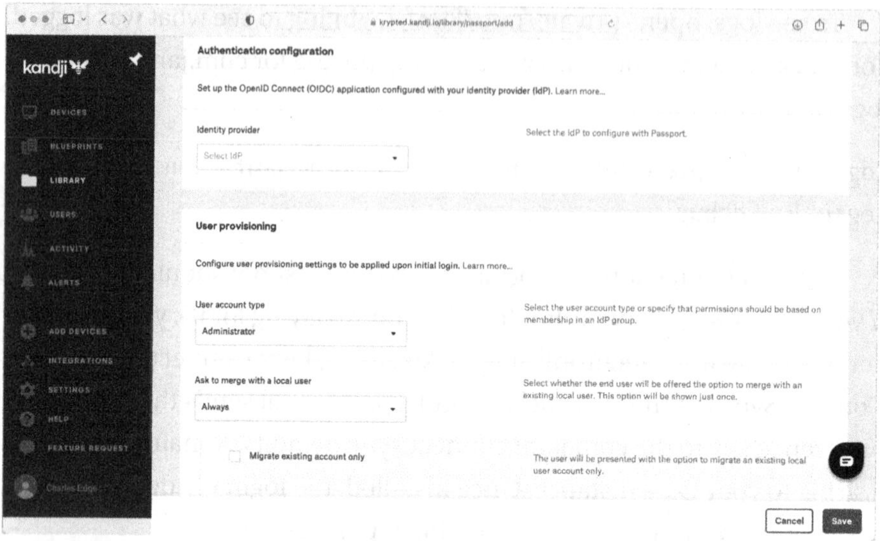

Figure 12-20. *Build Kandji Passport in the web interface*

Another option is what Apple calls Platform SSO, part of a more comprehensive strategy to deal with federated identities from Apple – documented at `https://developer.apple.com/documentation/authenticationservices`. As of the time of this writing, all of the platform single sign-on options are still in beta, and the only third-party vendor to work with it fully is Microsoft. This is built into the Microsoft Authenticator app for iOS and iPadOS devices and the Intune Company Portal for macOS-based devices. The Platform SSO extension is likely to be used by many other vendors as it's an extension, and on the MDM side, it's just a profile that can be easily configured.

com.twocanoes.xcreds.plist

com.twocanoes.xcreds

com.twocanoes.xcreds 〉 No Selection

Key	Type	Value
pfm_type	String	string
pfm_title	String	Local Username
pfm_description	String	When a user uses cloud login, XCreds will try and figure out the loc
pfm_default	String	
> Item 10	Dictionary	(5 items)
> Item 11	Dictionary	(5 items)
> Item 12	Dictionary	(5 items)
> Item 13	Dictionary	(5 items)
> Item 14	Dictionary	(5 items)
> Item 15	Dictionary	(5 items)
> Item 16	Dictionary	(5 items)
∨ Item 17	Dictionary	(5 items)
pfm_name	String	shouldShowSupportStatus
pfm_type	String	boolean
pfm_title	String	Show Support Status Message
pfm_description	String	Show message in XCreds Login reminding people to buy support.
pfm_default	Boolean	YES
> Item 18	Dictionary	(5 items)
> Item 19	Dictionary	(5 items)
∨ Item 20	Dictionary	(5 items)
pfm_name	String	shouldSetGoogleAccessTypeToOffline
pfm_type	String	boolean
pfm_title	String	Request Google Refresh Token
pfm_description	String	When using Google IdP, a refresh token may need be requested in a
pfm_default	Boolean	NO
> Item 21	Dictionary	(5 items)
> Item 22	Dictionary	(5 items)
> Item 23	Dictionary	(5 items)
∨ Item 24	Dictionary	(5 items)
pfm_name	String	CreateAdminUser
pfm_type	String	boolean
pfm_title	String	Create User as Admin
pfm_description	String	When set to true and the user account is created, the user will be a
pfm_default	Boolean	NO

***Figure 12-21.** Most of the tools have property lists to configure options, like this one for Kandji*

Use Azure AD for Conditional Access

Conditional Access is a feature of Azure Active Directory that controls access to cloud-based or SaaS apps based on where a device meets a number of conditions, such as whether the device has a security posture that meets the requirements of an organization. This is also available with Google's BeyondCorp (or BeyondTrust) service(s) and a number of other tools that isolate the security posture of a device before granting access to the user account to log in to any services.

Conditional Access allows an administrator to then build policies that are enforced at any point during the authentication and authorization process to access a resource. Gating access to content based on the security posture of a device is a growing requirement for any type of environment and is therefore a growing requirement for administrators of any device, including Apple devices. A number of MDM or identity products have then introduced features to allow for this, many leveraging the Microsoft APIs for Intune or Office 365 to gate access.

Each of those MDM developers has their own strategy and outcomes. Some have built their own app ecosystem, others have chosen to use proxies, or ZTNA (Zero Trust Network Access) solutions, where vendors pretend to be doing more complicated tasks than proxies. Some do a pure API-level integration with an identity provider or SaaS solution. Deciphering what is happening and exactly what outcomes to expect during the planning phase can then be a challenge as engineers navigate through marketing speak.

We'll start our review of Conditional Access integrations by looking at the Jamf and Intune integration. This integration allows organizations to make sure only trusted users on Macs that meet a given security posture are given access to applications or other resources owned by an organization. This is done by flowing information from Jamf Pro into the Microsoft Intune database, which Jamf Pro pushes there using the Microsoft Graph API. Based on smart group membership access, applications are set up in Azure Active Directory, and then if a device meets requirements, they are given access to those apps. Additionally, the Jamf Self Service app can put a machine into compliance if it falls out of compliance.

Configure the Jamf Integration with Intune

There are a few requirements to be aware of before configuring the Jamf Intune Conditional Access integration. The Jamf Intune integration requires an account to access a Jamf Pro instance. This account should also have Conditional Access privileges. Additionally, you'll need an account with Intune. Finally, you'll need devices running a minimum of macOS 10.11 in order for machines to be configured.

Once you've made sure that you meet the minimum requirements, open Jamf Pro and then click the Settings icon. Then click Conditional Access in the Global Management section of the page (Figure 12-22).

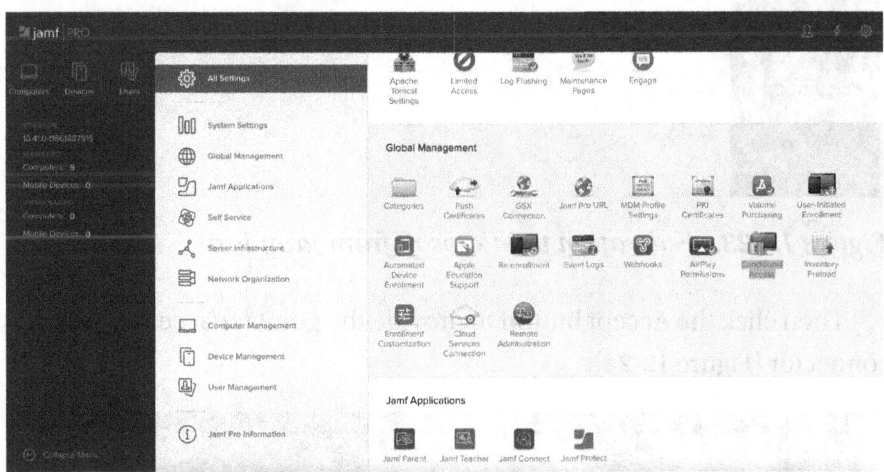

Figure 12-22. *Jamf Pro settings*

At the Conditional Access screen, click the Edit button. Here, you will have the following settings available. To begin the process of linking accounts, check the box for Enable Intune Integration for macOS. This enables the integration. When this setting is selected, Jamf Pro will send inventory updates to Microsoft Intune. Clear the selection if you want to disable the connection, but save your configuration once we're done.

Next, select the region of your Microsoft Azure Active Directory instance in the SOVEREIGN CLOUD field (Figure 12-23), which should by default be set to GLOBAL. Then click the "Open Administrator Consent URL" button to open the window to integrate with the Azure Active Directory instance. Once clicked, provide a username and password for the Azure Active Directory tenant where you have access to Conditional Access and click the Sign In button.

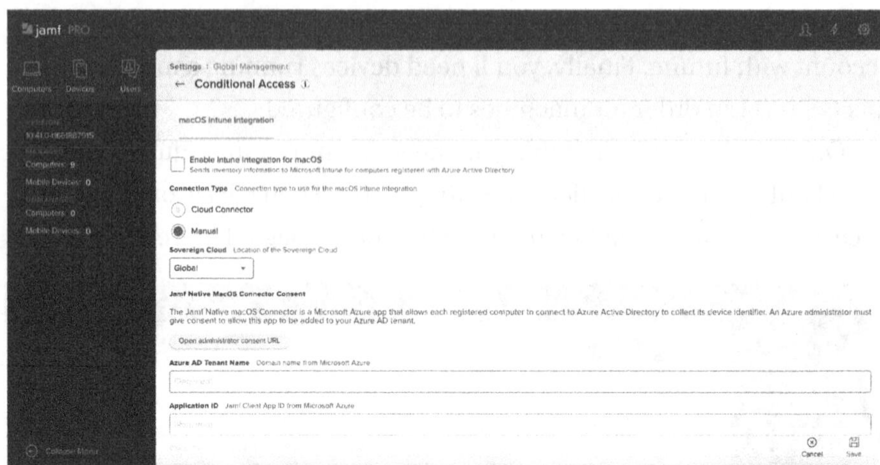

Figure 12-23. *Federation to Microsoft from Jamf Pro*

Then click the Accept button to provide the grant for accessing the connector (Figure 12-24).

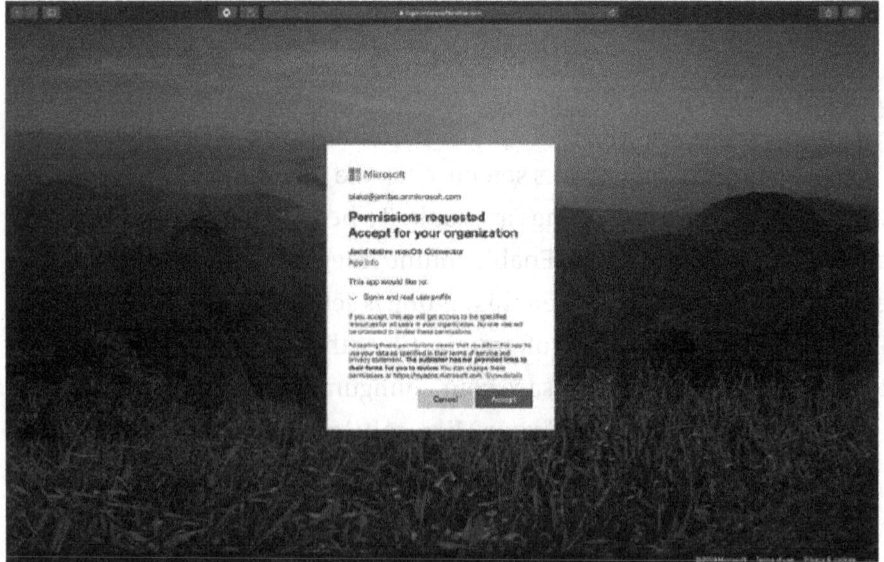

Figure 12-24. *Configuring the grant type*

Provided the connection is established, you'll then be prompted that the "App has been added." When the setup is initially established. Back at the Jamf Instance, the Jamf Native macOS Connector app is running, and you can then configure the rest of the settings. In the AZURE AD TENANT NAME section, provide the name of the Active Directory Azure tenant, and in the APPLICATION ID, provide the ID of the Jamf Client app from Microsoft Azure. Those settings are matched with the Name and Application ID from the Properties of the Connector in Azure, shown in Figure 12-25.

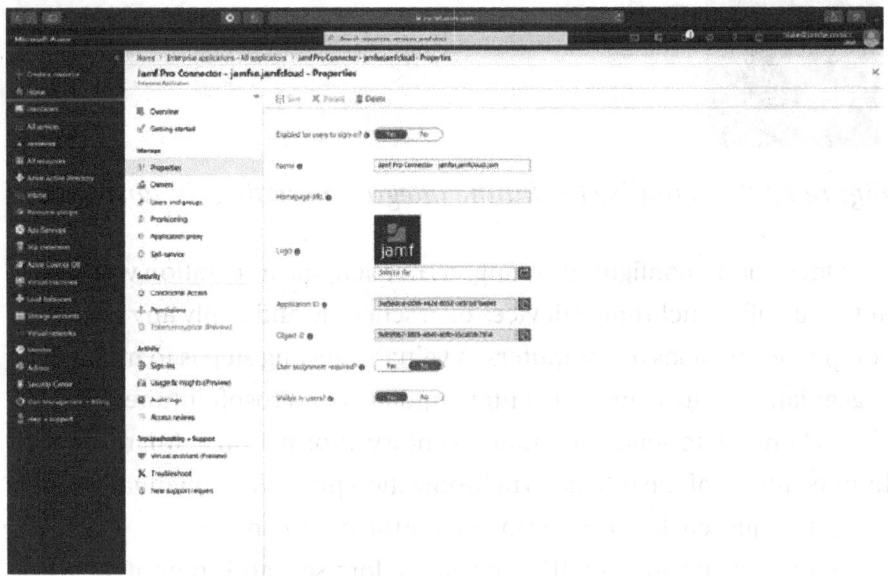

***Figure 12-25.** Configure the Jamf Pro Connector in Azure*

Finally, in the LANDING PAGE FOR COMPUTERS NOT RECOGNIZED BY MICROSOFT AZURE, the default here is the Jamf Pro Device Registration page or the standard page to add devices. Additionally, you can automatically deny access or provide a custom URL so you can script your own workflow to remediate devices (Figure 12-26).

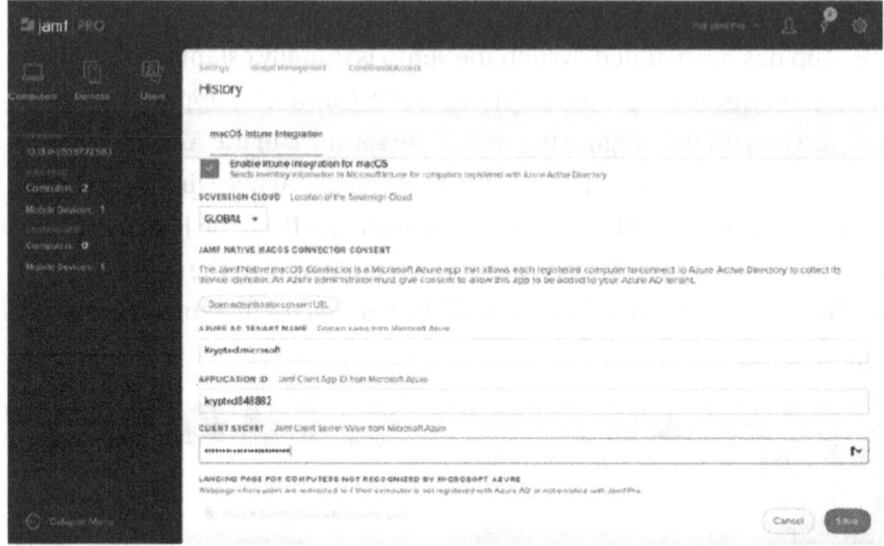

Figure 12-26. Finalize the Intune integration settings in Jamf Pro

Once you've configured settings as needed, the integration will automatically synchronize devices on a schedule and apply any necessary compliance policies to computers. A valuable testing step is to manually trigger Jamf Pro to send an inventory update to Microsoft Intune. This allows Jamf Pro to send computer inventory information to Microsoft Intune outside of the regular synchronization process. To manually send an update, just click the Send Update button once configured.

Azure Active Directory ID information for users and computers appears in the Local User Account category for a computer's inventory information in Jamf Pro. For more on setting up this integration, see `https://docs.jamf.com/10.24.1/jamf-pro/administrator-guide/Microsoft_Intune_Integration.html`.

Beyond Authentication

Now that we've gone through how common tools provision identity information through OAuth Connect and SAML, let's take a much more user-centric approach. Because an IdP is so integral to the future of device management, a number of device management vendors have chosen to release their own identity provider, hoping to reduce the friction required and build a better user experience for customers. MobileIron Access and VMware Identity Manager are two such products.

VMware Identity Manager works in conjunction with the VMware approach that in order to simplify the user experience, you want to provide users with one pane of glass to access web, mobile, SaaS, and legacy apps. Having a user provide credentials at provisioning time and then simply accessing those resources through Identity Manager allows VMware to save end users time and build a great user experience by using the Self Service App Store as a means to see all of that. Bolt multifactor authentication and the in-depth knowledge of what's on a device and how the device is configured that the device management piece brings in and you have a pretty complete solution. This is the goal of Workspace ONE, using the Workspace ONE Intelligent Hub. For more on Workspace ONE, see `https://docs.vmware.com/en/VMware-Workspace-ONE/index.html`.

Multifactor Authentication

Multifactor authentication combines two or more independent credentials to authenticate. Think of these as something the user knows, like a password; something the user is, like a fingerprint or Face ID verification; and something a user has, like a security token. This provides a layered defense. A password can be written on a sticky note. But the chances of the sticky note making it into the hands of someone who can unlock a phone through Touch ID and accept a prompt increase the security of that transaction.

There are a variety of factors that go into the need for multifactor authentication. Maybe a local password database gets compromised. Those passwords are often reused across a number of different sites. Messaging a phone when the password is used then reduces the risk that the password alone can give an attacker access to a given resource.

An early example might be swiping an ATM card (something you have) and then entering a PIN (something you know). A modern representation would be entering a username and password in a website and then entering a code sent to your phone via text message – or to make this process even simpler now, entering your Apple ID and then just tapping Allow on your phone. While Apple began to adopt multifactor authentication with iCloud, that's for accessing Apple services.

Many vendors are looking to give organizations access to similar levels of security. If you're reading this book, chances are you were exposed to an RSA SecurID in your career. This was the standard in token-based multifactor authentication for a long time. But why use physical tokens when we can replace the function that those provide with an app? Salesforce Authenticator and Microsoft Authenticator are two such apps.

Microsoft Authenticator

The Microsoft Authenticator app (available for iOS and Android) is used to sign in, back up, and recover account credentials and adds a two-step verification to the signing process for integrated products. Microsoft Authenticator also has the option to require biometric (Touch ID or Face ID) or a PIN code to get that second step for verification. The administrator can choose to require that or allow a user to configure it.

The Microsoft Authenticator app also supports one-time passcodes. Here, a time-based, one-time passcode secures an online account that's been configured to work with the TOTP standard, providing added security. An example of using this option would be an integration with GitHub. To configure GitHub for two-factor authentication, go to the

Settings page, then Security, and select "Personal settings" in the sidebar. Click Enable two-factor authentication and then select the option to "Set up using an app."

Make sure to keep the security codes when you're prompted with them. Your account is lost if you lose them. Like really, really lost. When you see the QR code, open the Microsoft Authenticator app, select "Add account," and then enter the text at the top of the site.

This process is similar to how you set up a SmartThings bridge to manage the lights in your home, various HomeKit-enabled devices, and other IoT-based authentication flows. The fact that you have a short amount of time to enter codes keeps the transactions secure, and the simplicity of the QR code workflow in exchange for a token keeps our coworkers from doing wonky things.

Finally, Microsoft Authenticator has the Apple Platform SSO extensions built in. As of the time of this writing, it's one of the only tools to support this new approach to SSO, and there aren't a lot of tools that work with it, but that should change over the course of the next few years.

MobileIron Access

MobileIron Authenticator is another such an app. MobileIron Access starts with using MobileIron Authenticator as a soft token app that replaces hard tokens with an automated setup experience that provides a one-touch activation process. Once configured, users verify login attempts with the app in much the same way that Apple prompts you on iCloud-enabled devices when you access various services for the first time on a device. Apple devices will push that notification through APNs and then aggregate information from security products, apps, the state of the device, and the user location.

This provides a framework for remediation workflows. So if a user violates a given policy, MobileIron Access will then silo the user into a group and gate access to various resources until the device no longer violates that policy. Users can run their own remediation flows and will be prompted on the device to perform given tasks that get the device back into a state where it can be trusted again.

All of this does require that each part of the ecosystem is aware of the type of transaction being performed when replacing a password with a push notification response. For example, if you're using OAuth to provide a single sign-on to a site, and that site will send a push notification to MobileIron Authenticator, then the site needs to have code in the authentication page that does that instead of prompting the user for the password. This would then put the task of brokering the OAuth token on MobileIron instead of on a handler that runs when the login button is clicked.

Putting the job of authenticating users into a new flow is more secure and provides the benefit that the single sign-on transaction can be based on the context of the user, device, and ecosystem requesting access; however, this can limit the vendors you work with.

For more on MobileIron Access, see `https://community.mobileiron.com/docs/DOC-4417` or `https://help.ivanti.com/mi/help/en_us/ACC/46/gd/Content/AccessGuide/About_multi_factor_authe.htm` for `MobileIron Authenticator`.

Conditional Access for Google Workspace

Google Workspace has an option for Conditional Access through their BeyondCorp Enterprise integration. As of the printing of this book, Google Workspace (formerly known as G Suite) doesn't allow for creating a device in Google Directory easily. This means that you would need to routinely manually upload a list of device serial numbers in order to get devices into Google Workspace. Once devices are in Google Workspace, you can build a Google Cloud Function that takes output from a webhook and changes the state of that device.

Tools like Kandji and others can integrate with a Google Workspace domain to do things like import user accounts, but that's using Google as an identity provider, not a Conditional Access provider - although similar functionality can be scripted among MDM providers.

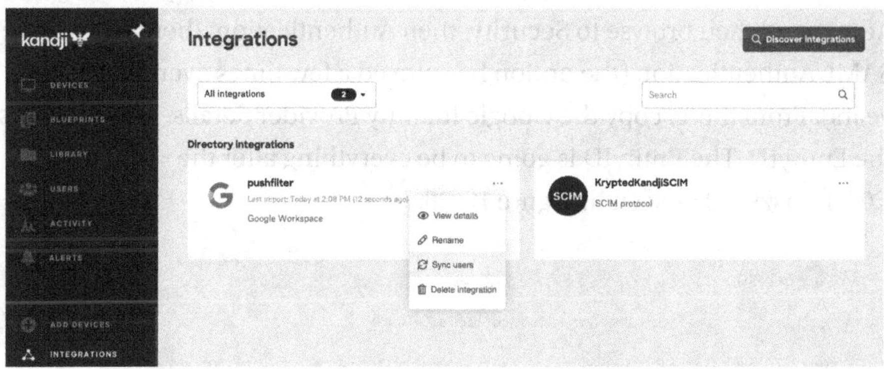

Figure 12-27. *Kandji integration with Google Workspace*

These and other directory integrations with other vendors don't get an organization all the way to a BeyondCorp integration. Instead, customers need to contact Google to buy BeyondCorp licensing or do manual integrations themselves. Once the environment is integrated with Google, so the status of a device can be seen in tools like Kandji, it can then be reported back to Google Workspace as needed. The easiest way to tackle that is to use Google's cloud offering, GCP (Google Cloud Platform), to script device trust manually. If the device doesn't meet the required attributes in the MDM or device management suite, then automate disabling accounts or restricting access to various resources.

Obtain Your CustomerID from Google Workspace

The first thing that's required to work with GCP is a valid login to `https://admin.google.com/`. Once logged in, a CustomerID will be necessary to programmatically connect. There are a few ways to grab a CustomerID from Google Workspace. This is important when configuring SSO or when interfacing between Google Workspace, G Suite, or GCP programmatically (through their lovely API).

The first and easiest way to obtain the CustomerID is to look at the web interface. This isn't the most intuitive. To find the key, open Google Admin and then browse to Security, then Authentication, then SSO with SAML Authentication (the option has moved a few times over the past few years). From there, copy the Google Identity Provider details. This includes the EntityID. The EntityID is going to be everything after the = such as C034minsz9330 as seen in Figure 12-28.

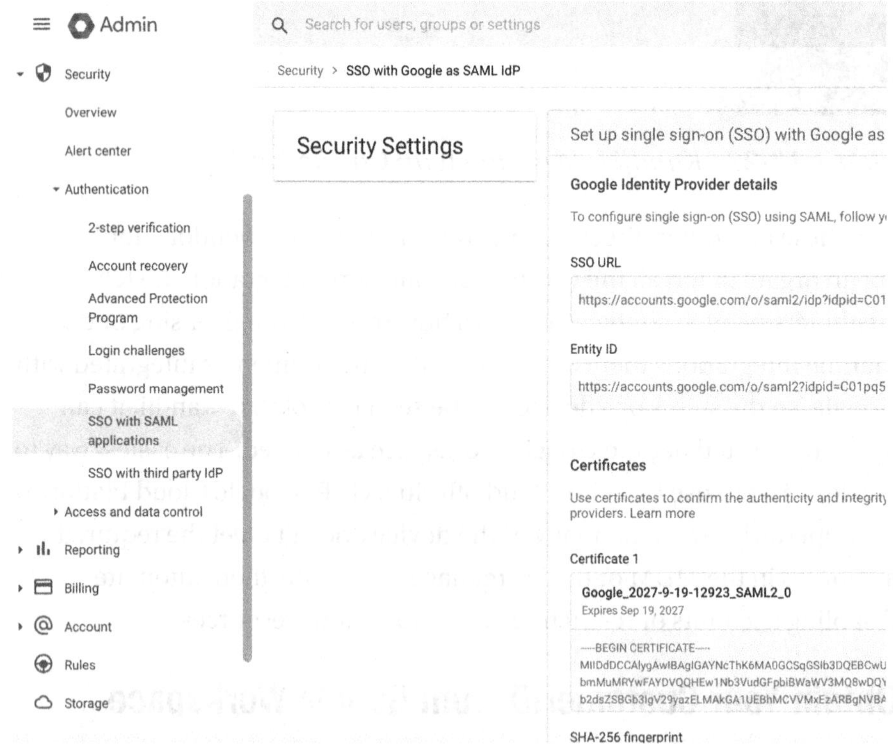

Figure 12-28. Obtain your Google URLs

While here, also grab the SSO URL and the certificates to secure communications. This key should not be rotated. Once you have the key, you can communicate with the Google API Gateway, for example:

```
curl 'https://www.googleapis.com/admin/directory/v1/
customers/$CUSTOMERKEY' \
--header 'Authorization: Bearer [$ACCESSTOKEN]' \
--header 'Accept: application/json' \
--compressed
```

Provision a Google Cloud Function Resource

Google Cloud Functions (GCFs) provide a streamlined method for running a simple microservice leveraging custom functions as well as SDKs for any Google service that can be imported into your script. Currently, node.js is the only nonbeta language you can build scripts in. Before you set up Google Cloud Functions to work with a Google Workspace domain, first provide the account of a developer with the appropriate permissions. Google Workspace has a number of features exposed to their API by importing SDKs into projects. As an example, the Admin SDK provides us with endpoints and classes that make developing microservices to perform actions in the G Suite admin portal easier. In this section, we'll import that SDK, although the tasks for importing other SDKs are similar.

Enable the Necessary APIs

To get started, open the Google Cloud Platform using the button in the upper left-hand corner and click APIs and Services (the names of these buttons change over time, but the screen should appear similar to that in Figure 12-29).

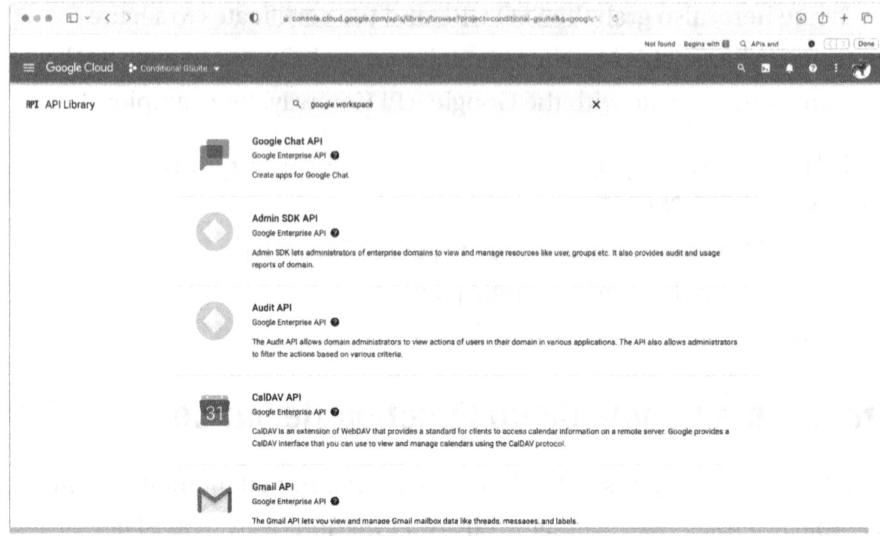

Figure 12-29. *Configure OAuth*

Next, click the Enable APIs and Services button in the dashboard. Under Credentials, provide the appropriate credentials for the app you're importing the SDK into. Search for Admin SDK API. From the entry for Admin SDK, made by Google, click Enable (Figure 12-33). Once enabled, you'll need to create a service account for your function to communicate with. Click Credentials (Figure 12-30).

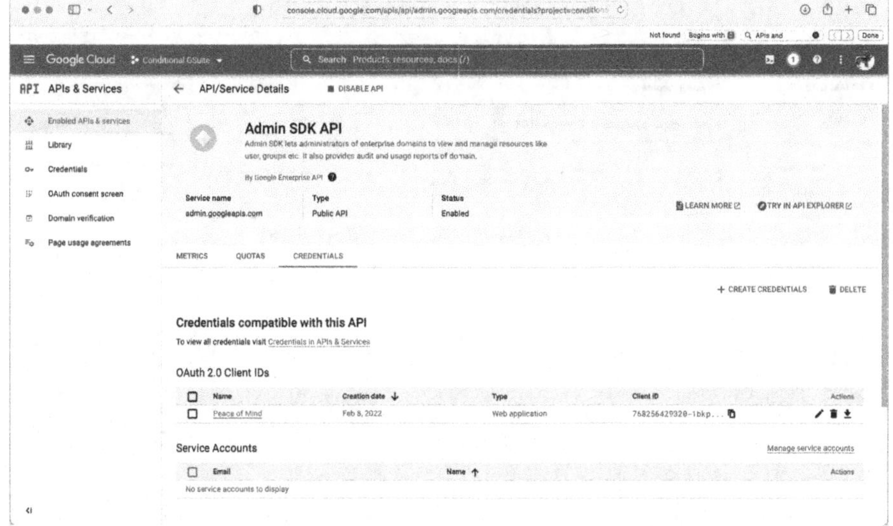

Figure 12-30. *Credentials for the Admin SDK*

Create a Service Account

Service accounts give you a JWT, useful to authenticate from a Google Cloud Function back to an instance of the Google Workspace Admin portal endpoints. To set up a service account, go to "IAM & Admin" using the button in the upper left-hand corner and click Service Accounts (Figure 12-31).

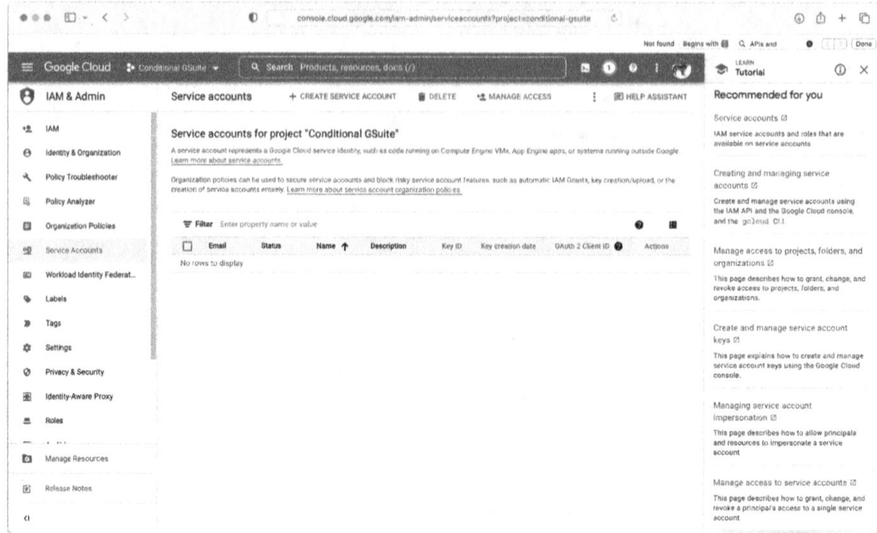

Figure 12-31. *View service accounts*

Click Create Service Accounts (Figure 12-32).

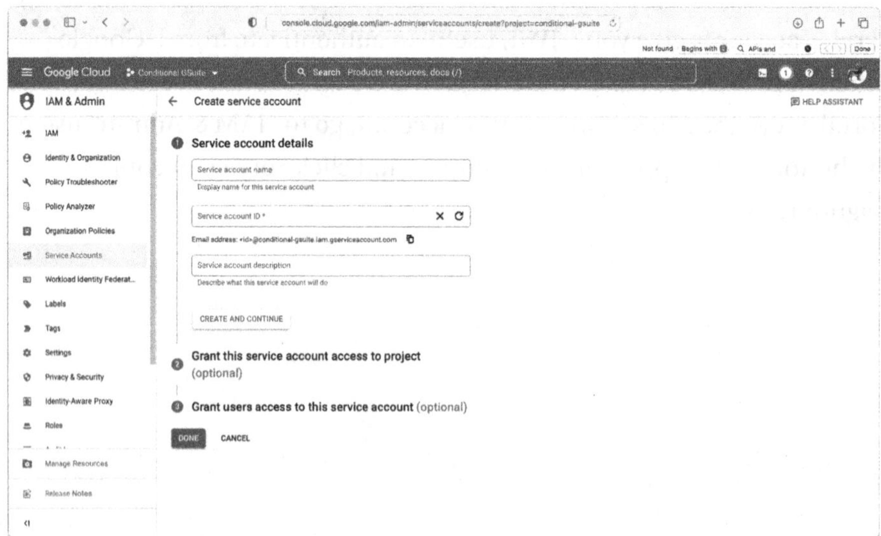

Figure 12-32. *Create a new Google service account for your Cloud Function*

Provide a project name and a location (if your organization uses locations); otherwise, leave that set to No Organization and click CREATE. Now that you've set up a project, let's create the actual function.

Create Your Google Cloud Function

The Google Cloud Function is then a microservice that can be called routinely, similar to the process that the Jamf Connect for iOS app performs (or any of the competitors). This might be sending some json from an app to perform a task from an app or sending a webhook to the function to perform an action. To get started with functions, click Cloud Function at the bottom of the Google Cloud Platform dashboard and then click Enable Billing. Given the word Billing is present, this will require a credit card, although less than a penny was spent writing this section of the book. If necessary, click UPGRADE.

The function API will also need to be enabled for billing, if it hasn't already been for the account used. To do so, click Enable API. Once all of this is done, there should be a button that says Create function. Click that and then you'll be able to provide settings for the function.

Settings include the following (Figure 12-33):

- **Name**: How the function is called in the admin panel.
- **Memory allocated**: How much memory the function can consume.
- **Trigger**: Most will use HTTP for our purposes.
- **URL**: The URL you use to call the function.
- **Source**: The code (typically node.js) that is run.

Note The package.json allows us to leverage this function in a multitenant fashion.

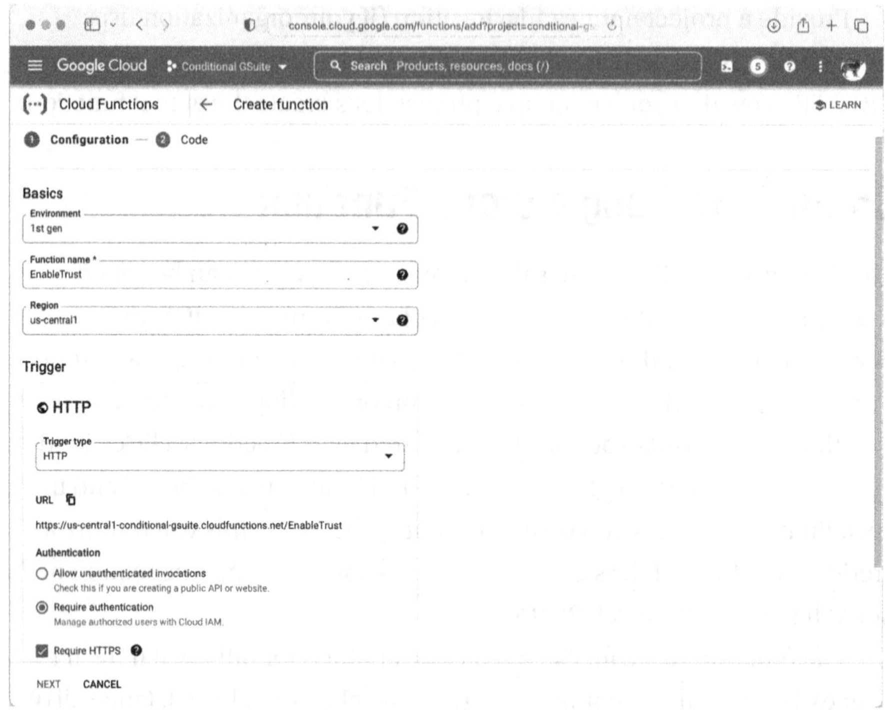

***Figure 12-33.** Create a Google Cloud Function*

Once enabled, you can hit the endpoint. To load a script, click Next and paste the script in so it's run when triggered (Figure 12-34).

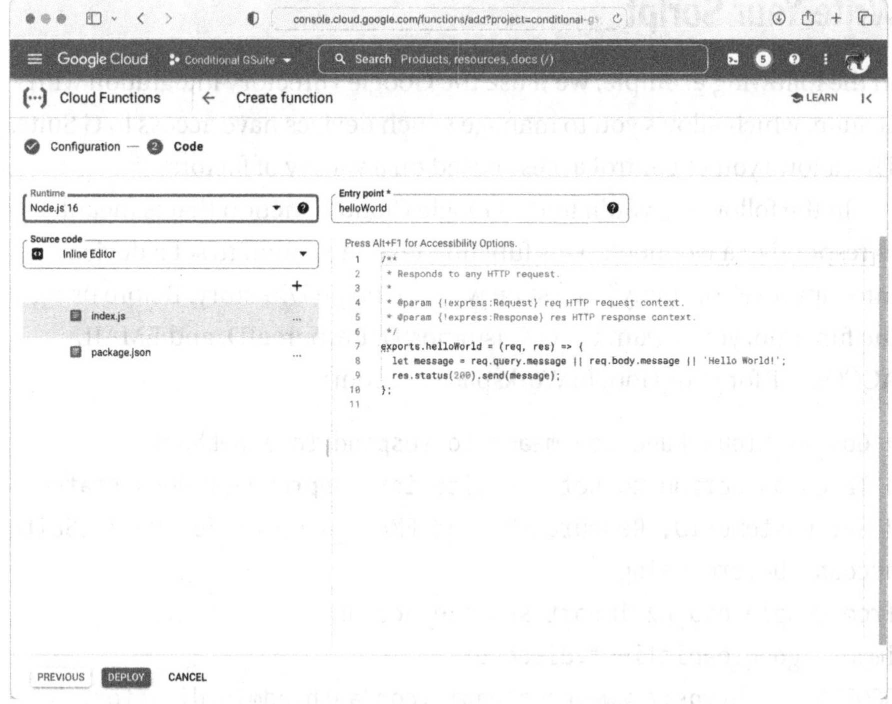

***Figure 12-34.** Add code to the function*

This is similar to how Amazon Lambda's run as well. To access the function once created, use curl to send a command to the URL provided earlier. If there's no header parameters you need to send, that could be as simple as

```
curl https://us-central1-alpine-canto-231018.cloudfunctions.
net/test-function
```

Now that we have a sample up, let's actually build a script we can paste into the function in the next section.

Write Your Script

In the following example, we'll use the Google Directory integration with G Suite, which allows you to manage which devices have access to G Suite. This allows you to control access based on a variety of factors.

In the following, you'll find a Google Cloud Function that is meant to respond to a webhook. This function takes an action to set a device into "approve" or "deny" as a state within Google Directory. Before using the function, you'll want to set CustomerID, ResourceID, and EMAIL_ACCOUNT for your Google Workspace account:

```
# Google Cloud Function meant to respond to a webhook
# Takes an action to set a device into approve or deny state
# Set CustomerID, ResourceID, and EMAIL_ACCOUNT for your GSuite
account before using
from google.oauth2 import service_account
import googleapiclient.discovery
SCOPES = ['https://www.googleapis.com/auth/admin.directory.
device.mobile']
SERVICE_ACCOUNT_FILE = 'auth.json'
EMAIL_ACCOUNT = '<INSERTTHEEMAILADDRESSHERE>'
def get_credential():

credentials = service_account.Credentials.from_service_account_
file(SERVICE_ACCOUNT_FILE, scopes=SCOPES)

delegated_credentials = credentials.with_subject(EMAIL_ACCOUNT)

# admin = googleapiclient.discovery.build('admin', 'directory_
v1', credentials=credentials)

admin = googleapiclient.discovery.build('admin', 'directory_
v1', credentials=delegated_credentials)
    return admin
def get_mobiledevice_list(admin, customerId):
```

```
results = admin.mobiledevices().list(customerId=customerId).
execute()
    mobiledevices = results.get('mobiledevices', [])
    print('mobile devices name and resourceId')
    for mobiledevice in mobiledevices:

print(u'{0} ({1})'.format(mobiledevice['name'],
mobiledevice['resourceId']))
    return results
def action_mobiledevice(admin, customerId, resourceId,
actionName):  # actionName: "approve", "block",etc
    body = dict(action=actionName)

results = admin.mobiledevices().action(customerId=customerId,
resourceId=resourceId, body=body).execute()
    return results
def main():
    admin = get_credential()
    customerId = '<INSERTTHECUSTOMERIDHERE>'
    resourceId = '<INSERTTHEJWTHERE>'
    action = "approve"
    #action = "block"
    mobiledevice_list = get_mobiledevice_list(admin,
    customerId)
    print(mobiledevice_list)
    action_mobiledevice(admin, customerId, resourceId, action)
    print ("Approved successfully")
if __name__ == '__main__':
    main()
```

The webhook will then output when a device is approved or blocked. This could be triggered by a number of services that are integrated with an MDM, a configuration management solution, a fully separate automation-only tool, etc.

Duo Trusted Endpoints

Another approach is what Duo Security does with their Trusted Endpoints product. Trusted Endpoints allows an administrator to configure a Trusted Endpoints policy. The Trusted Endpoints policy gates access from devices to applications. This is done based on whether a certificate is on the device. As an example, the integration shown at `https://duo.com/docs/jamf-jss` for Jamf checks that a Jamf enrollment certificate is on a device, and some apps are only accessible if so.

If the certificate is present, Duo checks the device information against the required policy settings, and if appropriate, the requestor receives access to protected applications (Figure 12-35).

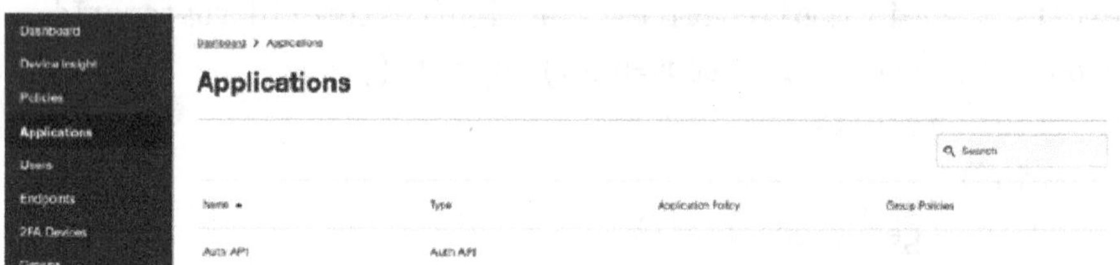

Figure 12-35. *The Duo Applications list*

The authentications are then tracked, and administrators can see traffic in the Duo dashboard (Figure 12-36).

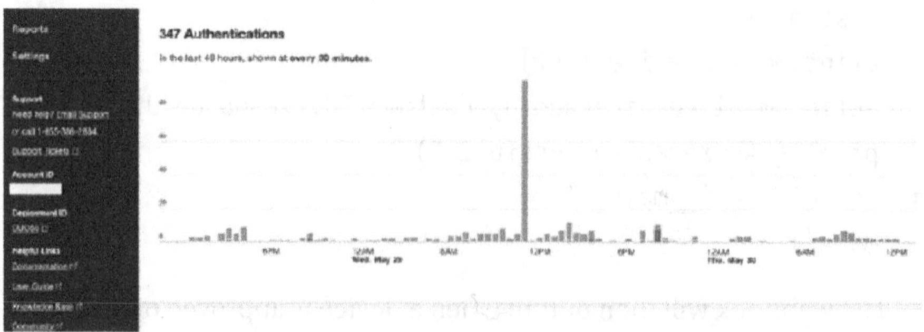

Figure 12-36. *Authentications in Duo*

Duo also has integrations with Sophos, MobileIron, LANDESK, Google G Suite, AirWatch/Workspace ONE, and a generic option for providing integration with management solutions they don't have an actual integration with (so some customization may be necessary).

Managed Apple IDs Continued

You use an Apple ID to access iCloud, install apps, and consume media in the Apple ecosystem. A Managed Apple ID is a type of Apple ID used to deploy apps and books as well as to configure devices. We'll cover how Managed Apple IDs are used in schools and business separately.

Managed Apple IDs also allow an administrator to accept Apple's terms and conditions on behalf of people who are usually not old enough to do so, like in schools. Managed Apple IDs that are provisioned through Apple School Manager (ASM) also come with 200GB of space in iCloud. These IDs should be unique, and many organizations create a subdomain just for them (e.g., appleid.company.com). But one of the most helpful is that Managed Apple IDs can be generated in bulk.

Managed Apple IDs in Schools

Managed Apple IDs require device supervisions and DEP enrollment. Once set up, administrators can assign VPP licenses to Managed Apple IDs for books and apps. However, students can't buy apps or books on their own. There are some teacher-centric options for Managed Apple IDs. Teachers can reset Managed Apple ID passwords through the Classroom app and collaborate with students in Keynote, Numbers, and Pages.

As mentioned, each Managed Apple ID should be unique (as with MAIDs for Apple Business Manager). This involves a unique username within a subdomain and not using an existing Apple ID. You can use modifiers (e.g., instead of using `john.doe@school.org`, you can use `john.doe+1@school.org`). This allows some options around moving an address for an existing Apple ID out of the way and then bringing it back. Or you could walk away from the old domain and move to `john.doe@appleid.school.org`.

Managed Apple IDs for Business

Apple announced Managed Apple IDs for Apple Business Manager at Managed Apple IDs are created for employees who sign in and manage functions of Apple Business Manager. Managed Apple IDs for Apple Business Manager are different. Managed Apple IDs in Apple Business Manager are to be used for managing tasks in Apple Business Manager only. There is no Apple Schoolwork or Apple Classroom app that users would require a Managed Apple ID for. There is no PowerSchool to source the accounts from.

There is also no extra 200GB of iCloud storage. This means the only things administrators do with those IDs are acquire content, supervise devices with device enrollment, and manage a handful of IT users that handle those roles. That doesn't mean that Apple will not change these capabilities in a future release, but for now there is likely little reason to add Azure federation if only IT teams are using a Managed Apple ID. For more on Apple Business Manager and Managed Apple IDs, see `https://help.apple.com/businessmanager/en.lproj/static.html#tes55db2af4a`.

Webhooks

A webhook is a small web trigger that, when fired, can easily send amount of small json to a web listener. Most modern software solutions support webhooks. They provide an easy way to trigger events from a piece of software to happen in another piece of software.

An example of this is when a smart group change happens in Jamf Pro, do something elsewhere. To start, you register a webhook in Jamf Pro by opening an instance of Jamf Pro, clicking Settings, clicking Global Management, and then clicking Webhooks (Figure 12-37).

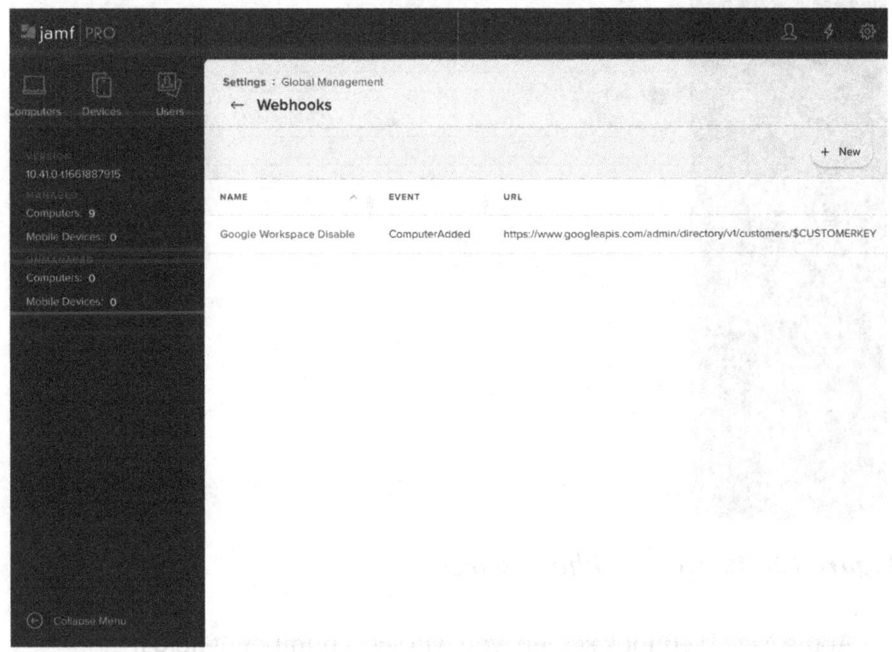

Figure 12-37. *Registering Webhooks*

From the Webhooks screen, click New (Figure 12-38).

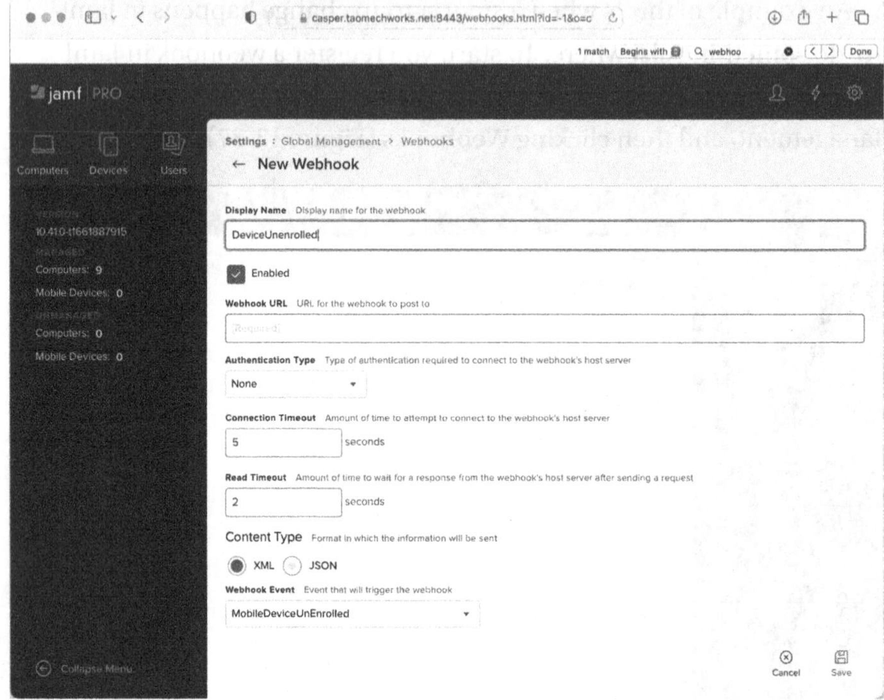

Figure 12-38. *New Webhook screen*

At the New Webhook screen, you will see a number of fields:

- **Display Name**: The name used to identify the webhook in Jamf Pro.
- **Enabled**: Check to enable the webhook; uncheck the box to disable the webhook.
- **Webhook URL**: The URL that the json or xml will be sent to (note that you'll need something at this URL to accept your webhook).
- **Authentication Type**: None is used for an anonymous webhook, and basic can be used to send a username and password to the webhook listener.

- **Connection Timeout**: How long the webhook will attempt to open a connection before sending data.
- **Read Timeout**: How long the webhook will attempt to send data for before it turns off.
- **Content Type**: Choose to send information via xml or json.
- **Webhook Event**: The type of event that Jamf Pro can send a hook based on.

The options for webhook events include

- ComputerAdded
- ComputerCheckin
- ComputerInventoryCompleted
- ComputerPatchPolicyCompleted
- ComputerPolicyFinished
- ComputerPushCapabilityChanged
- DeviceRateLimited
- JSSShutdown
- JSSStartup
- MobileDeviceCheckin
- MobileDeviceCommandCompleted
- MobileDeviceEnrolled
- PatchSoftwareTitleUpdated
- PushSent
- RestAPIOperation

- SCEPChallenge
- SmartGroupComputerMembershipChange
- SmartGroupMobileDeviceMembershipChange

An example of a full workflow would be what we did to trigger a Zapier action, documented at `http://krypted.com/mac-os-x/add-jamf-pro-smart-group-google-doc-using-zapier/`. Here, we look at sending smart group membership changes to a Google sheet so we can analyze it with other tools, a pretty standard use case.

Most management tools will support webhooks at this point. For example, SimpleMDM just improved support for webhooks as seen in Figure 12-39.

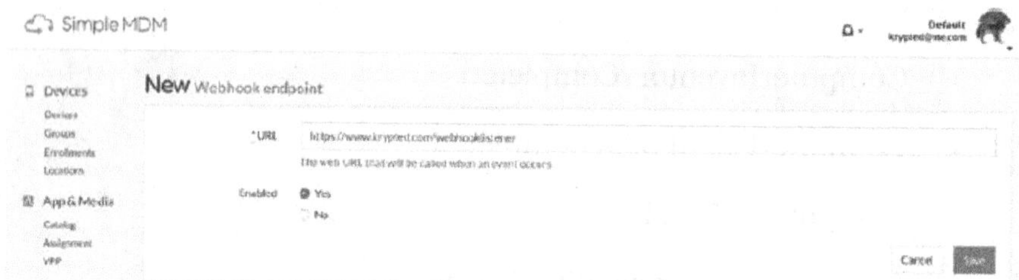

Figure 12-39. *SimpleMDM webhooks*

While webhooks make for a great enhancement to how you manage devices, they also represent a fundamental building block of technology: the callback URL (or URI), which we reviewed earlier in the chapter while describing the fundamental building blocks of tools like OpenID Connect and SAML which are the basis for all modern Federated Identity Providers.

Working with the Keychain

Keychain Access is an application that uses a small database in macOS that allows users to store secure pieces of information. It first appeared as a password manager in Mac OS 8.6 and has evolved ever since. A Keychain can contain a number of data types, including passwords, keys, certificates, and notes. You can interact with the keychain programmatically in macOS. This means that you have a number of options for pushing accounts and settings to devices from a centralized portal, app, or service.

The default user keychain is stored at ~/Library/Keychains/login.keychain, and the default system keychain is stored at /Library/Keychains/System.keychain. Each of these can have different strings in the name to indicate versions or use cases - and may appear multiple times if in use. You can most easily access the keychains using the Keychain Access application. Simply open the application from /Applications/Utilities and search for a site that you have stored information for, and you'll be able to see the entry in the keychain database (Figure 12-40).

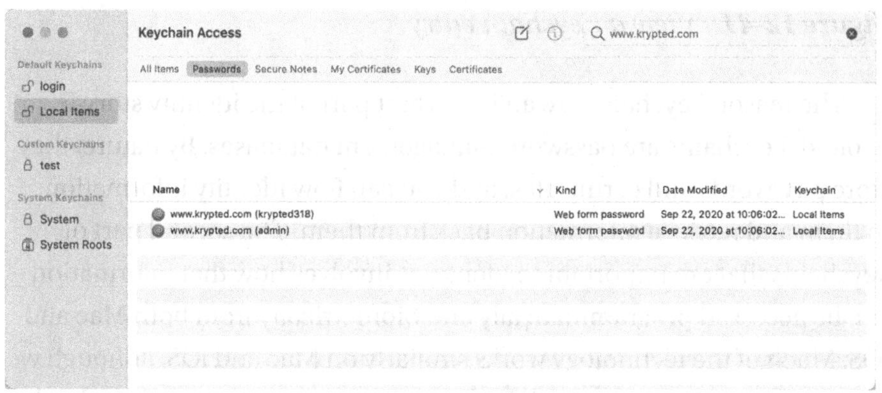

***Figure 12-40.** Keychains*

Double-click the keychain entry to see what's stored in that item, shown in Figure 12-41. Any passwords are encrypted, and you'll need to click Show Password to see the actual password.

Figure 12-41. View a Keychain entry

The reason keychains are an important part of the identity story is twofold: keychains are password management databases. By nature, they store passwords and certificates, and you can flow identity information to them and retrieve information back from them. The second part of keychains that are important to identities involves how that information can be accessed programmatically and biometrically from both Mac and iOS. Much of the technology works similarly on Mac and iOS, although we have more visibility into what's happening under the hood with tools when using a Mac, as we can see logs and we can view keys and passwords using Keychain Utility.

Accessing information programmatically is done using the security command. The security command is used to read from and manipulate the keychain database(s). Since there are multiple keychains, let's first look at a list of keychains using the security command in verbose mode (thus, the -v flag) and using the list-keychains verb:

```
security -v list-keychains
```

The output will be a list of the keychains on the Mac. You can also view the preferences file that shows the current users keychains by reading the ~/Library/Preferences/com.apple.security.plist file:

```
cat ~/Library/Preferences/com.apple.security.plist
```

The /Library/Preferences/com.apple.security.plist file is used to store information about the system default keychain and the order with which searches are done if there are multiples. You will need to unlock a keychain if you want to edit it, which is similar to decrypting the file that stores the database. To do so, use the unlock-keychain option followed by the path of the keychain:

```
security unlock-keychain ~/Library/Keychains/login.keychain
```

When prompted, provide the password (or do so via an expect script). You can put certificates and passwords directly in the keychain as well, using find-certificate to find a certificate, find-identity to find a certificate and a private key, find-generic-password to find a password for an app, and find-internet-password to locate a password to a website.

```
security add-internet-password -a krypted -s site.com -w
```

The command to do so is security, and the verb to add a password is add-internet-password. In the following example, we'll use a more mature incantation, using the -a to send the username again, but using the -D option to define the kind of password (the category label in Keychain), the -s which is a variable for the server address, followed by the path to the keychain:

```
sudo security add-internet-password \
    -a $username \
    -D "network password" \
    -r "smb " \
```

```
-s $server \
"/Library/Keychains/System.keychain" \
-W
```

Directly manipulating keychains should be considered a legacy workflow; however, in the absence of better APIs and options, sometimes it's the only option to get a task done. This is how some of the login tools work, to keep passwords in sync. The preferred modern way is to use keys with such workflows, as in how WebAuthn works. However, it's not uncommon to see machines with a keychain password that hasn't changed in five or seven years, so if the password for the IdP is in a keychain, this is a potential security risk.

Summary

IdPs are quickly replacing or augmenting the directory services solutions that became widely used in enterprises with the advent of Active Directory in the early 2000s. Tools like Azure Active Directory, Google Identity Access Management, Okta, OneLogin, JumpCloud, and PingFederate have now replaced some of the single sign-on functionality given the increasingly distributed nature of organizations and the increasing reliance on web apps. It's clear that thus far Apple programs to manage schools and businesses focus on Azure and Google - but these are open standards, so those may expand in the next few years.

As we showed throughout this chapter, federated identities are able to provide an added layer of security for the Apple platform. Those federated identities can have a layer of multifactor authentication (MFA), which is increasingly moving away from physical tokens and into a world where a "soft token" or app is used. This reduces the cost of MFA and lets our coworkers do more with that phone they increasingly have on them at all times. The beauty of those devices is also that they already have another layer of security: a face or fingerprint.

We see this industry in its infancy today. Some vendors may seem like they're getting big or getting acquired for large sums of money, but the technology is changing quickly. This pace of innovation is being caused by the rapid uptake in usage by key vendors but also by enterprises that see the quick shift to mobile endpoints as one of the largest potential security threats in their fleets. As you plan out how identity fits into your organization (or how the identity plan fits into the Apple fleet of devices), think about the end result. That result should be that data allowed on devices is gated by the security posture of the organization. When done right, admins can get granular control over this data while still providing a great experience for your coworkers.

We don't go into Zero Trust Network Access solutions (ZTNA) much in the chapter but instead look at the links between the IdP, Apple, and the devices - and expand some into Conditional Access solutions. ZTNA is a solution where traffic is routed through a tunnel and analyzed, and while it isn't the most private solution, it does give administrators the most telemetry into what happens on devices. Expect more large-scale integrations between ZTNA and device management based on that telemetry where there aren't yet holistic ecosystems in the future (we'll be happy to document them further once those are there even if the buzzwordy acronym changes).

Given that everything on the Apple platform is changing so fast, now that we've gone through how to deploy and manage Apple devices through the first 12 chapters of this book, we'll continue with projects like we just made with ZTNA and turn our attention to the future in Chapter 13.

CHAPTER 13

The Future of Apple Device Management

This book primarily focused on Apple device management techniques that are used on the macOS, tvOS, and iOS devices, with the exception of the areas where certain functionality is only available on a given platform today. That's because Apple has slowly brought the management story together for their platforms. This makes sense, considering the fact that each framework has to be maintained differently for each platform. That becomes a lot of development sprawl to maintain.

This isn't to say that the platforms will merge and that we'll see a unified operating system. But Apple does seem to trend toward a lot of similarities. That began with the Mac App Store and thus far led to a much more sandboxed Mac. It is impossible to know what the future holds. These and other changes can lead to a number of pretty informed assumptions about the future, based on what has happened in the past.

In Chapter 1, we covered how we got to where we are today. Throughout the main body of this book, we then looked at how to implement various options necessary for a successful Apple deployment. How does this impact you and why are we talking about the future, though?

This impacts each deployment as it saves hours or days previously spent to build something that got outdated in a year. That's why the book goes into the future of the platforms, to keep from repeating the

C. Edge and R. Trouton, *Apple Device Management*,
https://doi.org/10.1007/978-1-4842-9156-6_13

same mistakes and avoid future technical debt. In other words, think of the future long-term state of a given environment and all the attributes. Compare that to the current state and then prioritize each chunk of work to get from the new way to a new steady state. A tool that can help get that future state in mind is a balanced scorecard.

Balanced Apple Scorecard

Apple devices can act as a first-class citizen on any network. What emerged through the history laid out in this book is a collection of best practices, a tool chain that's commonly used, and a general philosophy (or one for each vendor or open source project in some cases).

One way to maximize impact is to take a step back and look at the ecosystem of an environment from the perspective of "what do I need for my environment?" To guide that observation, this section includes a scorecard to use, but consider the ecosystem of a given Apple environment more holistically. The scorecard for any two organizations is likely to be different than any others, and the development of a way to quantify how an organization tracks is likely best when it stems from a negotiation between all the stakeholders involved. That might include legal, compliance, human resources, and finance teams. Don't get entrenched in any opinions with the other stakeholders but do explain gently where their support is needed.

This scorecard provides a snapshot into the technology stack required by most organizations as well as the attributes of each in a simple dashboard that executives can understand. Many of the technologies in this scorecard might not be required by an organization at the time the scorecard is created but are likely to be required at some point in the future if not already, as the deployment (and organization) grows and becomes more visible - and even if they're never required, it's good to talk about them and just make sure that's the case.

Balanced scorecards can use four boxes in a document built in Excel, mind map tools, or any other tool available. They're usually a list of attributes that an organization cares about. In the following text, see a list of categories and some attributes to consider asking about. Most organizations won't adopt all of the technologies on this list, but most should at least have a discussion about each:

Access to the organization's network

- Network access controls
- 802.1x access
- Captive portal management
- Proxy access and PAC file distribution
- Centralized certificate, CA, and SCEP management
- Printer distribution and management
- Centralized font management
- VPN management and access

Access to organizational resources

- License tracking and reporting.
- All applications are available to Apple devices.
- Centralized collaboration suite access based on device state.
- All file servers and content management.
- Virtualization for any applications not available for the Mac, per job function.

Cradle to Grave device management

- A seamless unboxing and deployment experience (including imaging for legacy devices).
- Devices can be centrally managed.
- Automated application deployment.
- Standardized application packaging.
- Automated QA and User Acceptability Testing for patches and application updates.
- Dashboard that shows standard KPIs for the fleet.

Directory services

- Leveraging directory services for single sign-on (whether there's a trusted bind in the transaction or not)
- Integrated Identity Management with SSO and/or SAML providers
- Migrate directory services into a cloud solution and provide login window access to those directory services

Endpoint protection

- Antivirus
- Endpoint backup
- Centralized encryption management
- Centrally managed and auditable policies following NIST guidelines (e.g., password aging and complexity)
- Log analysis
- Application access controls (whitelisting)

- Threat management and mitigation
- Forensic snapshotting and antitheft
- Legal hold

World-class support

- Zero-touch assets that cover the most common tasks necessary to get your job done
- Support staff trained on managing devices
- Centralized auditable remote access
- Service desk software that is integrated with management platform
- User-controlled software deployment with automated approvals from management where needed
- Device state management
- Help menu providing easy access to tickets and standard support tools
- Automated proactive maintenance

Now there's something to cover at the next annual review! The point isn't to integrate everything, but to make sure to be cognizant of what is integrated, why, the priority of each, how to quantify the deployment, and ultimately how it makes the user experience better while protecting your organization. These should also be time bound and viable. It's usually not too smart to try and project the future of technology too far in the future, given that the industry moves so rapidly. But do look into the near-field future so there's no need to rebuild infrastructure just put into place last year.

The Tools

One of the most important aspects of device management is to choose the right tools. These typically have a direct correlation to labor costs as most are used to automate tasks. A large multinational enterprise needs different tools that can scale with their footprint; a small business may get crushed under the weight of tools that are purpose-built for, often codesigned by, and maintained for larger organizations. Most tools aren't a permanent decision, though. The antivirus, backup, collaboration, and file server access software are easily interchangeable. For a Mac, admins can also migrate between management solutions with a scripted workflow. However, migration between management solutions is more difficult for iOS devices. In order to move an iOS device from one Mobile Device Management solution to another, the devices typically need to be reenrolled and sometimes wiped (e.g., for supervised devices). This is the kind of migration not often undertaken, and so some vendor lock-in can occur.

Consider how tools interoperate to plan a switch or net-new installation as well. Many will build complex workflows that automate workflows. As an example, if antivirus definitions for a device don't get updated, there are prebuilt integrations that can revoke access to various resources and create a ticket in service desk software. This allows administrators to automate a number of their tasks as well as tasks for other teams, which reduces the need for more service desk and desktop support teams and reduces the possibility of human error.

Some vendors provide connections to solutions within their own portfolio (e.g., they may have an MDM and an antivirus tool that they sell). Others provide support for some third-party solutions, which allows administrators to have a consistent administrative experience across multiple tools. Some have mature APIs but no prebuilt integrations. The level of customization for each integration often requires more training to learn how to build tools but comes with more options and can therefore give administrators more flexibility in how they automate tasks. This trade-off is a consistent theme in any management stack. Bite off too much and not much gets done.

The reason there are so many options now is that the population of Apple devices out there warrants it. This allows niche vendors to offer more value to customers with solutions tailored to their needs. As the number of tools to manage various aspects of Apple devices has exploded, it's gotten harder to determine one that fits with each environment. Apple innovates at such a rapid pace that those in the space can't be everything to everyone. Picking the right vendor therefore requires research and a bit of diligence.

The future of Apple Consulting lies within the powers of the tools we use. There are so many options out there on the market to manage a fleet of Macs with. Choosing one and going all in helps, but you need to know when to pivot. Ask yourself if a tool is doing everything in its power to help administrators constantly maintaining it.

Justin Esgar, Founder and Organizer of ACES Conference

One aspect of choosing the right tools is to find solutions that keep current with Apple advances and maybe even think ahead to what Apple might be planning next.

The Near Future

This book has covered User Accepted MDM, User Accepted Kernel Extension Loading, Privacy Preferences Policy Control, and now Extensions in the System Preferences. Anyone who has paid attention throughout this book will note these really mean one thing: transparency for end users. The argument against some of these transparency alerts is that when prompted so often, users click accept every time they get prompted. This leads to a fine line between how to inform people and get their consent and how to best protect companies that issue devices to those users.

Administrators can do more to manage devices if they can prove ownership. Device supervision means proof that a device is owned by an organization. It doesn't mean that the developers who wrote supervision actually want organizations to spy on end users without their knowledge. This is nothing new. Apple Remote Desktop had a different icon in the menu bar when it was in use. But in those earlier days, it was much less likely an administrator could gain access to a credit card number, social security number, or personally identifiable information as easily as they can today. Further, if that data was remotely accessed, there wasn't nearly as much of a market for the data as there is today.

Privacy Controls

The biggest changes over the next few years will be to continue that trend, where users must consent to management that impacts their privacy, but not consent to changes that impact the management of features on a device. This might seem simple, but the balance between an organization's telemetry and how to provide privacy on devices is far more complicated. Organizations need to manage devices in a cost-effective manner, and a lack of centralized administrative capabilities actually requires a lot of deliberation and even a little backtracking here and there.

Keep in mind, Apple has changed the way devices are managed universally. They played nicely in a system led by Microsoft, but the challenges were different. Users didn't use desktops in a closed Local Area Network, they used phones and tablets on devices constantly connected to the Internet directly. They set aside 3–40 years of corporate IT dogma to improve security and privacy. This new theory of device management seems popular enough that Microsoft, Google, and others have slowly adopted most of the same options as well. Transparent management and privacy protections are what most of us want, and so we should assume our coworkers want the same, no matter how many support cases they file in a given month.

Being an Apple admin requires a little patience. Apple doesn't publish a road map that spans a decade like some vendors do. Apple doesn't guarantee that a given model of device will be available for five years. Apple also doesn't comment publicly on most of these features outside of the Worldwide Developers Conference (WWDC). This doesn't mean that individuals at Apple won't comment on what they're up to. What "Apple" tells their users, like any organization, is often just one person who talks about something with no information beyond their own circle within the company. "Apple" is a company of individuals, not a single organism. Anyone who is in a position that provides them access to privileged information about future plans likely isn't willing to risk that position.

"Apple" would love to tell people more. There are a number of questions that software developers and product managers at Apple haven't answered for themselves, much less written a single line of code for. And as they chart a new course for our industry, we have to expect that Apple will constantly be moving our cheese. Job security is a wonderful thing!

The Apple Product Lines

Anyone new to the Apple world would probably be surprised that Apple once distributed wireless access points, routers, 1U rack-mount servers, rack-mount RAID enclosures, and even a full server-based operating system called Mac OS X Server. In fact, Apple has built and sold server services since the introduction of the Mac.

Right around the time that Oracle bought Sun, Apple doubled down on their iOS investment and released the iPad. At the time, Apple reportedly had $64 billion in cash on hand and so could have purchased Sun with a relatively small investment in cash compared to what they had in reserves. But the iPad was a much smarter investment of those resources.

Apple started to spin down their own lines of servers and pull functionality out of the operating system that didn't align with a long-term vision at about that same time. Apple didn't try to be something they weren't anymore and sell enterprise servers. Instead, they parlayed their success with further investments into iPhone and the emergent iPad to become the wealthiest company in the world. Apple doesn't want to be a server company, and it's doubtful that more than a few people within Apple ever did.

Over the course of the next few years, Apple discontinued all dedicated server hardware and slowly slimmed down on the number of services in the Server operating system. First, they removed specialty services such as Podcast Producer and Xgrid, then groupware functionality such as Mail, Contacts, and Calendar services. These services were never going to rival Office 365 or Google Apps. Apple finally canceled the macOS Server project entirely in 2022. This allowed them to repurpose engineers to other teams and move faster on the client platforms.

Apple simplified their product offerings when they cut more than just the server hardware and software. Apple discontinued the Apple AirPort Base Station from the product line. This was another moment in the slow spin-down of various teams at Apple who had previously been tasked with owning the entire network stack. Apple made the AirPort since the early days of Wi-Fi, mostly out of a need to get good wireless options available for their own lines of computers. The AirPort devices were over four times the cost of base stations with similar specifications from competitors, but they were solid devices and relatively easy to set up and configure. At one point, that product line included a base station with integrated storage as well. The AirPorts were stable, rarely had issues, rarely needed updates, and had great range. But when similar devices started to plummet in cost, Apple shuffled resources to more profitable adventures, as they should have.

As with server hardware, Apple has removed devices that don't sell well to maximize their investment into the devices that sell like hotcakes. This is good business. Expect the trend to continue for one of the wealthiest companies in the world (if not, according to the day, the wealthiest company in the world). Consider how the Apple portfolio has changed since the early days. Apple divested the LaserWriter when there were other good options for printers users could buy. Apple made switches and network appliances as well, but don't need to at this point. Apple canceled these and their servers when the Return on Investment (ROI) calculations made it smart to do so, and they were no longer needed in the ecosystem.

If at first you don't succeed, try and try again. Apple tried to make mobile devices twice before they succeeded with the iPhone. There were more times, but they didn't leave Apple labs. The iPod to iPhone and iPad release will go down in business history books as one of the most important business decisions of all time. The MacBook sells well for a computer, although pales in comparison to the sales of iPhones and iPads. But pay attention to those annual reports and notice the lack of discussion about desktop computers and some Apple apps on the App Store (some of which have never been mentioned).

Apps

"There's an app for that" is now part of everyday vernacular, especially among those who work in the IT industry. Since the inception of the App Store, millions of apps have made their way onto the Apple App Stores and changed the way many organizations purchase and use software. Where organizations once needed to purchase large software packages that ran the business, the App Store has allowed people to buy smaller apps that do various tasks and string those workflows together either with built-in integrations or by linking various tools together with third-party automation solutions.

Evolutions in Software Design and Architecture

The ability to link disparate tools together is facilitated by a few trends in how software is architected. The first is that since the first iPhone was released, software has increasingly moved from client-side apps to web-based apps. This move has been to cut down on development costs, make software easier to deploy at companies, and allow software to be run on more and more platforms. Additionally, the more companies that have transitioned into web apps, the more engineers that are trained on how to develop for them and so the easier it has become to train engineers.

Another trend is microservices or a trend toward smaller code and so more easily run as functions in environments like Amazon's Lambda service, Google's App Engine, or a plethora of other options. These replace large monolithic structures of code that are hard to maintain and even harder to make parts of the code public (e.g., through APIs an app can consume). This allows a lot of different developers to work on various services collaboratively and not step on each other's toes. The move away from huge servers saves the organizations that embrace a microservice-based architecture millions of dollars in hosting fees.

Because so many companies need their software to interoperate, the authentication mechanisms have also evolved. Federated web identities allow two pieces of software to trade data on behalf of a user (e.g., with technologies like OAuth Connect and SAML) or admins (using tokens such as a JWT). The ability to have a federated identity means administrators can easily install plug-ins in software and automate tasks in their name. Where authentication was once handled by Kerberos or with local salted hashes, developers could now just import a library to do OAuth (or implement a microservice that handles that code) and easily be able to work with other vendors.

Another aspect of how software has evolved would be URL handlers. Websites have long looked at the http:// or https:// prefix to know that a URL represents a web page. Before that, URI schemes could include ftp://, smb://, or one of the originals referenced in the IETF specifications, gopher://. It turns out that an app can register that prefix as well, known as a URL handler, much the way that users once registered a file extension. This allows software hosted on the Web to open an app, receive data from the app, and send data to the app with deep linking. Most modern software solutions not only interpret URLs this way but then interact with microservices authenticated through a federated identity and so get away from monolithic structures that have too much logic built into them that cost an arm and a leg to rebuild every decade when programming languages change. Further, if a site is built in Java, Python, or a bevy of other languages, there are plenty of tools that allow admins to build once in those languages and compiled as native apps for Apple and Android (although a truly native Swift app is smaller and better in nearly every case).

The Evolution of Apple Software

The programming languages that Apple either distributes or designs have changed over the years. Apple has quickly iterated the tools and code used to create apps. This makes code more interchangeable between platforms. The fact that code has become smaller and more modular also means that bits of code can be shared more easily on social coding sites, such as GitHub. This means developers can build more, faster.

The languages have changed, but Apple has always distributed software used to develop other software (as do most operating system vendors). The tool most often used to build software for Apple devices today is Xcode. Xcode can be used to edit code for most any language, although a number of other tools are tailor-built for different languages. Over the years, we've had programming languages that include the following:

- Smalltalk was a language developed in 1972 with the last stable release in 1980.
- AppleScript is a language introduced in 1993 that can still be run on a Mac. AppleScript can be used with services, Automator, or invoked through shell scripts today and is meant to be used for simple automations.
- Objective-C took parts of Smalltalk messaging and added them to C and was the main programming language for NeXT and by virtue for subsequent Apple products until Swift was introduced.
- Swift is licensed under the Apache 2.0 license and has been available since 2014. Swift is now the language most often used to write tools for Apple devices, with many components reusable between tvOS, macOS, and iOS.
- Python, Bash, and even Perl are common scripting languages used on the Mac. These have been compiled and distributed with the operating system, although sometimes it pays (as with Python 3) to update to newer versions. Recently, Apple has begun to remove these from a default installation, so a native Swift app is in most cases the best bet to automate tasks if possible.

Cocoa and Cocoa Touch aren't languages, but APIs commonly imported into projects when a developer writes apps for Apple products. Cocoa apps are usually developed in Objective-C or Swift. Since Cocoa is an API, it can also be called from Python, Perl, Ruby, AppleScript, and a cornucopia of other languages with a bridge. Cocoa provides access to many of the built-in frameworks, and there are a number of projects that can be found to get other frameworks in projects. Package managers such as CocoaPods help keep them up to date and provide some build automation where needed, although Swift Packages are a better alternative for most.

Carbon was an API that helped bridge the gap from OS 9 to OS X. Carbon was never updated to 64-bit, so Carbon was deprecated in Mac OS X 10.8. Cocoa has been around for a long time, but don't expect it to disappear any time soon. Apple will also further restrict what lower-level functions can be accessed from Cocoa on the Mac in the future and continue to evolve Mac, iOS, and tvOS options for Swift.

In the first edition of the book, we said "Stay on the lookout for an eventual shift in what chips Apple uses on the Mac." These are all now ARM chips made by Apple, so Swift is easily portable between machines. This allows the same app to have different interfaces for how users interface with apps on different types of devices. The reason watchOS isn't mentioned earlier is that it's an extension that developers add into other apps and not truly a stand-alone device.

In addition to the tools Apple provides, organizations that want to develop cross-platform apps that don't require much of the native functionality found in Swift can use a number of different mobile development platforms such as Appcelerator, AppInstitute, AppMachine, AppMakr, Appery.io, Appy Pie, Bizness Apps, BuildFire, Como, Crowdbotics, GoodBarber, iBuildApp, Kony, PhoneGap, ShoutEm (Javascript), TheAppBuilder, Verivo, ViziApps, Xamarin, and Xojo. There are a lot of these, and each appeals to a specific use case - after all, each developer wrote theirs because they identified a gap in the market.

Low-code apps are a great gateway drug to test a thesis that any organization might have: an app will reduce the need to buy a third-party app/service, remove a barrier for adoption for the platform, or increase productivity. As the app gets more complicated, then it's likely to become too mature for a low-code type of solution such as those mentioned earlier. Additionally, the options each of these organizations is able to provide are limited to the options Apple makes available on the platform. However, to satisfy the needs of multiple platforms at once and be able to get an app out the door in days is often pretty much worth it, which explains why they remain popular.

Now that we've looked at developing apps, let's look at Apple apps and the future of each.

Apple Apps

The Server app is finally gone. But a few tools are still necessary to enable the Apple platforms. Apple Configurator was written by one of Apple's first employees in order to address problems he saw in the classroom. The tool has gone through several iterations over the years and has since become an integral part of the Apple management offerings, as seen in its use throughout this book. Other tools can do some of what Apple Configurator does, which we've covered in this book, but none have reached a level of maturity or official support where the loss of Apple Configurator would not negatively impact the ability to deploy iOS devices en masse. Therefore, there's little risk to developing workflows based on Apple Configurator. In fact, the product built on top of Configurator's command-line interface makes it seem like it will only become more necessary in the future, or the introduction of APIs that allow similar functionality in other apps might mean Configurator-type of functionality becomes parts of other apps.

Apple Remote Desktop (ARD) began life as Apple Network Assistant and has evolved over the years. As networks have become more complex, ARD is less useful than it once was. Today, there are a number of competitive products ready-made for remotely controlling devices, which include Bomgar, GoToMyPC, TeamViewer, Splashtop, and dozens of others on the app store. Additionally, for those on a LAN, there are dozens of options for VNC-based clients that can access the VNC server built into the Mac. ARD isn't useful for iOS or tvOS devices. Either ARD will get an update so it can connect over APNs or it will not likely be a product in the future now that there's a rich ecosystem of products that can do what it does. In the meantime, ARD should be used if the alternatives are cost-prohibitive or lack features needed, such as the ability to connect to devices remotely.

Apps that should be safe are those that empower the platform. Think of Xcode for software development and Apple Configurator for setting up and managing large iOS device deployments. There's not a strict ROI calculation to be done on these, and they're necessary for the third-party applications available for the platform to mature. Do expect them to evolve, though.

Productivity Apps

There are other apps as well, built into the operating system. These can come and go, based on technology changes. For example, when all Macs shipped with writable DVD drives, the iDVD app was necessary. Other apps have remained somewhat consistent over time, even if they're packaged differently than when they were first released.

iWork was introduced in 2005 and is a collection of desktop apps that Apple distributes to rival Microsoft Office and Google Apps. iWork includes Pages, Numbers, and Keynote. Initially sold for $79 per copy, iWork was then distributed for free with Apple devices manufactured after 2013 and later just made free for iCloud account holders, once online collaboration was added to the suite. It's important to note that Apple has had a suite of apps going back to 1984 with AppleWorks Classic, which would then be spun off into Claris and come back as AppleWorks, which reached End of Life in 2007 in favor of iWork. Microsoft Office is certainly the dominant player in word processors, spreadsheets, and presentation software, but Apple has maintained their own option since before the inception of the Mac and is likely to continue to do so in the future.

Professional (or prosumer as some are called) apps like GarageBand, Logic Pro, Final Cut Pro, and iMovie are also likely to stay and just get better with an infusion of options through various machine learning frameworks.

Apple Services

Apple has also long had a file distribution and sharing option. The Newton could ship documents out of Works and into an eMate add-on for At Ease. The Server app had file sharing, which has now been moved to a simple service provided by client computers. The cloud is a far more interesting topic for most enterprises. In 2000, Apple introduced iTools and in 2002 changed that to .Mac until 2008 and MobileMe until 2013. iCloud has been the successor to that evolution and bolts on a bunch of additional functionality, including

- **Activation Lock**: Locks devices from activating if they're wiped, without the iCloud account that was last registered on a device. The ability to bypass Activation Lock is a key feature of most MDM solutions.
- **Backup and restore**: Used to back up and restore iOS devices.
- **Back to my Mac**: Share screens and files with other computers that are using the same iCloud account. This service doesn't allow access to devices for accounts on different iCloud accounts and so is not a replacement for Remote Desktop.
- **Calendar**: CalDAV service provided by Apple to keep calendars in sync between devices and share calendars between devices.
- **Email**: Email service provided by Apple, with accounts in the domains me.com and/or icloud.com.

- **Find My Friends**: A geolocation service so friends and family members can share their location with one another and locate devices physically. Find My Friends is simply called Find Friends in the iCloud interface.
- **Find My Phone**: Allows you to geolocate your devices from other devices or from the icloud.com portal, where the option is called Find iPhone.
- **Handoff**: Allows you to continue tasks such as writing an email or viewing a website from one device to another. Currently works with Mail, Maps, Safari, Reminders, Calendar, Contacts, Pages, Numbers, Keynote, and any third-party apps that are developed to work with Handoff.
- **iCloud Drive**: File storage that is accessible between (and often synchronized to) any devices registered with the iCloud account and accessible from the iCloud.com web interface.
- **iCloud Keychain**: Synchronizes passwords between devices.
- **iCloud Music Library**: Adds any content you purchase from one device to automatically be downloaded to other devices.
- **iCloud Photos**: Synchronizes all photos and videos to iCloud (and so to each device that uses the service). Photos can then be placed into albums and shared to other Apple devices.
- **iWork**: Shared Pages, Numbers, and Keynote documents.
- **Messages**: Instant messaging service from Apple.

- **News Publisher**: If you've signed up, allows you to write articles for the Apple News app.
- **Notes**: Keeps content synchronized between the Notes app on computers, mobile devices, and the iCloud web interface.
- **Photo Stream**: Stores photos in My Photo Stream for 30 days (duplicative when using iCloud Photos).
- **Storage**: Each iCloud account gets 5GB of free storage and then provides upgrade plans up to 2TB of storage for syncing all files between Apple devices.

The most notable way of accessing many of these is by logging in to iCloud at icloud.com, as can be seen in Figure 13-1. But many are hidden as they are accessed on devices, such as the Backup and Restore feature, which you access by looking in that option on an iOS device.

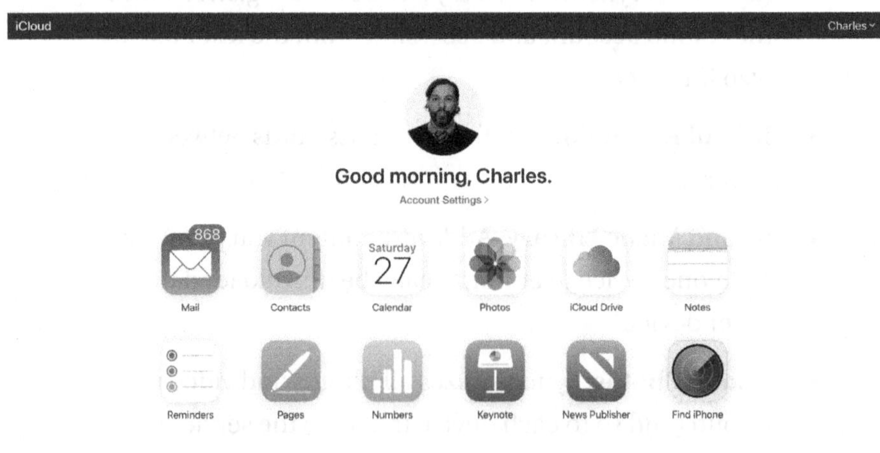

Figure 13-1. *iCloud.com home screen*

These services become more and more integrated into the operating system with each release. As an example, if the "Allow Handoff between this Mac and your iCloud devices" option in the General System Preference pane is enabled, Handoff is used to enable the Universal Clipboard to copy and paste text, photos, and other content between devices. Users can also send and receive iMessages from a Mac, answer calls on an iPhone from a Mac or Apple Watch, and have websites available in Safari that were opened on an iOS device. The frameworks available for developers also mean that technologies like Handoff appear in more and more apps. In the future, expect more and more services provided by Apple and third-party apps to make use of Handoff, given how much simpler it makes people.

The use of Bluetooth to provide an easy way to quickly transfer information between two devices isn't limited to Handoff. Apple Classroom makes use of Bluetooth to allow teachers to locate nearby devices assigned to their classes and provides teachers with the ability to open apps, browse to a specific website, lock devices, view screens, AirPlay the screen to another device, and set passwords on devices. These options are similar to (although a subset of) options in Apple Remote Desktop and expect to see more innovative uses emerge over the coming years (something we thought would happen with iBeacons but never really materialized).

Apple Device Management Programs

Apple School Manager, introduced in 2016, isn't required to use Apple Classroom, but it does give the option for Shared iPads, which is the first time we see multiuser iPads. It's also the first time we see Managed Apple IDs, which are used in Rosters in Apple School Manager. iCloud content is then synced to multiple users in much the same way it's done between Macs using iCloud Storage. Apple Classroom is also made better with an MDM solution that supports the Education profile payload.

Apple School Manager does more as well. Apple School Manager provides a portal for schools to manage Accounts (users), Classes (groups), Roles, MDM Servers that are used (or at least the token generation for servers), Automated Enrollment (the Device Enrollment Program), Device Assignments (which maps devices to users), Locations, Apps and Books (otherwise referred to as the Volume Purchase Program), and iTunes U, a service for accessing educational content through iTunes or the iTunes U app. Office 365 now has built-in integrations with Apple School Manager and expects more from Shared iPad and Managed Apple IDs in the future.

Managed Apple IDs initially came to Apple School Manager and can now be found in Apple Business Manager. Apple Business Manager is a portal similar to Apple School Manager but designed with less learning management in mind. While you can't yet use Managed Apple IDs to manage iCloud or the App Store for a given ID, expect this functionality to mature in the future.

If an administrator started out with the standard Volume Purchase Program and still has a number of VPP tokens, then those need to be migrated to Apple Business Manager, but probably with a support call to make sure it's all done correctly. The ability to purchase credits on a PO rather than use a credit card is a reason a number of companies will migrate to the platform, but make sure to understand exactly what happens with those VPP tokens before you do so in order not to orphan previous app purchases.

Automated Device Enrollment is the new name for DEP management. DEP should be migrated when possible in order to take use of the default DEP server option, which allows administrators to assign a different DEP server to each type of Apple devices, especially useful when there are multiple vendors to manage different types of devices (e.g., an MDM for iPhones and a different one for Macs). Apple Management accounts are consolidated, just make sure to work with each MDM vendor to best understand what impact to expect, given that each vendor might integrate the various services differently. That includes Apple Business Essentials, a cloud-hosted device management platform from Apple, introduced in 2022.

Getting Apps to Devices

One barrier to ship a new app is actually how to get the app out of Xcode and onto devices to test and then how to get that app onto the App Store. The first step to doing so is testing. Testing in iOS can be done using Xcode using the iPhone Simulator, manually distributing an .ipa file to a device (which is a bundle of compiled files that comprise an app), or through TestFlight.

TestFlight was founded in 2010 and acquired by Apple in 2014. TestFlight is provided to developers in the iOS Developer Program. TestFlight allows users to install and test apps before they are distributed through the App Store. Developers can see logs and review feedback from people who test apps as well. If an organization will build apps, then they likely at least need a working knowledge of TestFlight in order to support developers, who can use TestFlight to test up to 100 apps at a time. Don't expect TestFlight to go anywhere, so any time spent learning how it works is time well spent, and it helps you to understand how the App Store works a little more as well.

Once an app has been tested, it's time to distribute the app to devices. This can be done through web servers that distribute .ipa files for iOS and .app files for macOS. Any attempts to build internal or third-party app stores are typically linked to such a distribution model, and provided an app has been notarized, this isn't likely to go anywhere. The App Store options for distribution continue to evolve. Those options began with gift codes, moved to VPP, and then got the option for Business to Business (B2B) apps, but those aren't yet available for schools through Apple School Manager, and they aren't supported by all MDM solutions.

Distributing software for the Mac is a bit different. Software can be distributed as an .app bundle, through a package file (a .pkg file), or through the App Store. An .app bundle is easy to copy, simply compile from Xcode, and open the application. We've covered installing an app through the App Store thoroughly in this book, and that process is pretty well ironed out at this point. The process will change here and there as options mature, such as the ability to install an iOS app on a Mac. Packages are a bit more complex, although far simpler than App Store oddities.

A package file can be sent by a number of mechanisms. These include the installer command in scripts, the ability to open the package and run the installer (seen in Figure 13-2), headless when pushed by a package through ARD or an agent-based management solution or now through an MDM command provided the package is properly signed. Packages can be one of the most time-intensive aspects required to manage large fleets of Apple devices. New versions of software come out all the time, and many contain security updates. This can make it daunting to stay on top of the version of each piece of software deployed, especially as deployments grow.

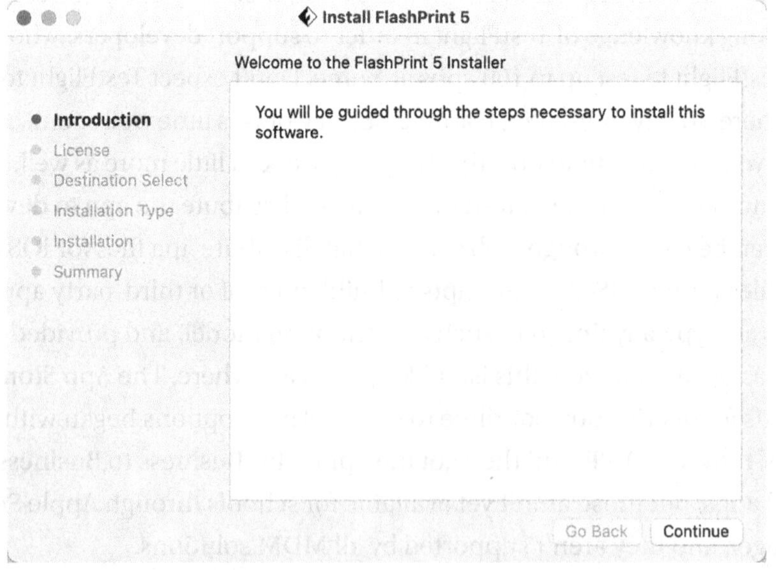

***Figure 13-2.** Installing software manually on the Mac*

Autopkg is an open source third-party solution that automatically builds packages. Anyone who hasn't begun to automate their package build train should. Some third-party management solutions provide packages for various software titles as well. Autopkg can also be integrated into management tools (e.g., via the JSSImporter project to get packages into Jamf Pro). Many large enterprises think they have a couple hundred apps deployed only to realize they actually have a couple of thousand once an inventory can be had from the MDM. All of this is why so many environments really just want to get all of their software from the App Store.

More and more software titles are distributed through the App Store. Apple makes $99 per year and 30% (although the number can vary) of all income generated through the App Store. As of 2018, Apple had sold over $130 billion worth of apps, a number that has doubled since then. This makes the App Store a considerable revenue generator for Apple. That caused many to wonder if all software would eventually have to be installed through the app store. Microsoft Office is used by nearly every company in the world and so runs on a lot of Macs. Office came to the App Store in 2018. While Office is only one of two million apps, it was a holdout for the Mac and along with other notable titles that moved to the App Store showed Apple chip away at apps not currently distributed through the App Store.

Just when it seemed as though all software was destined to the App Store, other App Stores began to emerge. These were slowed due to adjudication until they made it to the Supreme Court. The high court found against Apple in 2019. The two main vendors to look at if you're interested in what third-party app stores have to offer are GetJar, with 850,000 apps, and Appland with 135,000 apps.

Manage Only What Is Necessary

Most school districts in the early 2000s were obsessed with the dock experience on client computers. It was as though teachers and IT administrators in education environments just couldn't help but obsess over the fact that a user changing one of these was akin to the student spray painting "O'Doyle Rules" on the wall of the school. Schools would talk for hours about the various ways students found to break out of a managed environment to move the Dock or remove icons from the Dock.

One of the best use cases for management in education is to make devices simpler to use. That simple user experience on first-grade iPads will help the kids follow along with the teacher without getting overwhelmed. In an increasingly one-to-one world, don't obsess about the details. Children are really good with computers now. Show them how to use Spotlight to find the app they need instead of relying on the Dock - they'll thank you later.

So why manage the Dock at all? To make it easier to get started using a device. This is true for a lot of the other settings as well. It's not usually necessary to manage the background of iOS or Mac devices. It's appropriate in customer-facing devices like in Point of Sale environments, but rarely in a distribution of devices where every user has their own. The less petty settings that are managed, the more time can be spent on the things that really matter, like security.

Administrators need to manage certificates that allow devices to join networks, directory services settings, and the state of a device when it's provided to a user, so they can get to the things they need to get to most easily. This includes the ability to put the appropriate apps on devices, set the icons in an order that will provide for a good user experience, and provide any settings to help configure apps to access necessary resources. In other words, delight your coworkers rather than micromanage their experience (within whatever compliance guidelines are necessary).

But what does this have to do with the future of device management? It's important to consider the Apple philosophy in order to future-proof deployments. That philosophy is to protect privacy and enable users. Anything that is too far from what Apple engineers test in their own QA labs risks being made out of date with a small release. This isn't meant to be heavy-handed, just practical.

Sometimes, we have to pay attention to the trends involved and listen to what people from Apple tell us, even if what they say doesn't match with what we want to hear. For example, various representatives from Apple discouraged the use of MCX for a couple of years. Later, that functionality was deprecated in subsequent releases of the operating system. All workflows that leveraged MCX had to be rearchitected to use other, more modern techniques. This meant that some of the work was done twice. What can we expect next? Let's start with Agents.

The Future of Agents

The word "agent" can mean a few things, according to the audience. Will the future of Apple device management allow for LaunchAgents? LaunchAgents and LaunchDaemons will be around until probably at least `10.17`. They will likely become more and more restrictive, though. So expect some kind of signing infrastructure and potentially a vetting on behalf of a user in order to invoke them.

Some people refer to kernel extensions as "agents." It's more appropriate to call them "drivers," but we've seen enough that ***should*** be LaunchDaemons that we might as well just address them here. When the first edition of this book was written, Apple still allowed third-party kernel extensions. Those have all but been removed and replaced by extensions that are specific to a task and so can be sandboxed more easily. A list of extensions is available at `https://developer.apple.com/app-extensions/`. For example, if an app is to redirect network information, Apple developers want to make sure that the end user has agreed to that (or is at least aware of it); therefore, before the network extension is loaded into memory, the user is asked to approve of what is happening.

Apple does still use kernel extensions. To see a list of all active kernel extensions running on a host, use the following command:

```
kextstat
```

To see a list of the ones that are from third-party developers (likely none on modern computers):

```
kextstat | grep -v com.apple
```

Developers like to know a system is in a given state so they know their code will work as intended. The ability to run code with the privileges a kext receives though is not popular within Apple, nor is anything that has root access. First, users needed to approve kernel extensions. Then they needed to be signed and notarized. This is similar to what has changed with agents in the past few releases. They haven't gone away, but they have become more restrictive.

MDM is invoked by an agent called mdmclient. So there is no such thing as an agentless management solution. But it's easy to think of a scenario where administrators cannot manage anything Apple hasn't previously given access to manage via API endpoints, MDM commands, or profiles. This means less reliance on third-party agents, especially if users can see them in System Preferences and disable them. As the other management options are being trimmed back, consider how important mdmclient has become. At this point, anything that can be managed with the built-in MDM framework in macOS should be managed there; and anything managed in other ways should be reconsidered.

The term agentless comes from the fact that MDM is an Apple-supplied agent. Don't be overly concerned about losing any custom or third-party agents. Instead, if a task can be performed either with MDM or using an agent/script/command, do so with MDM.

Other Impacts to Sandboxing

The sandbox implementation on iOS and tvOS has always provided a locked down environment that only allows users to interact with systems in ways Apple explicitly allows for. Administrators have to work around this, which makes many deployments seem more logistically complicated than they are technically complicated. That is likely to remain consistent in the coming years as threats (not only to phishing attacks but to privacy and persistent threats) continue to evolve.

The base sandbox implementation in macOS restricts operations in a number of ways. Expect that restrictive nature to increase in the coming years. This doesn't mean that users won't be able to browse the filesystem with the Finder. But it does mean that we will have to change the way we think about why, when, and how we automate settings changes and software deployment. Rather than think about changing files manually, consider automation by deep-linking into an app using parameters passed to the URI, assuming the app has a URL handler registered. For example, a remote control solution called ISL can be opened and have various settings put into the app using the following parameters (e.g., when sent via an open command using Terminal on a Mac):

```
isllight://www.islonline.net/?cmdline=--on-load%20%22disable_
dashboard%3Dtrue%26disable_computers%3Dtrue%22%20--web-login%20
WEBTOKEN%20--connect%20TARGETCOID%20--computer-password-MD5%20
MD5PASSWORD
```

Rather than have preferences stored in a centralized repository, each app might eventually have to have its own preference file in the app bundle. And Managed App Config is how this is dealt with on iOS. Administrators can pass parameters to an app on a Mac similarly. Look for apps that can be configured in such a manner rather than reverting to edit defaults domains and learn how to do so in order to be in front of any changes that may come in the future.

In order to run, all apps should be signed. In order to install, all packages should be signed. In order to load, all kexts must be signed and notarized. The Notary service is a proof that Apple performed some checks that apps and kexts actually do what they say they do and no more. The added security isn't just a perception, it also means an app can have a hardened runtime, which lets an app run with additional security protections. This means developers need to follow a few specific rules though; most notably, they have to inform the user of every entitlement in use.

These entitlements are similar to the technology that came out of sandbox (.sb) files. Apple has enforced more sandbox technology on the operating system. Sandboxing does restrict what administrators are able to automate. For example, we can't write to /System and so can't automate tasks that called on resources nested in there in the past. As the platform becomes more widely used, it also becomes a more attractive target and needs those additional security measures to be enforced. These are all examples of parts of iOS technologies that moved into the Mac, which brings up the question: Will iOS and macOS merge?

iOS, macOS, tvOS, and watchOS Will Remain Separate Operating Systems

Apple has been clear that there are no plans to merge the operating systems. Instead, the message has been clear that each operating system is ready-built for a given purpose, and each is used on the appropriate type of device. This doesn't mean they won't merge someday, but it certainly means that we should plan deployments for the next few years with the assumption that they will remain separate. We should also watch for the barriers to fall in order to unify parts of the operating systems.

As mentioned earlier in the chapter, this isn't to say that many of the necessary frameworks necessary to enable each won't end up unified over time. There are far more apps for the iPhone than for any other app in Apple's portfolio of devices. And it stands to reason that if those apps can run on a Mac, the Mac is a more attractive device to purchase.

Apple planned for developers to be able to build a single app that works on the iPhone, iPad, and Mac by 2021 - that process has gone well so far. Marzipan, initially introduced at WWDC in 2018, meant one binary could run on any platform, but each still needs a different look and feel that is appropriate for the screen of the other platforms to be usable, thus enhancements to UIKit and SwiftUI. Apple then brought several of their iOS apps to 10.14, including Home, News, Stocks, and Voice Memos. This introduces a number of questions to look for answers to in the coming releases, which include

- How will these work with VPP?
- How will they react to containerization technologies like Managed Open-In, AirWatch Container, and the MobileIron AppConnect?
- Where are preferences stored and how are they loaded? Will Managed App Config play a larger role in the app ecosystem?

The third-party tools are all SDKs, and so the onus will be on developers to resolve any issues that Marzipan creates. The Mac seems to evolve more toward iOS, but there are ways iOS has evolved toward the Mac as well.

Will iOS Become Truly Multiuser?

The Mac didn't have multiple users for decades but has had multiple users for over 20 years at this point (officially since the release of 10.1 in 2001). iOS has always been a single-user operating system. The integration between Apple School Manager and Apple Classroom gave the first glimpse of what multiple users might look like on iOS devices.

Apple School Manager, using Managed Apple IDs, allows education environments to run different users on a single iOS device and provides a brief glimpse into what a multiuser iOS might eventually look like.

Each user can have an app shown or hidden. So apps can be on the device unbeknownst to a user, and when the device switches users, it just shows a different set of apps. This gets around the need to push apps to devices every time a user logs in. While Shared iPad is only offered in Apple School Manager today, Managed Apple IDs are now available in Apple Business Manager, and the future may hold a shared iPad for enterprises.

The impact, though, might not be that we have iPads in the hands of multiple people. The devices are just different. iPads cost less, are much more personal devices, and, other than niche use cases, have never needed the ability to have multiple users log in. The impact instead might be that users authenticate to access a device and then are able to better federate access between services with modern protocols such as OpenID Connect, SAML, and web tokens. The federated identity picture is still in its infancy on the Apple platforms.

Changes in Chipsets

The advent of the Intel in Apple devices saw Apple finally welcomed into many enterprises in ways Apple hadn't been welcomed in the previous decade. This allowed Apple to exploit the desires of many to have a choice rather than just use Microsoft, all the time. Ironically, once the platform finally caught on enough to be the darling of "innovative" leaders in enterprises, Apple began to move away from Intel.

Apple purchased PrimeSense for $350 million in 2013 in order to make the chips now used for Face ID. Apple purchased parts of chip maker Dialog for $650 million in 2018 (which brought in 300 engineers). Apple once owned part of the ARM alliance. Intel chips have had a number of pretty substantial security vulnerabilities over the past few years. It's also increasingly important for Apple to preemptively check that no changes have occurred to the firmware on chips.

Apple has switched things up before. Apple has made the A series of chips for iOS devices since 2007. The Intel transition in 2005 signaled a move from PowerPC, which resulted in a collaboration that had begun between Apple, IBM, and Motorola in 1991. But the shift led to a drop in apps for a short period. Some developers had to refactor to work with the new chips. Apple released the M1 MacBook in 2020 and the M2 MacBook in 2022. They also released a compatibility option called Rosetta 2 to allow for a simpler transition. To see a list of software that works with the M-series of MacBooks, see `https://isapplesiliconready.com/`.

Another chip that Apple touts is the T2, a security chip introduced in 2017 (the T1 was released the year before and brought Touch ID with it). The T2 runs its own operating system called bridgeOS, a derivative of watchOS. This is the basis for the secure enclave. The secure enclave is where encrypted keys are stored and locks down the boot process. The camera and microphone go through the T2 physically as do the encryption mechanisms for the SSD drives on a Mac, and so the T2 becomes important for FileVault. The T2 is likely to be embedded into all Macs at some point.

Universal adoption of the T2 (and subsequent releases) means that Apple suddenly has a lot of new options around Apple Pay, Face ID for the Mac, and a number of innovations we can't possibly have put together because we're not sitting in their design labs. What does this mean for those who need to plan an enterprise deployment of Macs with a three-year budget? It means if you have an option to buy a device with a T2 or without, it would be wise to spend a little more to get the T2-enabled device. Chips keep Apple from innovating as quickly as they'd like, so Apple is likely to continue to do more themselves. But the impacts to an enterprise are minimal, other than planning purchasing options to align with the desired life cycle of devices.

You're Just Not an "Enterprise" Company

Apple is not an "Enterprise" company. Those who have been in the Apple space for a long time have heard this throughout their entire careers. Other companies that are mentioned as not enterprise companies include IBM, Cisco, Microsoft, VMware, and the list goes on. It turns out that being "Enterprise" means doing the specific thing that a 200–200,000-person company wants a company to be doing at that moment. Many companies say they will do things, but not every business unit can do everything a company wants them to do all the time.

This isn't to say Apple hasn't become more and more "Enterprise"-friendly over the years. Engineers once said "you'll never be able to lock the home screen on an iPad," then tout that as a great feature, and later treat it as table stakes. We've gone from agent-based management that seemed barely tolerated on devices to a Mobile Device Management framework built just for centralized and streamlined management of devices. That framework is not ready to completely replace agents as has been made clear throughout this book. It gets closer every year, as teams at Apple identify each feature that organizations want to manage. That framework works when devices aren't on corporate networks.

Apple has a tool called Enterprise Connect. Apple has an enterprise sales team. Apple has an Enterprise professional services team. Apple has a number of executive briefing centers. The Apple CEO goes for long strolls with the CEO of IBM and has meetings with presidents of various countries. Apple built Exchange Active Sync policies into iPhone OS and, due to overwhelming needs from large customers, invented a whole new kind of management. Apple continues to integrate with the latest enterprise software, whether that's emerging SAML providers (including Microsoft), 802.1x network requirements, etc.

Sure, Apple is not an Enterprise company. But think about this: Apple is just getting started in the enterprise space, and as more enterprises adopt the platform, they're likely to become more and more enterprise focused.

Apple Is a Privacy Company

In this book, we've covered dozens of security features on iOS devices. These include Managed Open-In, SIP, certificate deployment, policies, application blacklisting, signatures, and so much more. Apple has had a number of slips with security over the years, such as when they accidentally showed a root password in clear text.

For the most part, these are just programming slips and mean Apple just needs to get better with Quality Assurance, especially in a time when competitors such as Microsoft do so well in that regard, which is amplified in the eyes of the security community. Growing so rapidly is hard, given that the more people who use software, the more weird things they do to that software - and the more bugs they find.

Security and privacy are different. Apple devices have great security, but they'll always be able to get better. In the face of so many privacy blunders by their competitors, one place where Apple shines is privacy. This privacy is seen and felt in all of the recent updates that frustrate Apple administrators. These block an administrator from performing various tasks.

The options for managing iOS devices over the years have opened up a lot of possibilities. iOS devices that are supervised can be managed in ways that we never thought would be possible in the iOS 4 era. All with privacy in mind. As an example, when Volume Purchase Program (VPP) apps are deployed, management solutions can push an app to an Apple ID. And if a user associates, the MDM can see the hash of the user that was used. But the MDM doesn't receive the actual Apple ID; thus, they protect the privacy of the end users. Expect questions like "what are the impacts to privacy" to come up with every new management feature provided.

This brings us to one of the most important concepts that emerged in the minds of the authors of this book. While not much may have changed in the ethos around device management at Apple, the need to keep users safe has grown exponentially. The hacker mentality that brought many

Mac administrators into the fold with the advent of Mac OS X creates danger for many standard users. And so many Mac Admins have left the platform to go manage Linux and other platforms. We all want different things out of our careers.

Summary

The only thing that is certain is change. The Apple platforms themselves change constantly, and so the way we manage them must change as well. The most important thing to ask about every new feature or change is how to manage a feature. And yet we need to manage features far less often than we might think.

Less is more. This doesn't mean don't manage anything on devices. It does mean that if a framework to manage features and settings in the operating system like MDM doesn't have an option that it's worth a second long and hard think about whether that should be managed long and short-term. A great example of this is how extensions can only be managed from within the app that instantiated an extension. Anyone who manages something that requires custom scripts should make sure to accept the fact that they'll own occasional changes as Apple changes the underlying tools (e.g., from bash to zsh or the need to install python, etc.) until that setting doesn't need to be managed any longer.

As we've shown in this book, Apple has had a consistent set of tools to manage devices since the inception of the Mac. Apple changes the tools to address IT industry trends or larger global security and privacy concerns. But the tools have always been there and in some cases still look similar to how they did in 1994. The name of the tools can change, the way they connect can change, and the way the tools manage settings can change over the years. Most were fairly static for decades, but began to change more quickly to address the invasion of privacy felt by many Apple customers given how ubiquitous technology has become. That's not likely to end any time soon.

APPENDIX A

The Apple Ecosystem

There are a lot of applications used to manage Apple devices in one way or another. Additionally, here's a list of tools, sorted alphabetically per category in order to remain vendor agnostic.

Antivirus and Malware Detection

Solutions for scanning Macs for viruses and other malware:

- **AVG**: Basic antivirus and spyware detection and remediation.
- **Avast**: Centralized antivirus with a cloud console for tracking incidents and device status.
- **Avira**: Antivirus and a browser extension. Avira Connect allows you to view device status online.
- **Bitdefender**: Antivirus and malware managed from a central console.
- **Carbon Black**: Antivirus and Application Control.
- **Cylance**: Ransomware, advanced threats, fileless malware, and malicious documents in addition to standard antivirus.
- **Jamf Protect**: Antivirus with threat hunting options.

C. Edge and R. Trouton, *Apple Device Management*,
https://doi.org/10.1007/978-1-4842-9156-6

- **Kaspersky**: Antivirus with a centralized cloud dashboard to track device status.
- **Malwarebytes**: Antivirus and malware managed from a central console.
- **McAfee Endpoint Security**: Antivirus and advanced threat management with a centralized server to track devices.
- **Sophos**: Antivirus and malware managed from a central console.
- **Symantec Mobile Device Management**: Antivirus and malware managed from a central console.
- **Trend Micro Endpoint Security**: Application whitelisting, antivirus, and ransomware protection in a centralized console.
- **Wandera**: Malicious hotspot monitoring, jailbreak detection, web gateway for mobile threat detection that integrates with common MDM solutions. Wandera is now a part of Jamf Private Access.

Automation Tools

Scripty tools used to automate management on the Mac (some of these are made obsolete by Apple Silicon, e.g., M1 or M2 chips):

- **AutoCasperNBI**: Automates the creation of NetBoot Images (read: NBI's) for use with Casper Imaging
- **AutoDMG**: Takes a macOS installer (10.10 or newer) and builds a system image suitable for deployment with Imagr, DeployStudio, LANrev, Jamf Pro, and other asr or Apple Software Restore-based imaging tools

- **AutoNBI**: Automates the build and customization of Apple NetInstall Images
- **Dockutil**: Command-line tool for managing dock items
- **Homebrew**: Package manager for macOS
- **Cakebrew**: Provides a pretty GUI for Homebrew
- **Jamjar**: Synergizes jamf, autopkg, and munki into an aggregated convergence that cherry-picks functionality from each product's core competency to create an innovative, scalable, and modular update framework
- **MacPorts**: An open source community initiative to design an easy-to-use system for compiling, installing, and upgrading either command-line, X11, or Aqua-based open source software on Macs
- **Precache**: Programmatically caches Mac and iOS updates rather than waiting for a device to initiate caching on a local caching server
- **Outset**: Automatically processes packages, profiles, and scripts during the boot sequence, user logins, or on demand

Backup

We highly recommend bundling or reselling some form of backup service to your customers, whether home, small business, or large enterprises. The flexibility to restore a device from a backup when needed is one of the most important things to keep costs at a manageable level and put devices back into the hands of customers in an appropriate time frame.

- **Acronis**: Centrally managed backups with image-based restores
- **Archiware**: Centrally managed backups to disk and tape with a variety of agents for backing up common Apple requirements, such as Xsan
- **Arq**: One-time fee cloud-based backups and unlimited storage
- **Backblaze**: Unlimited continuous backup with a 30-day rollback feature
- **Carbon Copy Cloner**: File- or disk-based cloning of files for macOS
- **Carbonite**: SaaS or local server–based backups of Mac clients
- **CrashPlan**: Backup to cloud and local storage with a great deduplication engine
- **Datto**: Local and cloud backup and restore, as well as cloud failover for various services
- **Druva**: Backup for local computers as well as some backup for cloud services
- **Quest Backup (formerly NetVault)**: Can back up Mac clients and Xsan volumes to a centralized tape or disk-based backup server
- **SuperDuper!**: Duplicates the contents of volumes to other disks
- **Time Machine**: Built-in backup tool for macOS

Collaboration Suites and File Sharing

Once upon a time, a Mac server was great for shared calendars, contacts, and email. But most businesses aren't going to want anything to do with the repercussions of potential downtime that can happen on a mail server. Nothing will get your hard-earned customers to fire you faster than an email outage. So while the Mac server is listed, consider cloud options, for optimal customer retention:

- **Atlassian**: Development-oriented suite including wiki (Confluence), issue tracking (Jira), messaging (HipChat), and other tools
- **Box**: File sharing in the cloud
- **Dropbox**: File sharing in the cloud
- **Egnyte**: Caches assets from popular cloud-based services so they're accessible faster on networks where they're frequently accessed
- **G Suite**: Shared Mail, Contacts, Calendars. Groupware, accessible from the built-in Apple tools, Microsoft Outlook, and through the Web
- **Kerio Connect**: Shared Mail, Contacts, Calendars. Groupware, accessible from the built-in Apple tools, Microsoft Outlook, and through the Web
- **Office 365**: Shared Mail, Contacts, Calendars. Groupware, accessible from the built-in Apple tools, Microsoft Outlook, and through the Web

CRM

Mac-friendly tools used to track contacts and communications with those contacts:

- **Daylite**: Mac tool for managing contacts and communications with those contacts
- **Hike**: Mac tool for managing contacts and communications with those contacts
- **Gro CRM**: iOS tool for managing contacts and communications with those contacts

DEP Splash Screens and Help Menus

Tools that make the DEP and service desk process more user-friendly by providing more information to users:

- **ADEPT**: Adds a splash screen for DEP enrollments so users can see what is happening on their devices
- **DEPNotify**: Adds a splash screen for DEP enrollments so users can see what is happening on their devices
- **HelloIT**: Customizable help menu so users can get information about their systems or IT support
- **MacDNA**: Customizable help menu so users can get information about their systems or IT support
- **Nudge**: Better alerts for things like software updates
- **SplashBuddy**: Adds a splash screen for DEP enrollments so users can see what is happening on their devices

Development Tools, IDEs, and Text Manipulators

Tools used when building scripts, writing and debugging software, and manipulating text:

- **aText**: Replaces abbreviations with frequently used phrases you define
- **Atom**: A modern text editor with bells and whistles that make it work like an IDE for common scripting languages
- **BBEdit**: A modern text editor with bells and whistles that make it work like an IDE for common scripting languages
- **Charles Proxy**: A proxy tool that can be used to inspect traffic so you can programmatically reproduce the traffic or reverse-engineer what is happening when trying to solve issues or build tools
- **CocoaDialog**: Creates better dialog boxes than with traditional tools like AppleScript
- **Coda**: An IDE and a modern text editor with bells and whistles that make it work like an IDE for common scripting languages
- **Dash**: Offline access to 150+ API documentation sets
- **Docker**: Containerization tool
- **FileMaker**: Rapid application development software from Apple

- **git**: Code versioning, merging, and tracking – and with GitHub, a repository to put code into and share code
- **Hopper Disassembler**: Disassembles binaries as part of reverse engineering and security testing
- **Microsoft Visual Studio**: An IDE for a variety of languages
- **MySQL Workbench**: Creates and edits MySQL databases and used to build complex queries
- **Navicat Essentials**: Creates and edits MySQL databases and used to build complex queries
- **Pashua**: Creating native Aqua dialogs from programming languages that have none or only limited support for graphic user interfaces on Mac OS X, such as AppleScript, Bash scripts, Perl, PHP, Python, and Ruby
- **Platypus**: Creates native Mac OS X applications from interpreted scripts such as shell scripts or Perl, Ruby, and Python programs
- **Script Debugger**: Tools like a dictionary explorer and more IDE-esque features for building AppleScript applications
- **Sequel Pro**: Creates and edits MySQL databases and used to build complex queries
- **Snippets Manager**: Collects and organizes code snippets
- **Sourcetree**: GUI tool for Git and GitHub

- **Sublime Text**: A modern text editor with bells and whistles that make it work like an IDE for common scripting languages
- **TextExpander**: Replaces abbreviations with frequently used phrases you define
- **TextWrangler**: A modern text editor with bells and whistles that make it work like an IDE for common scripting languages
- **Tower**: A modern text editor with bells and whistles that make it work like an IDE for common scripting languages
- **VisualJSON**: Simple JSON pretty viewer for the Mac
- **Xcode**: Apple tool for writing apps and scripts in common languages

Digital Signage and Kiosks

A lot of organizations have made a great little additional revenue stream by reselling or deploying these tools on behalf of their customers. Overall, it's a possible new revenue stream, and as an added bonus, you'll likely have an NFR (or not-for-resale copy of the software), so you can have pretty cool signage in your office (if you're into that kind of thing).

- **Carousel Digital Signage**: Runs Digital Signage from an Apple TV
- **Kiosk Pro**: Turns any iPad into a single-user kiosk tool, manageable via an API (e.g., with a Jamf Pro integration)
- **Rise Vision**: Runs Digital Signage from a Mac

Directory Services and Authentication Tools

Tools that provide primarily on-premises access to a shared directory of services and allow for single sign-on to those services:

- **Apple Enterprise Connect**: Tool sold through Apple that connects to Active Directory environments without binding to Active Directory
- **ADmitMac**: Adds support for fringe Active Directory requirements
- **JumpCloud**: Runs your directory service in the cloud
- **LDAP**: Open source directory service
- **macOS Server Open Directory**: Directory service installed in macOS Server that is based on OpenLDAP
- **Microsoft Active Directory**: Centralized directory service from Microsoft
- **NoMAD**: Connects clients to Active Directory environments without binding to Active Directory and has some other nifty features

Identity Management

Providers of predominantly SAML- or OAuth-based single sign-on solutions that federate security for Apple devices to access web-based services:

- **Apple Business Manager**: Federates Apple IDs with Azure AD identities and syncs users from Google Workspace
- **Centrify**: Provides federated login across common web services and other SAML-capable solutions, as well as

resolves common issues with Active Directory. Also has an integrated profile management tool for compliance

- **Duo Mobile**: Additional options in the realm of secure identity, with lots of great research going on in the Apple space
- **LastPass Enterprise**: Provides federated login across common web services and other SAML-capable solutions
- **Jamf Connect**: Jamf solution for improving the local experience when working with various Identity Providers
- **Microsoft Azure Active Directory**: Active Directory with Azure in the cloud
- **Okta**: Provides federated login across common web services and other SAML-capable solutions
- **OneLogin**: Provides federated login across common web services and other SAML-capable solutions
- **Ping Identity**: Provides federated login across common web services and other SAML-capable solutions

Imaging and Configuration Tools

Tools used to place devices into a given state or create that state. This includes traditional Macs, including tools, as well as those built for iOS.

- **Apple Configurator**: Configures iOS and tvOS devices en masse, automates MDM enrollment, and distributes data.
- **Blast Image Config**: Will no longer be developed, given the state of device imaging, but allows admins

to quickly restore and configure a Macintosh back to a known state (10.12.2 and below).

- **createOSXInstallPackage**: Creates an installer package from an "Install OS X.app" or an InstallESD.dmg (10.12.4 and below).
- **Deep Freeze**: Freezes the state of a Mac.
- **DeployStudio**: Free imaging server for Macs.
- **Google Restor**: Images macOS computers from a single source. It is an application intended to be run interactively on a machine.
- **Ground Control**: Mass deploys (and enrolls) iOS devices.
- **Imagr**: Replaces tools such as DeployStudio for many organizations without the requirement of needing to be run on OS X servers.
- **libimobiledevice**: Suite of tools to configure, inspect, wipe, etc., for iOS devices.
- **Winclone**: Creates Windows images for deployment onto Macs.

Log Collection and Analysis

Centralized logging has been a necessity for large, growing fleets of devices. Modern tools can store large amounts of logs from client computers and allow fast and complex searching so you can triangulate issues quickly and effectively. As an added benefit, you can also centralize logs for network appliances, allowing you to isolate the source of issues across an entire ecosystem of devices.

- **Elasticsearch**: Open source, very fast log analysis
- **RobotCloud Dashboard**: Provides more granular and intuitive visibility into devices managed by Jamf Pro
- **Splunk**: Big data log analysis
- **Tableau**: Big data analysis
- **Watchman Monitoring**: Mac-focused monitoring agent that inspects common third-party tools
- **Zentral**: Open source, built on Elasticsearch, but with hooks into lots of other tools and custom recipes for Mac logs

Management Suites

Tools used to manage settings on Apple Devices. Each is marked as MDM, Agent based, or both:

- **Addigy**: Agent and MDM based
- **AirWatch**: MDM and agent based
- **Altiris**: Agent based
- **Apple Business Essentials**: Light MDM for small business
- **BigFix**: Agent based
- **Chef**: Agent based
- **ConnectWise**: Limited agent-based Mac management focused on MSPs
- **FileWave**: MDM and agent based
- **IBM MaaS360**: MDM

- **Ivanti**: MDM and agent based
- **Jamf Now**: Small business-focused MDM
- **Jamf Pro (formerly Casper Suite)**: MDM and agent based
- **Jamf School**: MDM with a parent app
- **JumpCloud**: Agent based, directory based, and MDM
- **KACE**: Agent based
- **Kandji**: MDM with lots of prebuilt automations
- **Kaseya**: Agent-based Mac management for Managed Service Providers
- **Labtech**: Agent based
- **LANrev**: MDM and agent based (currently being retired)
- **Lightspeed Mobile Manager**: MDM
- **Meraki Systems Manager**: MDM
- **MicroMDM**: Open source MDM
- **Microsoft Intune** (MDM) and **SCCM** (agent based)
- **Manage Engine**: Agent based
- **Mobile Guardian**: MDM
- **MobileIron**: MDM
- **Mosyle**: MDM
- **Munki**: Agent based
- **NanoMDM**: Open source MDM

- **Parallels Mac Management for SCCM**: Agent-based SCCM plug-in for Macs
- **Profile Manager (macOS Server)**: MDM
- **Puppet**: Agent based
- **SAL**: Agent-based SaaS version of Munki, Puppet, Django, and SB Admin 2
- **SAP Mobile Secure**: MDM with integrations to other SAP products
- **Solarwinds MSP**: Agent based with integrated backup and ticketing for Managed Service Providers
- **Sophos**: MDM
- **TabPilot**: MDM

Misc

- **Jamf NetSUS**: Reposado packaged up for Jamf servers (no longer actively maintained)
- **InfineaIQ**: Peripheral management software
- **IT Glue**: Stores credentials and information about common IT tools in a SaaS-based database
- **Reposado**: An open source interpretation of the Apple Software Update Server
- **Sassafras Keyserver**: Centralized software license management server
- **ipaSign**: Programmatically resigns ipa files with a new key

Point of Sale

Similar to digital signage, but you might also operate a storefront or track customer data in one of these solutions:

- **Checkout**: Point of sale solution that can run on Apple devices
- **Lightspeed**: Point of sale solution that can run on Apple devices
- **PayGo**: Point of sale solution that can run on Apple devices
- **Posim**: Point of sale solution that can run on Apple devices
- **ShopKeep**: Point of sale solution that can run on Apple devices
- **Square**: Point of sale solution that can run on Apple devices
- **Vend**: Point of sale solution that can run on Apple devices

Print Servers

Printers jam, they break, the drivers seem to be rife with problems for every other operating system update, printers are often connected to via ad hoc networks (like Bonjour), and you often need special software to access the cool features. All in all, printers suck, but these tools might make them just a tad bit easier to use or, if not, help to account for who is using them so your customers can bill their departments back as much as possible:

- **PaperCut**: Printer cost accounting for the Mac
- **Printopia**: Allows for better printing from iOS devices

Remote Management

These tools allow you to take control of the screen, keyboard, and mouse of devices. We can't tell you which are the best, as that's different for every organization. But we can tell you that tools should typically be cross-platform and cloud based, prompt users for acceptance of the remote control session, and audit connections so we know who is taking over what devices.

- **Apple Remote Desktop**: Apple tool for remotely controlling other Macs, sending packages to Macs, and running scripts on Macs over a LAN or directly to an IP address
- **Bomgar**: Appliance that allows for cross-platform remote control of devices
- **CoRD**: RDP client
- **LogMeIn**: Cross-platform remote control utility
- **GoToMyPC**: Cross-platform remote control utility
- **Remote Desktop**: The official RDP client for the Mac
- **Remotix**: RDP and VNC server with lots of bells and whistles
- **Splashtop**: Works with iOS as well (with limitations)
- **TeamViewer**: Cross-platform remote control utility

Security Tools

Tools used to manage firewalls and FileVault and perform other tasks required to secure Macs, based on the security posture of a given organization:

- **Cauliflower Vest**: Stores FileVault keys on a centralized server
- **Crypt**: FileVault 2 Escrow solution
- **Digital Guardian**: Data loss prevention
- **Google Santa**: Binary blacklisting and whitelisting for the Mac
- **iOS Location Scraper**: Dumps the contents of the location database files on iOS and macOS
- **iOS Frequent Location Scraper**: Dumps the contents of the StateModel#.archive files located in /private/var/mobile/Library/Caches/com.apple.routined/
- **Little Snitch**: Provides information about what is accessing network resources and where those resources are
- **Objective-See**: 's KnockKnock, Task Explorer, BlockBlock, RansomWhere?, Oversight, and KextViewr, tools for finding more information about ports and services running on machines
- **Osquery**: Queries for information on Macs in a live, granular search
- **Portecle**: Creates and manages keystores, keys, certificates, certificate requests, and certificate revocation lists

- **PowerBroker**: Enables standard users on a Mac to perform administrative tasks without entering elevated credentials
- **Prey**: Tracks Mac and iOS devices if they're stolen

Service Desk Tools

These tools are for ticketing and ticket management. It's always great if you can pick one that actually integrates with both your billing solution and the various other techie bits you choose to use:

- **Freshdesk**: Case/ticket management that allows for automatic billing via Freshbooks
- **Salesforce Cases**: Case/ticket management that automatically integrates with Salesforce CRM
- **ServiceNow**: Case/ticket management with an expansive marketplace for integrations
- **Web Help Desk**: Case/ticket management
- **Zendesk**: Case/ticket management with an expansive marketplace for integrations

Software Packaging and Package Management

Tools for normalizing software for mass distribution on Apple platforms:

- **Autopkg**: Automates the creation of Mac software distribution packages using recipes
- **CreateUserPkg**: Creates packages that create local user accounts when installed (10.12 and below)

- **JSSImporter**: Connects Autopkg to Jamf Pro
- **Iceberg**: Creates Mac software distribution packages
- **InstallApplication**: Dynamically downloads packages for use with MDM's `InstallApplication`
- **Jamf Composer**: Creates Mac software distribution packages
- **Luggage**: Open source project to create a wrapper that makes pkgs for Macs so you can have peer review of a package by examining the diffs between versions of a Makefile
- **Munkipkg**: A simple tool for building packages in a consistent, repeatable manner from source files and scripts in a project directory
- **Pacifist**: A shareware application that opens macOS .pkg package files, .dmg disk images, and .zip, .tar, .tar.gz, .tar.bz2, and .xar archives and allows you to extract individual files and folders out of them
- **Payload-Free Package Creator**: An Automator application that uses AppleScript, shell scripting, and pkgbuild behind the scenes to create payload-free packages
- **QuickPkg**: Creates Mac software distribution packages
- **Simple Package Creator**: Creates Mac software distribution packages
- **Suspicious Package**: Views the contents of Mac software distribution packages
- **Whitebox Packages**: Creates Mac software distribution packages

Storage

Apple-focused solutions for sharing files:

- **Netatalk**: Better AFP connectivity to Windows and other storage platforms from a Mac
- **Promise**: Apple-vetted direct attached storage (DAS), storage area network (SAN), etc.
- **Synology**: Storage appliances tailored to working with the Mac
- **Xsan**: The built-in Apple SAN filesystem

Troubleshooting, Repair, and Service Tools

Tools used to fix logical problems with hard drives, check hardware for issues, repair various system problems, or just clean up a Mac:

- **AppCleaner**: Cleans up unneeded files on a Mac
- **AppleJack**: Repairs disks/permissions and cleans cache/swap files from single-user mode when a Mac can't fully boot
- **Bartender**: Manages items in the menu bar on a Mac
- **CleanMyDrive**: Drags and drops files directly to any drive, checks disk stats, and automatically cleans hidden junk from external drives
- **Data Rescue**: Data recovery tool for Mac
- **Disk Doctor**: Repairs logical drives and cleans up unneeded files
- **DiskWarrior**: Repairs logical volume corruption on Macs

- **Drive Genius**: Automates monitoring for hard drive errors, finds duplicate files, allows for repartition of volumes, clones volumes, performs secure erase, and defragmentation
- **Disk Inventory X**: Visual representation of what's on a logical volume in macOS
- **EasyFind**: Finds files, folders, or contents in any file without indexing through Spotlight
- **iStumbler**: Wireless discovery tool for Mac that can locate Wi-Fi networks, Bluetooth devices, and Bonjour services and perform spectrum analysis
- **GeekTool**: Puts script output and logs directly on the desktop of a Mac
- **Google Plan B**: Remediates Macs that fall out of a given state by performing a secure download of disk images and then putting the device into a management platform
- **GrandPerspective**: Visual representation of what's on a logical volume in macOS
- **Hardware Monitor**: Reads hardware sensor information on a Mac
- **Lingon**: Creates, manages, and deletes LaunchAgents and LaunchDaemons on macOS
- **Memtest OS X**: Tests each RAM module in a Mac
- **Nmap**: Advanced port scanning, network mapping, and network troubleshooting
- **Peak Hour**: Network performance, quality, and usage monitoring

- **OmniDiskSweeper**: Finds and removes unused files in macOS to conserve and reclaim disk space
- **OnyX**: Verifies the startup disk and structure of system files, runs maintenance and cleaning tasks, configures settings (e.g., for the Finder, Dock, Safari), deletes caches, and rebuilds various databases and indexes
- **Push Diagnostics**: Tests port and host access for APNs Traffic
- **Stellar Phoenix**: Mac data recovery tool
- **TechTool Pro**: Drive repair, RAM testing, and data protection
- **TinkerTool**: Graphical interface for changing preferences on a Mac that would otherwise need to be managed with the defaults command
- **Xirrus Wi-Fi Inspector**: Searches for Wi-Fi networks, conducts site surveys, troubleshoots Wi-Fi connectivity issues, locates Wi-Fi devices, and detects rogue apps

Virtualization and Emulation

Not all software runs on a Mac. Customers will have certain tasks that may require a Windows machine. You can use Citrix or a Microsoft Terminal Server to provide for that potential requirement. Or, especially if users need data from their Windows apps when offline, you can use a local virtualization tool.

- **Anka veertu**: Runs virtual machines on a Mac
- **Citrix**: Publishes Windows application sessions that end users connect to from a Mac using standard RDP clients

- **Parallels**: Runs virtual machines on a Mac
- **Microsoft Windows Terminal Server**: Publishes Windows sessions that end users connect to from a Mac using standard RDP clients
- **UTM**: Free virtual machine solution
- **vFuse**: Script to create a VMware Fusion VM from a DMG that hasn't been booted
- **VirtualBox**: Runs virtual machines on a Mac
- **VMware Fusion**: Runs virtual machines on a Mac

Honorable Mention

- **The MacAdmins Slack**: Join a community of 15,000 other admins charged with managing large fleets of Apple devices.
- **Apple Developer Program**: Sign up for a developer account in order to get access to beta resources and documentation not otherwise available.
- **Your Apple SE or local retail store**: A great resource for finding information!
- **Coffee**... lots and lots of coffee

APPENDIX B

Common Apple Ports

There are a number of ports used by Apple products. The following table lists examples of commonly used ports, along with basic information about the Apple services which use them. The following defines the meaning of each column of the table:

- **Port**: The number of the port to be used (from 0 to 65535).
- **TCP or UDP**: Whether communications use the Transport Control Protocol (TCP) or User Datagram Protocol (UDP) communications protocol.
- **Protocol**: The stringified name of the protocol to be used.
- **RFC**: The Internet Engineering Task Force (IETF) document number used to define how communications for the protocol flow. Check these to make sure they haven't been replaced with a newer document.
- **Purpose**: What the protocol is meant to do.

Note Some services will use more than one port.

C. Edge and R. Trouton, *Apple Device Management*,
https://doi.org/10.1007/978-1-4842-9156-6

Port	TCP or UDP	Protocol	RFC	Service Name	Purpose
7	TCP/UDP	echo	792	echo	–
20	TCP	File Transport Protocol (FTP)	959	ftp-data	–
21	TCP	FTP control	959	ftp	–
22	TCP	Secure Shell (SSH), SSH File Transfer Protocol (SFTP), and secure copy (scp)	4253	Ssh	Xcode Server (hosted and remote Git+SSH; remote SVN+SSH)
23	TCP	Telnet	854	telnet	–
25	TCP	Simple Mail Transfer Protocol (SMTP)	5321	smtp	Mail (sending email); iCloud Mail (sending email)
53	TCP/UDP	Domain Name System (DNS)	1034	Domain	–
67	UDP	Bootstrap Protocol Server (BootP, bootps)	951	Bootps	NetBoot via DHCP
68	UDP	Bootstrap Protocol Client (bootpc)	951	Bootpc	NetBoot via DHCP
69	UDP	Trivial File Transfer Protocol (TFTP)	1350	Tftp	–
79	TCP	Finger	1288	finger	–

80	TCP	Hypertext Transfer Protocol (HTTP)	2616	http	World Wide Web, FaceTime, iMessage, iCloud, QuickTime Installer, Maps, iTunes U, Apple Music, iTunes Store, Podcasts, Internet Radio, Software Update (OS X Lion or earlier), Mac App Store, RAID Admin, Backup, Calendar, WebDAV, Final Cut Server, AirPlay, macOS Internet Recovery, Profile Manager, Xcode Server (Xcode app, hosted and remote Git HTTP, remote SVN HTTP)
88	TCP	Kerberos	4120	kerberos	Kerberos, including Screen Sharing authentication
106	TCP	Password Server (unregistered use)	–	3com-tsmux	macOS Server Password Server
110	TCP	Post Office Protocol (POP3) Authenticated Post Office Protocol (APOP)	1939	pop3	Mail (receiving email)

(continued)

Port	TCP or UDP	Protocol	RFC	Service Name	Purpose
111	TCP/UDP	Remote Procedure Call (RPC)	1057, 1831	Sunrpc	Portmap (sunrpc)
113	TCP	Identification Protocol	1413	Ident	–
119	TCP	Network News Transfer Protocol (NNTP)	3977	nntp	Apps that read newsgroups
123	UDP	Network Time Protocol (NTP)	1305	Ntp	Date and Time preferences, network time server synchronization, Apple TV network time server sync
137	UDP	Windows Internet Naming Service (WINS)	–	netbios-ns	–
138	UDP	NetBIOS Datagram Service	–	netbios-dgm	Windows Datagram Service, Windows Network Neighborhood
139	TCP	Server Message Block (SMB)	–	netbios-ssn	Microsoft Windows file and print services, such as Windows Sharing in macOS
143	TCP	Internet Message Access Protocol (IMAP)	3501	imap	Mail (receiving email)

161	UDP	Simple Network Management Protocol (SNMP)	1157	Snmp	–
192	UDP	OSU Network Monitoring System	–	osu-nms	AirPort Base Station PPP status or discovery (certain configurations), AirPort Admin Utility, AirPort Express Assistant
311	TCP	Secure server administration	–	asip-webadmin	Server app, Server Admin, Workgroup Manager, Server Monitor, Xsan Admin
312	TCP	Xsan administration	–	Vslmp	Xsan Admin (OS X Mountain Lion v10.8 and later)
389	TCP	Lightweight Directory Access Protocol (LDAP)	4511	ldap	Apps that look up addresses, such as Mail and Address Book
427	TCP/UDP	Service Location Protocol (SLP)	2608	svrloc	Network Browser

(continued)

Port	TCP or UDP	Protocol	RFC	Service Name	Purpose
443	TCP	Secure Sockets Layer (SSL or HTTPS)	2818	https	TLS websites, iTunes Store, Software Update (OS X Mountain Lion and later), Spotlight Suggestions, Mac App Store, Maps, FaceTime, Game Center, iCloud authentication and DAV Services (Contacts, Calendars, Bookmarks), iCloud backup and apps (Calendars, Contacts, Find My iPhone, Find My Friends, Mail, iMessage, Documents, and Photo Stream), iCloud Key Value Store (KVS), iPhoto Journals, AirPlay, macOS Internet Recovery, Profile Manager, Back to My Mac, Dictation, Siri, Xcode Server (hosted and remote Git HTTPS, remote SVN HTTPS, Apple Developer registration), Push Notifications (if necessary)
445	TCP	Microsoft SMB Domain Server	–	microsoft-ds	–

464	TCP/UDP	Kpasswd	3244	kpasswd	–
465	TCP	Message Submission for Mail (Authenticated SMTP)		smtp (legacy)	Mail (sending mail)
500	UDP	ISAKMP/IKE	2408	Isakmp	macOS Server VPN service, Back to My Mac
500	UDP	Wi-Fi Calling	5996	IKEv2	Wi-Fi Calling
514	TCP	Shell	–	shell	–
514	UDP	Syslog	–	syslog	–
515	TCP	Line Printer (LPR), Line Printer Daemon (LPD)	–	printer	Printing to a network printer, Printer Sharing in macOS
532	TCP	Netnews	–	netnews	–
548	TCP	Apple Filing Protocol (AFP) over TCP	–	afpovertcp	AppleShare, Personal File Sharing, Apple File Service
554	TCP/UDP	Real-Time Streaming Protocol (RTSP)	2326	Rtsp	AirPlay, QuickTime Streaming Server (QTSS), streaming media players
587	TCP	Message Submission for Mail (Authenticated SMTP)	4409	submission	Mail (sending mail), iCloud Mail (SMTP authentication)

(continued)

Port	TCP or UDP	Protocol	RFC	Service Name	Purpose
600–1023	TCP/UDP	Mac OS X RPC–based services	–	ipcserver	NetInfo
623	UDP	Lights-Out Monitoring	–	asf-rmcp	Lights-Out Monitoring (LOM) feature of Intel-based Xserve computers, Server Monitor
625	TCP	Open Directory Proxy (ODProxy) (unregistered use)	–	dec_dlm	Open Directory, Server app, Workgroup Manager; directory services in OS X Lion or earlier Note: This port is registered to DEC DLM
626	TCP	AppleShare Imap Admin (ASIA)	–	Asia	IMAP administration (Mac OS X Server v10.2.8 or earlier)
626	UDP	serialnumberd (unregistered use)	–	Asia	Server serial number registration (Xsan, Mac OS X Server v10.3–v10.6)
631	TCP	Internet Printing Protocol (IPP)	2910	Ipp	macOS Printer Sharing, printing to many common printers
636	TCP	Secure LDAP	–	ldaps	–

660	TCP	Server administration	–	mac-srvr-admin	Server administration tools for Mac OS X Server v10.4 or earlier, including AppleShare IP
687	TCP	Server administration	–	asipregistry	Server administration tools for Mac OS X Server v10.6 or earlier, including AppleShare IP
749	TCP/UDP	Kerberos 5 admin/changepw	–	kerberos-adm	–
985	TCP	NetInfo Static Port	–	–	–
993	TCP	Mail IMAP SSL	–	Imaps	iCloud Mail (SSL IMAP)
995	TCP/UDP	Mail POP SSL	–	pop3s	–
1085	TCP/UDP	WebObjects	–	webobjects	–
1099, 8043	TCP	Remote RMI and IIOP Access to JBoss	–	rmiregistry	–
1220	TCP	QT Server Admin	–	qt-serveradmin	Administration of QuickTime Streaming Server
1640	TCP	Certificate Enrollment Server	–	cert-responder	Profile Manager in macOS Server 5.2 and earlier

(continued)

Port	TCP or UDP	Protocol	RFC	Service Name	Purpose
1649	TCP	IP Failover	–	kermit	–
1701	UDP	L2TP	–	l2f	macOS Server VPN service
1723	TCP	PPTP	–	pptp	macOS Server VPN service
1900	UDP	SSDP	–	ssdp	Bonjour, Back to My Mac
2049	TCP/UDP	Network File System (NFS) (versions 3 and 4)	3530	nfsd	–
2195	TCP	Apple Push Notification Service (APNS)	–	–	Push notifications
2196	TCP	Apple Push Notification Service (APNS)	–	–	Feedback service
2336	TCP	Mobile account sync	–	Appleugcontrol	Home directory synchronization
3004	TCP	iSync	–	csoftragent	–
3031	TCP/UDP	Remote Apple Events	–	Eppc	Program Linking, Remote Apple Events
3283	TCP/UDP	Net Assistant	–	net-assistant	Apple Remote Desktop 2.0 or later (Reporting feature), Classroom app (command channel)

3284	TCP/UDP	Net Assistant	–	net-assistant	Classroom app (document sharing)
3306	TCP	MySQL	–	mysql	–
3478–3497	UDP	–	–	nat-stun-port - ipether232port	FaceTime, Game Center
3632	TCP	Distributed compiler	–	distcc	–
3659	TCP/UDP	Simple Authentication and Security Layer (SASL)	–	apple-sasl	macOS Server Password Server
3689	TCP	Digital Audio Access Protocol (DAAP)	–	daap	iTunes Music Sharing, AirPlay
3690	TCP/UDP	Subversion	–	Svn	Xcode Server (anonymous remote SVN)
4111	TCP	Xgrid	–	Xgrid	–
4398	UDP	–	–	–	Game Center
4488	TCP	Apple Wide Area Connectivity Service		awacs-ice	Back to My Mac
4500	UDP	IPsec NAT Traversal	4306	ipsec-msft	macOS Server VPN service, Back to My Mac

(continued)

Port	TCP or UDP	Protocol	RFC	Service Name	Purpose
					Note: Configuring Back to My Mac on an AirPort Base Station or AirPort Time Capsule in NAT mode impedes connectivity to a macOS Server VPN service behind that NAT
4500	UDP	Wi-Fi Calling	5996	IKEv2	Wi-Fi Calling
5003	TCP	FileMaker – name binding and transport	–	fmpro-internal	–
5009	TCP	(unregistered use)	–	winfs	AirPort Utility, AirPort Express Assistant
5100	TCP	–	–	socalia	macOS camera and scanner sharing
5222	TCP	XMPP (Jabber)	3920	jabber-client	Jabber messages
5223	TCP	Apple Push Notification Service (APNS)	–	–	iCloud DAV Services (Contacts, Calendars, Bookmarks), Push Notifications, FaceTime, iMessage, Game Center, Photo Stream, Back to My Mac
5228	TCP	–	–	–	Spotlight Suggestions, Siri
5297	TCP	–	–	–	Messages (local traffic)

5350	UDP	NAT Port Mapping Protocol Announcements	–	–	Bonjour, Back to My Mac
5351	UDP	NAT Port Mapping Protocol	–	nat-pmp	Bonjour, Back to My Mac
5353	UDP	Multicast DNS (MDNS)	3927	Mdns	Bonjour, AirPlay, Home Sharing, Printer Discovery, Back to My Mac
5432	TCP	PostgreSQL	–	postgresql	Can be enabled manually in OS X Lion Server (previously enabled by default for ARD 2.0 Database)
5897–5898	UDP	(unregistered use)	–	–	xrdiags
5900	TCP	Virtual Network Computing (VNC)	–	vnc-server	Apple Remote Desktop 2.0 or later (Observe/Control feature)
		(unregistered use)			Screen Sharing (Mac OS X 10.5 or later)
5988	TCP	WBEM HTTP	–	wbem-http	Apple Remote Desktop 2.x Note: For more information, please also see `www.dmtf.org/standards/wbem`

(continued)

Port	TCP or UDP	Protocol	RFC	Service Name	Purpose
6970–9999	UDP	–	–	–	QuickTime Streaming Server
7070	TCP	RTSP (unregistered use), Automatic Router Configuration Protocol (ARCP)	–	Arcp	QuickTime Streaming Server (RTSP)
7070	UDP	RTSP alternate	–	Arcp	QuickTime Streaming Server
8000–8999	TCP	–	–	Irdmi	Web service, iTunes Radio streams
8005	TCP	Tomcat remote shutdown	–	–	–
8008	TCP	iCal service	–	http-alt	Mac OS X Server v10.5 or later
8080	TCP	Alternate port for Apache web service	–	http-alt	Also JBoss HTTP in Mac OS X Server 10.4 or earlier
8085–8087	TCP	Wiki service	–	–	Mac OS X Server v10.5 or later
8088	TCP	Software Update service	–	radan-http	Mac OS X Server v10.4 or later
8089	TCP	Web email rules	–	–	Mac OS X Server v10.6 or later
8096	TCP	Web Password Reset	–	–	Mac OS X Server v10.6.3 or later
8170	TCP	HTTPS (web service/site)	–	–	Podcast Capture/podcast CLI

8171	TCP	HTTP (web service/site)	–	–	Podcast Capture/podcast CLI
8175	TCP	Pcast Tunnel	–	–	pcastagentd (such as for control operations and camera)
8443	TCP	iCal service (SSL)	–	pcsync-https	Mac OS X Server v10.5 or later (JBoss HTTPS in Mac OS X Server 10.4 or earlier)
8800	TCP	Address Book service	–	Sunwebadmin	Mac OS X Server v10.6 or later
8843	TCP	Address Book service (SSL)	–	–	Mac OS X Server v10.6 or later
8821, 8826	TCP	Stored	–	–	Final Cut Server
8891	TCP	Ldsd	–	–	Final Cut Server (data transfers)
9006	TCP	Tomcat stand-alone	–	–	Mac OS X Server v10.6 or earlier
9100	TCP	Printing	–	–	Printing to certain network printers
9418	TCP/UDP	git pack transfer	–	Git	Xcode Server (remote git)
10548	TCP	Apple Document Sharing Service	–	serverdocs	macOS Server iOS file sharing
11211	–	memcached (unregistered use)	–	–	Calendar Server

(*continued*)

Port	TCP or UDP	Protocol	RFC	Service Name	Purpose
16080	TCP	–	–	–	Web service with performance cache
16384–16403	UDP	Real-Time Transport Protocol (RTP), Real-Time Control Protocol (RTCP)	–	connected, –	Messages (Audio RTP, RTCP; Video RTP, RTCP)
16384–16387	UDP	Real-Time Transport Protocol (RTP), Real-Time Control Protocol (RTCP)	–	connected, –	FaceTime, Game Center
16393–16402	UDP	Real-Time Transport Protocol (RTP), Real-Time Control Protocol (RTCP)	–	–	FaceTime, Game Center
16403–16472	UDP	Real-Time Transport Protocol (RTP), Real-Time Control Protocol (RTCP)	–	–	Game Center
24000–24999	TCP	–	–	med-ltp	Web service with performance cache
50003	–	FileMaker Server Service	–	–	–
50006	–	FileMaker Helper Service	–	–	–

APPENDIX C

Configure macOS Lab Virtual Machines with UTM

One of the most helpful tools to learn how to manage systems is to create virtual machines that can be freely experimented with while learning a new tool. This keeps the operating system of our "daily driver" or normal computer free and helps keep us from traveling around with three or four laptops to test how to use new technologies.

New virtualization tools come around every few years. Traditionally, Parallels, VMware Fusion, and a few others were the traditional favorites to use. Indeed, these still have the most options to tweak various settings. However, where many once used virtual machines on a Mac to run services full time, virtualization on the platform has now been relegated mostly to testing. As such, an inexpensive and fast tool that uses the latest frameworks from Apple is just as good as most others.

UTM is a virtualization tool available on the Mac App Store at `https://apps.apple.com/us/app/utm-virtual-machines/id1538878817?mt=12` with a GitHub at `https://github.com/osy`. UTM uses the new virtualization framework (documented here) from Apple, so runs the most modern virtualization stack currently available on a Mac. It also emulates

C. Edge and R. Trouton, *Apple Device Management*,
https://doi.org/10.1007/978-1-4842-9156-6

via the QEMU system emulation. It can run guest operating systems in Windows, Linux, etc. - emulating RISC, ARM, Intel, etc.

Installation of UTM from the App Store is easy. Once installed, open the UTM app and click the plus sign to create a new virtual machine. Here, there are options to Virtualize or Emulate. Given that we'll be installing a beta OS from Apple for this example (which for major OS releases or point releases is a fairly constant task at this point), we'll click Virtualize, as seen in Figure C-1.

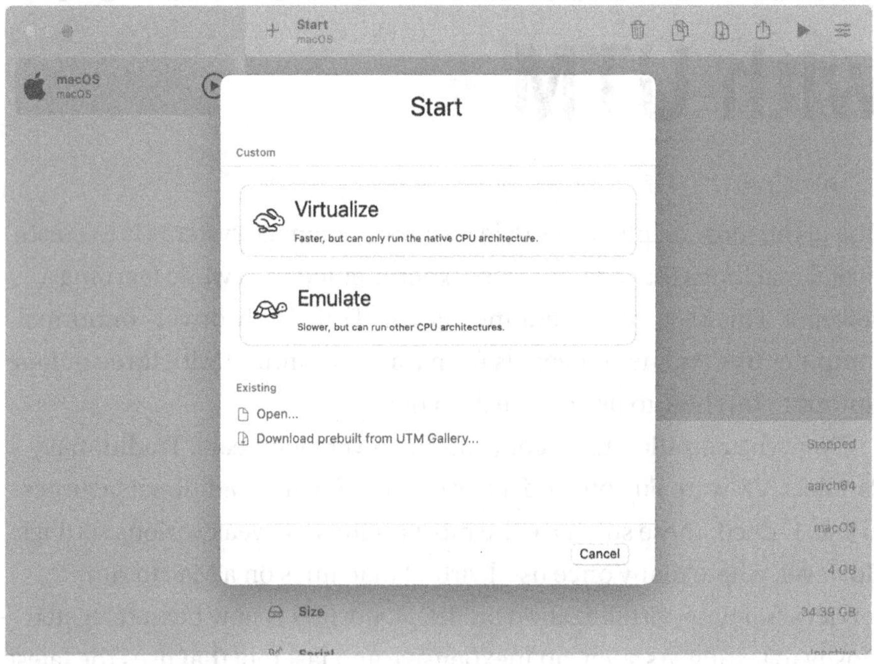

***Figure C-1.** The opening screen for UTM*

The list of operating systems will reflect those that can be run as virtual machines with the current architecture. For a Mac running macOS 12, 13, etc., this will be the first option, so click there (Figure C-2).

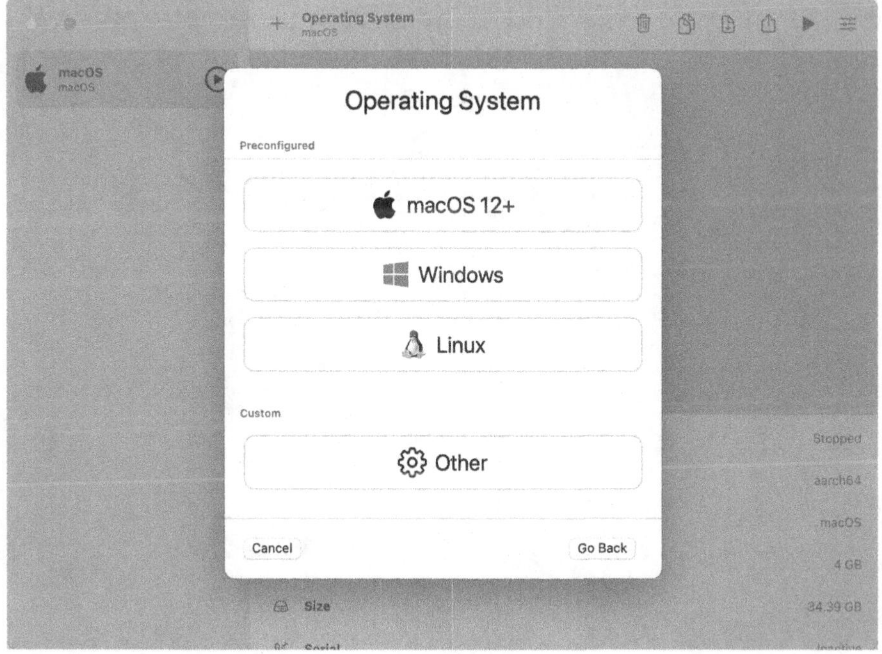

Figure C-2. *Selecting an operating system*

The next screen gives the option to either install the OS the host operating system is running or a different version of macOS via an IPSW (which is downloaded from Apple's Developer portal). Either click Continue, as seen in Figure C-3, for the same OS or click Browse and select the IPSW obtained from the Apple Developer portal.

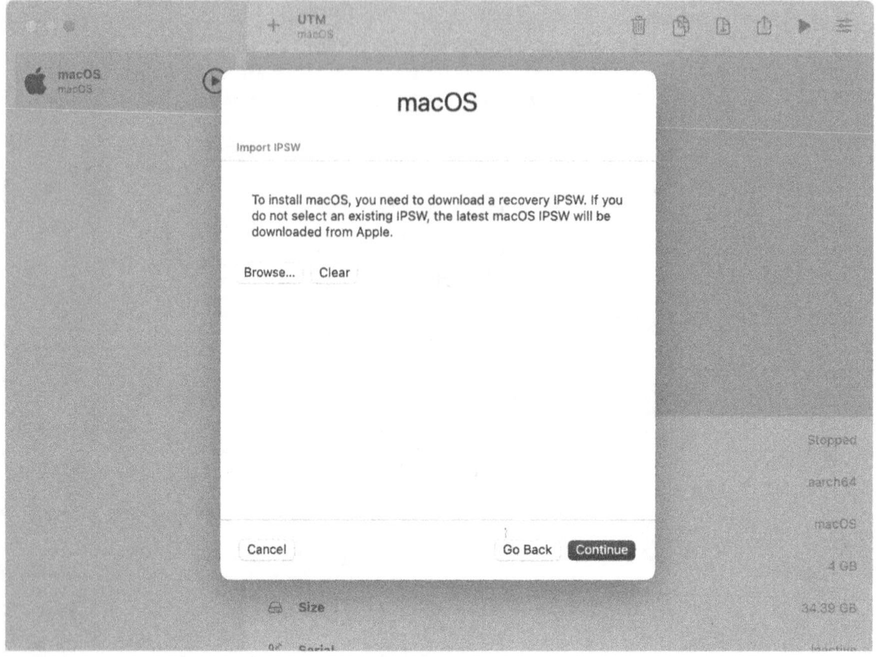

Figure C-3. *Select the IPSW (if needed)*

Once the IPSW is selected, choose the virtual hardware to allocate to the virtual machine. The defaults for Memory and how many CPU Cores should be fine for an initial experiment (and these can be changed later). Indeed, for most testing, the defaults will be more than enough to test functionality, especially with regard to hardware configurations. Click Continue, as in Figure C-4, once the settings are appropriately configured.

Figure C-4. *Configure how much Memory and how many CPU Cores*

The next screen decides how much space the virtual machine will occupy. This pulls the capacity from the available hard drive space for a machine. 64GB is a fine amount to start with (Figure C-5), but go below 32 and there may be some issues.

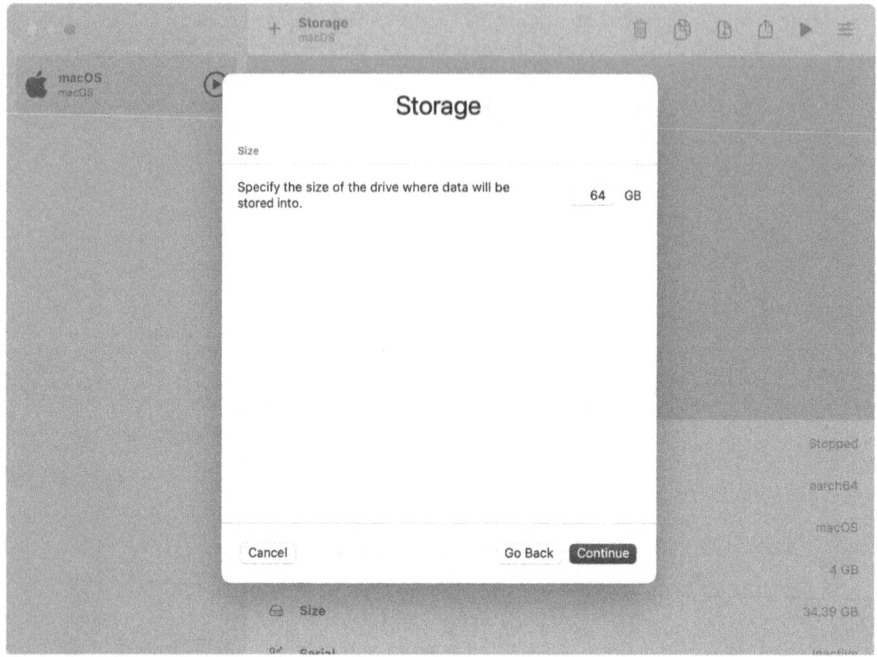

Figure C-5. *Select how much storage for the VM*

Review the information in the Summary screen, as seen in Figure C-6, and click Save to start creating the new virtual machine. Make sure the IPSW is the one to create the specific OS desired.

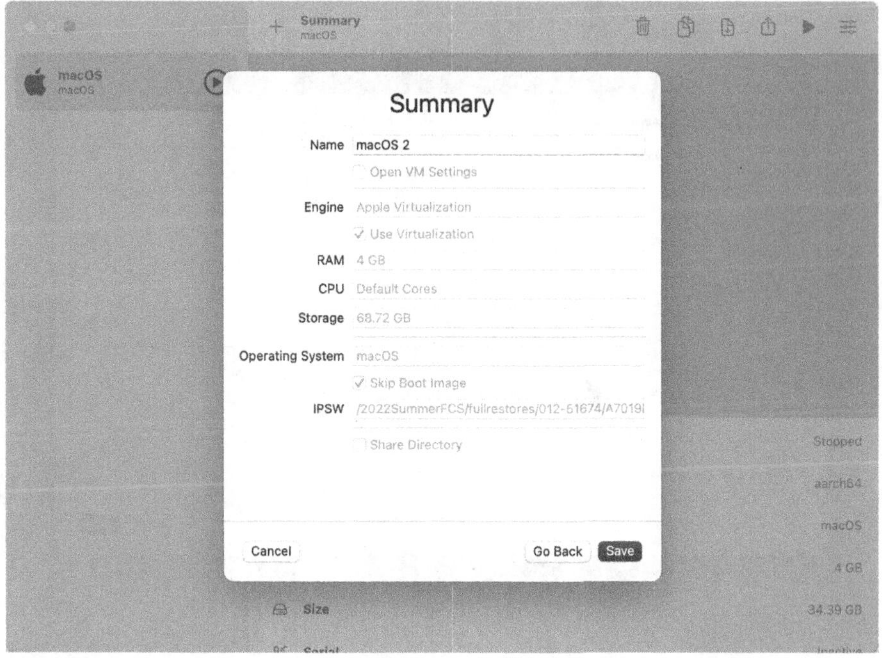

Figure C-6. The Summary screen

Once the VM has been created, select it in the left sidebar to see more settings available and click the icon in the upper-right corner to change any settings. The first option is the Information screen (Figure C-7), which just includes some information (I like to put the date I created a VM and a version number (or other naming schemes) in the Notes box).

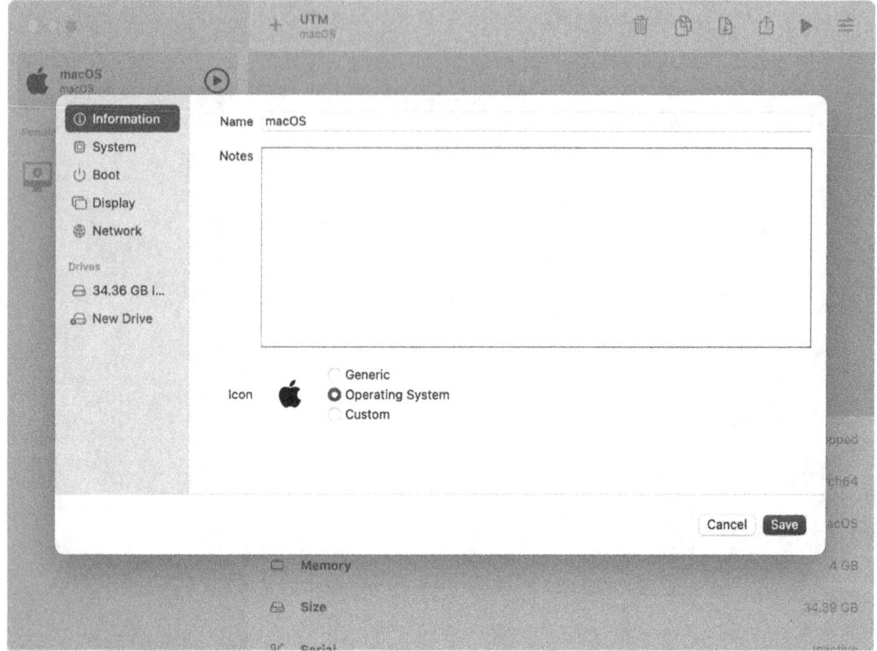

Figure C-7. *Settings for the VM*

The System option is where cores can be edited and memory added. Again, we wouldn't recommend below 4096 memory (see Figure C-8) for most uses.

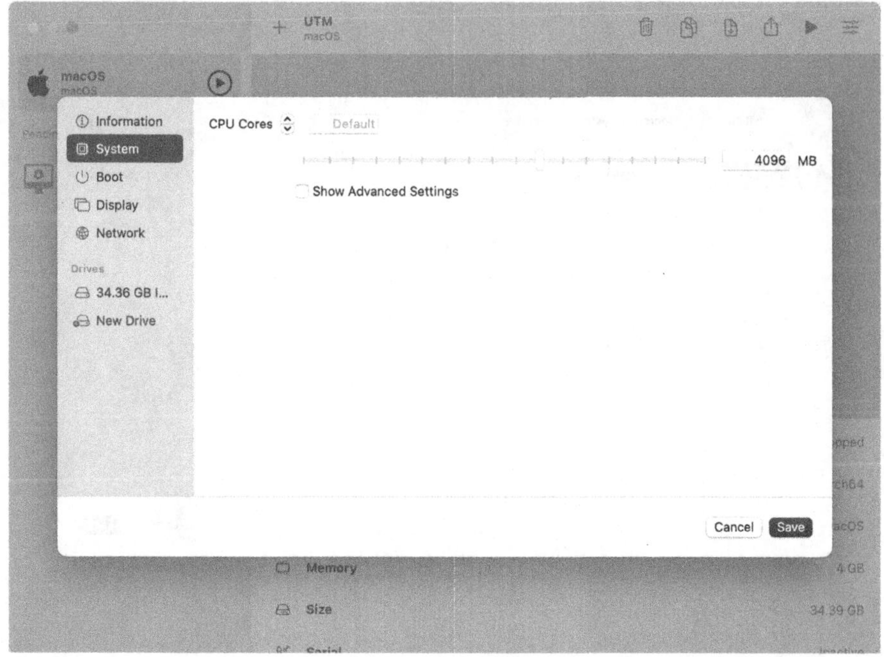

Figure C-8. ***Edit the System CPU and Memory settings as needed***

The Boot tab (Figure C-9) provides an option to name the guest OS (what is seen in UTM) and change the IPSW (best to just start a new guest OS though).

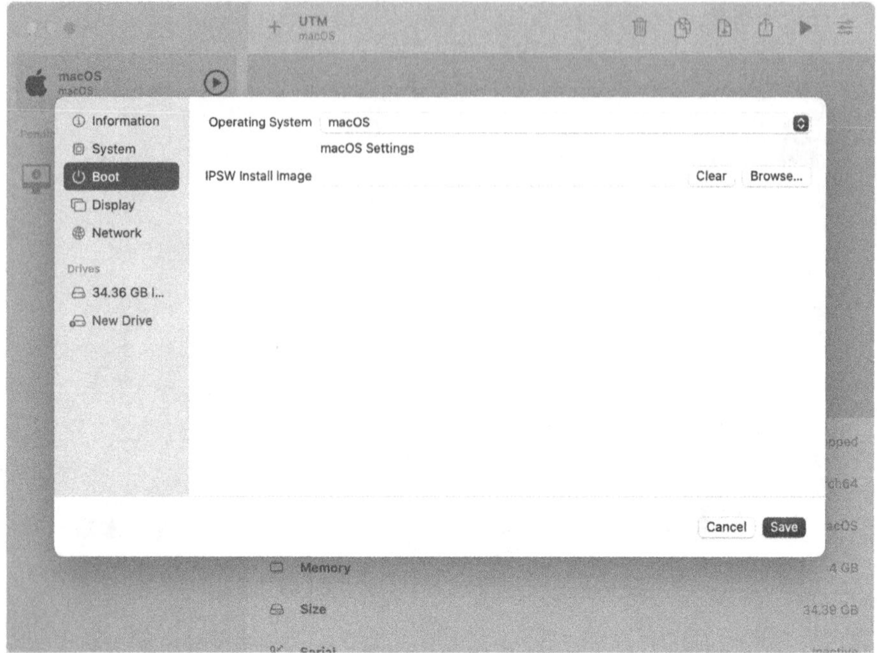

***Figure C-9.** Change IPSW settings as needed*

The Display option controls the graphics. This usually works well with the default settings, but can be improved if needed (Figure C-10). This can be helpful when moving a VM to a computer with a different display.

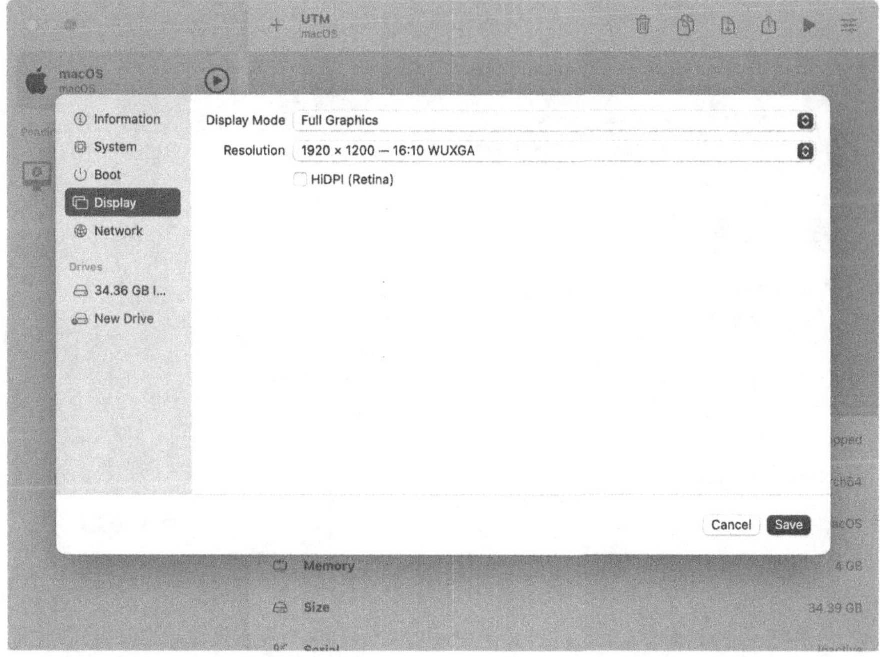

***Figure C-10.** Change graphics information as needed*

The Network screen shows the MAC address of the VM and provides options to communicate. The Shared option (Figure C-11) allows the guest and host operating systems to access the network interface and so work well. For dedicated services, consider the Bridged setting for performance purposes.

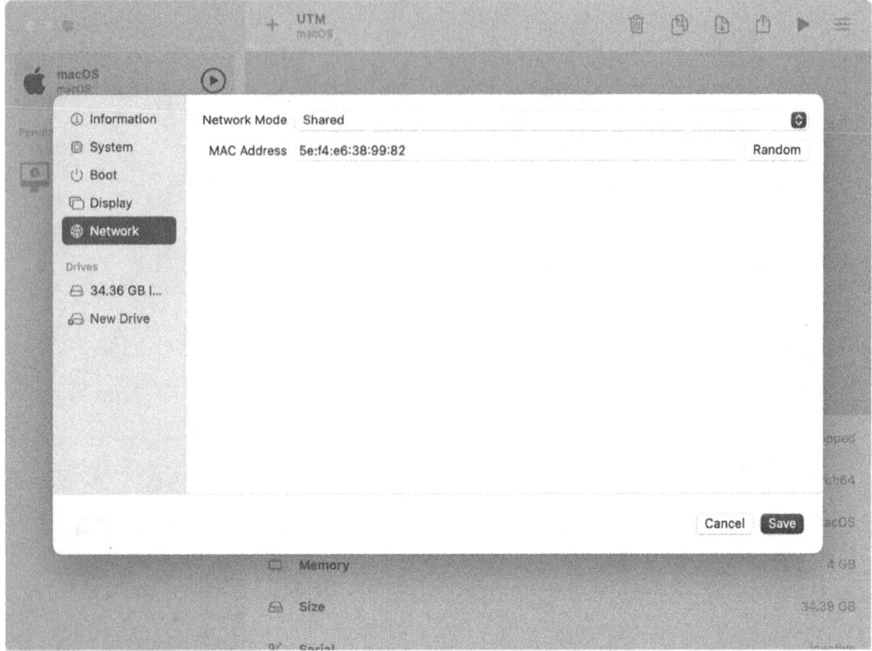

Figure C-11. *Edit the MAC address and network information*

The next options create image files for the VMs. If deleting one, use the Delete Drive option, or to add an additional volume into /Volumes, use the New Drive button. Keep in mind these are image files, so don't overcommit how much storage is available to boot the host OS and have a useful machine when not using VMs. Double-click the VM, and it should fire up and allow a user to run the startup process(es) and eventually log in, as seen in Figure C-12.

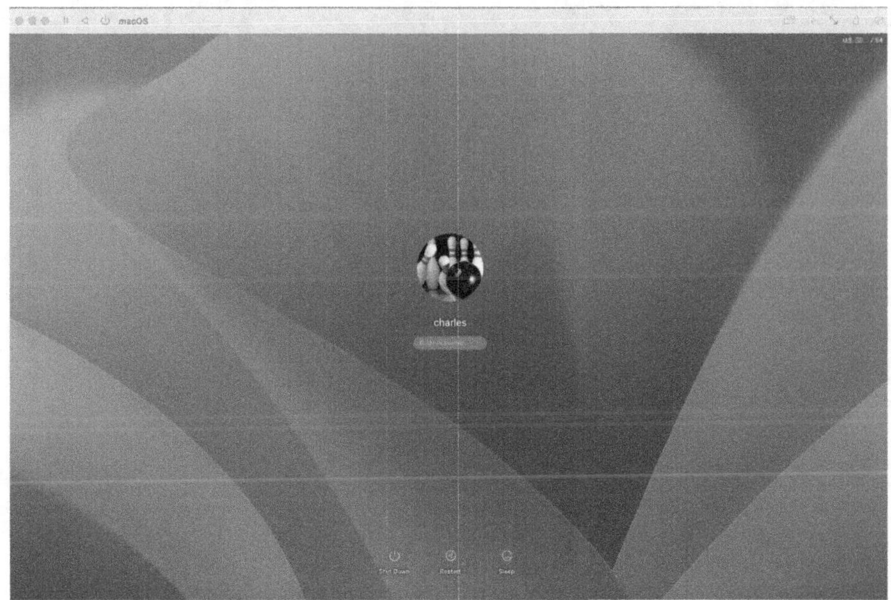

Figure C-12. *The VM then opens as needed (and can be paused from the top row of icons)*

In general, UTM is now one of those apps that should probably be a part of every Mac Admins toolbelt. It's great to have some more granular features with a VMware or a Parallels, but the ease of use and speed of UTM is unparalleled, which is impressive given it's so inexpensive. Further, there's a gallery of other interesting guest operating systems, like Mac OS 9.2.1! That's available at `https://mac.getutm.app/gallery/`.

The VMs can then be deleted or more created as new versions of operating systems come available.

APPENDIX D

Conferences, Helpful Mac Admins, and User Groups

A number of Mac admins are the only ones handling Apple devices in their particular company, school, or institution. If this is you, you are not alone. There are a number of conferences and user groups where you can get together with your colleagues and collectively solve your individual problems.

Conferences

ACES Conference

When: Summer

Where: United States

Link: `https://acesconf.com/`

Focus: Business-focused conference for Apple consultants

Why go?: If you are an Apple consultant looking to start or build your business, this conference provides great opportunities for networking and learning new ways to grow your company.

Addigy Summit

When: Winter

Where: United States

Link: `www.addigy.com/summit`

C. Edge and R. Trouton, *Apple Device Management*,
https://doi.org/10.1007/978-1-4842-9156-6

Focus: Mac admins who use Addigy for endpoint management

Why go?: If you're a Mac admin who uses Addigy, this vendor conference provides Addigy users with an opportunity to learn the latest ways to use this endpoint management tool to manage their Macs.

Command-IT

When: Winter

Where: France

Link: `www.command-it.fr`

Focus: Francophone Mac admins

Why go?: If you're a Mac admin whose first language is French, this conference speaks your language and covers the latest techniques in Mac administration.

Jamf Nation User Conference

When: Fall

Where: San Diego, California, United States

Link: `www.jamf.com/events/jamf-nation-user-conference/`

Focus: Mac admins who use Jamf Software's Jamf Pro or Jamf Now for endpoint management

Why go?: If you're a Mac admin who uses Jamf Pro or Jamf Now, this vendor conference provides Jamf users with an opportunity to learn the latest ways to use this endpoint management tool to manage their Macs.

Jamf Nation Roadshows

When: Various times

Where: Various countries

Link: `www.jamf.com/events/`

Focus: Mac admins who use Jamf Software's Jamf Pro or Jamf Now for endpoint management

Why go?: If you're a Mac admin who wants to go to Jamf Nation User Conference but can't go for various reasons, Jamf has a traveling conference that may be able to come to you.

Mac Admin and Developer Conference UK (MacADUK)

When: Winter

Where: London, England, United Kingdom

Link: `https://macad.uk/`

Focus: Conference for Mac admins and Apple developers

Why go?: If you're a Mac admin based in the United Kingdom, this conference covers the latest techniques in Mac administration and development techniques.

Mac AdminsUA

When: Summer

Where: Kyiv, Ukraine

Link: `https://macadmins.org.ua/`

Focus: Conference for Mac admins

Why go?: If you're a Mac admin based in Eastern Europe or Ukraine, this conference provides a variety of sessions for managing your Apple fleet.

MacDevOps YVR

When: Summer

Where: Vancouver, British Columbia, Canada

Link: `https://mdoyvr.com/`

Focus: Conference for Mac admins

Why go?: If you're a Mac admin who is interested in systems automation and DevOps, this conference provides a variety of sessions focused on those topics and how to apply them in a Mac-centric environment.

MacDeployment

When: Summer

Where: Calgary, Alberta, Canada

Link: `https://macdeployment.ca/`

Focus: Conference for Mac admins

Why go?: If you're a Mac admin based in Canada, this community-focused conference offers sessions on the current best practices for deploying and maintaining Macs in education and enterprise environments.

MacSysAdmin

When: Fall

Where: Göteborg, Sweden

Link: `https://macsysadmin.se/`

Focus: Conference for Mac admins

Why go?: If you're a Mac admin based in Europe, this conference covers the latest techniques in Mac administration from a global perspective.

Objective by the Sea

When: Fall

Where: Conference location changes annually

Link: `https://objectivebythesea.com`

Focus: Conference for Apple security and digital forensics

Why go?: If your focus is security or digital forensics in an Apple-centric environment, this conference offers a variety of sessions focused on the challenges of securing macOS and iOS.

Penn State MacAdmins Conference

When: Summer

Where: State College, Pennsylvania, United States

Link: `https://macadmins.psu.edu/`

Focus: Conference for Apple security and digital forensics

Why go?: If your focus is supporting Macs or iOS in education or enterprise environments, this conference offers a wide variety of sessions given by both vendors and community speakers.

Apple Worldwide Developers Conference

When: Summer

Where: San Jose, California, United States

Link: `https://developer.apple.com/wwdc/`

Focus: Conference for Apple development

Why go?: If your focus is developing software for Macs or iOS, this conference is your very best opportunity to learn the latest techniques and speak directly with Apple engineers and developers.

X World

When: Summer

Where: Sydney, New South Wales, Australia

Link: https://auc.edu.au/xworld/

Focus: Conference for Mac admins

Why go?: If you're a Mac admin based in Australia, this community-focused conference offers sessions on the latest techniques in Mac administration and development techniques.

Helpful Mac Admins

Allister Banks

Blog: www.aru-b.com

GitHub: https://github.com/arubdesu

Adam Codega

Blog: www.adamcodega.com/

Andrew Seago

GitHub: https://github.com/andrewseago

Andrina Kelly

GitHub: https://github.com/andrina

Ben Goodstein

GitHub: https://github.com/fuzzylogiq

Ben Toms

Blog: https://macmule.com/

GitHub: https://github.com/macmule

Bill Smith

Blog: https://talkingmoose.net/

GitHub: https://github.com/talkingmoose

Brandon Kurtz

Blog: https://bkurtz.io/

GitHub: https://github.com/discentem

Bryson Tyrrell

Blog: https://bryson3gps.wordpress.com/

GitHub: https://github.com/brysontyrrell

Calum Hunter

Blog: https://themacwrangler.wordpress.com/

GitHub: https://github.com/calum-hunter

Clayton Burlison

Blog: https://clburlison.com/

GitHub: https://github.com/clburlison

Darren Wallace

Blog: https://dazwallace.wordpress.com/

GitHub: https://github.com/Daz-wallace

Ed Marczak

Blog: www.radiotope.com/

GitHub: https://github.com/marczak

Emily Kausalik-Whittle

Blog: www.modtitan.com/

GitHub: https://github.com/smashism

Eric Holtam

Blog: https://osxbytes.wordpress.com/

GitHub: https://github.com/poundbangbash

Erik Gomez

Blog: https://blog.eriknicolasgomez.com

GitHub: https://github.com/erikng

Graham Gilbert

Blog: https://grahamgilbert.com/

GitHub: https://github.com/grahamgilbert

Graham Pugh

Blog: https://grpugh.wordpress.com/

GitHub: https://github.com/grahampugh

Greg Neagle

Blog: https://managingosx.wordpress.com/

GitHub: https://github.com/gregneagle

Hannes Juutilainen

GitHub: https://github.com/hjuutilainen

Howard Oakley

Blog: `https://eclecticlight.co`

Jeremy Reichman

Blog: www.`jaharmi.com/`

GitHub: `https://github.com/jaharmi`

John Kitzmiller

GitHub: `https://github.com/kitzy`

Joseph Chilcote

GitHub: `https://github.com/chilcote`

Karl Kuehn

Blog: `https://wranglingmacs.blogspot.com/`

GitHub: `https://github.com/larkost`

Michael Lynn

GitHub: `https://github.com/pudquick`

Mike Solin

Blog: `https://mikesolin.com/`

GitHub: `https://github.com/flammable`

Matthew Warren

Blog: `https://macblog.org/`

GitHub: `https://github.com/haircut`

Neil Martin

Blog: `https://soundmacguy.wordpress.com/`

GitHub: `https://github.com/neilmartin83`

Nick McSpadden

Blog: `https://osxdominion.wordpress.com/`

GitHub: `https://github.com/nmcspadden`

Patrick Fergus

Blog: `https://foigus.wordpress.com/`

GitHub: `https://github.com/foigus`

Pepijn Bruienne

Blog: `https://enterprisemac.bruienne.com/`

GitHub: `https://github.com/bruienne`

Per Olofsson

Blog: `https://magervalp.github.io/`

GitHub: `https://github.com/magervalp`

Randy Saeks

Blog: `www.rsaeks.com/`

GitHub: `https://github.com/rsaeks`

Rich Trouton

Blog: `https://derflounder.wordpress.com/`

GitHub: `https://github.com/rtrouton`

Richard Purves

Blog: `www.richard-purves.com/`

GitHub: `https://github.com/franton`

Ryan (Last Name Not Public)

Blog: `https://mrmacintosh.com`

Samantha Demi

Blog: `https://pewpewthespells.com/`

GitHub: `https://github.com/samdmarshall`

Sean Kaiser

Blog: `https://seankaiser.com/`

GitHub: `https://github.com/seankaiser`

Shea Craig

GitHub: `https://github.com/sheagcraig`

Stéphane Sudre

Blog: `http://s.sudre.free.fr/`

GitHub: `https://github.com/packagesdev`

Steve Yuroff

Blog: `https://swytechnotes.wordpress.com/`

GitHub: `https://github.com/swy`

Tim Perfitt

Blog: `https://twocanoes.com/blog/`

GitHub: `https://github.com/tperfitt`

Tim Sutton

Blog: https://macops.ca/

GitHub: https://github.com/timsutton

Tom Bridge

Blog: https://tombridge.com/

GitHub: https://github.com/tbridge

Victor Vrantchan

Blog: https://groob.io/

GitHub: https://github.com/groob

Yoann Gini

Blog: www.abelionni.com/

GitHub: https://github.com/ygini

User Groups and Meetups

Austin Apple Admins

Where: Austin, Texas, United States

Link: www.austinappleadmins.org

London Apple Admins

Where: London, England, United Kingdom

Link: https://londonappleadmins.org.uk/

MacAdmin Monthly

Where: New York, New York, United States

Link: www.macadminmonthly.org/

MacDMV

Where: Washington, District of Columbia, United States

Link: www.macdmv.com/

Philly Apple Admins

Where: Philadelphia, Pennsylvania, United States

Link: https://phillymacadmins.com

Apple Admins of Seattle and the Great Northwest

Where: Seattle, Washington, United States

Link: www.meetup.com/Seattle-Apple-Admins/

Sydney Mac Admins Meetup

Where: Sydney, New South Wales, Australia

Link: `www.meetup.com/Sydney-Mac-Admins/`

Twin Cities Mac Admins Group

Where: Minneapolis, Minnesota, United States

Link: `www.mspmacadmins.org/`

APPENDIX E

Set Up a Test Okta Account

We're using Okta in this chapter because their trial accounts are simple to set up, and it's easy to get started. Most identity providers are similar. Okta is a solid IdP, but the concepts in this chapter should be easily portable to other providers as well. The Okta screens are succinct, but the terms used can vary from provider to provider.

To set up an account, go to Okta.com and click Try Okta. You'll then be prompted for a domain to set your account up on. Fill in the fields requested and click the Create Account button. You'll then get an email.

Once you have an Okta account, log in, and at the Getting Started with Okta screen, click the Add App button to link your first app to Okta (Figure E-1).

C. Edge and R. Trouton, *Apple Device Management*,
https://doi.org/10.1007/978-1-4842-9156-6

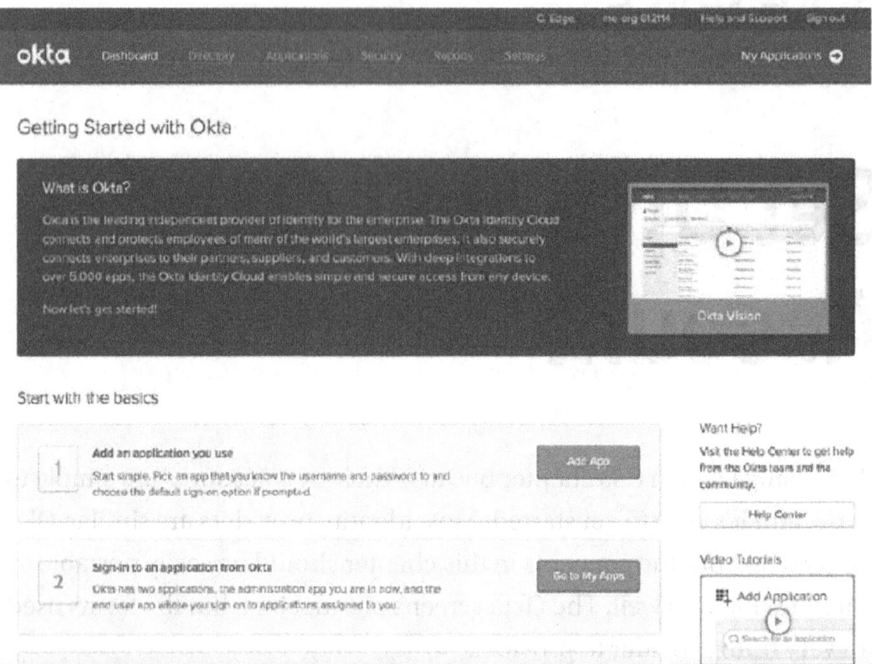

***Figure E-1.** Set up an Okta trial account*

At the Add Application screen, search for the name of the tool you'd like to add. In Figure E-2, we'll use Jamf Pro.

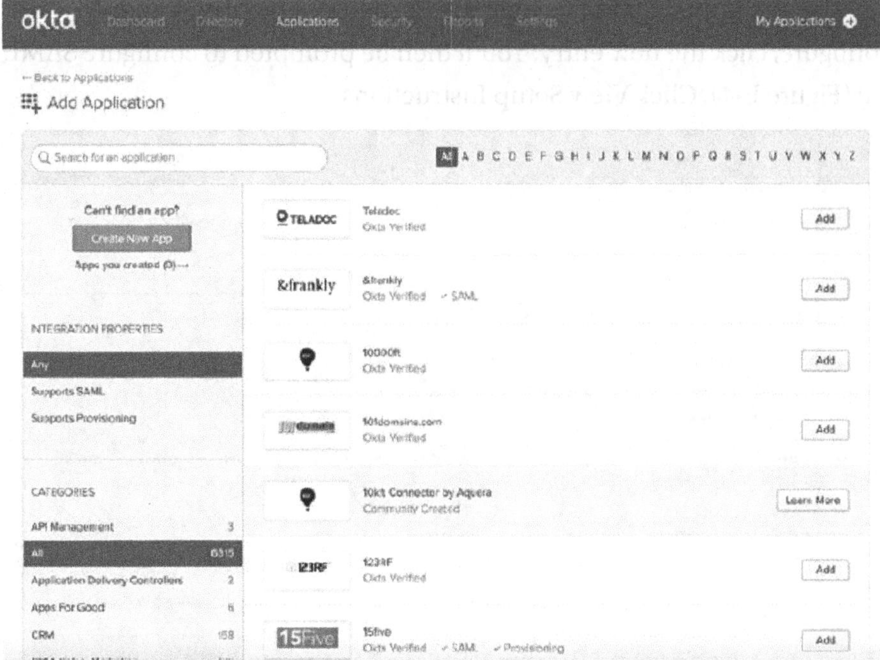

Figure E-2. *Add a web application in Okta*

When the app appears, click Add, as shown in Figure E-3. Note that if an app is using SAML, it will say as much!

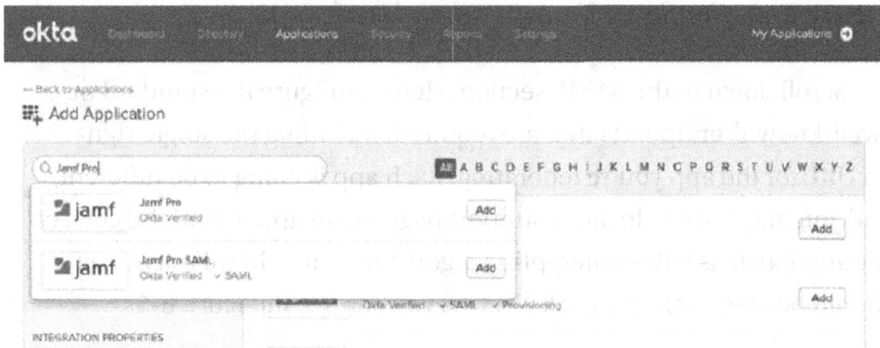

Figure E-3. *Selecting the application to add*

The app is then added to your app list and can be configured. To configure, click the new entry. You'll then be prompted to configure SAML 2.0 (Figure E-4). Click View Setup Instructions.

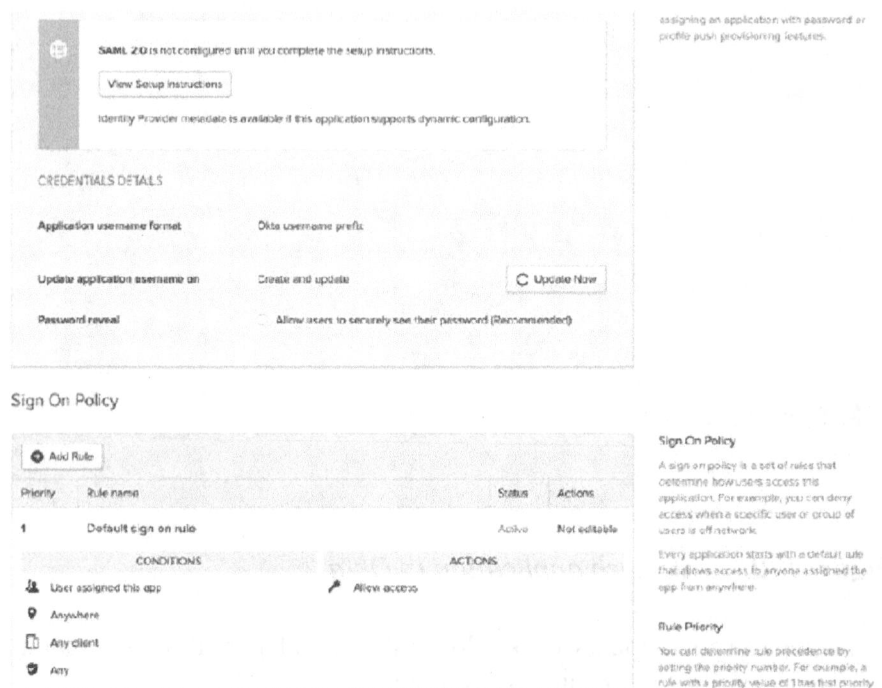

Figure E-4. *Configure the sign-on and credentials*

Scroll down to the SAML section. Here, configure the standard or "well-known" endpoints that are required, including the single sign-on URL for the app you're federating. Each app is going to be different, and you may have to locate a support page for an app to find the correct settings (such as URLs, encryption algorithms, etc.). In this case, you should be able to simply click Next, as you can see in Figure E-5.

SAML Settings

Edit

GENERAL

Single Sign On URL	https://jamf.jamfcloud.com/saml/SSO
Recipient URL	https://jamf.jamfcloud.com/saml/SSO
Destination URL	https://jamf.jamfcloud.com/saml/SSO
Audience Restriction	https://jamf.jamfcloud.com/saml/metadata
Default Relay State	
Name ID Format	Unspecified
Response	Signed
Assertion Signature	Signed
Signature Algorithm	RSA_SHA1
Digest Algorithm	SHA1
Assertion Encryption	Unencrypted
SAML Single Logout	Disabled
authnContextClassRef	PasswordProtectedTransport
Honor Force Authentication	Yes

Figure E-5. *SAML settings for federation*

Click Assignments. Here, you configure each user that has access to federate their account. Many will work with Just-in-Time (JIT) provisioning or SCIM (System for Cross-domain Identity Management), so accounts can be provisioned on the fly as they appear in a directory service and deprovisioned, respectively.

JIT and SCIM are separate standards that make this kind of management easier. JIT provisioning creates users in a service provider the first time they log on, based on information in a SAML assertion. SCIM is a standard that automates the flow of identity metadata between domains. Accounts can be provisioned in one system and show up in another, with additional attributes such as fields and group memberships being automatically assigned in the process, or gated based on a grant type for the specific service provider accessing the identity. While we're selecting a user manually in Figure E-6, it's worth noting that provisioning can be automated provided both the service provider and identity provider support the ability to do so.

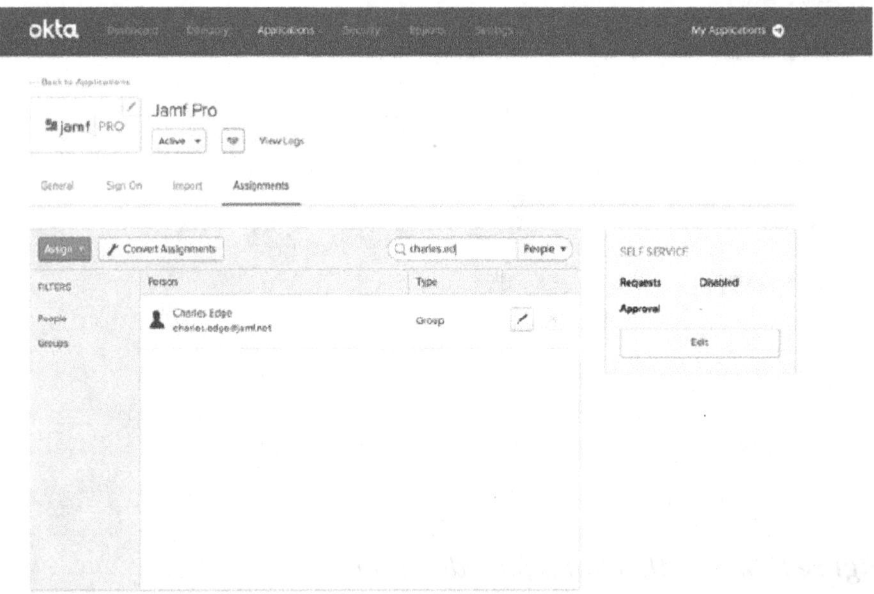

Figure E-6. *Configuring the application for a user*

Next, open your Okta domain on a computer you haven't tested before. You'll then be prompted to install the Okta browser plug-in (Figure E-7).

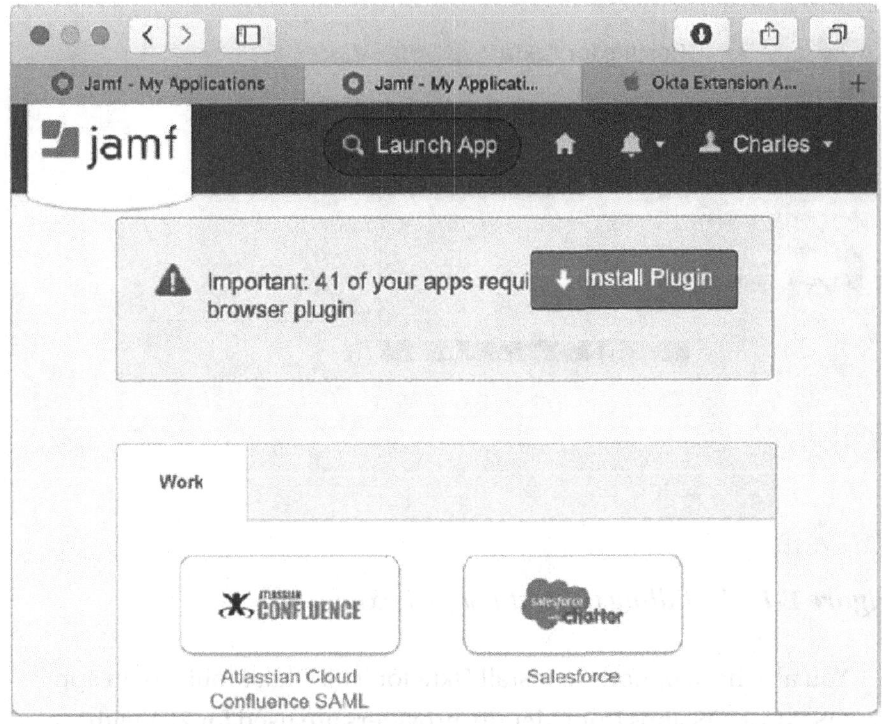

***Figure E-7.** Logging in to Okta*

Most identity providers offer an app that helps them to get around certain service provider or client computer limitations on a platform basis. For example, Okta provides a plug-in to allow password injection for services that cannot be federated over any delegated authentication protocol. This is a free download from the Safari Extension store. To download the Safari Extension for the Mac, open Safari and search for Okta (or use the link provided earlier). Simply click the Install button, or if the extension has already been installed, click Update (Figure E-8).

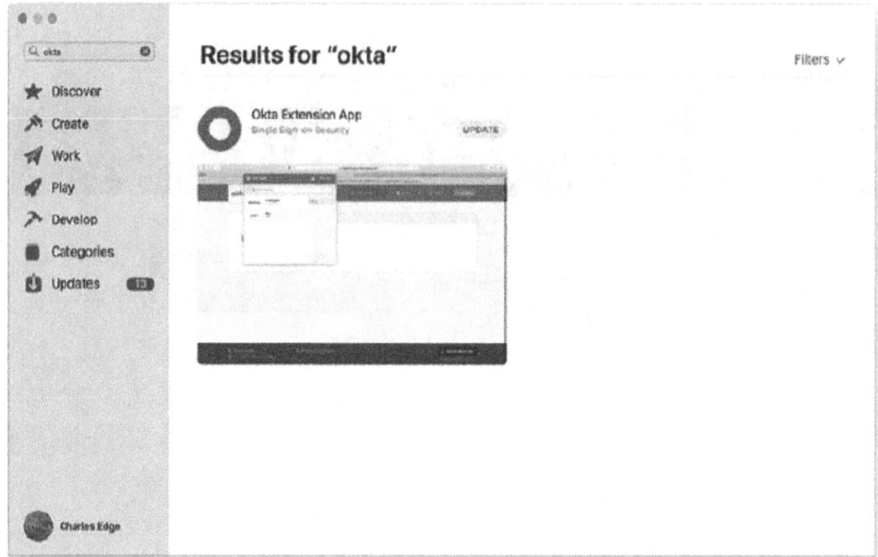

Figure E-8. *Installing the Okta Safari Extension*

You also have options to install Okta for iOS. Okta Mobile is an app for iOS. Most iOS apps from identity providers are used for 2FA with push notification or OTP. The launcher apps that attempt to federate authentication is an option most provide, but not really useful given that none of the iOS solutions have matured to the point where users will love it. We hope new options in how OAuth is handled on the platform help to improve this user experience after iOS 15 is released.

This process was for federating an administrative screen, but the process is similar for other self-service and app store solutions - and most apps should follow a similar pattern for federating. Once federated, look at some SAML responses to get a better understanding of how modern single sign-on works.

Index

A

C. Edge and R. Trouton, *Apple Device Management*, https://doi.org/10.1007/978-1-4842-9156-6

B

C

D

J

K

L

M

N

O

T

U

V

W

X

Y

Z

Printed in the United States
by Baker & Taylor Publisher Services